Studies in Church His

31

THE CHURCH AND CHILDHOOD

Frontispiece Madonna and Child, Tewkesbury Abbey, nave. Photo by courtesy of the Vicar and Churchwardens of Tewkesbury Abbey.

THE CHURCH AND CHILDHOOD

PAPERS READ AT
THE 1993 SUMMER MEETING AND
THE 1994 WINTER MEETING OF
THE ECCLESIASTICAL HISTORY SOCIETY

EDITED BY

DIANA WOOD

PUBLISHED FOR
THE ECCLESIASTICAL HISTORY SOCIETY
BY
BLACKWELL PUBLISHERS
1994

First published 1994

Blackwell Publishers
108 Cowley Road, Oxford OX4 1JF, UK

238 Main Street
Cambridge, Massachusetts 02142, USA

British Library Cataloguing in Publication Data

A CIP catalogue record for this book is available from the British Library.

Library of Congress Cataloguing-in-Publication Data

ISBN 0631 19586 6 hb
0631 19587 4 pb

Typeset in 11 on 12 pt Bembo
by Pure Tech Corporation, Pondicherry, India
Printed in Great Britain by
Hartnolls Ltd, Bodmin, Cornwall

IN MEMORY OF JOAN M. PETERSEN

CONTENTS

CONTENTS

CONTENTS

PREFACE

The theme chosen by Professor Janet Nelson for the year 1993–4, The Church and Childhood, is a particularly apt one, given that 1994 is the United Nations Year of the Family. It is also one which has resulted in a record-breaking number of communications and evoked a wide variety of historical responses, theological, theoretical, educational, economic, artistic and literary, liturgical and musical, ranging in time from the Holy Innocents to the twentieth-century Sunday-school children of Purley. This being so, the editor's job in selecting papers for publication was harder than ever, and once again I can only apologize to those who had to be omitted. The papers published here are the main papers delivered in the summer of 1993 and in January 1994, and a selection of the communications presented in July.

The Society owes a great debt of gratitude to the staff of Manchester College, Oxford, where the summer conference was held, and in particular to the Revd Dr Ralph Waller, the Principal, Mrs Margaret Alderson, the Bursar, and to Dr Rowena Archer, the Tutor for Graduates, all of whom went out of their way to make us welcome, to make the conference enjoyable and memorable, and to ease the burden of organization. Our thanks are also due, once again, to King's College London for its hospitality in January.

One of the most exciting themes of the summer conference was the participation of children in the liturgy, drama, and music of the Church. In anticipation of this the July conference opened with solemn choral Evensong at the Church of St Mary Magdalen, Oxford, at which an introit, 'Out of the Mouths . . .', specially composed for the Society by Vincent Packford, the Director of Music, was given its first performance: this is published as an appendix to this volume. The conference ended appropriately with the sound of children's voices, those of the girls of the Hildegard Choir, directed by Lucy Haigh, and accompanied by William Gatens, performing a beautiful concert of sacred music in the chapel of Manchester College. The Society would like to thank all those concerned.

As editor I should like to add my personal thanks to Blackwell Publishers, especially to Ann McCall and to Clare Braithwaite, who have ensured the smooth passage of the volume through the press, and to all those members who have helped me so much over the years by chairing sessions of communications.

The news of the death of Joan Petersen, one of the contributors to this volume, was received with great sadness by the Society. The book is therefore dedicated to her memory.

Diana Wood

LIST OF CONTRIBUTORS

BERNARD ASPINWALL
Senior Lecturer in Modern History, University of Glasgow

JANE BAUN
Research Student, Department of History, Princeton University

ISTVÁN P. BEJCZY
Research Assistant, Department of History, Catholic University of Nijmegen

CLYDE BINFIELD
Reader in History, University of Sheffield

BRENDA M. BOLTON
Senior Lecturer in History, Queen Mary and Westfield College, University of London

RUTH B. BOTTIGHEIMER
Associate Professor, State University of New York, Stony Brook

GILLIAN CLARK
Lecturer in Classics, University of Liverpool

T. N. COOPER
Research Fellow in History, University of Sheffield

WILLIAM COSTER
Lecturer in History, Bedford College of Higher Education

FRANÇOISE DECONINCK-BROSSARD
Professor, University of Paris X

JOHN DORAN
Research Student, Royal Holloway and Bedford New College, University of London

MARTIN R. DUDLEY
Lecturer, Simon of Cyrene Theological Institute, London

DOROTHY ENTWISTLE
Research Associate, Department of Education, University of Edinburgh

ANTHONY FLETCHER
Professor of Modern History, University of Durham

GRAHAM GOULD
Lecturer in Early Church History, King's College London

JOAN GREATREX
Bye Fellow, Robinson College, Cambridge

SUSAN HARDMAN MOORE
Lecturer in Reformation Studies, King's College London

PAUL A. HAYWARD
Research Student, St John's College, Cambridge

WALTER HILLSMAN
Member of the Faculty of Music, University of Oxford

W. M. JACOB
Warden of Lincoln Theological College

OLIVER LOGAN
Lecturer in History, University of East Anglia

ANDREW MARTINDALE
Professor of Visual Arts, University of East Anglia

ROB MEENS
Visiting Scholar in the History Faculty, University of Cambridge

STUART MEWS
Reader in Theology and Religious Studies, Cheltenham and Gloucester College of Higher Education

JANET L. NELSON
Professor of Medieval History, King's College London

VINCENT H. PACKFORD
Director of Music, St Mary Magdalen's Church, Oxford

THE LATE JOAN M. PETERSEN
Formerly Editor, SPCK

SHULAMITH SHAHAR
Professor of Medieval History, Tel-Aviv University

LIST OF CONTRIBUTORS

ELIZABETH SIBERRY

BRIAN STANLEY
Lecturer in Church History, Trinity College, Bristol

ALEXANDRA WALSHAM
Research Fellow, Emmanuel College, Cambridge

DIANA M. WEBB
Lecturer in History, King's College London

ABBREVIATIONS

Abbreviated titles are adopted within each paper after the first full citation. In addition, the following abbreviations are used throughout the volume.

ActaSS	*Acta Sanctorum*, ed. J. Bolland and G. Henschen (Antwerp, etc. 1643 ff.)
AFP	*Archivum Fratrum Praedicatorum* (Rome, 1931 ff.)
AHR	*American Historical Review* (New York, 1895 ff.)
AnBoll	*Analecta Bollandiana* (Brussels, 1882 ff.)
BJRL	*Bulletin of the John Rylands Library* (Manchester, 1903 ff.)
BL	British Library, London
BN	Bibliothèque nationale, Paris
CChr	*Corpus Christianorum* (Turnhout, 1953 ff.)
CChr. SG	*Corpus Christianorum, series Graeca* (1974 ff.)
CChr. SL	*Corpus Christianorum, series Latina* (1953 ff.)
CSEL	*Corpus scriptorum ecclesiasticorum Latinorum* (Vienna, 1866 ff.)
DNB	*Dictionary of National Biography* (London, 1885 ff.)
DublR	*Dublin Review* (London, 1836 ff.)
EHD	*English Historical Documents* (London, 1953 ff.)
EHR	*English Historical Review* (London, 1886 ff.)
GCS	*Die grieschischen christlichen Schriftsteller der ersten drei Jahrhunderte* (Leipzig, 1897 ff.)
InR	*Innes Review* (Glasgow, 1950 ff.)
JEH	*Journal of Ecclesiastical History* (Cambridge, 1950 ff.)
JMedH	*Journal of Medieval History* (Amsterdam, 1975 ff.)
LCL	*Loeb Classical Library* (London and Cambridge, Mass., 1900 ff.)
MGH	*Monumenta Germaniae Historica inde ab a, c. 500 usque ad a. 1500, ed. G. H. Pertz et al. (Hanover, Berlin, etc., 1826 ff.)*
MGH. A	*Antiquitates* [see *MGH, PL*]
MGH. Cap	*Capitularia regnum Francorum* (1883–97) [= *MGH, L*, sectio 2]
MGH. Conc	*Concilia* (1893 ff.)
MGH. Ep	*Epistolae* (1887 ff.)
MGH. F	*Fontes iuris Germanici antiqui* (1869 ff.) ns (1933D ff.)
MGH. L	*Leges* (in folio) (1835–89) — 1. Sectio: *MGH. LNG* — 3. Sectio: *MGH. Conc*
MGH. LNG	*Leges nationum Germanicarum* (1886 ff.) = *MGH. L* sectio 1
MGH. PL	*Poetae Latinae medii aevi* (1880 ff.) [= *MGH.A*]
MGH. SRG	*Scriptores rerum Germanicarum in usum scholarum* . . . (1826–32), ns (1922 ff.)
MGH. SRL	*Scriptores rerum Langobardicum et Italicarum s. VI–IX* (1878)
MGH. SRM	*Scriptores rerum Merovingicarum* (1884–1920)
MGH. SS	*Scriptores* (in folio) (1826–1934)
MS	*Medieval Studies* (Toronto, 1939 ff.)

ABBREVIATIONS

nd	no date
np	no place
NH	*Northern History* (Leeds, 1966 ff.)
ns	new series
os	old series
PaP	*Past and Present. A Journal of Scientific History* (London, 1952 ff.)
PBA	*Proceedings of the British Academy* (London, 1904 ff.)
PG	*Patrologia Graeca*, ed. J. P. Migne, 161 vols (Paris, 1857–66)
PL	*Patrologia Latina*, ed. J. P. Migne, 217 + 4 index vols (Paris, 1841–61)
PS	*Parker Society* (Cambridge, 1841–55)
RBen	*Revue Bénédictine de critique, d'histoire et de littéraire religieuses* (Maredsous, 1884 ff.)
RS	*Rerum Brittanicarum medii aevi scriptores*, 99 vols (London, 1858–1911) = *Rolls Series*
SC	*Sources chrétiennes*, ed. H. de Lubac, J. Danielou et al. (Paris, 1941 ff.)
SCH	*Studies in Church History* (London/Oxford, 1964 ff.)
SCH. S	*Studies in Church History, Subsidia* (Oxford, 1978 ff.)
TRHS	*Transactions of the Royal Historical Society* (London, 1871 ff.)
VCH	*Victoria County History* (London, 1900 ff.)

INTRODUCTION

The year 1993 was one in which child abuse recurrently captured the headlines: a local authority challenged a child-minder's right, delegated from the parents, to smack children in her charge; a child's right to 'divorce' its natal family was acknowledged, and the acknowledgement disputed; the news that scientists had enabled a fifty-nine-year-old to give birth evoked revulsion in some, delight in others; and when two Liverpool children were found guilty of murdering a two-year-old, horror mingled with vengeance as the media examined the nation's soul. On all these matters leading churchmen were asked to pronounce—which, in turn, provoked further intense public argument. And so, in 1994, the Year of the Child, the theme of the Church and Childhood has acquired a topicality not entirely foreseen by its deviser. Marina Warner in the third of her 1994 Reith Lectures, on children as angels, and as monsters, thought-provokingly set these pressing contemporary issues in a wider cultural context. In this collective quest for understanding, ecclesiastical historians, too, have things to offer: a sense of the time-boundness of particular attitudes towards childhood and of particular uses, and abuses, of children; at the same time, an awareness of theological implications in matters of public policy, a feel for underlying rhythms, and discontinuities, in Christian concern with childhood, and hence a capacity to assess and contextualize changes, continuities, and recurrences in the treatment of the living child in societies which, no longer (if they ever were) homogeneously Christian, still recognizably inherit so much of Christian traditions.

The history of Christian, and ecclesiastical, ideas and images of childhood is shot through with ambiguity. Children have been represented as innocent, hence peculiarly apt vessels for the Spirit; they have been seen as weak, hence peculiarly susceptible to sin and diabolical temptation. Children have been declared martyrs and saints; yet Christian adults, profoundly anxious about perverse and foolish infants, wild boys and girls, have set themselves to train and discipline children's minds and bodies. Children have been conscientiously beaten throughout the

Christian centuries—and as conscientiously cherished. They have been instruments of social cleansing, symbolic and practical, in a variety of historical contexts. Source of nurture and of discipline alike, the Church has made institutional provision for children. Persons childless by profession have 'engendered' new generations for the Church, undertaking quasi-parental responsibilities, and experiencing much of the joys, and sufferings, of parenthood. Ecclesiastically run schools and youth organizations, foundling hospitals and orphanages, have helped in the socialization and control of children to create godly societies, and to reinforce patriarchy and gender division within the home. Yet ecclesiastical organizations, themselves recruiting from the converted, have also supported children in revolt against family constraints, and upheld the individual choices of such youthful rebels. This volume, then, is replete with varieties, ambivalences, and contradictions. Well-drilled choristers jostle with prophetic critics. Silent victims take their places alongside vociferous vessels of supernatural power. Throughout run complex counterpoints of ecclesiastical prescription and practice, of parental love and fear, and, last but not least, on the part of children themselves, of passivity and active appropriation.

Our subject, inevitably, receives uneven geographical coverage: nearly all the contributions deal with European churches, and there is a further heavy tilt (especially in reference to the modern period) towards British ones. Within this ambit, though, both genders, and all stages from babyhood to adolescence, are embraced. The range is ecumenical, with the attitudes of Greeks and Latins, Catholics and Protestants, Anglicans and Dissenters, all claiming attention. Every period from the Early Church to the twentieth century is represented. So large and diverse a collection constitutes an editorial challenge: I want to take this opportunity, on the Society's behalf, to thank Diana Wood most warmly for doing, as ever, an exemplary job.

Remarkably, in all this diversity, several themes emerge as leitmotivs that give unity to the volume. The first is the child's dual role as passive object of ecclesiastical concern and active religious subject. Gillian Clark points out that while the Early Church shouldered the burden of social control, it offered some children, girls as well as boys, the chance to assume responsibility for their own religious life. The late Joan Petersen shows aristocratic Roman girls acquiring, through Christianity, the equivalent of tertiary education. Even the system of child oblation, widespread in the Middle Ages, did not preclude an element of individual choice: John Doran underlines a significant shift towards emphasizing consent in canonical thought from the twelfth century on. Sixteenth-century Jesuits had, as Oliver Logan notes, a special interest in maintaining the freedom of youths to declare a religious profession, even at the cost of challenging paternal authority. Alexandra Walsham and Susan Hardman Moore present remarkable case-studies of child prophets in Reformation England: children manipulated by their elders, who nevertheless themselves assumed a certain authority.

A second, partially related, theme, and similarly loaded with ambiguity, is that of the Holy Innocents. Paul Hayward explores the contested meanings of 'becoming like little children' (cf. Matthew 8.3) and explains how, in the reforming milieux of the eighth and ninth centuries, the Innocents were invested with a new function as exemplars of active virginity. Shulamith Shahar decodes the rites, and readings, of the late medieval Feast of the Holy Innocents, when (and certainly not coincidentally) in a carnivalesque inversion of social order the boy bishop took temporary control of 'his' church. In fifteenth-century Toul, he and his chorister companions would process through the streets dressed as girls to collect money from neighbouring religious women and from layfolk. These unruly cross-dressing children evoke the child sprites and trick-or-treaters of Hallow-e'en and St Nicholas Day. Walter Hillsman recalls a variation of this theme in Lancashire parishes just within living memory: on School Sermons Sunday 'Little (Girl-)Singers' in white dresses and shawls were the star turn, subverting the norm of male monopoly of choral performance. In the later Middle Ages, games castigated as 'foolish and noxious' were transmuted, as Martin Dudley explains, into suitably solemn liturgical performances in which boys symbolized the 144,000 redeemed virgins of the Book of Revelation.

The story of the Innocents is one of appalling suffering; and a third, and linked, recurrent theme is that of child death. Here, Graham Gould suggests, patristic theologians confronted a fundamental problem of theodicy: how could infants have deserved to die? Augustine's answer—that all were tainted by original sin—was not adopted by Gregory of Nyssa, who considered the possibility that dead children experienced spiritual growth in a future life. Jane Baun discusses Byzantine responses (in which humanity defied logic) to the related theological problem of the deaths of unbaptized babies. In the eighteenth century, Françoise Deconinck-Brossard shows Philip Doddridge, dissenting preacher and bereaved father, clinging to faith, but advocating inoculation against smallpox.

On to the bodies of children were mapped the hopes, fears, and fantasies of adults. In early medieval penitentials, Rob Meens traces parental guilt at failure to protect their offspring from harm, alongside clerical sympathy for parental predicaments. Yet the penitentials may reflect, at the same time, a certain displacement of that guilt in the punishment of children for lack of bodily control. István Bejczy finds the baby's refusal of the breast recurring in later medieval saints' lives as the mark of the holy infant: it is not far hence to the food-rejecting girl visionaries of the seventeenth century. Clerical advisers in every period warned parents against sparing the rod; and while in every generation, it seems, there were spoiled children to be deplored, the association of child bodies with wickedness seems to have been especially frequent in the early modern period when witch-beliefs flourished. Beating was prescribed as a means of expelling evil. In practice, Anthony Fletcher suggests, while some fathers invested this task with patriarchal symbolism, many could not bring themselves to beat their sons, instead offloading this task on to schoolmasters. Nevertheless, Reformation and Counter-Reformation moralists buttressed paternal authority in closely similar ways to create holy households that were miniatures of the well-ordered state. On the whole, there was optimism about what careful child-rearing could achieve. Andrew Martindale invites us to re-view the visual evidence, from the thirteenth century onwards, for a new realism in the depiction of children, including the Christ-child, in art—a product of Christian Aristotelianism's 're-evaluation of the human senses'. Martindale, like several other contributors to this volume, suggests some important qualifications to Philippe Ariès's famous thesis of a 'child-less' Middle Ages.

Anxious concern for children's welfare is documented in a variety of milieux. Brenda Bolton argues that solid fact underlay the pious legend of Innocent III's pastoral care of abandoned babies. Yet concern, once translated into collective, institutional action, could never be quite disinterested. In late medieval Italian cities, the friars can be seen, thanks to Diana Webb's careful deconstruction of miracle stories, ensuring that saintly supply of child protection kept pace with buoyant parental demand. William Coster's analysis of sixteenth-century Yorkshire wills, while reaching the important negative conclusion that godparental responsibilities are rarely mentioned, amply documents parental provision, spiritual as well as the material, for their offspring. Bernard Aspinwall's Glasgow Catholic school-teachers toiled, from the later nineteenth century into the twentieth, to improve the lives of their pupils—materially, by providing them with footwear, mentally, by (*inter alia*) promoting Celtic F.C.—while constructing them as model Ultramontanes. In another, leafier, part of the wood, Clyde Binfield's Congregationalists in suburban Surrey were offering middle-class children a 'Purley way' which led, through active involvement in church services of their own (the Montessori-trained deaconess who designed these was, in her way, a virtuoso), to firmer Congregationalist commitment as adults, in a pluralist religious world. Methodists' promotion of juvenile support for missionary work had, as Brian Stanley reveals, financial as well as spiritual benefits clearly in view. Stuart Mews's Kilburn Sisters could hardly avoid in some sense 'using' the children they cared for, defending the Sisterhood's reputation against detractors whose vested interests were as characteristic of the 1890s as were their anxieties about young persons' sexuality. W. M. Jacobs shows eighteenth-century charity schools conscientiously managed by Anglicans, lay and clerical (brutal school-teachers could be summarily dismissed), but at the same time well patronized by the bourgeoisie as a source of apprentice labour and a means of instilling a religion which taught the future servant 'that tho' his master's eye may sometimes be off yet the Eye of his Master which is in Heaven never is . . .'.

A different kind of social pressure brought about successive manipulations of their sacred material by compilers of children's Bibles: Ruth Bottigheimer unravels a skein of 'improvements' and erasures applied to the Old Testament story of Jael (Judges 4–5)—revealing some unexpected national differences (and perhaps helping clear the Swiss of the charge of misogyny!). Focusing on the late nineteenth and early twentieth centuries, Elizabeth Siberry reveals a similar plasticity in children's stories of heroic boys on Crusade, while Dorothy Entwhistle's examination of books deemed fitting Sunday-school prizes for children in this period throws up some surprising choices alongside predictable ones. Gender constitutes an important axis of these last three papers.

Through most of the Western Church's history, the voices of boy children have been in demand to augment the musical beauty of holiness. Late medieval English cathedrals made careful arrangements to ensure quality performance, as Joan Greatrex shows for Norwich, and T. N. Cooper for Lichfield. Walter Hillsman, after looking back to a nineteenth century in which choristers' wearing of surplices excluded female participation for decades, looks forward to a twenty-first century when girl choristers can play a full part alongside boys and adults. Sadly Joan Petersen has not lived to see that century. The cause of the girl choristers was dear to her heart, and she loved the musical offerings which were among the greatest delights of the 1993 summer meeting. Joan's combination of learning and humanity typifies her contribution, over many years, to our Society as it does, I confidently believe, our Society itself. This volume is dedicated to her memory, with our respect and affection.

Janet L. Nelson

THE FATHERS AND THE CHILDREN

by GILLIAN CLARK

I

A Theban once came to abba Sisoes, wanting to become a monk. The old man asked him whether he had anyone in the world. He said, 'I have a son.' The old man said to him, 'Go, throw him into the river, and then you shall be a monk.' When he went off to throw him in, the old man sent a brother to stop him. The brother said, 'Stop: what are you doing?' He said, 'The abba told me to throw him in.' So the brother said, 'But now he has told you not to.' He left him and went to the old man, and he became a proven monk because of his obedience.[1]

ABBA SISOES clearly did not intend the father to drown the son, so perhaps he was making the obvious point that someone with family commitments is not in a position to be a monk. But if that was his point, the would-be monk failed to understand it, and continued to believe that a man who gave such an order was worth following. Nor was the would-be monk rebuked for failing to understand: instead, he was accepted because of his unquestioning obedience.

This is an extreme case, but it is not the only occasion when patristic writers hold up for admiration adults who leave children so as to lead a religious life, or who commit children to a religious life about which the child has not been consulted. When the ascetic Abraham found himself responsible for a seven-year-old niece, he enclosed her in a little cell next to his own and trained her as an ascetic. A monk who had yielded to temptation, and who had become the father of a son, brought the son back to share his cell. Simeon the Mountaineer, evangelizing an untaught village, took one third of its children as the nucleus of two monastic communities. Some of the children wept, some

[1] Sisoes, 10, *PG* 65, col. 393; see further Graham Gould, *The Desert Fathers on Monastic Community* (Oxford, 1993), p. 55.

were silent. Only two families refused to part with their children—and those children soon died.[2] These, perhaps, were people under great economic constraint, who could not offer the children in their charge anything but the village or the monastic cell. But the most striking examples come from the combination of strong-minded aristocrats and brilliant writers in fourth-century Rome.

At some time after the mid-century, aristocratic Roman women were inspired to lead the ascetic life. The inspiration came from stories of the desert; Jerome suggests that the stories were told by Athanasius and his companions in exile, but if so, it took some time for their influence to be felt.[3] Marcella and her friends, who pioneered the ascetic lifestyle, opted for 'house asceticism', making a personal desert of austerity or enclosure within a great house, and either refusing to marry or remaining as widows. But Melania the Elder started a new trend. She was widowed at twenty-two; she had had several miscarriages, and two of her sons died soon after their father. Early in the 370s, she left her only surviving son in Rome while she went on pilgrimage to Egypt and the Holy Land. She was absent for at least twenty-five years.

It is not clear how old this son, Valerius Publicola, was when she left him. Paulinus of Nola, a relative as well as a fellow ascetic, portrays her as a widow with one surviving baby, and comments approvingly on her decision to leave. 'She loved her child by neglecting him, and kept him by giving him up.' He makes a comparison with the readiness of Abraham to sacrifice Isaac. Melania may, in fact, have stayed long enough to see her son embarked on a public career. He seems to have grown up a conventional Roman aristocrat. According to Paulinus, he had a deep sense of religious devotion, and practised charity without committing himself to the ascetic life. He may have consulted Augustine about religious problems in his North African estates.

[2] The story of Maria, niece of Abraham, is included in Sebastian Brock and Susan Ashbrook Harvey, *Holy Women of the Syrian Orient* (Berkeley, 1987). The monk who brought back his son: cited by Peter Brown, *The Body and Society: Men, Women and Sexual Renunciation in Early Christianity* (London, 1989), p. 230. Simeon the Mountaineer: Susan Ashbrook Harvey, *Asceticism and Society in Crisis: John of Ephesus and the Lives of the Eastern Saints* (Berkeley, 1990), pp. 96–7.

[3] Jerome, *Letter* 127.5, *CSEL*, 56, pp. 149–50; but he dates the influence too early: see Elizabeth A. Clark, *The Life of Melania the Younger* (New York and Toronto, 1984), p. 93.

But for the biographer of his daughter, the younger Melania, Publicola featured only as an obstacle.[4]

Melania the Younger was compelled to marry by her parents, who wanted heirs: she was either their only, or their only surviving, child. At fourteen she married the seventeen-year-old Pinianus, also heir to a great Roman fortune, and asked him to live with her in chastity. He said they must first provide heirs; but when, in the early years of the fifth century, they produced a baby daughter, they promptly dedicated her to virginity. This need not imply separation from the child, for she could—had she lived beyond infancy—have led a religious life in her parents' house, never leaving it to marry. It did imply that this child would not devote her life to perpetuating the family and its inheritance. Perhaps they would have behaved differently with a son. We do not know, because their baby son died at birth, Melania nearly died too, and Pinianus was sufficiently distressed to vow himself to post-marital celibacy.[5]

Meanwhile Paula, another member of the aristocratic network, had likewise done her duty and produced children, persevering until, after four daughters, she achieved a son. But once she was widowed she too sailed away to the holy places. Jerome makes a fine rhetorical picture of the children on the quay at Ostia, stretching out their hands, weeping and pleading with their mother to return: the little son, whose age is not specified, and the daughter ready for marriage, who may not have been more than twelve. He focuses on the heroic mother: 'She raised dry eyes to heaven, overcoming devotion [*pietas*] to her children by devotion to God.'[6] The pleading children are stage props enhancing the effect. This is all extremely hard to take.

There must have been reasons why committed Christians thought it right to behave like this to children, and why others were expected to admire them for it. What was it about their theology, or about their society, which made them do so? Christianity preached the need to put devotion to God before

[4] For problems in the tradition about Publicola, see Clark, *Life of Melania*, pp. 86–90. Paulinus, *Letter* 29.9 and 45.3, *CSEL*, 29, pp. 251 and 381–2.

[5] *Life of Melania* 2, 6 (Clark, *Life of Melania*, p. 30). For 'post-marital celibacy' and the lively debate on marriage and celibacy in late fourth-century Italy, see David G. Hunter, 'Resistance to the virginal ideal in late fourth century Rome: the case of Jovinian', *Theological Studies*, 48 (1987), pp. 45–64.

[6] Jerome, *Letter* 108.6.3, *CSEL*, 55, p. 311.

family ties, and in the early Christian centuries the choice sometimes did require separation from children, as when Perpetua handed over her baby son before her martyrdom, or Agathonice declared before hers that God would take care of her son.[7] In the fourth century, the conflict between family duty and religious commitment might express itself in refusal to marry or to take on social responsibilities. But surely those who are parents, and who are not actually facing martyrdom, should not abandon dependent children? Basil's mother, Emmelia, evidently agreed: she finished the job first, seeing four sons and four daughters safely established in marriage, careers, or the Church, before joining her eldest daughter in house asceticism. Augustine spoke very sharply to Ecdicia, who decided to adopt the religious life without thought for her husband and son.[8] Perhaps the Roman examples show the eccentricity of an urban aristocracy.

On the other hand, some modern theories about parental attitudes to children in imperial Rome are quite as sensational as any of these examples. Perhaps the Roman mothers should be seen as extreme cases of a general indifference, or even hostility, to children. So there is reason to ask the classic question: what difference did Christianity make? Christianity proclaimed a saviour, born as a baby, who taught that the kingdom of heaven belonged to those who were like little children. Christians baptized in adulthood were not only, in a familiar image, reborn, but were taught to think of themselves as newborn, as infants in need of the most basic feeding and training. This ought to have made a difference to the way adults thought about children. But child-rearing practices are resistant to change, and the most influential Christian writers and teachers were themselves successful products of Roman elite culture and education. Did Christian teaching transform inherited ideas about children, and consequently the experience of childhood?[9]

7 See further Stuart G. Hall, 'Women among the Early Martyrs', in Diana Wood, ed., *Martyrs and Martyrologies*, *SCH*, 30 (1993), p. 7.

8 Augustine, *Letter* 262, *CSEL*, 57, pp. 621–31.

9 For other perspectives on this question, see Thomas Wiedemann, *Adults and Children in the Roman Empire* (London, 1989); Sarah Currie, 'Childhood and Christianity from Paul to the Council of Chalcedon' (Cambridge Ph.D. thesis, 1993).

II

The parent-child relationship has to be seen in its cultural context. It is said that present-day children in different cultures, given a sentence beginning 'I love my mother but . . .', will complete it differently. Western Europeans add, 'but I hate the way she nags about my room', or some such complaint. Children in southern Asia add, 'but I can never repay all that I owe her.' Children in the patristic period were expected to have the second reaction.

Parents had to ensure that their children were fed and clothed and looked after, educated as far as was practicable, established in a career or a marriage, and given their fair share of the inheritance which would allow the next generation to survive. If natural affection and parental duty failed, there was no welfare net and no state-subsidized education. Welfare provision was not an acknowledged responsibility of the state: it depended on private charities, which were sometimes, but not consistently, reinforced by directives or gifts from the emperor. So it was literally true that children owed their life and upbringing to their parents, and the extent of the debt was made clear in law and in social practice.

The father had begotten his children, and at their birth had accepted the responsibility of rearing them. He was not bound to do so. His *patria potestas*, that is, his power as a father to take decisions which were legally binding on his children, extended to having his newborn child put out of the house *sanguinolentus*, still bloodstained from the birth and denied the most basic care. He could also sell his children into slavery for a fixed term when he felt unable to provide for them otherwise. Hence there were ten-year-old prostitutes in Constantinople in the time of Justinian, and Augustine's tasks as a bishop included finding out about the legal position of children who had been sold. Could a freeborn father sell children into permanent slavery? If a child whose labour had been sold for a fixed term became legally independent on the death of the father who had made the sale, was he or she bound to complete the term? Could a mother sell her child's labour if the father had died?[10]

[10] Justinian, *Novella* 14.1 (in *Corpus iuris civilis*, ed. T. Mommsen and P. Krueger, 16th edn (Berlin, 1954) [hereafter *Corpus iuris civilis*]; Augustine, *Letter* 24*, *CSEL*, 88, pp. 126–7.

When the child survived within the family to marriageable age (which in law was as early as presumed puberty, twelve for girls and fourteen for boys), the father decided whom his daughter, or even his son, should marry. It was, after all, his property which would be given in dowry or nuptial donation, and the object of the exercise was to provide him with grandchildren.

The mother had carried and given birth to the child at risk of her own life. Sometimes she had nursed the child herself, at further cost to her health and energy, instead of finding a wet-nurse. She might well meet part of the costs of upbringing and career; she too had money to leave; and she might be the person on whom the child was most dependent. Late Roman law-codes increasingly gave legal recognition to the bond between mother and child, overriding the traditional principle that a woman has no *potestas* over any member of her family, not even her own child. If the father died, a mother, or even a grandmother, who was prepared to take an oath not to remarry was regarded as the most suitable guardian of the child's interests.[11]

This was a practical, rather than emotional, concern for a child's well-being. Roman law provided for the children of a marriage broken by death or divorce, but the object was to ensure that they would not lose their inheritance because a stepmother or stepfather diverted it, or because their mother remarried and favoured her new family at their expense—this seems to be regarded as a quite usual shift of interest. Nothing is said about the emotional stability of the child. So the elder Melania, and Paula, could be said to have fulfilled their maternal duty in that their children had guardians to protect their inheritance. Paula, according to Jerome, had handed over her property to her children.[12] They had made proper provision.

Jerome presents both Paula and her children as distressed by the parting, but it is unlikely that the departure of a mother caused an emotional void in her children's lives. Social and economic conditions of course varied immensely, but it does seem clear that in any household which could afford slaves, one

[11] On the legal position, see further Gillian Clark, *Women in Late Antiquity* (Oxford, 1993).
[12] Jerome, *Letter* 108.6, *CSEL*, 55, p. 312.

of the primary slave tasks was child-minding. The care of small children is messy, time-consuming, and (except for the most devoted) often tedious: a typically servile task, by Graeco-Roman standards. A child might form a close and lifelong bond with one particular nurse, or might have more diffuse emotional links with a nurse or nurses, a *paedagogus* (the slave who escorted a child to school), and various 'uncles' and 'aunties' within or linked to the household.[13] School-books, designed to train children in the correct use of language, show the child's social world as seen by adults:

> I go out of my bedroom with my tutor [*paedagogus*] and my nurse to greet my father and mother. I greet them both and kiss them both. I go to find my writing kit and my exercise book and give them to my slave. Then everything is ready. Followed by my tutor, I go out of the house and set off to school.
>
> I make my way through the portico which leads to school. My school fellows come to meet me. I greet them and they greet me back. I come to the staircase. I go up the stairs quietly. I raise the curtain and greet the assistant teachers. I greet the master and he kisses me.[14]

Father, mother, and teacher are formally greeted with a kiss, a sign not so much of affection as of social connection (assistant masters do not rate a kiss); nurse, tutor, and slave attendant are the child's everyday companions. It may have been just as well that children did not usually depend on one care-giver, for they were quite likely to lose a parent by death or separation, or to find themselves part of a new household.

The case for emotional distance between parent and child can be strongly put, and has influenced interpretations of Late Antique asceticism. Arranged marriage, early childbearing, painful and dangerous childbirth, the abandonment of newborn babies, the practices of swaddling and wet-nursing can all be used

[13] Evidence on family structures in the late Roman republic and early Empire is collected by Keith Bradley, *Discovering the Roman Family* (Oxford, 1991) and Suzanne Dixon, *The Roman Mother* (London, 1988).

[14] Cited from Keith Hopkins, 'Everyday Life for the Roman Schoolboy', *History Today*, 43 (October 1993), p. 26. See also Carlotta Dionisotti, 'From Ausonius' schooldays? A schoolbook and its relatives', *Journal of Roman Studies*, 72 (1982), pp. 83–125.

to argue that parents and children were at best unlikely to form a strong emotional bond. At worst, it may be concluded, the experience of marriage and child-rearing was so much resented that parents had no wish to repeat it themselves or to see it repeated by their children. They wished instead to reclaim their own and their children's bodies from the constraints of civic and family duty. Perhaps, therefore, parents would not be unduly distressed if they were separated from their children by entering, or seeing the children enter, a religious community. Perhaps mothers, supported by Christian teaching on the merits of celibacy, wanted to repress the sexuality of their sons because they had been unable to repress, or to welcome, the sexuality of their husbands. Perhaps they were anxious to spare their children what they themselves had suffered, and therefore encouraged the children—particularly daughters—to choose virginity.[15]

The argument for emotional distance starts from the supposition that when child mortality rates are high, parents simply cannot afford to make an emotional investment in the child. This reaction is understandable in late twentieth-century Westerners, for whom the loss of a child is (mercifully) so rare, and so devastating, an experience that they wonder how parents survived when it was common. But the evidence from Graeco-Roman Antiquity makes it impossible to generalize about how parents felt. Some parents clearly suffered, and expressed, grief for their loss. One deservedly famous example, from the early second century, is Plutarch's consolation to his wife for the loss of their little daughter Timoxena.[16] They had wanted a daughter. She was named after her mother, and she was a delightful child, who used to bring her dolls for her nurse to breast-feed. Plutarch commends his wife for not giving way to grief, either on the death of their daughter or on the earlier deaths of two little sons, but he takes it for granted that both of them felt it. Some parents also chose to commemorate a dead child. Again, the evidence is

[15] Aline Rousselle, *Porneia: On Desire and the Body in Antiquity* (Eng. trans., Oxford, 1988), made dramatic use of medical and legal material. The impact can be seen in Brown, *Body and Society*. Peter Garnsey, 'Child-rearing in ancient Italy', in D. I. Kertzer and R. P. Saller, eds, *The Family in Italy from Antiquity to the Present* (New Haven and London, 1991), pp. 48–65, helpfully surveys the range of modern study, and moves the discussion away from psychohistory and the irrecoverable emotions of parent and child.

[16] Plutarch, *Moralia* 609 (*LCL*, *Plutarch* 7, pp. 586–8).

not conclusive, partly because the material depends on excavation and chance survival, and partly because funeral customs varied over time, between urban and rural districts, and between areas of the Roman Empire. A recent survey suggests that parents rarely commemorated infants but increasingly, in the fourth and fifth centuries, commemorated children, and that Christians seem more concerned to do so than non-Christians; but that the choice to commemorate did not depend only on the strength of parental feeling.[17]

It is also natural to wonder about the emotional response of women to pregnancy and childbirth when they had chosen neither the father of their child nor (in all probability) the time of pregnancy.[18] Some Christian texts argued for virginity by presenting marriage, childbirth, and child-rearing as revolting and oppressive. Other Christians vigorously disagreed, but the case for resentment can be put very strongly.[19] Girls were expected to marry a bridegroom chosen by their father or, if he had died, by another close relative or guardian; they could (in law) reject the chosen bridegroom only if he was mentally defective. Marriage was legally valid when the girl was twelve. There is some evidence that among some social groups the preferred age of marriage was later, but not enough to show that Christians generally postponed marriage to the late teens or early twenties.[20] Young men might be unwilling to take on the responsibilities of parenthood, and pregnancy might be the result of legalized rape, occurring in a body which had not yet finished its own development. In the opinion of the first-century gynaecologist Soranus, a girl who has just reached puberty is capable of conception, but is not yet physically ready for pregnancy and childbirth. Soranus' writings were widely used, but it was still assumed that a twelve-year-old girl was reaching the time for marriage, and doctors

[17] Brent Shaw, 'The cultural meaning of death', in D. I. Kertzer and R. P. Saller, eds, *The Family in Italy*, pp. 66–90.

[18] There is much debate on whether contraceptive medicines had any effect: for a recent optimistic view, see John. M. Riddle, *Contraception and Abortion from the Ancient World to the Renaissance* (Cambridge, Mass., 1992). But respectable women were not supposed to use such things: see further Clark, *Women*, pp. 84–8.

[19] See further Hunter, 'Resistance'.

[20] Brent Shaw, 'The age of Roman girls at marriage: some reconsiderations', *Journal of Roman Studies*, 77 (1987), pp. 30–46.

continued to prescribe for girls who had not reached puberty at the expected time.[21]

Childbearing women could have emotional support in labour, but little or no effective pain relief. If the baby was difficult to deliver, they risked death from exhaustion and haemorrhage; the baby might have to be dismembered *in utero* to save the mother; and even after a successful delivery a woman might die from puerperal fever. Modern demographers disagree about the rate of maternal and perinatal death, but the mother's danger was generally acknowledged.[22] Even if a woman and her baby survived the birth, she was not certain of keeping her child. Midwives were trained to assess which babies were healthy enough to be 'worth rearing', and fathers had the legal right not to accept even a healthy child into the family. It is impossible to assess how many newborns were abandoned at birth (the modern term 'exposure' translates the Latin *expositio*, 'putting out'). Pessimists among modern scholars emphasize the high figures of abandonment available from later periods, for instance, in the records of foundling hospitals, and the repeated denunciations of exposure by late Roman emperors as well as by Christian preachers. Optimists argue that such denunciations show strong social pressure against exposure. They also suggest that in some social contexts, exposure might, in effect, be informal adoption, and that exposure was most often practised by the desperately poor in order to give their children some chance of survival, even if it was as a slave. (One argument used by Christian writers against exposure was that a father might, in years to come, recognize or even make use of his son as a male prostitute in the local brothel.) Leaving a baby in the porch of a church, or offering an older child to a monastery, might be an attempt to give the child the best life available.[23]

But suppose the mother did bear a living, healthy child who was accepted by the father? 'As for the children brought into the world by these women, it was recognised throughout the

[21] Soranus, *Gynecology* 1.8.33 (Eng. tr. by Owsei Temkin, Baltimore, 1956); see further Clark, *Women*, p. 80.

[22] For the debate on maternal and perinatal mortality rates, see Tim G. Parkin, *Demography and Roman Society* (Baltimore, 1992), pp. 93–4, 103–5.

[23] See further John Boswell, *The Kindness of Strangers: the Abandonment of Children in Western Europe from Late Antiquity to the Renaissance* (Harmondsworth, 1988); Clark, *Women*, pp. 48–50; Parkin, *Demography*, pp. 95–8.

Mediterranean that their mothers cared very little for them.' This spectacular conclusion by Aline Rousselle is not supported by the reference she gives, namely, a mildly chauvinist comment by Soranus that mothers in the city of Rome are not as careful as Greek mothers, but try to make the children walk before they are ready.[24] But it is true that child-rearing practices might not encourage the formation of a close bond between mother and child. Although breast-feeding was one of the signs of a devoted mother, many women who were able to breast-feed chose to use wet-nurses. Some mothers had other things to do (these might include another pregnancy), others said that childbirth was exhausting enough without adding lactation. Mothers who followed the advice of Soranus would not breast-feed for perhaps the first three weeks after birth, until their bodies had recovered from the disruption of childbirth.[25] This delay might make bonding less likely, especially when physical contact was restricted because the baby was swaddled. Swaddling was believed to help the limbs to grow straight, but there are modern (not ancient) theories about its psychological effect: perhaps the child grows up with internalized constraint and little capacity for making relationships. But, again, it is difficult to generalize. Soranus complains about women who give small babies two or three baths a day because it sends them to sleep, and himself recommends loosening the swaddling-clothes as soon as the baby feels reasonably firm, and sooner if the child is chafed by them.[26] Wet-nursing, too, did not necessarily mean that the mother lost contact with the child, for babies were not farmed out: the nurse was carefully chosen and was expected to live in, or at least, in the case of nurses who were paid to rear foundling children in Egypt, to bring the child for regular inspection.[27] It is perhaps safest to conclude that parents brought up their children as seemed best, or as seemed obvious, in the circumstances, and that most could be relied on to aim for their children's well-being. The next question is what they thought that meant.

[24] Rousselle, *Porneia*, p. 46; the reference is to Soranus, *Gynecology* 2.44. Soranus may in fact have observed, but not understood, the effect of rickets in crowded urban conditions.

[25] Ibid., 2.11.18.

[26] Ibid., 2.16.30, 2.19.42.

[27] On the use of wet-nursing and swaddling, together with the abandonment of newborn babies, as 'barometers' of parental feeling, see Garnsey, 'Child-rearing', p. 49.

III

Childhood, Philippe Ariès suggested, is a recent invention. That is, parents were not indifferent or hostile to their children, but they did not spend much time attending to children and did not expect child development, or the child's perspective on life, to be particularly interesting. They saw children as adults in the making, not as individuals with a distinct experience of life and a developing understanding of the world. These claims find some support in Graeco-Roman perceptions of childhood.

The stages of childhood were described in very general terms. Seven and fourteen were significant ages, marked by second dentition and by puberty, as well as by interesting numbers. Roman law reflected the general assumption that a seven-year-old had emerged from babyhood. A law of 426 says that, for the purpose of entering on an inheritance, an *infans* is under seven years old; this may also be the age limit for the *infans* who was not liable for a murder charge, on the grounds of *innocentia consilii*, 'harmlessness of intent'.[28] Seven-year-olds could respond to Bible stories, and did not need proxies at baptism. 'At that age children can lie and speak the truth, acknowledge and deny: so when they are baptized they can already give back the *symbolum* themselves, and reply for themselves to the questions.'[29] But there is a great difference (at least, there is to those who actually look after children) between six weeks and six months, six months and six years. In Latin, an *infans* may be anything from a baby, who literally cannot speak, to a child who does not yet count as a *puer*. In Greek, a *brephos* is a young baby, but *nêpios* is as wide-ranging as *infans*. Within the category of 'childhood' Latin has a *parvulus/a* as well as a *puer/puella*, Greek has a *paidion* as well as a *pais*, but at what age does a 'little child' become a child? The end of childhood was also unclear. After *pueritia* came *adulescentia*, but 'adolescence' could last through the twenties, or even longer if the *adolescens* was still in the power of his father. A male child whose father had died was freed from guardianship on

[28] *Justinian's Code* 6.30.18 pr.; *Digest* 48.8.12 (in *Corpus iuris civilis*). *Digest* 48.10.22 says that a child who has not yet reached puberty (*impuber*) cannot be held to have engaged in deliberate fraud.

[29] Jerome, *Letter* 128.3, *CSEL*, 56, pp. 158–9; Augustine, *On the nature and origin of the soul* 1.10.12, *CSEL*, 60, p. 312.

reaching puberty, but lawyers differed on whether there should be a fixed time, the completion of the thirteenth year, or a physical check. Males and females continued to have a *curator* (administrator) until the age of twenty-five; but the Emperor Leo, sensibly commenting that people mature at different rates, allowed for some flexibility.[30]

Inexact vocabulary does not in itself prove lack of attention to children: even in modern English an infant may be a baby or an infant, as distinct from a junior, in primary school. It may be just good sense not to make clear distinctions between one life-stage and the next. As Augustine said (without putting an age to it), '*Infantia* did not leave—where did it go?—but it was not there, for I was no longer an *infans* who could not speak, but a talking *puer*.'[31] But the representation of children in art may also suggest that childhood was seen in general terms, and children as adults in the making. There is a standard sequence of images on Roman children's sarcophagi: the baby, probably swaddled, being nursed or handed to the mother; the young child with a pet or a toy; the older child, in formal dress and holding a scroll, practising a speech before an approving father. Sometimes children are represented with what seems to be startling incompetence, as scaled-down adults or with baby faces on adult torsos. Again, this might suggest a failure actually to look at children. The reason may be severely practical: the sculptor has done a rush job, recarving only the head on a ready-made bust. But why did the parents not object? Perhaps there is a deliberate attempt to represent the dead child as the adult he or she should have become.[32]

Literary representations of children also present problems. When Prudentius constructs a child martyr, the indications of age are contradictory. The child is not long weaned, an innocent suckling, and when he is beaten, the blows draw more milk than blood. He is also nearly seven years old and fluently professes his

[30] Justinian, *Institutes* 1.23 pr.; Leo, *Novella* 28 (in *Corpus iuris civilis*). On legal rules about pre-pubertal children, see further Chris Jones, 'Women, Death and the Law', in Diana Wood, ed., *Martyrs and Martyrologies*, *SCH*, 30 (1993), p. 25. Further examples of generalizing references to age in T. Carp, '*Puer senex* in Roman and medieval thought', *Latomus*, 39 (1980), pp. 736–9.

[31] Augustine, *Confessions* 1.8.13, *CChr. SL*, 27, p. 7.

[32] Diana Kleiner, 'Women and family life on Roman funerary altars', *Latomus*, 46 (1987), pp. 552–3. See further Janet Huskinson, *Children's Sarcophagi from Imperial Rome: their Decoration and its Social Importance* (Oxford Monographs in Classical Archaeology, 1994 forthcoming), to whom I owe the comment that Christian sarcophagi may use the same motifs (biblical scenes, the Good Shepherd, Christ the teacher) for children as for adults; but the evidence is difficult to assess.

Christian faith. But it would be naïve to suppose that Prudentius is just confused about children. He juxtaposes the *infans* Barulas, the inarticulate child, with the rhetor Romanus, whose martyrdom speaks more eloquently than all his words, even when his tongue is torn out: the child speaks, out of the mouth of a babe and suckling, a testimony to natural understanding of Christ.[33] Similarly, Prudentius provides a girl martyr, Eulalia, who is almost ready for marriage (so presumably not yet twelve) but has never shown an interest in the childish things which girls put away on marriage. She is precociously ready to challenge a proconsul with a declaration of faith, inviting the torture which is promptly applied. As a literary construct, Eulalia has to be a fragile virgin, triumphing over physical violence and the dubious pleasure it affords to spectators—and perhaps also to readers of Prudentius.[34] Her commitment to God allows her to overcome the double weakness of childhood and femaleness.

Perhaps, then, both visual art and literature display not so much a culpable ignorance about children as an overriding concern for adult qualities already present in the seemingly undeveloped child. This is certainly true of biography, whether Christian or non-Christian. The parentage of the subject is noted, and sometimes the influence of some famous teacher or philosopher. There is no attempt to describe the physical and cultural setting in which the child grew up, or the development of his (or, for Christian biography, her) character. But there may be an anecdote in which the child displays the qualities of the future adult.[35] In Christian biography, instances of precocious saintliness were welcome, as foreshadowings of greatness had been in non-Christian biography. Ambrose told his family that they should kiss his hand just as they kissed the hands of visiting bishops. Athanasius was found on the beach playing

[33] Prudentius, *Peristephanon* 10, *CChr. SL*, 126, pp. 352–7: see further Cynthia Hahn, 'Speaking without Tongues: the martyr Romanus and Augustine's theory of language in illustrations of Bern Burgerbibliothek Codex 264', in Renate Blumenfeld-Kosinski and Timea Szell, eds, *Images of Sainthood in Medieval Europe* (Ithaca and London, 1991), pp. 161–80.

[34] Prudentius, *Peristephanon* 3, pp. 278–85. I have profited from an exchange of papers on this subject with Elizabeth Castelli.

[35] See further Christopher Pelling, 'Childhood and Personality in Greek Biography', in Christopher Pelling, ed., *Characterization and Individuality in Greek Literature* (Oxford, 1990), pp. 213–44; Gillian Clark, *Augustine: The Confessions* (Cambridge, 1993), pp. 46–8.

baptisms (he was the bishop). Caesarius of Arles also had something to explain.

> When he was seven years old or a little older, the holy and venerable Caesarius never hesitated to make gifts to the poor of the garments he wore. Often, when the blessed man had been seen by his parents returning home half naked, and was questioned under threat of punishment about what he had done with his clothes, he would only respond that they had been carried off by passers-by.[36]

It can never have been easy to bring up a saint.

Interest in the potential adult may be explained by one simple fact: childhood was in practice short. If a twelve-year-old girl is ready for marriage, then the sooner she displays adult qualities, the better. Boys might have longer to prepare themselves for adult life, but the successful public speaker and official had to train himself in self-control as well as technical competence.[37] There was no time to spare for mistaken choices and changes of direction. Young men were known to be reckless and difficult, but stormy adolescence was likely to meet repression rather than sympathy—something which may help to explain the appeal of the ascetic life as a justification for defying social rules:

> Anulinus the proconsul said, 'How old are you?'
> Maxima replied, 'Am I the daughter of a magus, as you are a magus?'
> Anulinus the proconsul said, 'How do you know I am a magus?'
> Maxima replied, 'Because the holy Spirit is in us, but in you the devil shows himself.'
> Anulinus the proconsul said, 'I adjure you by the living God to tell me how old you are.'
> Maxima replied, 'May the sides of your limbs be shattered. I am fourteen.'[38]

[36] Ambrose: Paulinus, *Life of Ambrose* 2.4, *PL* 14, col. 30. Athanasius: Rufinus, *Ecclesiastical History* 1.14, *PL* 21, col. 487. Caesarius: *Life of Caesarius* 3, tr. W. Klingshirn, *Caesarius of Arles: Life Testament, Letters* (Liverpool, 1994).

[37] See further Peter Brown, *Power and Persuasion in Late Antiquity* (Wisconsin, 1992), pp. 35–61.

[38] *Passio of Maxima, Secunda and Donatilla*, *AnBoll*, 9 (1890), pp. 112–13. I am indebted to Dr Maureen Tilley for introducing me to these texts. On teenagers and Roman categories, see further M. Kleijwegt, *Ancient Youth: the Ambiguity of Youth and the Absence of Adolescence in Greco-Roman Society* (Amsterdam, 1991); E. Eyben, *Restless Youth in Ancient Rome* (London, 1993).

Self-professed virgins, according to Jerome, went around in scruffy black clothes, their hair straggling from under inadequate veils; the general effect was remarkably sexy. This, like the aggressive tone of Maxima, sounds familiar.[39] But the choice of the religious life might be made at an even earlier age. Macrina was twelve when her fiancé died. Asella chose virginity at the age of ten—someone took seriously a ten-year-old declaring, 'I'm never going to get married and I don't want any children.' Even more impressive is the case of Eupraxia:

> 'Eupraxia, my little lady, do you love our convent and all the sisters?' And she replied, 'Indeed, my lady, I do.' . . . 'Between us and your betrothed, whom do you love best?' The girl replied: 'I have neither known him nor he me; I have known you and I love you.' . . . 'But no-one can remain here unless she has dedicated herself to Christ.' To which the girl replied: 'Where is Christ?' The deaconess gladly showed her an icon of the Lord, and Eupraxia, turning towards her, said to the deaconess: 'Truly, I also dedicate myself to my Christ, and I will no longer go with my lady mother.'

Eupraxia was seven, sitting on the deaconess's knee.[40] Her lady mother may well have felt that the response of a seven-year-old in such circumstances should not determine her future.

One of the questions put to Basil, to elicit a response included in his *Rule*, was the age at which a religious profession should be accepted. Both the question and the response illuminate fourth-century attitudes to children. Basil replied that, since Jesus had said 'Suffer the little children to come to me, and forbid them not' (the Latin translation uses *infantes*), all times of life were suitable. The profession of virginity would be firm from the beginning of adulthood, that is, the age considered suitable for marriage: by law and convention, this would be twelve, but in a canonical letter Basil preferred sixteen or seventeen. Children should be accepted into the community with the good will of their parents; preferably, the parents would offer the child, with witnesses. Such children would need careful guidance and observa-

[39] Jerome, *Letter* 117.7, *CSEL*, 55, p. 430; see further Clark, *Women*, p. 116.

[40] Jerome, *Letter* 24.2, *CSEL*, 54, p. 215: 'still wrapped in the swaddling-clothes of infancy, and having scarcely completed her tenth year.' *Life of Saint Eupraxia*, cited from Brown, *Body and Society*, pp. 275–6.

tion, and might, when they grew up, prove to be unsuited to the religious life.[41]

IV

Childhood, then, was a relatively short period, perhaps not very much differentiated, in which children were expected to defer to their parents' wishes, and were approved for displaying the qualities they would need in adulthood. Christianity did make a difference here, in that children might be supported in making decisive choices at a young age, even against the wishes of their parents. Admittedly, the choices were of a kind acceptable to at least some influential adults, but it was still a new option. Ambrose tells the story of a girl who rushed forward and seized the altar to declare her commitment to virginity. 'What would your father have said?' demanded her furious guardian. 'Perhaps he died so that I could make this choice', she retaliated. Augustine rebukes parents who resist the wish of their sons or daughters to be servants of God, and reply, 'Even if it costs your salvation, by God, you shall not do what you want but what I want!' The spiritual father could be invoked against the earthly father who wanted obedience and grandchildren.[42]

There were real problems for Christian parents, and for Christian teachers who were usually childless, who wanted to educate children as Christians. Should they prepare a child for world-renouncing ascetic Christianity, or for a more ordinary life as parent and citizen? How could they tell which they ought to do, or how the child would turn out? Not all parents were as single-minded as Melania and Pinianus, prepared to dedicate a baby to virginity. Theodoret was conceived in answer to prayer, a longed-for heir, born after years of infertility, to a mother who had renounced all worldly finery. The holy men who prayed for his conception had told his mother to think of him as Hannah did of Samuel: 'So long as he lives, I have lent him to the Lord.' She took him on regular visits to them. Even so, it was not

[41] Basil, *Rule* 7.1–4, in the translation by Rufinus, *CSEL*, 86, pp. 38–9; Canonical Letter 199.18, *PG* 32, col. 720.

[42] Ambrose, *On Virgins* 1. 65–6, *PL* 16, col. 218; Augustine cited by F. van der Meer, *Augustine the Bishop* (London and New York, 1961), pp. 214–15.

certain that he would renounce his worldly status. 'Daniel used to say "That boy will be a bishop". But old Peter would not agree with him, knowing how much my parents doted on me. Often he used to put me on his knees and feed me grapes and bread.'[43] Theodoret did become a bishop, and so did Gregory Nazianzen, who had been dedicated by his mother before and after his birth, but both might have been monks or local notables instead. Parents were told that they left their children a better inheritance by charitable giving than by heaping up riches, but that did not solve the practical questions: how much pocket-money to give a schoolboy son, what clothes an almost-marriageable daughter should wear. And children who might after all grow up to be part of the social system had to be prepared for their role in it.

All parents were concerned for *paideia*, the formation of the child as an educated and well-mannered member of adult society, who gave the right signals about his or her social class and education by correct use of language and deployment of cultural allusions. 'We buy cakes for them, and give them pocket-money, asking only one thing of them: that they should go to school now.'[44] Basil made a rather cursory attempt to deal with the most obvious problem, that the traditional *paideia* depended on the close study of non-Christian classics.[45] Christian education, in a society only superficially Christian, was another question. Basil acknowledged a debt to his mother and grandmother, who had herself been taught by Gregory Thaumatourgos.[46] Augustine's experience, at a lower social level, was different. His mother was devout but theologically untrained, and he thought that his parents, Christian mother and non-Christian father, were chiefly concerned for him to do well at school. His mother was anxious about fornication, but not to the point of tying him down by an early and undistinguished marriage.[47] He had been made a

[43] Theodoret, *Religious History*, *PG* 82, col. 1380d.

[44] John Chrysostom, *Homily 4 on Colossians*, *PG* 62, col. 329. I owe the reference to this illuminating homily to Pauline Allen and Wendy Mayer, 'Computer and homily: accessing the everyday life of early Christians', *Vigiliae Christianae*, 47 (1993), pp. 260–80: a sample of material from a database which should provide much more information on children.

[45] Basil, *Advice to Young Men: Homily 22*, *PG* 31, cols 564–89.

[46] Basil, *Letter* 223, *PG* 32, col. 825.

[47] Augustine, *Confessions*, 2.3.5–8, pp. 19–21.

catechumen as a baby, and used to be taken to church to receive the sign of the Cross and the offering of salt, but he makes no mention of any teaching or preaching. Catechesis was supplied when the catechumen decided to be baptized, and that was usually in adulthood.[48] But what provision was made for teaching those who were made catechumens, or actually baptized, as infants?

The task seems to have been left to parents. When John Chrysostom turns his attention to Christian education, he does not suggest that the Church will supply some equivalent of Sunday school. In some moods he exhorts parents to send their sons to the monastery for education in a safe environment.[49] But in one sermon he tackles the problem of bringing up a Christian child—a boy—in the city.[50] Girls, he notes in an afterthought, are really the mother's business, but the same principles apply. Christian fathers, he says, should impose basic moral rules: no swearing, no disparagement of others, no unfair treatment of slaves. This can be done in two months, once the ground rules are established. Sons should be protected from bad influences, but this should not be merely negative: hymns should replace unsuitable songs, Bible stories should replace romances. He offers an example, a lively retelling of Cain and Abel, complete with advice on presentation and reinforcement. When the father is sure his son knows the story, he should take the boy to church on a day when it will be read. 'Then you will see the boy jumping with delight, because he knows the story and the others do not.' Other stories are more suitable for a later age, and the threat of hell-fire is not to be used before the boy is fifteen and at risk from desire. The child should not grow used to being beaten: it is better to use the fear rather than the fact of beating, and to assure the boy of his father's pride and affection, and later of the bishop's approval and the congregation's interest. The promise of a lovely bride is to be used as an incentive, so that the

[48] This is the assumption Augustine makes in *On Catechizing the Uninstructed* (*De catechizandis rudibus*: *CChr.SL*, 46, pp. 115–78), advice addressed to a deacon at Carthage: the problem for the catechist is different educational levels, not different ages.

[49] Rousselle, *Porneia*, pp. 134–5, notes the fourth-century evidence that boys in monasteries might be at risk of sexual abuse.

[50] John Chrysostom, *On Vainglory and the right way for parents to bring up their children*, tr. in M. L. W. Laistner, *Christianity and Pagan Culture in the later Roman Empire* (Ithaca, 1951).

boy will wish to be worthy of her. John Chrysostom, himself childless, seems very much aware of what might actually work with children at different ages. The childless Jerome, writing about the education of Paula's granddaughter, engages in what one can only hope her parents recognized as rhetorical fantasy on the theme of the pure and sheltered virgin—though even he sees the need for praise and reward.[51] It is noticeable that children are not expected to be inspired by the thought of the child Jesus (nor their parents by fantasies about the home life of the Holy Family). When the Christ-child is represented in Late Antique art, it is usually as a small-scale adult sitting upright on Mary's knee: the message is concerned with the Incarnation, not with childhood. The stories of Jesus' own childhood which circulated in the apocryphal 'infancy gospels' were concerned with the power of this exceptional child and certainly not intended as models for other children.[52]

The main concern of both Jerome and John Chrysostom is to protect the growing child from corrupting influences while he, or she, acquires the necessary education. Here again Christianity may have made a difference, for the distinctive quality of children, in the inherited Graeco-Roman culture, was not innocence, but unreason. In both Christian and non-Christian texts, irrationality is something to be outgrown. Small children know no better than to be frightened of masks and bogeymen (or, more often, bogeywomen) and shapeless lumps of wool. Nurses tell them silly stories, which they believe, but grown-ups must dismiss. The characteristic tone of such stories appears in the unexpected setting of a martyr text. A Donatist family has been arrested, and the proconsul would prefer to release its youngest member, the child Hilarianus. This child, like Prudentius' infant martyr, has some characteristics of the very young, and some of the older child who does declamation at school:

> When he was asked, 'Did you follow your father or your brothers?', suddenly a youthful voice was heard from the

[51] Jerome, *Letter* 107, *CSEL* 55, pp. 290–305: for a more sympathetic account of this letter, see Joan Petersen, 'The Education of Girls in Fourth-century Rome', pp. 29–37, below, and Graham Gould, 'Childhood in Eastern Patristic Thought', pp. 39–52, below.

[52] The Christ-child in art: see further Currie, 'Childhood', pp. 206–22. The apocryphal gospels: E. Hennecke, W. Schneemelcher, and R. McL. Wilson, eds, *New Testament Apocrypha*, 2 vols (London, 1963), 1, pp. 392–401.

> small body, and the boy's narrow chest was fully opened to confess the Lord as he replied, 'I am a Christian, and of my own free will I assembled with my father and my brothers'. It was the voice of his father Saturninus coming through the child's sweet lips, and following it a tongue confessing Christ the Lord as in his brother's example. The fool of a proconsul did not realize that in the martyrs he was fighting not people, but God, and did not recognize the giant spirit in the childish years. He thought he could frighten the boy with the terrors of infancy. 'Well then', he said, 'I'll cut off your hair and your nose and your ears and that's how I'll send you away.'[53]

Children also show unreason in that they quarrel over trivial things and mind about games; they cannot control fits of anger or greed.

> There is irrationality—great irrationality—and great lack of reasoning at that age, so it is not surprising that a small child is dominated by anger. Often, if they bump into something or fall, they will hit their knee in rage, or kick over a stool, and in that way their pain is relieved and their anger subsides.[54]

Like other irrational creatures, children had to be controlled and coerced by beating. Even a freeborn child was subject to the same punishment as a slave. (The same word, Greek *pais* and Latin *puer*, could be used for both child and slave, but the point is the slave's subordination, not the child's.) Beating was the feature of schooling most strongly remembered by adults: in the poems of Ausonius and Prudentius it becomes almost a shorthand expression for schooldays.[55] Usually it was trivialized by adults. Philosophers used the comparison with childish fears of masks and bogeys and beatings to make adults ashamed of their own anxieties: when the adults developed their reason further, they would see that worries about illness or death or powerful enemies were equally irrational. But Augustine remembered, and took seriously, the child's perspective on beatings at school.

[53] *Acts of the Abitinian Martyrs* (Donatist version), *PL* 8, col. 699.

[54] John Chrysostom, *Homily 4 on Colossians*, *PG* 62, col. 329. On passions in children, see further Gould, 'Childhood'.

[55] Ausonius, *Letter* 22, ed. S. Prete (Leipzig, 1978); Prudentius, *Preface* 7–9, *CChr. SL*, 126, p. 1.

In the *Confessions*, he inverts the philosophic comparison: a child's fear of beating is analogous to an adult's fear of torture, and the parents' dismissal of such fears is as incomprehensible as indifference to the torture of a loved one. Augustine declines to see childhood as a pre-adult phase of life, its terrors merely irrational and its wrongdoing to be taken lightly as something the child will grow out of when the power of reason develops.[56]

Christian teaching might be expected to challenge the image of the child as irrational pre-adult in need of coercion and instruction, since Jesus had made children an example for his followers: 'Suffer the little children to come unto me, and forbid them not, for of such is the kingdom of heaven' (Matt. 19.14). But in what respect were children exemplary? Interpretation of this text drew on the prevailing discourse of childhood. John Chrysostom explains it as follows (as often, his preaching style is not entirely clear):

> Why did the disciples scare off the children? Because of status (*axiôma*). So what did he do? Teaching them [the disciples] to be moderate, and to trample worldly conceit, he takes them [the children] and puts his arms round them and promises the kingdom to such as these (he said this before). So we, if we want to be heirs of heaven, shall try to acquire this virtue with great diligence. For this is the height of virtue, to be sincere with understanding. This is the angelic life. For the soul of a little child is pure from all the passions. He does not bear a grudge against those who have hurt him, but he approaches them as friends, as if nothing had happened. However much his mother whips him, he looks for her and values her above all others. If you showed him a queen with her diadem, would he not prefer his mother, dressed in rags, and choose to see her in those rather than the queen in her finery? He knows how to distinguish what is his and what is alien to him not by wealth and poverty, but by love. He does not want more than he needs, but only to take his fill from the breast, and then let go of the nipple. The little child is not distressed by the same things as we are—a fine in money, things like that—or made happy by the same

[56] Augustine, *Confessions* 1.9.14–15, 1.7.11, pp. 8–9, 6.

> transient things as we are, and he is not excited by the beauty of bodies. That is why he said 'For of such is the kingdom of heaven', so that we should achieve by choice what children have by nature.[57]

Children, then, are an example to adults in that passions do not take root in them, and in that they are uncorrupted by false worldly values. This is not to say, as a general principle, that children are admirable. John Chrysostom is thinking of little children, those in the category of the *nêpios* or *infans*, and ranges from babes in arms to toddlers. More important, the child is not an example of the angelic life, for that requires understanding, not just single-mindedness and freedom from distraction by desires. The unreasoning child is innocent; the adult must use reason to recover innocence. But how long does the innocence of childhood last? Augustine remembered his childhood and watched babies. He refused to say that even the youngest child was free from *concupiscentia*, the basic human drive to dominate and possess. A tiny baby may want no more than the milk he needs, which, by God's providence, his mother and nurses need to give him: there is a perfect match between his wishes and theirs, but not for long. A baby screams, wanting his mother and nurses to do what he wants; a baby watching another being fed is pale with jealousy. It seems an unduly harsh assessment. The baby cannot know that it would not be good for him to be fed whenever he wants, or that there will be plenty of milk for him when the other baby has finished. He will learn to behave better. But Augustine wants to know why he should be like that in the first place, if young children are innocent. He regards children as innocent only in the etymological sense: a child is *in/nocens*, harmless in that he is unable to harm, not in that he has no harmful desires.[58] A child can sin:

> We are not dealing here with rather bigger children, to whom some people are unwilling to ascribe sin in the strict sense until the beginning of the fourteenth year, when they reach puberty. We would be right to believe this, if there

[57] John Chrysostom, *Homily on Matthew* 62.4, *PG* 58, cols 600–1. 'He said this before' presumably refers to Matt. 18.1–5.

[58] Augustine, *Confessions* 1.6.8, 1.7.11, pp. 4, 6.

> were no sins except those committed by the genitals. But who would dare to affirm that theft, lies and perjury are not sins, except someone who wants to commit them with impunity? Yet childhood is full of these, even though it does not seem advisable to punish them in children just as in adults, because the hope is that as the years are added in which reason grows stronger, they will be better able to understand salutary rules and to obey them more willingly.[59]

Theft, lies and perjury—cheating—are Augustine's dominant memories of himself as *puer*.

> Is *that* the innocence of childhood? It is not, Lord; it is not, I pray you, my God. This is what continues as age advances, from tutors and schoolteachers, nuts and balls and pet birds, to prefects and kings, gold and land and slaves, just as greater penalties succeed to the cane. So, our king, it was an image of humility which you approved in the stature of childhood, when you said, 'Of such is the kingdom of heaven'.[60]

Is childhood an exemplar of innocence, or a reminder of low status in relation to God? It depends what you expect to see in childhood, and especially in babies, as a basic truth about human nature. The 'cradle argument', which is still going strong, suggests that children too young to be socialized reveal what human nature is really like. In his debate with Julian of Eclanum, Augustine quoted Cicero:

> Cicero says that a human being is brought into life by nature, not as by a mother but as by a stepmother, with a body naked, fragile and weak, a soul distressed by troubles, abject before fears, feeble before work, liable to lusts, in whom nevertheless, as if buried, there is a divine spark of intelligence and mind.[61]

Cicero, he said, did not understand why, because he had not read Scripture and did not know about original sin.

John Chrysostom envisaged humans born with a natural immunity to destructive passions. The immunity is depleted as the

[59] Augustine, *Literal Interpretation of Genesis* 10.13.23, *CSEL*, 54, p. 557.
[60] Augustine, *Confessions* 1.19.30, p. 17.
[61] Hennecke, Schneemelcher, and Wilson, *New Testament Apocrypha*, 1, pp. 392–401.

child grows, but may be re-established. Augustine envisaged humans born infected with sexually transmitted sin. Both theories told adults how to think about themselves. But did they have an effect on children? There might be implications for the upbringing of children, if parents were able to control what their children were taught, and how they were disciplined, both at home and at school; but social, as well as theological, factors would have to be taken into account. Augustine's own experience of childhood was different from John Chrysostom's, and almost certainly more authoritarian. Their mothers were different in character: John Chrysostom's mother was widowed early, whereas Augustine's father survived into his son's adolescence. School at Antioch was not like school at Madauros. We do not know how children saw themselves or how they experienced childhood. Children's voices reach us, even in Augustine's memories, only as selected and transmitted by adults.

V

In one respect, Christianity did revalue childhood, by revaluing adulthood in relation to childhood. Adults, in Graeco-Roman tradition, had been distinguished from children by their superior reason and self-control, and their affirmation of power over themselves and their lives. Philosophers taught that reason is the aspect of human beings which is closest to God, and that the exercise of reason is the route to eventual oneness with God: *nêpiotês*, being like a *nêpios* or very young child, meant just 'silliness'. But in Christian imagery adults could be urged to identify themselves as newborn babes, naked in the rebirth of baptism, wrapped in pure robes, fed on the milk of basic instruction because they were not yet ready for solid food. Thus 'our dear Nepotianus, like a crying baby, a child untrained, was all at once born to us from the Jordan'; and Arsenius, who had been tutor to the sons of an emperor, could say that he had not yet learned the ABC of an illiterate peasant who was his spiritual superior.[62]

[62] Nepotianus: Jerome, *Letter* 60.8.2, *CSEL*, 54, p. 557; see further J. H. Scourfield, *Consoling Heliodorus* (Oxford, 1993), on this passage. Arsenius: 6, *PG* 65, col. 89. On Christians as infants, see further Clement of Alexandria, *Paedagogus* 1.5–6, *PG* 8, cols 261–312.

This imagery of helpless ignorance and dependence contributed to the priest's, or bishop's, fatherly control of the adult flock he nurtured. Parenting was revalued, or rather devalued: childlessness was no longer a human tragedy but a superior choice. The spiritual childbearing of the virgin or celibate, male or female, who bore spiritual fruit or nurtured converts, was exalted above the physical childbearing and breast-feeding of a woman who would have preferred not to marry or who had succumbed to physical desire. Ambrose, wrote Paulinus of Nola to Augustine, is my father in that he raised me up.[63] Begetting and bearing children was held to be enmeshed in desire and carnality and the transmission of sin, whether genetic or environmental; attempting to provide for your children showed worldly concerns; parental authority must give way before the choice of virginity. But if adults were urged to see themselves differently, how much had changed for children?

Christianity made a difference to children's lives in much the same way as it made a difference to women's lives. For some, it offered possibilities which were unimaginable in a pre-Christian world. It offered a radically new option, that of dedicating a life to God and of living it in a single-sex community. It supported children who chose that option despite resistance from their families, and could thus give children an escape-route from indebtedness to their parents and obedience to family purposes. It argued that the weakness and fear characteristic of childhood could be overcome by commitment to God. So children might find at least some of their choices taken seriously; and behaviour which would otherwise have been interpreted as frankly naughty might be acknowledged as prophetic. Children might even dream, like Radegund, of dying as martyrs, or of being acknowledged as the spiritual equals of adults.[64] Desperate parents, too, had a new option. Oblation was not just a continuation of abandonment, since the child was entering a structured and purposeful way of life, in which at least a minimum of care would be provided, and at best love and education. Christianity

[63] Paulinus, *Letter* 3.4, *CSEL*, 29, p. 16. The appropriation of childbearing goes back to Plato; on the appropriation of nursing imagery, see Gail Corrington, 'The milk of salvation: redemption by the mother in late antiquity and early Christianity', *Harvard Theological Review*, 82 (1989), pp. 406–13.

[64] Venantius Fortunatus, *Life of Radegund* 2: conveniently translated in JoAnn McNamara, ed., *Sainted Women of the Dark Ages* (Durham, North Carolina, 1992), p. 71.

could also function as a new kind of constraint. Children might be made to feel themselves corrupt and sinful, or they could be forced to enter a religious lifestyle for which they were not suited, and in which they might suffer cruelty disguised as chastisement, or sexual abuse. But the child who fought his or her way to the monastery, and the child victim of religiously inspired neglect, are extreme cases. In the kingdom of God there may be neither child nor adult—though St Paul did not say so—just as there is neither slave nor free, male nor female. In the later Roman Empire, the three basic household hierarchies remained in place. Schools continued to teach the traditional culture; some families put church on Sunday and attendance at martyr feasts in place of the traditional sacrifices and festivals. For most children, life was not very different.

University of Liverpool

THE EDUCATION OF GIRLS IN FOURTH-CENTURY ROME

by THE LATE JOAN M. PETERSEN

THERE is little direct evidence about the education of girls in classical times and Late Antiquity. Our conception of what provision was available has to be based chiefly on an examination of the material relating to the education of adult women and to the early training of little girls of four or five years of age. For the second half of the fourth century we are fortunate in possessing the testimony of three Christian writers on the subject of the education of mature women: Palladius, Gerontius of Jerusalem, and Jerome. Nevertheless, we need to be aware of their limitations. All three writers deal with women of a narrow social class, members of the wealthy Roman aristocracy, who were attempting to live a disciplined and austere monastic life, the majority of them against the incongruous background of their family mansions on the Aventine Hill, which was then a fashionable residential district. They were perhaps in the tradition of those earlier learned and cultivated aristocratic Roman ladies, recalled by Cicero,[1] and exemplified by the daughter of his friend Atticus, who provided her with a tutor even after her marriage, and by Hortensia, the daughter of the orator Hortensius, who was trained by her father in public speaking, and who even made a speech in the Forum against a tax assessment.[2] For information about the early training of little girls in fourth-century Rome we are indebted to the letters of Jerome, but this evidence, as we shall see, has certain limitations.

Two difficulties confront us when we examine the evidence provided by our three Christian writers: in the first place, none of them describes the educational process by which these ladies achieved so high a degree of cultivation and learning; secondly, the advice which Jerome gives about the training and education of little girls is intended for child oblates, consecrated to God

[1] M. Tullius Cicero, *Brutus*, ed. and tr. G. L. Hendrickson, *LCL* (1939), 210–12, pp. 178–81.
[2] Quintilian, *Institutio oratoria*, ed. and tr. H. E. Butler, *LCL* (1921), bk i, ch. 1, pp. 22–3.

even before their birth, and is, in any case, suspect, because much of it has been culled from an earlier writer.

Melania the Elder was a contemporary of Jerome, for she was born about 342, but predeceased him, as she died in 410. She and her granddaughter, Melania the Younger, were women of immense wealth, comparable in modern times to the great American heiresses of the earlier years of this century. Palladius portrays her as a woman of strong character and considerable administrative ability, who founded a monastery in Jerusalem, where she lived for twenty-seven years. As evidence of her intellectual prowess he tells us that she was a very learned lady, who studied far into the night and went carefully through the works of all the ancient commentators. She read 'millions' of lines of Origen, Gregory, Stephen, Pierios, Basil, and other very erudite authors. Melania was no desultory reader, but a scholar who went laboriously through each book seven or eight times, so as to gain a mastery of its subject.[3] Her aim was not self-aggrandizement or even self-improvement, but the achievement of union with Christ by means of her studies. 'She made herself into a bird of the spirit and was able to soar away on her journey to Christ.'[4] Besides having a good command of Greek, she had obviously received a good scholarly training to enable her to study in so disciplined a manner, but how, when, or where she acquired it, we do not know.

Her granddaughter, Melania the Younger, was married at fourteen years of age, in accordance with the normal fourth-century practice, but in view of her attainments, she must have received tuition after her marriage. A devoted student of the Bible, she first read through the Old Testament and then the New Testament three or four times a year, making extracts of what was sufficient for her own needs, and providing her fellow Christians with copies which she had written out herself.[5] According to Gerontius, she wrote, without mistakes, 'in little notebooks'; her reading matter was not only the Scriptures but also homilies and the lives of the Fathers.[6] If she read aloud in

[3] Palladius, *Historia Lausiaca*, 55.3, ed. W. J. M. Bartelink, *Vite dei sa santi*, 2 (Milan, 1974), pp. 252–3.
[4] Ibid.
[5] Gerontius, [*Vita S. Melaniae Iunioris*] *Vie de sainte Mélanie*, ed. D. Gorce, *SC*, 90 (1962), pp. 198–9.
[6] Possibly an early example of a topos; Radegund had a similar predilection for holy men; see Venantius Fortunatus, *Vita*, 8, *MGH. SRM*, 2, p. 367.

Greek, it sounded like her native language; if she read in Latin, it seemed as though she knew no Greek.[7] She enjoyed the society of 'saintly and distinguished bishops', particularly those who were famous for their learning, so that she might make good use of her time with them in questioning them about divine sayings.[8] She also found pleasure in meeting some of the Desert Fathers, but this seems to have been derived from receiving their spiritual counsel rather than the fruits of their learning.[9]

In the world of Late Antiquity—and indeed for centuries afterwards—it was considered a great compliment to tell a woman that in character and intellect she resembled a man. Palladius classes both Melania the Elder and Melania the Younger among 'certain women with masculine qualities, to whom God granted the grace to carry on struggles equal to those undertaken by men'.[10] Gerontius, too, classes Melania the Younger in this same category of honorary males: 'It can truthfully be said that she was a woman of more than average feminine ability and that she had acquired a masculine, or rather, a heavenly cast of thought.'[11]

Of the various ladies in the circle surrounding Jerome, those of most interest from our point of view are Marcella, Paula the Elder, and her daughters, particularly Eustochium. Marcella and Paula the Elder were widows and the others spinsters. Marcella was the leader of a group of feminine ascetics, living the religious life on a domestic basis in Rome. According to Jerome, she learned of the religious life from the great Athanasius himself, when he was in exile in Rome between 340 and 346.[12] As she was then only a child of about twelve years old, this has sometimes been questioned, but it is quite likely that at this impressionable age she may have heard Athanasius preach or even have

[7] Gerontius, *Vita*, 23v, pp. 174–5.

[8] Ibid., 26, pp. 180–1.

[9] Ibid., 39, pp. 200–1.

[10] Palladius, *Historia*, 41.1, pp. 210–11.

[11] Gerontius, *Vita*, 40, pp. 176–7.

[12] The first exile of Athanasius was at Trier, 335–7 (*contra Arianos* 87, *PG* 23, col. 408) and the second, at Rome, 340–6 (*de synodis*, 26, *PG* 26, col. 72). See also Socrates, *Historia ecclesiastica*, 4.23, *PG* 67, col. 520; Jerome, *Ep.* 127.5, *CSEL*, 56, p. 149. For a discussion on the origins of feminine monasticism in Rome see P. Schmitz, 'La première communauté des vierges à Rome', *RBen*, 38 (1926), pp. 189–95; G. D. Gordini, 'Origine e sviluppo del monachesimo a Roma', *Gregorianum*, 37 (1956), pp. 220–60; R. Lorenz, 'Die Anfänge des abendländischen Mônchtums im 4. Jahrhundert', *Zeitschrift für Kirchengeschichte*, 77 (1966), pp. 12–18.

met him.[13] These women, in their own homes on the Aventine, practised rigorous fasting, wore coarse and squalid clothing, and renounced baths (except when ill) and hairdressing. Above all, they shunned sex. It was represented to young girls growing up in their circles that virginity was the highest form of virtue. Marriage was tolerated because it was the sole means of replenishing the supply of virgins.[14]

Originally Paula had been a member of Marcella's group, but by the time of her first meeting with Jerome she was the centre of an independent circle of ascetics, which included her daughters, Blesilla, Paulina, Eustochium, and Rufina. Blesilla and Paulina both married, but Blesilla's husband soon died. She then underwent a conversion experience, which led her to forsake the smart set of Rome for life in the maternal monastery. Paulina predeceased her husband, Pammachius, a man who was both wealthy and religious, although he was many years her senior. Eustochium was the daughter dearest to Jerome, because she chose a life of virginity of her own accord.

Both Marcella and Paula were keen students of the Bible, but their approach was very different. Marcella was clearly an able woman with a down-to-earth outlook. She demanded and obtained from Jerome lengthy explanations of Hebrew and other words that baffled her. He went to great lengths to satisfy her searching mind. In letter 25, for example, he expounds the ten names of God given by the Jews.[15] In other letters he explains the meanings of *alleluia*, *amen*, *maranatha*, and *selah* and *amen* in the Psalms.[16] He also explains what an *ephod* and *teraphim* were.[17] Marcella also had an interest in theology: in letters 41 and 42 he tries to arm her with arguments against the teachings of the Montanists and Novatianists.[18] Before long he found himself conducting a course of Bible study for a group of enthusiastic women students and giving some of them, at any rate, Hebrew lessons.

[13] See Jerome, *Ep.* 127.5, *CSEL*, 56, p. 149.
[14] Jerome, *Ep.* 22.20, *CSEL*, 54, p. 170.
[15] For the ten Hebrew names of God, see Jerome, *Ep.* 25, *CSEL*, 54 pp. 218–20.
[16] For *alleluia, amen* and *maranatha*, see *Ep.* 26, *CSEL*, 54, p. 221; for *amen* and *selah* in the Psalms, see *Ep.* 28, *CSEL*, 54, p. 229 (cf. ibid., pp. 232–42).
[17] For *ephod* and *teraphim*, see *Ep.* 29, *CSEL*, 54, pp. 232–42.
[18] Jerome, *Epp.* 41, 42, *CSEL*, 54, pp. 311–21.

Paula was a student of a different type from Marcella. Though not lacking in intellectual ability, she was of a more romantic disposition. She preferred a more allegorical style of biblical exegesis, of the type practised by the School of Alexandria. This must have been particularly congenial to Jerome, since he was at this time engaged in the study of the works of Origen. Like Marcella, Paula headed a Bible-study group, which Jerome called her *domestica ecclesia.*[19] She practised an ardent, Christocentric devotion. Ultimately she knew much of the Bible by heart and set herself to learn Hebrew, so that she might understand it better. Indeed, she became proficient at chanting the Psalms in that language. Jerome's translation of Origen's homilies on St Luke's Gospel was made, he tells us, at the urgent request of Paula and Eustochium.[20] At their request, too, he followed it with commentaries on Ecclesiastes, Philemon, Ephesians, and Titus. His commentary on Galatians was compiled at the request of Marcella. How much Greek these ascetics knew we cannot judge. Their motives for study were primarily religious, to deepen their own spiritual lives by a better understanding of the Bible, which they believed could best be achieved by reading it in the original languages.

We now need to examine how far Jerome's advice on the training and education of little girls was likely to set them on the road to achieve the high state of intellectual and spiritual development achieved by the two Melanias and by the ladies on the Aventine Hill. Much of this advice in contained in letters 107 and 128,[21] addressed to Laeta, the wife of Paula's son, Toxotius, and mother of Paula the Younger, and to Gaudentius, the father of Pacatula, respectively. These letters, as we have already seen, have certain limitations as sources.

Passages in letter 107 and letter 128, which may probably be assigned to 400 and 412 respectively, are sometimes cited as evidence for the existence of a more gentle side to Jerome's character, which is a contrast to that of the author of the stern regime laid down for older virgins, such as Eustochium and Demetrias. Play for children like Paula and Pacatula must be

[19] Jerome, *Ep.* 30, *CSEL*, 54, p. 238.
[20] For the homilies, see *GCS*, 49, 1.
[21] Jerome *Ep.* 107 (to Laeta), *CSEL*, 55, pp. 290–305; *Ep.* 128 (to Gaudentius), *CSEL*, 56, pp. 156–62.

educational. Little Paula is to be given a set of ivory or box-wood letters from which to be taught the alphabet. This is to be learned by both little girls, but Paula's educational programme is to be set out in more detail. She is to learn the names of the letters and the importance of alphabetical order. Rhymes may be used to aid her memory, and the letters should be jumbled up, so that she may learn to sort them out correctly. She is to learn to write through an adult guiding her hand in forming the letters on a wax tablet. Alternatively, she should be supplied with a wax tablet with the shapes of the letters cut in it. Small prizes are to be given for good spelling.[22] Gaudentius is even given hints as to suitable rewards for Pacatula's efforts: cakes, a sweet and sticky drink of honey mixed with water, sweets, a little bunch of flowers, a glittering trinket, or an enchanting doll. Everything possible must be done to make study attractive; a distaste for it, once acquired, is difficult to eradicate. The child must learn to love what she is obliged to recite, for example, the Psalms.

Unfortunately these charming pictures of young children growing up are evidence not for Jerome's enlightened views on their upbringing and education, but for his knowledge of the writings of Quintilian. Most of what he says in these two letters about their early training can be found in the first books of the *Institutio*.[23]

Jerome's contribution, as distinct from Quintilian's, is more consistent with what we know of his character from other sources and shows little understanding of children. Since Paula was consecrated to God before birth, her relationship with her mother must be comparable to that of Samuel to Hannah or of John the Baptist with Elizabeth.[24] She must be brought up differently from other children. She may certainly be fondled by her maternal grandmother, but she must be trained to think often about her paternal grandmother, Paula, and her aunt Eustochium, far away in Palestine, and should be encouraged to long to join them.[25] Not for her are pierced ears and ear-rings,

[22] Ibid.; cf. Quintilian, *Institutio*, bk i; ch. 1, 26–7; 20, pp. 32–5, 28–31.
[23] Jerome *Ep*. 128.1, *CSEL*, 56, p. 157; see n. 22, above.
[24] Jerome *Ep*. 107.3, *CSEL*, 55, pp. 292–3.
[25] Jerome, *Ep*. 107.13, *CSEL*, 55, p. 304.

cosmetics, tinted hair, high heels, silk dresses, gold chains, pearl necklaces, and other jewellery.[26] The child oblate, Jerome advises Gaudentius, is to be deprived of her linen garments and wrapped in a dark cloak. This is preferable to the practice of allowing her to dress like other people and hoping that she will be so sickened by an excessive shower of personal possessions that she will reject them.[27] The advice about personal adornment seems a little premature for girls of four or five years old. It seems as though Jerome used his letters often as vehicles for his own thoughts and opinions, without always paying attention to the needs of the recipient.

Jerome has some advice to offer on the choice of nurses and teachers for the very young. Nurses are evidently a great source of harm, if not carefully chosen. They may be addicted to strong drink and gossip and to speaking incorrectly, and even if of good character, they must be kept from mingling with worldly persons, whose habits may infect them and, through them, their charges.[28] Paula is to have a male tutor of approved years, life, and learning. A really cultured man will not be ashamed of teaching the rudiments of knowledge to a kinswoman or a virgin of good birth; Aristotle did not think it beneath him to teach Alexander the Great when a child.[29] Paula is also to have some kind of chaperone and spiritual mentor, an aged virgin of approved faith and chastity, who can instruct her by word and example to get up at night to recite prayers and psalms, sing hymns in the morning at the third, sixth, and ninth hours, and to do battle for Christ.[30] One wonders whether he does not see himself and Eustochium in these roles, should Laeta, her mother, agree to exporting the child to Palestine, as he hopes. Pacatula, however, is apparently to have a full-time governess-companion, a lady 'not much given to wine, idleness, and tittle-tattle'.[31] It is likely that Pacatula's governess rather than a distinguished male tutor is the kind of instructor normally provided for the daughters of upper-class families. Here again, in the discussion of the

[26] Jerome, *Ep.* 107.5, *CSEL*, 55, p. 296.
[27] Jerome, *Ep.* 128.2, *CSEL*, 56, p. 137; cf. *Ep.* 24.3, *CSEL*, 54, pp. 215–16.
[28] Jerome, *Ep.* 107.4, *CSEL*, 55, p. 295.
[29] Ibid., p. 294; cf. Quintilian, *Institutio* I. 1. 23.
[30] Jerome, *Ep.* 107.9, *CSEL*, 55, p. 300.
[31] Jerome, *Ep.* 128.4, *CSEL*, 56, pp. 160–1.

choice of attendants to care for children, we find that Jerome is heavily indebted to Quintilian.[32]

Jerome's educational programme for Paula can hardly be described as liberal. Her days are to be spent largely in Bible study. Her treasures are to be not silks and jewels but unadorned manuscripts of the Scriptures. The basis of her Christian life is to be found in the Psalms, which she is to know by heart, and in those books of the Bible which were then believed to have been written by Solomon. She is to derive a rule of life from Proverbs, to learn to despise the world from Ecclesiastes, and to follow the examples of patience and virtue supplied by Job. After this, she may enrich her mind by studying the Gospels and Acts. Not before she has learned by heart the Prophets, the Heptateuch, the Books of Kings, Chronicles, Ezra, and Esther is she to read the Song of Songs. The apocryphal writings are to be avoided, but she may take pleasure in the works of Cyprian, Athanasius, and Hilary.[33]

The only provision for manual work is spinning, which may be begun at an early age, and sewing. Paula is apparently to make her own clothes from non-luxurious materials, simply to keep her body warm and to cover it decently.[34] Opportunities for fresh air and exercise appear to be confined to occasional visits to churches and shrines, always accompanied by her mother.[35] Her confined, indoor life will lead to a loss of looks, but this is regarded as desirable.[36]

This severe programme of education must surely represent an ideal rather than a practical syllabus. There was a general feeling that the traditional secular curriculum of the Greek and Latin classics was not suitable for Christian girls. Gregory of Nyssa in his life of his sister, St Macrina, describes the education which he would like her to have had, but judging by his *de anima et resurrectione*, which takes the form of a dialogue between Gregory and Macrina, it was not the education which she in fact received.[37] In the same way, Jerome devises an elaborate scheme of

[32] See above, n. 22.

[33] Paula's programme: Jerome, *Ep.* 107.12, *CSEL*, 55, pp. 302–3. Pacatula's programme: *Ep.* 128.4, *CSEL*, 56, p. 160.

[34] Pacatula: *Ep.* 128, *CSEL*, 56, p. 107; Paula: *Ep.* 107.10, *CSEL*, 55, pp. 301–2.

[35] Ibid., 11, *CSEL*, 55, p. 302.

[36] Jerome thought a pale, sickly appearance desirable for a virgin, e.g., *Ep.* 22.17, *CSEL*, 54, p. 164.

[37] Gregory of Nyssa, [*Vita sanctae Macrinae*] *Vie de sainte Macrine* 3, ed. P. Maraval, *SC*, 178 (1971), pp. 148–51; cf. *de anima et resurrectione, PG* 46, col. 21.

Bible study for Paula the Younger, though one suspects that such Roman ladies as managed to acquire a good education were brought up on the traditional curriculum, first with their little brothers at home at the elementary stage, and then, if they were fortunate, with a master who had himself been trained in it hired by their parents. The rhetorical studies, which corresponded to a university course today, were completely closed to women, since they prepared students for careers as lawyers or civil servants, for which they were ineligible.

By the end of the fourth century the Church had settled down to a period of respectability and conformity with worldly standards. It was this kind of spiritual and intellectual climate which lay behind the development of monasticism. It was the Church, paradoxically, in the person of Jerome, which caused a gentle wind of change to blow where women's education was concerned. Gradually it became acceptable for some women, at any rate, to spend their time in prayer and study instead of pursuing an empty round of social duties. Advanced Bible study, under Jerome or some other priest, could supply them with a form of tertiary education for which some of them were obviously well fitted.

London

CHILDHOOD IN EASTERN PATRISTIC THOUGHT: SOME PROBLEMS OF THEOLOGY AND THEOLOGICAL ANTHROPOLOGY

by GRAHAM GOULD

THE writings of the Early Church concerning childhood are not extensive, but in the works of a number of Eastern Christian authors of the second to fourth centuries it is possible to discern some ideas about childhood which raise important problems of Christian theology and theological anthropology. The theological problem is that of the question posed for theodicy by the sufferings and deaths of infants. It is harder to give a brief definition of the anthropological problem, but it is important to do so because to define the problem as the Eastern Fathers saw it is also to identify the set of conceptual tools—the anthropological paradigm—which they used to answer it. These are not, naturally, the concepts of modern anthropology and psychology. Applied to patristic thought, these terms usually refer to speculations about the composition and functioning of the human person or the human soul which belong to a discourse which is recognizably philosophical and metaphysical—by which is meant that it is (though influenced by other sources, such as the Bible) the discourse of a tradition descending ultimately from the anthropological terminology of Plato, Aristotle, and the Stoics. Patristic anthropology seeks to account for the history and experiences of the human person as a created being—the experience of sin and mortality in the present life, but also of eternal salvation and advancement to perfection in the image of God.

In patristic terms, the anthropological problem of childhood is that of defining the condition of childhood in terms of three interrelated factors: firstly, the development of a child's soul in terms of its possession, or lack, of faculties such as reason and desire (ἐπιθυμία) which are among the components of the human soul as they were commonly understood; secondly, the extent to which a child's soul is open to the same temptations, desires, or passions as that of an adult; thirdly, the extent to which children are capable of understanding religious ideas and precepts or may be held to deserve reward or punishment for their actions.

The materials for an answer to these questions are to be found in several different types of patristic writing. Firstly, there are comments on the biblical metaphor of childhood as a description of the Christian life, especially in Matthew 18.1–5 and 19.14. In explaining what these metaphors convey, patristic authors reveal something about their understanding of what it is that is distinctive, in moral or religious terms, about the condition of childhood as opposed to maturity. Secondly, there are treatises on the education of children. These contain ideas about the differences (in their use of reason and other faculties) between children and adults. Finally, there are writings which are relevant to the first, theological problem of childhood—the problem posed by infant suffering for belief in divine providence and justice.

The late second-century author Clement of Alexandria was probably the first Eastern patristic author to discuss the implications of the biblical metaphor of childhood. His view is summarized in a comment on the terms which Jesus uses to refer to his disciples:

> And that he calls us chickens Scripture testifies: 'As a hen gathers her chickens under her wings'. Thus we are the Lord's chickens, the Word thus marvellously and mystically describing the simplicity of childhood (ἁπλότητα τῆς ψυχῆς εἰς ἡλικίαν παιδικήν). For sometimes he calls us children (παῖδας), sometimes chickens, sometimes infants (νηπίους), and at other times sons, and 'a new people', and 'a recent people'. 'And my servants shall be called by a new name'; a new name, he says, fresh and eternal, pure and simple, and childlike and true, which shall be blessed on earth.[1]

Childhood, the beginning of biological life, is thus a symbol, applied to Christians, of the beginning of a new religious life of discipleship in a condition of childlike (παιδικός) simplicity, freshness, and purity. These are aspirations which Clement's

[1] *Paedagogos*, i, 5, ed. O. Stählin, *GCS*, 12, 3rd edn (Berlin, 1972), p. 98; tr. in *The Ante-Nicene Fathers* [hereafter *ANF*], 2, p. 212b (altered); Matt. 23.37; Isa. 65.15–16.

gnostic opponents (perhaps drawing on one of the more negative biblical images of childhood in I Corinthians 13.11) cite as evidence of the childish (παιδαριῶδες) and contemptible character of ordinary Christian teaching.[2] But for Clement they are the conditions of a new freedom of approach to God. The childhood of Christians is a condition of liberation from the sins of unconverted adult life:

> We, then, who are infants, no longer roll on the ground, nor creep on the earth like serpents as before, crawling with the whole body about senseless lusts (ἀνοήτους ἐπιθυμίας); but, stretching upwards in soul, loosed from the world and our sins . . . we pursue holy wisdom, although this seems folly to those whose wits are sharpened for wickedness. Rightly, then, are those called children who know him who is God alone as their Father, who are simple, and infants, and guileless.[3]

Christ the παιδαγωγός, the tutor or child guide of Christians, is himself called a child (Isaiah 9.6), and for Christians to be children is thus to be formed in Christ's image and guided, as his little ones, by his perfect discipline.[4]

Clement's Alexandrian successor Origen (d. 253/4) adopted a similar position on the freedom of children from irrational desires. But Origen's view is more precisely formulated than Clement's, and seeks to illustrate the absence of the passions (πάθη) in childhood with examples drawn from observation of children's behaviour. Unlike Clement, he is concerned not just with the biblical metaphor of childhood but with the anthropological problem of childhood itself. In his commentary on Matthew 18.2 he writes that a child 'has not tasted sexual pleasures (ἀφροδισίων) and has no conception of the impulses of manhood (ἀνδρικῶν κινημάτων)'.[5] Thus a Christian who becomes like a

[2] Ibid., i, 6, p. 104. Clement's adoption of the term νήπιος is notable in view of its negative use by Paul. For a gnostic exegesis of the Pauline text see Elaine Pagels, *The Gnostic Paul: Gnostic Exegesis of the Pauline Letters* (Philadelphia, 1975), p. 80.

[3] Ibid., i, 5, pp. 99–100; tr. in *ANF*, 2, p. 213a–b (altered).

[4] Ibid., p. 104.

[5] *Commentary on Matthew*, xiii, 16, ed. E. Klostermann, *GCS*, 40 (1935), pp. 219–22; translated in *ANF*, 10, p. 484 (altered). The remaining quotations are from the same chapter and the same page of the translation.

child is one who 'mortifies the lusts of manhood (τὰ ἀνδρικὰς ἐπιθυμίας), putting to death by the spirit the deeds of the body.'

What is true of children's freedom from the temptations or desires associated with adult sexuality is true also of 'the rest of the passions and infirmities and sicknesses of the soul, into which it is not the nature of children to fall, who have not yet fully attained to the possession of reason.' These passions of the soul (as opposed to the body) include anger, grief, fear, and the pride and conceit and distinctions of worth which adults display, or make between people, on grounds of birth, wealth, 'or any of those things which are thought to be good, but are not.' The fear which young children experience, for example, is not the same thing which adults know when they are frightened of something or someone wicked, but a different kind of experience to which the name of fear has conventionally been given; for, 'In the case of children there is a forgetfulness of their evils at the very time of their tears, for they change in a moment, and laugh and play along with those who were thought to grieve and terrify them.'

The assertion that children 'have not yet fully attained to the possession of reason (μηδέπω συμπεπληρωκότα τόν λόγον)' occurs twice in the course of Origen's comments. Both the passions and the rational power of deliberation and choice to resist them are thus seen as developing concomitantly in children with increasing age. This does not mean that Origen commits himself to the view that reason is wholly absent in a child: to do so would create problems for his belief that the rational mind (νοῦς) is the ontological core of the human person which pre-exists its entry into the body.[6] The sense of the verb πληρῶν must be the complete development, or complete manifestation, of something

[6] Though Origen argues in *De principiis*, II, ix, 3–7, ed. P. Koetschau, *GCS*, 22 (1913), pp. 166–71, that the degree to which human souls sinned before they entered the body accounts for the apparently arbitrary diversity of their sufferings and opportunities in the present life, he never, so far as I have been able to discover, suggests that an infant's freedom from the passions may be compromised by the extent of its sinfulness in its previous existence. The nearest approach to such a view appears to be in *Homilies on Leviticus*, viii, 3, ed. W. A. Baehrens, *GCS*, 29 (1920), pp. 396–8, where Origen suggests that the practice of infant baptism proves that even in infants there is something to be forgiven. But here too he appears to be referring to evil contracted in a previous existence and not to any capacity for personal sin in an infant. Elsewhere he states categorically that no sin is imputed to infants, who are not 'under the law' (Rom. 3.19) because they as yet have no power of decision between right and wrong: *Commentary on Romans*, iii, 2 and 6, ed. Caroline P. Hammond Bammel, *Der Römerbriefkommentar des Origenes* (Freiburg im Breisgau, 1990), pp. 208, 223 (also *PG* 14, cols 930C–D, 939A).

previously unexercised or hidden. Origen probably associates the development of reason and the passions in children with the development of speech—the term λόγος is of course appropriate to both. He gives an estimate of the age at which the passions begin to manifest themselves when he observes that distinctions of wealth or birth are not understood by children up to three or four years old. It is at an older age that children begin to be 'affected towards those passions which exalt the senseless (ἀνοήτους)'. These are the irrational passions, whether those associated with the adult body or with the soul itself, which it is necessary for Christians, in the various terms used by Origen and Clement, to strive to transcend or mortify by attaining to a childlike, passionless, condition of soul, according to the biblical metaphor. Even if in children, writes Origen,

> there is anything corresponding to the passions, these are faint, and very quickly suppressed, and healed in the case of children, so that he is worthy of love, who, being converted like children, has reached such a point as to have, as it were, his passions in subjection like children.

Speculations about the extent to which children are subject to the passions, or about their development of the use of reason, seem to be largely absent from later Greek patristic writings.[7] The inclusion of a few relevant comments is one of the things which makes the work of the Antiochene theologian John Chrysostom (d. 407), *On Vainglory and on the Education of Children*[8] perhaps the most interesting representative of the genre of patristic educational treatises. On the other hand, most of this work is about moral principles that are as applicable to adults as to children, and much of its advice makes no specific reference to the condition of childhood. It takes the form of a discussion first of the control of the senses and then of the different virtues and temptations of the soul according to its commonest philosophical analysis into reason (called by Chrysostom τὸ λογιστικόν or ἡ φρόνησις), ἐπιθυμία, and the third element of θυμός—irascibility or impulsiveness.[9] When Chrysostom discusses the condi-

[7] The foremost Christian anthropological writing of the late fourth century, Nemesius of Emesa, *On the Nature of Man*, *PG* 40, cols 508–818, contains no significant discussion of children.

[8] Ed. A.-M. Malingrey, *SC*, 188 (1972).

[9] Ibid., chs 26–63 (the senses); chs 64–87 (the parts of the soul).

tion of childhood, he first notes that the origin of evil habits which are so hard to eradicate later in life lies in the fact that insufficient care is taken by parents and tutors to impress on children the values of virginity, restraint σωφροσύνη, despising wealth and vainglory (this supplies the formal link between the two parts of the treatise), and obedience to Scripture.[10] A child is in a favourable condition for education in these virtues as it is not yet involved in the contest for worldly success and so has no occasion for arrogance or blasphemy.[11] The infant soul is tender (ἁπαλὴν) and can be impressed with the principles of good behaviour while it is still fearful.[12] Intemperance (ἀκολασία, the opposite of σωφροσύνη) is the passion which most damages the souls of the young; before a child comes to experience this, it must be trained to be sober and vigilant, to pray, and to set the sign of the Cross over all it says and does.[13]

If there is a suggestion here that children are to be regarded as psychologically free of harmful passions until a certain age (as opposed to merely lacking the opportunities which adults have to indulge them), then Chrysostom does not explore the idea any further. He does suggest that ἐπιθυμία begins to become a problem at about the age of fifteen,[14] but this is because in this context he uses ἐπιθυμία as a term for sexual desire, so that the observation is linked to physical rather than psychological development. Ἐπιθυμία—whether still thought of as sexual or not is unclear—is also said to affect boys more than girls, who are more prone to τὸ φιλόκοσμον καὶ ἀνεπτερωμένον (flightiness).[15] Here, however, we find Chrysostom using the word women (γυναιξί), indicating that he is again indulging in a general moral comment, not identifying a problem specifically connected with the passions or ἐπιθυμία of children.

Chrysostom also fails to take explicit note of any differences between adults and children in his sections on the other two elements of the soul, θυμός and φρόνησις.[16] But he does have

[10] Ibid., ch. 17.
[11] Ibid., ch. 29.
[12] Ibid., ch. 20.
[13] Ibid., ch. 22.
[14] Ibid., ch. 76.
[15] Ibid., ch. 90.
[16] Ibid., chs 66–75 (θυμός), chs 85–7 (φρόνησις). What Chrysostom says about θυμός, that it should be moderated rather than eliminated (ch. 66), could apply to any age. Origen's view that children

some ideas about the age at which children are ready to understand religious teachings which help to fill some of these gaps. In a homily on Ephesians 6.1–4, he explains that this text speaks to children in a concise manner appropriate to their inability to follow lengthy arguments. Further, in commanding them to obey their parents, the epistle does not promise them the kingdom of Christ as a reward, 'since it is not for that age to hear these things (οὐ γὰρ ἐστι τῆς ἡλικίας ἐκείνης ταῦτα ἀκούειν), but he [Paul] promises what the infant soul most wishes to hear—that it will have a long life.'[17] If young children can desire a long life, Chrysostom must think that they can understand the notion of a reward that goes beyond purely immediate gratification, and therefore that they are capable, though in an immature way, of the use of reason, even if the idea of eternal life is beyond them (or otherwise deemed too holy or too dangerous to explain to them at an early age, whatever exactly Chrysostom may mean). This is consistent with the work *On Vainglory*, which suggests that biblical stories inculcating the idea of rewards for virtue should be used in the very earliest stages of education.[18] Teaching about sin and punishment should start at ten, eight, or less; understanding of the New Testament and grace belongs to a later stage of development, and the threat of hell should be saved until the age of fifteen.[19] Chrysostom also says (here without any indication of what age is meant) that children are quite capable of devotion and compunction in prayer—it is the (moral) condition of the soul, not its age, which determines this capacity.[20]

With these remarks of Chrysostom should be compared a comment of Basil of Caesarea (d. 379) to the effect that non-Christian Greek literature is suitable as a preliminary training of the soul for those who, because of youth, are not yet able to understand the depth of the mind of Scripture.[21] This remark is vague compared with Chrysostom's account, and really only

---

are free from anger and grief might be taken to imply the absence from their soul of θυμός, but Origen does not use the term in this context, and elsewhere expresses reserve about the validity of the tripartite division of the soul derived from platonist anthropology: *De principiis*, III, iv, 1 (p. 264).

17 *Homily on Ephesians 6. 1–4*, 1, *PG* 62, col. 149.

18 *On Vainglory*, chs 39–46, 51.

19 Ibid., ch. 52.

20 Ibid., ch. 80.

21 *Homily 22: To Young Men on how to profit from Greek Literature*, 2, *PG* 30, col. 565D.

serves to emphasize the scarcity of serious treatments of child development in the educational treatises of the Fathers.[22]

Some more precise remarks than Chrysostom's on the development of sexual desire in children are found in a work of Basil of Ancyra (d. *c.*364). Basil does not suggest an age at which sexual desire commences, but he does remark that while children are still sexually immature (ἀτελῆ . . . πρὸς τὴν φυσικὴν ἐνέργειαν), 'the law of sin is at rest.' It may be said that ignorance of the sexual act (ἄγνοιαν . . . τῆς φυσικῆς πράξεως) belongs to the body at this stage of life, even though nature has an inbuilt tendency towards what is appropriate to it—as can be seen from the example of irrational animals, which require no education in order to engage in sexual unions.[23] The implication that children are morally innocent of the experience of sexual passion is not obviated by Basil's following observation that children may be observed *imitating* the sexual act.

A point to be noted is Basil's assumption that the phrase 'the law of sin' can be equated with sexual desire: in Romans 7.25, though associated with the flesh, it does wider duty than sexual sin. This restriction is analogous to Chrysostom's use of ἐπιθυμία specifically for sexual desire. This meaning of ἐπιθυμία also seems to be present in Origen's use of the word in the instance which has been quoted.[24] To place an emphasis on sexual desire among the desires associated with the body which are absent from children, as Origen does, has the effect of including by implication the sexual innocence of children among the things which the metaphor of childhood is intended to convey about the Christian life. Clement, by contrast, does not emphasize sexual desire in this way (though no doubt he would include sexual desires in a list of the irrational passions avoided by Christians). In this respect he is unlike his Western contemporary Tertullian, who makes this use of the metaphor of childhood quite explicit.[25]

Chrysostom's contemporary Jerome (d. 420) was the author of

[22] Basil's remark might indeed be seen as no more than a debating point offering a *post hoc* justification of the fact that the early education of the socially privileged Christian would inevitably be based on the classical curriculum.

[23] *On Virginity*, 65, *PG* 30, col. 801B–C.

[24] See above, p. 42: τὰς ἀνδρικὰς ἐπιθυμίας.

[25] *De monogamia*, 8, ed. Paul Mattei, *SC*, 343 (1988), pp. 166–8.

two well-known letters advising on the education of young girls who had been dedicated to virginity by their parents.[26] Jerome does not believe that a very young child, capable only of playing on its mother's knee, of being attracted to food, and of being amused by children's tales, will be responsive to the message of the Bible.[27] Young children need to be accustomed to learning by the provision of regular rewards.[28] But—a view closely echoing Chrysostom's—habits of restraint in diet and behaviour must be inculcated from the start, when children are still easily influenced to good or evil (*in utramque partem*) by their parents, tutors, or companions.[29] Children are not to be permitted any indulgences which they will have to renounce later on, on the specious grounds that it is better for them to have desired them and learnt to renounce them than not to have had them and to carry on desiring them.[30] This is more a moral and theological point—a child dedicated to God must not have its vocation spoilt by careless parents, but must 'remain in the condition of life in which it was called' (I Corinthians 7.24)—than an educational or psychological one. Jerome sees parents as fully responsible for ensuring that the development of their children in virtue does not go astray: they will surely be punished by God if they fail to offer their child for baptism, or having dedicated it to God, prove negligent in its upbringing in virtue.[31] Chrysostom makes the same point firmly too: one's own virtue is not sufficient for salvation; one is responsible for that of one's dependants (wife or children) as well.[32]

In Jerome's view, the age at which a child will be ready to begin the study of Scripture is seven, by which time it will have learnt 'scire quid taceat, dubitare quid dicat'—that is, it will have attained some understanding of the difference between truth and falsehood, or some sense of shame at being in

[26] Letters 107, *PL* 22, cols 867–78; and 128, *PL* 22, cols 1095–9.

[27] Letter 128, 1, cols 1095–6.

[28] Ibid., col. 1096.

[29] Letters 107, 8, col. 874; 128, 3a, col. 1098; quotation from 128.

[30] Letter 128, 2–3, cols 1096–8.

[31] Letter 107, 6, cols 873–4.

[32] *Homily on Ephesians 6.1–4*, 4, col. 154. For the same emphasis on parental responsibility cf. Chrysostom, *Against those who oppose the Monastic Life*, iii, 3–4, *PG* 47, cols 354–6, and another late fourth-century work of Antiochene provenance, *Apostolic Constitutions*, iv, 11, ed. F. X. Funk (Paderborn, 1905), pp. 231–3.

error.[33] Like Chrysostom, then, Jerome can be said to have made an attempt (though not as fully as Chrysostom) to answer the part of the patristic anthropological question of childhood which deals with the capacity of the infant soul for religious understanding or moral development. But neither author associates these observations with a theory of the infant soul placed in the context of a more general anthropological theory of reason and the passions. In this respect, Clement and Origen's discussions of the freedom of the infant soul from passion remain unique in the Eastern Early Church.

The theological problem of childhood which was mentioned at the beginning of this paper was treated most fully among the Eastern Fathers by Gregory of Nyssa (d. *c.*395) in his work *On Infants' Early Deaths*.[34] In one sense the scope of this work is limited. Gregory is not concerned to provide an answer to the problem of evil in general—of why there is evil and suffering at all in a world created and governed by a good God. His concern is with the problem of accounting for the unequal treatment of human beings in a way consistent with divine justice.[35] Why is it that, in a world where everything which happens is dependent on God's will, the lives of some human beings are prolonged into old age, while others suffer and die as infants (as a result of natural causes, exposure, or deliberate killing), without having had an opportunity to share in any of life's pleasures (τῶν κατὰ τὸν βίον ἡδέων)?[36] Yet in order to answer this question, Gregory believes that it is necessary to set the phenomenon of infant deaths in the context of a general understanding of the nature and destiny (ὅτου χάριν ἦλθεν [ἡ ἀνθρωπίνη φύσις] εἰς γένεσιν) of the human person.[37] In this sense, Gregory's work is a wide-ranging one which exemplifies his originality as a theologian.[38]

[33] Letter 128, 3a, col. 1098.

[34] Ed. Hadwig Hörner, *Gregorii Nysseni Opera*, 3, 1 (Leiden, 1987), pp. 67–97; references are given by page and line number. There is a translation in *The Nicene and post-Nicene Fathers*, 2nd series, 5, pp. 372–81.

[35] For Origen's response to this problem see above, n. 6.

[36] *On Infants' Early Deaths*, p. 72, line 11 – p. 73, line 12.

[37] Ibid., p. 76, 20–3.

[38] For a fuller account of Gregory's arguments than is possible here see the various papers contained in J. C. M. van Winden and A. van Heck, eds, *Colloquii Gregoriani III Leidensis 18/23-IX-1974 Acta* (Leiden, 1976).

Gregory regards it as self-evident that an infant who dies cannot have done anything in the world which would deserve any reward or punishment in the future life.[39] Anyone who claims that after death an infant will receive from God the same recompense (ἀντίδοσις) as the good must face two contrary arguments: firstly, this is not consistent with divine justice, which requires that only those who do things which deserve the kingdom of heaven should receive it;[40] secondly, if infants did receive the same reward as the good after death, this would mean that it was better to die in a state of unreason as an infant[41] than to live a longer life which would inevitably involve either a difficult struggle to avoid the pollution of evil and acquire virtue, or the penalty of receiving after death the painful recompense due to a life of sin.[42]

Gregory's eventual answer to this problem is to say that an infant who dies will receive a reward, for it is natural to human beings, who were created in God's image, to participate in (μετέχειν) the divine nature to which they are akin.[43] Uniquely among God's creatures, human beings belong both to the intelligible or spiritual (νοητόν) world and to the sensible or material (αἰσθητόν) one.[44] Together with the angels (which belong only to the spiritual world), their purpose is to ensure that God is praised throughout both parts of creation by intelligent beings who possess the power of seeing or knowing him (ἐν πάσῃ τῇ κτίσει διὰ τῆς νοερᾶς φύσεως . . . δοξάζεσθαι . . . διὰ τῆς αὐτῆς ἐνεργείας, λέγω δὲ διὰ τοῦ πρὸς τὸν θεὸν βλέπειν).[45]

But in this life it is easy for the soul to become clouded by ignorance of the true good and to be impeded from its purpose.[46]

[39] *On Infants' Early Deaths*, p. 74, 1–12.

[40] Ibid., p. 74, 15–22.

[41] Cf. ibid., p. 73, 7–8 for the view that reason is undeveloped in infants.

[42] Ibid., p. 75, 1–13.

[43] Ibid., p. 79, 21–4.

[44] Ibid., p. 77, 23 – p. 78, 23.

[45] Ibid., p. 78, 24 – p. 79, 1.

[46] Ibid., p. 80, 2–10. Ignorance of God is a defect or privation in the human relationship with God whose origin is difficult to account for (p. 80, 11–20). Gregory's reluctance to attempt to explain the origin of evil in general is apparent here, though he clearly believes that the partly material nature of human beings, however essential to their role in creation as a bond between the material and spiritual worlds, is also what interferes with their spiritual capacity for knowledge of the creator; cf. *On the Lord's Prayer*, 2, *PG* 44, cols 1165B–68C. What we experience as evil is not a substance or positive quality but an absence of knowledge, goodness, and being, an inevitable consequence

A human being has two options—either to purify himself of ignorance by a struggle for virtue and receive the reward that his nature deserves, or to allow himself to be trapped by pleasures and denied a share in what naturally belongs to him.[47] Infants who die have not had time to have their souls, created for contemplation of God, clouded by ignorance through a life in this world, but neither have they had the same opportunities as those who have lived a life of virtue to apprehend God through his creation.[48] Infants cannot, then, expect to receive the same reward, immediately, as those who have struggled to attain virtue during the course of this life. In the future life they must be content with a gradual growth in knowledge of and participation in (γνῶσιν τε καὶ μετουσίαν) God until they are ready to receive the full reward.[49] But they are in a far better position than those who have lived an evil life in this world, who will undergo an infinite period of purgation (εἰς ἄπειρον παρατείνεται ἡ διὰ τῆς καθάρσεως κόλασις) in the future life.[50]

By means of this argument, Gregory disposes of any suggestion that what each human soul receives in the future life is not in perfect proportion to its spiritual condition. But the original question was why some die as infants while others survive. Gregory's answer to this is that through his foreknowledge of the character of every person, God in his love of humanity (φιλανθρωπία) may see fit to end the lives of people of a particularly evil disposition as infants, in order to prevent the full development of their evil passions.[51] Perhaps he does this especially in the case of children of virtuous parents out of kindness to them.[52] The implication is that these souls will be in a better condition as a result of dying as infants than if they had survived to live an evil life. The argument, though of a more obviously apologetic character than the discussion of the destiny of human

of our existence at a greater distance from God, and hence at a lower level of being, than that of the purely spiritual world.

[47] *On Infants' Early Deaths*, p. 82, 21–8.

[48] Ibid., p. 82, 28 – p. 83, 4; p. 85, 9 – p. 87, 6.

[49] Ibid., p. 84, 21 – p. 85, 6.

[50] Ibid., p. 87, 10–12. The use of this phrase may indicate an equivocation between the idea of eternal punishment and that of purgation as the experience of the wicked after death; generally Gregory seems to favour purgation (e.g. p. 73, 15–17).

[51] Ibid., p. 88, 1–8; p. 90, 12–19.

[52] Ibid., p. 93, 2–10, 12–14.

nature, is equally illustrative of Gregory's concern to show that the life accorded to each person in this world is proportioned by God to provide the maximum opportunities for attaining a state of blessedness in the life to come. Gregory is aware of some of the shortcomings of this argument and recalls the fact that no final answer to the question is to be expected; but, since nothing that God does is governed by chance or irrationality, it is to be believed that, whether the reasons for the deaths of infants are known or not, they happen for the best.[53]

In writing this work Gregory did not think it necessary to discuss the issues connected with the passions in children or their moral and religious development which preoccupied Origen, Chrysostom, and Jerome. This is largely because Gregory starts from the assumption that it is the death of newborn infants, in whom the question of sin or responsibility simply does not arise, that poses a theological problem. But apart from their intrinsic interest, there are good reasons for giving space to Gregory's arguments in this paper. Study of patristic thought on the condition of childhood has tended to focus on the argument between Augustine and Pelagius and on the background to their views in earlier patristic thought.[54] Augustine saw the sufferings of children as evidence of their inheritance of original sin, and argued that the baptism of infants was a necessary condition (despite the absence of any capacity for personal sin in a child who had not yet reached the age of reason and will) of their salvation should they die. The physical and mental weaknesses and ignorance of their own condition in which children are immersed, which lead them even to resist the application to them of the saving sacrament of baptism, can only be described as a corruption of nature which is part of the penalty of original sin.[55]

[53] Ibid., p. 93, 10–12; p. 93, 18 – p. 94, 2. The main objection to the argument is that some of the wicked are apparently allowed to survive into old age. To this Gregory replies that (a) some of those who die as infants might, if they lived, have been even more evil than the most notorious of actual sinners (p. 93, 14–18); (b) the evil acts of the wicked are used by God to the greater good (pp. 94, 2 – 95, 17); (c) the wicked survive so that in the future life, the good will know of the sufferings undergone by the wicked and will form a greater awareness of the value of their own reward as a result (pp. 95, 22–96, 14). Gregory regards the first of these arguments as speculative, but the other two as securely grounded in Scripture.

[54] For a recent survey see Elizabeth A. Clark, 'From Origenism to Pelagianism: elusive issues in an ancient debate', *Princeton Seminary Bulletin*, 12 (1991), pp. 283–303.

[55] See, e.g., Augustine, *De peccatorum meritis et remissione et de baptismo parvulorum*, i, 63–9, *PL* 44, cols 146–50.

It is not necessary to be among those who reject the Augustinian tradition of thought on grace and the sacraments in its entirety in order to agree that Gregory's arguments add a valuable alternative perspective to the stock of Christian theological reflection. Gregory's understanding of evil and ignorance of God is not free of pessimistic or dualist traits;[56] but it avoids the extreme pessimism and apparently unavoidable determinism of Augustine's involvement of every human being in the *massa peccati* of corrupted human nature as a result of the sin of the one individual, Adam. Gregory's failure to mention baptism and its incorporation of the individual into the body of Christ in whom salvation is effected and sin and death overcome is no less one-sided than Augustine's single-minded defence of the necessity of the sacrament for the salvation of infants; but Gregory's teaching also has a positive emphasis on the providence of God, who, though the possibility of an eternal purgation for sinners is not ruled out, so expresses his care for every individual that we can be sure that what we achieve in the present life does not end our chances of ultimately attaining to salvation and knowledge of God. The deaths of unbaptized infants are seen not as an eternal waste of human potential, but as only one stage (albeit in each case a tragic and perhaps inexplicable one) in the process by which God may bring all human beings to the fulfilment of their nature in the enjoyment of participation in his life.

King's College London

[56] See above, n. 46.

CHILDREN AND CONFESSION IN THE EARLY MIDDLE AGES*

by ROB MEENS

THE handbooks for confessors known as penitentials are, I shall argue, an important source for our knowledge of early medieval attitudes on the part of churchmen and others towards children.[1] These texts, basically lists of sins with the prescription of an appropriate penance for each iniquity, can be said to reflect widespread practices and ideas. They originated in the Irish and British Churches in the sixth century and spread from there over all of Western Europe, where they remained in use until the twelfth century.[2]

In these texts children are mentioned in two ways. Either they are affected, in one way or another, by someone else's misdeed, or they confess their own offences. Children who sin are never called *infantes*; mostly they are labelled *pueri*. While *infantia* seems to accord with the classification, best known from the work of Isidore of Seville, that includes children up to seven years in this group, *pueritia* seems to span a wider range, maybe from seven to

*Research for this paper was made possible by a generous grant from the *Niels Stensen Stichting*. I would like to thank Rosamond McKitterick and Janet Nelson for their helpful comments on an earlier version of this paper.

[1] See Maria Guiseppina Muzzarelli, 'Le donne e i bambini nei libri penitenziali: regole di condotta per una società in formazione', in Benedetto Vetere and Paolo Renzi, eds, *Profili di donne. Mito, immagine, realtà fra medioevo ed età contemporanea* (Galatina, 1986), pp. 145–92, who focuses on the relationship between mother and child. It is a pity she does not give sufficient account of the textual history of these texts. Craig B. McKee, 'Les enfants et la pénitence avant Latran IV (1215). De ludis puerilibus', *La Maison-Dieu*, 172 (1987), pp. 89–106, is, as the author himself admits (p. 90), 'une incursion superficielle dans le sujet'.

[2] For a general introduction to these texts see Cyrille Vogel, *Les 'Libri Paenitentiales' =Typologie des sources du moyen âge occidental*, 27 (Turnhout, 1978); A. J. Frantzen, *The Literature of Penance in Anglo-Saxon England* (New Brunswick, NJ, 1983), and Raymund Kottje, 'Busspraxis und Bussritus', *Segni e riti nella chiesa altomedievale occidentale, Settimane di studio*, 33 (1987), pp. 369–95.The Irish penitentials are edited by Ludwig Bieler, *The Irish Penitentials, with an appendix by D. A. Binchy, Scriptores Latini Hiberniae*, 5 (1963) [hereafter Bieler]; most of the texts still have to be consulted in F. W. H. Wasserschleben, *Die Bussordnungen der abendländischen Kirche* (Halle, 1851) [hereafter Wasserschleben], and Hermann J. Schmitz, *Die Bussbücher und die Bussdisciplin der Kirche* (Mainz, 1883, repr. Graz, 1958) [hereafter Schmitz I], and *Die Bussbücher und das kanonische Bussverfahren* (Düsseldorf, 1898, repr. Graz, 1958) [hereafter Schmitz II].

twenty years of age, in monasteries even to twenty-five years. In monasteries, where we expect a more developed educational system, *infantia* and *pueritia* seem to become expanded.[3] The texts emanating from *dicta* spoken by Theodore of Canterbury speak of *infantes monasterii* who are fourteen years old, and of twenty-five-year-old *pueri monasterii*.[4]

Other terms seem to have been used more indiscriminately. A *parvulus* can be a young child who dies without baptism, or a child of ten already capable of stealing. *Parvoli infantes* are held to be capable of sexual activity, and a *parvulus* can be twenty years of age.[5] The terms *filius* and *filia* are not used to specify a certain age, but only refer to a relationship with the parents. As we would expect, the mother appears normally in relation to young children, whereas the father is mentioned when the *patria potestas* is at stake, at moments when children want to make decisions of their own concerning marriage or entry into the religious life.[6] The Theodorian traditions deal extensively with the limitations of the father's authority. From this it is clear that somewhere around the age of fifteen a boy is held to be capable of acting independently. At that age he could enter a monastery without his father's permission. For girls this moment seems to have come somewhat later in life, for they could make their own decision to enter a monastery or have a say in the choice of their

[3] Possibly, however, we are dealing here with the 'long *pueritia*', that combines the Isidorian *infantia*, *pueritia*, and *adolescentia* in one class: see Adolf Hofmeister, '*Puer, iuvenis, senex*. Zum Verständnis der mittelalterlichen Altersbezeichnungen', in Albert Brackmann, ed., *Papsttum und Kaisertum. Forschungen zur politischen Geschichte und Geisteskultur des Mittelalters Paul Kehr zum 65. Geburtstag dargebracht* (Munich, 1926), pp. 287–316, esp. pp. 296 and 304.

[4] *P. Theodori Capitula Dacheriana* [hereafter *ThD*], C. 57; *P. Theodori Canones Cottoniani* [hereafter *ThCo*], C. 196, ed. Paul Willem Finsterwalder, *Die Canones Theodori Cantuariensis und ihre Überlieferungsformen* (Weimar, 1929) [hereafter Finsterwalder], pp. 244 and 283; and *P. Theodori Canones Basilienses* [hereafter *ThB*], C. 86c, ed. Franz B. Asbach, *Das Poenitentiale Remense und der sogen. Excarpsus Cummeani: Überlieferung, Quellen und Entwicklung Zweier kontinentaler Bußbücher aus der 1. Hälfte des 8. Jahrhunderts* (Regensburg, 1975) [hereafter Asbach], Anhang, p. 87; on the Theodorian traditions see R. Kottje, 'Paenitentiale Theodori', in *Handwörterbuch zur deutschen Rechtsgeschichte*, 3 (Berlin, 1984), cols 1413–16.

[5] *Parvulus* and baptism: *Paenitentiale Vinniani* [hereafter *PVinn*], C. 47–8, ed. Bieler, p. 92, and *P. Parisiense*, II, C. 47, ed. Schmitz II. p. 330; stealing *parvulus*: *P. Sangallense*, II, *C.* 25, ed. Schmitz II, p. 347 and *P. Cummeani* [hereafter *PCumm*], I, 13, ed. Bieler, p. 112; sexually active *parvuli* and a twenty-year-old *parvulus*: *P. Parisiense*, II, C. 53 and 55, ed. Schmitz II, p. 330.

[6] Raoul Manselli, 'Vie familiale et éthique sexuelle dans les pénitentiels', in G. Duby and J. Le Goff, eds, *Famille et parenté dans l'occident mediéval* (Rome, 1977), pp. 363–78, esp. pp. 366–8.

future husbands only at the age of sixteen, seventeen, or even eighteen.[7]

It is more difficult to determine exactly what children the texts are talking about. Penitentials originated in a monastic context, and the early texts have a clear monastic imprint. They often provide for confessions made by monks, clerics, and the laity. As we have seen, some texts specifically mention children attached to a monastery: oblates or other commended children.[8] It is often hard to establish if the texts aim primarily at confessions made by children in the care of the monastery or also at confessions of other children. We may ask ourselves, however, if it is not as difficult for us to make this distinction as it was for the users of these manuals. Is it not possible that sentences, originally designed for children attached to a monastery, were used with regard to other children as well?

Of course, these texts only tell us something about people who came to confess, or of whose sins confessors gained knowledge. Not much is known about the frequency of confession in the early medieval period. The great number of penitentials, and manuscripts with these texts, written in this period suggests, however, that confession was not uncommon.

INFANTES

In the later Middle Ages theologians and authors of didactic works held children younger than seven to be incapable of sin.[9] The fact that *infantes* are never mentioned as sinners, but only in the context of a confession made by someone else, accords well with this view. In general, the production of offspring is

[7] *ThD*, C. 166; *P. Theodori. Canones sancti Gregorii papae* [hereafter *ThG*], C. 43 and 186; *P. Theodori Discipulus Umbrensium* [hereafter *ThU*], II, xii, 37, ed. Finsterwalder, pp. 251, 256, 270, and 330–1. On this see Mayke de Jong, *Kind en klooster in de vroege middeleeuwen. Aspecten van de schenking van kinderen aan kloosters in het Frankische Rijk (500–900)* (Amsterdam, 1986), p. 60.

[8] On these, see De Jong, *Kind en klooster*, Patricia Quinn, *Better than the Sons of Kings: Boys and Monks in the Early Middle Ages, Studies in History and Culture*, 3 (New York, 1989); and M. Lahaye-Geusen, *Das Opfer der Kinder. Ein Beitrag zur Liturgie-und Sozialgeschichte im Hohen Mittelalter, Münsteraner Theologische Abhandlungen*, 13 (Altenberge, 1991).

[9] Shulamith Shahar, *Childhood in the Middle Ages* (London and New York, 1990), pp. 24–5.

seen as the sole justification for sexual activity.[10] Hence it is only natural that the penitentials severely penalize any attempt at abortion.[11]

Infanticide, another practice aimed at reducing the number of children, is also frequently mentioned in penitentials. Together with her statistical analysis of the polyptych of St Germain-des-Prés, this was the basis on which Emily Coleman built her case of a widespread practice of infanticide, especially in regard to little girls, in the early Middle Ages.[12] Although her analysis of the polyptych has been rightly criticized,[13] the frequency with which the practice of infanticide is mentioned in penitentials indeed attests to an established custom. The fact that penitential canons specify special circumstances in which infanticide might have taken place, such as to hide fornication or in cases of poverty,[14] refutes the argument that these canons bear no resemblance to reality, but are 'theoretical catalogues of offences'.[15]

A striking case is the discussion of infanticide in the recently discovered *Paenitentiale Oxoniense II*, a text from the eighth century which may have been composed by St Willibrord.[16] This penitential is a highly original text and may thus be held to reflect contemporary concerns. It treats infanticide in four canons. The first one imposes a penance of forty days on a woman who kills

[10] *PVinn*, C. 46, ed. Bieler, pp. 90–2. On the importance of this canon for all later penitentials, see Raymund Kottje, 'Ehe und Eheverständnis in den vorgratianischen Bussbüchern', in W. van Hoecke and A. Welkenhuysen, eds, *Love and Marriage in the Twelfth Century* (Leuven, 1981), pp. 18–40, at pp. 32–3.

[11] See John T. Noonan, *Contraception. A History of its Treatment by the Catholic Theologians and Canonists* (Cambridge, Mass., 1966), pp. 152–70; B. Honings, 'L'aborto nei libri penitenziali irlandesi. Convergenza morale e divergenze pastorali', in Maria Muzzarelli, ed., *Una componente della mentalità occidentale: Penitenziali nell' alto medioevo* (Bologna, 1980), pp. 155–84; and Maria Muzzarelli, 'Il valore della vita nell'alto medioevo: la testimonianza dei libri penitenziali', *Aevum*, 62 (1988), pp. 171–85, esp. p. 178.

[12] Emily R. Coleman, 'L'Infanticide dans le haut moyen age', *Annales. Economies, sociétés, civilisations*, 29 (1974), pp. 315–35.

[13] David Herlihy, *Medieval Households* (Cambridge, Mass, and London, 1985), pp. 64–8.

[14] For infanticide to hide fornication, see, e.g., *P. Ps.-Gregorii*, C. 17, ed. Franz Kerff, 'Das Paenitentiale Pseudo-Gregorii. Eine kritische Edition', in Hubert Mordek, ed., *Aus Archiven und Bibliotheken. Festschrift für Raymund Kottje zum 65. Geburtstag* (Frankfurt am Main and Bern, 1992), pp. 161–88, at p. 177. Leniency towards a poor woman (*mulier paupercula*) who kills her child: *ThU*, I, xiv, 26, ed. Finsterwalder, p. 309.

[15] L. Milis, 'Het kind in de middeleeuwen. Beschouwingen over onderzoek en methode', *Tijdschrift voor Geschiedenis*, 94 (1981), pp. 377–90, at p. 382.

[16] On this text see Ludger Körntgen, *Studien zu den Quellen der frühmittelalterlichen Bußbücher = Quellen und Forschungen zum Recht im Mittelalter*, 7 (Sigmaringen, 1993), pp. 90–205, and Rob Meens, 'Willibrord's boeteboek?', *Tijdschrift voor Geschiedenis*, 106 (1993), pp. 163–78.

(*suffugauerit*) her child deliberately before it is baptized (*infantem gentilem*). Apart from the original formulation and the light penance, this canon is the regular one we should expect to find in a penitential. The other three deal with the special case in which a woman following the army (*in hostem*), probably as a captive, gives birth to a child and subsequently kills it. Here the text makes a remarkable distinction between killing the child before or after it is accepted by the mother. The act by which the mother accepts the child seems to have consisted of lifting the child from the floor and feeding it. The text accommodates itself in a way to this ritual act, for it decrees that if the child has not yet been accepted, the guilty woman may do penance as much or as little as she pleases, whereas if the slaying took place after lifting and feeding the child she has to do penance for twenty-eight weeks, in this text the normal penance for murder in peacetime.[17] If, however, a woman does not accept her child because she wants to hide her infidelity from her husband, she has to perform a thirty-five-week penance.[18] From other sources we know that there existed a similar ritual of accepting a child among the Frisians, and that they also regarded it as rightful to kill a child before this took place.[19]

It seems, therefore, that this penitential reflects an established custom among the Frisians of killing children at birth. We should, however, bear in mind that these canons were never repeated thereafter. They seem to have been designed for the period right after conversion, and the accommodation to this non-Christian ritual of accepting a child seems to have disappeared to make way for the ritual of Christian baptism. In the Christian view the Frisian attitude was turned on its head. For whereas in Frisian custom it was less harmful to kill a child that

[17] *P. Oxoniense II*, Oxford, Bodleian Library, MS Bodl. 311 [hereafter *POxon*], fols 76v–77r; canon 31: 'Si autem mulier in hostem peperit infantem et eum⟨non⟩sustulerit a terra nec captauit ad infantem, illa ieiunet quantum uoluerit.' Canon 32: 'Si autem mulier in hostem peperit infantem et tulerit eum a terra et lactauit sibi in filium et iterum proiecit eum nolendo, ille ieiunet ebdomada xxviii.' Canon 33: 'De eam qui in hostem inuitum proicit infantem. Si autem mulier inuitus proicit infantem, siue quia non potuit eum portare uel nutrire, illa non est culpanda, sed tamen ieiunet ebdomada III.' Murder in peacetime, canon 6, fols 72v–73r.

[18] *POxon*, C. 34, fol. 77r: 'Si autem mulier christiana peperit infantem et non sustulit eum a terra, ut non laboret, neque nutriat infantem, ut non uidetur⟨tur⟩pes uel infidelis coram proprio maritu suo, ille ieunet ebdomada XXXV.'

[19] Körntgen, *Studien*, pp. 186–90. Cf. *Lex Frisionum* V, 2, ed. *MGH. F* 12, p. 46; *Vita Liudgeri*, I, 6–7, ed. W. Diekamp, *Die Geschichtsquellen des Bistums Münster*, 4 (Münster, 1881), pp. 10–11.

had not been accepted by a formal rite, in Christian doctrine it was considered a graver offence to kill a child that was not yet baptized, because it had not been given a chance to save its soul.

Penitentials frequently mention the case of parents suffocating their child by accident.[20] Probably this was caused by the fact that parents and children slept together in the same bed. It is not clear if this was the normal practice or if parents took children into their own bed only for feeding or warmth. Even in eighteenth-century Flanders, where cradles were a normal piece of furniture, we find preachers warning against the dangers of taking children into your bed because you might thereby suffocate them.[21] Only one penitential, however, speaks about a cradle: the text with Frisian connections I referred to earlier. It deals with the case of the 'cot death'. If a wife puts her baby in the cradle (*cuna*), or in another place where she is accustomed to lay down the child, and later finds it dead, she is not to blame.[22] This text also gives us the most sophisticated treatment of the case of suffocating a child. It distinguishes between five instances, moving from the most innocuous to the most serious. The first case is that in which a mother finds her dead child next to her in bed, without being sure the child has died because of her. In that case the woman should fast for four weeks to cleanse her soul.[23] If she is sure the child died because of her, but did not cause this on purpose, the penance is increased to fourteen weeks. If the child was not baptized she has to fast twice as long. If the mother was drunk at the time, the penance increases to twenty weeks if the child has received baptism, and to thirty-five if it dies without. The most severe penance, forty weeks, is finally imposed for suffocating a child intentionally.[24]

[20] For a treatment of similar cases in the later Middle Ages see Shahar, *Childhood*, pp. 129–31.

[21] H. Storme, 'Kerkelijke alarmkreten over kinderversmachting door het bij zich in bed nemen van zuigelingen (XVIe–XVIIIe eeuw)', *Handelingen van het Genootschap voor geschiedenis gesticht onder de benaming Société d'émulation de Bruges*, 125 (1988), pp. 471–87.

[22] *POxon*, C. 28, fol, 76v: 'De eam, qui in cunam mortuum inueniet. Si autem posuerit infantem suum secundum consuetudinem siue in cuna siue in alio loco et inuenerit eum mortuum, non iuxta se, sed si incidi, ubi consuetudinem habebat [habebebat, MS] infans iacere, non est mulieri culpa.' Cf. Körntgen, *Studien*, p. 190, esp. n. 676.

[23] *POxon*, C. 25, fol. 76r: 'De mulieris: si inuenerit iuxta se infantem mortuum, si non tenet eam conscientiam eius ut per eam mortuum fuisset infans, sed tamen ad purificandum animam suam ieiunet ebdomada IV.' Cf. Körntgen, *Studien*, p. 186.

[24] *POxon*, C. 26–30, fols 76r–v.

This subtle treatment of the suffocation of children is not repeated anywhere else. Other penitentials only make the distinction between children who die in this way after having received baptism and those who die without it, and between the acts committed accidentally and those done in negligence through drunkenness. In some cases not only the mother is blamed, but also the father.[25]

These canons reflect the high mortality rate among young children. This was, according to Ariès, one of the main reasons for the absence of a 'sentiment de l'enfance' in medieval Europe. Though Ariès's thesis has encountered sharp criticism from medievalists,[26] a canon from Theodore's penitential may point to a certain indifference towards the death of young children. This canon recalls that 'many say' that it is not permitted to say Mass for children younger than seven. Though the background of this canon remains unclear—it could well be to do with young children's inability to sin—this could be regarded as a sign of absence of grief at the death of a young child. Theodore, however, explicitly allows Mass to be said for young children, and thus seems to reflect concern for the salvation of young children after death.[27] A canon forbidding parents to mourn in an excessive way, by cutting their hair and lacerating their faces with a sword or with their nails, also suggests that there existed an emotional bond between parents and children, though it is not clear if this canon speaks of very young, or already adult, children.[28]

A major concern in the penitentials involves the case in which a child dies without baptism. Finnian calls this a great offence (*magnum crimen*).[29] The responsibility for this can lie either with the parents of the child or with the priest who should have administered the sacrament. Parents were expected, so it seems, to take care that their children received baptism before the age

[25] See, e.g. *P. Parisiense*, II, C. 18, *P. Hubertense*, C. 19, and *P. Burchardi*, C. 182–3, ed. Schmitz II, pp. 342, 335, and 449. The question if, and why, a mother had to do penance after suffocating her child unintentionally was amply discussed in the ninth century, though without reaching a satisfactory conclusion: see Gerhard Schmitz, 'Schuld und Strafe. Eine unbekannte Stellungnahme des Rathramnus von Corbie zur Kindestötung', *Deutsches Archiv*, 38 (1982), pp. 363–87.

[26] See, e.g., Herlihy, *Households*, pp. 126–6, Shahar, *Childhood*, pp. 1–4.

[27] *ThU*, II, v, 7, ed. Finsterwalder, p. 319.

[28] *POxon*, C. 40, fol. 78r. Cf. Körntgen, *Studien*, p. 190. For the adoption of this canon in several later works see ibid. p. 116.

[29] *P. Vinniani*, C. 47, ed. Bieler, p. 92.

of three, because after that the required penance increased significantly.[30]

In penitentials we also find reflections of real concern about the well-being of living children. In the Theodorian traditions we find a canon that imposes a penance on a woman who places her child in an oven or on the roof to cure it from fever.[31] The heavy penance imposed seems to imply some sort of magical connotation here, but the canon at least reflects a mother's care for the health of her children. This canon is repeated in many penitentials of a later age.[32] This need not mean that this 'magical' cure was applied in many places, but the canon could have been used as a guide-line for priests in imposing a penance on women using any sort of magical means to ensure the health of their offspring. In the penitential written by Burchard of Worms, around the year 1000, we find another magical rite to secure a child's health. Here the child is pulled through a tunnel made from earth to make it stop crying.[33]

Only in later penitentials do we see more demands being addressed to parents to take care for the well-being of their children. Interesting in this respect is the eleventh-century *Paenitentiale Pseudo-Fulberti* which prescribes a penance of one year for parents of a child who has fallen and died. At first sight the text seems puzzling, but variant reading in the manuscripts show us what was meant. The canon seems to deal with children younger than six, who have been baptized, and who have fallen into water (*in aquam*), into a pit (*in foveam*), or have encountered

[30] *PCumm*, II, 32–3 and (X), 19–20, ed. Bieler, pp. 116 and 128, *ThG*, C.103 and 161–2; *ThCo*, C.23; *ThU*, 1, xiv, 28–9; *ThB*, C. 79a–b, ed. Finsterwalder, pp. 268, 272, 310, and Asbach, Anhang, p. 86. Cf. *P. Vindobonense B*, XI, 14 (= Cummean); *Excarpsus Cummeani*, VI, 30; *P. Remense*, VIII, 39 and 66–9; *P. Sangallense tripartitum*, II, 4; *P. Merseburgense A*, 111; *P. Vindobonense B*, XXXIII, 30 (= Theodor); *P. Capitula Iudiciorum*, IV, 2; *P. Vallicellianum*, I, 8; *P. Parisiene*, I, C. 59–60; *P. Ps.-Fulberti*, C. 12 (ed. Kerff, p. 30); *P. Burchardi*, C. 164, 180, 185.

[31] *ThG*, C. 117; *ThU*, I, xv, 2; *ThCo*, C. 148; ed. Finsterwalder, pp. 264, 280, 310. *P. Vallicellianum*, I, 92; *P. Parisiense*, I, C. 21.

[32] E.g., *Excarpsus Cummeani*, VII, 14; *P. Remense*, IX, 15; *P. Sangallense tripartitum*, II, 34; *P. Merseburgense A*, C. 99; *P. Vindobonense B*, XXXIV, 14; *P. Capitula Iudiciorum*, XVI, 4.

[33] *P. Burchardi*, C. 179, ed. Schmitz II, p. 448. Aron Gurevich, *Medieval Popular Culture: Problems of Belief and Perception* (Cambridge and New York, etc., 1988), p. 83, links this up with the healing power attached to the earth, 'a very characteristic trait of agrarian beliefs'. Cf. *P. Arundel*, C. 97, ed. Schmitz I, p. 464, and *P. Ps.-Ecgberti*, written in Anglo-Saxon, IV, 16, ed. J. Raith, *Die altenglische Version des Halitgar'schen Bussbuches (sog. Poenitentiale Pseudo-Ecgberti)* (Darmstadt, 1964), p. 55. Muzzarelli, 'Le donne', p. 182, cites the last text in the Latin translation as it is given in Wasserschleben.

another dangerous situation (*in periculum*).[34] The *Paenitentiale Parisiense I*, which is of the same period, has a similar canon, but only speaks of a child that has drowned in water.[35] In the penitential of Burchard of Worms a penance of three years is imposed on a woman who has placed her child near a fire, so that the child was killed by boiling water from a kettle that was hung there by someone else. It is not the person who boiled the water who is to blame, Burchard says, but the mother who has put her child in such a dangerous place. For it is her responsibility to take care of the child during the first seven years of its life.[36]

PUERI

Until now we have looked at what adults may have confessed about their behaviour towards children. But what did children confess themselves? As has been said, we only read about older children, mostly designated as *pueri*, making confessions. In general, it is said in several prefaces to the penitential books that a confessor when imposing a specific penance should use his discretion. The prescribed penances were not meant to be applied mechanically, as some historians seem to think, but should be adapted to the age, sex, intelligence, and occupation of the sinner.[37] So, already, in principle, we should expect a confessor to mitigate the penance in the case of sinning children. But apart from this general rule, certain canons give explicit suggestions for a gentle treatment of children. These canons treat cases of theft, talking in a manner that was not allowed, fighting, and several forms of sexual conduct. It is therefore reasonable to assume that older children were regarded as inclined to be attracted by these activities.

[34] *P. Ps.-Fulberti*, C. 11, Franz Kerff, 'Das sogenannte Paenitentiale Fulberti. Überlieferung, Verfasserfrage, Edition', *Zeitschrift de Savigny-Stiftung für Rechtsgeschichte. Kanonistische Abteilung*, 73 (1987), pp. 1–40, edition on p. 30. Cf. apparatus, pp. 31–2. The similar cases Kerff mentions on p. 36 are not similar, because they imply an appeal to superstitious beliefs.

[35] *P. Parisiense*, I, C. 64. This parallel with *P. Ps.-Fulberti*, C. 11 is not noticed by Kerff. For the dating of this text, see Rob Meens, 'Fragmente der Capitula episcoporum Ruotgers von Trier und des Scarapsus Pirminii', *Deutsches Archiv*, 48 (1992), pp. 167–74, at p. 168.

[36] *P. Burchardi*, C. 174, ed. Schmitz II, p. 447.

[37] Pierre J. Payer, 'The Humanism of the Penitentials and the Continuity of the Penitential Tradition', *MS*, 46 (1984), pp. 340–54, esp. pp. 342–6.

Most of the canons on children's sins derive from the penitential of Cummean, written in Ireland in the seventh century. This text has a strong monastic imprint. Later texts using these canons are much more secular in character. As said before, this may have led to the use of these canons for other children than those in the monasteries. One of the topics addressed here is theft. Canons regarding theft committed by *pueri* are included in the sections on gluttony and avarice, and in chapter 10, devoted to sinning boys. The penances vary from seven to forty days. In one canon the penance is explicitly said to be mitigated according to the age and intelligence ('ut est aetas uel qualitas eruditionis') of the sinner.[38]

Cummean devotes a whole chapter to the (sinful) playing of boys (*de ludis puerilibus*). It is the only penitential that does this, though canons from this chapter were adopted in numerous later penitentials. Some canons of Cummean's chapter, however, refer to adults.[39] Most of the sins this chapter deals with are of a sexual nature. The canons treat rather innocent activities, like kissing, or imitating sexual acts, which have to be cured by light penances ranging from six *superpositiones*, special fasts, to twenty days of fasting. More serious offences are also included here, such as bestiality and anal intercourse. It is uncertain whether the penance of one hundred days for a boy who takes Communion after having sinned with an animal is meant only to apply to taking Communion in this state of sin, or also as a penance for the sin of bestiality itself.[40] Anal intercourse requires a two years' penance, while adults committing the same offence should perform a three or four years' penance.[41] A boy of ten, who is

[38] *PCumm*, I, 13, III, 1–2 and (X), 10, ed. Bieler, pp. 112, 116 and 128. For an example of theft and confession by a boy, see the *Old Irish Life of Brigid*, ed. W. Stokes, *Lives of Saints from the Book of Lismore* (Oxford, 1890), p. 196.

[39] *PCumm*, (X), 3, 12–14, 19–20 are in fact directed at adults. Quinn, *Boys and Monks*, p. 160, assumes however that all canons are meant for boys.

[40] *PCumm*, (X), 5: 'Puer qui sacrificio communicat peccans cum pecode, centum diebus'; ed. Bieler, p. 128. Cf. Pierre J. Payer, *Sex and the Penitentials: the Development of a Sexual Code, 550–1150* (Toronto, 1984), p. 44. The canon of Finnian, to which Payer refers, is in fact not Finnian's but a canon from Cummean's penitential incorporated in the *P. Vindobonense B*, which Bieler mistakenly included in his edition of Finnian's penitential; see Rob Meens, 'The Penitential of Finnian and the textual witness of the Paenitentiale Vindobonense B', *MS*, 55 (1993), pp. 243–55, esp. p. 251.

[41] *PCumm*, (X), 15, ed. Bieler, p. 128, Cf. *ThU*, I, ii, 4–7, ed. Finsterwalder, p. 290, with harsher penances, but a similar mitigation for boys.

sexually abused by an older person (*a maiore*) or, as the *Paenitentiale Pseudo-Bedae* suggests, by an older boy (*a majore puero*), has to perform a penance, even if he has not consented to the act.[42] This seems to agree with the view that penitentials do not take intention into account, but it is more likely that this has something to do with ideas on ritual purity. It was thought that sexual activities caused some kind of spiritual pollution, which, for example, made a person unfit to approach the altar. A penance had to be performed to restore a person to his former state of purity.[43]

These canons seem to focus on boys in a monastery. This is very clear from the provision concerning a boy who has only recently left 'the world' and wishes to fornicate with some girl. If he does not fulfil his desire his penance will be twenty days, if he is polluted by his desire it rises to a hundred days, and if they fornicate together, as is usual, so says Cummean, a penance of a year is required.[44] In Theodore's penitential, however, the penance for sexual offences is mitigated for boys, without it being clear that the canons deal with boys in a monastery.[45] The same text, however, contains a canon that explicitly allows children to eat meat. This points to the specific alleviations made for children in the monasteries.[46]

Apart from sins of a sexual nature, Cummean in his chapter on children's offences mentions sins connected with talking, though it remains unclear whether it is aimed at talking without supervision or at sins that remain words and are not put into practice. This sin of talking required the same penance, three

[42] *PCumm*, (X), 9, ed. Bieler, p. 128. *P. Ps.-Bedae*, III, 32, ed. Wasserschleben, p. 223. Cf. Payer, *Sex*, p. 42, who suggests that a penance is here imposed for educational purposes; Quinn, *Boys and Monks*, pp. 163–4, draws attention to the possible therapeutic effects of the imposition of a penance. Though it may have had this effect, I do not believe that this was the intention of this canon.

[43] Rob Meens, 'Het heilige bezoedeld. Opvattingen over het heilige en het onreine in de vroegmiddeleeuwse religieuze mentaliteit', in P. Bange and A. G. Weiler, eds, *Willibrord, zijn wereld en zijn werk. Voordrachten gehouden tijdens het Willibrordcongres Nijmegen, 28–30 september 1989* (Nijmegen, 1990), pp. 237–55, esp. pp. 244 and 249.

[44] *PCumm*, (X), 17: 'Puer de saeculo ueniens nuper cum aliqua puella fornicari nitens nec coinquinatus, XX diebus; si autem coinquinatus est, C diebus; si uero, ut moris est, suam compleat uoluntatem, ann(o) peniteat'; ed. Bieler, p. 128. Quinn, *Boys and Monks*, p. 163, n. 19, interprets this passage as referring to a sexual sin committed before entry into the monastery; Bieler's intepretation of *nuper* as an adverb relative to *ueniens* and not *nitens* seems, however, most probable.

[45] *ThU*, I, ii, 7 and 10, ed. Finsterwalder, p. 290. The reference to Basilius in 7 might, however, imply a monastic context.

[46] See Quinn, *Boys and Monks*, pp. 91 and 127–8.

superpositiones, as the sin of disobedience to the rulings of the elders (*statuta seniorum*), which again brings a monastic environment to mind.[47] Hitting each other is another offence associated with children. Little ones (*parvuli*) are corrected by seven days of penance, older children by twenty days, and adolescents, finally, by forty days.[48] This chapter also includes a penalty for eating things that were not meant to be consumed, such as parts of their own skin or excrement (*urinam stercoraue*). This was severely penalized. It is unclear, however, if this canon was meant especially for children, for the text itself makes no allusion to them.[49]

* * *

It is clear that confessors did not apply the same sentences to children as to adults. Apart from the general rule to adapt the penance to the person of the sinner, they also, in cases where children might be implied, mitigated the prescriptions given in the canons themselves. The sins most generally mentioned with regard to children concern sexual offences and theft. The canons that mention children in the confessions of others reflect the high mortality rate among young children. Of course, penitentials give a biased account of human behaviour, for they highlight moral wrongs. We should not forget, however, that they also show us the ideals that the confessors tried to achieve: priests should provide baptism; parents were to take care of their children; infanticide should be abolished, and children should live in chastity and obedience. In the penances they prescribe, the authors of these texts, furthermore, often show a humaneness that is not always recognized by modern historians. But if, even after these remarks, a gloomy picture of early medieval children may persist, we should remember the words of that most sensitive historian, the Venerable Bede, writing in his famous letter to

[47] *PCumm*, (X), 1: 'Pueri soli sermocinantes et transgredientes statuta seniorum iii superpositionibus emendantur'; ed. Bieler, p. 126, who translates: 'Boys talking alone', but 'boys only talking' seems also possible.

[48] *PCumm*, (X), 21, ed. Bieler, p. 128.

[49] *PCumm*, (X), 18, ed. Bieler, p. 128. Cf. *Excarpsus Cummeani*, I, 38, and *P. Capitula Iudiciorum*, XXIII, 3, ed. Schmitz II, p. 608, two penitentials from the eighth century that gained wide diffusion, where this canon is presented among other regulations on food, without any reference to children.

Egbert of York, of people who are not tainted by sin and thus may receive the holy sacrament: 'There are innumerable blameless people of chaste conduct, boys and girls (*pueri ac puellae*), young men and maidens (*iuvenes et virgines*), old men and women (*senes et anus*), who could without a grain of doubt participate in the celestial mysteries every Sunday.'[50]

History Faculty,
University of Cambridge

[50] *EHD*, 1, pp. 807–8.

SUFFERING AND INNOCENCE IN LATIN SERMONS FOR THE FEAST OF THE HOLY INNOCENTS, *c.* 400–800

by PAUL A. HAYWARD

IT has long been recognized that medieval representations of the Holy Innocents are much concerned with the horrendous cruelty of their passion. They are often cited as evidence that the Church, putting a high priority on loving parenthood, attempted to raise the standard of Christian childcare,[1] and it is indeed clear that their rhetoric depends upon a degree of sympathy for suffering children. This paper aims to suggest, however, that the history of this theme shows how the construction of their sanctity was influenced by the changing place of childhood in matters of theology and spirituality. It will show, I hope, that the emphasis on the Innocents' suffering needs to be seen in the context of the Origenist controversy, that there was an erosion of this theme's importance in later representations of the infants, and that this shift reflected a desire on the part of monastic authors to adapt the now established cult of the Innocents to new-found spiritual needs.

An emphasis on the suffering of the Holy Innocents can be traced to late fourth- and fifth-century accounts of their martyrdom. The poet Prudentius, for example, has heads dashed upon stones, vomiting their eyes and splattering milk-white brains across the ground.[2] This was a period of much increased interest in the story manifested, above all, in the establishment of an annual feast in both East and West, and in the composition of sermons for its celebration.[3] (There survive at least thirteen fifth-

[1] Recent examples include J. Boswell, *The Kindness of Strangers: the Abandonment of Children in Western Europe from Late Antiquity to the Renaissance* (Harmondsworth, 1988), p. 177; M. M. McLaughlin, 'Survivors and Surrogates: Children and Parents from the Ninth to the Thirteenth Century', in *The History of Childhood*, ed. L. De Mause (New York, 1974), p. 133; I. H. Forsyth, 'Children in Early Medieval Art: Ninth through Twelfth Centuries', *Journal of Psychohistory*, 4 (1976), pp. 34–5.

[2] Prudentius, 'Liber Cathemerinon', 12.116–20, ed. H. J. Thompson, *The Poems of Prudentius*, 2 vols (London, 1939–53), 1, p. 108.

[3] The origin of the feast in the West may be placed in the early fifth century (although belief in the sanctity of the Innocents is much older: see n. 57 below), as the oldest reliably attributable sermon (Maximinus the Arian (*fl.* 420s), 'In natale infantum' = 'Sermones de sollemnatibus', 8, ed.

and sixth-century Latin sermons for the feast, although the way in which sermons for Christmas and especially Epiphany continue to 'cover' the infants' story until the seventh century suggests that it was some time before a separate celebration became established everywhere.)[4] These sermons certainly devote much eloquence and space to graphic description of the passive suffering of both infants and mothers, and occasionally fathers. In virtually every text the infants are ripped from their mothers' breasts:[5] one sermon speaks of an *infantile bellum* in the homes of the infants, their cries and tears attacking their mothers' senses.[6]

R. Gryson, *Scripta Arriana Latina, CChr. SL*, 87 (1982), pp. 69–72) seems to have been composed then, while the earliest evidence of its celebration on 28 December is supplied by the early sixth-century 'Calendar of Carthage': see 'Kalendarium antiquissimum ecclesiae Carthaginensis' in *PL* 13, cols 1219–30, at col. 1228, dated by H. Leclercq, 'Kalendaria', *Dictionnaire d'archéologie chrétienne et de liturgie*, 8.1, cols 642–5. The earliest extant Greek sermon for the feast is Basil of Seleucia (d. 468), *Oratio* 27: see F. Scorza Barcellona, 'La celebrazione dei Santi Innocenti nell'omiletica greca', *Bollettino della Badia greca di Grottaferrata*, ns 29 (1975), pp. 105–35. It should also be noted that the liturgical celebration mentioned in the fourth-century 'Itinerarium Egeriae', section 42.1–8, R. Franceschini and R. Weber, eds, in *Itineraria et Geographia*, 2 vols, *CChr. SL*, 175–6 (1965), 1, p. 84, is unlikely to have been a feast of the Holy Innocents: see A. Bastiaensen, 'Sur quelques passages de l'Itinerarium Egeriae', *AnBoll*, 108 (1990), pp. 272–4.

4 This much is the burden of F. Scorza Barcellona, 'La celebrazione dei Santi Innocenti nell'omiletica latina dei secoli IV–VI', *Studi Medievali*, 3A ser., 15.2 (1974), pp. 705–67, an exhaustive survey which identifies twelve pre-seventh-century sermons for their feast, and another three Christmas sermons and twenty-three sermons for Epiphany in which the infants are 'covered'. J. Lemarié, 'Nouvelle édition du sermon pour les saints innocents', *AnBoll*, 99 (1981), pp. 137–8, edits a further sermon of probable late fifth- or sixth-century African origin, but his attempt in 'Le sermon Mai 193 et l'origine de la fête des ss. Innocents en Occident', ibid., pp. 135–50, to show that a Carolingian homily (Pseudo-Augustine, 'Sermo Mai 193', ed. ibid., pp. 141–2) derives from a now lost sermon for the feast by Chromatius of Aquileia (d. 408) rests upon mistaken assumptions about the transmission of this text. 'Sermo Mai 193' is an abbreviated version of an eighth-century sermon (now preserved in Munich, Bayerische Staatsbibliothek, MS clm 6233, fols 121v–125r and Cologne, Diözesan and Dombibliothek, MS 171, fols 17v–20v, and discussed in detail below) whose text precludes the verbal parallels on which the argument rests. See R. Étaix, 'Le sermonnaire d'Hildebold de Cologne', *Recherches Augustiniennes*, 23 (1988), p. 117.

5 See, for example, Pseudo-Augustine, 'Sermo 218', section 2, ed. *PL* 39, col. 2150; 'Sermo 219', section 2, ed. *PL* 39, col. 2151; 'Cum uniuersus mundus', cols 24–5 and 35, ed. J. Lemarié, 'Nouvelle édition', pp. 137–8, and so on. See also Prudentius, 'Liber Cathemerinon', 12.101–4, ed. Thompson, p. 108. I know of only one sermon which deploys the topos of active maternal encouragement to martyrdom, a standard scene in the lives of infant-martyrs: namely, 'Sermo Caillau-Saint-Yves 2, app. 77' = 'Sermo Mai 149', section 2, ed. *PLSupp.*, 2.1246. On the ideological function of this scene, which relates to the desire to promote Christian teaching in the home, see my forthcoming study, *The Idea of Innocent Martyrdom in Earlier Medieval England.*

6 Pseudo-Augustine, 'Sermo Mai 111 [in epiphania Domini]' = 'Sermo Caillau-Saint-Yves 2, app. 21', section 2, ed. *PLSupp.*, 2.1212.

This theme may not have been the only interpretation which patristic writing on the Holy Innocents bequeathed to the early medieval Church,[7] but it does seem to have been one of the most influential. For this corpus of materials includes a half-dozen or so sermons which may well have been instrumental in communicating this theme to later periods: those by Archbishop Peter Chrysologus of Ravenna (d. *c.* 450), that by Caesarius of Arles (d. 542), and four others falsely attributed to Augustine.[8] These sermons were disseminated through the most widely known early medieval homiliaries, including that complied by Paul the Deacon and that associated with Alan of Farfa.[9] Later authors, such as the Old English Martyrologist[10] and Ælfric of

[7] Notice should be made, for example, of the argument, derived from Cyprian of Carthage, *Ep.* 58.6, ed. G. Hartel, *CSEL*, 3.2 (1871), p. 661.21–7, that the massacre is a sign that no Christian should expect to escape persecution as even *infantia innocens* was martyred for Christ's sake. This theme was known in northern Europe through the letter itself, through excerpts made to provide a reading for the feast of the 'Infantes' in the early eighth-century Gallican Lectionary of Luxeuil, ed. P. Salmon, *The Lectionary of Luxeuil (Paris MS Lat. 9427): Édition et Étude comparative*, 2 vols = *Collectanea Biblica Latina*, 7 and 9 (Rome, 1944–53), 1, p. 17; see also A. Wilmart, 'La lettre LVIII de saint Cyprien parmi les lectures non bibliques du lectionnaire de Luxeuil', *RBen*, 28 (1911), pp. 228 and 230). It was also known through a Donatist sermon falsely attributed to Optatus of Milevi, which takes it as its central theme: Pseudo-Optatus, 'In natali infantum [*recte.* Christi], qui pro domino occisi sunt', ed. A. Wilmart, 'Un sermon de saint Optat pour la fête de noel', *Revue des sciences religieuses*, 2 (1922), pp. 282–91. This sermon is preserved in a ninth-century manuscript from the Benedictine Abbey of Weissemburg: Wolfenbüttel, Herzog August-Bibl., MS Weissemburg 4096, fols 8v–12r. See R. Grégoire, *Homéliaires liturgiques médiévaux*: *Analyse de manuscrits* = *Biblioteca degli 'Studi Medievali'*, 12 (Spoleto, 1980), pp. 394 and 401.

[8] Peter Chrysologus, 'Sermo 152' = 'De herode et infantibus', ed. A. Olivar, *Sancti Petri Chrysologi. Collectio Sermonum*, 3 vols, *CChr. SL*, 24–24A–24B (1975–82), 3, pp. 947–57, and 'Sermo 153', ed. *CChr. SL*, 24B, pp. 956–7; Caesarius of Arles, 'Sermo 222', ed. G. Morin, *Sancti Caesarii Arelatensis, Sermones*, 2 vols, *CChr. SL*, 103–4 (1953), 2, pp. 877–81); Pseudo-Auguste,'Sermo 218', ed. *PL* 39.2149–50, 'Sermo 219', ed. *PL* 39.2151–2, and 'Sermo 221', ed. *PL* 39.2154–6; and Pseudo-Augustine, 'Sermo Caillau-Saint-Yves 2, app. 79', ed. A. Caillau, *S. Augustini Hipponensis Episcopi Opera Omnia*, 24bis (Paris, 1842), pp. 418–24, a sermon which survives in four distinct recensions: see J. Machielsen, *Clavis Patristica Pseudigraphorum Medii Aevi: Opera Homiletica*, 2 vols, *CChr. SL*, 1A–1B (1990), nos 1487, 1717, 1733, the most widely known of which is that attributed to John Chrysostom in the Homiliary of Paul the Deacon, ed. *PL*, 95.1176–7.

[9] For Paul the Deacon (in which 'Herod and the Infants' by Peter Chrysologus is attributed to Bishop Severianus), see Grégoire, *Homéliaires liturgiques médiévaux*, pp. 436–7; for Alan of Farfa, see ibid., pp. 148–9 and 234. The only subsequent homily to approach these in 'popularity' seems to be Bede, 'De ss. Innocentibus' = 'Homeliarum evangelii libri III', 1.10, ed. D. Hurst, *Bedae Venerabilis. Opera Exegetica, CChr. SL*, 122 (1955), pp. 68–72.

[10] Compare 'Old English Martyrology', 27 Dec., ed. G. Kotzor, *Das altenglische Martyrologium*, Bayerische Akademie der Wissenschaften Philosophisch-Historische Klasse Abhandlungen – Neue Folge, Heft 88, 2 vols (Munich, 1981), 2, pp. 7–8, with Peter Chrysologus, 'De Herode et infantibus', 2.14–16 and 8.73–80, ed. *CChr. SL*, 24B, pp. 949–50 and 954. See also J. E. Cross, 'The Use of Homilies in the *Old English Martyrology*', *Anglo-Saxon England*, 13 (1985), pp. 109–11.

Eynsham,[11] draw heavily upon them without significantly modifying their central theme. These sermons yield, more to the point, clues as to the causes of interest in the suffering of the Holy Innocents. This much is especially true of 'Herod and the Infants' by Peter Chrysologus.

The sermon falls into two halves. The first (sections 1–5), making a moral point, develops the theme of Herod's obscene cruelty towards the infants in order show how terrible and all-consuming are envy and spite. Herod's anger did not stop, for example, at violating maternal love and tenderness: he sends his soldiers to attack the mothers' embrace, and to test their swords between tender breasts.[12] The second half relates the helpless-suffering theme to issues of grace and divine justice. Chrysologus' first concern is to vindicate Jesus from the charge that he deserted those whom he knew were being hunted down and martyred in his place. Christ, he argues, did not condemn his soldiers; instead, he promoted them. He enabled them to have a triumph without having to live, he gave them a victory before having to fight, and so on.[13] Chrysologus asserts, in other words, that their death was not an injustice allowed by Christ. Developing the theme further, he argues that both the infants *and* their mothers were blessed by their passion, because it conferred on them the grace of baptism:

> They live, they live, who live for the truth, who are worthy to die for Christ. Blessed are the wombs that carried such as them; blessed are the breasts which gave suck to such as them. Blessed are the tears which were shed for them and conferred on the weeping ones the grace of baptism. For, by one gift, but in different ways, the mothers were baptized in their tears and the infants in their blood; the mothers suffered in the martyrdoms of their sons. For the sword which cut off

[11] Compare Ælfric, 'In natale innocentium infantium', 118–23, ed. D. Whitelock, *Sweet's Anglo-Saxon Reader in Prose and Verse*, 15th ed. (Oxford, 1967), p. 73, with Peter Chrysologus, 'De Herode et infantibus', 8.72–80, 83–5, ed. *CChr. SL*, 24B, pp. 954–5. Ælfric also used Caesarius of Arles, 'Sermo 222' and Pseudo-Augustine, 'Sermo 218': see C. L. Smetana, 'Ælfric and the Early Medieval Homiliary', *Traditio*, 15 (1959), pp. 184–5.

[12] Peter Chrysologus, 'Sermo 152', section 2.14–16, ed. *CChr. SL*, 24B, pp. 949–50. Compare also, 'Cum uniuersus mundus', lines 15–16, 21–2 and 25–6, ed. J. Lemarié, 'Nouvelle édition', pp. 137–8; Pseudo-Augustine, 'Sermo Caillu-Saint-Yves 2, app. 77' = 'Sermo Mai 149', section 2, ed. *PLSupp.*, 2.1246.

[13] Peter Chrysologus, 'Sermo 152', section 7.57–69, ed. *CChr. SL*, 24B, pp. 953–4.

> their sons' limbs, reached the hearts of the mothers: thus it is inevitable that they will be consorts in their reward, as they were companions in their passion.[14]

He even suggests that the infants, in their naïvety, rejoiced at the arrival of their executioners.[15] His final point, moreover, is that the combination of their incapacity as infants and their sanctification is certain proof that sancity is not earned by merit, but conferred by grace alone. For there is no *voluntas* or *arbitrium* in small boys: in them *natura* is held captive.[16] Their martyrdom, in other words, demonstrates the truth of the Augustinian interpretation of grace and baptism.

The other sermons are also, in their various ways, concerned to vindicate the suffering of these infants. Most simply assert one or more of these explanations: that the brevity with which they passed from this life to heaven was a great blessing;[17] that their ignorance made them incapable of knowing that they were suffering;[18] and, that the massacre was a great wonder of Christ by which infancy was allowed to overcome its limitations and witness for the faith.[19] Pseudo-Augustine's Sermon 219, for example, is full of rhetoric to this effect:

[14] Ibid., section 8.72–80, pp. 954–5. See also section 8.83–5, p. 955. The idea that they were baptized in their mothers' milk and by their very baptism is anticipated by Chromatius of Aquileia: see 'Sermo 14' = 'De paraclyti sanatione et de baptismo', section 2.32–41, eds R. Étaix and J. Lemarié, *Chromatii Aquileiensis Opera, CChr. SL*, 9A (1974), pp. 62–3.

[15] Peter Chrysologus, 'De Herode et infantibus', section 8.50–83, ed. *CChr. SL*, 24B, p. 954. See, likewise, Pseudo-Augustine, 'Sermo Caillau-Saint-Yves 2, app. 77' = 'Sermo Mai 149', section 1, ed. *PLSupp.*, 2.1245–6: they died without the pain of martyrdom, 'because even if they loved their mothers, the unknowing infants were mutilated unjustly: the conscience of the unknowing infants did not care about the sword of the persecutor, because they were rejoicing with Him, innocents of the saviour in flight [to Egypt]'.

[16] Peter Chrysologus, 'De Herode et infantibus', section 9.86–9, ed. *CChr. SL*, 24B, p. 955. His other sermon for the feast is much shorter, but its central point is essentially the same: see 'Sermo 153', section 2.24–9, ed. *CChr. SL*, 24B, p. 957.

[17] See, for example, 'Cum uniuersus mundus', lines 6–7, 38, 43–7, ed. J. Lemarié, 'Nouvelle édition', pp. 137–8; Augustine, 'Sermo 199 [in epiphania Domini]', section 1, ed. *PL* 38.1027, and 'Sermo dubius 373', 3, ed. *PL* 39.1664.

[18] See, for example, Augustine, 'Sermo 199 [in epiphania Domini]', section 1, ed. *PL*, 38.1027: it was happier for them than for the Magi, since they, not yet being capable of confessing Christ, could suffer for him in their ignorance without knowing the terror of Herod. See also Leo the Great, 'Tractatus 32', section 3.64–74, ed. A. Chavasse, *Sancti Leonis Magni Romani Pontificis Tractatus Septem et Nonaginta, CChr. SL*, 138–138A (1974), 1, pp. 165–9, at p. 168, who develops this idea.

[19] This might be said to be the central theme of the sermon attributed to John Chrysostom in the Homiliary of Paul the Deacon, ed. *PL* 95.1176–7. On this theme, see also Leo the Great, 'Tractatus 32', section 3.64–74, ed. *CChr. SL*, 138, p. 168.

> *Happy* is their age, which could not yet acknowledge Christ, but which was worthy to die for him; . . . Blessed was their birth, because they found everlasting life at the entrance of this present life. They ran, indeed, from their beginning of entry into daylight to a trial and resulting salvation; and from this end they began forthwith on the beginnings of eternity [and so on].[20]

These sermons seem, in short, much concerned to assert that the massacre of the infants was ultimately to their and their mothers' benefit and, as a wondrous miracle of divine grace, to the glory of Christ *despite the suffering involved.*

Not all of these sermons are as carefully Augustinian as Peter Chrysologus, but it seems clear that all approach the subject of the Holy Innocents from the direction of the Pelagian controversy, in which the question of infant suffering was an acutely topical issue. In essence, the problem was that the manifest suffering of children was difficult to reconcile with the belief that God was utterly just, without adopting either an 'Origenist' position on the origin of the soul, or a determinist position which denied both the power of God and the existence of a free will that gave significance to moral endeavour.[21] In Augustine's later works, for example, the suffering of infants is certain proof of his solution to the problem, the doctrine of 'original sin'. He argued that the sufferings of infants were explained by a legacy of sin which they had contracted at birth through the flesh of their parents.[22] For Julian of Eclanum, on the other hand, this was no solution to the problem: a just God would never allow infants to suffer for sins contracted not by their own volition but through others;[23] and a God who denied human beings the opportunity

[20] Pseudo-Augustine, 'Sermo 218', section 2, ed. *PL* 39.2150, and quoted in Pseudo-Eusebius, 'De epiphania Domini et de Innocentibus', section 4.75–85, ed. Fr. Glorie, *Eusebius Gallicanus. Collectio Homiliarum*, 3 vols, *CChr. SL*, 101–101A–101B (1970), 1, no. iv, p. 48.

[21] On the importance of this issue, see further E. A. Clark, *The Origenist Controversy: The Cultural Construction of an Early Christian Debate* (Princeton, N. J., 1992), pp. 194–247, esp. pp. 194 and 238. See also F. Refoulé, 'Misère des enfants et péché originel d'après saint Augustin', *Revue Thomiste*, 63 (1963), pp. 341–62.

[22] See Augustine, 'De peccatorum meritis et remissione et de baptismo parvulorum', i.9.9, 24.34, and iii. 2.2, ed. C. F. Urba and J. Zycha, *CSEL*, 60 (Vienna, 1913), pp. 10–11, 34, and 130, arguing against the Origenist view that souls committed sins in heaven prior to being born, which he finds implausible and contrary to scripture. See also i.22.31 and iii.9.17, pp. 29–30 and 143.

[23] Julian, 'Ad Turbantium', in Augustine, 'Contra Julianum', ii.1.2, ed. *PL*, 44.673. See also Augustine, 'De nuptiis et concupiscentia', ii.27.44, ed. C. F. Urba and J. Zycha, *CSEL*, 42 (1902), pp. 297–8.

to choose good by rendering their very being defective at the moment of birth was hardly a just God.[24] But for Augustine, to exempt infants from sinfulness was to impugn divine justice, since there was no other way of accounting for their sufferings.[25] 'Original sin' is, in addition, the only justification for infant baptism—a practice which was, he claimed, the apostolic doctrine of the Church. If all must be baptized, then all must be sinful.[26]

Given the great deal of discussion of the place of infant suffering in the divine order that was going on in the early fifth century, it is easy to see why the sermon writers focused upon the sufferings of the Holy Innocents and formulated their commentary around questions of justice. Moreover, that the emergence of the feast was bound up with the problem of theodicy is suggested by Augustine's tract *On Free Will*. This is an early work in which he argues, among other things, that the miseries of infants have a beneficent purpose known only to God. God may, he suggests, reserve some special reward for infants whose suffering has aroused the faith of their parents:

> Although they have performed no good act, they have nevertheless endured these sufferings without having committed any sins. Nor is it without reason that the church commends for veneration as martyrs, even the infants who were slain when the Lord Jesus Christ was being sought out for destruction by Herod.[27]

Augustine was later to retract this argument because it implied that it was possible for unbaptized infants to escape damnation.[28]

[24] Ibid., ii.13.27 and 27.44, pp. 280 and 298.

[25] Augustine, 'Contra Julianum "Opus imperfectum" ', iii.236.34–56, ed. M. Zelzer, *CSEL*, 85 (1974), pp. 349–50, and 'Contra Julianum', iii.3.8, ed. *PL* 44.705–6.

[26] Augustine, 'Contra Julianum', vi.5.11, ed. *PL* 44.705–6; 'De nuptiis et concupiscentia', ii.29.51, ed. *CSEL*, 42, pp. 307–8; 'De origine animae hominis' = *Ep.* 166.9.28, ed. A. Goldbacher, *CSEL*, 44 (1904), pp. 584–5. For infant baptism as the apostolic custom of the Church, see Augustine, 'De Genesi ad litteram', 10.xxiii.39, ed. J. Zycha, *CSEL*, 28.1 (1894), p. 327.1–4; 'De baptismo', 4.xxiv.31, ed. M. Petschenig, *CSEL*, 51 (1906), p. 259.2–4. But notice also that, as Julian pointed out ('Ad Turbantium', in Augustine, 'Contra Julianum', vi.13.40, ed. *PL* 44.843), Augustine's idea of 'original sin' implies that baptism is not a completely efficacious rite, since Christians cannot escape transferring this legacy to their children through baptism. The Pelagians, on the other hand, held that baptism created completely new beings (Clark, *The Origenist Controversy*, pp. 210, 220).

[27] Augustine, 'De libero arbitrio', iii.23.68.231, ed. W. M. Green, *Sancti Augustini Opera*, pt. 2.2, *CChr. SL*, 29 (1970), p. 315.

[28] Augustine, *Ep.* 166.7.18–19, ed. *CSEL*, 44, pp. 571–4; and 'De dono perseverantiae', 11.27, 12.30, ed. *PL* 45.1009–10. See Clark, *The Origenist Controversy*, pp. 229, 235, 241.

But there is the definite suggestion here that some early fourth-century churches promoted the cult of the Holy Innocents because 'their existence' had a bearing upon the problem of suffering and divine justice, even though the precise sense of that bearing is not specified.

Once Augustine's solution to the problem had crystallized, moreover, there was a powerful reason for insisting that these infants were indeed martyrs.[29] Pelagians could always argue that they had been saved by their own innate infant innocence. The logical implication of Augustine's theory of original sin, on the other hand, is that these infants were damned unless sanctified by divine grace, since, living before the inception of the new dispensation, they were not baptized Christians.[30] The event's association with Jesus would seem to have been crucial. To fail to assert that they had been sanctified by some exceptional act of grace would be to associate the Incarnation of Christ, and the Christmas story, with a cruel injustice against children. Vindicating the episode from this charge and accommodating it to the Augustinian view of infancy and grace are, indeed, what the fifth-century sermons seem to be about.[31]

That, furthermore, the cult of the Holy Innocents was promoted to this end is implied by the opening paragraphs of the sermon by Caesarius of Arles. Today's feast, he argues, shows us that the grace of benediction filled the blessed infants as much as iniquity abounded against them. Stretching the sense of the biblical account, he argues that Rachel (a symbol for Judah) 'did not need to be consoled' (Matthew 2.18), not because she was inconsolable, but because she was not sorry for them. It is only the foolish who think that the Holy Land was left bereft by the loss of its infants: rather, she was blessed by this, and she never

[29] Some confirmation of this point is supplied by Augustine, 'Sermo dubius [de epiphania Domini] 373', section 3, *PL* 39.1664–5, where he argues that those who doubt the custom of baptizing infants question the martyrdom of the infants. Note also 'De Genesi ad litteram', 10.xxiii.39, ed. J. Zycha, *CSEL*, 28.1 (1894), p. 327.4–6. Here Augustine argues that it is important to baptize infants, because, as the first age to witness for Christ, their age carries great importance.

[30] A point noted by Leo the Great: 'Tractatus 31', section 3.56–8, ed. *CChr. SL*, 138, p. 163: Christ bestowed the dignity of martyrdom on those on whom he had not yet spent his redeeming blood.

[31] For an early African solution, see Quoduultdeus of Carthage (*size4fl. c.* 428–39), 'Sermo de symbolo II', iv.65–9, ed. R. Braun, *Opera Quoduultdeo Carthaginiensi Episcopo tributa, CChr. SL*, 60 (1976), pp. 335–49, at p. 340): 'Christ vouched for them as they had died for Christ, vouched for them so that they were cleansed of original sin with their own blood. They were born to death but returned straight to life.'

lamented her sons. Thus the anniversary of the infants' death is an occasion not for grief, but to honour those who were killed for Christ's sake, not to weep, but to give due veneration.[32] He goes on, in addition, to discuss other issues concerning suffering and justice (that the wicked never profit from persecution; that suffering in the midst of evil is infinitely better than being wicked, and so on),[33] as though these issues naturally follow from the subject of the Holy Innocents.

Bede's sermon, written in the early eighth century, shows the continuing relevance of this issue. He argues that we must not mourn their deaths (some manuscripts add 'unjust' deaths)[34] as much as we should rejoice that they have attained the palm of righteousness. Like Caesarius, Bede attempts to explain away Rachel's sorrow: her laments signify the mourning due from the Church to its saints, but they do not indicate, he asserts, that 'she wished them to return to the world, so that they might bear its strife with her.'[35] In heaven, 'Rachel will not bewail her children, but "God will wipe away every tear from her eyes", and give them the voice of joy and of eternal salvation in their tabernacles.'[36] The suffering of Rachel and the mutilation of the infants should not, in other words, become an occasion for regret but a cause for celebration. Bede's sermon also reflects, however, a shift to a more 'medieval' way of looking at the Holy Innocents. He is, for example, much more interested than earlier writers to set out the literal, and sometimes the figurative, significance of each detail in the story.[37] Bede is, moreover, concerned with ascetic themes: the fact, he writes, that little children were killed indicates that martyrdom comes through the virtue of humility, for it is not possible to give a soul for

[32] Caesarius of Arles, 'Sermo 222', sections 1–2, ed. *CChr. SL*, 104, pp. 877–8.

[33] Ibid., sections 3–5, pp. 878–7.

[34] See Bede, 'De ss. Innocentibus', 120, ed. *CChr. SL*, 122, p. 71n.

[35] Ibid., 31–7, p. 69. The point is repeated at 121–6, p. 71.

[36] Ibid., 154–8, p. 72, quoting Rev. 7.17 and 21.4.

[37] See esp. ibid., 1–89, pp. 68–70. Haimo of Auxerre, 'De ss. Innocentibus', ed. *PL* 118.75–82, is organized to the same end, taking its narrative from Rufinus' translation of Eusebius, 'Historia Ecclesiastica', i.6–8, ed. E. Schwartz and Th. Mommsen, *Eusebius Werke*, 2, *Die Kirchengeschichte [mit] der lateinischen Übersetzung des Rufinus*, Die griechischen christlichen Schriftsteller 11, 1–3 (1903–9), 1, pp. 63–9, and its exegesis mainly from Bede. On Haimo's homiliary, see H. Barré, *Les homéliaires carolingiens de l'école d'Auxerre: Authenticité – Inventaire – Tableaux comparatifs – Initia = Studi e Testi* 225 (1962), pp. 146–60.

Christ unless you are converted and become like unto little boys.[38]

It is true, of course, that this point was far from new. Leo the Great, having touched on other issues in his earlier accounts of the Holy Innocents, arrived at this argument in his seventh sermon for Epiphany (written in 452). He explains that this feast promotes for our imitation the model of infancy, not just in the form of the infant Saviour who was adored by the Magi, but also in the *form* of the infants who, begotten at Bethlehem at the time of his birth, became consorts of his passion *per communionem aetatis*.[39] He goes on to cite Matthew 18.3 ('Unless you be converted and become as little children, you shall not enter the kingdom of heaven'), and to develop this commandment with some enthusiasm:

> Christ loved infancy, master of humility, rule of innocence, model of gentleness. Christ loved infancy, to which he directed the behaviour of their elders, to which he humbled the age of the old and to which example he urged them, in order to sublimate them to the eternal kingdom.[40]

But, like most fifth-century commentators on Matthew 18.3, Leo reduces the scope of this imperative to imitation of an *image* displayed by children. He cites I Corinthians 14.20 ('Brethren, do not become children in sense; but in malice be children, and in sense be perfect'),[41] and defines the aspects of childhood to which Christ was referring with a list of a 'outward' and largely negative virtues, such as the facility for the immediate return to an *attitude* of peacefulness after a commotion, for never remembering an offence, and so on.[42] All of this is a patristic commonplace which reflects an unease with the implications of Matthew

[38] Bede, 'De ss. Innocentibus', 4–5, ed. *CChr. SL*, 122, p. 68, after Matt. 18.3. For an allusion to this passage in Haimo of Auxerre, 'De ss. Innocentibus', see *PL* 118.79A. See also 'Sermo Casinensis 3', p. 38, ed. *PLSupp*. 2.1322, a sermon of similar date (?), where the 'sinlessness' of the infants becomes an exhortation to self-mortification.

[39] Leo, 'Tractatus 37', section 4.77–83, ed. *CChr. SL*, 138, pp. 200–4, at p. 203. Compare 'Tractatus 31' (written in 441), section 3.61–8, pp. 163–4, where Leo takes Christ's infancy as an exhortation to humility, but not the martyrdom of the infants which he also describes.

[40] Ibid., section 3.48–64, pp. 202–3.

[41] The influence of this passage is stressed by C. Gnilka, *Aetas Spiritalis: Die Überwindung der natüralichen Altersstufen als Ideal frühchristlichen Lebens* = *Theophaneia*, 24 (Bonn, 1972), pp. 106–11.

[42] Leo, 'Tractatus 37', section 4.68–73, ed. *CChr. SL*, 138, p. 203.

18.3,[43] and is closely allied to Augustine's view that children are 'innocent' only in so far as bodily incapacity prevents them from sinning.[44] Leo takes care, in short, to avoid saying that Jesus singled out the infants to be martyrs because they were especially virtuous in themselves. The innovative aspect of medieval versions of this argument is that they show no misgivings about stressing the Innocents' inward purity and virtue.

This tendency is well illustrated by a sermon preserved in an eighth-century Bavarian manuscript (today, Munich, Bayerische Staatsbibliothek, MS clm 6233, fols 121v–125r) and in the early ninth-century homiliary of Archbishop Hildebald of Cologne (Cologne, Diözesan and Dombibliothek, MS 171, fols 17v–20v).[45] The sermon addresses the issue of their place in the sacramental order by arguing that the infants were baptized like others who pleased God with their complete faith and good works before the time of Jesus, such as the thief who was crucified with Christ.[46] But having invoked the topos that they prefigure all other martyrs, and having placed them before Peter and Paul in martyrdom,[47] the author argues that the Lord singled out infants for this special honour, because he loved the *innocentia*

[43] The desire to limit the application of the verse comes through most clearly in Ambrose, 'Expositio Evangelii Secundum Lucam', viii.57–9, ed. M. Adriaen, *Sancti Ambrosii Mediolanensis Opera, CChr. SL*, 14 (1957), pp. 319–20, and as developed by Maximus of Turin, 'Sermo 54', sections 1.18–2.49, ed. A. Mutzenbecher, *Maximi Episcopi Taurinensis. Collectio Sermonum, CChr. SL*, 23 (1962), pp. 218–19. Here Jesus himself is made the 'child' whose example was being referred to. The meaning of this exegetical tradition is discussed in my forthcoming study, *The Idea of Innocent Martyrdom*.

[44] See Augustine, 'Confessiones', 1.vii.11.19–20, ed. L. Verheijen, *Sancti Augustini Opera, CChr. SL*, 27 (1981), p. 6. Augustine's belief in the innate adult nature of children is eminently compatible with the doctrines of original sin and infant baptism: see J. J. O'Donnell, *Augustine, Confessions: Introduction, Text and Commentary*, 3 vols (Oxford, 1992), 2, p. 44.

[45] This sermon is nowhere printed in full, but Lemarié, 'Le sermon Mai 193', pp. 141–2, edits an abbreviated text (see further, n. 4 above), while J. E. Cross, 'The Insular Connections of a Sermon for Holy Innocents', in M. Stokes and T. Burton, eds, *Medieval Literature and Antiquities for Basil Cottle* (Cambridge, 1987), pp. 61–6, has shown that this sermon was used by the author of a homily preserved in, amongst other manuscripts, an eleventh-century Bury St Edmund's homiliary: today, Cambridge, Pembroke College MS 25, fols 19v–21r, ed. ibid., pp. 69–70.

[46] Munich, Bay. Staatsbibl. MS clm 6233, fol. 124r.

[47] Ibid., fol. 122v. See also 'Sermo Mai 193', section 3.24–7, ed. Lémarie, 'Le sermon Mai 193', p. 142. For the topos that the infants prefigure all the martyrs, see Pseudo-Optatus, 'In natali infantum', section 4.37–8 and 40, ed. Wilmart, 'Un sermon', p. 283; Prudentius, 'Liber Cathemerinon', 12.129–32, ed. Thompson, 1, pp. 108–10; Chromatius of Aquileia, 'Tractatus VI, in Matthaeum 2.13–18', section 2.63–74, ed. *CChr. SL*, 9A, p. 222; Caesarius of Arles, 'Sermo 222', section 2, ed. *CChr. SL*, 104, p. 878. In Bede, 'De ss. Innocentibus', 1–3, ed. *CChr. SL*, 122, p. 68, their deaths 'signify' the passions of all Christ's martyrs.

of little children and wanted us to follow their example.[48] Here the author cites Matthew 18.3, and reproduces some conventional patristic line on the meaning of Christ's imperative: children are to be imitated because they do not delight at the sight of a beautiful woman, nor are they ambitious, nor do they begrudge anything, and so on. [49] In this sermon, however, the author adds material stressing their inward purity. The infants were those, he writes, 'whom the Lord chose for their innocence, as little boys are unsullied and pure.'[50] The homily gives the notion of *innocentia* a definite sexual connotation, moreover, by quoting from Apocalypse 14.1–5, the Epistle read during their Mass in the Roman Rite from the eighth century at the latest.[51] These verses define the Innocents as members of the one-hundred and forty-four thousand arranged about the throne of the Lord in Heaven. Thus the homily argues that,

> The infants are those who 'have washed their robes and have made them white in the blood of the lamb' and 'follow the lamb whithersoever he goeth'; that is, they follow Jesus Christ the son of God through all the kingdom of heaven and sing the new song that no one is able to sing who has been defiled with women, and no part of the kingdom of heaven is closed to them.[52]

[48] Munich, Bay. Staatsbibl., MS clm 6233, fol. 122v, reproduced with some rearrangement or order in 'Sermo Mai 193', section 4.28–30 and 33–5, ed. Lémarie, 'Le sermon Mai 193', p. 142.

[49] Munich, Bay. Staatsbibl., MS clm 6233, fol. 122v–123v. The author is probably following the form given by Jerome, 'Commentariorum in Mattheum', iii. 18.4.500–5, ed. D. Hurst and M. Adriaen, *Hieronymi Presbyteri Opera Exegetica, CChr. SL*, 7 (1969), p. 157, who seems to have derived the idea from Hilary of Poitiers, 'Commentarius in Matthaeum', xviii. 1, ed. J. Doignon, *Hilaire de Poitiers sur Matthieu*, 2 vols, *SC*, 254 and 258 (1978–9), 2, pp. 74–5.

[50] Munich, Bay. Staatsbibl., MS clm 6233, fol. 122v: 'Hiis sunt quos eligit Dominus quorum innocentia sicut paruulorum pura et munda est.' This idea is deleted in 'Sermo Mai 193', but expanded in 'Omelia in Natale Innocentium', lines 54–9, ed. Cross, 'A Sermon for Holy Innocents', p. 69.

[51] The earliest known Roman lectionary, the eighth-century Comes of Würzburg, has this lection. See G. Morin, 'Le plus ancien "Comes" ou lectionnaire de l'Eglise romaine', *RBen*, 27 (1910), p. 47 (item xiii). See also the tenth-century Corbie (and St Germain-des-Pres) 'Liber Comitis', item vii, ed. W. H. Frere, *Studies in the Early Roman Lectionary*, 3, *The Roman Epistle Lectionary = Alcuin Club Collections*, 32 (London, 1935), p. 2.

[52] Munich, Bay. Staatsbibl., MS clm 6233, fol. 124r. Note, again, that whereas 'Sermo Mai 193' eradicates all reference to Apocalypse 14.1–5, the more radical later sermon, 'Omelia in Natale Innocentium', ed. Cross, 'A Sermon for Holy Innocents', p. 69.47–9, adds a further reference to Apocalypse 14.4. See also lines 70–9, p. 70.

This leads, finally, to the evidence of the Roman liturgy, for the use of these verses, and of the title *Holy Innocents*, is confined to this rite.[53] It is impossible to say when the Roman Church began to use these verses or the title, given that the earliest Gospel lectionaries and homiliaries are all of eighth-century date; but it may well be significant that it is virtually unknown for sermons to quote these verses before the eighth century.[54] It is possible that their use was introduced relatively late, making them another indication of a growing tendency to see the martyred infants as examples of active virginity; but this is a matter requiring further investigation. For now it is worth noting that the oldest extant prayers for the feast take up the same themes as the patristic sermons. The two fifth-century Mass sets preserved in the *Leonine Sacramentary* focus, for example, upon the grace which enabled the infants to confess before they could speak, which granted them a passion before Christ's Passion, and so on.[55] Their martyrdom is here a great benefaction of divine mercy precisely because, moreover, Christ would not allow those who had suffered in his name to perish, even though they had had no experience of that which deserves glory.[56]

The fifth and sixth centuries were, in conclusion, the most formative period in the development of the cult of the Holy

[53] The Gallican Rite used the title *infantes*, while employing readings from Jer. 31.15–20, Rev. 6.9–11, and Matt. 2.1–23; Salmon, ed., *The Lectionary of Luxeuil*, 1, pp. 18–20; J. Mabillon, 'De liturgica Gallicana libri tres', *PL* 72.176, the Mozarabic rite the same title (under 8 January), while employing readings from Jer. 31.15–20, Heb. 2.9–3.2, and Matt. 2.16–23 (see J. Perez de Urbel and A. Gonzalez y Ruiz-Zorilla, eds, *Liber commicus*, 2 vols, *Monumenta Hispaniae sacra, series liturgica*, 2–3 (Madrid, 1950–5), 1, pp. 47–9). In the Armenian Lectionary the readings for their feast are Matt. 2.16–18, Acts 12.1–24, Heb. 2.14–18, and Ps. 103. See the table in J. Wilkinson, tr., *Egeria's Travels to the Holy Land*, rev. edn (Jerusalem, 1981), p. 272, item 55. See also L. Duchesne, *Christian Worship: Its Origins and Evolution*, 5th edn (London, 1919), p. 268, n. 4.

[54] I know of only one potentially early sermon (namely, 'Sermo Casinensis 3, p. 38', ed. *PLSupp.*, 2.1320–3) which alludes to Rev. 14.1–5, but it is likely to be relatively late. As Scorza Barcellona, 'La celebrazione dei Santi Innocenti', pp. 760–1, points out, most early sermons mention Ps. 78.10–11 and Rom. 8.35 when refering to the Lections for that day (see, for example, Pseudo-Augustine, 'Sermo Caillau-Saint-Yves 2, 87', section 2, ed. *PLSupp.*, 2.1101, also citing Apocalypse 6.9–10). Bede, 'De ss. Innocentibus', 127–57, ed. *CChr. SL*, 122, pp. 71–2, draws heavily upon Apocalypse 7.9–17, implying, perhaps, that they and not 14.1–5 supplied the epistle in the early eighth-century Northumbrian church.

[55] 'Sacramentarium Veronense', nos 1284–93, ed. L. C. Mohlberg, *Sacramentarium Veronense* (*Cod. Bibl. Capit. Veron. LXXXV* [80]) = *Rerum ecclesiasticarum documenta, series maior*, Fontes 1 (Rome, 1956). These prayers would seem to date from the mid-fifth century, but see further, E. Bourque, *Étude sur les sacramentaires romains*, pt, 1, *Les textes primitifs* = *Studi di Antichità Cristiana*, 20 (Vatican, 1948), 1, esp. p. 143.

[56] Ibid., no. 1286, p. 165. See also no. 1291, pp. 165–6.

Innocents. Belief in the sanctity of the infants seems to have arisen by the end of the second century,[57] but the decisive contribution to medieval interpretations of its significance came in the later patristic period. For the literary and artistic traditions established at this time made an emphasis on their terrible suffering a requirement of later representations of their martyrdom. This emphasis was, however, a reflection of the priority which arguments about the suffering of infants had in the theological controversies of the period. Later authors, less interested in these issues, give increasing space to the nature of the infants' sanctity, holding up their *innocentia* as an exhortation to humility and active virginity. But, in so doing, they were building upon earlier formulations of the infants' sanctity which arose from a quite different agenda, and which rested upon an essentially negative view of their holiness. For references to the murdered infants' *innocentia* in fifth- and sixth-century sermons refer to their 'apparent' innocence alone: their physical inability to commit actual sin, their harmlessness, and their naïvety.[58] Whether later authors were aware that their inclination to stress the inner purity of the Holy Innocents was in conflict with the subtler implications of these earlier formulations is far from clear—their notion of infant innocence is, ironically, not dissimilar to that of Pelagius and Julian of Eclanum. But, whatever the case, it is certain that the construction of the Holy Innocents' sanctity is a product of religious, not 'social', concerns.

St John's College,
Cambridge

[57] This belief is a premise in rhetorical arguments advanced by both Irenaeus of Antioch and Cyprian of Carthage: see Irenaeus, 'Adversus Haereses', 3.16.4, A. Rousseau and L. Doultreleau, eds, *Irénée de Lyon Contre les Hérésies Livre III*, 2 vols *SC*, 110–11 (1974), 2, p. 304; Cyprian of Carthage, *Ep.* 58.6, to the Congregation of Thibaris, ed. *CSEL*, 3.2, p. 661.21–7. See also M. A. Fahey, *Cyprian and the Bible: a Study in Third-Century Exegesis* (Tübingen. 1971), pp. 203–4.

[58] See, for example, Peter Chrysologus, 'De Herode et infantibus', esp. section 8.82–3, ed. *CChr. SL*, 24B, p. 955.

PARENTS, CHILDREN, AND THE CHURCH IN THE EARLIER MIDDLE AGES*
(*PRESIDENTIAL ADDRESS*)

by JANET L. NELSON

THE titles of Ecclesiastical History Society conferences have sometimes presented the Church as part of a pair that carries more than a hint of contradiction: the Church and War; the Church and Wealth. Well now: the Church and Childhood? Ecclesiastical Historians and Childhood? I can't help recalling Heloise's rhetorical question: 'What harmony can there be between pupils and nursemaids, desks and cradles?'[1] Last year we reminded ourselves that the blood of the martyrs is the life of the Church: this year and, more fortunately placed than Heloise, I'm confident that we'll show the multifarious ways in which flesh-and-blood children have been part of that life. 'The Church' is shorthand: not only do we have to speak of many churches, but of many varieties of ecclesiastical attitude, of conflicts of ecclesiastical interest, of juxtapositions and negotiations between clerical and lay (for parents, too, are members of the Church), and, in all the above, of change. Equally subject to change and variety is the other element in this year's pair. Although the stages of a child's development are biological, physiological, perhaps psychological givens, and genetically programmed, childhood itself is a construct, culturally determined. As historians, it's our job to historicize it: identify the phases and modes and variations in its construction, its adaptation, and its lived experience.

I want to pay homage at the outset to Philippe Ariès, who first pointed out the fundamental importance of childhood as a historical subject.[2] He was wrong about the Middle Ages: he

*For a generous supply of references and helpful suggestions on themes dealt with in this paper I should like to thank Andrew Louth, Michelle Lucey, Jane Martindale, Rob Meens, Julia Smith, and, especially, Mayke de Jong.

[1] Heloise, as reported by Abelard, *Historia Calamitatum*, tr. B. Radice, *The Letters of Abelard and Heloise* (Harmondsworth, 1974), p. 71.

[2] P. Ariès, *L'enfant et la vie familiale sous l'ancien régime* (Paris, 1960), tr. R. Boldick, *Centuries of Childhood* (Harmondsworth, 1973).

mistook the absence of handbooks on child-rearing for lack of concern with child-rearing, instead of looking in medical treatises for relevant material; focusing on artistic representations of children as miniature adults, he ignored a mass of textual evidence, from Isidore onwards, for the recognition of childhood as a human stage with specific characteristics and needs; he neglected varieties of class and place, and of shifts *within* the medieval centuries; and he underestimated the love of medieval parents for their offspring.[3] Ariès, to be frank, fell into our professional vice of locating the Other in the period before the one he knew most about. But he opened new vistas for researchers on any and every period. Appreciative yet critical, we can go on to investigate historically-specific ways in which parental attitudes to children were manifested in different times, and within different social contexts. As ecclesiastical historians, we seek to identify within the Christian tradition the contributions of the Church, its personnel, its theorists, its institutions, to the processes whereby childhood was defined, moulded, embodied, and used. It was not only for the Church that parents produced children—though churchmen often taught 'the order of married persons' to that effect. But the Church did condition the manifestations of parental feeling; and in societies polarized between rich and poor, noble and low-born, the Church preached ideas about childhood which transcended, and perhaps modified, a social reality in which some children (like some adults) were so much more equal than others. For their part, parents, which is to say the vast majority of the laity, exerted a steady pressure on the Church to express, reinforce, sacralize their attitudes to and treatment of children, and hence the process of social reproduction itself. Parents and churchmen acted upon each other to construct what childhood should be:

[3] See P. P. A. Biller, 'Marriage patterns and women's lives', in P. J. P. Goldberg, ed., *Woman is a Worthy Wight. Women in English Society c.1200–1500* (Stroud, 1992), pp. 60–107, at p. 65; R. Samuel, 'Reading the signs: II. Fact-grubbers and mind-readers', *History Workshop Journal*, 33 (1992), pp. 220–51, at pp. 220–31; also K. Arnold, *Kind und Gesellschaft in Mittelalter und Renaissance* (Paderborn and Munich, 1980); S. Wilson, 'The myth of motherhood a myth: the historical view of European child-rearing', *Social History*, 9 (1984), pp. 181–98, and D. Alexandre-Bidon and M. Closson, *L'Enfant à l'ombre des cathédrales* (Paris, 1985), pp. 234–5; and, with further references, S. Shahar, *Childhood in the Middle Ages* (London, 1990), pp. 1–6 and p. 260 at n. 7. Like all the above, the fine paper of M. McLaughlin, 'Survivors and surrogates: parents and children from the ninth to the thirteenth centuries', in L. de Mause, *The History of Childhood* (London, 1976), pp. 101–82, is most valuable on the eleventh century, or later.

generation upon generation of real children constituted the great laboratory in which the work went on.

'Exultavit Maria in sacratissimo puerperio, exultat ecclesia in filiorum suorum generationis specie.' ('Mary exulted in her most holy childbearing; and the Church exults in the substance of the bringing to birth of her children.') Thus a baptismal prayer in an eighth-century sacramentary linked typologically the central event in Christian history, the birth of Mary's child, with the Church's reproduction of itself.[4] To become a Christian is to be born again: to become as a little child.[5] The earliest liturgies of Christian initiation were replete with the symbolism of motherhood, childbearing, birth, and infancy. From the fourth century onwards, the generalized practice of infant baptism gave the metaphor a new dimension. As part of the preliminary rituals of baptism in the Gelasian Sacramentary, the acolyte asked for the children's names to be called out, first the boys, then the girls.[6] They were written down on a list, just like the new members of the E.H.S., as read out by the Secretary at our AGM. The Church named, and claimed, its own. In blessing newlyweds that they might multiply the human race, in celebrating the birth of a child, in invoking the gift of fertility that the barren wife might bring forth offspring—and in the early medieval liturgy there were prayers for all these eventualities—the earlier medieval Church firmly distanced itself from dualism.[7] The flesh as well as the spirit was God-given. God was *nascentium genitor*—the Father of those who are born. Humanity had been created in order to multiply. Children were among God's *beneficia*—a blessing among blessings.

Before baptism, babies were exorcized: 'Audi maledicte satana . . . cum tua victus invidia tremens gemensque discede!' 'Hear, accursed Satan. Depart in defeat, trembling and groaning, and take your envy with you! Let there be nothing in common

[4] *Sacramentary of Angoulême*, ed. P. Saint-Roch. *Liber Sacramentorum Engolismensis. Manuscrit B.N. Lat. 816. Le Sacramentaire Gélasien d'Angoulême, CChr. SL*, 159 (1987), p. 117.

[5] Matt. 18.3–6.

[6] *Gelasian Sacramentary*, ed. L. C. Mohlberg, *Liber sacramentorum romanae aecclesiae ordinis anni circuli = Rerum ecclesiasticarum documenta. Series Maior*, Fontes 1 (Rome, 1960), no. 284, p. 42. The elements of this rite are datable to the sixth and seventh centuries: A. Chavasse, *Le Sacramentaire Gélasien* (Tournai, 1959), pp. 155–76.

[7] *Sacramentary of Gellone*, ed. A. Dumas and J. Deshusses, *Liber Sacramentorum Gellonensis, CChr. SL*, 159 (1981), nos 406, 407, 408, pp. 411–17.

between you and the servants of God.'[8] Baptismal exorcism was explained thus by a ninth-century theologian: 'Savage power is exsufflated [referring to the ritual of blowing evil away from the catechumen]. The malign spirit must flee, yielding place to the Holy Spirit, so that the Devil recognizing the Cross, the sign of his own slaying, now on what had been his own vessel, knows that that vessel belongs to someone else.'[9] But the child, even once baptized, strengthened by anointing for the fight against sin, remained weak, irresolute, vulnerable. Here is 'the time of infancy' as presented by an eighth-century hagiographer:

> a trouble to parents, nurses, other children in the same age-group, liable to the uncontrolled sexuality (*lascivia*) of young children, exposed to the nonsensical chatter of matrons, to the silly stories of the common folk, to the stupid moans of peasants, and (last but not least) to the imitating of different cries of various kinds of birds which children of that age are wont to do.

The hagiographer's point is—of course—that the list covers all that the future saint was *not*. Guthlac succumbed to none of those temptations.[10] Cuthbert, by contrast, 'up to his eighth year, which is the first year after the end of infancy, could devote his mind to nothing but the games and uncontrolled behaviour [*lascivia* again] of children. Like the infant Samuel, he did not yet know the Lord.'[11]

The dualism that seems to lurk—still—in so much early medieval Christianity, the sense of matter itself as base, provoked not only a horror of sexual activity and of the reproduction that ensued, but a perception of infancy and childhood as paradigms of physicality and wilfulness. Take Augustine's retrospective on his own boyhood:

[8] *Gelasian Sacramentary*, ed. Mohlberg, no. 294, p. 44; *Ordo Romanus XI*, ed. M. Andrieu, *Les ordines romani du haut moyen âge*, 5 vols, *Spicilegium sacrum lovaniense. Etudes et documents*, 11, 23, 24, 28, 29 (Louvain, 1931–61), 2 (1948), p. 422. See H. Kelly, *The Devil at Baptism. Ritual, Theology, and Drama* (Cornell, 1985), ch. 12. For the dating of Ordo Romanus XI, see below, p. 102, n. 91.

[9] Hrabanus Maurus, *De clericorum institutione*, 1, 27, *PL* 107, cols 311–12. For exorcized infants as symbolic demoniacs, see Kelly, *The Devil at Baptism*, p. 151.

[10] *Felix's Life of Guthlac*, ch. 12, ed. B. Colgrave (Cambridge, 1956), p. 78 (the translation is mine).

[11] *Bede's Life of Cuthbert*, ch. 1. tr. B. Colgrave, *Two Lives of Saint Cuthbert* (Cambridge, 1940), p. 154 (my translation), with reference to 1 Sam. 3.7. The *levitas* of youthful play is castigated further on in the same chapter, p. 156; cf. the even more critical comments on children's *scurilitas*, especially with reference to hand-stands, in Bede's source, the *Anonymous Life of Cuthbert*, ch. 3, ibid., p. 64.

> Dependent on the authority of my parents and the direction of adult people . . . 'what miseries I experienced'. . . . If ever I was indolent in learning, I was beaten. . . . Adult people, including even my parents. . . , used to laugh at my stripes, which were at that time a great and painful evil to me . . . .We [boys] were at fault in paying less attention than was required of us to writing or reading. . . . As a boy, I played ball-games, and that play slowed down the speed at which I learnt letters . . . . I sinned by not doing as I was told by my parents and teachers [who, Augustine did not fail to observe, were themselves 'engaged in adult games'].[12]

The rot had set in with birth itself:

> Who reminds me of the sin of my infancy? For 'none is pure from sin before you, not even an infant of one day upon the earth' [Job 14.4–5]. Who reminds me? Any tiny child now, for I see in that child what I do not remember in myself. What sin did I then have? Was it wrong that in tears I greedily opened my mouth wide to suck the breasts?

Augustine's answer is 'Yes'. 'The feebleness of infant limbs is innocent, not the infant's mind.'[13]

These perceptions had theological consequences: for Augustine the baby's dependence was a perfect image of the person's dependence on God. A man deluded himself if he thought he could ever be free of that—could ever be, in the Pelagian phrase, *emancipatus a deo*, as a son was 'freed', in Roman family law, from his father's *potestas* when he came of age. Nor could human life on earth ever be free of sin. Baptism cleansed original sin, yet actual sin, that is, sin caused by wilful acts of self-defilement, would surely follow.[14] The medieval meanings of *puerilitas* and *pueriliter* were pejorative, as in modern English 'puerile' or 'childish'. Medieval Latin, as far as I know, had no equivalent for our 'childlike'. Early medieval penitentials classified special vices as those to which *pueri* were liable—stealing, sexual play, quarrelling, lack of control in speaking: sins which, if unchecked,

[12] Augustine, *Confessions*, I, chs viii–x, tr. H. Chadwick (Oxford, 1991), pp. 11–12. See B. Shaw, 'The family in Late Antiquity: the experience of Augustine', *Pap*, 115 (1987), pp. 3–51.

[13] Augustine, *Confessions*, I, ch. xi, p. 9.

[14] P. Brown, *Augustine of Hippo* (London, 1967), pp. 365–6, and 'Late Antiquity', in P. Veyne, ed., *A History of Private Life*, I (Cambridge, Mass. and London, 1987), pp. 292–311.

could produce real wickedness in later life (even if not necessarily suggesting that children as such were excessively wicked).[15] Holy children acted in ways that were the very reverse of normal child behaviour.

The essential corrective to children's weaknesses was assumed to be corporal punishment. On this subject, Late Antique Christianity, despite its heavy investment in bodily control, apparently continued pagan belief and practice without laying any special new emphasis on them.[16] The Rule of St Benedict prescribes 'for every age and degree of understanding its appropriate measure of discipline' and therefore 'as often as faults are committed by boys or by youths (*pueri vel adolescentiores aetate*) . . . let them be punished with severe fasts or chastised with sharp blows (*ieiuniis nimiis aut acris verberibus*), in order that they may be cured.' 'Those who make mistakes in the oratory' are to be punished, 'but boys (*infantes autem*) for such faults shall be whipped.'[17] Throughout the earlier Middle Ages, the chastisement of children in the cloister, as in the home, was evidently commonplace, if not specially emphasized in prescriptive texts. An eighth-century Lombard legislator threatened punishment for a male guardian who struck his ward dishonourably (*battederit turpiter*) 'unless she is still a child and, in honest discipline (*pro honesta disciplina*), he is trying to show her a woman's work or is correcting her evil ways just as he would do with his own daughter.' Abelard in the early twelfth century could assume an association of teaching with beating so axiomatic for contemporaries that he beat Heloise 'to avert suspicion'.[18]

And yet, the notion of childhood purity, of innocence, appears in early medieval contexts. In all legal systems there has to be some determination of the age of responsibility, of consent. The framers of early medieval laws took the view that the child was irrational, hence incapable of choosing wrong, hence not liable

[15] Cf. Rob Meens's contribution to the present volume, above pp. 53–65; and for ordinary children perceived as wicked, see J. Leclercq, 'Pédagogie et formation spirituelle du Ve au XIe siècle', *Settimane di Studio di Centro Italiano di Studi sull'alto medioevo, Spoleto*, 19 (1972), pp. 255–90, at p. 283.

[16] P. Brown, *The Body and Society* (New York, 1988) is silent on this subject.

[17] *Rule of Benedict*, ed. and tr. J. McCann (London, 1969), chs 30, 45, pp. 80, 106.

[18] *Liutprandi Leges* (731), ch. 120, ed. F. Beyerle, *Leges Langobardorum* 643–866, 2nd edn (Witzenhausen, 1962), p. 157, tr. K. F. Drew, *The Lombard Laws* (Philadelphia, 1973), p. 197; Radice, *Letters of Abelard and Heloise*, p. 67. For beating in secular and monastic contexts, see e.g. below, pp. 95, 113.

for criminal acts,[19] and not required to swear oaths. The Franks laid down that 'little boys (*parvuli*) who have not reached the age of reason are not to be compelled to swear oaths as the Burgundians make them do.'[20] The age of majority approximated to the age of puberty, when sexual difference became evident, and when gender difference was socially acknowledged.[21] Churchmen in the earlier Middle Ages sometimes espoused the idea of childhood innocence—though usually in clearly gendered form. Isidore of Seville derived the word *puer* from *puritas*. A little boy, he wrote, had four virtues that an adult man lacked: 'He doesn't bear rancour; he doesn't persist in anger; he's not susceptible to a beautiful woman; and he doesn't think one thing and say another.'[22] Gregory the Great imagined Heaven thronged with *infantes* and *parvuli* whose innocence had ensured immediate entry there after death.[23] According to Theodore's Penitential, 'many' denied that Mass should be said for children who had died below the age of seven: presumably the 'many' thought under-sevens to be pre-rational, hence incapable of choosing sin.[24] Bede told Archbishop Ecgbert that even 'those considered more devout' took Mass only thrice a year, yet 'there are countless boys and girls, young men and virgins, old men and women' who could 'without any shadow of doubt receive Communion every Sunday', the assumption here clearly being that the old and the young—interestingly, females as well as males—are uncontaminated by sexual pollution.[25] In monastic contexts, too,

[19] 'If a boy under twelve commits a crime, no fine is required from him', *Lex Salica*, 34, *MGH.LNG*, IV, 2, ed. K. A. Eckhardt (Hanover, 1969), p. 72. But a capitulary of Louis the Pious in 819, *MGH. Cap*, I, ed. A. Boretius (Hanover, 1883), no. 142, p. 293, clarifies this: an *infans* who steals someone else's property (*res*) must appear in court before the count, and though not liable to a fine, must pay compensation.

[20] *MGH. Cap*, 1, no. 22, ch. 64, p. 58 (*rationabilis aetas*), cf. no. 28, ch. 45, p. 77.

[21] The secular legal notion of majority was gendered: women did not swear oaths of fidelity. By contrast, canon law on consent, whether for entry into religious life or for marriage, was gender-blind.

[22] Isidore, *Etymologies*, XI, 2, 10, ed. W. M. Lindsay, 2 vols (Oxford, 1911), 2 (unpaginated); *Quaestiones* XL, 54, *PL* 83, col. 207: 'non laesus meminit; non perseverat in ira; non delectatur pulchra femina; non aliud cogitat vel aliud loquitur'. The latter passage (note that all four virtues are negative ones) was quoted by Bede and many others. For its patristic source, see Gillian Clark, above, p. 22.

[23] *Dialogues*, IV, 18, ed. A. de Vogüé, 3 vols, *SC*, 251, 265 and 266 (1978–80), 3, p. 72.

[24] Theodore, *Penitential*, II, v. 7, ed., P. W. Finsterwalder, *Die Canones Theodori Cantuariensis und ihre Uberlieferungsformen* (Weimar, 1929), p. 319.

[25] Bede, *Epistola ad Ecgbertum*, ch. 15, ed. C. Plummer (Oxford, 1896), p. 419, tr. D. Farmer, *Bede, Ecclesiastical History and Letter to Egbert* (Harmondsworth, 1990), p. 348.

childhood could be assigned a privileged status. Benedict wanted all members of the community to be called together when important business had to be done—all, because 'God often reveals to the younger what is better.'[26] Early medieval miracle stories show pre-adolescent children, boys as well as girls, within convent precincts without offence: something impossible for adult men.[27] In a wide variety of situations, young children, *pueri*, *infantuli*, but with the occasional *puella*, were thought especially suitable for *sortes biblicae*—divination by opening the Bible at random.[28] The Church, here as elsewhere, may well have borrowed from pre-Christian ideas: in eighth-century Frisian Law, judgement could be sought by divination, and this was performed in church, in the absence of a priest, by 'an innocent boy' choosing between blessed and unblessed tally-sticks placed on the altar.[29] In a difficult episcopal election at Orleans, the name of the future St Aignan was chosen from a raft of names on *breves* by a little boy 'not yet talking' (*necdum loquens*), but suddenly endowed with the gift of speech.[30] In the church of Llancarfan in the late eleventh century, the community claimed the right to judge wrongs done to it: in the absence of twelve suitable monks, judgement could be declared by 'twelve virgin boys'.[31]

The ambiguity inscribed in the Church's attitude to childhood is evident in the motif of the *puer-senex*: the tiny child with the wisdom of an old man.[32] In Bede's *Life of Cuthbert*, this is actually juxtaposed to the image of infant wilfulness.

26 *Rule of Benedict*, ch. 3. p. 24: 'Saepe iuniori Dominus revelat quod melius est'. Cf. also P. Riché, 'L'enfant dans la société monastique au XIIe siècle', in Riché, *Instruction et vie religieuse dans le Haut Moyen Age* (London, 1981), ch. 19. On monastic views of childlike innocence, see the forthcoming book of Mayke de Jong.

27 *Vita Sanctae Geretrudis, Miracula*, ch. 11, ed. B. Krusch, *MGH.SRM*, II (Hanover, 1888), p. 470, tr. J. A. McNamara and J. Halborg, eds, *Sainted Women of the Dark Ages* (Durham, NC and London, 1992), pp. 233–4; *Vita Austrebertae*, ch. 16, *ActaSS*, 10 Feb., p. 422, tr. McNamara and Halborg, pp. 315–16.

28 P. Courcelle, 'L'enfant et les sorts bibliques', *Vigiliae Christianae*, 7 (1953), pp. 194–220.

29 *Lex Frisionum*, 14, 1, *MGH.LNG*, III, ed. K. von Richthofen (Hanover, 1863), p. 667. Courcelle, 'L'enfant', p. 200, n. 21 discerns 'a newly-Christianized ancient Indo-European custom'.

30 *Vita Sancti Aniani III*, ch. 2, ed. A. Theiner, *Saint Aignan et le siège d'Orléans par Attila* (Paris, 1832), p. 34, cited in Courcelle, 'L'enfant', p. 202, n. 28. T. Head, *Hagiography and the Cult of the Saints. The Diocese of Orleans, 800–1200* (Cambridge, 1990), pp. 35–7, in a careful discussion, assigns this Life to the (late) ninth century.

31 *Vita Cadoci*, ch. 16, ed. A. W. Wade-Evans, *Vitae Sanctorum Britanniae et Genealogiae* (Cardiff, 1944), p. 60: 'parvulis pueris virginibus cum mulieribus haut coinquinatis'. For this reference, I am very grateful to Wendy Davies, who comments that this text probably incorporates earlier material.

32 On the *puer-senex* in Christian hagiography, see E. R. Curtius, *European Literature and the Latin Middle Ages*, tr. W. R. Trask (London, 1952), pp. 98–105, noting the contrast between classical

> As a boy (*puer*) Cuthbert was devoted to making a lot of noise and to jumping, running, brawling and gambolling about contorting his limbs contrary to their natural state (*contra congruum naturae statum*): it was one of the little ones (*puerulі*) aged about three who began to exhort him with the gravity of an old man: do not indulge in idle games. . . . Nor is it to be wondered at that a little boy's wantonness (*parvuli lascivia*) could have been repressed through a little boy (*per parvulum*), for 'out of the mouths of babes and sucklings thou hast perfected praise.'[33]

In a ninth-century saint's Life, a wicked bishop sets the holy man an impossible task: make that abandoned infant, only three days old, declare before us all (the scene is a public one) the truth about his paternity. The baby begins to speak: 'My father's the bishop. . .'.[34] In the twelfth-century *Life of Stephen of Obazine* (a saint who was in the habit of disciplining the children in his community 'by beating them around the head so hard that the noise could be heard some distance away' for such offences as inattention during the monastic office), there are stories of *pueri* whose purity approached that of the angels.[35] The conceptions of childhood underlying these stories seem to oscillate between extremes, because children's behaviour was taken to indicate good or bad supernatural power: on the one hand, lack of control suggested diabolical influence, on the other, weakness and unpretentiousness suggested access to the divine. Either way, the child was channel, vessel, sign of power beyond him/herself. That transparency was exploited in legal or political as well as moralizing contexts.

The ambiguity within early medieval perceptions of childhood remained unresolved, to become embroiled in doctrinal problems. Early in the twelfth century the heretic preacher Henry of Lausanne allegedly taught that children who died before the years of discretion could be saved without baptism. This may

(positive) and Christian (negative) constructions of childhood. Shahar, *Childhood*, p. 16, points out that hagiographers using this topos 'implicitly rejected' young children.

33 *Bede's Life of Cuthbert*, ch. 1, ed. Colgrave, pp. 156, 158, citing Ps. 8.3.

34 *Vita Sancti Goaris*, ch. 7, ed. B. Krusch, *MGH.SRM*, 4 (Hanover, 1902), p. 418. For this motif, see W. Berschin, *Biographie und Epochenstil im lateinischen Mittelalter*, 3 (Stuttgart, 1991), pp. 71–4.

35 *Vita Stephani Obazinensis*, ed. M. Aubrun (Clermont-Ferrand, 1970), ch. 16, 47–9, pp. 68, 170–3 (with citation of I Cor. 14.20).

have implied the argument that children came innocent into the world.[36] Henry allegedly based his views on two Gospel verses, Mark 10.14: 'Suffer the little children to come unto me, for of such is the kingdom of God', and Matthew 18.2–3: 'Unless you be converted and become as little children, you shall not enter the kingdom of heaven.' The orthodox response to Henry insisted, of course, on the necessity of infant baptism, yet accepted the idea of a time-period between the washing away of original sin, and the incurring of actual sin 'because little children have not sinned actually, since they have not attained the age of reason'.[37] The *parvuli* were the under-sevens. Henry further buttressed his argument against infant baptism by citing Mark 16.16: 'He that believeth and is baptized shall be saved'. 'For', Henry argued, 'someone cannot believe who has not yet reached the age of believing or not believing (*aetas credendi vel non credendi*).' The response of Henry's interrogator—and it brings us to the heart of the three-way relationship which is my subject in this paper—was to insist that 'a person can be saved by the faith of another. . . . The faith of parents benefits children: this is shown by the story of the woman of Canae, who by her faith merited that her daughter be saved [Matt. 15.22–8].'[38] This is an argument about vicarious faith, about parents, children, and the Church. It is an argument that goes back via Alcuin and Isidore to Augustine. In having children baptized, in promising on their behalf, parents themselves participated in the whole Church's regeneration. 'Children are not offered so much by those who are carrying them in their arms as by the whole community of the saints and the faithful.'[39]

36 See the thought-provoking discussion of R. I. Moore, *The Origins of European Dissent* (London, 1977), pp. 99–101. Orthodox views on original sin were well established in the earlier Middle Ages: see J. Gross, *Geschichte des Erbsundendogmas. Ein Beitrag zur Geschichte des Problems von Ursprung des Ubels*, 4 vols (Munich, Basle, 1960–72), 1.

37 'Parvi . . . actualiter non peccaverunt, cum sint infra annos rationales': from the account by the monk William of his debate with Henry, ed. R. Manselli, 'Il monaco Enrico e la sua eresia', *Bulletino dell'Istituto storico Italiano per il medio evo*, 65 (1953), pp. 36–62, at p. 48.

38 Ibid., p. 50: 'Baptizantur autem parvi fide baptizantium vel in fide parentum, immo generaliter in fide totius ecclesie. In fide autem alterius posse salvari, si bene voles intelligere, ex multis auctoritatibus habes evangelii . . . Fidem parentum liberis similter prodesse, mulieris chananee testimonium, que fide sua, sicut ait Evangelista, filiam suam sanari meruit evidenter ostendit.'

39 Augustine, *Epistola ad Bonifacium*, Ep. 98, 5, ed. A. Goldbacher, *CSEL*, 34 (1895), p. 526. See further B. Jussen, *Patenschaft und Adoption im frühen Mittelalter. Künstliche Verwantschaft als soziale Praxis* (Göttingen, 1991), p. 147.

In the earlier Middle Ages, the Church accommodated its rituals to the needs of parents. Fathers and, especially, mothers were encouraged to bring their sick children to seek cures at the shrines of saints. There are dozens of affecting stories about the healing of children, some explicitly opposing the power of the saints to 'pagan magic'.[40] (Many mothers may well not have troubled overmuch about the distinction: the cult of the dog-saint Guinefort suggests they did not in the thirteenth-century Lyonnais.[41]) Bishop Theodulf instructed priests to give extreme unction to dying children—*ipsis quoque pueris*: penance was needful for them too, and the Devil ever on the lookout for prey.[42] Although the earlier medieval service-books offered no special funeral rite for dead children, they could be commemorated in monastic liturgy; and churchmen produced touching epitaphs on the dead offspring of noble and royal parents. Here is an example:

In this tomb a pretty little girl lies buried
Her name was Adelaide of the holy river
To whom Charles was the father, powerful by twin diadems
Noble by nature, very strong in arms.
She was born near the lofty walls of Pavia
when her powerful father seized the Italian domains.
But hastening towards the river Rhone she was taken from the threshold of life
and the heart of her mother is wounded with sorrow from afar.
She died on the point of seeing her father's triumphs.
Now she holds the blessed domains of the Eternal Father.[43]

40 See J. L. Nelson, 'Les femmes et l'évangélisation au IXe siècle', *Revue du Nord*, 68 (1986), pp. 471–85, esp. pp. 480–1; and 'Women and the Word', *SCH*, 27 (1989), pp. 53–78, at pp. 67–8.

41 Cf. J.-C. Schmidt, *Le saint lévrier. Guinefort, guérisseur d'enfants depuis le XIIIe siècle* (Paris, 1979).

42 Theodulf of Orleans, *Second Set of Capitula*, X, 31, ed. P. Brommer, *MGH. Capitula Episcoporum*, I (Hanover, 1984), pp. 182–3.

43 Paul the Deacon, *Gesta Episcoporum Mettensium*, ed. G.H. Pertz, *MGH.SS*, II (Hanover, 1829), p. 267. I am very grateful to Guy Halsall for allowing me to use his unpublished translation. For other examples of the commemoration of children who had died in infancy, see epitaphs by Sedulius Scottus and Milo of St-Amand, ed. L. Traube, *MGH.PL* III (Berlin, 1896), pp. 201, 677–8; cf. also G. Tellenbach, 'Uber die ältesten Welfen im West- und Ostfrankenreich', in Tellenbach, ed., *Studien und Vorarbeiten zur Geschichte des grossfränkische Adels* (Freibach, 1957), pp. 335–40; R. Louis, *Girard, comte de Vienne*, 3 vols (Auxerre, 1946), 1, pp. 49–50. For royal

The epitaph of Charlemagne's baby daughter Adelaide is stylish, but not merely conventional; and (though the poet mentions only the mother's sorrow) perhaps to be set alongside Einhard's comment about Charlemagne's far from conventional grief at the deaths of his adult sons.[44]

There were episcopal attempts to prescribe and sometimes to change parental practices. Archbishop Wulfad of Bourges commended breast-feeding, rather than using wet-nurses, to the women of his diocese, who, he thought, cared too much for their own figures. Wulfad did not, however, discriminate between boy babies and girl babies.[45] Where such differentiation does clearly occur is in the evidence of peasant practice (uninfluenced by those peasants' monastic lord?) conveyed in the early ninth-century Polyptych of St-Victor, Marseille: here nurslings are separately listed, and it is clear that boy babies were breast-fed for twice as long as girl babies—two years instead of one.[46] Very uneven sex ratios are detectable in the peasant households recorded in the Polyptych of St-Germain-des-Prés; and even if these are attributable, at least in part, to the landlord's under-recording of girls, widespread peasant recourse to female infanticide seems a plausible inference. Yet the one case documented—and it concerns a foiled attempt—is set in a pagan Frisian context.[47] Here churchmen laid responsibility for infanticide on the mother rather than the father. It was the poverty of *pauperculae*—women of slowly status, poor little women—that sometimes drove them to have abortions, or to kill newborn babies. That account might be taken of mitigating circumstances, and reduced penances prescribed, is evidence of some ecclesiastical sympathy for the plight of such women.[48] Certainly the Church condemned infanticide without any sex-discrimination

---

child-saints, see D. Rollason, *Saints and Relics in Anglo-Saxon England* (London, 1989), pp. 118–19; and, in comparative context, G. Klaniczay, *The Uses of Supernatural Power* (London, 1990), pp. 79–94.

44 *Vita Karoli*, ch. 19, ed. G. Waitz, *MGH.SRG* (Hanover, 1911), p. 24.

45 Wulfad, *Pastoral Letter*, ed. E. Dümmler, *MGH.Ep*, VI (Berlin, 1902), pp. 188–92, at p. 191.

46 E. Coleman, 'Infanticide in the early Middle Ages', in S. M. Stuard, ed., *Women in Medieval Society* (Philadelphia, 1976), pp. 47–71, at p. 60. Cf. also D. Herlihy, *Medieval Households* (London, 1985), pp. 64–8.

47 *Vita Liudgeri*, I, chs. 6–7, ed. G. H. Pertz, *MGH.SS*, 11 (Hanover, 1829), p. 406.

48 G. Schmitz, 'Schuld und Strafe. Eine unbekannte Stellungnahme des Rathramnus von Corbie zur Kindestötung', *Deutsches Archiv*, 38 (1982), pp. 363–87; P. J. Payer, 'The humanism of the Penitentials', *MS*, 46 (1984), pp. 340–54.

where the babies were concerned, and pre-pubertal girls, as virgins, enjoyed immunity from misogyny's fire.

Ecclesiastical notions of seemliness and bodily control may account for the near-total absence of reference to funerary practice in the case of dead children: a ninth-century canon prohibits the showing of excessive grief by bereaved persons in general.[49] This concern, and an elaborate attempt to reconcile contradictory codes of behaviour, appears in Hucbald of St-Amand's *Life of Rictrude*, written early in the tenth century.[50] Rictrude had lived in the seventh century: the widow of a noble Frank, she had founded the convent of Marchiennes. Hucbald wrote up the Life for the tenth-century community of Marchiennes, and also for the local bishop. The Life's purpose was partly pastoral: to offer the convent's inmates and patrons a model of Christian conduct. Rictrude and her husband, according to the Life, followed the command of Genesis 1.28: 'Be fruitful and multiply.' The couple had four children, a son and three daughters. When her husband was killed, the son became a priest, while Rictrude and all her daughters entered the convent.

> In those days, the youngest daughter died. . . . She departed with the annual cycle of the turning year, on the sacrosanct solemnity of the Lord's birth, that is, Christmas Day. . . . What did Rictrude do then? With her mind running in two contrary directions, did she rejoice, or did she mourn? While the whole world listened to the angel intoning, 'Behold I bring you good tidings of great joy', Rictrude had her dead daughter before her eyes. But did she give in to the natural sorrow of her condition? No, the strength of the manly mind within her overcame her womanly feelings. Sadness for her daughter's death was not allowed to enter where the birth of Life was celebrated. The burial was completed, but the mourning of the loved one was postponed. The three days of Christmas were celebrated, and on the fourth day, when Holy Church recalls the Massacre of the Innocents and the misery of their bereft mothers, Rictrude knew what she

[49] T. H. McNeill and H. Gamer, *Medieval Handbooks of Penance* (New York, 1939), p. 294; and cf. ibid, indicating that 'excessive' mourning over kin (*parentes*) occasioned particular concern.

[50] H. Platelle, 'Le thème de la conversion à travers les oeuvres hagiographiques d'Hucbald de Saint-Amand', *Revue du Nord*, 68 (1986), pp. 510–31.

> should do. There is a time for all things under heaven: a time for joy, a time for tears. 'Now', she said, 'I will follow the example of the mothers of the Holy Innocents for whom mourning is heard today. They are like my own little girl-innocent (*mea innocentula*). And now it is permissible to mourn her', and she asked for a private place to mourn so that her grief might be satisfied.[51]

In Hucbald's pastoral message the theme of childhood innocence offered the framework for a scale of priorities, and a context in which the loss of a child could be made sense of: religious duty mirrored, yet took absolute precedence over, personal concerns, just as the public rhythm of the liturgy controlled Rictrude's conduct in private life. In her case, the community had absorbed the family.

The ninth-century noblewoman Dhuoda presented another model of parental conduct. Her handbook for her fifteen-year-old son was a work of spiritual guidance unmediated, for once, by monastic authorship or influence. Dhuoda, in fact, showed no interest in monasteries; and while she had something to say about priests, she herself oversaw her son's religious education, directed his spiritual exercises, and urged him to ensure that his baby brother in due time would read her book.[52] Here is a well-documented early medieval case of loving as well as responsible parenting. Dhuoda also enjoined responsibilities on the younger generation: her book ends with instructions for the epitaph to be placed on her tomb and the inscribing of her name in the list of the family dead to be liturgically commemorated by her sons. William, her first born, apparently had the book among his personal possessions at the time of his death.[53] If he had indeed absorbed only part of its message, then one dedicated noble mother had ensured that her child was taught very much more than those Christian fundamentals, the Lord's Prayer and the Creed. Dhuoda could assume extensive familiarity with Scripture; she could recommend frequent use of the sign of the Cross with imprecations borrowed from the liturgy;[54] she could

[51] *PL* 132, ch. 13, cols 8xx–x; tr. McNamara and Halborg, *Sainted Women*, pp. 210–11.
[52] Dhuoda, *Manuel*, 1, 7, ed. P. Riché, *Dhuoda, Manuel pour mon fils*, *SC*, 225 (1975), p. 116.
[53] Ibid., Riché, Introduction, p. 49.
[54] Ibid., pp. 128–9, with Riché's n. 5.

prescribe daily prayer, Bible-reading, and meditation. Dhuoda evidently practised what the Church preached. The bishops who were her contemporaries set new standards of parental duty, but, no doubt realistically, expected most of aristocratic mothers who were in charge of great households and so were in a position to provide basic religious training for their dependants' children as well as for their own.[55] Dhuoda's repeated exhortations to her 'handsome and lovable son'[56] in the imperative mood suggest the lesson of filial obedience to herself as mother. Yet Dhuoda certainly taught William 'a religion of paternity': that is, to obey his father as lord, an obligation that took precedence even over fidelity to the king.[57] If Dhuoda said nothing about physical chastisement, that was presumably because it was the father's department. When churchmen urged parents to teach their children obedience, the sanction was physical violence: 'For it is easier for children to bear parental beatings than to risk the wrath of God.'[58] There was to be no sparing of the paternal rod. The family, or the influence of a noble household, offered the best means of imparting Christian fundamentals to the vast majority of children.

Bishop Riculf of Soissons urged rural priests to have schools for boys—but never to admit girls alongside them for fear of *mala conversatio*.[59] It's far from clear, however, that anything like parish boy's schools (let alone coeducational ones) existed in the early Middle Ages. A few large monasteries with rural outliers may indeed have provided schooling for boys intended for the religious life: the evidence is ample in the case of Fulda. A widespread network of 'external schools' in which monasteries educated boys destined for secular life has, however, recently, and with some justification, been dismissed as retrospective wishful thinking on the part of modern ecclesiastical pedagogues.[60] Yet for such boys, low-born as well as high-born, and for girls too,

55 Jonas of Orleans, *De institutione laicali*, ii, chs 14, 16, *PL* 106, cols 192–5, 197; Council of Meaux-Paris (845), ch. 77, ed. W. Hartmann, *MGH.Conc*, III (Hanover, 1984), p. 124.

56 Dhuoda, *Manuel*, I, 7, p. 114.

57 Ibid., III, 1–3, pp. 134–49; cf. Riché, Introduction, p. 27.

58 Theodulf of Orleans, *Capitula* 1, 33, *MGH.Capitula Episcoporum*, I, ed. P. Brommer (Hanover, 1984), p. 131; Radulf of Bourges, *Capitula*, ch. 23, ibid. p. 251; Jonas of Orleans, *De institutione laicali*, II, ch. 14, *PL* 106, cols 192–5.

59 *PL* 131, col. 20—the unique reference to girls at school is a prohibition!

60 M. Hildebrandt, *The External School in Carolingian Society* (Leiden, 1992).

monasteries could perform a kind of educational function analogous to that of secular lordship, and in conjunction with the efforts of families. At the abbey of St-Riquier, in the early ninth century, elaborate processions at Easter and Christmas were drawn up seven abreast and ordered by age, gender, and class: after the clergy came members of the *scola laicorum puerorum* (the lay boys, who were the sons of the local nobility and expected, no doubt, to grow up to the perform military service for the abbey) carrying banners, then noblemen, then noble women; then came the crosses of the *forinseci*, the peasantry 'outside' the monastic centre: these were led by 'boys and girls who know how to sing the Lord's Prayer and the Creed and other things which we have ordered them to be taught'. The text goes on to explain that these boys and girls were unlettered but had had help from the [boys in the] *scola* and from the women's workshops so that they were able to learn the chants by heart. This implies the oral transmission of Christian fundamentals to low-born by high-born boys, and by women (?mothers) to girls among the working population of the monastery's lordship. The *forinseci* boys and girls *sine litteris* were the offspring of the 'peasant families which are settled in that place.'[61] Thus, in interestingly gendered fashion, and overseen by the monastery's leadership, this particular younger generation could learn to be Christians by regular participation in Christian rites. Thus, too, ecclesiastical stage-managers, in the early Middle Ages as in other periods, saw to the self-representation of local communities by including children in cultic performance. Such practices may have been widespread, though they are rarely recorded. In 590, when Rome was ravaged by plague, Gregory the Great organized a whole series of penitential processions, consisting of clergy and priests; abbots and monks; abbesses and nuns; children; lay men; widows; married women—a significant ordering by religious status and gender, from most to least pure.[62] At least in Rome, the classical symbolic link between childhood and a bright future was not lost: apparently inspired by the *adventus* ceremonials of Late

[61] Ibid., pp. 80–5, 144–5; cf., for a different interpretation, R. McKitterick, 'Town and monastery in the Carolingian period', *SCH*, 16 (1978), p. 101. *Scola* here means 'troup', not 'school'.

[62] Gregory of Tours, *Libri Historiarum*, x, 1, ed. B. Krusch and W. Levison. *MGH-SRM*, 1 (Hanover, 1951), pp. 480–1.

Antiquity, Pope Hadrian I arranged for children waving palm-branches to welcome Charlemagne into the city in 774.[63]

* * *

In the rest of this paper I want to look more closely at two specific earlier medieval forms of collaboration or collusion between parents and churchmen, in which Christian children were involved not only—or even primarily—as ends in themselves, but as means to other, adult-centred, ends. Children were the blank sheet on which parents and churchmen inscribed needs and desires and strategies. They were the blue-print in which designs for the future were embodied. On the one hand, parents exploited ecclesiastically-constructed rites and rules to create mutually-supportive social relationships with churchmen and with other laypeople. On the other hand, churchmen themselves, whose institutions could thrive only through external recruitment and support, accepted children as vicarious penitents, offerings for their parents' sins.

First, then, baptism formed a key point of intersection between the family and the Church. During the period between the eighth and the tenth centuries it assumed more elaborate liturgical forms, and an altogether higher profile in the self-representation of Christian culture, than it had ever had before. One consequence of the tremendous interest in the rites of Christian initiation in the Carolingian period was to highlight childhood as a period of socialization into the Christian life. There was a political dimension here in the early Middle Ages, for this was still a heroic age of expansion and conversion. Just as Charlemagne insisted on Christianity for all those under his government, so he made baptism the *rite de passage* for entry into his people—the *populus christianus*. Pagan Saxons were baptized at the point of the sword; and then forced to pay tithes to the Frankish Church.[64] Conquerors are wise if they concentrate on winning the hearts and minds of the younger generation of the conquered elite. If the imposition of a new religion is central to the conquest, then the education of babes and sucklings may

[63] M. McCormick, *Eternal Victory* (Cambridge, 1987), pp. 370, 373; cf. p. 149.

[64] Alcuin, Ep. 111, *MGH.Ep*, IV, ed. E. Dümmler (Berlin, 1895), pp. 159–62. Alcuin disapproved, however, of forced conversion.

be an indispensable instrument of acculturation thereafter. The Spaniards found this in the sixteenth century in Latin America, where they took away the sons of the caciques and had them brought up by the Franciscans.[65] In the thirteenth century, when the Danish archbishop of Lund was spreading Danish political influence in the eastern Baltic, 'He took the children of the Livonian aristocracy as hostages and sent priests out to preach.'[66] And in ninth-century Saxony, where indigenous nobles had been forced to convert to Christianity, their sons were bought up, and sometimes permanently placed, in Frankish monasteries: within a couple of generations, a Saxon monk-poet was thanking Charlemagne for leading the Saxons to Christ.[67]

Late in his reign Charlemagne, himself in his sixties—a *senex* surrounded at Aachen by a growing tribe of *pueri* and *puellae*, his own children and grandchildren[68]—became extremely concerned about religion. In characteristically peremptory style, '*Nosse volumus* . . . We want to know', he told his bishops, 'either through yourselves in person or through written reports, what is the meaning of baptism, what is said in the rite itself, and what is renounced.' Charlemagne's *renovatio* now assumed a new dimension. 'We need to consider whether we are really Christians—hence to inspect the lives and conduct of our people (*nostri*).'[69] When Charlemagne said 'We want to know', bishops jumped—and no fewer than sixty-one separate texts commenting on the significance of baptism are the still-surviving evidence of that response.[70] Charlemagne's preoccupation with baptism had an educational purpose that was at the same time a means of social control: children were to be uniformly initiated and socialized in Christian virtues—pre-eminently the virtues of obedience, and fidelity to the Carolingian regime. It was not only

65 R. C. Trexler, 'From the mouths of babes: Christianization by children in sixteenth-century New Spain', in J. Davis, ed., *Religious Organization and Religious Experience = Association of Social Anthropologists Monograph*, 21 (London, 1982), pp. 115–36.

66 See R. Bartlett, *The Making of Europe* (Harmondsworth, 1993), p. 290.

67 P. Godman, *Poetry of the Carolingian Renaissance* (London, 1985), pp. 344–5, lines 687–94. For the Fulda community, see below, pp. 110–11.

68 J. L. Nelson, 'La famille de Charlemagne', *Byzantion*, 61 (1991), pp. 194–212.

69 *MGH.Cap*, 1, no. 71, p. 161.

70 S. A. Keefe, 'Carolingian baptismal expositions', in U.-R. Blumenthal, ed., *Carolingian Essays* (Washington, 1983), pp. 169–237; and D. A. Bullough, 'Alcuin and the Kingdom of Heaven', ibid., pp. 1–69, reprinted in Bullough's collection of papers, *Carolingian Renewal* (Manchester, 1991), pp. 161–240.

for the newly-converted Saxons that the Christianity of the Frankish Church was in some sense a *ritus dominorum*.[71]

The pre-Christian ritual of the first hair-cutting, or beard-shaving, survived in Christianized form in the eighth century as a prayer 'for those who cut their beards for the first time' (*pro his qui prius barbam tundunt*).[72] This ritual functioned as a rite of coming-of-age. And it was for boys only. It established a kind of paternal relationship between the man who performed, or organized, the hair-cutting, and the boy whose hair was cut.[73] There is a significant coincidence between the disappearance of that ritual, and the newly-elaborated rituals of Christian initiation; and it is tempting to think that the Christian rituals replaced the hair-cutting. What was new? First, Christian initiation was available for girls as well as boys, and while hardly gender-blind—all the service-books prescribe for the boys to be dealt with first, the girls afterwards—its forms were more or less identical for boys and girls.[74] Second, Christian initiation did not function as a boy's coming-of-age ritual, for although confirmation was detached from baptism, the child was normally confirmed within a few years of being baptized.[75] The whole weight of the newly-elaborated Christian rites fell on early childhood. For most people, the symbolic moment of adulthood was now presumably postponed until marriage, which, judging from our scanty available evidence, was often relatively late—for boys, eighteen or over—and its timing in the hands of fathers.[76] There was certainly no necessary association with the legal age of majority (though for boys, at least those of high birth, that link

[71] Hrabanus Maurus, *Liber de oblatione puerorum*, *PL* 107, col. 432.

[72] *Sacramentary of Angoulême*, no. 2057, p. 313.

[73] See R. Bartlett, 'Symbolic meanings of hair in the Middle Ages', *TRHS*, ser. 6, 4 (1994), forthcoming.

[74] Though for an interesting gender-difference, see Kelly, *The Devil at Baptism*, pp. 208–9: where the exorcism, *Audi maledicte* (above, p. 83) is said over the boys, for the girls there is 'simply a petition that God may free them as he did Susannah from the crime falsely charged against her'.

[75] A. Angenendt, 'Bonifatius und das *Sacramentum initiationis*. Zugleich ein Beitrag zur Geschichte der Firmung', *Romische Quartalschrift für christliche Altertumskunde und Kirchengeschichte*, 72 (1977), pp. 133–83; J. Lynch, *Godparents and Kinship in Early Medieval Europe* (Princeton, 1986), pp. 210–13.

[76] This is implied, for instance, in the *Vita Eptadii presbyteri Cervidunensis*, ch. 3, ed. B. Krusch, *MGH.SRM*, III (Hanover, 1896), col. 187: the Saint's parents started to arrange a marriage for him when he was twenty. Krusch dated this Life (of a sixth-century bishop of Auxerre) to the eighth century, but it may be older.

may have been made through ritual investiture with weapons).[77] Between childhood and marriage lay adolescence, the mid-to-late teens: 'the dangerous age'.[78] Paternal authority thus remained in force throughout these years. Acute tensions between fathers and sons are a well-documented feature of the royal families of the earlier Middle Ages.[79] This may have been a more general phenomenon. Certainly, the elaboration of a political and social hierarchy depended in this period on the strengthening of patriarchy—through what (as we've seen) was a religion of paternity.[80] In other words, the Church was willing to bolster paternal authority, not only insisting heavily on the subordination of children, but institutionalizing it within ecclesiastical rites and structures.

Here godparenthood played a key role.[81] For although in a sense godparents might replace natural parents, they could at the same time reinforce parental authority. They were, after all, chosen by the natural parents. Fathers may have seen godparents as potential protectors of their offspring, especially vulnerable female offspring. Such an obligation is implied, and negatively reinforced, by Gregory the Great's story of a man who raped his god-daughter and died within days, after which his body burned to ashes in his grave: social and spiritual obliteration was the horrendous outcome of a horrendous crime.[82] The godparent-godson tie could ease father-son tension, while affirming the older generation's authority. The fact that spiritual relationships were often formed between close kin of the same sex—for instance when a man stood godfather to his own nephew—fur-

[77] J. L. Nelson, 'Ninth-century knighthood: the evidence of Nithard', in C. Harper-Bill, C. Holdsworth and J. L. Nelson, eds, *Studies in Medieval History presented to R. Allen Brown* (Woodbridge, 1989), pp. 255–66, esp. pp. 263–4.

[78] *Narratio de monacho Cenomanensi, PL* 129, col. 1266: see below, p. 113. Cf. Council of Aachen (816), ch. 135, *MGH. Conc.* II, ii., ed. A. Werminghoff (Hanover, 1908), p. 143, on recruits to canonical life: 'nihil incertius quam vita adolescentium'. Cf. IV Council of Toledo (633), ch. 24, *PL* 84, col. 374.

[79] R. Schieffer, 'Väter und Söhne im Karolingerhause', in *Beiträge zur Geschichte des* Regnum Francorum, Beihefte der *Francia*, 22 (Paris, 1990), pp. 149–64.

[80] Above, p. 95.

[81] For what follows, I am much indebted to two fine recent studies: Lynch, *Godparents and Kinship*, and Jussen, *Patenschaft und Adoption*.

[82] *Dialogues*, iv, 33, ed. de Vogüé, iii, p. 110. On the problem of female vulnerability in tenth-century Saxon noble households, see K. Leyser, *Rule and Conflict in an Early Medieval Society: Ottonian Saxony* (London, 1979), p. 64.

ther underlines their function in defusing intra-familial conflict, at any rate among the social elite.[83] Uncles could be wicked: to have an uncle as your godfather was to increase the chances of his acting, instead, as your *nutritor et amator*.[84] There are several instances of such arrangements in and between royal families.[85] Although in such cases a godchild might inherit from a godfather, a crucial aspect of fictive kinship was that inheritance was no intrinsic part of it. Here, in some modern societies, has been found 'amity free of jural pressures'.[86] In early medieval Latin Christendom, here was social power unmediated, and uncomplicated, by property rights.

Godparents mattered, in principle, at all social levels. An eighth-century pastoral handbook from Alamannia urged: 'Those children whom you have received in baptism, know that you stand as their sureties (*fideiussores*) before God. Teach them, castigate them, and correct them . . .'.[87] Frankish bishops stressed godparents' duty to know the Creed and the Lord's Prayer, and to teach these to their spiritual offspring.[88] Amalar of Metz assured Charlemagne, 'We test godfathers and godmothers to see if they can recite the Lord's Prayer and the Creed, as we instructed them previously they should do.'[89] Among the earliest texts in Old High German are confession formulae for non-performance of godparental duties, and a ninth-century pastoral exhortation which includes instructions to godparents on what

83 For similar points in the context of modern Mediterranean societies, see J. Pitt-Rivers, 'The Kith and the Kin', in J. Goody, ed., *The Character of Kinship* (Cambridge, 1971), pp. 89–105, at p. 102, and *The fate of Shechem or the Politics of Sex. Essays in the Anthropology of the Mediterranean* (Cambridge, 1977), ch. 3.

84 Dhuoda, *Manuel*, viii, 15, pp. 320–3: Dhuoda tells her son to pray for, and to offer Masses and alms to the poor, for his uncle Theuderic 'qui te, ex meis suscipiens brachiis, per lavacrum regenerationis filium adoptavit in Christo'.

85 J. L. Nelson, *Charles the Bald* (London, 1992), see Index, under 'spiritual kinship'.

86 Pitt-Rivers, 'The Kith and the Kin', pp. 96–8, 101–3.

87 Pirmin, *Dicta de singulis libris canonicis scarapsus*, ch. 32, ed. U. Engelmann, *Der heilige Pirmin und sein Pastoralbüchlein* (Sigmaringen, 1976), p. 76. (Note, again, the close association of teaching and castigating.) Lynch, *Godparents and Kinship*, p. 189, comments on the influence here of Caesarius of Arles.

88 Ghaerbald of Liège, *Second Set of Capitula*, ch. 3, ed. Brommer, *MGH. Capitula Episcoporum*, i, p. 26, with references at n. 4 to numerous other ninth-century examples of similar episcopal insistence. Herard of Tours, *PL* 121, col. 768, told priests to ensure that godparents 'have the Lord's Prayer and the Creed by heart, in their own language, and understand them too'. See also Jonas of Orleans, *De institutione laicali*, i, 6, *PL* 106, col. 133.

89 Amalar, *Epistola ad Carolum imperatorem de scrutinio et baptismo*, ch. 40, ed. J. M. Hanssens, *Amalarii episcopi opera liturgica omnia*, 1 = *Studi e testi*, 138 (Vatican City, 1948), p. 246.

they must teach, and a reminder of their responsibility for their godchildren's faith on the Day of Judgement.[90] Changes in the liturgy in the Carolingian period underscored this obligation.[91] Sponsors now came to play a more conspicuous, and vocal, role than in earlier rites. Godparents carried the infants in parts of the service;[92] godparents' names were recited at the scrutinal Masses that preceded baptism,[93] and made the sign of the Cross over the infants;[94] godparents said the responses for the infants during the baptism itself; and godparents stood ready, towels in hand, to receive the new-baptized from the font.[95] By the tenth century, godparents were being required to recite the Creed, and to renounce Satan and his works, on their godchildren's behalf, as part of the baptismal liturgy.[96] (Such vicarious action had long since been justified by Isidore: 'Since infants were damned by the sin of another, they can be saved through another's profession of faith.')[97] The Romano-Germanic Pontifical directed that if the child was still an infant, he/she was to be carried in the sponsor's right arm, but if the child was old enough to stand, then during the confirmation-rite, she/he was to stand with one foot on the foot of the godparent.[98] The symbolic message surely was of godparental responsibility for guiding the child's footsteps.

A system of such fictive kin-ties, elaborated by the eighth century, was backed in the Carolingian period by the Church's extension of the incest taboo to cover spiritual kin. It would be misleading to depict this development in terms of a conjuncture

90 Confession formulae: ed. E. von Steinmeyer, *Die kleineren althochdeutschen Sprachdenkmaler* (Berlin, 1916), pp. 309–64; *Exhortatio*, eds K. Muellenhoff and W. Scherer, *Denkmäler deutscher Poesie und Prosa aus dem VIII–XII Jhdt*, 1 (Berlin, 1892), pp. 200–1. For the cultural context, see C. Edwards, 'German vernacular literature: a survey', in R. McKitterick, ed., *Carolingian Culture: Emulation and Innovation* (Cambridge, 1993), pp. 141–70, esp. pp. 145–6.

91 See J. D. C. Fisher, *Christian Initiation: Baptism in the Medieval West* (London, 1965), pp. 58–69. *Ordo Romanus XI*, dated by Andrieu to *c.* 600, has been convincingly re-assigned to the eighth century: see Lynch, *Godparents and Kinship*, pp. 171 and 290.

92 *Ordo Romanus XI*, chs. 12, 17, 20, 23, 98, ed. Andrieu, pp. 420, 421, 422, 423 and 446.

93 Ibid., ch. 34, p. 425.

94 Ibid. chs. 7–16, pp. 419–21; ch. 24, p. 423.

95 Ibid., ch. 98, p. 446: 'et sunt parati qui eos suscepturi sunt cum linteis in manibus eorum'.

96 *Ordo Romanus L*, ed. Andrieu, 5 (Louvain, 1961), no. 99, ch. 337, p. 93. See Lynch, *Godparents and Kinship*, pp. 301–2, 304.

97 *Etymologies*, vi, xix, 56.

98 *Pontificale Romano-Germanicum, Ordo ad baptizandum infantes*, ch. 38, ed. C. Vogel and R. Elze = *Studi e testi*, 227 (Vatican City, 1963), pp. 163–4: 'maiores vero pedem ponunt super pedem patrini sui.'

of historically separate forces—an accommodation of clerical to lay requirements, whereby the Church somewhat belatedly, even grudgingly, yielded to the pressures of 'Frankish popular culture'.[99] Nothing suggests ecclesiastical misgivings about the social bonds involved in spiritual kinship: in fact, it looks as if churchmen were themselves much involved in sponsoring, in the Merovingian as in the Carolingian period. For it was not only the godfather, but also the officiant at baptism, who became the child's spiritual father—and, crucially, the *compater* (co-father) of the child's natural father. *Compaternitas* was the relationship that eighth-century popes keenly sought with the new Frankish dynasty of the Carolingians—so keenly, indeed, that in at least one case the pope sounded impatient for the birth of a new prince or princess, which would provide the occasion for renewing this bond with the Frankish king.[100] *Compaternitas* had important social implications: one *compater* could call on another for help. Nor was it only through baptism that the link was made: it arose from confirmation too. A ninth-century example was Alfred of Wessex, confirmed as a four-year-old by Pope Leo IV, who thus became his spiritual father, and, at the same time, co-father of Alfred's father, King Æthelwulf. Thanks to the existence of the English *schola* in Rome, the West Saxon King had the means to lend the Pope effective military support.[101]

The spiritual bond between godparents and natural parents could be created through baptism, but also through confirmation, or by the rituals of the catechumenate which were the preliminary to baptism. According to an eighth-century penitential with widespread influence in England and on the Continent, 'There can be the same [spiritual] father for all these, but that is

[99] See Lynch, *Godparents and Kinship*, pp. 193–4, 218. Jussen, *Patenschaft und Adoption*, p. 281, is rightly critical of the suggestion of opposed 'popular' and 'clerical' cultures here, but perhaps exaggerates Lynch's commitment to such a model.

[100] *Codex Carolinus* 14, *MGH. Ep*, III, ed. W. Gundlach (Berlin, 1892), p. 511. (A literal raising from the font was not necessary—the rite could be performed by proxy.) For this relationship in the eighth century, see Angenendt, 'Das geistliche Bündnis der Päpste mit den Karolingern (754–796)', *Historisches Jahrbuch*, 11 (1980), pp. 1–94.

[101] Nelson, 'The Problem of Alfred's royal anointing', *JEH*, 18 (1967), pp. 145–63, repr. in Nelson, *Politics and Ritual in Early Medieval Europe* (London, 1986), and 'The Franks and the English in the Ninth Century revisited', in P. Szarmach and J. T. Rosenthal, eds, *The Preservation and Transmission of Anglo-Saxon Culture* (Binghampton, NY, 1994), forthcoming.

not the custom. Instead different fathers receive [the children] for each occasion.'[102] This certainly reflects 'the impulse to multiply occasions for sponsorship'. The reasons behind the impulse, and the ways in which such relationships functioned, can be inferred from the complaint of a ninth-century moralist: 'Many become godfathers not for the salvation of the child received but for worldly reasons . . '.[103] Social support, and, at aristocratic level, political benefits, were the consequences of godparenthood for the adults involved—and these explain the inflation-rate of such relationships. A story from Ravenna made the benefits explicit in an urban milieu exceptional for the ninth century: 'Two men wanted to make a partnership (*foedus*) between themselves', and so one suggested to the other that he take his son as godchild, 'so that we are fathers together, you the carnal and I the spiritual one'. And so it was done.[104] Here the child became the instrument of a social relationship primarily between co-parents. It seems a short step thence to the kind of *compadrazgo* that flourishes today in parts of Mexico, where apparently if no child is available, the two *compadres* sponsor something else—a truck, or a TV set.[105]

Why should the Church oppose spiritual relationships? They created *caritas*—the basis of social peace. There were freely chosen rather than socially imposed. Individual churchmen could choose and use them. The Church itself could use them for pastoral purposes: the responsibilities of godparents for spiritual teaching were increasingly insisted on as the Carolingian Reforms took effect. In the calculations of the adults involved, the child him- or herself might be quite secondary, strictly

[102] So, Lynch, *Godparents and Kinship*, p. 214, commenting on the so-called *Canones Theodori*, ii, 4, 8, ed. P. Finsterwalder, *Die Canones Theodori Cantuariensis und ihre Überlieferungsformen* (Weimar, 1929), p. 317.

[103] Jonas of Orleans, *De institutione laicali*, i, 6, *PL* 106, col. 133.

[104] Agnellus of Ravenna, *Liber Pontificalis ecclesiae Ravennatis*, ch. 30, ed. O. Holder-Egger, *MGH.SRL* (Hanover, 1878), p. 294, cited by Jussen, *Patenschaft und Adoption*, pp. 26, 296–7. Jussen may well be right in surmising that 'Kaufleute' made this *foedus*, though Agnellus does not make this explicit.

[105] Lynch, *Godparents and Kinship*, pp. 195–6, n. 118, citing H. G. Nutini and B. Bell, *Ritual Kinship: the Structure and Historical Development of the Compadrazgo System in Rural Tlaxcala*, 2 vols (Princeton, 1980–4)—though Lynch himself, pp. 72–4, registers caution about the use medieval historians might make of this and other anthropological work. See also the important methodological contribution of Jussen, 'Le parrainage à la fin du moyen âge: savoir public, attentes théologiques et usages sociaux', *Annales ESC*, mars–avril 1992, pp. 467–502.

instrumental. The benefits sought by the adults initially affected them, and only secondarily the children. Familial bonds were the model; and the child took his/her place within that matrix. Co-parenting could entail co-operation between men and women: it was precisely because godfathers and biological mothers expressed their relationship with a kiss that monks had to be forbidden to form such spiritual ties 'for monks are not to kiss any woman whatsoever'.[106] Repeated injunctions indicate that the prohibitions were not observed. With the extension of the incest taboo to spiritual kin, exogamy became, so to speak, more exogamous, expanding the circle of those bound in relations of peace and mutual support. The formation of spiritual kinship could even, it was thought (or hoped), constitute grounds for divorce. A rather typically misogynistic allegation of ninth-century bishops was that some fraudulent women sponsored their own children at confirmation so that they could then separate from their husbands.[107] Again the intended outcome affected the adults involved—and the child was the means to an end. In short, the focus of spiritual kinship in the earlier Middle Ages was on co-parenthood rather than filiation, on the interests of parents, rather than those of children. Naming practices reflected parental, specifically paternal, choice, and at the same time extremely limited ecclesiastical influence.[108] It was only later in the Middle Ages that most parents gave their children Christian names, and so sought to provide them with personalized heavenly, as well as earthly, protectors.

* * *

In the last part of this paper, I want to turn to another type of earlier medieval interaction between parents, children, and the Church. And I'll introduce it by briefly considering royal children, for whom some information exists even in this 'source-

[106] Lynch, *Godparents and Kinship*, p. 193.

[107] Council of Châlons (813), *MGH. Conc*, ii (Hanover, 1906), i. p. 279.

[108] H.-W. Goetz, 'Zur Namengebung in der alamannischen Grundbesitzerschicht der Karolingerzeit. Ein Beitrag zur Familienforschung', *Zeitschrift fur die Geschichte des Oberrheins*, 133 (1985), pp. 1–40; and *Leben im Mittelalter* (Munich, 1986), pp. 37–8. The nature of early medieval documentation scarcely ever permits inferences about possible naming after godparents.

poor period'.[109] This is how Alfred's biographer depicts his upbringing of his son Edward and his daughter Ælfthryth:

> The two were at all times fostered at the royal court under the solicitous care of tutors and wet-nurses. . . . Nor amid the other pursuits of this present life which are appropriate to the nobility are these two allowed to live idly and indifferently, with no liberal education, for they have attentively learned the Psalms, and books in English, and especially English poems (*carmina saxonica*), and they very frequently make use of books.[110]

This cheerfully coeducational picture is modelled on, yet significantly different from, Einhard's account of the upbringing of Charlemagne's sons and daughters.[111] But other court milieux, whatever their spiritual dangers, were also presented as child-friendly. Louis the Pious, aged three, was crowned King of Aquitaine by the pope in Rome. Louis' biographer makes the only early medieval allusion I know of to a push-chair: the *cunarum gestatorium* in which the little king was brought to Orleans for his ceremonial adventus into his new kingdom.[112] Here is a court poet's vignette of the three-year old Charles the Bald stealing the show at a great liturgical occasion (the royal family is processing into church) in June 826: 'Ahead of his father, the lovely boy Charles resplendent in gold merrily goes, pattering with his feet across the marble floor.'[113] Alfred, who liked to appear to his contemporaries an ideal family-man, wrote briefly of children in one of his own works: when he wanted to drive home the point that only fools and evil persons fail to aim at what wins praise, he gave an example of his own: 'Look, children when they can only just walk strive after credit and renown, riding on sticks and playing many games in which they

109 I borrow, and enlarge, the label from one who knows the period best: K. Schmid, 'Unerforschte Quellen aus quellenarmen Zeit: Zur *amicitia* zwischen Heinrich I und dem westfränkischen König Robert im Jahre 923', *Francia*, 12 (1984), pp. 119–47.

110 Asser, *De rebus gestis Ælfredi*, ch. 75, ed. W. H. Stevenson (Oxford, 1904), p. 58. (Note the present tense: Asser was writing in 893.)

111 Einhard, *Vita Karoli*, ch. 19, p. 23: 'first', all of them learned *liberalia studia*, 'then' they proceeded to gendered pursuits, the sons to riding and martial exercise, and daughters to textile work.

112 Astronomer, *Vita Hludowici Imperatoris*, ch., 4, ed. G. H. Pertz, *MGH. SS*, ii (Hanover, 1829), p. 607.

113 Ermold le Noir, *In Honorem Hludowici Pii*, ed. E. Faral, *Poème sur Louis le Pieux* (Paris, 1932), lines 2300–1, p. 176.

imitate their elders.'[114] Such appreciation of the efforts of toddlers accurately reflects the political world of the ninth century. The establishment of dynasties required the acceptance of, and ecclesiastical backing for, the succession of child rulers. It was now that the bishops of several kingdoms of Western Christendom took a leaf out of the popes' book, and themselves invented and conducted rituals designed to secure dynastic continuity: by consecrating selected princes to kingship.[115] But there was a negative side to dynastic policy: namely, the exclusion of princes surplus to requirement. Here, too, ninth-century churchmen had a key role to play, by performing other kinds of ritual: consecrating to clerical orders, and tonsuring.[116] The offering of a son to the Church meant his removal from the circle of heirs to the royal title. He was paid off with a share of the family inheritance; and spent the rest of his days supporting the family's well-being through prayer.

Royalty were special. But among the nobility, too, the practice of oblation became a key element in the *entente* between parents and the Church. A recent fascinating book has treated oblation as a variety of child-abandonment.[117] Fascinating, but wrong-headed: for parents in offering their children did not abandon them, nor did the children abandon their parents.[118] It was in the Carolingian period, once again, that the liturgy of oblation was elaborated, and its purpose thus made clear:

> The father brings his son to the altar. The son has in his hand an offering and a petition. [The father says:] 'It was sanctioned by the old law that parents handed over their sons,

[114] *King Alfred's Old English Version of the Consolations of Boethius*, tr. W. J. Sedgefield (Oxford, 1900), p. 124.

[115] Nelson, *Politics and Ritual*, chs 10 and 12.

[116] Nelson, 'A tale of two princes: politics, text, and ideology in a Carolingian annal', *Studies in Medieval and Renaissance History*, 10 (1988), pp. 105–41, at pp. 108–10, and 'The Franks and the English', forthcoming.

[117] J. Boswell, *The Kindness of Strangers. The Abandonment of Children in Western Europe from Late Antiquity to the Renaissance* (Harmondsworth, 1988); see also '*Expositio and Oblatio*. The abandonment of children and the ancient and medieval family', *AHR*, 89 (1984), pp. 10–33.

[118] See J. H. Lynch, *Simonaical Entry into Religious Life* (Columbus, Ohio, 1976); C. Bouchard, *Sword, Miter and Cloister: Nobility And the Church in Burgundy (980–1198)* (Ithaca, 1987); P. Quinn, *Better than the Sons of Kings: Boys and Monks in the Early Middle Ages* (New York, 1989). See further M. Bull, *Knightly Piety and the Lay Response to the First Crusade* (Oxford, 1993), esp. pp. 116–25; and above all, the forthcoming English translation (1994) of M. de Jong, *Kind en Klooster in de Vroege Middeleeuwen* (Amsterdam, 1986).

with offerings, to serve joyfully in the temple of the Lord. Thus I have no doubt that this shows an example to us in a way that brings salvation (*salubriter*) when we do the same with our sons, and that it is right and just to give back our fruit to our creator. Therefore I hand over my son with an offering [of bread] in his hand wrapped in the altarcloth, enclosed in my hand, in which I have this document, to the name (*nomen*) of the saint whose relics are herein and to this present abbot. I do this before witnesses according to the Rule intending this to be permanent so that from this day forth my son shall not be able to withdraw his neck from the yoke of the Rule.'[119]

A ninth-century commentator on the Rule of Benedict explained that this ritual worked by analogy: the offering which the child clutched in his hand, the bread-offering, became the Eucharist, and in the same way the child was the sacrifice to the Lord. The Old Testament holocaust, the 'burnt offering', was the prototype for the offering of the living human child.[120] The child entered the community. The *petitio*, the document recording the gift, entered the archive. There it functioned as an *aide-mémoire* to the other gift, unmentioned in the ritual, the gift of property which, in fact, went with the child.

The principle underlying this was that of reciprocity: the gift which demanded a counter-gift, in this case, a divine one. This was sometimes understood in a quite particular sense, as when the seventh-century Northumbrian king Edwin promised his daughter as a thank-offering for victory;[121] or when in the late tenth century, the Ottonian princess Adelaide entered the convent of Quedlinburg as a propitiatory offering in a time of famine and plague.[122] (In this latter episode the offerer was not Adelaide's long-deceased father but her younger brother, Otto III. Patriarchy moves in mysterious ways.) The underlying idea was evidently not peculiar to the Carolingian period. What was new

119 M. Stratmann, *Hinkmar von Reims als Verwalter von Bistum und Kirchenprovinz* = *Quellen und Forschungen zum Recht im Mittelalter*, 6 (Sigmaringen, 1991), pp. 72–8, with oblation-formula at p. 73, n. 7.

120 Hildemar, *Expositio in regulam sancti Benedicti*, ch. 59, ed. M. Mittermuller (Regensburg, 1980), p. 549. See M. de Jong, 'In Samuel's image. Child oblation and the Rule of St Benedict in the early Middle Ages (600–900)', *Regulae Benedicti Studia*, 16 (1987), pp. 69–79.

121 Bede, *Historia Ecclesiastica*, ii, 9, ed. Plummer, p. 99, tr. Farmer, p. 119.

122 Leyser, *Rule and Conflict*, pp. 89–90.

then was the ritual which underlined the donor's role, that is, normally the father's role, in the offering: his hand enclosed, and literally moved, that of the child. The oblation at the same time constituted a legal transaction—hence, was recorded in a legal document, duly witnessed. Is the sacrifical principle to be understood as an 'archaic' one?[123] There is a danger in that term of suggesting something pre- and even un-Christian, hence that the Church was accommodating something alien to it. Early medieval Christianity need not be seen as in some way compromised, or debased, by accepting, as with oblation, the magicality of the sacrificial gift that expects a return. (If it *is* seen thus, then Christianity has been, and still is, compromised in the understanding of most of its practitioners.)[124] Specific to the earlier medieval period, and especially to the ninth to tenth centuries, was the socially-approved institutionalization in the Latin West of the parental gift of the living child. This belonged in a social context: of familial identities, dynastic consciousness, narrower descent-lines, localized bases defined less as family seats than as family monasteries. The gift of the child to a church was a sacrifice: but it was also a transaction that mediated, and reinforced, the relationship between the parent on the one hand, and the church (in the sense of *this* church) and the saint and his/her local representatives on the other. The transfer of the child's *hereditas* sealed the bond between the two contracting parties. But the bond would exist, at the relatively high social level where these practices are documented, even without that transfer. Aristocratic fostering offers a relevant comparison; and Hrabanus noted, as a touch of contemporary colour to a picture largely derived from a classical source, that 'today youths are brought up in the households of magnates'.[125] The elite of the Frankish world, then, were very familiar with the use of boy-children to consolidate, and perpetuate across the generations, the links between lords and men.

[123] Cf. Angenendt, *Das Frühmittelalter. Die abendlandische Christenheit von 400 bis 900* (Stuttgart-Berling-Koln, 1990), pp. 43–5. I am very grateful to Arnold Angenendt, and other participants, for exploring this question at the colloquium on 'Religion and Power in the Early Middle Ages', held at Wassenaar, Netherlands, in October 1993. Mayke de Jong put all of us in her debt by organizing the colloquium and contributing very substantially to the fruitfulness of our discussions.

[124] See M. Douglas, *Natural Symbols*, 2nd end (London, 1973).

[125] Hrabanus, *De procinctu romanae militiae*, ch. 3, ed. E. Dümmler, *Zeitschrift für deutsches Alterthum*, 15 (1872), pp. 443–51, at p. 444. (Hrabanus' work draws heavily on Vegetius.)

In practice, then, oblation worked to forge, and reinforce, on-going relationships between landed families and particular churches. Dynasties, in fact, were consolidated around cult-sites, and families defined themselves as founders and/or patrons of churches in which their ascendants and close collaterals (*genealogia*), and their descent-line (*progenies*), would be permanently commemorated. To offer a boy to such an institution was to plan for the future. Girls were different, remaining at the heart of the family. They could be kept at home, or set up in what were, in effect, house-convents, which often lived no longer than their original inmates. The fact that there could be house-nuns, but not house-monks,[126] reflected (*inter alia*) the firmer institutional definition of male communities. The oblation of boys, each bringing his gift of property, was the essential way to achieve the maintenance of the monastery's personnel, its economic base, and its long-term survival. Where evidence is plentiful over a lengthy timespan, as at Cluny, it is possible to see parental strategies operating over the generations to benefit family and monastery alike.[127] Fulda offers another well-documented case for the ninth century.[128] Benefactors and inmates existed over time in symbiotic relationship, with oblation as the central link. The same names recurring over the generations indicate continuities in the constellation of local landed families, who were Fulda's main patrons. One such name seems especially revealing: *Sibigelt*—which apparently derives from *Sippe geld*—'family offering'.[129] The name can stand for the function of every oblate. And the extant lists of names of the dead for whom prayers were said confirms the delivery of the spiritual benefits desired by donors. The sacrifice of the child brought its reward to the parents. They could be confident of Heaven—where a ninth-century visionary saw 'boys writing lists of the names of those who would be saved'.[130] Parents could also be confident of 'their'

[126] As pointed out by H. Fichtenau, *Living in the Tenth Century: Mentalities and Social Orders*, tr. P. J. Geary (Chicago, 1991), pp. 114–15.

[127] See esp. B. Rosenwein, *To be the Neighbour of Saint Peter* (Ithaca, 1989); and also J. B. W. Nightingale, 'Monasteries and their patrons in the Dioceses of Trier, Metz and Toul, 850–1000' (Oxford D. Phil. thesis, 1988).

[128] E. Freise, 'Studien zum Einzugsbereich der Klostergemeinschaft Fulda', in K. Schmid et al., *Die Klostergemeinschaft von Fulda im früheren Mittelalter*, vol. 2.3 (Munich, 1978), pp. 1003–1269.

[129] Ibid., pp. 1086–8.

[130] *Annales de Saint Bertin*, s.a. 839, eds F. Grat, J. Vielliard and S. Clémencet (Paris, 1964), p. 29.

monastery's support on earth, as ally or patron. On high days and holy days they would visit. Permanent proximity meant continuing contacts with sons who had been oblated, but certainly *not* abandoned.

No social system ever functioned perfectly. Many charters granting land to monasteries show that what monasteries feared (though, in fact, this seems rather seldom to have happened) were familial second thoughts—or rather, the revocation of a gift by the donor's kinsman or descendant. And suppose an oblate himself demanded his 'freedom'? One such case (and this is a great rarity) was that of the Saxon monk Gottschalk. It centred around the twin issues of his personal *libertas*, and the land—his *hereditas*—which he had brought to the monastery of Fulda.[131] Gottschalk argued, when he reached maturity, that the oblation which had cost him his freedom was invalid. I shall not say much more about Gottschalk's argument, because it was a specifically Saxon argument: that is, it depended on legal technicalities about Saxon free status and the need for Saxon witnesses to a Saxon's legal acts. Many Saxon youths had been offered to Fulda by their parents in the immediate aftermath of Frankish conquest. The situation was a peculiar one in time and space: a short-term product of imperialism. Nevertheless, the Abbot of Fulda, Hrabanus Maurus, saw Gottschalk's case as a challenge to the ideology of oblation: Hrabanus therefore set out that ideology in the clearest possible terms. The parallel was with baptism, when promises were made on children's behalf: 'The faith . . . of those who offer is acceptable to God, as Scripture shows, just as in the Holy Church, the baptism of little ones is done through the faith and commitment of the parents.'[132] 'It is one thing for an equal to be handed over by an equal; another thing entirely for an inferior to be handed over by a superior.'[133] The case for oblation rested on parental authority: the capacity of the parent to act for the child—and to make a gift of him to God. Oblation is a classic case of the early medieval Church's adaptation to its environment: yet, at the same time, ecclesiastical practice reacted back on that environment. The Church reinforced the parental

[131] Freise, 'Studien', pp. 1021–9; and, especially, de Jong, 'In Samuel's image'.

[132] *Liber de oblatione puerorum, PL* 107, col. 428 (my translation). Cf. the translation of substantial extracts of this text by Boswell, *Kindness of Strangers*, pp. 438–44, at p. 443.

[133] Ibid., col. 425. Cf. Boswell's translation, p. 441.

authority that overrode the wills of offspring and achieved the practical outcome of substantial benefit to ecclesiastical institutions. Hrabanus, incidentally, had to argue for 'parental' authority because his biblical proof-text was I Samuel i. 24–8, which described the offering of the infant Samuel to the temple—by his mother. In Hrabanus's world it was the father who offered. Hrabanus meant to defend patriarchy.

Hrabanus's neglect of the child's willingness or unwillingness was not universally shared by early medieval churchmen. On the contrary, there were contemporaries of Hrabanus who, while acknowledging fathers' rights to offer their sons, insisted that those sons themselves 'should not be unwilling'.[134] No one at this period made clear, however, how and when the unwillingness should be expressed. As a result, the provisos were ineffective. In the ninth century, and until the twelfth, Hrabanus's view prevailed, as far as we can tell. Once a child had been cloistered in early childhood, 's/he could not leave and marry on reaching puberty.'[135] Oblation clearly did (as Boswell stresses) limit the number of heirs, and, to that extent, resembled abandonment in its effect. For some aristocratic families in this period (and social context needs specifying as clearly as possible), this was utility of a kind. Yet parents' *expressed* aims were religious. Through child oblates, early medieval parent-power was converted into religious power. Oblation became unacceptable from the twelfth century onwards, not for the materialist reason that it had become less functional—if anything, demographic growth should have made it more so, in terms of noble-parental strategies—but for the ideological reason that it outraged new attitudes (now translated into canon law) to personal choice and action.[136] Yet the twelfth-century canonists found ammunition in Carolingian texts—which suggests that in the very heyday of oblation, parental, and ecclesiastical, attitudes to children had left characteristically ambiguous marks.

* * *

134 Council of Mainz (829), *MGH. Conc*, ii, 2 (Hanover, 1908), 50, p. 602: 'neminem debere invitum fieri monachum'. See the comments of Boswell, *Kindness of Strangers*, p. 246.

135 Council of Worms (868), ch. 22, Mansi, 14, col. 873, cited by Boswell, *Kindness of Strangers*, p. 248.

136 For these changes in the High Middle Ages, see N. Berend, 'Une invisible subversion: la disparition de l'oblation irrévocable des enfants', in *Médiévales* (1994), forthcoming. My thanks are due to Nora Berend for kindly letting me read this illuminating paper in advance of publication.

I want to end this paper by briefly considering not the social but the personal, not fathers but sons, not planners but victims. Two case-histories convey—or at least refract—something of the experiences of children themselves. The first, dating from about 870, is that of Rigramnus, a noble Frankish youth from Le Mans.[137] His uncle, a canon of the cathedral, wished to dedicate the boy to the life of a secular cleric. The boy's mental anguish manifested itself in terrible stomach pains, until he eventually revealed that he had already been offered by his father, now deceased, to the monastic life, and this, the boy himself insisted, was what he himself wanted, 'so that his father's soul might be saved from peril of breaking his vow'. The boy stuck to his guns, despite the fury of his uncle, who regarded the life of a monk as thoroughly inferior to that of the cathedral canon. 'How', he demanded of his nephew, 'could you want the life of pigs in a vegetable garden? What about the pleasures of hunting, and the voluptuous touch of women?' But the boy kept to his monastic vow, for five years—until his uncle on his deathbed made a final attempt to lure him away, and this time succeeded.

The second case is from St-Gall, in Alamannia. It is the story, centring on events in 876, of a young man named Wolo.[138] He was a noble oblate at St-Gall, an adolescent, the son of a count. He was restless, and a wanderer—*inquietus et vagus*. The dean and the abbot had tried to cope with his *aversio* in the usual way, that is 'with words and with beatings' (*verbis verberibusque*), but to no avail. The writer here offered a revealing comment: 'St-Gall accepted only nobles, and the more noble often tended to go astray (*nobiliores saepe aberrabant*).' Wolo's parents came to visit, very concerned for their son, evidently to urge him to reconcile himself to monastic life; but like the monastery's leaders, the parents were unsuccessful. One day, at dawn, the devil appeared to the abbot and warned him that some evil would befall the community. When the abbot passed on the warning, only Wolo was sceptical: 'Old men always dream stupid things!' But as a

[137] *Narratio de monacho Cenomanensi ad canonicam vitam et habitum converso, PL* 129, cols 1263–8. I am grateful to David Ganz who some years ago drew attention to this neglected text in a paper read to the Anglo-American Conference of Historians in London. The dating problem must be left for future consideration.

[138] Ekkehard (iv), *Casus Sancti Galli*, ch. 3, ed. D. I. von Arx, *MGH. SS*, ii (Hanover, 1829), pp. 99–100.

precaution, the boys were forbidden to go outside the monastic enclosure. Later that same day, as Wolo sat copying out Scripture, he reached the words, '. . . and he began to die' (John. 4.7). Suddenly he leapt up and began to climb the monastery's bell-tower, 'so that he could see, though not allowed to walk there, the mountains and the fields, and thus assuage his wandering soul.' Then, as his climb took him directly above the altar of the Virgins, 'by Satan's impulse, so it's believed, he fell and broke his neck.' Wolo in his dying words was able to reveal his innermost fear: he wanted to be taken not to the infirmary but to the altar of the Virgins, 'for they [the Virgins] know that however wicked I was in other respects, I never had intercourse with a woman.' The story's sequel, focusing predictably on the abbot's reaction, makes it fairly clear that Wolo was a suicide.[139] Here, then, we glimpse the psychological pressures to which at least some oblates were subjected. In this case, there can be little doubt that the oblate was an unwilling one.

Both Rigramnus and Wolo were objects of parental (and in Rigramnus's case, avuncular) concern and control. Both struggled to find their own identity, pitting their wills against their elders. No doubt these are extreme cases; but it is at the extreme that we can gauge the weight of combined parental and institutional pressure. Parents needed to have their children in churches; churchmen needed to keep them there, and to impose on them rules of stability and sexual ethics completely at odds with those of the world. With and through those children worked adult interests and adult *ententes*. Parents and churchmen made of those children the ties that bound. But what did it mean to *be* the tie that bound? The voices of the children are audible only through the words of adults, who were themselves (as Augustine had pointed out) 'playing games'. The stories of Rigramnus and Wolo remind us that earlier medieval childhood could involve not games, but tragedies that were all its own.

King's College London

[139] H. F. Haefele, '*Wolo cecidit.* Zur Deutung einer Ekkehard-Erzahlung', *Deutsches Archiv*, 35 (1979), pp. 17–32; see also M. Borgolte, 'Conversatio cottidiana. Zeugnisse vom Alltag in frühmittelalterlicher Überlieferung', in H. U. Nuber et al., *Archäologie und Geschichte des ersten Jahrtausends in Südwestdeutschland = Freiburger Forschungen zum ersten Jahrtausend in Südwestdeutschland*, 1 (Sigmaringen, 1990), pp. 295–385, at pp. 327–9.

THE FATE OF BABIES DYING BEFORE BAPTISM IN BYZANTIUM*

by JANE BAUN

In the city of the Laodikaians lived a devout, pure, and blameless priest. To this priest one night the local governor came in urgent haste, pressing him to rise up and baptize his child, whose breath was already beginning to fail. Leaping up right away, the priest ran into the church. But while he was preparing the water and the holy oil the child died, before it could be baptized.

Taking the child, the priest placed it in front of the font and said to the attendant angel, 'To you, my fellow servant, angel of God, I say: by the authority that Christ gave us to bind and loose in heaven and upon earth, restore the soul of the child in the body until I shall baptize it, lest it depart unenlightened into that age. For my Master and yours knows that I was not careless, but when I was called, I ran straight away.' When the priest had spoken, the child returned to life. He then baptized it, kissed it, and said, 'Go, child, into the kingdom of heaven.' And immediately the child fell back asleep in the Lord.[1]

THIS medieval Greek edifying tale, of the type labelled by the Bollandist fathers 'de baptismo pueri mortui', was a perennial favourite in Byzantine anthologies of popular religious stories.[2] It also appears in two major 'question and answer' collections on canon law and church practice, first in the seventh-century compilation of Anastasios, Abbot of Sinai, and again, five centuries later, in that of Michael Glykas.[3] I have chosen, however, to paraphrase the version as told in a humbler

* I am indebted to Bishop Basil Rodzianko and Dr Joseph Munitiz, S. J., and also to Professors Peter Brown and Judith Herrin, for their patient endurance and many helpful suggestions.

[1] *Theognosti Thesaurus*, ed. Joseph A. Munitiz, *CChr.SG*, 5 (1979) [hereafter *Thesaurus*] XV[2], 5, pp. 129–30.

[2] F. Halkin, ed., *Bibliotheca Hagiographica Graeca*, 3rd edn, 3 vols (Brussels, 1957), no. 1444x.

[3] As cited in Munitiz, *Thesaurus*, pp. lxxiii–iv, who places its probable origin in the seventh-century Anastasian corpus.

and later source: a mid-thirteenth-century handbook of religious instruction known as The Treasury (*Thēsauros*). *The work's priest-monk compiler, Theognostos, frames our story with stern admonitions to parents and priests regarding the grave dangers of letting children die unbaptized.*

The Laodikaian baby experienced a narrow escape and a happy ending. But what if a more conventional priest, or a less co-operative angel, had been on duty that evening? What if as-yet-unbaptized 'baby x', like so many other Byzantine infants, had not been miraculously revived, but had remained prematurely, irrevocably, dead? I should like to explore the moment that might have come next, when the disconsolate parents asked the priest what would happen to their child.

If our priest had been a post-Augustinian, Western, Catholic priest, his task would have been much more straightforward. Thanks to the challenges of Pelagius, the Western Church had been compelled at an early stage to work the issue out in detail.[4] Even if later theologians and pastors departed gradually from the strictures of a purely Augustinian formulation, still, the debate was well established, the terms were known, and a geographical location, limbo, eventually evolved to contain those awkward in-between souls, worthy neither of punishment nor of reward.

What did our Orthodox priest, however, have to fall back on? As far as I have been able to determine, nothing so definite and three-dimensional as the Western version.[5] In fact, most Orthodox treatments of the question, from the Byzantine period to the present day, take pains to distance themselves from the Augustinian tradition of thought on original sin, human nature, judgement, and purgatory.[6] But for our hypothetical priest and parents, the question was not merely an academic exercise in original sin and eschatology, but rather a matter of immediate ritual and existential consequence, of spiritual life and death.

[4] For the centrality of the fate of babies to the Pelagian controversy, see Elizabeth A. Clark, *The Origenist Controversy: The Cultural Construction of an Early Christian Debate* (Princeton, NJ, 1992), pp. 194–244. I am indebted to Gary Hansen for this reference.

[5] A judgement echoed by Bishop Kallistos Ware, in his *The Orthodox Church* (New York, 1980), p. 229, n. 2.

[6] For 'the Latin doctrine of purgatory' as a sore point between East and West, see John Meyendorff, 'Theology in the Thirteenth Century: Methodological Contrasts', in J. Chrysostomides, ed., *Kathegetria: Essays presented to Joan Hussey* (Camberley, 1988), p. 403, with n. 20.

Accordingly, Byzantine canonists treated the question of the proper timing of infant baptism frequently and with great seriousness. It appears in some form in most Byzantine *responsa* collections, and serves as the opening problem in two important late eleventh-century texts, the 'Questions' attributed to the deacon Peter, chartophylax under Alexios Komnenos, and the 'Solutions' of the Patriarch Nicholas III Grammatikos.[7]

The usual ritual intervals to be observed between birth and baptism varied. Canonists most often advised either an eight-day period, taking the circumcision and naming of the infant Jesus as a model, or a forty-day hiatus, after which the mother, newly churched, could attend the ceremony.[8] But almost all the canonists, after describing the norm, hasten to add that infants who were sickly or in mortal danger were to be baptized immediately. The entire ritual, consisting of multiple anointings, exorcisms, blessings, and perambulations, did not need to be performed if death were feared imminent, but only the rite's core, three total immersions in water with invocation of the Holy Trinity.[9] Baptism could if necessary be performed in the home. Symeon, Archbishop of Thessalonike in the early fifteenth century, encouraged priests to be in attendance at the actual birth, in case of emergency.[10]

A few witnesses, such as the ninth-century Nikephoros the Confessor, would allow monks or any Orthodox Christian layman in good standing to perform baptisms in an emergency.[11] But this option is always treated as a desperate last resort. More typical perhaps is the case of the Laodikaian governor already mentioned, who, in spite of the increased risk to his child, preferred the church to the kitchen sink.

The possibility of the child's mother, the attending midwife, or any other laywoman's performing an emergency baptism,

[7] 'Petrou Khartophylakos erōtēmata', in G. Rhallēs and M. Potlēs, eds, *Syntagma tōn theiōn kai hierōn kanonōn*, 6 vols (Athens, 1852–9) [hereafter RP.*Syn.*], 5, p. 369. J. Darrouzès, 'Les Réponses de Nicolas III à l'évêque de Zètounion', in Chrysostomides, ed., *Kathegetria*, p. 336.

[8] Eight days: Symeon of Thessalonikie, *On the Holy Sacraments* [hereafter Sym.Thess.], 60, *PG* 155, cols 209–12; forty days: Peter the Chartophylax, in RP.*Syn.*, 5, p. 369. Current Eastern Orthodox practice tends toward forty days; cf. Fr Paul Lazor, ed., *Baptism*, Dept. of Religious Education, The Orthodox Church in America (New York, 1972), pp. 21–2.

[9] Sym.Thess., 63, *PG* 188, col. 228. See also Balsamon and Zonaras' commentaries on Apostolic Canon no. 50, *PG* 137, cols 138–42.

[10] Sym.Thess., 58, *PG* 155, col. 208.

[11] Nikephoros the Confessor, canons (2nd ser.) 6, 7, in RP.*Syn.*, 4, p. 431.

strongly attested in the medieval West, does not feature prominently in the East.[12] A theological explanation for the lack of evidence might be sought in the medieval Byzantine insistence on the ritual impurity of women for forty days after childbirth, and also during menstruation. Most canonists considered feminine ritual impurity a serious impediment even to receiving the sacraments, let alone administering one.[13]

Ritual and canonical complexities combined with a generally high infant mortality rate ensured that the possibility of a baby's dying before baptism was an ever-present threat in Byzantium. And so, as we would expect, the problem arises frequently in canon law. But it arises most often with reference to the moral and theological predicament of the parents only. It is to the nature and duration of their penance that the canonists attend, not to the fate of the babies themselves.

The standard penance in such cases is recorded in the canons of John the Faster. Of the actual writings of John, Patriarch of Constantinople from 582 to 595, almost nothing has survived, but the numerous works attributed to him formed one of the most widely-copied and quoted bodies of penitential and canonical texts in the Byzantine Church.[14] The 'Johannine' tradition dictates that parents whose children die unbaptized through negligence be excommunicated for three years. During this period they are to practise the severe form of fasting known as *xerophagy*, pray on bended knees, weep profusely, give alms, and perform forty metanies (acts of repentance) each day.[15] If the child dies at seven days or younger, the period is shortened to forty days.

Both this text and later commentaries upon it focus entirely on the parents: the urgency consists in putting *them* right with God for their sin of negligence. Nowhere is the suggestion found that the parents' penance might benefit the unfortunate child itself, might affect its progress in the other world. But what about the infant? Could its parents do anything to help it, or discover anything about the fate of its soul? Could its infant sins be shriven? Did it have sins? Did it still have a soul?

[12] For the West, see Shulamith Shahar, *Childhood in the Middle Ages* (London, 1990), pp. 49–50.
[13] Timothy of Alexandria, questions 6, 7, in RP.*Syn.*, 4, pp. 334–5.
[14] Complete corpus in *PG* 88, cols 1889–1918.
[15] John the Faster, canon 24, in RP.*Syn.*, 4, p. 443.

This last question, I believe, holds the key to our dilemma. Elizabeth Clark has observed of the Pelagian controversy that much of Augustine's great labour in refuting Pelagius—and in explaining what happens to unbaptized babies who die—can be traced to a failure (or refusal) to formulate a consistent doctrine of the origin of the soul.[16] It is, of course, unrealistic to expect our Byzantine canonists to have responded to concrete pastoral problems with lengthy and abstract theological explanations. In any case, the bitterly divisive controversies over 'Origenist' ideas in the Eastern Church, from the fourth to the sixth centuries, had perhaps rendered the origin and transmission of souls a highly sensitive topic. Yet had our canonists had access to a definitive teaching on the origin of the soul, their task of counselling bereaved parents might have been much more straightforward.

Byzantine texts of all kinds, perhaps reflecting this theological gap, present a uniformly bleak (if not blank) picture on the fate of such infants. In a phrase from the *Thēsauros* found throughout the Orthodox literature on the problem, from Gregory of Nazianzus in the fourth century to the present day, the unbaptized infant is 'worthy neither of the kingdom nor of punishment'.[17] But of what exactly these infant souls *might* be worthy, none of the Fathers, ancient or modern, speculates.

This was not due to lack of interest: priests and people continued to ask variations on the theme. An unknown questioner of Anastasios of Sinai went straight to the point: 'Whither do they depart, the innocent five- or four-year-old children of Jews and the unbaptized: to judgement, or to paradise?'[18] The seventh-century Abbot of Sinai's response is a masterful early demonstration of the tension produced when pastoral necessity confronted theological ambiguity on this issue. Citing 'the Prophets', Anastasios says he does not believe that God visits the sins of the fathers upon the children any more, and so the innocent children of sinners clearly do not go to Gehenna (his word). But do they then attain paradise? Our abbot seals his

[16] Clark, *Origenist Controversy*, pp. 197, 221, 232–9, 244.

[17] Gregory of Nazianzus, *Oration* 40, *PG* 36, cols 381–9; for a strikingly similar nineteenth-century view see Cyril, Patriarch of Constantinople, tr. in Charles Stewart, *Demons and the Devil: Moral Imagination in Modern Greek Culture* (Princeton, NJ, 1991), p. 196.

[18] Anastasius of Sinai, Question 81, *PG* 89, col. 709 (no. 9 of the original Anastasian questions).

response tersely: 'But it is not good to probe into the judgements of God.'

Byzantine theologians, canonists, and exegetes, feeling that they had neither biblical warrant nor theological justification for the certainty that gradually evolved in the West, always stop short of the precise definition and evocative description that people craved. There are no pictures, gentle or terrible, no intimations of neutral resting-places between reward and punishment, there is no 'discretion'. No amount of prayer, fasting, or weeping is suggested as able to ease the consequences for the child of its parents' sin of omission.

Even the authors of popular visionary texts, who usually gratified the laity's need to know certain things that the bishops could not or would not reveal, provided no niche for these infants. The middle Byzantine *Apocalypse of Anastasia*, a pious nun's visionary journey to the other world, is full of babies: baptized babies who die under three years old throng the throne of the Almighty, as do the Holy Innocents, who have been baptized in the blood of their martyrdom.[19] Unbaptized innocents, however, are nowhere to be found, though their parents are greatly in evidence. In fact, the punishment of negligent parents and godparents forms one of the longer stops on Anastasia's tour.[20]

Anastasia is taken beyond the third gate of heaven and shown two pools. The first is the source of the River Jordan, on whose banks John the Baptist stands, transformed into a priest. The second pool, immense, teems with parents and baptismal sponsors of children who died before baptism. The Archangel Michael explains that the inhabitants of these pools are being punished, but Anastasia does not describe any particular suffering or torment, and we are not given to know whether the punishment is everlasting. The Palermo redaction of the vision, more prone to theatrical effects, adds pitch, sulphur, and darkness to the scene, but still stops short of torment. It is significant that the pool is located not in hell, which Anastasia visits later, but in heaven: authorial ambivalence at the parents' fate? Conspicuously missing from Anastasia's journey, however, so detailed in most

[19] *Apocalypsis Anastasiae*, ed. Rudolf Homberg (Leipzig, 1903), p. 5.
[20] Ibid., p. 9.

other ways, are the actual babies, without whom the unhappy adults would not be in the pool at all.

The thirteenth-century didactic handbook with which we began, the *Thēsauros* of the priest-monk Theognostos, provides the fullest discussion I have found. Theognostos's exegesis of John 3.5 is unambiguous:

> Concerning those who die unbaptized, it is impossible to falsify the divine voice, for he said, 'Truly, truly I say to you, unless one be born from water and spirit, he shall not enter the kingdom of heaven'. Thus the impious are handed over from darkness into darkness when they die, just like not-yet-fully-formed babes from the womb. In Hades and in annihilation they receive the punishment in store for them. . . . It is not possible for one who does not bear upon him the seal of rebirth of baptism to be known as Christ's, and to attain salvation. For this same reason, unbaptized infants are worthy neither of the kingdom nor of punishment. Of how great a penalty for their children, then, do parents become the cause, if from carelessness they rob them of divine baptism, and through this also of the kingdom of heaven![21]

What keeps such a child from the kingdom? The strict Augustinian would answer, original sin. The Eastern Church, however, has approached original sin from a different angle. Orthodox theologians are agreed with St Paul that death, corruption, and sin came into the world through Adam, and are still with us. But the actual *guilt* for Adam's fall is not transmitted personally to each mortal as a judicial sentence, only the *effects* of that fall, which are mortality, and the inclination toward sin and disobedience.[22] Our unbaptized deceased infants do not fail to enter the kingdom because they bear a guilt burden of inherited sin, as in the Augustinian formulation—which would imply a moral identity of sorts—but because, I would argue, their unbaptized state means they have no identity at all, whether moral, personal, or spiritual.

This hypothesis is possible because baptism, for the Byzantines, signified far more than a simple ritual initiation into church

[21] *Thesaurus*, XV^2, 4, lines 617–24, 633–7.

[22] John Meyendorff, *Byzantine Theology: Historical Trends and Doctrinal Themes* (New York, 1979), pp. 143–6.

life. The sacrament, considered the only true source of Christian being and identity, worked a radical transformation on the innermost soul. Nowhere is this understanding more completely or beautifully presented than in a fourteenth-century treatise, entitled *Concerning the Life in Christ*. This series of discourses on sacramental theology by the lay theologian Nicholas Cabasilas is still considered normative by Orthodox today.[23]

Baptism, asserts Cabasilas, is literally the beginning of existence for the Christian soul: those who were formerly nothing receive being itself, and begin to exist truly for the first time.[24] In an almost Platonic sense, to the extent that they are conformed to the ideal, which is Christ, they receive true being. The soul is molten gold, silver, or bronze, given form by the sculptor; it is soft wax or lead, receiving the imprint of Christ as from a seal.[25] Before baptism, the soul is formless matter, like the stuff of creation before God's word gave it shape and name. A modern analogy might be with a computer disk, which cannot function within a system until it is formatted. Like the unformatted disk, the unbaptized soul can neither receive information nor respond to commands within its (Christian) 'operating system'.

The Christian soul is given form, however, not through some mechanical process, but in a manner consonant with the mystery of the Incarnation. Theognostos builds on a time-honoured patristic analogy in describing the rebirth of baptism: the child receives human form in its mother's womb, but can receive spiritual form only in the spiritual womb, the font of baptism.[26] The unbaptized child, however, has not yet been reborn as a child of God, and so its heavenly Father is not bound to acknowledge it as his own.

Hence the urgency of the question: parents who allow their child to die unbaptized have, it seems, denied it the chance to be a person at all in the eyes of God. This is perhaps why John the Faster, and the later patriarch Nicholas Grammatikos, both con-

[23] Nicolas Cabasilas, *La Vie en Christ*, ed. Marie-Hélène Congourdeau, *SC*, 355, 2 vols (1989); English tr. C. J. de Catanzaro, *The Life in Christ* (Crestwood, NY, 1974). The late Father John Meyendorff made extensive use of Cabasilas in his now standard *Byzantine Theology*.

[24] Cabasilas, *Vie en Christ*, i, 19, ii, 8; 1, pp. 94–5, 138.

[25] Ibid., ii, 11–13; 1, pp. 140–2.

[26] *Thesaurus*, XV^2, 4, lines 628–37, p. 129.

sider it together with abortion, smothering, and abandonment of children; it is, in effect, spiritual murder.[27] Here, if I am correct in my reading of the sources, are free will and moral responsibility carried to a terrible extreme.

Can it be that parents may simply annihilate a soul created by God, just as humans may destroy other parts of God's creation? From the sixth century to the thirteenth, the reasoning of John the Faster, Nicholas Grammatikos, and Theognostos, taken to its logical conclusion, seems to arrive at this position. Of course, the possibility of rhetorical hyperbole to raise the moral stakes, in the model of the Sermon on the Mount, must be taken into consideration. Much of the harshness of the authors and compilers of canonical and apocryphal texts no doubt derives from a fervent desire to impress the importance of baptism indelibly upon the minds of all parents, pastors, and godparents who might be tempted to slacken their vigilance.

Certainly, few Orthodox pastors or theologians would adopt quite this line today, that unbaptized infants simply cease to exist, and most likely few Byzantine pastors explicitly did so in the past. Yet it is at least a possible explanation for the sources' seeming refusal to discuss the topic in detail, for the grave anxiety expressed in the apocryphal visionary literature, and for the utmost seriousness with which the canonists treat the issue of parental penance.

The existence—or non-existence—of the child, theologically and culturally, was also inextricably linked with its having a name. Cabasilas highlights the baptismal day as the day that God first knows us by name: 'It is equally for this reason that the salvific day of baptism is also the name day for Christians: for on this very day we are modelled and configured, and our unshapen and indefinite life receives a shape and a definition.'[28]

Symeon of Thessalonike also stresses the importance of the name, and the moral responsibility of parents to choose their child's name (and with it, his or her heavenly patron) thoughtfully. Each child should receive its own name, just as Jesus did on the eighth day. 'Don't', Symeon admonishes his priests, 'just

[27] John the Faster, 'Exerpta', *PG* 88, col. 1933D; Nicholas Grammatikos, in Darrouzès, 'Réponses', p. 336.

[28] Cabasilas, *Vie en Christ*, ii, 14, lines 1–5; 1, p. 144.

baptize them all John and Mary, the way some simpletons and ignorant persons say.'[29]

Anthropological field work carried out in twentieth-century Greece on the creation of the personal, corporate, and eschatological identity of the child is of special value, for here we see these seemingly 'medieval' and 'abstract' theological ideas on being and naming played out in the flesh. Neither Symeon of Thessalonike nor Nicholas Cabasilas would be surprised at the conclusion of the anthropologist Charles Stewart, when he observes that 'The naming of a child at baptism marks one of the most important performative utterances in Greek culture.'[30]

Between birth and baptism, the rural Greek infant is traditionally not called by name. A Christian name has been chosen, but its use is avoided as inauspicious. Unbaptized infants occupy a liminal, not clearly defined, status between animal and human, nature and society; they are referred to variously as snake-like creatures, as 'male baby' or 'female baby', or in the neuter. As they are especially susceptible to demonic activity, in one village it was considered prudent to spit three times in such a baby's direction upon meeting it.[31] It is only after the infant's baptism, with its exorcisms, prayers, anointings, and rituals, that the villager (and, if my reading of the theological texts is correct, God as well) knows exactly what and who this new being is.[32]

Abhorring ambiguity, Greek villagers advanced a number of theories, some with antique pedigrees, as to the fate of the infant who died before baptism.[33] The child's soul might be claimed by the Devil or sent on a long, wandering journey; it might reappear to see its family, or torment the priest who neglected to baptize it. Each of these explanations is worthy of consideration, but none, of course, could be offered in good conscience by a priest—of any period or confession.

Our priest's final resort, I think, would have to be to the Orthodox willingness to leave some issues to the limitless and unfathomable mind and heart of God. If the Western Catholic genius inclines toward cataphatic theology, affirming and defi-

[29] Sym.Thess., 60, *PG* 155, col. 209B.
[30] Stewart, *Demons*, pp. 213–14.
[31] Ibid., pp. 55, 208.
[32] Ibid., p. 214; Sym.Thess., 61, *PG* 155, cols 212–14.
[33] Stewart, *Demons*, p. 196.

ning what can be said about God, perhaps the Eastern Orthodox genius can be said to tend toward apophatic theology: some things simply cannot be said or known about God's ways. The divine intelligence works through mysteries beyond normal human speech and perception, and can begin to be understood only by going beyond human rational categories.

Set in such a theological context, the seeming Eastern Orthodox 'failure' to provide a niche for its deceased unbaptized babies does not imply any lack of concern for them or their parents. On the contrary: Byzantine pastors were obsessed, first, with trying to prevent the problem, and then, with trying to formulate an appropriate pastoral response. But that pastoral response was limited to the pastor's immediate cure: the souls of those still on earth, the bereaved parents standing in front of him. As for the departed child, unless the priest had a direct line to an angel (as in the edifying tale with which we began) there was nothing that he could do for it. He could only remind the parents of what *could* be known with certainty—the infinite compassion and love of the Creator for all his creatures.

Princeton University

OBLATION OR OBLIGATION? A CANONICAL AMBIGUITY*

by JOHN DORAN

THE practice of oblation, the giving of children to a religious community to be brought up and educated, is as old as monasticism itself.[1] Oblation was a means by which parents were able to dispose of unwanted offspring and be fairly confident that they would be cared for by others.[2] However, there were never any clear guidelines laid down by the Church with respect to oblation, and the confusion over the status of an oblate was never to be satisfactorily settled. Even the great effort put into removing ambiguities in canon law in the twelfth and thirteenth centuries failed to clarify the technicalities of oblation. This was because there was no agreement on the nature of oblation from the start.

The practice of the Eastern Church with respect to oblation is best summed up by St Basil the Great, in his *Regulae Fusius Tractatae*.[3] He took oblation for granted, noting that a child was easily moulded to the religious life, and stipulated no minimum age at which a child should be received, but he did insist that those under the care of their parents were to be received before witnesses.[4] More importantly, Basil was anxious that a child oblate should be questioned strictly when he reached the age of sixteen or seventeen as to whether he wished to be professed. He

* I should like to thank the committee of the Ecclesiastical History Society for the generous award of a bursary which enabled me to attend the summer conference and present this paper.

[1] On oblation, see M. P. Deroux, 'Les origines de l'oblature bénédictine', *Révue Mabillon*, 17 (1927), pp. 1–16, 81–113, 193–216; J. E. Boswell, '*Expositio* and *Oblatio*: the abandonment of children and the ancient and medieval family', *AHR*, 89 (1984), pp. 10–33; M. de Jong. 'Growing up in a Carolingian monastery: Magister Hildemar and his oblates', *J MedH*, 9 (1983), pp. 99–128; P. Riché, 'L'enfant dans la société monastique du xiie *siècle', Pierre Abélard, Pierre le Vénérable: Les Courants Philosophiques, Littéraires et Artistique en Occident au Milieu du XIIe Siècle. Actes et Mémoires du Colloque International, Abbaye de Cluny, 2 au 9 Juillet, 1972: Colloques Internationaux du Centre National de la Recherche Scientifique, no. 546* (Paris, 1975), pp. 689–701; S. Shahar, *Childhood in the Middle Ages* (London, 1990), esp. ch. 9, 'Education for service in the secular church and in the monastery', pp. 183–208; D. Knowles, *The Monastic Order in England* 940–1216 (Cambridge, 1963), pp. 418–22, 634–5; *Dictionnaire de Droit Canonique*, ed. R. Naz (Paris, 1935–65), 1, p. 324.

[2] Boswell, '*Expositio*', p. 17.

[3] *PG* 37, cols 905–1051, at cols 953–4.

[4] Ibid., col. 951.

then had to demonstrate perseverance in the religious life and was only to be professed after much pleading. This final profession was irrevocable.[5] Clearly the tradition of the Church was in favour of the oblation of children, but the giving of a child was not considered a definitive act. Certainly with St Basil we can see that the abbot of a community was to have the final say as to whether or not a child oblate should be professed when he came of age. This was very much in the spirit of early monasticism. The abbot was not to be forced to retain unsuitable monks in his monastery.

There was no consensus about the nature of oblation in the West. The Rule of St Benedict assumed that there would be children in the monastery.[6] The relationship between the boys and their elders was summed up in the Rule: 'Let the juniors, then, honour their seniors; let the seniors love their juniors.'[7] St Benedict did not mention anything about oblates being allowed to leave the monastery upon their majority. Indeed, their profession was not mentioned, because the act of oblation, during which the hand of the child, together with his *carta*, were placed in the corporal and offered at the Mass along with the bread and wine, also served as the profession.[8] Benedict even provided for the *carta* to be written on behalf of a child who was unable to write his own.[9]

The overriding principle behind the Rule of St Benedict, with its horror of the *gyrovague*, was *stabilitas*.[10] There is evidence that attitudes were hardening in the West in general. Gregory the Great exalted the clergy, recalling scriptural passages in which priests were referred to as angels and gods.[11] The Fourth Council of Toledo in 633 ruled that a person became a monk either by the gift of his parents or by his own profession.[12] Either way, should he secede from the monastery he was to be anathematized

[5] Ibid., cols 715–32; *Epistola CXCIX: Amphilioco de canonibus*, col. 719.
[6] J. McCann, ed. and tr., *The Rule of Saint Benedict in Latin and English* (London, 1952). On oblates, see chs 30, 45, 49, 63, and 70, pp. 80, 96, 106, 142, 144, 156.
[7] Ibid., ch. 63, p. 142.
[8] Deroux, 'Oblature bénédictine', p. 15.
[9] Ibid., p. 15.
[10] Ibid., pp. 14–15.
[11] *PL* 132, cols 390–1, 392. *Reginonis Prumiensis Abbatis de ecclesiasticis disciplinis et religione christiana.*
[12] J. D. Mansi, *Sacrorum conciliorum nova et amplissima collectio*, 31 vols (Florence and Venice 1757–98) [hereafter Mansi], 10, cols 611–50, at col. 631, canon 49.

as an apostate.[13] The Tenth Council of Toledo in 655 decreed that a child could not be given against his will after his tenth year. However, the oblation of a child who had not reached his tenth year was irrevocable.[14]

In spite of conciliar decrees and the Rule of St Benedict, however, in practice the treatment of the nature of oblation was left to the discretion of the abbot of each house. Before the ninth century there was no conception of a Benedictine 'order'. Each monastic community was free to follow any combination of the ancient rules, and all of them would have owned texts of the Greek and Latin Fathers.[15] Moreover, the majority of communities remained small, somewhere around the figure of twelve monks envisaged as ideal by Benedict, of whom only two or three would be children.[16] The monastic community before 800 was much more like a family unit. So although the Rule of St Benedict treated oblation as irrevocable, it is likely that the older tradition was followed in practice.

With the Carolingians the situation changed dramatically.[17] Angilbert, Abbot of Saint-Riquier, one of those involved in the reforms begun by Charlemagne, revealed the new conception of monasticism in his *Institutions*, written at the beginning of the ninth century. He pointed out with pride that the munificence of the founder of his abbey had provided for a congregation of 300 monks, together with at least 100 boys in the monastic school.[18] They were to join the monks in divine service and so contribute to the salvation of the abbot and of his successors. The boys were to live under the same habit as the monks and to receive the same food. These boys were the guarantee of the continuation of the abbey and they were considered to be monks already. There was no mention of what to do should one of them wish to leave the monastery or even of when to profess them. The *Institutes* represent the Carolingian conception of Benedic-

[13] Ibid., col. 632, canon 55.

[14] Ibid., 11, cols 23–46, at cols 36–7, canon 6.

[15] J. Leclercq, *The Love of Learning and the Desire for God* (London, 1961), ch. 6, 'The ancient traditional spirituality', pp. 111–38; Knowles, *The Monastic Order*, pp. 3–15, 16.

[16] Deroux, 'Oblature bénédictine', p. 16.

[17] On the Carolingian reforms see R. McKitterick, *The Frankish Church and the Carolingian Reforms, 789–895* (London, 1977); Knowles, *The Monastic Order*, pp. 25–8.

[18] K. Hallinger, ed., *Corpus consuetudinum monasticarum*, I (Siegburg, 1963) [hereafter *Corpus I*], pp. 283–303, at p. 291.

tine monasticism. Indeed, as far as the Latin Church was concerned, this was henceforth to be the only form of monasticism. The reform continued under Benedict of Aniane, and the main result was that the Rule of St Benedict became the only rule, to which uniformity was to be ensured. It is significant that we only begin to find controversy about oblation after the Carolingians had imposed this more rigorous adherence to the Rule of St Benedict.

The confusion over the precise nature of oblation was reflected at the Council of Mainz in 829, which, in a return to an earlier discipline, decided that Gottschalk of Orbais, who had been given to the monastery of Fulda as a child, should be allowed to leave, since he was unhappy there as an adult.[19] However, his abbot, Rabanus Maurus, appealed to the Emperor, and Gottschalk was forced to remain. His unhappiness led eventually to imprisonment under suspicion of heresy. In order to counterbalance the decision of the Council of Mainz, Rabanus wrote his *Liber de oblatione puerorum*, in which he somewhat ingenuously claimed the authority of the Fathers in favour of irrevocable oblation and denounced those who sought to uphold the liberty of the oblate.[20] Rabanus insisted that the vow was taken by the child and could not be broken without guilt. Moreover, the monastic life was instituted by God, not man, and those who attacked its practices were suffering from a form of madness.[21] More texts had been added to the argument in a period when there was no accepted universal authority.

The commentary on the Rule written by Hildemar at Civate between 845 and 850 showed the results of the Carolingian reforms.[22] The overwhelming concern of Hildemar was to ensure that oblates were guarded constantly and unrelentingly. He said relatively little about the novitiate, but concentrated on the oblates, perhaps reflecting the growing practice of ordaining oblates to the priesthood.[23] In the much larger monastic communities of the ninth century the oblates formed a class apart

[19] Boswell, '*Expositio*', p. 26. Deroux, 'Oblature bénédictine', p. 90.

[20] *PL* 107, cols, 419–40.

[21] Ibid. cols 421, 419.

[22] See especially M. de Jong, 'Magister Hildemar'.

[23] Knowles, *The Monastic Order*, p. 19; de Jong, 'Magister Hildemar', pp. 122–3.

from the rest of the monks. When they entered the adult hierarchy, however, it was the date of their oblation which determined their seniority, and there is evidence that this led precisely to that *superbia* of monastic priests which St Benedict had wished to avoid, with disputes growing between oblates and the *conversi*, who entered the community as adults.[24] Hildemar noted that banishment could only be used for adult converts. If an oblate disrupted the community he was to be imprisoned, since his complete ineptitude in the world would lead him inexorably into sin.

In 868 the Council of Worms repeated the judgement of the Fourth Council of Toledo that a monk was made by the dedication of his parents or by his own will.[25] In 895 an important distinction was drawn by the Council of Tribur, which stated that a monk was not be allowed to leave if he had consented originally to his oblation. If he had been against his oblation, he should be allowed to leave at the age of twelve.[26] Canon 24 of this council stated that a monk given by his parents, who had begun to sing and read in church, was bound to stay.[27] This phrase is ambiguous, and historians are divided over its meaning.[28] It may simply mean that an oblate had taken his place among the adult monks. Dom Leclercq, however, has shown that the *lectio divina* was more than just the pursuit of learning; it was a combination of physical and mental discipline which was considered almost as a sacrament of prayer.[29] The ambiguity surrounding oblates continued.

The Second Synod of Aachen in 817 had expressed some anxiety about oblates.[30] Canon 17 stated that when an oblate was offered to an abbey at the altar by his father and mother there must be lay witnesses.[31] Furthermore, the boy himself, once he had reached the age of reason, must confirm this oblation. This decree was placed in the statutes of a number of monasteries in

[24] Deroux, 'Oblature bénédictine', p. 105; de Jong, 'Magister Hildemar', p. 122.
[25] Deroux, 'Oblature bénédictine', p. 91.
[26] Mansi, 18a, cols 129–66, at col. 144, canon 23.
[27] Ibid. cols 144–5, canon 24.
[28] Leclercq, *The Love of Learning*, pp. 89–91; Boswell, '*Expositio*', p. 26.
[29] Leclercq, *The Love of Learning*, pp. 89–91.
[30] *Corpus I*, pp. 469–81.
[31] Ibid., pp. 473–81, at p. 477, canon 17. Deroux, 'Oblature bénédictine', p. 89.

the ninth century.[32] However, there is ample evidence that the principle that an oblate should have the right to leave the monastery when he reached the age of reason was not adhered to by many Benedictine houses. The schooling and training of oblates represented a substantial commitment of resources by an abbey in the education of its future monks. It is understandable that an abbot should try to prevent oblates leaving his house. The great abbey of Cluny was reputed to profess boys and men after only a few days.[33]

The conflicting rulings on oblation were a symptom of the more general confusion over the nature of authority in the Church that led to the revival of interest in both Roman and canon law initiated by the reformers of the eleventh century.[34] At the instigation of the popes, the archives of the Roman Church were explored in the search for ancient, and therefore authoritative, texts of canons. Stephan Kuttner has defined the period of the revival of jurisprudence as starting before 1100 and lasting into the 1230s.[35] This period was characterized by the attempt of reformers to create a truly Christian society, with the pope at its head as the supreme law-giver.[36] The legislative authority of the pope was the means by which the whole of society was to be renewed.[37] The popes expressed their judgements in the form of decretal letters, and these were intended to supplement and, where necessary, to remove ambiguity in the ancient decretals.[38] However, the confusion of authorities which had ruled on the subject of oblation was such that the compilers of canonical collections were unable to reconcile them. Moreover, the popes themselves, after their authority had been vindicated, were able only to juggle authorities in dealing with specific cases. They were unable to provide any definitive ruling.

[32] *Corpus I*, pp. 529, 549, 560.

[33] Knowles, *The Monastic Order*, p. 419.

[34] S. Kuttner, 'The revival of jurisprudence', in R. L. Benson, G. Constable and C. D. Lanham, eds. *Renaissance and Renewal in the Twelfth Century* (Oxford, 1982), pp. 299–323, at p. 303.

[35] Ibid., p. 304.

[36] J. Rambaud-Buhot, 'Le Decrèt de Gratien, legs du passé, avènement de l'âge classique', in M. de Gandillac and E. Jeauneau, eds, *Entretiens sur la Renaissance du* 12e siècle (Paris, 1968), pp. 492–506, at p. 496.

[37] G. Tellenbach, *Church, State and Christian Society at the Time of the Investiture Contest* (Oxford, 1940), p. 137.

[38] Kuttner, 'Revival of jurisprudence', p. 310.

The compilation made by Master Gratian at Bologna in about 1140, which is called the *Concordance of Discordant Canons* in the oldest manuscripts, was the first canonical collection to be accorded almost universal authority.[39] In what was essentially a guide to the actions proper to the clerical and the lay state, the *Decretum*, as it became known, reflected the results of the eleventh-century reform movement in its heightened reverence for the clerical state.[40] The desire to ensure that the clergy would reflect their exalted calling was a principal concern. Gratian included a number of canons with direct reference to oblates. The oblation of infants, when they were brought to the altar to be handed over, was to be done in the presence of lay witnesses, in order to preclude the opportunity for the evil speech of the worst sort of men.[41] Three canons made it plain that nobody was to be professed as a monk or given holy orders before the age of fourteen; that no child was to be forced to make a vow before he had attained the age of reason;[42] that no one under the age of fourteen should take a vow;[43] and that vows should be accompanied by strict fasting to reflect the sincerity of the candidate.[44]

The popes saw the enforcement of neglected canons as their duty.[45] The collection of decretals drawn up at the instigation of Gregory IX in 1234, with the express intention of providing definitive answers to problems made contentious by the judgements of conflicting authorities,[46] revealed that the popes of the previous century had taken note of Gratian's canons. However, the popes seem to have been wary in their approach to oblation, with the result that a good deal of confusion was reflected in their judgements.

The *Decretals* used specific cases dealt with by popes or general councils in order to clarify the law of the Church on a given

39 Rambaud-Buhot, 'Le Decrèt de Gratien', pp. 498–9; Kuttner, 'Revival of jurisprudence', p. 311.

40 I. S. Robinson, 'Gregory VII and the Soldiers of Christ', *History*, 58 (1973), pp. 169–92, at pp. 169–70.

41 *PL* 187, col. 1105. C.20 q.2 c.4.

42 Ibid., cols 1155–6, C.22 q.5 c.14.

43 Ibid., col. 1156, C.22 q.5 c.15.

44 Ibid., col. 1156, C.22 q.5 c.16.

45 K. Leyser, 'The polemics of the papal revolution', in B. Smalley, ed., *Trends in Medieval Political Thought* (Oxford, 1965), pp. 42–64, at p. 55.

46 *Decretales Gregorii IX*, ed. A. Friedberg, *Corpus iuris canonici*, 2 (Leipzig, 1879), cols 6–928 [hereafter *Decretales*]. On the purpose of the collection, see Gregory's bull *Rex pacificus*, in *Les Régistres de Grégoire IX*, ed. L. Auvray (Paris, 1896–1955) [hereafter *Reg. GIX*], 1. cos 1125–6, no. 2083.

question. In the section dealing with those who live under a rule and those going into religious orders, it is apparent that the intention of the papacy was to settle the question of oblates and novices. The first decretal in this section was a canon of the Council of Mainz of 813 which simply stated that nobody was to be given the tonsure unless he was of legitimate age and was willing to receive it.[47] If a boy was given the tonsure before he was of legitimate age, his parents were required to reclaim him before the passage of a year and a day by appealing to the prince or his agent or their own bishop.[48] Should they fail to do this, he was to remain a cleric. If he was above the legitimate age, and was forcibly given holy orders, either he or his parents were to appeal. Again, if there was no appeal within a year and a day he was to remain a cleric. This text shows that having attained the legitimate age, that is, fourteen years, did not necessarily make the boy an adult, or rather that it did not free him from the tutelage of his parents. This reflects the lack of consensus generally on stages of childhood and adolescence.[49]

The vow was central to the act of oblation, and the question of vows was dealt with in the *Decretals*. The authority of the pope to dispense from vows or to commute them was established. Alexander III absolved a cleric from a crusading vow taken when he was a boy.[50] A decretal of Pope Hormisdas was included to establish that a son must ratify vows sworn on his behalf by his father when he comes of age.[51] A decretal of Innocent III maintained that a boy was unable to contract a valid marriage because although he might have been able to say the words, he would not be able to understand them.[52] In the same way a betrothed child was allowed to renounce a vow taken on his behalf when he came of age.[53] It is clear that the principle was accepted that a child was incapable of making a vow, but in the matter of oblation there were scriptural precedents which would have especially impressed monks, whose lives were spent learn-

[47] *Decretales*, 3. 31. 1, col. 569.
[48] Ibid., 3. 31. 2, col. 569.
[49] Isidore's definition was given in *Decretales*, 4.2.3, col. 673; see Shahar, *Childhood*, pp. 21–31.
[50] *Decretales*, 3.34.2, col. 589.
[51] Ibid., 4.2.1, col. 672.
[52] Ibid., 4.1.25, col. 670.
[53] Ibid., 4.2.8, col. 675.

ing the Bible by rote, and who had an especially biblical imagination.[54]

The question of coercion into orders was dealt with in a number of decretals. Alexander III wrote to a canon of Civitate ordering him to investigate an appeal from a boy who claimed that he, together with other boys under fourteen years of age, had been seduced by a monk of Monte Foliano into immediately assuming the religious habit there.[55] The boy at once regretted what he had done, and his parents came without delay and took him home. He had been at the monastery for only one night, but the monks of Monte Foliano and others were preventing him from marrying a girl to whom he had already been betrothed. Alexander stated the broad principle that nobody should be professed without a probationary year or before he had reached fourteen years of age. Even after profession a man was free to leave a house within three days without prejudice. The person in question was to be allowed to marry the girl and was not to be hindered by the monks or anybody else in those parts. In a letter to the Bishop of Ely, Alexander stated that when a monk had been professed he might not return to his former state and was not to be given any preferment in secular churches, since his soul would be endangered if he contradicted the vow he had sworn to God.[56] Should he wish to leave, he was to go to a house observing a less strict rule. The principle was repeated that a novice might leave during his probationary year, since, as Alexander pointed out, the Rule says that such men should go away in their own clothing. Another letter of Alexander, to the Bishop of Benevento, deals with a certain Guiboldus, who had been professed as a monk at Roson because he was afraid of his grammar teacher.[57] He left the monastery within a year, while he was still under fourteen years of age. For six subsequent years he had immersed himself in worldly vanities and had lived as a vagabond. Alexander instructed the Bishop to inquire into the case. If all should prove to be as described, the Bishop was to declare the profession void and to publicize this in the area. However, if it should prove that the boy had been given by his

[54] Leclercq, *The Love of Learning*, pp. 93–4.
[55] *Decretales*, 3.31.8, col. 571.
[56] Ibid., 3.31.9, col. 570.
[57] Ibid., 3.31.11, col. 572.

parents as an oblate, or that he had consented after he was fourteen to the profession he had taken earlier, he was to be forced to return to the same monastery or to another rule. Here we see the note of confusion which had always surrounded oblation. St Benedict had regarded oblation as an exercise of the *patria potestas* of Roman Law,[58] a definitive act, and this conception is reflected in Alexander's equation of the parental oblation with the consent of a fourteen-year-old. If the boy had not been given by his parents he was to be absolved. So a boy could not offer himself without the consent of his parents, but their offering of him was definitive, his own objections resulting in nothing more than the concession of a move to a community observing a less harsh regime. A letter of Clement III throws more light on the status of a parental oblation.[59] A nun who maintained that she had been placed in a convent against her will and professed before she was twelve years old, and who afterwards had left the convent and had been made pregnant by a soldier, was to be forced to return to the convent, because Clement was not satisfied that the profession had been performed against her will. She had not protested at the appropriate time. Clement expressly stated that this judgement was in no way to prejudice the ruling of Leo the Great that a girl placed in a convent by her parents was to be free to leave if she so wished once she had reached the age of intelligence. 'She who has free will is not to be forced to follow the will of her parents.' It is clear that the parental oblation in this case was not considered definitive. The woman was forced to remain a nun because she did not leave when she had the opportunity, thus giving her consent. It should also be remembered, however, that a nun was not a member of the clergy. The almost excessively legalistic attitudes towards boy oblates arose because of conflicting opinions over their clerical status.[60]

The nature of parental authority over the future adult was brought into question by a decretal of Celestine III.[61] A certain knight, having been cured of a severe illness, took himself and his son to the monastery from which he held his land and forced his

[58] Deroux, 'Oblature bénédictine', p. 15.

[59] *Decretales*, 3.31.12, cols 572–3.

[60] See, for example, de Jong, 'Magister Hildemar', p. 119.

[61] *Decretales*, 3.31.14, col. 573.

son to become a monk at the same time as himself. The boy did not like the severity of the rule practised at the monastery and absconded within ten weeks. He then began to demand the goods of his father from the abbot. The boy's relatives had sworn that he had been under age and unwilling when he was professed. Celestine ruled that if the boy had, in fact, been unwilling to be professed and had left the monastery when he had attained the age of reason, he was to be considered free and was not to be compelled to return. Moreover, he was free to demand the goods of his father, which belonged to him by succession. The crux of the matter is the question of whether the child was willing to be received in the monastery originally. It appears that the act of oblation made by parents was a recognition of the will of the child to be consecrated to God. Thus, while they may remove him within a year, they cannot do so after this period, no matter what age he might be, and not at any time after he has reached the age of fourteen. This was confirmed in a decretal of Innocent III, in which he noted that different authorities had expressed diverse judgements on the matter. Inserted after a decretal stating that nobody was to be professed without having spent a probationary year at a monastery,[62] this decretal stated that a distinction was to be made between someone who really wanted to change his life and to become a member of the family of God and someone who was merely curious and was trying out the monastic life.[63] The latter was to be allowed to leave during his probationary year without incurring any prejudice, but before he went he was to be questioned about what he really wanted. The former, however, was not to be allowed to leave the religious life. He was able only to go to a community observing a more relaxed rule. This is a reversal of the counsel of St Basil: his oblate had to plead to get in; Innocent's had to beg to get out. The following decretal gives us a better idea of what Innocent intended here.[64] A man who had been sent to a monastery while under age and had left within his probationary year was not to be hindered in the promotion to orders and benefices. However, if he had reached the age when he would have been wise enough to know what he was doing—remember the child

[62] Ibid., 3.31.16, cols 574–5.
[63] Ibid., 3.31.20, col. 577.
[64] Ibid., 3.31.21, col. 577.

was still under fourteen—the fact that he had assumed the religious habit without protest would be evidence that he had really intended to change his life, and he should thus be sent to live under a more relaxed rule. The idea that a child who was willing to be professed was to be forever bound to the religious life was given a special emphasis in the *Decretals* of Gregory IX.

In order to tidy up the whole question of the probationary year and its implications, Honorius III ruled that anybody who had worn the religious habit for more than a year was to be considered a monk.[65] Gregory IX decreed that the habits of monks and novices were to be distinct, in order to remove ambiguity and confusion.[66] We have already seen that it was not only monks, but people in the area who had tried to prevent the boy from Monte Foliano from marrying. Since the reform of the eleventh century the laity had been encouraged to put pressure upon those clergy whose morals were found wanting. There is an echo of this in a decretal of Gregory IX, which demanded that fugitive monks who proved unwilling to return to their houses and do penance were to be excommunicated publicly in the churches of the area until they returned to their place.[67] This was a measure of last resort because of the risk of bringing the clerical order into disrepute, but it shows that the laity was considered to be an effective spur to the apostate monk to regularize his position.

Before his *Decretals* appeared, Gregory IX had begun a thorough reform of the Benedictine monks.[68] In 1231 he wrote to Cluny pointing out that its present practices needed reforming.[69] An annual general chapter of the whole order was henceforth to take place each year, in the presence of four Cistercian abbots, acting as advisers. Cluniac houses were told to observe the customs of Cîteaux in a range of disciplinary matters. Among the orders given to the Cluniacs by Gregory was that they were not to receive anyone as a monk who was less than fifteen years of age.[70] In a letter of 1234 Gregory again stated the principle that a

[65] Ibid., 3.31.22, col. 578.
[66] Ibid., 3.31.23, col. 578.
[67] Ibid., 3.31.24, col. 578.
[68] *Reg. GIX*, cols 317–18. Auvray suggests that the need for reform is shown in the following letters in the registers: nos 1288, 1289, 1492, 2385, 2504, 2551, 2689, 2710, 2750, 2836, 2933.
[69] *Reg. GIX*, 1, no. 745, cols 469–74.
[70] Ibid., no. 745, cols 469–74, at col. 473.

probationary year was to be given according to the Rule or, rather, as he pointed out, according to Gregory the Great's alteration of the Rule, which had originally allowed for a probationary period of three years.[71] This letter stated that the lack of any fixed practice in dealing with the novitiate in general was the source of many doubts arising among the faithful, and Gregory noted that there had been a variety of responses from his predecessors. He stated explicitly that he wanted to provide for the health of souls as well as to remove the scope for scandal by decreeing that those who left the monastery in the year before their profession were to be allowed to return to their former state. However, even here Gregory was unable to remove the ambiguity over oblation once and for all. Having stated that before profession novices were free to leave he added the clause, 'unless it had been clearly apparent that they had wanted to change their lives and to serve God for ever in religion.' Ironically, Gregory followed this by ordering that novices should be distinguished from monks by their habits, stating that this would completely remove any ambiguity. Perhaps this was wishful thinking.

It was in his ordinances and statutes for Black monks that Gregory IX showed his most determined efforts at reform. In two slightly different redactions of the same text, called the Ordinances in 1234 and the Statutes about twenty months later, Gregory decreed a wholesale reform of the Order[72] through closer observance of the Rule of St Benedict, and most of the decrees dealt with ensuring that the monks would live a life of true poverty, chastity, and obedience. However, in the case of novices the Pope laid down some interesting guide-lines. As soon as anybody was admitted to the monastery it was to be made clear by the abbot or prior that a year was to be spent on probation before profession.[73] This year was strictly a voluntary agreement and implied no contract or obligation for either party. If the novice wanted to leave he was free to do so within this year. The harshness of the life was to be clearly explained to the novices, and the Rule was to be read and explained to them

[71] Ibid., no. 572, cols 364–5.

[72] 'De statutis monachorum et monialium nigri ordinis', *Reg. GIX*, 2, no. 3045, cols 319, 321, 323, 325, 327, 329, 331; 'Ordinatione monachorum nigrorum', ibid., no. 3045 *bis*, cols 320, 322, 324, 326, 328, 330, 332.

[73] Ibid., col. 319.

three times during the course of the year. Later Gregory stated that because in many monasteries the regular reading of the Rule in the chapter house was not understood by the *minores*, it was at once to be explained to them in the vernacular by the reader or by someone delegated by him.[74] The present constitutions were also to be explained annually to the monks.[75] Elsewhere Gregory instructed his legate to see that an abbot was appointed to the abbey of St Ouen, in Rheims, who would give frequent theology lessons to the monks and explain the Rule to them.[76] Nobody under the age of fifteen was to be admitted to the monastery, but should this happen, the boys were to make no vows or promises.[77] In the second redaction, which we must consider to be Gregory's definitive pronouncement on the matter, this age was set at eighteen years.[78] If anyone should decide not to be professed after the first year, he was quickly to go away.[79]

The concern of the papacy with eradicating abuses and potential embarrassments for the Church in the Benedictine system of receiving oblates should not obscure the fact that the system was essentially a successful one. Once a recognized probationary period was accepted, and the scandal of coercion was removed, the system worked well. The popes recommended the Benedictine practices with regard to oblates to many of the new orders which appeared in the thirteenth century.[80] The Benedictines remained, however, the only major order to support a population of children. The appearance of new orders and the decline in the number of oblates from the twelfth century onwards represented a return to a pre-Carolingian model of monasticism. This was also the effect of the reforms of Gregory IX, since they restored the final decision over profession of oblates to the abbots of individual houses. It was left to their judgement to decide whether a novice had really desired to change his life. Thus, on

[74] Ibid., col. 327.
[75] Ibid., col. 331.
[76] Ibid., 1, no. 2163, col. 1162.
[77] Ibid., 2, no. 3045 *bis*, col. 319.
[78] Ibid., no. 3045, col. 320. See cols 317–18 for Auvray's comments.
[79] Ibid., 2, no. 3045, col. 319.
[80] *Dictionnaire de Droit Canonique*, 1, p. 324.

a modest scale, the irrevocable oblation introduced by St Benedict survived to be dealt with by the Council of Trent.[81]

Royal Holloway and Bedford New College.
University of London

[81] Knowles, *The Monastic Order*, p. 421, wrongly asserted that the Fourth Lateran council of 1215 outlawed the practice of oblation. In fact, the council had nothing to say on the matter.

THE *SACRA INFANTIA* IN MEDIEVAL HAGIOGRAPHY*

by ISTVÁN P. BEJCZY

I

IN his *De civitate Dei*, Augustine stated that anyone who wants to lead a good and Christian life must necessarily have lived in sin in his life up to then.[1] It is quite conceivable that Augustine had his own course of life in mind when writing these words; he never made a secret of his own sinful youth, as is clear from the *Confessiones*. None the less, his statement is expressed in the form of a general rule.

Many medieval saints' lives seem to accord with Augustine's statement. The saint repents after a life of sin and henceforth leads a model Christian life until the day of his death. Thus the eventual victory of Christianity over the forces of evil was demonstrated.[2]

However, there are also many *vitae* that follow a different pattern. The saint is sometimes supposed to have been perfect in every respect from childhood onward. He was born a saint rather than becoming one through a process of 'spiritual maturation'. Stories about such precocious saints have not escaped notice in modern scholarship.[3] Following E. R. Curtius, the phrase *puer*

*I should like to thank Mayke de Jong, Rob Meens, Shulamith Shahar, and, especially, Rosamond McKitterick for their comments on this paper.

[1] *De civitate Dei*, xv, 1, *Opera omnia, CChr.SL*, 14, 2 (1960), pp. 453–4; cf. *Confessiones*, I, vii, 11, *Opera omnia, CChr.SL*, 27 (1981), p. 6.

[2] Cf. Ehrhard Dorn, *Der sündige Heilige in der Legende des Mittelalters = Medium Aevum, Philologische Studien*, 10 (Munich, 1967).

[3] Donald Weinstein and Rudolph M. Bell, *Saints and Society. The Two Worlds of Western Christendom* (Chicago and London, 1982), pp. 19–47; Michael Goodich, 'Childhood and adolescence among thirteenth-century saints', *History of Childhood Quarterly*, 1 (1973–4), pp. 285–309, reiterated almost verbatim in *Vita perfecta: the Ideal of Sainthood in the Thirteenth Century = Monographien zur Geschichte des Mittelalters*, 25 (Stuttgart, 1982), pp. 82–99. On the role of the child in medieval hagiography, see also Shulamith Shahar, 'Infants, infant care and attitudes towards infancy in the medieval lives of saints', *Journal of Psychohistory*, 10 (1983), pp. 281–309.

senex is sometimes used to denote the topos;[4] in hagiography, expressions such as as *quasi senex* and *cor gerens senile* are used.[5] The use of the phrase *puer senex*, however, presents some difficulties. Not only is the *puella senex* unfortunately disregarded, but the phrase is also too inspecific. As has been pointed out by Weinstein and Bell, there is a significant distinction to be made among stories about holy children: some children seem to be really holy from their birth onward. Others live like normal children until about their seventh year, but then subject themselves to a severe discipline, of which penance is an important aspect.[6] Stories of the latter category could still be brought into line with Augustine's statement, even though repentance comes very early in life. The phrase *sacra infantia* is used here to denote the infancy of children who seem to be born saints.[7]

In this article attention will be devoted to a specific hagiographical feature which brings *sacra infantia* into strong relief: that of the saint's refusal to be suckled when a baby. In the next paragraph a survey will be given of the distribution of this feature in medieval Latin hagiography. After that I shall go more deeply into some details that I consider typical of the feature. I do not aim at an exhaustive treatment: this would need to be done for every *vita* separately, within its own context. The observations given below, however, may throw light upon the tradition in which the particular tales dealing with *sacra infantia* stand.

[4] Ernst Robert Curtius, *Europäische Literatur und lateinisches Mittelalter* (Bern and Munich, 1948), pp. 108ff. On the ancient, especially Greek origins of the topos, see Elena Giannarelli, 'Il paidariogeron nella biografia cristiana antica', *Prometheus*, 14 (1988), pp. 279–84.

[5] The phrase *quasi senex* in the *vita* of Anthony Pilgrim Manzoni (*AnBoll*, 13, p. 417); *cor gerens senile* in Gregory the Great (*Vita Benedicti* = *Dialogi* 2, ed. Umberto Moricca (Rome, 1924), p. 71), and the *vitae* of Louis of Toulouse (*AnBoll*, 9, p. 283) and Hedwig of Poland (*ActaSS*, Oct. viii, p. 225). The Christ-child, however, 'est puer atque senex', according to Fulcoius Beluacensis, (*Utriusque*) *De nuptiis Christi et Ecclesiae libri septem*, ed. Mary Isaac Jogues Rousseau (Washington, DC, 1960), vi, 353, p. 115*.

[6] Weinstein and Bell, *Saints and Society*, p. 26.

[7] The term *sacra infantia* appears in the *vita* of Louis of Toulouse (*AnBoll*, 9, p. 283). The term *infans sanctus* was probably unknown in the Middle Ages: see André Vauchez, *La Sainteté en occident aux derniers siècles du moyen âge, d'après les procès de canonisation et les documents hagiographiques* (Rome, 1981), p. 595, n. 67.

II

In hagiography, tales about the refusal to take the breast are first and foremost associated with Nicholas of Myra. As one reads in the first Latin *vita* of Nicholas, translated from the Greek about 880 by Johannes Diaconus of Naples, he refused to be suckled more than once on Wednesdays and Fridays: 'Coepit binis in hebdomada diebus, quarta scilicet et sexta feria, semel bibere mammas; et hac vice contentus, tota die sic permanebat.'[8]

With this behaviour, also mentioned by later authors such as Vincent of Beauvais[9] and James of Voragine,[10] Nicholas became a 'trend-setter' for many other saints in medieval hagiography. Similar stories are told, for example, in the Lives of the following saints:[11]

- Albert the Hermit (12th century) [*ActaSS*, Jan. I, p. 402];
- Catervus of Tolentino (11th century or before) [*AnBoll*, 61, pp. 16–17][12]
- Cunegond of Poland (d. 1292) [*ActaSS*, Jul. V, p. 674];
- George of Suelli (d. 1117?) [*ActaSS*, Apr. III, p. 217];
- Leo of Rouen (9th century) [*ActaSS*, Mart. I, p. 94];
- Nicander (12th century) [*ActaSS*, Sept. VI, p. 89];
- Procula (11th or 12th century) [*Les petits Bollandistes. Vies des saints*, 8, p. 189];[13]
- Raymund Nonnatus (d. 1279?) [*ActaSS*, Aug. VI, p. 729];
- Roche (14th century) [*ActaSS*, Aug. III, p. 400];
- Stephen of Die (d. 1208?) [*ActaSS*, Sept. III, pp. 186, 188].

[8] Johannes Diaconus of Naples, [*Vita Nicolai*], ed. Angelo Mai, *Spicilegium Romanum* (Rome, 1840), 4, p. 326. For the Greek text, see Gustav Anrich, *Hagios Nikolaos. Der heilige Nikolaos in der griechischen Kirche*, 2 vols (Leipsig, 1913–17).

[9] Vincent of Beauvais, *Speculum historiale* (Douai, 1624; repr. Graz, 1965), xiii, p. 67.

[10] James of Voragine, *Legenda aurea vulgo Historia Lombardica dicta*, ed. Th. Graesse (Breslau, 1890; repr. Osnabrück, 1965), p. 22.

[11] For the sources mentioned here I am partly indebted to C. Grant Loomis, *White Magic: an Introduction to the Folklore of Christian Legend* (Cambridge, Mass., 1948), p. 141 n. 102, referred to by Charles W. Jones, *Saint Nicholas of Myra, Bari and Manhattan* (Chicago and London, 1978), p. 383, n. 6, as well as to Weinstein and Bell, *Saints and Society*, pp. 24–5.

[12] Weinstein and Bell mention Nicholas of Tolentino (*Saints and Society*, p. 24); however, there is no such story about him. Perhaps they have, by mistake, merged Nicholas of Myra and Catervus of Tolentino into one saint?

[13] *Les petits Bollandistes. Vies des saints*, 15 vols (Paris, 1866–9), [hereafter *PB*].

Of Cunegond and Nicander it is said, in so many words, that their behaviour resembles that of Nicholas. Roche and George are said to have contented themselves with only one feed on Wednesdays and Fridays, Catervus on Fridays only, Raymund on Fridays and Saturdays; it is safe to assume that the life of Nicholas served as a source of inspiration for their *vitae*, too. In the cases of Albert, Leo, and Stephen, the connection with Nicholas is less obvious. Finally, as to Procula's *vita*, the edition used here gives only a paraphrase in French, stating that Procula, following the lead of 'certain other saints', restricted herself to only one feed on Tuesdays and Thursdays (*sic*). I shall use the term *lactatio*, coined by C. W. Jones, for this type of narration.

A special case is the *vita* of Juliana of Cornillon (d. 1258) [*ActaSS*, Apr. I, pp. 443–4], who is said to have fasted on Wednesdays and Fridays, following Nicholas. She did this, however, not as a baby but when she was five years old.

In a different context the refusal of breast-feeding also occurs in the *vitae* of:

- Canid (5th century) [*ActaSS* Jun. II, p. 277];
- Catharine of Sweden (d. 1381) [*ActaSS*, Mart. III, pp. 503–4];
- Gonçalvo of Amarante (d. 1259) [*ActaSS*, Jan. I, p. 642];
- Robert of Chaise-Dieu (d. 1067) [*PL* 171, col. 1507];
- Ursuline of Parma (d. 1410) [*ActaSS*, Apr. I, p. 722].

Canid always abstained from the right breast of his mother, and if she had had a delicious meal, he abstained from the left one as well. Catharine refused to take her mother's breast, or those of other women, if they had had sexual intercourse shortly before. Robert refused to take the breast because his nurse prostituted herself, Ursuline turned away from her adulterous nurse, and Gonçalvo refused to be suckled until he had been taken to church and had been shown the statues of other saints.[14]

Lactatio and similar stories are connected with male as well as female saints of very different backgrounds. For the most part, these saints lived in the later Middle Ages, though the *lactatio*

[14] The *vita* of Berachius is slightly out of tune. He is reputed to have been suckled in the convent, where he was brought when a baby, although not on a breast but on his patron's right ear-lobe, yet, for all that, growing like any other baby (*ActaSS*, Feb. ii, p. 834).

story recurs in the Lives of some post-medieval saints as well.[15] Although a survey of the dates of the *vitae* is not easily given, none of them seems to have originated before the twelfth century.[16] It seems safe to state that the feature of the baby saint's refusal to be suckled, originally related to the *vita* of Nicholas of Myra only, took a sudden upsurge in the twelfth and thirteenth centuries so as to become a stock subject of hagiographical imagination in later periods.

III

The popularity of the tales on refusing the breast in hagiography from the twelfth century onwards could be related to the tendency towards a more positive evaluation of childhood in the later Middle Ages. According to several authors, the image of the child valued for its own sake began to take shape between 1100 and 1300, and the role of childhood was becoming greater in literature, in art, and, above all, in hagiography.[17]

The apparent increasing attention to childhood and the more positive evaluation of it do not in themselves explain the particular depictions of childhood attached to the saints mentioned above in hagiography. However, the *vita* of Rose of Viterbo (thirteenth century) throws a special light on *sacra infantia* in general and on *lactatio* in particular. The opening words of the *vita* (the final version of which dates from the fifteenth century) read as follows:

[15] Thus, e.g., in the *vitae* of Veronique of Mercatello (seventeenth century, *PB*, 8, p. 220), and of Posadas (eighteenth century, *PB*, 11, p. 274).

[16] The *vita* of Robert dates from the twelfth century, just as the Greek version of Nicander's life; the Latin version inserted in the *ActaSS* was written in the seventeenth century. The *vitae* of Catervus, Juliana, and Stephen date from the thirteenth century, that of Leo from the fourteenth or fifteenth, those of Ursuline 1472 (sources from the first half of the century), Cunegond 1475 ('ex antiquo manuscripto'), Roche 1478 (older sources), and Catharine from the fifteenth. In 1586, the presumably contemporary life of Gonçalvo was printed; the life of George, 'ex antiquo manuscripto', in 1597. An Italian version of Albert's life, originally from the fourteenth century or before, was published in 1600 (the *ActaSS* cite it in Latin). The information given on Raymund is drawn from a Spanish sermon printed in 1676. The data concerning Canid's life were translated from the Greek *Menaia*. I have been unable to data Procula's *vita* (see *ActaSS* Supplementum, Auctuaria Octobris, 127*–8*).

[17] Klaus Arnold, *Kind und Gesellschaft in Mittelalter und Renaissance = Beiträge und Texte zur Geschichte der Kindheit* (Paderborn and Munich, 1980); Pierre Riché, 'L'Enfant dans la société chrétienne aux

> Aeternus autem rerum conditor, ut ait Apostolus, ante mundi constitutionem electos praedestinavit, et praedestinatos ad suum regnum vocavit sola gratia, nulla necessitate seu meritis precedentibus. Quae quidem gratia in sanctis et electis . . . demonstrata est dudum in quibusdam, antequam progrederentur ex utero, ut Hyeremia et Joanne Baptista, qui in adventu Domini exultavit in utero. In quibusdam vero demonstrata fuit ab ipsis ipsorum cunabulis, ut patuit in beato Nicolao, qui die, quo natus fuit, stetit in pelvi, et bino hebdomadae die coepit non sugere mammas. In quibusdam aliis apparuit haec gratia in pupillari aetate . . . sicut etiam patuit suo modo in hac puella virgine Rosa . . . ut, dum esset trium annorum . . .[18]

On the basis of the information that this passage contains I shall try to determine the place of the *sacra infantia* in medieval imagination.

Two issues demand attention. In the first place, the signs of being chosen accorded to the saint as a foetus, as a baby, and as a very young child are all bracketed together. An *infans* leading a holy life is considered just as miraculous as the manifestation of grace in an unborn child. The *sacra infantia*, as an example of which *lactatio* is mentioned in relation, again, to Nicholas of Myra, demonstrates the alliance of the saint to God in a way that apparently was looked upon as extraordinary by medieval spectators as well.

The passages in hagiography concerning the refusal of the breast confirm this view. George of Suelli was almost a divine child in the eyes of the people around him: 'Quae res [scil. *lactatio*] tantam ingessit sapientibus admirationem, ut infantem illum non humanum quidem, sed divinum putarent.' In the case of Nicholas of Myra, Procula, Catharine of Sweden, and Ursuline of Parma the refusal to be suckled was primarily understood as a sign of their future sanctity. 'Manum Dei jam in eo operari cernentes', the parents of Stephen of Die connected the *lactatio* of their son with the story about John the Baptist. Leo of

XIe–XIIe siècles', in *La cristianità dei secoli XI e XII in occidente: coscienza e strutture di una società* = *Miscellanea del Centro di Studi Medioevali* 10 (Milan, 1983), pp. 281–302; Weinstein and Bell, *Saints and Society*, p. 20. A more circumspect view is expressed in Shulamith Shahar, *Childhood in the Middle Ages* (London, 1990).

18 *ActaSS*, Sept. II, p. 434.

Rouen's refusal to take the breast of his mother was regarded as such an 'admirandum spectaculum' that it was shown to the King of France. Ursuline's behaviour was accounted 'mirabile', Stephen of Die's was 'fere incredibile'; 'O mira principia! Sanctitatis exordia!' it reads in the rhymed version of his *vita*. In connection with the *lactatio* of Nicholas of Myra, his hagiographer commented: 'Quis, immense Deus, quis umquam mortalium audivit talia?'

The refusal of the breast can even be considered a miracle proper. Thomas Aquinas, who adopted his formula from Augustine,[19] described a miracle as 'aliquid arduum et insolitum supra facultatem naturae et spem admirantis proveniens', brought about by God.[20] From the passages quoted above it can easily be inferred that the *sacra infantia* falls in with all elements of this definition. In the *vita* of Gonçalvo of Amarante the refusal of the breast is indeed called a 'miraculum'.

In the second place, it is quite notable that in Rose's *vita*, divine grace is identified as the sole relevant agent, 'nulla necessitate seu meritis precedentibus'. According to this *vita*, sanctity is not attained gradually in a process of spiritual maturation, but is a given fact. The saint's personal merits have no bearing on it: sanctity is a status conferred by God, and sometimes it is bestowed upon a person as early as during conception. The *sacra infantia* seems indeed to disagree with Augustine's vision as paraphrased at the beginning of this article.

It is possible to find support for this break in high scholasticism. The necessity of a sinful youth preceding a holy life seems not to have been endorsed by the most important theologians. Although Thomas Aquinas asserted on several occasions that it was not impossible that divine *misericordia* brought the sinner closer to salvation by means of his own sin, he denied that one should suppose this happened of necessity.[21] Accordingly, the schoolmen recognized in so many words the possibility of saints never having come into contact with evil at all. Though Bonaventure remarked, 'An ignoras, quod multi de sanctis peccaverunt?' he also added: 'Omnes enim, quotquot modo cum Deo

[19] *De utilitate credendi*, *PL* 42, col. 90.

[20] *Summa Theologiae*, ed. iussu impensaque Leonis XIII [hereafter: ed. Leon.], I, cv, 7.

[21] Ibid., I.II, lxxix, 4; ibid., II, i, 3 ad 3; *In IV libros Sententiarum*, *Opera omnia*, 1, ed. Robertus Busa (Stuttgart and Bad Cannstatt, 1980), III, i, 1, 3 ad 5, p. 260.

regnant, vel olim sicut nos peccaverunt, vel saltem peccare potuissent, si eos divina clementia a peccato non praeservasset; quia, cuicumque donatum est, ut peccare penitus non potuerit, non est hoc naturae, sed caelestis gratiae.'[22] The same thought is voiced by Thomas Aquinas: 'tam angelus quam quaecumque creatura rationalis, si in sua sola natura consideretur, potest peccare; et cuicumque creaturae hoc convenit ut peccare non possit, hoc habet ex dono gratiae, non ex conditione naturae.'[23] The *sacra infantia* seems implicitly to be acknowledged by these words: it was not described as a result of the saint's nature, but as an effect of divine grace—just as had been advanced in the *vita* of Rose of Viterbo.

Indeed, in hagiography this vision seems to be have been followed as far as the refusal to take the breast is concerned. In his rhymed life of Nicholas, Robert Wace writes about the *lactatio*, 'Si l'out Deus de sa grace empli.'[24] Hilbert of Le Mans reported that Nicholas ran counter to nature in this respect: 'repugnans legi naturae jejunia observavit.'[25] *Lactatio* is presented as a product of grace in the *vitae* of Albert the Hermit: 'Mox vero singularis Dei erga illum gratia eluxit'; and of Catharine of Sweden: 'Ejus futurae sanctitatis et puritatis indicia divina gratia demonstravit.' As a final example, the following passage from the *vita* of Robert of Chaise-Dieu makes clear that not the child, but rather God, is responsible for the refusal of the breast: 'Mulier enim illa [the wet-nurse] meretrix erat, et ob hoc infans, cum lac respueret, damnabat peccatum; nesciebat utique quid damnaret, sed Dei virtus etiam in nescientibus operatur.'

Perhaps it could be inferred from another fact as well that divine grace was held responsible for the *sacra infantia*. Although, according to the *vita* of Rose, grace could make itself felt even before the saint's birth, the view that grace did not enfold man until the moment of his baptism was generally accepted. In those cases in which, in the *vitae* mentioned above, the saint's baptism is recorded at all, it precedes the mention of the child's refusal to take the breast—although it may reasonably be assumed that the

[22] Bonaventure, *Soliloquium*, *Opera omnia*, 8 (Quaracchi, 1898), i, 27.

[23] *Summa Theologiae*, ed. Leon., I, lxiii, 1.

[24] Robert Wace, *La Vie de Saint Nicholas par Wace, poème religieux du XIIe siècle = Etudes Romanes de Lund*, 5, ed. Einar Ronsjö (Lund and Copenhagen, 1942), l. 67.

[25] Hilbert of Le Mans, *In dedicatione Ecclesiae Sancti Nicolai sermo* 6, *PL* 171, col. 751.

baby was also suckled before its baptism. Examples of this can be found in the *vitae* of George of Suelli, Gonçalvo of Amarante, and, especially, Catervus of Tolentino: 'Puer ergo baptisato et divinis sacramentis susceptis, parentes protinus baptisati cum tota familia infantulum allactari fecerunt et enutriri [. . .] at in ipsa lactis enutritione [scil. on a Friday] abstinebat a lacte et a cunctis corporeis alimentis.' This description of the chain of events almost suggests some kind of causal connection between baptism and *lactatio*. Only in the Latin paraphrase of the Greek life of Canid is baptism mentioned after *lactatio*.

IV

Finally, I should like to point to the fact that the *sacra infantia* appears to fit very well into the image of medieval hagiography that has been outlined, notably by Aron Gurevich. According to Gurevich, hagiography presented, above all, tangible, concrete manifestations of God's will on earth, by which popular needs were satisfied; the abundance of miracles attributed to the saints were the most important result of that. The power to bring about miracles was even considered a principal criterion for sanctity.[26] The *sacra infantia* was an exquisite means of setting the saint apart from other people in a most visible way; the refusal of the breast was a striking and very concrete example of the alliance between the saint and God, and was indeed accounted a miracle that demonstrated the sanctity (or the future sanctity) of the child in question.

Whether in the case of the *sacra infantia* a particular popular need was satisfied is an issue that falls outside the scope of this article. The tales about the *sacra infantia* definitely had a marked effect on part of the medieval public at least. 'Quam impotens Nicolaus jacens sub ubere! quam potens abstinens ab ubere!', Peter of Celle exclaimed.[27] As an illustration of holiness, *sacra infantia* is also miraculous in its expedience.

Catholic University of Nijmegen

[26] Aron J. Gurevich, *Mittelalterliche Volkskultur* (Munich, 1987; originally Russian, Moscow, 1981), pp. 68–124.
[27] Peter of Celle, Sermo 79, *PL* 202, col. 880.

'RECEIVED IN HIS NAME': ROME'S BUSY BABY BOX

by BRENDA M. BOLTON

INNOCENT III, a proud and learned Roman pope, was well acquainted with the history and literature of the Rome of earlier days.[1] He would have been aware of the prophecy given by Virgil in the *Aeneid* that when the foaming Tiber appeared to run as a river of blood disaster was foretold.[2] In his own day the River Tiber gave him a clear message of a real disaster actually taking place. Far too frequently the fishermen of Rome drew in their nets only to find not a harvest of fish, but the tiny corpses of babies. These had been thrown naked to meet their deaths in the waters of the Tiber. Rome, of course, was by no means a stranger to the problem of abandoned babies. The great legend of the City's origins with the suckling of the babes who were to become its eventual founders was given a daily reminder since, under the portico of the Lateran Palace, was the famous bronze statue of the *Lupa* or *She-Wolf.*[3] In spite of the serious damage caused by a thunderbolt in Antiquity, which had left the Wolf's feet broken and destroyed the group of the twins,[4] the 'Mother of the Romans', as she was known, had come to represent papal jurisdiction over Rome, as well as the nourishing of its children.[5] The River Tiber had always been available for

[1] *Sermo XXII in solemnitate D. Apostolorum Petri et Pauli, PL* 217, cols 555–8. M. Maccarrone, 'Innocenzo III, prima del pontificato', *Archivio della Società Romana di Storia Patria*, 20 (1942), pp. 3–78, at p. 16, n. 6, 'Troviamo citazioni di Orazio, Ovidio, Giovenale, Severino Boezio'.

[2] Virgil, *Aeneid*, book vi, lines 86–8; compare Enoch Powell's speech at Birmingham, 21 April 1968, 'I am filled with foreboding. Like the Roman, I seem to see the River Tiber foaming with much blood.'

[3] C. Dulière, *Lupa Romana: Recherches d'iconographie et essai d'interpretation* (Brussels, 1979), pp. 21–43; Master Gregory, *The Marvels of Rome*, ed. and tr. John Osborne (Toronto, 1987), pp. 36, 96–7; P. Borchardt, 'The sculpture in front of the Lateran as described by Benjamin of Tudela and Master Gregorius', *Journal of Roman Studies*, 26 (1936), pp. 68–70.

[4] R. Krautheimer, *Rome: Profile of a City, 312–1308* (Princeton, 1980), pp. 192–7; A. Venturi, 'Romolo e Remo di Antonio Pollaiolo nella lupa capitolina', *L'Arte*, 22 (1919), pp. 133–5; R. Schofield, 'Giovanni da Tolentino goes to Rome: a description of the antiquities of Rome in 1490', *Journal of the Warburg and Courtauld Institutes*, 43 (1980), pp. 246–56.

[5] *PL* 217, col. 557, 'ubi duo fratres . . . Remus et Romulus, qui urbem istam corporaliter condiderunt . . . ibi duo fratres . . . Petrus et Paulus . . . civitatem istam suis patrociniis tucantur'.

the disposal of the many unwanted infants. Why, then, should the macabre catch of the fishermen of his time have been received by Innocent III as a matter in need of his most urgent attention? It might have been that there were more babies than usual. Population pressure was affecting Rome, and, as elsewhere, social problems were increasing with consequent effects on newborn children.[6] What evidence then can be found to link Innocent with Rome's Baby Box as a way of remedying such a dreadful situation?

The Hospital of Santo Spirito is the starting-point. In his papal role and even earlier, through curial responsibilities, Innocent was aware of the need for new large hospitals, which were required by the populations of the growing towns. The Hospital of the Order of St John in Jerusalem provided the outstanding model.[7] Before 1187, some 2,000 sick male and female pilgrims were being taken in annually and cared for within its compound.[8] As Lotario, Cardinal-Deacon of SS Sergio e Bacco, Innocent had personally witnessed the granting of privileges to a European-based hospital of the Order of St John at Sigena on 3 June 1193, which followed the hospital model provided by Jerusalem.[9] The *maisons-Dieu* in France were also similarly influenced.[10] One such was at Montpellier. There Innocent's attention was particularly caught by the Hospital of Saint-Esprit, founded in about 1174, by Guy of Montpellier at Pyla-Saint-Gely, close by the city walls.[11]

[6] John Boswell, '*Expositio* and *Oblatio*: the abandonment of children and the ancient and medieval family', *AHR*, 89 (1984), pp. 10–33, and *The Kindness of Strangers: the Abandonment of Children in Western Europe from Late Antiquity to the Renaissance* (New York, 1988), esp. pp. 322–63. Compare Richard B. Lyman Jnr, 'Barbarism and Religion: Late Roman and early Medieval Childhood', in Lloyd de Mause, ed., *The History of Childhood* (London, 1976), pp. 75–100, and S. Shahar, *Childhood in the Middle Ages* (London, 1990).

[7] J. Delaville le Roulx, ed., *Cartulaire général de l'Ordre des Hospitaliers de St Jean de Jérusalem (1100–1310)*, 4 vols (Paris, 1894–1906) [hereafter *Cartulaire*]; J. Riley-Smith, *The Knights of St John in Jerusalem and Cyprus c. 1050–1310* (London, 1967); Jean Richard, 'Hospitals and Hospital Congregations in the Latin Kingdom during the first period of the Frankish Conquest', in *Outremer: Studies in the History of the Crusading Kingdom of Jerusalem*, ed. B. Z. Kedar, H. E. Meyer and R. C. Smail (Jerusalem, 1982), pp. 89–100.

[8] John of Würzburg, *Descriptiones Terrae Sanctae ex saeculo VIII, IX, XII et XV*, ed. T. Tobler (Leipzig, 1874), p. 159; Timothy S. Miller, 'The Knights of Saint John and the Hospitals of the Latin West', *Speculum*, 53 (1978), pp. 709–33.

[9] *Cartulaire*, 1, 947, pp. 598–9.

[10] Louis Le Grand, 'Les Maisons-Dieux, leurs statuts au xiii siècle', *Revue des questions historiques*, 40 (1896), pp. 95–134.

[11] P. Brune, *Histoire de l'Ordre Hospitalier du Saint-Esprit* (Lons-le-Saunier-Paris, 1892); A. Fliche, 'La

In a letter of 22 April 1198, Innocent praised Guy's foundation, which 'shone out' like a star amongst the new hospitals.[12] It was an outstanding example of piety and the exercise of hospitality through the distribution of alms. The Pope had heard 'from the lips of many' that there 'the hungry were fed, the poor clothed, the sick cared for'. There, too, the Gospel was preached. The abundance of consolation given so much more than matched the misery suffered that the Master and brothers of the hospital were 'not just the protectors of these unfortunates but also their servants'. In recognition of their devotion the Pope specially empowered the brothers of Saint-Esprit to erect oratories and cemeteries. He also ordered local bishops not to hinder in any way the 'pious liberalities' of the faithful on behalf of the hospital. On the following day, 23 April, the bull *Religiosam vitam* took the hospital into papal protection and confirmed Guy's profession to the religious life.[13] The status of an *ordo* was given both to Guy and to his brothers, so that henceforth they were able to live according to a form of rule, *secundum rationabiles institutiones*. Other houses belonging to this new *ordo* were listed as Millau, Clapier, Mèze, Brioude, Barjac, Largentière, Marseille, and Troyes to the north. Beyond the Alps, in Rome itself, were two more—the hospice across the Tiber, next to S. Maria in Trastevere, and S. Agatha *in introitu urbis Rome*. All these were to be subject to the authority of the head of the Order at Montpellier.

Bearing these examples in mind, the site chosen by Innocent for his Roman hospital foundation was to be that of the abandoned Saxon School, with its associations as the former pilgrim hostel for the English nation.[14] He also utilized the nearby church of S. Maria in Saxia, where several kings of Wessex were

vie réligieuse à Montpellier sous le pontificat d'Innocent III (1198–1216)', *Mélanges Louis Halphen* (Paris, 1951), pp. 217–24; M. Revel, 'Le rayonnement à Rome et en Italie de l'ordre du Saint-Esprit de Montpellier', in *Cahiers de Fanjeaux*, 13, *Assistance et charité*, ed. M.-H. Vicaire (Toulouse, 1978), pp. 343–55; B. Rano, 'Ospitalieri di Santo Spirito', *Dizionario degli Istituti di Perfezione*, 6 (Rome, 1980), cols 994–1014.

[12] O. Hageneder and A. Haidacher eds, *Die Register Innocenz' III*, Band I, *Pontifikatsjahr 1198/99* (Graz and Cologne, 1964), 95, pp. 139–40 [hereafter *Register*]; *PL* 214, cols 83–4; *Regesta pontificium Roman – orum inde ab. a post Christum natum 1198 ad 1304*, ed. A. Potthast, 2 vols (Berlin, 1874–5, repr. Graz, 1957) [hereafter Potthast], I, p. 96.

[13] *Register* I, 97, pp. 141–4; *PL* 214, cols 85–6; Potthast I, 102.

[14] W. Levison, *England and the Continent in the Eighth Century* (Oxford, 1946), pp. 39–44.

buried. This *zenodochium* had been Innocent's responsibility as Bishop of Rome, and so prime a site could not be allowed to remain under-utilized for long.[15] Since before the beginning of Innocent's pontificate, the *Schola Saxonum* had stood derelict and ripe for development.[16] With characteristic enterprise, Innocent proceeded to gather resources for the foundation of his hospital. In November 1201, Renaud de Bar, Bishop of Chartres (1182–1217), was persuaded to donate the third part of a prebend from his church to the hospital.[17] In addition, Innocent's letter *Cupientes proplurimis*, of 10 December 1201,[18] led to the acquisition by the new hospital of property which had formerly belonged to S. Maria in Saxia, consisting of various lands and churches.

On 19 June 1204,[19] a detailed and eloquent preface set out what Innocent believed to be the aim and purpose of his hospital. These were those corporeal works of mercy which would be particularly rewarded on the Day of Judgement: feeding the hungry; giving drink to those who thirst; welcoming homeless strangers; clothing the naked; visiting captives in prison, and helping those who have suffered during their lifetime. The brothers of the hospital were not to be content merely to visit the sick, but they were also to provide material care for all those unfortunates, including abandoned children. Like Abraham and Lot, the brothers felt that, in so doing, they would have the honour of giving hospitality to the angels.[20] The benefits of hospitality are listed, together with the need for the renunciation of riches, which might otherwise lead to perdition: all an admirable exchange—the perishable goods of this world in return for the eternal goods of the next. On behalf, therefore, of his predecessors, of his successors, and of the cardinals, Innocent announced the building of the Hospital of Santo Spirito. It was to be a most favoured place for the exercise of hospitality, so that

[15] P. de Angelis, *L'Ospedale di Santo Spirito in Saxia*, 2 vols, 1. *Dalle origini al 1300*; 2. *Dal 1301 al 1500* (Rome, 1960–2).

[16] J. C. Robertson, ed., *Materials for the History of Thomas Becket, Archbishop of Canterbury*, 7 vols, *RS* (London, 1875–85), 5 (1881), pp. 64–5.

[17] De Angelis, *Santo Spirito*, 1, pp. 379–80; *PL* 215, col. 1334, 11 November 1207. Compare *Cum vacetis operibus*, 14 June 1217, cited by De Angelis, *Santo Spirito*, 1, p. 211.

[18] Ibid., 1, pp. 211–14, 380–1.

[19] *PL* 215, col. 380.

[20] Ibid., col. 377.

the poor might be received, the sick tended, and other works of charity performed.[21]

To ensure that the spiritual administration of the hospital was adequately carried out, at least four clerics professed by the Order were always to be in attendance. Santo Spirito was given primacy in the Order and was joined to Saint-Esprit in Montpellier. Guy, named as its Master, was to rule the two foundations on either side of the Alps and was to visit both annually.[22] Provision was made that any future election would depend upon whether Guy died in Rome or in Montpellier.[23] The task of the Master was to manage the finances of the foundations, and he was entrusted with the entire spiritual administration, being responsible only to the pope.[24]

Innocent's Rule for Santo Spirito must have undergone several revisions.[25] The primitive text, part of which is dated to 1213, is associated with two cardinals, Stephen, Cardinal-Deacon of S. Adriano (1216–28) and later Cardinal-Priest of S. Maria in Trastevere (1228–54)[26] and Rainier of Viterbo, Cardinal-Deacon of S. Maria in Cosmedin (1216–50).[27] Stephen was none other than Innocent's own nephew, the son of his brother Richard.[28] He was close to his uncle and had accompanied him on the preaching campaign for the Fifth Crusade in the summer of 1216.[29] Innocent's design for the hospital and its future implementation could not therefore have been left in safer hands. Stephen and Rainier were entrusted with subsequent compilations of the hospital's Rule, possibly between 1228 and 1250. The wisdom they showed in organization and reform at Santo Spirito led to them being used on another occasion by Gervase, Abbot of Premontré, in the matter of S. Maria *de Parvo Ponte* at Brindisi.[30]

[21] Compare Luke 7. 22.

[22] *Bullarium diplomatum et privilegiorum Sanctorum Romanorum Pontificium*, 3, ed. F. Gaude (Turin, 1858), pp. 320–3, for Honorius III's Bull of 13 May 1217 dissolving this union.

[23] *PL* 215, cols 378–80.

[24] Ibid., cols 1270–1 and 1424.

[25] *PL* 217, cols 1129–58.

[26] W. Maleczek, *Papst und Kardinalskolleg von 1191 bis 1216* (Vienna, 1984), pp. 195–201.

[27] Ibid., pp. 184–9.

[28] M. Dykmans, 'D'Innocent III à Boniface VIII. Histoire des Conti et des Annibaldi', *Bulletin de l'Institut historique belge de Rome*, 45 (1975), pp. 19–211, especially 44–6.

[29] M. Maccarrone, *Studi su Innocenzo III Italia Sacra* 17 (Padua, 1972), pp. 8–9, 135–8.

[30] C. L. Hugo, *Sacrae antiquitatis monumenta* (Etival, 1725), Letter XXII, pp. 26–7, 'per litteras vestras

Out of the 105 articles of the Rule followed by the brothers at both hospitals, more than one-third have since been identified as literal borrowings from the Rule of the Hospital of St John at Jerusalem.[31] It seems possible, therefore, that the primitive Rule of Saint-Esprit and Santo Spirito was an adaptation of that of St John well before the early thirteenth century. The two or three chapters of the original Rule referring specifically to children are most relevant. Chapter 41, *De orphanis nutriendis et feminis praegnantibus*,[32] simply states that abandoned children, *proiecti*, will be looked after by the hospital, whilst pregnant female paupers will be freely received into its care. Chapter 59, *De cunabulis puerorum*,[33] applies to a slightly different group of children, this time those born in the hospital to female pilgrims. These children were to be placed in individual cradles so that they could sleep alone, lest any accident by overlaying or crushing occurred. Renaud, Bishop of Chartres, is the link here. He seems to have been aware of the little cradles provided at the hospital in Jerusalem by the Statutes of Roger des Molins in 1182[34] and could well have been the driving force behind their introduction at Santo Spirito.[35]

Evidence on the founding and work of the Hospital of Santo Spirito can be deduced by the study of a series of frescos still existing in the hospital itself.[36] These draw attention to Innocent III's connection with the babes drowned in the Tiber. They are to be found in the Corsia Sistina, a vast hall of more than 350 feet in length, which is the largest ward of the hospital. The walls of the Corsia Sistina, named after Sixtus IV (1471–84), who rebuilt it about 1471–5, are decorated with a double row of frescos by Antonio da Viterbo (*c.* 1476). These show the relationship between the foundation of the hospital and papal patronage. It is a narrative cycle, depicting both the historic growth and day-by-

quas in hac parte multum esse efficaciam habituras'; A. De Leo, *Codice Diplomatico Brindisino*, I (492–1299), pp. 62–3, 70–2.

[31] Le Grand, 'Les Maisons-Dieux', pp. 105–6.

[32] *PL* 217, col. 1146.

[33] Ibid. col. 1148.

[34] 14 March 1182, 'Cet si establi que petiz bers fucent fait por les enfans des femes pelerines qui naissent en la maison, si que il gisent à une part soul, et que li enfant alaitant n'en aient aucun ennui por le mesaise de lor mere', *Cartulaire*, p. 426.

[35] Ibid., p. 719, for the meeting of 1185 between Renaud de Bar and Roger des Molins at Chartres.

[36] Eunice D. Howe, *The Hospital of Santo Spirito and Pope Sixtus IV* (Baltimore, 1978).

day work of the institution. The fresco cycle records three aspects which are relevant to the babes in the river. As was to be expected, the contemporary patron, Sixtus IV, is well to the fore, but also, and naturally of considerable interest, are the three representations of the hospital's first founder, Innocent III.[37] On the east wall is the particular depiction which suggests his link with the babes. It had been placed by Antonio da Viterbo in a position accessible to the widest conceivable range of visitors at the time. This central position indicates that, of all the fresco stories, this was the one with a message in constant need of reiteration, namely, that succour was to be given to the innocent victims of sin. This important fresco, set by the Tiber, shows a group of mothers engaged in infanticide by throwing into the river their unclothed and unwanted offspring. Obviously the time which elapsed between the delivery of the babies and their deposition in the Tiber needed to be minimal and so was often done in the full light of day. A second scene depicts two fishermen drawing in their net with its catch of three drowned babies. The fishermen are shown using their creels to carry the corpses to the Pope. Innocent throws up his hands in horror at being so confronted. His distraught countenance and upraised hands display his abhorrence at what is before him. It surely must have been so horrible as to disturb his sleep, and he may have recalled an earlier vision in one of his dreams.[38] This is also depicted by Antonio da Viterbo. Innocent is told by an angel to erect a hospital on the banks of the Tiber. The Pope responds, and in a subsequent scene is shown riding up on his white horse to inspect the progress of the building works.

The next stage of the search for evidence is best undertaken with the help of Professor Bergami, the current Hospital Administrator.[39] When prevailed upon he will show with pride the evidence of the founding Pope's charitable concern for children in general and his practical solution to the problem of the *expositi*, the abandoned infants. Set into the wall, just to the left of the main entrance to the hospital, is the Rota Box, a rotating turntable with an iron grille through which a small, newly-born

[37] Ibid., pp. 336–41.
[38] Ibid., p. 201.
[39] My gratitude to Professor Bergami for privileged visits on 24 September 1988 and 29 September 1990.

baby might be inserted.[40] The baby, instead of being drowned or abandoned, thus ended up on a little mattress in the box behind the grille, placed there for its safe reception to face its life in the world. The sound of the Rota turning or the child crying—or most likely both—often alerted an attendant, who would collect the child, without being aware of the identity of the person or persons who had deposited it through the grille. The Baby Box is certainly there today. It was certainly there in the time of Sixtus IV, when the hospital was rebuilt, but any attempt to link the first box to Innocent III can be met only with the most tenuous evidence. However attractive the possibility might be, the connection between the Box and the Pope was largely a legend which the fifteenth century certainly played to the full, with little regard to the evidence.[41]

The legend seems to have been already widely disseminated before the fifteenth century.[42] A specific manuscript decoration from at least the late thirteenth or early fourteenth century associated Innocent III with the hospital. The *Book of the Rule* or *Liber Regulae*,[43] from about 1290 to 1320, is a superb codex of 248 folios, containing more than fifty miniatures.[44] Amongst these are several representing the legendary facts which induced Innocent to found the hospital—the macabre catch in the Tiber, the Pope's dream, and the angel's revelation. These were currently the beliefs of 1386, when Jacob Twinger of Königshofen attributed the foundation of the hospital to Innocent's desire to prevent the killing of unwanted infants.[45] In the mid-fifteenth century, Philip III the Good, Duke of Burgundy (1419–67), commissioned a series of twenty-two miniatures to commemorate the foundation of the Hospital of Saint-Esprit at Dijon, about 1204, by his predecessor, Duke Odo III (1193–1218).[46]

[40] Brune, *Saint-Esprit*, p. 288.

[41] Ibid., p. 38, 'il paraît avoir frappé bien vivement l'imagination populaire car sa fondation finit par revêtir le charactère d'une légende aux traits merveilleux.'

[42] Howe, *Santo Spirito*, p. 203.

[43] Rome, Archivio di Stato, MS 3193; A. Canezza, *Liber Regulae Hospitalis S. Spiritus in Saxia de Urbe*, IV Congresso Internationale degli Ospedali, 19–26 Maggio 1935, XIII (Rome, 1936); A. F. La Cava, *Liber Regulae S. Spirito, Studi di storia della medicina*, 6 (Milan, 1946).

[44] Canezza, *Liber Regulae*, pp. 7–8.

[45] Jacob Twinger, *Strassburger Chronik* (Strasbourg, 1871), p. 569.

[46] Dijon, Archives of Saint-Esprit, A4; G. Peignot, 'Histoire de la fondation des Hôpitaux du Saint-Esprit de Rome et de Dijon', *Memoires de la Commission des Antiquités du Department de la Côte-d'Or*, 1 (1838), pp. 17–70.

The first ten miniatures from Dijon depict the same sequence of events as for the founding of the Hospital of Santo Spirito—from sinful mothers tossing their babies into the Tiber to Innocent III's institution of the Hospital Order. It is unlikely that the Dijon illuminations served as a direct model for the Corsia Sistina frescos.[47] The settings are French Gothic and have more in common with the local Burgundian style than with anything Roman. They can be dated quite precisely between the granting of a Jubilee privilege to the Order by Nicholas V in 1450 and the death of Duke Philip in 1467.[48] The two series, the *Liber Regulae* and the Dijon miniatures, would seem to have been dependent on some common text, as yet undocumented. Both could have been modelled on fresco scenes from the old Hospital of Santo Spirito, *vetustate pene collapsum* by the time of Sixtus IV.[49] His predecessor, Eugenius IV (1431–47), was the first fifteenth-century pope to revive papal patronage of the hospital,[50] and his renovations may well have included just such a fresco cycle. Exact details of the projects commissioned by Eugenius IV or Nicholas V (1447–55) may never be known, as the literary sources for the hospital narrative pre-date Sixtus's own biography. It is perfectly possible that the Dijon miniatures at least were dependent on an older cycle.[51]

The fifteenth-century Life of Sixtus IV states quite clearly that 'Cruel mothers were killing their illegitimate offspring by throwing them off the bridge into the Tiber where they were caught up in the nets of the fishermen.'[52] As late as 1570, Albert Bassanus, a Pole, in his history of the Order, further embellished this legend. Guided by a heavenly voice, Innocent III had been led to the banks of the Tiber to inspect the bodies of more than 400 dead babies. In 1653, Ascanio Tamburini, Abbot of Vallombrosa, reproduced the account without comment, but added the more reasonable assertion that the hospital's task was to care for 'the

[47] Howe, *Santo Spirito*, pp. 204–7.

[48] Ibid. p. 234, n. 41.

[49] Vatican, MS Cod. Urb. 1023, fols 11b–12a.

[50] Vatican, MS Lat. 9026, fol. 64a.

[51] Howe, *Santo Spirito*, pp. 206–7.

[52] Vatican, MS Cod. Urb. 1023, fol. 11a, 'Qualiter ex damnatu coitu progenitos in lucem veniant, crudeles matres diversimode erucidant. Qualiter infantes de Ponte in Tiberim proiecti a Piscatoribus rete pro piscibus capiuntur.'

sick and pilgrims and for abandoned children and babies'.[53] Sixtus IV, himself a Franciscan, felt a great reverence for Innocent, who had granted approval to Francis of Assisi. Howe has pointed out that there were no precedents for biographical scenes commissioned by a living patron, but Sixtus wished to create a legend in his own day.[54] 'Never before had a pope seen fit to depict his own life from birth to death as a succession of laudatory acts.'[55] The presence of three depictions of the great pope, Innocent III, would have enhanced this—prestige by association! The frescos of Sixtus's early life display a continuous hagiographical sequence—from his mother's vision of her unborn child in a Franciscan habit; his birth near Savona in 1414; his baptism; severe illness; his vesting with the Franciscan habit in order to cure him, and to his infantile blessing of the people in the piazza at Savona.[56] In all these the stress emphatically is upon images of a rewarding childhood.

No contemporary frescos of a like nature exist for Innocent III. Other means will have to be used to try to discover those spiritual and philosophical beliefs which underlay his actions in regard to the poor, the sick, and the helpless, the babies and children in general, and the role to be played by the hospital.[57] He appears to pass through three developmental stages—as cardinal presenting a learned text, as pastoral pope concerned with the saving of souls, and as Bishop of Rome imbued with the *vita apostolica*. These need to be tackled chronologically, even though all were to have formative influences on his ultimate position.

First, as a cardinal who may have felt that publication was an essential qualification for advancement. Between about 1190 and 1198[58] he wrote three interesting works, *De miseria humanae*

[53] *PL* 217, cols 1129–30, where an extract from Tamburini's history is reproduced. Also A. Tamburini, *De Iure Abbatum et aliorum praelatorum*, 2 vols (Lyon, 1640), 2, Disputatio xxiv, Quaest. IV, p. 367: 'Ad Tiberim se contulit et laxatis retibus, prima vice octaginta septem, secunda vero trecentos et quadraginta extraxit infantes abortivos.'

[54] Howe, *Santo Spirito*, pp. 207–20.

[55] Ibid., p. 207.

[56] Ibid., pp. 342–50.

[57] Brenda Bolton, ' "Hearts not Purses": Innocent III's Approach to Social Welfare', *Through the Eye of a Needle: Judeo-Christian Roots of Social Welfare*, ed. Emily Albu Hanawalt and Carter Lindberg (Missouri, 1994), pp. 123–45.

[58] He was created Cardinal-Deacon of SS Sergio e Bacco between 3 June 1189 and 8 January 1190.

conditionis,[59] *De sacro mysterio altaris*,[60] and *De quadripartita specie nuptiarum*.[61] Of relevance here is his *De miseria*, with its concern for the human condition. In the first few pages of this ascetic treatise he deals with the evil world into which the young were unfortunately born to suffer the sins of their fathers.[62]

This work, written between 25 December 1194 and 13 April 1195, became one of the most popular and influential works of the Middle Ages.[63] Now seen by some as a 'mirror' revealing the Curia and its corruption,[64] this was only the first of a projected two volumes. The misery of the human condition was intended to be complemented by another, *On the Dignity of the Human Condition*, but this was never completed. No evidence has been found as to its proposed contents.

In *De miseria*, Lotario discourses upon the weak, sad, and sinful condition of the child. From the moment of its conception in sin and lust, the Cardinal sees the child condemned to bear the transgressions of its parents. 'Happy is the child', he says, 'who dies before it is born, experiencing death before knowing life.'[65] In this passage he particularly mentions children with deformities, singled out as they were for ridicule. He then reflects that all children are born weak, unable to speak or understand, or even to crawl on all fours.[66] Indeed, children are less well equipped than animals, who at least can walk soon after they are born. The weakness of the child is further demonstrated when it is born crying, which expresses the misery of its own nature and the world into which it has entered. Lotario cannot resist at this stage indulging in a little sophisticated punning, obviously meant to appeal to his clerical readers. Boys are born saying 'Ah', while girls cry 'E' or '*Eu*'.[67] '*Eu*' and 'Ah' are a play on the name of Eve

[59] *PL* 217, cols 701–46; *De miseria humane conditionis*, ed. M. Maccarrone (Padua, 1955); *On the Misery of the Human Condition*, ed. Donald R. Howard and tr. Margaret M. Dietz; *De miseria condicionis humane*, ed. Robert E. Lewis (Athens, GA, 1978).

[60] *PL* 217, cols 774–914.

[61] Ibid., cols 922–68.

[62] Lewis, *De miseria*, pp. 93–105.

[63] R. Bultot, 'Mépris du monde, misère et dignité de l'homme dans la pensée d'Innocent III', *Cahiers de civilisation médiévale*, 4 (1961), pp. 441–56, esp. p. 442.

[64] J. C. Moore, 'Innocent III's *De Miseria Humanae Conditionis*: a *Speculum Curiae*?', *Catholic Historical Review*, 67 (1981), pp. 553–64.

[65] Lewis, *De miseria*, p. 103, lines 2–4.

[66] Ibid., p. 103, lines 15–18.

[67] Ibid., p. 104, lines 1–19.

or Eva, both interjections expressing the magnitude of sorrow or great pain caused by childbirth. He cites Rachel's death who, whilst dying of this agony, named her son 'Benoni, that is, son of pain', which, incidentally, Jacob quickly changed to Benjamin. There was, too, the sorrow of the child Ichabod, representing 'the glory hath departed', so named by his mother, the wife of Phineas (one of the two disreputable sons of Eli), who was killed at the time when the Philistines captured the Ark of the Covenant. No greater disaster could have been faced by the Israelites. In this early work, Lotario seems to have had little regard for any action that might be needed to ease the pain and suffering of the child born from sin.

In his second stage of development, as pope and pastor, one of Innocent's first tasks was to clarify important and complex matters concerning the spiritual well-being of his flock. The baptism of infants as soon as possible after their birth[68] raised important issues. In a letter of 1201 to Humbert, Bishop of Arles,[69] which entered into the *Decretals* of Gregory IX, Innocent argued strongly against those who asserted that baptism was conferred uselessly on infants who were dying in such numbers every day. He considered baptism an essential pastoral duty to ensure the child's passage into Heaven, having received Christ's salvation.[70] But for the grace of God these little ones would have perished eternally. The saving of souls was even more important than the saving of bodies. The Baby Box was an ideal solution, for it allowed for both. Yet Innocent was bound to approach the 'Babes in the Tiber' problem as would all priests: had these children already been baptized or not? The anonymity which the Box was designed to encourage raised at least the practical problem of finding this out. If, by chance, the custodian of the Baby Box heard footsteps outside, he was immediately to rush to put the question: 'Has this child been baptized?'[71] Failing an

[68] J. D. C. Fisher, *Christian Initiation: Baptism in the Medieval West* (London, 1965), pp. 109–12.

[69] Humbert de Aquaria (1190–1202), *Gallia Christiana*, 1 (Paris, 1715), pp. 564–5. For the letter see H. Denzinger, *Enchiridion symbolorum, definitionum et declarationum de rebus fidei et morum*, 10th edn. (Freiburg, 1908), pp. 180–2.

[70] For similar views, see Innocent's Advent Sermon VII, *PL* 217, cols 341–6, especially cols 343–4. Compare O. Pontal, *Les Statuts Synodaux Français du xiiie siècle* I. *Les statuts de Paris et le synodal de l'Ouest (xiii siècle)* (Paris, 1971), p. 140; Boswell, *Kindness of Strangers*, pp. 322–5.

[71] Brune, *Saint-Esprit*, p. 288.

answer, exposed children were to be baptized, just in case, and their souls would be saved.[72]

It would be a mistake, in considering Innocent III's actions, to neglect any acknowledgement of his social awareness. He was, above all, a pastoral pope, and the building of the hospital was evidence of this, as was the care he gave to pilgrims coming to Rome. Many of these pilgrims were pregnant women, whose babies added to the demands for child-care in Rome. Each pilgrim baby was provided with its own separate cradle, thus protecting it from being overlaid by its worn out pilgrim mother.[73] There was, after all, room at the inn!

Many harrowing tales exist about the mishaps and injury to infants, including those where babies were frequently suffocated or squashed. Innocent had to adjudicate as pope in one such heart-rending case. On 2 May 1207 he wrote to the Bishop of Lubeck and his suffragans about the case.[74] 'H', a priest, had come personally to see him with a tearful confession. Entering the house of his niece, with whom he had to arrange the payment of a debt, the priest apparently sat down, at her invitation, on a heap of clothing placed near the communal seat. Under this seat a certain sick little child, entrusted to the care of his father (no less), had been placed there to sleep. No sooner had he sat down than his niece hastened to warn him of the child beneath the clothing, whereupon the priest in horror leapt up from the place where he had been sitting. Alas, it was too late. Whether because of the weight of the clothing, or the gravity of the illness, or whether because the priest had crushed the child by sitting on him, the babe was found to be dead. The priest 'H' had come to the Pope, not presuming to perform any of the functions of his office until he received forgiveness. Innocent's judgement in this case was that the man had not gravely sinned, but that penance should be performed in a manner compatible with the event.

This third and fundamental aspect brought about by Innocent's social awareness in regard to children would have developed from his support for the *vita apostolica*, the movement which had arisen out of the spiritual ferment of the twelfth

[72] Boswell, *Kindness of Strangers*, pp. 322–5.
[73] *PL* 217, col. 1118.
[74] *PL* 215, cols 871–72.

century. With such spiritual inspiration, Innocent would constantly have had in mind the Gospels and the sayings of Jesus. There, in Matthew[75] and Mark,[76] he would have found the advice to 'suffer little children . . . because of such are the Kingdom of Heaven.' This demanded an approach to children by others than those in the parental relationship, which was perhaps not at all common at the time. What Christ had said was certainly as unexpected in apostolic times and in the early years of the Church as it would have been in Ancient Greece and Rome. It is not clear when Christ's injunction—not to offend against his little ones—became a guiding principle for the Church, but by the turn of the twelfth century some attempts were obviously being made. These seem to have been irregular, often ineffective, perhaps not truly 'Gospel based', and more concerned with the consequences to the parents of their sin than to the foundlings themselves. Innocent III can hardly have been the first, although his anonymous biographer would like us to believe so. This biographer does not mention the Baby Box specifically, but devotes much space to Innocent's support for such causes as Santo Spirito. Indeed, Innocent's overall expenditure on poor orphans, on widows, and the younger sons of impoverished nobles was estimated at the staggering sum of 5,000 pounds in the first ten years of the pontificate.[77] This most pious pope not only allowed, but positively encouraged the very poor children of Rome to come to his own table after meals so that they could eat up the remaining food.[78]

Innocent certainly took the words of Christ as the basis for his actions, as he became increasingly aware of the needs of poor children in general and abandoned babies in particular. What better could the Church to than to receive these little children in his name, so receiving Christ himself and he who sent him? Perhaps the legends of the fifteenth century had more basis in fact than we imagine. The Hospital of Santo Spirito is well documented, but the episode of the Baby Box less so. A deeper examination of the spiritual beliefs underlying Innocent's ac-

[75] Matt. 18.2–6; 19.13–15.
[76] Mark 9.36–7, 42; 10.13–16.
[77] *Gesta* CL, col. ccxxviii.
[78] *Gesta Innocentii P.P.III, PL* 214, ch. CXL, col. cc.

tions may be a logical first step towards finding the evidence we seek.

Queen Mary and Westfield College,
University of London

THE ALMONRY SCHOOL OF NORWICH CATHEDRAL PRIORY IN THE THIRTEENTH AND FOURTEENTH CENTURIES*

by JOAN GREATREX

IN 1535 the monks of Norwich Cathedral Priory made the following report:

> Each year there are thirteen boys dwelling within the monastery and receiving free instruction in the *scola grammaticalis* or 'almery scole'. They are also given food and clothing, which costs us 26*s.* 8*d.* per head per annum. In addition a master is provided to teach the boys, together with a servant to attend to their other needs; the former is paid an annual stipend of 53*s.* 4*d.*, and the latter 20*s.* This school was founded by Herbert, the first bishop of the see of Norwich and the founder of the monastic cathedral community.[1]

This statement makes it clear that the monks believed in a foundation date for the school not later than 1119, the year of Bishop Herbert de Losinga's death.[2] The question is, what evidence exists to confirm the veracity of this firmly held conviction, which must have been passed on by each successive generation of monks for at least a significant portion of the intervening four centuries? Unfortunately, there is as yet no definitive answer, but some clarification is now possible; this will permit us to suggest a partial reconstruction of the process by which the monks' belief

*I wish to thank Barbara Dodwell, Barbara Harvey, and Paul Cattermole for their helpful comments and suggestions after reading an earlier draft of this paper.

[1] J. Caley and J. Hunter, eds, *Valor Ecclesiasticus, Record Publications*, 6 vols (1810–34), 3, p. 287. This statement, paraphrased here, was made necessary by the Act of Supremacy, which required from every religious house a detailed account of all regular expenditures that could be regarded as charitable. Fifteen years earlier a monk had informed the bishop during a visitation that the number of boys was down to only eight: A. Jessopp, ed., *Visitations of the Diocese of Norwich, AD 1492–1532* = Camden Society, ns 13 (1888), p. 192.

[2] For details of the foundation of both cathedral and monastery, see B. Dodwell, 'The Foundation of Norwich Cathedral', *TRHS*, ser. 5, 7 (1957), pp. 1–18.

was gradually transformed, as they continued to look back on their ever-lengthening past, and as the collective memory blurred the distinction between child oblates and poor scholars, both dwelling in the monastery and receiving education at the monks' expense.[3] Losinga's personal concern for the teaching of the young in the cloister was probably the result of his own excellent education as a young monk at the Norman abbey of Fécamp. There is one reference in his correspondence which reveals that boys were already being taught by the Norwich monks even before construction of the cathedral had been completed. In a letter to Prior Ingulph he expressed the desire, on his return, to check up on their progress: 'Volo, rediens, gaudere . . . de custodia et doctrina puerorum.'[4] These boys were no doubt the child oblates for whom Archbishop Lanfranc had legislated only a few years before in his Monastic Constitutions for Christ Church Cathedral Priory, where he described them as *pueri* or *infantes*. He ordered that their reading was to be supervised by a master, and they were expected to take part with the cantors in singing the Palm Sunday antiphons.[5]

Several examples of the boys' musical activities at Norwich occur in MS, 465 of Corpus Christi College, Cambridge, commonly known as the Norwich Customary.[6] It was probably written about 1260, although it was based on an earlier exemplar from Fécamp, contemporaneous with Losinga. We cannot be certain that all the observances in the Customary continued to be followed in the mid-thirteenth century at Norwich; and yet it seems reasonable to assume that most of it remained in force as written, since, with a number of minor modifications and addi-

[3] St Benedict prescribed the form for the ceremony of child oblation in ch. 59 of his Rule, and he also laid down regulations for the care and training of the children in chs 30, 37, 39, 45, 63, 70; Abbot Justin McCann's edition, *The Rule of St Benedict* (London, 1952), provides both the Latin and English text.

[4] R. Anstruther, ed., *Epistolae Herberti de Losinga, primi episcopi Norwicensis* (London and Brussels, 1846; reprinted New York, 1969), p. 33. In another letter he addressed the *adolescentes*, ibid., p. 99: 'Adolescentes, non dedignemini vestri pedagogi correctionem, et praeparate absentes quid meae praesenti condignum respondeatis.' However, these were possibly *juvenes* or young monks.

[5] D. Knowles, ed., *The Monastic Constitutions of Lanfranc* (London, 1951), pp. 4, 21, 31, 23–4, where the word *incipiet* when used in the context of the office probably meant 'intone'.

[6] This manuscript, which is mainly concerned with liturgical practice, has been transcribed and edited by J. B. L. Tolhurst, *The Customary of the Cathedral Priory of Norwich* = *Henry Bradshaw Society* (London, 1948) [hereafter, *Norwich Customary*].

tions, it was still in use as late as 1311.[7] The Fécamp original would have understood the *pueri* to have been the child oblates, who had virtually ceased to exist by the late twelfth century.[8] However, in their place, at some uncertain date, there must have appeared small numbers of boys, probably of local origin, who came to the monastery for education, and not necessarily as future candidates for the monastic life. By or before 1260, therefore, the rubrics applying to *pueri* must have come to signify the latter rather than the former type. These, then, like Lanfranc's *pueri*, would have processed with their masters on Palm Sunday and sung the antiphons. The Customary also laid down that a boy should begin the litany on the Vigil of the Feast of St John the Baptist, the antiphon *Placebo* at Vespers on All Saints, and the *Dirige domine* at Lauds on All Souls'.[9]

A stray Norwich document, in the form of a single loose leaf of parchment, which has recently come to light among the muniments of Worcester Cathedral Priory, proves beyond doubt the existence of an almonry school during the priorate of William de Kirkby (1272–88/9), similar to that described by the monks in their statement of 1535. It is unique in being the earliest known reference to such schools, whose origins have previously been dated some twenty or thirty years later,[10] apart from one brief allusion of Archbishop Winchelsey in 1299 to the maintenance of 'pauperes scolares . . . sicut antiquitus' in the almonry school of Rochester Cathedral Priory.[11] Until now the chapter ordinance of 1314 for the almonry school at Ely Cathedral Priory contained the earliest provisions known.[12]

Both the Norwich chapter ordinance in this manuscript and that of Ely have certain features in common, but only the former specifies the number of boys eligible. There were to be places for

[7] The introduction to the *Norwich Customary* discusses these problems in some detail, ibid., pp. xiii–xix.

[8] D. Knowles, *The Monastic Order in England* (Cambridge, 1966), pp. 421–2, where the main reasons for their disappearance are attributed to the improved facilities for education outside the cloister and to changes in ecclesiastical legislation.

[9] Tolhurst, *Norwich Customary*, pp. 76, 135, 187.

[10] The Worcester document is Worcester Cathedral Muniment [hereafter WCM] B. 680.

[11] This Rochester reference occurs in an injunction issued by the archbishop after a visitation, R. Graham, ed., *Registrum Roberti Winchelsey, Cantuariensis archiepiscopi. AD 1294–1313*, 2 vols, Canterbury and York Society (1952–6), 2, p. 841.

[12] S. J. A. Evans, ed., *Ely Chapter Ordinances* = Camden Society, 3rd series, 64, *Camden Miscellany*, 17 (1940), pp. 38–9.

thirteen 'clerici, elegantis stature, pauperes et ad erudiendum habiles', to whom a master and a servant were assigned, the former to instruct them 'in literatura et in moribus', and the latter to look after their other needs. Should one of the boys lose interest in his studies and require repeated correction for misconduct, he was to be dismissed after the third warning and another boy be found to take his place. The selection of apt pupils for the Norwich, as for the Ely, school was carefully regulated, but the concerns expressed were different. In this document the Norwich chapter named the subprior and almoner as the examining board for applicants, who were to be judged according to three criteria: only boys who proved to be 'competentis forme, habilis ad studium et pauper' would be accepted. At Ely the chapter's concern was with the nomination of candidates by the monks and outsiders, the limitation of the study period to four years, and the actual admission procedures, matters which were dealt with at Norwich some years later and which will be considered below. The Norwich servant, in this earliest known ordinance, was to be responsible for procuring the boys' alms, that is, for collecting supplies of food and drink from the leftovers on the monastic tables for distribution to his charges; and the almoner was himself to be responsible for setting aside enough bread of the quality served to the monks to satisfy the appetites of master and boys.[13]

The unique and the most interesting aspect of the Norwich ordinance relates to the musical involvement of the boys, and may be the earliest indication of the existence of a song school, even if only in a rudimentary form. Because of the lack of any earlier evidence, the introduction of boys into liturgical choirs has generally been regarded as occurring during the final quarter of the fourteenth century.[14] However, it now seems certain that almonry boys at Norwich, possibly only those with musical ability, were being trained in singing as well as in grammar in the last quarter of the thirteenth century; and, as such, they may

[13] It was normal Benedictine practice to collect the 'broken meats' from the refectory for distribution among the poor; this included the almonry boys as well as the old and sick who were cared for within the monastery precincts or nearby, and also the poor at the monastery gates.

[14] Roger Bowers, 'Choral institutions within the English Church: their constitution and development, 1340–1500' (University of East Anglia, Ph.D. thesis, 1975), p. 4086. I am grateful to Dr Bowers for his perceptive comments and suggestions while this paper was in progress.

provide the link of continuity with the child oblates of Lanfranc's day and the *pueri* of the Norwich Customary. On Sundays and feast days these boys were to be occupied with their lessons from the beginning of Matins to the end of Mass, after which their presence was required in the Church of St Mary in the Marsh, the parish church within the monastic precincts. There they were to sing the chant at divine service (*divinis*), half of them on one side (? of the choir) and half on the other, reading and intoning the psalms (*legentes et psallentes*) to the best of their ability. These must have been the precursors of the *clerici beate virginis* or *clerici beate Marie*, who are not named before the late 1370s.[15] The ordinance under discussion cannot be mistaken for a foundation charter. Like the later ordinance at Ely, it was a regulatory measure necessitated by an increase of laxity, a decline in standards or perhaps some failure of responsibility on the part of the almoner.

A few of the practical details of the day-to-day running of the almonry school emerge in the surviving accounts of the obedientiaries, especially those of the almoner, the earliest of which are almost contemporaneous with the ordinance. The master of the boys, for example, first occurs in 1297/8, when he received a gift of 12*d.* from the obedientiary known at Norwich as the master of the cellar.[16] In 1308/9 the master's name was Thomas Lilie; two years later he or his successor was paid an annual stipend of 13*s.* 4*d.* by the almoner, who also spent 27*s.* 3*d.* on cloth for the *pauperes clerici*.[17] This makes it clear that the boys were provided with clothing as well as with bed and board. Lists of food purchases for the boys and the other members of the almoner's household regularly included meat, poultry, fish, eggs, cheese, milk, and butter, candles, and occasionally tablecloths, crockery, and mats.[18] With the addition of bread and the left-overs from the monastic fare, the boys' diet appears to have been adequate and, by the standard of their day, nutritious.

[15] These *clerici* appear as such on the almoner's accounts in 1378/81 and 1389/90; Norfolk Record Office [hereafter NRO], DCN 1/6/18–20, 23; in 1390/1 they were *clerici sancte Marie*, ibid., 1/6/24.

[16] NRO, DCN 1/1/13; the master of the cellar was the equivalent of the bursar or treasurer at other Benedictine houses.

[17] NRO, DCN 1/1/19, 1/6/9.

[18] NRO, DCN 1/6/10 (1328/9), DCN 1/6/12 (1339/40); these items are headed '*custus puerorum et familie*'.

Although none of these *pauperes clerici* can be identified by name, the collation of scattered references provides further details of their presence and of some of their activities within the cathedral community; inevitably, this will amount to a delineation of the setting and of the group as a whole rather than of the individual boys, but it is well worth pursuing. First, then, who were the clerks of St Nicholas, whose earliest appearance in the Norwich records was in 1302/3, when they received a gift of 6*d*. by order of the prior?[19] There is no doubt that these were the almonry boys in another guise, which was associated with the festivities surrounding their election of one of their number as bishop and the accompanying reversal of roles on St Nicholas's or Holy Innocents' Day. At Durham gifts were regularly entered on the obedientiary accounts for the bishop of the almonry boys or of the almonry, but this appellation never occurs at Norwich.[20]

Again, who were the clerks mentioned in 1308 in one of Bishop Salmon's injunctions to the cathedral priory? He stipulated that when monk priests who were saying private Masses lacked clerks to assist them as servers, the almoner was to draw up a weekly rota to enable him to choose three of the almonry clerks, 'ad hoc habiles et potentes . . . qui in ministrando mature se gerant et honeste.' They were to be in attendance for this purpose from the hour of Matins until the end of High Mass, after which they were to resume their studies for the rest of the day without further distraction.[21] In these clerks we almost certainly find some of the more mature almonry boys being called on to assume another function, on account of the shortage or unavailability of any clerical servants who were employed by the sacrist and other obedientiaries and would probably have been accustomed to perform this duty. At Durham in the early

[19] NRO, DCN 1/1/16.

[20] J. T. Fowler, ed., *Extracts from the Account Rolls of the Abbey of Durham*, 3 vols, Surtees Society (1898–1901) [hereafter *Account Rolls of Durham*], 1, p. 212, 2, pp. 385, 574 and many other references. The conclusive evidence for their identity at Norwich is found in the early-fifteenth-century sacrist's accounts: on the feast of the Trinity in 1400/1 it was the clerks of St Nicholas who received gifts of gloves for their participation in the special ceremonies attached to the celebration of the cathedral's dedication, but in 1405 and 1406 similar entries name the almonry boys as the recipients, NRO, DCN 1/4/44, 47, 48.

[21] NRO, DCN 92/1. These injunctions have been transcribed, not always accurately, by E. H. Carter, *Studies in Norwich Cathedral History* (Norwich, 1935), where this article is found on pp. 21–2.

fifteenth century five boys received 4*s*. each for assisting at the monks' private Masses.[22] Whether this came to be regarded as normal practice or as a temporary necessity that came to stay cannot be determined, as there is no clear reference in any of the surviving Black Monk Chapter legislation.

At an unknown date, after the Black Death and probably prior to 1378/9, there appears to have been a change of policy with regard to admissions to the almonry school at Norwich.[23] Only about two or three years before the epidemic struck, Bishop Bateman visited the cathedral priory, and laid down that the monks were in future to propose names only according to a strict system of rotation, based on the order of seniority in chapter. Furthermore, he stressed that only the poor among their relatives (*pauperes eorum consanguinei*) would be eligible.[24] The need for this regulation, and for the Ely chapter ordinance with similar restrictions but of an earlier date, suggests that places in these two almonry schools had become highly competitive, as Dr Meryl Foster found to be the case at Durham by the early fourteenth century.[25] To relieve the pressure of a growing demand for places, and possibly to ease the burden of financial stringency, the Norwich monks decided to open the school to fee-paying boarders, the children of parents who had previously been excluded by the poverty clause.[26]

[22] W. A. Pantin, *General and Provincial Chapters of the English Black Monks, 1215–1540*, 3 vols = Camden Society, 3rd ser., 45, 47, 54 (1931–7), 3 (54), p. 281; Fowler, *Account Rolls of Durham*, 2, p. 406 Knowles states that before *c.*1150 the older child oblates acted as the servers: *The Religious Orders in England*, 3 vols (Cambridge, 1948–59), 2, p. 294; lay brethren or *conversi*, where they existed, would also have performed this duty.

[23] There are no surviving almoner's accounts between *c.*1355 and 1378/9.

[24] C. R. Cheney, 'Norwich Cathedral Priory in the fourteenth century', *BJRL*, 20 (1936), p. 112; this contains a transcription of the injunctions from the original which is now Manchester, John Rylands Library, Latin MS 226, and from Cambridge, Corpus Christi College, MS 370 which is a contemporary copy.

[25] Evans, *Ely Chapter Ordinances*, pp. 38–9, dated 1314; M. R. Foster, 'Durham Cathedral Priory 1229–1333: Aspects of the Ecclesiastical History and Interests of the Monastic Community' (Cambridge, Ph.D. thesis, 1979), pp. 181–2. Dr Foster has found evidence to suggest the existence of an almonry school at Durham in the early thirteenth century, ibid., p. 181.

[26] Financial stringency, or indeed financial prosperity, is difficult to gauge because of obedientiary accounting methods which were subject to change; moreover, the variable headings, frequent rearrangement of individual entries and only a partial and therefore misleading record of transactions hinder interpretation and warn against hasty judgement. However, a few relevant facts should prove helpful: the almoner's account of 1378/9 (NRO, DCN 1/6/18) follows a thirty-year gap and records that he was then carrying a deficit of £38 (which had probably been accumulating over a number of years) on an income of only £71; his income was decreasing and his expenses rising

There is no record of the selection process applied to this new group of boys—probably musical aptitude played a part—but a few of their family names have been preserved in the records between 1378/9 and 1436/7. To judge from this small sample, they were drawn, not surprisingly, from 'the landed and burgess classes of Norfolk and Norwich'.[27] For example, in 1378/9 the sons of William Elys and John de Beverle spent twelve weeks in the almonry school, for which their parents paid 10*d.* per week for each of them for bed and board (*pro mensa*). The boy Repp lodged for the same length of time, but the charge was only 9*s.*, while Charleton remained only six weeks for a fee of 5*s.* The master of the boys received his usual stipend of 13*s.* 4*d.*, but the only identifiable expenditure for the boys' maintenance was 3*s.* 3*d.* for purchases of food to alleviate their diet in Advent and Lent.[28] The following year the Beverle boy spent thirty-two weeks in the school, and Elys forty-one weeks.[29] These two continued their studies for a third year during which Beverle was only absent for one week; and one new boy arrived.[30] Unfortunately these lists of fee-paying boarders were not continued during the next twenty years, but with the appointment of a new almoner in 1401/2 the names of four boys were recorded, at least two of whom were in the school two years later.[31] Some of the many surviving fifteenth-century almoner's accounts continue to include names of those who paid for their board and lodging in the almonry, and a few are identified as *filii*, but these probably never numbered more than three or four; it may be that this policy of charging fees continued only until about 1437, after which the lists of names cease. The extent of the resulting

---

during the second half of the fourteenth century; the cost of maintaining his household (*custus puerorum et familie*) was about £6 in 1354/5 (ibid., 1/6/17) and had increased to £15 (*custus familie*) in 1379/80 (ibid., 1/6/19), but these figures must be treated with caution because of the changes and rearrangements referred to above.

[27] Paul Cattermole in Richard Harries, Paul Cattermole, and Peter Mackintosh, *A History of Norwich School, King Edward VI's Grammar School at Norwich* (Norwich, 1991), p. 7. The names occur in 1407/8, 1409/10, between 1419 and 1427 and in 1436/7, NRO, DCN 1/6/36, 39, 46–57, 62.

[28] NRO, DCN 1/6/18. The obvious conclusion is that the boys were considered as full members of the almoner's *familia* and therefore rarely distinguishable from the others in his household.

[29] NRO, DCN 1/6/19.

[30] NRO, DCN 1/6/20. There are only two known relatives of monks, both of whom were fee-paying boarders rather than poor relations: the nephew of Brother Richard Helyngton between 1420 and 1422 and the nephew of the Prior of the dependent cell of Yarmouth in 1422/3; in the latter case the Prior himself paid the fees, NRO, DCN 1/6/47, 48, 50.

increase in numbers in the almonry school cannot be determined, but it seems unlikely that, apart from a few possible occasions, the total ever rose above twenty. Numbers in other monastic almonry schools are too rarely stated for any meaningful comparison to be made, and the simultaneous provision of free places and of those for which charges were levied is, I believe, a phenomenon unique to Norwich among the cathedral priories.[32]

The location of a schoolroom in the precincts is known only by a single reference to its door in 1387/8, when the communar, who was paying for repairs, described it as being next to the entrance of the great hall; this implies that it opened on to the west range of the cloister.[33] The almonry buildings, within which the boys were housed, were further to the south-west, near St Ethelbert's Gate, and on the site now referred to as Almary Green. The extent to which the adjacent church of St Mary in the Marsh was used by the boys remains a mystery, apart from the single reference in the thirteenth-century ordinance, but it may not have been sheer coincidence that the master of the almonry school in 1425/6 was also the rector.[34]

Discernment, when applied to the study of the past, requires the historian to be wary of the deception which lurks behind apparent clarity. In this particular context there are two danger-spots which should be given a brief consideration. Both arise from the ambiguity of the Latin terms employed, and our inability to get behind the actual words to the minds of those who wrote them and to know the extent to which they were concerned to be precise and consistent. The word *clerici* has already

[31] NRO, DCN 1/6/30, 31; the two were the sons of Robert Martham and of Wastwyk.

[32] The number of boys at Glastonbury abbey in 1377 was reported to have been thirty-nine: N. Orme, *English Schools in the Middle Ages* (London, 1973), p. 244. At Westminster Abbey there were twenty-eight boys in 1385/6 and twenty-two in 1389/90: Westminster Abbey Muniments 23712, 23716 (I owe this reference to Miss Harvey).

[33] NRO, DCN 1/12/33. In 1436/7 the almoner bought a key for the door of the school '*iuxta claustrum*', ibid., 1/6/62. We have no assurance that this was the schoolroom used by the boys rather than by the novices; perhaps it was shared, since there is record of the Winchester boys and novices sharing the same master in the sixteenth century: Winchester Cathedral Muniments, Priory Register III, fol. 83v. Writing in the mid-twelfth century, Thomas of Monmouth ascribed to the boy martyr St William of Norwich, after his temporary burial in the chapter house, the desire 'to rest awhile in the chapter house among the boys', and M. R. James concluded that lessons may have been taught there; if so, this was surely a temporary measure: A. Jessopp and M. R. James, eds, *The Life and Miracles of St William of Norwich* (Cambridge, 1896), pp. xx, 187.

[34] NRO, DCN 1/12/51. St Mary in the Marsh presumably served as the parish church for those lay officials and servants of the priory who lived within the precincts.

served to illustrate this point by its use as an alternative to *pueri* in the clerks of St Nicholas and the clerks of St Mary.[35] The terms were presumably interchangeable when applied to boys who were old enough to be clerks in minor orders. There were, however, other *clerici* living within the precincts, some of whom can at times be identified, as members of the sacrist's *familia*, for example.[36] These clerks or boys, now identified more clearly, also performed a number of useful tasks at Norwich, among which were sweeping the cloister and, on at least one occasion, assisting the precentor in producing the books for the monks' Lenten reading.[37]

The other main source of confusion alerts us to the simultaneous presence of two groups of schoolboys, although in all probability there were never two separate and distinct schools. The distinguishing feature is that one group received special musical training in addition to other instruction. These were taught to take part in some of the liturgical services, and at Norwich came to be known as *clerici beate virginis* or *clerici beate Marie*, as already noted.[38] It has generally been accepted that the song or choir schools of the late fourteenth and early fifteenth centuries developed from the almonry schools; in the thirteenth-century Norwich ordinance we have confirmation of this common origin, but at an earlier date, and possibly at a time when all the boys received some instruction in music in addition to their other lessons. When Bishop Wakering, before his death in 1425, appointed seven almonry boys to sing antiphons daily after Vespers before the high altar (*altis vocibus decantandas*), he was no doubt calling on those who had been set apart and trained to

[35] *Garcio*, another word for boy, was generally used for a young page boy or servant, but the *garciones elemosinari[e* at Winchester in 1316/17 were the almonry boys: G. W. Kitchin, ed., *Compotus Rolls of the Obedientiaries of St Swithun's Priory, Winchester*, Hampshire Record Society (1892), p. 401; cf. S. J. A. Evans, 'Ely almonry boys and choristers in the later Middle Ages', in J. Conway Davies, ed., *Studies Presented to Sir Hilary Jenkinson* (London, 1957), p. 159.

[36] In 1363/4 and later years the sacrist regularly employed several and these were sometimes referred to as *clerici ecclesie*, or individually as *clericus capelle Marie* or *clericus beate Marie*, *clericus crucis* and so on according to their various responsibilities, NRO, DCN 1/4/35, 36, 42, 46.

[37] For sweeping in the 1430s and later years, NRO, DCN 1/12/57 (as *pueri*), 1/12/59 (as *clerici*). The precentor's account for 1352/3 contains the following entry: 'In ostens[atione librorum in quadrages[ima duobus pueris custod[ientibus libros ix d', ibid., DCN 1/9/6. The rule concerning the monks' Lenten reading comes from St Benedict himself; see McCann, *The Rule of St Benedict*, pp. 111–13.

[38] See above n. 15.

enhance the musical settings used in the liturgy.[39] Bishop Wykeham had had the same group in mind a few years before, when he drew up the arrangements for his chantry chapel in the nave of Winchester Cathedral.[40] However, unlike Winchester, with its informative records, those at Norwich give little indication of the extent of the musical involvement of the boys or, indeed, of the monks or of paid cantors in the Lady Chapel; and unlike Ely, Worcester, and elsewhere, there is no sign that a separate office of Master or Custos of the Lady Chapel was ever instituted.[41] Although there is an occasional reference to the *pueri beate Marie* in the almoner's accounts, it may be that the attempt to maintain and support a permanent choir for the daily singing of the Lady Mass did not long survive the disastrous fire of 1463.[42] After that date the chapter was preoccupied with an expensive restoration programme to replace the spire and the presbytery vault, and it seems that no one was found to succeed John Scarlet, the cantor, who for about twenty years had been in charge of the Lady Mass.[43]

In his research into the medieval origins of the present Norwich School, Dr Cattermole found a close connection between the cathedral almonry school and the city school, which was under episcopal patronage. Both seem to have been thriving institutions in the fourteenth and early fifteenth centuries, both were known as grammar schools, and at least one headmaster is known to have moved from the former to the latter in the early fifteenth century.[44] By the early sixteenth century, however, almonry boys were being sent to the episcopal school, a fact

[39] NRO, DCN 4/5, and also Wakering's will in E. F. Jacob, ed., *The Register of Henry Chichele*, 4 vols., Canterbury and York Society (1937–47), 2, p. 312.

[40] J. Greatrex, ed., *The Register of the Common Seal of the Priory of St Swithun, Winchester, 1345–1497*, Hampshire Record Series, 2 (1979), p. 22.

[41] However, there was a *magister altaris Marie* under the sacrist's authority as early as 1293, NRO, DCN 1/4/11.

[42] There are several references to the almoner's payments to the launderer for washing the boys' surplices, for example, in 1425/6 (NRO, DCN 1/6/55) and in 1436/7 (ibid., 1/6/62). A stimulating article on the medieval music and choir at Winchester, based on extensive research in the Winchester Cathedral archives by Dr Roger Bowers, will appear shortly in *JEH*.

[43] He occurs regularly on obedientiary accounts between 1442/3 and 1455/6, NRO, DCN 1/12/60, 66, and the Lady Mass continues to be recorded as an expense until 1469/70, DCN 1/12/70.

[44] In July 1403 M. John Hancok was appointed headmaster of the episcopal school but by 1423 he had moved to the almonry school, while continuing to be in charge of the episcopal school through a deputy, NRO, DN Reg. 3/6, fol. 298v, DN Reg. 4/8 fol. 155 and Cattermole, *Norwich School*, pp. 16–17.

which may explain the lament about the lack of a grammar master in the monastery and the dwindling number of almonry boys noted above.[45]

Although many regrettable gaps in the records still remain, and other new documents may come to light to alter the perspective from which we now view the Norwich almonry school, recent scholarly investigation has shown that the almonry and episcopal schools were not functioning in isolation. The fourteenth-century city was a flourishing centre of higher learning, in which all four mendicant houses co-operated and played a leading role, their *studia* attracting an international reputation. Direct evidence for Benedictine participation is lacking, but the scholarly pursuits and achievements of Norwich monks are well attested during this century.[46] The priory sent at least forty monks to university, approximately a third of whom returned with degrees, and several became widely known as theologians and preachers.[47] It would be surprising if none of these had received any elementary instruction in the almonry school before making a commitment to the monastic life,[48] and remarkable, too, if, although unlikely to have been officially involved in the teaching, they displayed no interest in and exerted no influence on its curriculum. For its part, the school, in the fourteenth century at least, must have shared in this educational vitality; and the monks who maintained it were in this way making their contribution to the local programme of more advanced studies by concerning themselves with instilling the rudiments of learning and stimulating young minds on the bottom rung of the academic ladder.

[45] The lack of a grammar master to teach the monks was reported at a visitation in 1514, Jessopp, *Visitations*, p. 77, and see n.1 above.

[46] W. J. Courtenay, *Schools and Scholars in Fourteenth-Century England* (Princeton, 1987), pp. 106–11. There is evidence of a cathedral school at Worcester in the fourteenth and fifteenth centuries which provided public lectures in theology by university trained monks: J. Greatrex, 'Benedictine monk scholars as teachers and preachers in the Later Middle Ages: evidence from Worcester Cathedral Priory', *Monastic Studies*, 2 (1991), p. 217.

[47] For example, Thomas Brinton, later bishop of Rochester, Adam Easton, cardinal priest of St Cecilia, John de Mari and John Stukle; see J. Greatrex, 'Monk students from Norwich Cathedral Priory at Oxford and Cambridge, *c.* 1300 to 1530', *EHR*, 106 (1991), pp. 555–83, especially the appendices, pp. 579–83.

[48] Noting the fact that in 1468 four former pupils of the almonry school of Canterbury cathedral were clothed as monks, Prof. Knowles suggested that this was a frequent occurrence but rarely recorded, *Religious Orders*, 2, p. 296, and quoting W. G. Searle, 'The chronicle of John Stone, monk of Christ Church, 1415–1471', *Cambridge Antiquarian Society*, no. 34 (1902), p. 106.

There is one surviving Norwich manuscript of the fourteenth century, which must have been a manual for all those with responsibilities in the almonry school; it is Vincent de Beauvais' *De puerorum nobilium erudicione*, which provides chapters on reading, writing, moral instruction, discipline, and social behaviour, devotes a section to the training of adolescents, and urges moderation in correction.[49]

The fact that the schooling provided by the monks of Norwich and of other Benedictine houses was limited to a very small number of boys at any one time does not mean that the monastic contribution in the field of medieval education was negligible. The high standard of teaching attained by the almonry schools was explained by Professor Orme as due to the presence of graduate masters and excellent libraries.[50] The Norwich sources rarely name the masters, and the title *magister* does not necessarily imply a university qualification.[51] However, the monastic library was well stocked and presumably frequented by instructors and mature scholars as well as by the monks; and in the thirteenth and fourteenth centuries, as we have seen, the cathedral priory was in the mainstream of educational development in the city. Finally, let us be clear that schools within the cloister, open to those not already dedicated to the monastic life, are extrinsic to the Benedictine vocation. Providing instruction and care for the young must, therefore, be considered as one of the monastic works of charity; and it was one which, in the Middle Ages, the monks were uniquely competent to perform.

Robinson College,
Cambridge

[49] The volume is now Cambridge, Corpus Christi College MS 325; I am grateful to the Master and Fellows of the College for permission to consult it.

[50] Orme, *English Schools*, pp. 249–51.

[51] Vincent de Beauvais' treatise was owned by Brother John de Strattone senior in the early fourteenth century and he may have been one of the monk instructors; see n. 49 above.

FRIENDS OF THE FAMILY: SOME MIRACLES FOR CHILDREN BY ITALIAN FRIARS

by DIANA M. WEBB

AT some time in the 1320s, the Sienese master Simone Martini painted an altar-piece celebrating the Hermit friar Agostino Novello.[1] Agostino, who had died at the convent of San Leonardo al Lago, near Siena, in 1309, is shown surrounded by illustrations of four of his posthumous miracles (see plates 1 and 2, pp. 198 and 200, below). Of these, three were performed on behalf of children. The exception, at upper right, shows the deliverance of a knight who, riding in a desolate mountainous landscape, has fallen beneath his horse. Top left, we see the rescue of a child from mauling by what is presumably a wolf. Below, a child falls into the street from a wooden balcony when one of its slats gives way; not only does he suffer no injury from the fall, but Agostino seizes the falling slat in mid-air and prevents it from hurting him. Bottom right, an infant suffers head injuries when he falls from his cradle, but his aunt kneels to make a vow to Agostino, and in the lower register we see the fulfilment of the vow: robed as a little Augustinian friar and carrying a taper, the child is carried by his nurse to give thanks, followed by his mother and his aunt, who carries another taper.

These miracles can be closely paralleled, as we shall see, by similar miracles performed for children by other saints, including mendicants, in the Italian cities and elsewhere at just this period. It is beyond dispute that most saints, at all periods, did some miracles for children, sometimes a lot of them;[2] it is the concentration of them in this altar-piece that is noteworthy. We do not know who the patron of the altar-piece was, or whether the subject-matter stemmed from a personal interest. Perhaps, Martindale suggests, it was simply fashionable at the time, and he

[1] A. Martindale, *Simone Martini: Complete Edition* (Oxford, 1988), pp. 33–4, 211–14 and pls 75–81. *Vita* and miracles in *ActaSS*, Maii 4, 614–24; four further miracles in a life printed by R. Arbesmann, 'A Legendary of early Augustinian saints', *Analecta Augustiniana*, 29 (1966), pp. 44–7.

[2] See the general comments of S. Shahar, *Childhood in the Middle Ages* (London, 1992), pp. 145–7.

points out that Simone also depicted miracles for children in his frescos of St Martin at Assisi and his altar-piece in honour of St Louis of Toulouse.[3] In both cases these are resuscitations of dead children, which establish the credentials of the saint by recalling their prototype among Christ's own miracles. Several such resuscitations were included among the miracles detailed in the bull of canonization of Louis of Toulouse.[4] What strikes the eye in the Agostino Novello altar-piece is, rather, the domestic setting of an Italian city and the evocation of the day-to-day hazards of a small child's life in that setting.[5] In the next decade the Lorenzetti brothers extended this Sienese interest in genre painting, but Simone's depiction of Agostino's miracles and their setting were not products of purely artistic fashion. Two of the three miracles are described in detail in extant written sources,[6] and similar stories were being told about other *beati*, at Siena and elsewhere.

Agostino's Sienese contemporary, the Servite Joachim (d. 1305), for example, performed four of his fourteen recorded miracles for children, and they are rich in interesting detail. He cured a child whose finger had been bitten off by a dog, and prevented injury to another who fell from a window while watching a joust.[7] Quantitatively, a more striking testimony to mendicant solicitude for children is contained in the list of 133 miracles performed at Bologna by the Augustinian Simone da Todi between 22 April 1322, two days after his death, and 7 July 1325.[8] The notaries who transcribed the miracles, in three parallel processes, invariably recorded the time of life of the beneficiary (*puer/puella*, *juvenis*, *homo/femina*, or *mulier*) and frequently their exact age as well. As they seem to have been fairly consistent in their usage, it is possible to be confident, even where no exact age is given, into what age range the beneficiary falls. Only young persons under the age of fourteen are denoted *puer* or

[3] Martindale, *Simone Martini*, pp. 212–14 and n. 6, pls 19, 36. The father of the child revived by Louis bears an image, not of the child, but of the saint himself as bishop in thanksgiving.

[4] *ActaSS*, Augusti 5, p. 791. Cf. below, n. 21.

[5] M. Seidel, 'Condizionamento iconografico e scelta semantica: Simone Martini e la Tavola del Beato Agostino Novello', in *Simone Martini, atti del convegno*, L. Bellosi, ed. (Florence, 1988), pp. 81–6.

[6] Martindale, *Simone Martini*, p. 212, gives the texts and references.

[7] *Vita ac legenda Beati Ioachimi Senensis*, ed. P. M. Soulier, *AnBoll*, 13 (1894), pp. 393, 395. For the other miracles, see below, pp. 191, 192.

[8] *ActaSS*, Aprilis 2, pp. 818–31.

puella. The term *infans* does not occur, but there are a few *pueri parvi*. At fourteen the young person becomes a *juvenis* (the word *adolescens* is not used), and by twenty-three a young woman is a *femina* or a *mulier*. The youngest *homo* who is assigned an age is twenty-five.

If we adhere to the notaries' narrow definition of children, we find that Simone performed 60 of his 133 miracles for this age-group (45.1 per cent). Of these, seventeen at least were under-fives. Two of his 'epileptics' were, in fact, infants suffering from convulsions, and he also saved two very small children who ran out into the road and were crushed by ox carts.[9] If we modify the categories used by the notaries and class *juvenes* of fourteen to sixteen as 'children', the relevant number would rise to 69 (51.9 per cent), including 40 boys and 29 girls. If we go a step further and include all the miracles Simone did for *juvenes* between fourteen and twenty-one, the total for young persons reaches 77. Even allowing for the greater prominence of this age cohort in pre-industrial populations, Simone was giving them more than their fair share (57.9 per cent) of his thaumaturgic attentions.

This proportion is, it must be said, rather exceptional. There are over 230 distinct miracles recorded for the Dominican Ambrogio Sansedoni of Siena (d. 1287) among the published material.[10] It looks as if 73 of them involved children, perhaps a more normal percentage at around 31 per cent. Exact comparisons, whether between friar and friar or between mendicant and non-mendicant miracles, are difficult, because miracle collections differ not only in their exactitude as to ages, which are frequently not recorded at all, but in their choice of terms and of dividing-lines between life-stages. Among Ambrogio's miracles was the cure of a fifteen-year-old boy who is called *puer*.[11] It seems safe to assume that where in collections of this date and type a young person is called *puer* or *puella*, he or she was at most sixteen years of age. Where a beneficiary is described only as *filius* or *filia* of another person, exactitude is unattainable, although it is sometimes possible to infer that a parent is reporting a miracle on behalf of a child. We possess a notarized record of 99 miracles

[9] Ibid., pp. 828, 829, 823–4, 827.
[10] Ibid., Martii 3, pp. 181–251.
[11] Ibid., p. 234.

done by Zita of Lucca, beginning on 28 April 1279;[12] many of her clients are described simply as 'sons' and 'daughters', and only if we make the rather generous assumption that most of these were children can we hazard that children constituted about 28 per cent of the total clientele. The layman Henry of Bolzano performed 362 recorded cures, mostly of orthopaedic conditions, for a period after his death at Treviso in June 1315. There is no indication of the ages of the beneficiaries at the time of the cure, but it is often noted that their condition dated from the cradle or a very young age.[13] Eleven had been living with injuries sustained as a result of falls in infancy—from a cradle, a staircase, or somebody's arms. Henry's miracles centred on the cathedral of Treviso, which reaped the benefit because the local Augustinians, whom he had frequented in life, had allegedly not accepted him for burial;[14] Zita's on the baptismal church of San Frediano, in Lucca, which was served by a community of regular canons. The miracles recorded for Simone da Todi, as for Ambrogio Sansedoni, Agostino Novello, and Joachim of Siena, mostly belong to a similar context of local churches frequented by a populace who require help with day-to-day problems. When a few years after Zita's death the prior was persuaded by her miracles to translate her to a new tomb, he consulted first with the Franciscans and Dominicans, and the cult subsequently owed much to the preaching of the mendicants.[15] Relations between the friars and other clergy may not always have been so harmonious, but they served, indeed often competed for, the same market.

There is certainly no *prima facie* justification for supposing that miracles done by friars were distinctive in terms of number, type, or the clientele they benefited. The point that seems to be illustrated by Simone Martini's altar-piece is subtly different. By the 1320s the friars had been putting down roots in urban society for the better part of a century. The Dominicans and Franciscans

[12] Ibid., Aprilis 3, pp. 510–27.

[13] Ibid., Junii 2, pp. 376–91. Eighty- five clients had suffered conditions from birth, and another sixty 'from the cradle', 'from infancy' or 'childhood' or from a specified young age. Many more, who are described only as having suffered for so many years, may have suffered from childhood.

[14] Reported as hearsay by Henry's biographer, Pietro Dominico, Bishop of Treviso, a canon of the cathedral in the saint's lifetime: ibid., p. 371.

[15] Ibid., Aprilis 3, p. 508; A. Vauchez, *La Sainteté en occident aux derniers siècles du moyen âge* (Rome, 1981), pp. 246–7 and n. 187.

were still publicizing their mission by adding to the number of their canonized saints, with Louis of Toulouse (1317) and Thomas Aquinas (1323). Even when a saint had long been canonized, the work of compiling and circulating miracles continued: sixty years after Peter Martyr's canonization in 1253, the Dominican chapter general held at London in 1314 ordered the collection of his miracles, and many of them are dated to the first two decades of the fourteenth century.[16] Brother Recuperatus, one of a syndicate of Sienese Dominicans who had originally written Ambrogio Sansedoni's Life at the command of Honorius IV, compiled a new summary of his life and miracles some time after 1318.[17] The promoters of the Augustinian Nicolas of Tolentino (d. 1305) succeeded in obtaining a canonization process in 1325, although it did not bear the desired fruit until 1446.[18] It was also in the 1320s that Simone da Todi performed his miracles and that the cults of Agostino, Joachim, and Ambrogio Sansedoni, and also the Franciscan tertiary Pier Pettinaio, were officially recognized by the commune of Siena.[19] Simone's Agostino Novello altar-piece was painted when the mendicant influence on Italian urban society was arguably at its height.

In life, saints varied in their enthusiasm for miracle-working. For some it was a hallmark of their style, while Antony of Padua was one who did not seek a reputation as a wonder worker, but had it energetically forced upon him after death.[20] Nor were posthumous miracles necessarily consonant with the saint's characteristics in life. The youthful friar-prince Louis of Toulouse, who in life was a model of withdrawal from the world rather than pastoral engagement with it,[21] and who is reported to have

[16] Printed with Ambrogio Taegio's sixteenth-century compilation of the saint's Life, *ActaSS*, Aprilis 3, pp. 686–719. On the reliability of these texts, A. Dondaine, 'Saint-Pierre-Martyr: Etudes', *AFP*, 23 (1953), pp. 66–162.

[17] *ActaSS*, Martii 3, pp. 210–41. I have cited Ambrogio's miracles principally from this source.

[18] *Il processo di canonizazzione di S. Nicola di Tolentino*, ed. N. Occhioni (Rome, 1984). Several miracles are included in the life printed in *ActaSS* which are not in the canonization process.

[19] A. Vauchez, 'La Commune de Sienne, les Ordres Mendiants et le Culte des Saints. Histoire et enseignements d'une crise (novembre 1328–avril 1329)', *Mélanges de l'Ecole Française de Rome*, 89. ii (1977), pp. 757–67.

[20] Vauchez, *Sainteté*, p. 617, citing L. de Kerval, *L'évolution et le développement du merveilleux dans les légendes de saint Antoine de Padoue* (Paris, 1906). Cf. A. Thompson, *Revival Preachers and Politics in Thirteenth-Century Italy: the Great Devotion of 1233* (Oxford, 1992), pp. 90, 108, 213.

[21] Vauchez, *Sainteté*, pp. 398–9. The miracles are edited in *Analecta Franciscana*, 8 (1951), pp. 275–331, but I have cited here the old text in *ActaSS*, Augusti 5, pp. 775–822.

refused to kiss his own mother because she was a woman, expended a great deal of spiritual energy *post mortem* in reviving stillborn children at the behest of parents, and even on one occasion granted abundant milk to a woman who had been unable to feed two previous babies.[22] By contrast, Ambrogio Sansedoni was an acknowledged specialist, both before and after death, in the care of a distinct group among the young, *puellae* of marriageable age, whose well-being was of increasing concern to the public authorities of the Italian cities in the later medieval period. He was not even above rescuing bungling brothers who had promised their sister to two different suitors from the consequences of their own incompetence.[23] A newly married girl, who was terrified lest her husband discover her epilepsy, was delivered; a Florentine girl, betrothed to a young man, appealed to Ambrogio for the cure of an ulcer on her side, knowing him to be the *advocatus virginum*.[24]

To dismiss thaumaturgic potency as a mere contrivance of the Orders and the ecclesiastical authorities to promote the cult would fail to convey the full context in which the veneration of these saints unfolded. Miracles performed a variety of propaganda and pastoral functions; many made explicit the fact that the Church's power in society depended on its ability to answer the needs of the ordinary lay public. In all but extraordinary circumstances[25] miracles of healing were the most interesting to that public. Men and women wanted healing for themselves, but perhaps they wanted it even more for their children. Many, if not most, such miracles were, in effect, done for parents, not only in the technical sense that it was they, rather than the children, who prayed for the cure and made the appropriate vow of offering or pilgrimage, but because their distress at the child's suffering was relieved, as well as the suffering itself.

[22] *ActaSS*, Augusti 5, p. 817. Agostino Novello enabled the widowed mother of a poor girl who had borne a baby daughter, but had neither milk nor the money to hire a wet-nurse, to produce enough milk herself to feed her granddaughter: ibid., Maii 4, p. 621.

[23] Ibid., Martii 3, p. 200. Another very similar miracle is described on pp. 235–6.

[24] Ibid., pp. 223, 198. For Ambrogio's concern in life with the well-being of *virgines nubiles*, see p. 193. It was the fame of his own virginity which attracted petitioners of both sexes and apparently gave him the power both to bring about marriages which had seemed impossible and prevent others which seemed inevitable. Every year *iuvenculae nubiles* made offerings at his tomb 'ut in matrimonio sancto digne se copulare possent'.

[25] For example, Thompson suggests, during the 'Alleluia' of 1233: *Revival Preachers*, pp. 115–17.

Parental concerns which were catered for by miracles began, sometimes, before the actual birth of children. The relief of sterility was an essential component of the saint's art, which generated a number of model stories, and so, too, was the granting of children who survived to mothers who had had a run of stillbirths or miscarriages. Peter Martyr's miracles include three tales of women, one a noblewoman of Cyprus and two inhabitants of Ascoli in the Marche, who had been granted children in one or other of these circumstances. All had vowed that if a male child were born to them they would do everything in their power to ensure that when the time came he entered the Order of Preachers. Alas, moved, by the beauty of their children, these foolish women went back on their vows, with distressing results.[26] Saints commonly intervened to avert the hazards of childbirth and to ensure that a baby lived long enough to be baptized. Louis of Toulouse frequently did so, and in several instances we are told how long the child in fact survived.[27] Less commonly, the saints assuaged parents' anxieties about the earthly well-being of children if their own life or livelihood was threatened. One client of Simone da Todi, seized in the chest by 'the affliction called *Noli-me-Tangere*', had been advised to go to the shrine of St Antony of Vienne, a specialist in epidemic disease. Evidently distressed at the thought of what would become of his four children, he applied instead to Simone, and when he received his cure presented images of the children at the tomb.[28] Ambrogio Sansedoni cured a woman of a severe fever, and she took as many images as she had children to the shrine.[29]

Peter Martyr's terms for the relief of childlessness could obviously be interpreted as recruitment devices. Clients of the friars could properly promise only to *try* to induce their sons to enter an order. A Sienese mother, when her son developed a severe fever, appealed to Ambrogio Sansedoni and explicitly promised her best efforts to make the child a Preacher.[30] It is not always made so clear, however, that the child was morally committed. Margarita of Siena had had four boy babies die with convulsions,

[26] *ActaSS*, Aprilis 3, pp. 705–7.
[27] Ibid., Augusti 5, pp. 817–18 for examples.
[28] Ibid., Aprilis 2, p. 831.
[29] Ibid., Martii 3, p. 224.
[30] Ibid., p. 226.

and when she bore a girl, who at six days old developed the same affliction, she vowed several acts of devotion to Ambrogio, among them that she would robe this daughter and all other children she might have in the Dominican habit and present them at the altar.[31] Simone Martini, like the text he was following, was describing a ritual that would from time to time be enacted in the churches of Siena and elsewhere.

The authors of miracle stories naturally often evoked the emotions of parents. A woman of Ascoli was saddened, after the death of four children, both because of their deaths and because she was becoming hateful to her husband. She was inspired to appeal to Peter Martyr when she heard of a miracle he had wrought for a woman of Flanders in a similar predicament. This woman, too, bearing a fourth dead child, realized that her husband was beginning to hate her.[32] In 1314, at Montpellier, the father and mother of an apparently stillborn son together persisted in supplication to Peter, while everyone around urged them to bury the child. In 1319, a grandmother, 'perceiving the sorrow of the father' at an apparent stillbirth, volunteered to take the infant to the saint's shrine.[33] To suggest that the mothers in such cases felt the simple emotions of loss and sorrow, while the fathers were concerned only with family pride and maintaining the lineage, would seem a risky speculation. Fathers are sometimes seen enacting a distinctive and energetic role in the nurturing of sickly children. A child of Ascoli had been crippled from infancy and unable to stand. His mother, preparing a herbal bath for him, asked Peter Martyr that he might be enabled to walk once a year. Her husband rebuked her for imposing any limit, and tested the efficacy of their faith by calling to the boy to come to them from across the room.[34] The better part of a century earlier, a native of Padua, called Pietro, was carrying his crippled and epileptic four-year-old daughter through the streets when he met St Antony and begged a blessing of him. This was no instant miracle. On his return home Pietro began to force the child to walk round the house on a wheeled support (*curriculo sustentatam*)

[31] Ibid., p. 223; there is another account on p. 197, and a notarial instrument recording the miracle, p. 204.
[32] Ibid., Aprilis 3, pp. 706, 708.
[33] Ibid., p. 710.
[34] Ibid., p. 714.

until she could manage by herself. She was also cured of her epilepsy.[35] Another Paduan father had tried to straighten his eleven-year-old son's left foot, deformed since birth, by strapping it to splints; it was the child's mother who took him as a suppliant to Antony's shrine.[36]

Mothers, who were responsible for the day-to-day care of their children, sometimes implored the saints for help for fear of the reactions of their husbands if they returned to the house to find a child dead, sick, or injured. A mother left her three-year-old only son, 'whom she loved tenderly', asleep in bed while she went to church; he awoke while she was out, began to cry at finding himself alone, and fell, breaking his arm, in trying to climb out of bed. The mother 'greatly feared lest her husband, who was in the country, should on his return find the child thus injured and punish her for not taking care of him.' A vow to Joachim of Siena removed the difficulty.[37] This unrelenting domestic responsibility generated hazards of its own, for urban and rural families alike. A little girl in the Paduan countryside drowned in a ditch while her mother went to get fire from a neighbouring house.[38] Nicolas of Tolentino rescued a child who, while his mother was doing the washing, fell into a mill-race and actually became lodged in the mill-wheel. Ambrogio Sansedoni, too, delivered a child who was mangled by an animal-powered mill.[39]

The predicament of the pious woman, at home with her infant but fretting to hear a famous preacher, generated a topos. One version concerns a village housewife who had her child near her while she heated water in a cauldron for a bath. Hearing that Antony of Padua was about to preach in the neighbourhood, she was so eager to hear him that, thinking she had put the child in the basin, presumably the one intended for the bath, in fact popped him into the cauldron. Returning from the sermon, she was asked by the neighbours where the child was, and remembered only that she had left him near the fire. Tearing her hair,

[35] Ibid., Junii 2, p. 721.

[36] Ibid., p. 719.

[37] *Vita*, p. 394.

[38] *ActaSS*, Junii 2, p. 721.

[39] Ibid., Septembris 3, p. 661; *Il processo*, pp. 263–4; *ActaSS*, Martii 3, p. 226. For similar hazards documented in English manorial court records, see B. Hanawalt, *The Ties that Bound* (Oxford, 1986), pp. 175–8.

she rushed into the house accompanied by half the neighbourhood, to find him sitting in the cauldron, playing in the boiling water.[40] Small wonder that San Bernardino later counselled housewives not to leave their household chores unattended to in order to hear sermons.[41]

Once they had surmounted the perils of their first few hours and days, and presuming they did not fall victim to maternal absence of mind, children tended to require a great deal of straightforward healing, although it was not out of the question that a young person, usually a girl, might develop the symptoms of mental illness. Simone da Todi cured one demoniac who was only eleven,[42] and there are others, simply called *puellae*, among the clients of other saints. Boys were especially prone to injuries received at play, and they were likely to constitute the groups of children in the streets who were sometimes ridden down by runaway horses or carts. Boys were more liable to fall from great heights, drown in ditches, or receive injuries in the course of mock fights. It was both sententious and true to observe that children's play often turned into real fights; in one such case, head injuries received by a small boy seemed to require surgery, which both parents dreaded *propter pueritiae teneritudinem*, until Ambrogio Sansedoni intervened.[43] The juvenile clients of Joachim of Siena included several whose typically childlike behaviour had got them into trouble: the six-year-old who was walking along the road with a loaf of bread and nibbling at it, 'as children do', when a dog attacked him and bit off his finger; the child at Forlì who leaned out too far, *pueriliter*, while watching a joust from a window; another six-year-old, who was trying to pick flowers over a ditch just outside Siena, also leaned over too far, 'ut mos puerorum est'.[44] Six was a dangerous age: Ambrogio Sansedoni had to rescue the same incorrigible six-year-old from the consequences of two different accidents.[45]

There is, to repeat, nothing about any of these miracles that is peculiar to the late medieval period or environment, urban or

[40] Ibid., Junii 2, pp. 728–9.

[41] I. Origo, *The World of San Bernardino* (London, 1963), p. 46.

[42] *ActaSS*, Aprilis 2, p. 825.

[43] *ActaSS, ASB* Martii 3, p. 238.

[44] *Vita*, pp. 393, 395, 395–6.

[45] *ActaSS*, Martii 3, p. 239.

rural, or to mendicant saints. That mendicant saints performed them was a sign of the friars' implantation in their working environment. They sought to establish themselves as purveyors of pastoral care, and the cult of a mendicant saint depended in large part on the relationship of a church with a community of ordinary laypeople. The observations of human behaviour, including child behaviour, that appear in miracle stories, and even the occasional comment on the stages of child development, express a necessary awareness of the life-cycle and family problems. A child of Ascoli who was cured by Peter Martyr could not stand upright, 'although he had reached the age at which children usually walk'; a twenty-month-old boy whom Ambrogio Sansedoni cured was judged to have reached the age at which he should have been able to walk upright. It transpired that he had 'lost his name'; he should have been called Ambrogio. Another of Ambrogio's clients was a little girl of thirty months, 'who from her birth had progressed as girls of her age were accustomed to'; then an illness had arrested her development and paralysed her from the waist down.[46]

Like most saints, mendicant saints ministered first and foremost to a local clientele. A boy in the Camporeggio district of Siena, near the Dominican church, was buried when a cellar collapsed on him. He was dug out completely unhurt and said that he had seen Brother Ambrogio protecting him from the weight of the rubble. The curious thing was that no one present had invoked the saint's aid or commended the boy to him; but,

> as he was of the neighbourhood of the Friars Preachers, that is Camporeggio, where the aforementioned father is especially and frequently celebrated, it seems that he takes a special care of the inhabitants: nor, in their necessity, does he wait for prayers or promises, since he receives the sacrifice of their praise without ceasing.[47]

A woman dwelling near the Basilica of St Antony, at Padua, carelessly left her twenty-month-old son near a water-butt. Finding him drowned in it, she set up a howl which brought the neighbourhood running, including some of the brethren,

[46] Ibid., Aprilis 3, p. 714; Martii 3, pp. 231, 219.
[47] Ibid., p. 239.

together with workmen who were doing repairs in the church. They commiserated with the mother, but (as if put in mind of it by their presence) she vowed to the saint that she would give to the poor the weight of the child in wheat if he was delivered.[48]

The saint, in such contexts, is both wonder worker and local patron, operating from the shrine where his body lies, the focus for his community and the devotions of the neighbourhood. By apparent contrast, few of the stories of Peter Martyr's posthumous miracles focus on his principal shrine at the church of Sant' Eustorgio, in Milan. His relics were widely dispersed among altars in Dominican churches, and he exerted his miraculous powers from Cyprus to Ireland. The sense of neighbourhood, however, is present in many of these stories, too; the neighbourhood is that of the church and the Dominican community, wherever it may be. Many miracles, predictably, are done for layfolk who are clearly already linked with the friars. The five-year-old son of a certain noble of Montpellier, who had been long childless, died and was taken to the Preachers for burial. The grief-stricken mother, 'accompanied by a horde of matrons, against the custom of the country', invaded the church and induced the brethren to join with her in supplication. At Metz, a woman who had borne seven short-lived children, and was again pregnant, was counselled by a kinsman who had become a Preacher and had just been posted to the local convent. She vowed to call the baby Peter (a common promise), and to present him annually with fitting offerings at the shrine, to observe Peter's feast, and hear the office and sermon. The woman of Ascoli who was reluctant to give the healthy son she had at last had to be a friar found that he fell sick, with a severe swelling in his throat, when she again went back on her vow. She was in the act of applying a poultice to the swelling when some of the brethren came round on a parish call, *visitationis gratia*, and urged her to seek the saint's help once more.[49]

The story which perhaps most vividly evokes this parochial atmosphere concerns the woman of Narni who found her three-year-old son dead in his bed. Fearing that she would be accused of negligence by her husband, she told her serving-maid to take

[48] Ibid., Junii 2, p. 738.
[49] Ibid., Aprilis 3, pp. 709, 711, 706–7.

the child's body to the Preachers' church. She placed it inconspicuously beneath the altar of Peter Martyr (it was the octave of his feast). The mother told her husband that she had sent the child to a kinsman's home for some medicine. On the third day afterwards, the child revived and toddled happily into the refectory, where some of the brethren recognized him. Thinking he had been left behind in the church after Vespers, they sent word to the mother to send her servant to collect him.[50]

We are not, perhaps, much nearer to explaining precisely why Simone Martini depicted Agostino Novello as a special protector of children; but miracles of the type he depicted were in the established repertoire of the saint of the period. The friars competed with the secular clergy and with one another to provide the care which attracted the alms and loyalties of the populace. Because children mattered to the people, they had to matter to the friars.

King's College London

[50] Ibid., pp. 708–9.

THE CHILD IN THE PICTURE: A MEDIEVAL PERSPECTIVE

by ANDREW MARTINDALE

THE subject of this paper is the child in art about the year 1300. Some years ago, while studying the Tuscan painter Simone Martini (active *c.* 1310–44),[1] I noticed that he painted what seemed to be an unusually large number of scenes involving children; and I was curious to know whether this was as special or as interesting as at first appeared. As my knowledge increased, the subject broadened to involve the more general issue of change. Around 1300, images of children become more lively, more human, and more probable. Simone's painting forms a part of that change; and the question was 'What happened and why?' Other scholars have commented on this general problem;[2] but although it is possible to criticize their approaches, the issue of 'change' remains. Moreover, although the analysis and explanation of change are exercises common to all historians, the special problem of the visual arts is the integration of the world recorded by texts and documents with that recorded by the visual sources. The connections are often obscure; and, in order to clarify the issues, this paper will begin with some description.

In about the year 1325, Simone Martini painted an altar-piece[3] celebrating the person and miracles of the recently deceased Augustinian Hermit Agostino, called in religion Agostino

[1] The study appeared as *Simone Martini* (Oxford, 1988). Throughout this paper, frequent recourse is had to it – not because it contains all the answers, but because it is a source both of illustrations and of further bibliographical references.

[2] In particular, P. Ariès, *L'enfant et la vie familiale sous l'Ancien Régime* (Paris, 1960). For further discussion, see below pp. 205–6.

[3] For information on this altar, including the relevant miracle texts, see Martindale, *Simone Martini*, pp. 211–14. The main additional writing consists of the two contributions of M. Seidel: 'Questioni iconographichè', in A. Bagnoli and L. Bellosi, eds, *Simone Martini e 'chompagni'* (Florence, 1985), part of the catalogue entry for this altar-piece which was exhibit no. 7; see pp. 68–72. This contribution is particularly concerned with the representation of Agostino. See also 'Condizionamento iconografico e scelta semantica. Simone Martini e la tavola del Beato Agostino Novello', in L. Bellosi, ed., *Simone Martini, atti del convegno* (Florence, 1988), pp. 75–80. This contribution is more concerned with the interpretation of the miracles and the civic context of the altar-piece.

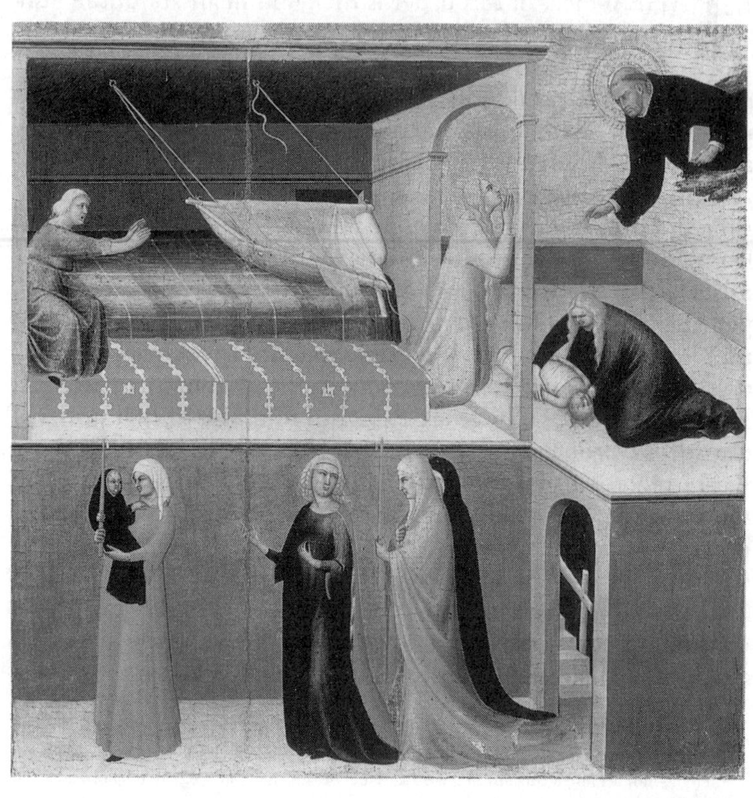

Plate 1 Simone Martini, *Miracle of the Blessed Agostino Novello: the Child who fell out of his Cradle*, Siena, S. Agostino. Photo: author.

Novello to distinguish him from the putative founder of the Order. One of the scenes (plate 1) shows an episode 'in which a six-month-old child was the victim of what would now be called an 'accident in the home'. As the nurse was lulling him to sleep in his cradle, one of the strings supporting the cradle broke and the child was propelled head first into a wall. At that point his head was described in the text of the miracle as like a bun (*guastella*).[4] Fortunately the mother's sister-in-law, who was apparently a woman of action, took the matter in hand. She got the head back into some sort of shape, remodelling it 'like wax'; while she was doing this, she vowed the boy to the Blessed Agostino, promising that if the boy survived, he would be offered on the altar of the saint, clothed like an Augustinian brother. Agostino heard the prayer and interceded for the tiny tot. The boy recovered, and the mother carried him to the church, 'just as had been promised'.

This charming story has several points of interest. There are, for instance, several miracle stories in which the parents in some manner 'vow their child to the saint'. Quite often the vow is to place the child actually on the saint's altar. It is not clear to me what the 'liturgy' for this was. I have always assumed the model to have been the Presentation of Christ in the Temple, and that the child was then redeemed back with an offering.[5] In any case, Simone's picture shows the youngest member of the Paganello family on his way to the ceremony dressed in a diminutive Augustinian habit. The painting illustrates a not infrequent event in progress.[6]

[4] The *Grande dizionario della lingua italiana* gives *guastella* as a *specie di focaccia*. The child's head must have seemed round and soft because the sister-in-law reshaped it 'like wax'.

[5] See here the paper given by Joan Greatrex, above, pp. 169–81, in which she alludes to the change from the custom of giving children as oblates. This change occurred during the twelfth century and is relevant to the discussion of the type of education on offer by the late thirteenth century at Norwich Cathedral Priory.

[6] For other examples of children being offered to the saint, see Margaret of Cortona: Fra Bevegnati, *Leggenda della vita e dei miracoli di Santa Margarita da Cortona* (Vicenza, 1978), pp. 341–6; Agnes of Bohemia: J. Nemec, *Agnese di Boemia* (Padua, 1987); Louis of France: P. B. Fay, *Les miracles de Saint Louis de Guillaume de Saint-Pathus* (Paris, 1931), p. 20. This occasion was rather more complicated since an initial vow both of a visit to the tomb of St Louis and of the girl victim to the saint ('je vos veu ma fille et la vous doins et vour promet que des or en avant ele n'aura autre mire que vous') was followed by further visits during which the malady gradually abated.

The custom seems to have developed post-1250, and is not to be confused with the earlier custom of giving small children as oblates. Among the miracles of St Francis there is what appears to be an intermediate stage where an eight-year-old boy, miraculously spared from beneath a mound of collapsed masonry, entered the order at the age of fourteen (*Legenda Maior. Miracula* III. 5).

Plate 2 Simone Martini, *Altar-piece of the Blessed Agostino Novello*, Siena, S. Agostino. Photo: University of East Anglia.

This painting belongs to a large panel, tripartite in form, and containing in the centre the figure of the *Beatus* with, to the right and left, representations of four posthumous miracles, two on each side (plate 2). The relevance of these to the theme of the conference is that three of the four involve children; and that represents a very high proportion for a single altar-piece. Normally, where space permits, the social spread of miracles is varied to suggest the accessibility of the saint to a variety of people. Thus in the famous and extensive late-thirteenth-century cycle dedicated to St Francis at Assisi, the posthumous miracles involve a doubting pope, a man who had been mugged, a dying woman with an unconfessed sin, and a penitent heretic. When all allowance has been made for the change of venue and 'audience', the concentration of children in the Simone altar remains exceptional; and the question arises whether this reveals anything about Agostino Novello, about Simone, about Siena—or, indeed, about the early fourteenth century. In fact, it opens up questions about the place of children in this sort of hagiography.[7]

Of the altar-piece itself nothing is known before the sixteenth century; and the first description comes only in the 1630s.[8] The original context and form have, nevertheless, been reconstructed. In the seventeenth century it was said to have been set above the coffin containing the body of the saint—the coffin itself being decorated with four scenes from his life. It has reasonably been suggested that the surviving stone shrine of S. Raniero, at Pisa, gives some idea of the original layout.[9] Dating from the first decade of the fourteenth century, that structure, originally set over an altar, consists of a sarcophagus, decorated with scenes from S. Raniero's life, surmounted by a canopied relief, which serves as an altar-piece. Moreover, the slightly unusual shape of the Simone altar-piece can be explained with reference to a predella panel painted by the fifteenth-century artist Sassetta.[10] From all this it seems likely that the Agosti-

[7] The issue is given more detailed attention in the paper offered at the conference by Diana Webb, 'Friends of the family: some miracles for children by Italian friars', pp. 183–95, above.

[8] It was only attributed to Simone Martini in the early nineteenth century. See Martindale, *Simone Martini*.

[9] M. Seidel, 'Condizionamento'.

[10] The panel is reproduced in a paper by H. van Os, 'Due divagazioni intorno alla pala di Simone Martini per il Beato Agostino Novello', in Bellosi, *Simone Martini*, pp. 81–6. It should be said that the author emphasizes the special characteristics of the tripartite design of the Simone altar-piece

no Novello altar was originally set above the saint's sarcophagus and in a shallow niche against a lateral wall of the conventual church of St Augustine of Hippo, in Siena.

The saint himself will be little known outside Siena.[11] Matteo da Tarano was almost certainly of central Italian origin. He trained to become a brilliant canon lawyer and served at the Staufen court in south Italy. He took part in the disastrous Battle of Benevento in 1266, but escaped to Sicily, where he retired from the world, joining the Augustinian Hermits. Although he moved thence *incognito* to a hermitage near Siena, his distinguished origins were eventually discovered. He was summoned by the General of the Order to Rome to assist in revising the Constitution of the Order. Nicholas IV made him Apostolic Penitentiary; and in 1298 he was elected General of the Order. He was seen to have managerial qualities. He was never, however, happy in that position—which he resigned in 1300, retiring to a hermitage at S. Leonardo al Lago, near Siena, where he died in 1309. This mini-biography is necessary as background to the four scenes which once adorned his sarcophagus. The first showed him lying ill in Sicily and sending his servants to seek out the *Dominican* friars, whom he was considering joining. The second scene showed the servants returning miraculously, if mistakenly, with two Augustinian Hermits (which they did three times in succession). In the third he was seen being received into the Order; and in the fourth he was shown being consecrated priest.[12]

Unfortunately these four scenes are lost. It is not known whether they were painted by Simone; and, indeed, since they were first described in 1638, it is not even certain that they belonged to the original structure. Assuming for the present that that was the case, the overall selection of scenes must appear surprising.

A recent explanation has suggested that the whole complex of altar, shrine, and altar-piece may be explained in terms of Sienese

---

which make it different from those seen in the predella panel. He suggests connections with goldsmiths' work and the design of reliquaries.

[11] Martindale, *Simone Martini*, p. 212. For a more complete biography, see *Biblioteca Sanctorum* (Rome, 1961–9).

[12] Or so the seventeenth-century Visitors were told. Agostino was shown being 'invested' with a chasuble (*planetam*).

civic and religious politics.[13] It is true that during the late thirteenth and early fourteenth centuries it was common for Italian communes to take in hand their local saints and to exalt the material presence of their remains. Siena was no exception; and Agostino Novello followed hard on the heels of Andrea Gallerani (d. 1251) and Ambrogio Sansedoni (d. 1286).[14] During the 1320s Agostino's position was debated in the city council; and although he was a 'foreigner' by birth, it was formally decided (1329) that his day should be celebrated by the council. Stylistically Simone's painting fits quite well into the 1320s; and a final step in this train of thought is to suggest that the altar was part of a deliberate Augustinian attempt to 'naturalize' Agostino and to turn him into *civis noster*.[15] In support of this it has been pointed out that the miracles are set in a local context—street, countryside, domestic dwelling; and that this suggests the unity of the saint with the civic context.[16]

It must be said that the sarcophagus scenes discourage this idea. Agostino had a number of important connections with Siena. In particular, he revised the constitutions of the ancient Ospedale della Scala and devised a uniform for the Master.[17] In a complex designed to emphasize the role of the saint in the city, some reference to this might have been expected; but the four scenes from his life refer only to his career in the south of Italy and to his joining the Augustinian Order.[18]

[13] M. Seidel, 'Condizionamento', *passim*.

[14] And others–see Van Os, 'Due divagazioni'; and Seidel, 'Condizionamento'.

[15] Seidel, 'Condizionamento', p. 79.

[16] As noted by Seidel in *Simone Martini e 'chompagni,'* (Florence, 1985), p. 72.

[17] Jordan of Saxony said, 'Fuit hospitalitatis auctor', persuading a rich Sienese, Dominus Restaurus, to become head of the hospital and to commit his wealth to it. Agostino obtained privileges for the hospital from Rome. He gave the brothers an *ordo* and a *modus* of life; and he decreed how the Master should be dressed. See *Acta SS*, 19 May, p. 618.

[18] Two of the four lost scenes related to the manner in which he came to join the Order. Traditions relating to a saint's choice of a particular order or institution were displayed in other instances, since it could be the matter for curious enquiry. A celebrated case would have been the tomb of Ogier the Dane at the monastic church of St Pharamond at Meaux (destroyed at the French Revolution). For an account of Ogier's choice of St Pharamond, see Dom Toussaints du Plessis, *Histoire de l'église de Meaux* (Paris, 1731), pp. 73–7. For an illustration of the monument, see W. Sauerlander, *Gothic Sculpture in France* 1140–1270 (London, 1970), p. 396. The more recent story of St Nicolas of Tolentino may also be cited (see below, p. 212).

To this should be added the fact that the altar itself was almost certainly built with funds given by the Tolomei family.[19] A member of that family had recently patronized Simone's brother-in-law Lippo Memmi in S. Gimignano.[20] Thus a further commission from within the same family group seems entirely plausible; and, in general, it seems more satisfactory to see this ensemble as a privately-sponsored commission paid for by the Tolomei and devised in conjunction with the Augustinian convent. This, of course, still fails to provide an answer to the question 'Why so many child miracles?'

It must be emphasized that miracles involving children are themselves common. This point emerged clearly during the conference.[21] It is the *choice* here which remains unexplained—although the reasons are likely to be uncomplicated—for example, the patron liked children, or had lost a child, or was the beneficiary of one or more of the miracles, and so on. Justifiable emphasis has been laid on the need to take the likely 'audience' into account. Yet, while this would account for the official 'tone' and choice of the posthumous miracles of St Francis at Assisi, as against the possibly more *gemütlich* atmosphere of a side-chapel in S. Agostino at Siena, it would not so easily account for the choice of a child miracle for both Simone's St Louis altar and his St Martin chapel.

A further unexpected 'child' miracle may be noted at this point—the raising of the daughter of Jairus, which is one of the surviving scenes on the Westminster Retable. This seems to be of particular significance. For if the need was simply to illustrate Christ's power to raise the dead, the normal exemplar would have been the scene of the raising of Lazarus. The illustration of Jairus's daughter is excessively rare. The Westminster Retable

[19] On this see the recent work of M. Butzek in P. A. Riedl and M. Seidel, eds, *Die Kirchen von Siena* (Munich, 1985), pp. 210–12. The Tolomei 'interest' dates from the very early fourteenth century—in fact to a will of 1307; and the Tolomei claimed a family burial place in front of the altar. The process by which the remains of Agostino came to rest on their altar is not known; nor is it known what liturgical arrangements were in position in the fourteenth century (this only becomes clear in 1413 when the family agreed to pay an annual rent in return for a daily Mass).

[20] The well-known *Maestà* in the *sala di Dante*, painted by Lippo Memmi 1317–18, was commissioned by Nello di Mino Tolomei, *podestà* and *capitano del popolo*. See Martindale, *Simone Martini*, p. 17, for comment and bibliography.

[21] In the paper presented by Diana Webb, see pp. 183–95.

has recently been re-examined;[22] and this has resulted in the most constructive attempt yet to provide meaning and focus to an iconography which is agreed by all to be extremely opaque. Moreover, the telling point is made that the very novelty of altar-pieces as liturgical objects about 1270 may well have meant that there were still no governing 'norms' for their imagery. Nevertheless, the riddle of Jairus's daughter remains—the only unequivocal child miracle, it may be noted, to be performed by Christ;[23] and the reasons for its selection are as elusive as the reasons for the selection of the child miracles in the cases of Saints Louis and Martin. In the absence of contemporary comment, the least complicated explanation may well be the correct one. The ability to summon a person back from the dead has, for obvious reasons, always exercised a powerful appeal. Arguably the power to summon small children back from the dead (or, indeed, to rescue them from the jaws of death) quite irrationally sharpens that appeal. There can be few things more emotionally dissolving than the two words *Talitha cumi*; and perhaps the significance of all these stories is that, in a most poignant way, they provide messages of hope.

Thus much for description and context. In studying the altar-piece—and precisely because of its emphasis on children—it is hard to ignore an argument which has developed over the last thirty years, since the publication of Philippe Ariès' book *L'enfant et la vie familiale sous l'Ancien Régime*. Ariès was much impressed by the considerable development of representations of the family and the child in the sixteenth and seventeenth centuries. They posed a problem because demographically the conditions of life did not substantially change before the industrial era; yet he could find little or no evidence for such concerns in the literature and painting of the medieval period. He therefore concluded that they did not exist; and that the historian is confronted by an evolution in attitudes with a gradual and

[22] By Paul Binski, 'What was the Westminster Retable?', *Journal of the British Archaeological Association*, 140 (1987), pp. 152–74.

[23] According to Mark 5.42, the girl was 12 years old. There are a few miracles in which a 'son' (filius) is cured but the age is not specified. See for instance John 6.46–54. The son of the widow of Nain is described as *adolescens* (Luke 7.14).

relatively late emergence of an interest in the whole process now known as 'growing up'.[24]

Ariès was right in one respect and wrong in another. To take the second first, it is certain as a result of recent research that throughout much of the 'Middle Ages' there existed some sort of intellectual *schema* which enabled people to comprehend, tabulate, and comment on the whole process of infancy, childhood, and adolescence.[25] The evidence for this is so overwhelming that it must require some sort of modification of Ariès' thesis. The main criticism is that Ariès ignored 'immutable and universal elements' in the process of caring for and socializing children which are likely to be present at most times and in most ages—and which were indeed present in the Middle Ages if one bothers to read the evidence; and it is arguable that alongside Ariès' sense of evolution, one should place something akin to a set of constants of basic human care and nurturing and of intellectual understanding.

Ariès was, nevertheless, right about the images—which do indeed change.[26] A casual comparison of images of the Madonna and Christ-child from different centuries and different countries leaves no doubt that the range of appeal was extraordinarily varied. Ariès is correct, too, in observing that convincing representations of tiny children and babies are hard to find before about 1280. If, therefore, one has reservations about his explanation of change, one is still left with the evidence for change on one's hands.

A tension between what is constant and what evolves is, of course, present in most historical investigations; and it may be helpful at this point to return to the Agostino Novello altar which in itself illustrates some of these tensions. It is, to begin with, necessary to know more about his *vita* and miracles, since the selection of illustrations was—obviously—entirely dependent on the material available.

[24] Ariès speculated that the high infant mortality rates made it initially unbearable to become emotionally bound up in the early stages of childhood. One of the main catalysts for change was the increasing development of educational programmes and theories.

[25] In this respect, the outstanding contribution is Shulamith Shahar's *Childhood in the Middle Ages* (London, 1990). During the conference her paper underlined the richness of the medieval material: see pp. 243–60 below.

[26] It is very difficult to distil Ariès' view of the precise chronology of these changes. In this paper the focus is on the period around 1300; but Ariès' examples tend to sweep across the centuries.

Agostino was not very much in demand for his miraculous powers. Where St Francis has about 200 recorded miracles,[27] Henry VI of England over 150,[28] and even William of Norwich over 100,[29] Agostino Novello has a mere thirteen.[30] They constitute a mixed bag of disasters—two people who fell into pits (one full of water); a man who swallowed a snake; a young mother who lacked milk for her child; a boy with an ulcer; a young man with some ill-defined malady *in parte inferiori*; a woman whose hand was pierced with a needle; a smith who blinded himself by pouring molten lead accidentally into a container which had water in it; and a boy with deformed feet. There are also the four miracles on the altar-piece—the miracle of the collapsed cradle and of the boy falling from the first-floor balcony; the child savaged by either a wolf or the fourteenth-century equivalent of a rottweiler; and literally the 'odd man out' on this altar-piece, the unknown man who was apparently crushed by his horse in a riding accident (his horse appears to have stumbled from a high mountain path into a ravine). Where they exist, the texts are informative. That relating to the collapsed cradle has already been cited at the start of this paper; and the account of the miracle of the child who fell from the balcony makes it clear that the potential disaster was to be found in the collapsing woodwork of the broken parapet. It is a pity that there is no text for the remaining two miracles—though it is possible (bearing in mind that Agostino had died only in 1309) that they were related to Simone *viva voce*.

It will be clear from this that the wonders wrought through the intercession of Agostino were miscellaneous in character. One curiosity is that six of the thirteen can be claimed to be concerned with small children. That might lead one to wonder whether there was anything in Agostino's life or character which led him to be perceived as having a special affinity with 'the young'. There is no evidence to support such a speculation—but

[27] See any edition of the *Legenda Maior* of St Bonaventure.

[28] P. Grosjean, *Henrici VI Anglae Regis Miracula Postuma* (Brussels, 1935).

[29] A. Jessop and M. R. James, *The Life and Miracles of St William of Norwich by Thomas of Monmouth* (Cambridge, 1896).

[30] The textual position is mildly complicated and unexpected since, for even such a small number of miracles, there are two independent fourteenth-century sources. The altar-piece draws one miracle from each source and supplies two miracles for which there is no text. See Martindale, *Simone Martini*, p. 212.

this leads to one of the 'constants' of hagiographical devotion which is perhaps worth comment.

On a superficial view, it might be supposed that people would deposit their problems at the feet of saints who, on the evidence of their lives, might be expected to have some sort of specialized or insider knowledge of the problem in question. The expectation would be that that saint could give a more reasoned and sympathetic account of the issues involved at the seat of the Almighty. In practice, this did not happen. There is no reason to suppose that people took academic problems to the shrine of St Thomas Aquinas at Naples; nor fishing or maritime problems to the tomb of St Peter in Rome.[31] Moreover, the answer is not far to seek. Since the Almighty may be supposed to be infinitely powerful and infinitely knowledgeable, he will need no special explanations of any of the problems which assault humans. Consequently most saints get a totally miscellaneous sequence of problems brought to them. There is nothing in Henry VI's life which might lead us to suppose that he was capable of coping with serious injury on the football field, although his miracles contain the earliest surviving account of a game of football.[32] There is nothing in the life of St Louis of Toulouse to suggest that he might be useful in helping the fishermen of Marseilles to increase their overnight catch, though that is one of the things for which they sought his help.[33] And what is one to suppose to have been the feelings of St Louis of France when he perceived a widow using one of his discarded hats to charm the floodwaters of the River Seine, which were threatening to engulf her late husband's wine cellar?[34] A belief in the thaumaturgic powers of

[31] This is rather different from the placing of a whole craft, profession or association *under the protection* of a particular saint—St Luke for painters, St Eligius for goldsmiths, Our Lady of Loreto for airline pilots, St Francis for the Planning, Environmental and Ecological Institute for Quality Life, etc.

[32] Grosjean, *Henrici VI*, pp. 159–60.

[33] On this, see 'Processus canonizationis et legendae variae Sancti Ludovici OFM episcopi tolosani'. *Analecta Franciscana*, 7 (1951). This contains an account of the miracles of the saint apparently drawn from the records kept (presumably by the sacristan) at the shrine (see p. xlviii). Of the 211 miracles, the large majority refer to physical ailments. But two (no. 167, p. 318, and no. 204, p. 329) refer to fishing difficulties. One of the problems was the shame brought on by lack of success. In the second of these two cases, the fisherman vowed that he would offer at the shrine *unum thonum de cera*. After making this promise, he threw his net into the sea 'et in uno ictu extraxit novem thonos, stupentibus et admirantibus qui astabant'. Within the same area of activity, St Louis' recovery of a stolen fishing boat may also be noted (no. 181, p. 322).

[34] P. B. Fay, *Les Miracles de Saint Louis*, pp. 140–2. Aelis l'Aveniere was the widow of Enoul, one of St Louis' esquires; and her late husband had acquired some of St Louis' hats (decorated with

St Louis' hats—a belief, it should be said, justified by events—must probably remain *hors de concours*. The point here is that most saints were appealed to in every conceivable situation.

A further 'normal' aspect of Agostino's miracles is their character. Anyone reading large numbers of miracle stories, is soon likely to have a sense of *déja vu*. If the miracles of Agostino are at all unusual, it is probably because of their concentration on 'events' rather than 'conditions', particularly as regards children. Child miracles would appear to be concerned mostly with problems with which the child was born—deformity, deafness, dumbness, blindness. If there is an 'event', it usually takes the form of a sudden and unexplained illness.[35] Simone indeed painted two such miracles. The altar-piece dedicated to St Louis of Toulouse contains in its predella a scene (plate 3) in which a small child is raised from its sick-bed after the father (?) had vowed a wax image of St Louis to the Saint himself.[36] A further infant miracle is to be found among the frescos of St Martin (plate 4), in the lower church of S. Francesco at Assisi—although here the wonder wrought by the saint is to some extent upstaged by the expressions of the spectators.[37] Many of Agostino's miracles concerned 'active' rather than 'passive' problems; but there is little that is unusual. People who fall into pits or wells, those who suffer from ulcers or sores, those born with deformities—there is little unexpected here. Even the tale of the person who swallowed a snake is to be found again among the miracles of William of Norwich.[38] To that extent, the Agostino Novello altar-piece reminds one of the constants both of existence and of hagiography.

---

peacock's feathers) at some point when the king had renewed all his hats. It should be said that the church authorities severely forbade Aelis to use the hat in this way when she first suggested it. She nevertheless went ahead privately with the experiment, aided and abetted by a servant. The result was a success—and a miracle which was duly placed in the 'official' records of William of St-Pathus. I am much indebted to Christopher Hohler for first drawing my attention to this splendid story.

[35] For an astonishing tally of sick children, see the miracles of fifteenth-century S. Giacomo della Marca in G. Caselli, *Studi su S. Giacomo della Marca pubblicati in occasione del II centenario della sua canonizzasione* (Ascoli Piceno, 1926).

[36] Martindale, *Simone Martini*, pp. 193–4.

[37] Ibid., p. 176.

[38] Jessop and James, *William of Norwich*, pp. 189–91. See also G. Caselli, *Studi su S. Giacomo della Marca*. The eighty-ninth miracle concerns a boy aged six who vomited up 'vermem rubeum et magnum praeter solitum'. Exactly what got inside these people is not clear. Poisonous snakes seem most unlikely; large tapeworms or something similar are more likely.

Plate 3 Simone Martini, *Miracle of St Louis of Toulouse*, from the St Louis Altar-piece, Museo Nazionale di Capodimonte, Naples. Photo: author.

Plate 4 Simone Martini, *Miracle of St Martin of Tours*, Chapel of St Martin, S. Francesco, Assisi. Photo: University of East Anglia.

Yet the altar-piece is also a reminder of change, since the very collection of miracles is significant. Recent scholarship has emphasized the increasing necessity after about 1200 of evidence of miracles as proof of sanctity—especially with any view to official canonization.[39] They became, in effect, a sort of thirteenth-century performance-indicator. There is no evidence that canonization at Rome was ever contemplated for Agostino (he was eventually beatified in 1759). There is, however, no doubt that he was venerated locally as a saint—he is painted here with a halo; and the collecting around him of miracles was and is evidence of that sanctity.

The altar-piece also indicates another and rather different sort of change, since this genre of liturgical object was itself relatively recent around 1320.[40] The format of the altar-piece is based on one first used in a number of panels celebrating St Francis (the earliest dating to 1228).[41] By the end of the thirteenth century it was being used in other contexts; and it is difficult to know whether here in Siena any special allusion to St Francis was intended. But painted retables as such were a relatively new invention, the earliest surviving dated example being from 1215.

Analysis of the changes observed by Ariès is seriously hampered by a shortage of images. In any case, in many major saints' lives, such as that of St Francis, children go almost unnoticed; and the number of times that relevant episodes are *illustrated* is tiny. One may instance the story of the child Nicolas of Tolentino, who was attracted to the Augustinian Hermits by the preaching of Reginaldo (plate 5).[42] There is also a picture of a posthumous miracle of St Nicolas of Bari, involving a small child who goes to answer a knock on the door in the middle of a feast (plate 6). He meets a stranger, dressed as a pilgrim and seeking alms, who lures him out of the house—and who turns out to be the devil in disguise. The devil murders the boy, but on the

[39] See especially A. Vauchez, *La Sainteté en occident au derniers siècles du moyen âge* (Rome, 1981), and B. Ward, *Miracles and the Medieval Mind* (Aldershot, 1987).

[40] For a recent account of this development see particularly H. van Os, *Sienese altarpieces 1215–1450*, vol. 1 (Groningen 1984).

[41] They are illustrated *passim* in E. B. Garrison, *Italian Romanesque Panel Painting: an illustrated index* (Florence, 1949).

[42] The cycle has been described and analysed by J. Gardner in 'The *cappelone di S. Nicola* at Tolentino: some functions of a fourteenth-century fresco cycle', in W. Tronzo, ed., *Italian Church Decoration of the Middle Ages and Early Renaissance*, 1 (Bologna, 1989), pp. 101–17.

Plate 5 Anonymous Artist of the second quarter of the Fourteenth Century, *The Attraction and Reception into the Augustinian Order of St Nicolas of Tolentino*, Tolentino, S. Nicola. Photo: University of East Anglia.

Plate 6 Pietro Lorenzetti, *Miracle of St Nicolas of Bari*, Florence, Gallerie Nazionali di Firenze. Photo: author.

intercession of St Nicolas he is restored to life. Such scenes are nevertheless few.[43]

Yet in attempting to build up a visual picture of the treatment of and attitudes to children during the period, the real stumbling-block is the Bible itself. For the vast majority of religious illustration is based on biblical stories; and in manuscript after manuscript and church after church it is these that form the foundation for any form of pictorial adornment. If, however, one asks what child stories are available for pictorial treament, the results are not very promising. The Old Testament is dominated by kings, warriors, and prophets;[44] and the New Testament, for different reasons, is not much more productive. Christ as a baby in a stable or cave with or without the shepherds or Magi is, of course, extremely common. There follows the Flight into Egypt and the Massacre of the Innocents. But, as the writer of the late thirteenth-century *Meditationes Vitae Christi* pointed out, apart from the episode of Christ disputing with the Doctors in the Temple at Jerusalem at the age of twelve, nothing is known about Christ's life between the return to Nazareth and the start of his ministry at the age of 30.[45] It is, of course, possible to have recourse to the apocryphal infancy gospels. These stories were known in the Middle Ages and they are occasionally illustrated.[46] However, they have never found much favour in orthodox circles.[47] For they depict Christ as a capricious and

[43] The painting is in the Uffizi, Florence. See L. Marcucci, *Gallerie Nazionali di Firenze. I dipinti toscani del secolo XIV* (Rome, 1965), pp. 161–3. For the text of the miracle, see the *Legenda Aurea* of Jacopo da Voragine, ed. T. Graesse (Dresden and Leipzig, 1846), p. 28.

[44] The number of child stories in the Old Testament and Apocrypha is small. Moreover the age of some of the 'children' is not always clear—e.g., the young Isaac, David, or Tobias. Certifiable children are uncommon and where they emerge (e.g. to taunt the prophet Elisha) they are seldom the subject for illustration.

[45] The Latin text of the *Meditationes* was printed under St Bonaventure's name in *Sancti Bonaventuri . . . opusculorum Tomus Primus* at Lyons in 1647. I have used F. le Bannier, *Méditations sur la vie de N–S Jésus-Christ* (Arras, 1873), whose text is based on the Lyons edition. In the present context, see Ch. XIII, 'De reditu domini ex Aegypto' (p. 43): 'Exinde autem usque ad duodecimum aetatis annum pueri Jesu, aliquid non legitur de ipso.' Also Ch. XV, 'Quid dominus fecit a duodecimo anno usque ad tricesimo' (p. 47): 'Nec in scripturis reperitur quod in toto iste tempore aliquid fecerit.'

[46] They occur occasionally in the course of manuscript decoration. See, in particular, BL, Egerton MS 2781 where some of the infancy 'events' occur (very unusually) as parts of the main cycle of pictures (*c.* 1340).

[47] Some of the gospels are printed in M. R. James, *The Apocryphal New Testament* (Oxford, 1924). A useful summary of these extraordinary stories is to be found in A. S. Rappoport, *Medieval Legends of Christ* (London, 1934). See particularly Ch. VI, 'The early childhood of Christ', pp. 107–41.

sometimes vindictive child; and I know of virtually no instance of them being used in the decoration of a church.[48]

It should be said that, by contrast, the apocryphal stories dealing with the childhood of the Virgin have been treated with considerably more respect.[49] They were regularly used as a source of information for her life between her miraculous conception and the Annunciation. There is, moreover, a long tradition of comment on the Virgin's childhood; and although this yields relatively few episodes suitable for illustration, there are a number of pictures of Mary as a girl—for instance, weaving the purple and scarlet veil for the Temple.

Nevertheless, the tally of possible illustrative material remains small; and, in practice, most investigations of this kind are based on that commonest of subjects, the Virgin holding the infant Christ-child. In this, those looking for 'development' or 'evolution' have to avoid a number of traps or pitfalls. Variations may relate to confusions within the theology of the subject matter. There is, for instance, an ancient but persistent tendency to make the infant Christ look like a manikin (plate 7). There is a certain logic to this, since Christ was God made Man; and this view of his position is still very much alive in the great wall-painting of the Virgin and Child in Majesty painted about 1315 by Simone Martini in the council chamber in Siena (plate 8).[50] Here a fairly robust and knowing Christ-child blesses the city rulers and, as the source of justice, tells them (on the parchment scroll held in his hand), 'Love justice, ye who judge the earth'—the opening words of the Book of the Wisdom of Solomon.

Humanizing images suggesting a more lively relationship between mother and child antedate this fresco by twenty to thirty years. There can, therefore, be no question of a smooth transi-

[48] Some of the visual evidence is to be found in A. Horton, *The Child Jesus* (London, 1975). One of his illustrations is indeed a piece of church decoration. It shows the incident in which the boy Jesus makes a dove of clay which turns into a real bird and flies away. The context is the twelfth-century ceiling of the church of St Martin, Zillis (Graubünden, Switzerland); and the remoteness of the church merely underlines the unusualness of the scene.

[49] The stories are mainly derived from the so-called Proto-Evangelium of St James which is to be found in James, *Apocryphal New Testament*, pp. 38–49. They are to be found *passim* in the *Legenda Aurea*; but for a recent view of the legendary material available in the Middle Ages, see W. Scase, 'St Anne and the education of the Virgin: literary and artistic traditions and their implications' in N. Rogers, ed., *England in the fourteenth century* = Harlaxton Medieval Series, 3 (Stamford, 1993), pp. 81–96.

[50] Martindale, *Simone Martini*, pp. 204–9.

Plate 7 Anonymous Artist of the first half of the Thirteenth Century, *Madonna degli Occhi Grossi*, Siena, Museo dell'Opera del Duomo. Photo: author.

Plate 8 Simone Martini, *Maestà* (detail), Siena, Palazzo Pubblico. Photo: author.

tion from one iconographic type to another; and this should perhaps caution against assuming a smooth evolution in attitudes.[51] Yet even further caution is needed. One of the most famous 'types', the so-called *glykophilousa*, is a very ancient importation from Byzantium. It acquired a relatively early currency and was, for instance, known by about 1240 to Matthew Paris.[52] A further 'type', known again in England by about 1250, is the *Maria Lactans*. It occurs in the Amesbury Psalter, where a decidely unbaby-like Christ is feeding at his mother's breast.[53] This should act as a reminder that meditation on the role of the Madonna as a mother as well as a queen evolved rapidly in the twelfth century, especially in the area of influence of the Cistercians and of St Bernard—who was privileged in a vision to receive a few drops of the Virgin's milk.[54]

Moreover, in the matter of the baby Christ, certain practices grew up in the early thirteenth century which encouraged imaginative participation in the Christmas story—in particular the cult of the Christmas crib.[55] The most famous manifestation of this is probably the event in the life of St Francis at Greccio. According to the legend, St Francis celebrated Christmas Eve Mass in 1223 over a crib complete with live animals and real hay. A privileged spectator, John of Greccio, saw sleeping in the crib a very beautiful and real child.[56]

It is against this background that the humanization of the Virgin and Child image should be set. The change, nevertheless, went far beyond the mere importation or popularization of earlier ideas. By the end of the century, one finds the Christchild walking around on the Virgin's knee (plate 9) and reaching up to touch her face (plate 10). The theme of lactation gradually becomes more common. The child acquires a degree of expression unknown at an earlier date (plate 11). The child also begins

[51] Cf. P. S. Gold, *The Lady and the Virgin* (Chicago and London, 1985).

[52] See London, BL, MS Royal C VII, fol. 6r.

[53] Oxford, All Souls College, MS Lat. 6, fol. 4v.

[54] For the whole development of the devotion to Mary during this period, with particular reference to England, the reader is referred to two very substantial papers by N. Morgan: 'Texts and images of Marian devotion in thirteenth-century England', in M. Ormrod, *England in the Thirteenth century* = Harlaxton Medieval Studies, 1, pp. 69–103; and 'Texts and images of Marian devotion in fourteenth-century England', in Rogers, *England in the fourteenth century*, pp. 34–57.

[55] H. van Os, *Simiolus*, V (1972), pp. 5–19, 'The Madonna and the mystery play' discusses the subject with further references.

[56] See St Bonaventure, *Legenda Maior*, Cap. X. 7.

Plate 9 Anonymous Artist of the late Thirteenth Century, *Madonna and Child*, Turin, Galleria Sabauda. Photo: University of East Anglia.

Plate 10 Duccio, *Crevole Madonna*, Siena, Museo dell'Opera del Duomo. Photo: University of East Anglia.

Plate 11 Ambrogio Lorenzetti, *Madonna and Child*, Siena, S. Agostino. Photo: author.

Plate 12 Lippo di Benvieni, *Madonna and Child*, Florence, Carlo degli Alessandri Collection. Photo: University of East Anglia.

to lose his clothes; and during the fourteenth century occasionally appears, in effect, naked (there is usually a piece of totally transparent drapery round his waist—plate 12).

The sense of a human relationship waiting to be explored is not confined to Italy. In the north, one of its earliest manifestations is likely to be the famous statue of the Madonna and Child on the *trumeau* of the south portal of Amiens Cathedral (*c.* 1230–40) where the mother smiles at the child. This acts as a reminder of the precociousness of northern sculptors in the exploration of human expression. Although the 'smile' seems in the main confined to the north, the mobile child achieved a wider currency. Indeed, on a boss in the nave vault of the abbey church at Tewkesbury (*c.* 1340), there is a charming scene in which the Virgin appears to be teaching Christ to walk (see frontispiece).[57]

It is hard to interpret these changes, since they receive no direct explanation in contemporary texts. They seem, nevertheless, to be part of a general development in which the world of experience became increasingly important in the interpretation of the biblical stories and in the conduct of personal piety. In Italy the most compelling piece of evidence for this is the late thirteenth-century treatise already referred to, known as the *Meditationes Vitae Christi*—written by a Franciscan for a woman, probably a Clarissite or a Tertiary.[58] The introduction is in part an injunction to use the imagination in meditating on the Bible story.

> You should not suppose that we may be able to meditate on all the things which it is understood that Christ said or did, or that they were all written down. Indeed I for greater emphasis shall narrate things thus as if they had been so, just as it may be piously believed that they were happening or had happened. And I shall use various imaginary representations which my mind has in different ways conceived.

What he is saying, in effect, is that it is permissible to fill in the gaps in the Gospel story by projecting the imagination. The

[57] For the development in England, see Morgan, 'Marian devotion', *passim*.
[58] See n. 45 above.

treatise throughout demonstrates how this works in practice, since the reader is constantly invited to imagine the feelings of those involved and to reconstruct the sort of things they thought and said. Thus of Mary's first days with the newborn child, the writer says,

> See with what reverence and care and with what fear she handled him whom she knew to be her God; and how with bended knee she took him and placed him in the cradle; with what joy and confidence and motherly authority she embraced him, kissed him, hugged him and delighted in him whom she knew to be her son; how curiously she looked at him in the face and looked at every part of his most sacred body.

The writer further enjoins us to imagine St Joseph with the Christ-child on his knee and being made to laugh.[59]

There was a limit to this type of imaginative reconstruction, and the unknown writer was careful to say that everything had to be grounded in Scripture. Thus, as already noted, he refused to attempt to fill in the missing twelve years of Christ's childhood, observing only that he had heard from those who had visited Nazareth that one could still see the fountain whence the boy Jesus carried water to his mother—and this was significant for his purposes because it showed that the Holy Family was too poor to employ servants.[60]

Thoughtfulness concerning the nature of childhood and the role of the child spilled over into other scenes and episodes in the biblical and sacred stories. In a fresco in the Baptistery at Parma (*c.* 1270), the boy Baptist sets out for the wilderness, escorted by an angel, and armed with his ABC on a scroll.[61] Children take part in the scenes of the Road to Golgotha and the Crucifixion (*c.* 1340).[62] At Assisi, children form part of the crowd to witness St Francis renouncing his father (*c.* 1290); and in a further version

[59] Le Bannier, *Méditations*, p. 31–2 (Ch. X, 'De morae dominae apud praesepe'). The devotional texts available in England complement this development—see especially Morgan, 'Marian devotions', *passim.*

[60] Ibid., p. 43, Ch. XIII, 'De reditu domini ex Aegypto'.

[61] P. Toesca, *Il battistero di Parma* (Milan, 1960), plate XXI.

[62] Martindale, *Simone Martini*, plates 119 and 120, pp. 171–3.

deriving from the first,[63] they actually throw stones at St Francis (*c.* 1340).[64]

There is one image which requires particular comment as a result of recent controversy—that is, the Virgin holding the naked Christ. It must be stressed that this image is unknown before 1300 and remains rare throughout the fourteenth century. Nevertheless, its appearance signifies change and should indicate some shift in thought. That there was some fresh perception of nudity receives some small support from contemporary texts. The *Meditationes* have already been quoted to the effect that Mary looked curiously (*curiose*) at Christ as she held him—and not merely at his face, but at every part of his body. Angela da Foligno (who died in 1309) related a vision in which the Virgin had let her hold the Christ-child in her arms—at first swaddled and then *totus nudus*.[65] It seems plausible that nudity was thought appropriate, granted that babies entered the world naked. It has, however, been argued recently that one is dealing here not merely with a more life-like view of babies, but with a far more fundamental theological argument concerning the gender and sexuality of Christ.[66]

It is very difficult to form a judgement on this matter. Of course, Christ's sexuality has formed the subject of muted comment at most times. It is difficult to avoid some sort of observation in a discussion of the Circumcision;[67] and it is also relevant to discussion of Christ's chastity. Moreover, a totally nude child

63 L. Marcucci, *Gallerie Nazionali di Firenze*, pp. 56–62 and plate 310. The scene is attributed to Taddeo Gaddi and formed part of the decoration of a relic cupboard formerly in S. Croce, Florence. It was probably painted *c.* 1330. In a scene of the Road to Golgotha painted probably a little earlier in the church of S. Maria Donnaregina in Naples, children throw stones at Christ.

64 Two very unusual Byzantine images may be noted at this point, both in the church of the Chora, Constantinople, and therefore datable *c.* 1320. See P. A. Underwood, *The Kariye Djami* (New York, 1966), 1, pp. 68–72 and 2, plates 104 and 114 for respectively the scenes of the first steps of the Virgin and of Joachim and Anna caressing the Virgin. The first of these illustrates an episode in the Proto-Evangelium of St James (see note 49). The second, dubbed by the author a Byzantine innovation of the thirteenth century, remains unexplained.

65 P. Doncoeur and F. Pulignano, *Le livre de la bien-heureuse Angèle de Foligno* (Toulouse, 1925), pp. 131–2.

66 L. Steinberg, *The Sexuality of Christ in Renaissance Art and in Modern Oblivion* (London, 1983).

67 This event, apart from being the first of the Sorrows of the Virgin, was also held to be the first occasion on which Christ shed blood for mankind. It was normal to stress or to assume the child's meekness. However, there is at least one representation in which the Christ-child struggles—see the scene which forms part of the huge Embriachi altar-piece given *c.* 1400 by the Duc de Berry to the nunnery of Poissy (it is now in the Louvre).

is evidence that God was in Christ made Man—and wholly Man—in a way that a partially draped, semi-naked child is not. The problem is that, as far as I am aware, there is no surviving comment from the period 1250 to 1350 to support any sort of a discussion of these questions. One is not told, for instance, what thoughts passed through the mind of Angela da Foligno. It is true that in the fifteenth century the emphasis on Christ's nudity and on his genitalia becomes much more emphatic—there is more to explain. But it remains very rare in the earlier period;[68] and to the extent that it appears to be almost entirely confined to single devotional images, it seems to have remained the subject of private contemplation. There appears to be no large public altar-piece before about 1400 displaying either a totally nude or a diaphanously swathed Christ-child.[69] My inference from this is that it was considered indecorous as a public subject, but permissible in the privacy of the home. But it is not clear to me whether the development begins in the wake of thoughts about sexuality and gender—or simply about maternity and infancy.

Where then does this leave the theme of the conference—the Church and Childhood? It seems to be the case that in the imagery of the period around 1300, childhood receives a new dimension. It has been suggested that this runs parallel to a new type of personal devotion in which men and women were encouraged to imagine in all its detail the human circumstances of the Gospel story. As the writer of the *Meditationes* wrote in his preface, 'If you wish to draw profit from this, show yourself present at those things which are said to have been done or spoken by Christ as if you are hearing them with your ears or seeing them with your eyes.'[70] This amounted to a new pragmatism; and this sense of human experience being brought to bear on sacred events has resonances in other areas of existence and activity. For the thirteenth century is in one of its aspects

[68] Contrary to Steinberg's view, *Sexuality of Christ*, p. 146, the 'token covering of the Child's nudity by transparent garments or veils' is not a motif common 'throughout the Trecento' though it seems to appear more frequently towards the end of the century. A totally nude Christ-child appears frequently in late fourteenth-century Bohemian painting and sculpture.

[69] The pieces of a polyptych of *c.* 1340 by Lippo di Benvieni survive in which the figure of the Christ-child (see here plate 12) is swathed in a diaphanous piece of drapery (see R. Fremantle, *Florentine Gothic Painters* (London, 1975), plate 54, where the altar-piece is reconstituted). This polyptych is not large; and its original context is unknown.

[70] Le Bannier, *Méditations*, p. 4, Proemium.

characterized by the re-evaluation of Aristotle; and it is the century in which information provided by the senses was given a new importance and a new validity. In Italian painting, this pragmatism is also found in the imitation of the effects of light and in the exploitation of effects of perspective.[71] There are also a number of bold tricks of illusion in which painters intruded into the 'real' world objects which did not in reality exist.[72] In northern sculpture, pragmatism took a quite different turn in the realistic foliage to be found carved in many churches and cathedrals.[73] In architecture, it is to be found in the advance 'realization' of buildings in terms of detailed plans and elevations. Architectural concepts were no longer merely a gleam in the master mason's eye.[74] Thus in many different ways 'ideas' were brought down to earth and matched against the 'realities' of existence. It would be difficult to argue that there is anything here sufficiently organized or coherent to be called a 'movement';[75] but it seems at least arguable that, somewhere along the way, there ought to be a link, however distant, between the close observation of the botanical world and the observation of the movements of a child.

[71] J. White, *The Birth and Rebirth of Pictorial Space*, 2nd edn (London, 1967); P. Hills, *The Light of Early Italian Painting* (New Haven, 1987).

[72] In large-scale decoration, the most famous of these are probably Giotto's fictive 'chapels' in the Arena Chapel at Padua (*c.* 1305); and Pietro Lorenzetti's fictive bench in the Lower Church at Assisi (*c.* 1315–20). Both the upper and the lower churches at Assisi are, of course, full of illusionistic tricks which the painters have played with the 'real' architecture. The later (1340s) secular decorations in the papal palace at Avignon may also be noted.

[73] Extensive comment on the identification and symbolism of the thirteenth-century foliage carving in France and Germany is to be found in L. Behling, *Die Pflanzenwelt der mittelalterlichen Kathedralen* (Cologne and Graz, 1964). The author is, however, as interested in the parallel developments both in scholastic philosophy and in natural science (especially botanical taxonomy and description); and she quotes at length from the writings of Albertus Magnus and Thomas Aquinas.

[74] See the essay by W. Schöller, 'Le dessin d'architecture à l'époque gothique' in R. Recht, ed., *Les battisseurs des cathédrales gothiques* (Strasbourg, 1989), pp. 227–35.

[75] Writing about the botanical sculpture carved on the thirteenth-century capitals of Southwell Minster in *The Leaves of Southwell* (London and New York, 1945), N. Pevsner argued eloquently and elegantly for the presence of a 'spirit of the age' to which these common manifestations might be imputed (see especially pp. 63–5). This is good Hegelian doctrine and, despite the restrictions of his context (the King Penguin Books were not intended to contain more than short essays), Pevsner went on to explore a little how this concept might be perceived to operate in the thirteenth century. It makes interesting reading, demonstrating both the strengths and the weaknesses of the deductive approach to history.

In the course of this paper some attention has been given to the imaginative observation devoted both to the theme of the Madonna and Child and to the interpretation of child miracles. It is true that innovative ideas may in time generate their own stereotypes, and this is particularly true of subjects such as the Virgin and Child. To conclude, therefore, on the theme of novelty and freshness, something will be said about one of the most remarkable pictures of the entire fourteenth century—namely, the painting which since about 1820 has been at Liverpool and is commonly called the 'Holy Family'.[76] The narrative basis for this picture is recounted in Luke 2. 41–51. At the age of twelve Christ went with Mary and Joseph to Jerusalem for the feast of the Passover. At the moment of return the family got separated; and after three days the parents found Jesus disputing with the theologians in the Temple. Mary said to Jesus, 'Son, why hast thou dealt with us thus? Behold thy father and I have sought thee sorrowing . . .'; and he said to them, 'How is it that ye sought me? Wist ye not that I must be about my father's business?' '. . . and he went down with them and came to Nazareth: and he was subject to them.' The scene of 'Christ among the Doctors' is extremely common in Christian iconography. It carried with it a number of lessons, including the evidence of divine wisdom and understanding immanent in the young boy. The scene of the return to Nazareth is rather less common. However, it too carried with it a message—of Christ's willing subjection to his parents. Where it occurs, it is, as far as I know, always a sequel to the earlier episode.[77]

In 1342 Simone Martini was commissioned to paint what appears to have been in its isolation a unique piece of subject-matter—the episode 'in between' (plate 13). It is important to emphasize the physical isolation of the Liverpool 'Holy Family'. There is no evidence that it ever formed part of a sequence—for instance, by being attached to any adjacent panels. The frame is unmarked for attachments; and the back is painted to look like marble. One is quite certainly meant either to hold this in one's hands; or to contemplate it propped up, perhaps on a stand or on

[76] Martindale, *Simone Martini*, pp. 51 and 190–1.

[77] Such a pair of paintings is to be found in the right transept of the lower church of Assisi (perhaps *c.* 1310). A rustic version of the same pair is to be seen among the wall-paintings of St George, Rhäzüns (eastern Switzerland) from *c.* 1360.

Plate 13 Simone Martini, *Holy Family*, Liverpool, Walker Art Gallery. Photo: author.

a table-top. The moment chosen does not portray either the wise Christ or the submissive Christ. It is clear what point has been reached in the story since the words accompanying Mary's gesture are written in the book which is open on her knee: 'Fili, quid fecisti nobis sic?' Christ has not yet replied—his book is closed; and the painter appears momentarily to have caught a defensive, defiant Christ, confronted by plaintive parents.

Further explanation of this painting would proceed beyond the purposes of this paper.[78] It has indeed been observed that the subject is, in effect, one of the Seven Sorrows of the Virgin.[79] This still fails to explain why this Sorrow has been extracted from the series and made the subject of such special attention. Moreover, there are no signs of original ownership, and the only reasonable certainty is that in 1342 it was done for a wealthy member of or visitor to the papal court at Avignon. The purpose of introducing it now is to offer a substantial postscript to the present subject. There is indeed a 'child in the picture', albeit a child on the verge of growing up; and the 'perspective' is that of the early fourteenth century rather than the 'Middle Ages'. The very quality and quirkiness of the painting may seem to raise problems. Arguably, just as hard cases are supposed to make bad law, exceptional achievements make poor general history. However, this may, I think, be seen as an exceptional example of the general change at which I have been looking. There is nothing like this a century before; and the challenge, of course, is to accommodate such a dramatic development alongside those 'constants' of care, concern, and attention, which certainly existed, and to which attention was drawn earlier. Perhaps in the end this is not such a problem. For what I have suggested is that the changes have as their setting not some fundamental psycho-social upheaval, but the thirteenth-century rediscovery or re-

[78] Further comment will be found in A. Martindale, 'Innovazioni di Simone Martini: i problemi di interpretazione' in Bellosi, ed., *Simone Martini, atti de convegno*, pp. 233–6. One of the most influential meditations on this whole episode was the treatise *De Iesu Puero duodenni*, long believed to be by St Bernard but in fact by Aelred of Rievaulx. See A. Hoste and C. H. Talbot, *Aelredi Rievallensis Opera Omnia* (Turnholt, 1971), pp. 245–78. Aelred's expostulation on the reunion reads 'Tene, o dulcissima Domina, tene quem diligis, rue in collum eius, amplectere, osculare, et triduanam absentiam eius multiplicatis deliciis recompensa.' Thus Aelred conjures up a picture of Mary falling on Christ's neck and giving him a passionate hug. This does not resemble very much the Liverpool painting and merely emphasizes its singularity.

[79] Pointed out to me by Christopher Hohler.

evaluation of the human senses and human experience. This had many different facets; but in the present context, these new perceptions may be seen not to contradict but to be superimposed on and to have enhanced those 'constants'. This at least seems to be one of the ways of interpreting these 'children in the picture'.

University of East Anglia

NATALIS INNOCENTUM: THE HOLY INNOCENTS IN LITURGY AND DRAMA

by MARTIN R. DUDLEY

> It has come to our knowledge, not without grievous amazement and displeasure of heart [Bishop Grandisson wrote to the clergy of Exeter Cathedral and of other collegiate churches in his diocese before Christmas 1360] that for these past years and some years preceding, at the most holy solemnities of Christ's Nativity, and the feasts of St Stephen, St John the Apostle and Evangelist, and the Innocents, when all faithful Christians are bound to busy themselves the more devoutly and quietly in praise of God and in Church Services, certain Ministers of our aforesaid Church, together with the boys, not only at Matins and Vespers and other hours, but also (which is more detestable) during the solemnity of the Mass have rashly presumed, putting the fear of God behind them, after the pernicious example of certain Churches, to associate together within the Church itself and play certain foolish and noxious games, unbecoming to clerical honesty.[1]

THE Bishop's strictures did not extend to the feast of the Circumcision—the *Festum Asinorum*—and, from the evidence provided by the customaries of French cathedrals, we can assume that, though disorder appears to have been commonplace throughout the period, the focus of his criticism was the feast of the Holy Innocents, falling on the third day within the octave of the Nativity. He was not opposed to the appropriate liturgical celebration of the feast, and his Exeter *Ordinale*, issued in 1337, provides, as do the Sarum books, for the full ceremonies of the day, including the appearance of the *episcopus puerorum* during Vespers of St John and throughout the Innocents' Day itself.[2] Grandison's point is most particular

[1] John Grandisson, Bishop of Exeter, *Register*, p. 1213. Translation in G. G. Coulton, *Life in the Middle Ages* (Cambridge, 1967), 1, pp. 99–100.

[2] The English liturgical texts cited here are drawn from the following: *Ordinale Exoniensis*, ed. J. N. Dalton, *Henry Bradshaw Society*, 37 (London, 1909); *Breviarium ad usum insignis Ecclesiae Sarum*, ed. F. Procter and C. Wordsworth (Cambridge, 1882); *The Sarum Missal*, ed. J. Wickham Legg

and concerns the way in which the original and lawful intention of the liturgy is destroyed: 'That which was first invented to excite and increase the devotion of the faithful is by such disorders converted—or rather perverted—to the irreverence and contempt of God and his Saints, not without guilt of blasphemy.'[3] He was representative of a new type of bishop, who saw the Church's liturgy serving her needs and saw that, if this was to be possible, the levels of meaning within the symbolic matrix of a feast or series of feasts needed to be limited and controlled. The feast of Corpus Christi, definitively established, after earlier unsuccessful attempts, by Grandisson's patron, Pope John XXII, provided a model for this.[4] Older feasts are like a virgin forest; the more modern ones like an artistically-kept flower garden.[5] The liturgy of the feast of the Holy Innocents had grown without restraint and operated on a variety of levels, apparently unrelated, but indissolubly linked.

The story of the slaughtered infants of Bethlehem is part of the account in the second chapter of St Matthew's Gospel of the birth of Jesus and the visit of the Magi. The narrative has four distinct but related parts. In the first, the Magi come to Jerusalem to enquire where the child is born and receive an answer from Herod. In the second, they deliver their gifts to the child. In the third, an angel appears to Joseph warning him that Herod is searching for the child to destroy him, and so he is to take the child and his mother and flee into Egypt. In the final section, Herod, infuriated that he has been tricked by the Magi, orders that all children in and around Bethlehem who are two years old or under are to be killed. The section concludes with the words of the prophet Jeremiah (31.15):

> A voice was heard in Ramah,
> wailing and loud lamentation,
> Rachel weeping for her children;
> she refused to be consoled,
> because they are no more.

(Oxford, 1916); *Ceremonies and Processions of the Cathedral Church of Salisbury*, ed. C. Wordsworth (Cambridge, 1901).

[3] Grandisson, *Register*, p. 1213.

[4] M. R. Dudley, 'Liturgy and Doctrine: Corpus Christi', *Worship*, 60, no. 5 (1992), pp. 417–26.

[5] P. Parsch, *The Church's Year of Grace*, 4 (Collegeville, 1959), p. 18.

The parts were early separated. The feast of the Epiphany, introduced into the West in the fourth century, became primarily a celebration of the visit of the Magi. The Gospel at the Mass concluded with the words *reversi sunt in regionem suam.*[6] Some evidence suggests that the Innocents were, for a relatively short time, commemorated on the Epiphany,[7] but the calendar of Carthage indicates that the commemoration of the death of the infants was observed there, in the fifth century, on 28 December.[8] Matthew 2.13–15, recounting the appearance of the angel to Joseph and the instruction to flee, was read at the Mass of the Innocents; there was no separate liturgical commemoration of the flight into Egypt, though in due course it found dramatic form at the conclusion of the *Officium stellae.* Irenaeus shows that the infants were venerated as martyrs in the West[9] (though that does not mean there was a separate liturgical commemoration), and the feast almost certainly entered the Western liturgy in the course of the fifth century; that is, after the Epiphany. In devotional terms, the way had been prepared by the poetry of Paulinus of Nola and Prudentius.[10]

In the *Sacramentarium Veronense*, the so-called *Leonine Sacramentary*, there is full provision for two Masses for the feast *In natale Innocentum*, in set XLII.[11] Emmanuel Bourque thinks that the first part of this set may be earlier than 400.[12] In the Gelasian Sacramentary, copied around 750, the feast *In natali Innocentium* appears on 28 December, and Cyrilla Vogel holds that the furthest we can push it back is into the sixth century.[13] The Gregorian Sacramentary notes, in a number of manuscripts, that the stational Mass was at St Paul's outside the Walls, where an

6 Matt. 2.12.

7 E.g., Leo the Great, *Sermon* 31, On the Feast of the Epiphany, which is largely concerned with the Innocents: *A Select Library of Nicene and Post-Nicene Fathers of the Christian Church*, ed. P. Schaff and H. Wace, series 2, 12 (Grand Rapids, 1976), pp. 144–5.

8 *PL* 13, cols 1219–30.

9 Irenaeus, *Adversus haereses*, III, xvi, 4 (*PG* 7).

10 Paulinus, *Carmina*, xxxi, 587, *CSEL*, 30 (1894), and Prudentius, *Cathemerinon*, xii, 93–140, M. P. Cunningham, ed., *CChr.* 126, (1966) from which the Tridentine office hymns were drawn. Note Duchesne's reservations about dating the introduction of the feast from hymns and sermons: *Christian Worship: Its Origin and Evolution* (London, 1923), p. 268 n. 3.

11 L. C. Mohlberg, ed., *Sacramentarium Veronense* (Rome, 1956), pp. 164–6.

12 E. Bourque, *Etude sur les Sacramentaires Romains* (Rome, 1949), p. 137.

13 C. Vogel, *Medieval Liturgy: an Introduction to the Sources*, rev. and tr. W. G. Sharp and N. K. Rasmussen (Washington DC, 1986), pp. 64–9.

early tradition held that five bodies of the infants were buried in a sarcophagus beneath the apse.[14] There are sermons of Fulgentius and of Caesarius of Arles which showed that Gaul and Africa celebrated the *Natale Infantium*—the title *innocentum* or *innocentium* was used only in Rome and Milan[15]—on the 28th, though in the Spanish Mozarabic rite it was, more appropriately, on 8 January. Its position, after the Nativity but before the celebration of the coming of the Magi on the Epiphany, is a result of the complex development of this part of the liturgical calendar, and it gave some medieval commentators pause for thought. In the thirteenth-century *Summa de officiis ecclesiasticis* of Guy d'Orchelles we find the argument that the massacre took place a year after the birth of Jesus, and hence after the Epiphany![16]

The curious liturgical nature of the feast is evident in both the Mass and the Office. There are Mass texts in all the sacramentaries, but they are not identical, and there was clearly some early development. Three collects appear in the Gelasian; two are drawn from the Veronense; only one of them—*Deus, cuius hodierna*—appears in the Gregorian Sacramentary and makes its way into the Sarum Missal, the Missal of Pius V, and, with slight amendment, that of Paul VI. It is the Gelasian *super oblata* that is used at Salisbury,[17] and the Gregorian one in Rome; but it is the Gregorian post communion that appears in all subsequent missals, and those of the earlier sacramentaries disappear. The selection of texts is one of the mysteries of medieval liturgical development.

Though within the octave of the Nativity, the Mass of the Innocents was celebrated in violet vestments, with dalmatic and tunicle, but without the *Gloria in excelsis*, *Credo*, and *Alleluia*, unless it was a Sunday, in which case it was celebrated as a double of the first class, in red vestments, as on any martyr's day. 'The Church puts on the garments of mourning today', said one commentator.[18] This practice of keeping the feast without joyful

[14] J. Deshusses, ed., *Le Sacramentaire Grégorien*, 1, 3rd edn (Fribourg, 1992), Parsch, *Church's Year of Grace*, 1, p. 226.

[15] The Western titles are listed by P. Bruylants, *Les Oraisons du Missel Romain* (Louvain, 1952), p. 8. They include *in natali Innocentum, natale Innocentum, natalis Innocentum*; the Missal of 1570 entitles it *In festo sanctorum Innocentium.*

[16] Guy d'Orchelles, *Summa de officiis ecclesiasticis*, V. L. Kennedy, ed., *MS* 1 (1939), pp. 39–40.

[17] It also appeared in the first Mass in the Veronense.

[18] Mother St Paul, *Nativitas Christi* (London, 1948), p. 12.

accompaniment was known to the commentator Amalarius of Metz in the ninth century.[19] It reveals a degree of ambiguity about the status of the Innocents which is not found in the Office and a marked contrast with the ceremonies of the boy bishop. A number of arguments were advanced for the variations.[20] First, though they are martyrs, they died before Christ and so descended into hell. Joyful chants were used on Sunday, because of the residual understanding of every Sunday as the Day of Resurrection, and on the octave day, celebrated after the Sunday, for, having descended into hell, they were raised up by Christ.[21] Some commentators found additional difficulties with the festive nature of the commemoration of the beheading of John the Baptist, whose death was also pre-Paschal.[22] Second, we are sorrowing along with the mothers of the children. Third, the children could not be called victorious, because they had not fought, but they were innocent and unstained.[23]

There is conflict on each of the days following Christmas between the nature of the three feasts and the celebration of the Nativity. The feasts themselves overlap—second Vespers of St John is the first Vespers of the Innocents, within the octaves of St Thomas (celebrated on 21 December), the Nativity, and St Stephen. The liturgy could easily have become confused and incomprehensible, but the creativity that marks so much of the medieval liturgy produced a simple and effective solution. At second Vespers of Christmas Day, there was a procession to the altar of St Stephen; on St Stephen's Day, to the altar of St John or of the Apostles, and on St John's Day, the procession went to the altar of the Holy Innocents, or, if that was lacking, the altar of the Holy Trinity.[24] It was during the procession that the *episcopus puerorum* moved into primary place. As the deacons had the honour of singing the antiphons and responsories on the feast

[19] Amalarius of Metz, *De ecclesiasticis officiis*, i, 41 and iv, 37, in J. M. Hanssens, ed., *Amalarii episcopi opera liturgica omnia*, 3 vols (Vatican City, 1948–50). See also Bernhold of Constance, *Micrologus*, *PL* 151, cols 1005–6, and Honorius of Autun, *Gemma anima*, *PL* 172, cols 646f.

[20] A full account of the arguments is given in B. Gavanto and C.-M. Merati, *Thesaurus sacrorum rituum* (Venice, 1749), pp. 351–2.

[21] Bernhold of Constance, *Micrologus*, *PL* 151, cols 1005–6.

[22] John Beleth, *Summa de ecclesiasticis officiis* in H. Douteil, ed., *CChr.CM* (1976), 41A, p. 133.

[23] Durandus, *Rationale divinorum officiorum* (Lyons, 1672), pp. 461–2.

[24] At Bayeux, the procession went to the altar of St Nicholas: *Ordinaire et coutumier de léglise cathédrale de Bayeux*, ed. U. Chevalier (Paris, 1902), p. 69.

of Stephen and the priests on that of St John, so the boys of the choir exercised that right for the Innocents' Day. Bishop Grandisson provides that the boy bishop shall begin the responsory *Centum quadraginta*, drawn from the fourteenth chapter of the Apocalypse. In Exeter and Salisbury the boy bishop received the *baculum episcopi* during the antiphon *Princeps ecclesiae*; he gave the blessing in a special form at the end of the procession, but at Compline it was given in the usual pontifical form. At Bayeux the procession went to the altar of St Nicholas, and there the boy bishop, in full pontificals, began the same responsory, and thereafter presided at every liturgy except the Mass. The *Officium puerorum* ended in England as it had begun. At Vespers the responsory *Centum quadraginta* was intoned by a boy solo; the other boys sang the verse. The final antiphon before the procession to the altar of St Thomas Becket was *Princeps ecclesiae*, after which the bishop again blessed the people. None of this was specifically connected, as at Bayeux (and Coutances), with the *Deposuit* of the Magnificat. We are not entirely sure what happened there, but it seems that the *baculus* was given to someone else from the choir of boys, creating thereby a new bishop. But the *Ordinarium* says 'si habent novum episcopum', he is to be taken to the altar to receive the mitre, staff, and cape, so it appears that the office sometimes changed hands at this point, and the boy bishop gave way to the bishop-elect. Nevertheless, this *Deposuit* ceremony of handing over the *baculus pastoralis* should not be confused with that of the handing over of the Precentor's staff, the *baculus choralis*, or the *baculus stultorum*,[25] associated with the feast of the Circumcision.

The office contained, therefore, unusual ceremonies, and they certainly do not all relate to the observance of the liturgical feast itself. They were not favoured by all. Pierre de Roncevaux, Archbishop of Bordeaux, presided over a council at Cognac (*Copriniacense*) in 1260. In its second canon it not only prohibited, on pain of excommunication, dances held in church on the Innocents' Day and the 'multae rixae, contentiones, et turbationes', but also the custom of choosing someone on that day who is given the title 'bishop'.[26] Grandisson, as we have seen,

[25] The difficulties of liturgical reconstruction of the rites are explored by P. Pickett in the programme notes included in *Pickett's Pageant: eight centuries of early music*, book 1 (London, 1989), and in the booklet accompanying the recording of *The Feast of Fools* (London, 1992).

retained the boy bishop, continued the practice of him giving a full pontifical benediction, and gave a specific interpretation to the ceremonies, but he too wanted an end to disorders and mockeries. The Council of Basle, in its twenty-first session, found time to consider these practices and wanted an end to them all:

> Turpem etiam illum abusum in quibusdam frequentatum Ecclesiis quo certis ani celebritatibus, nonnulli cum mitra, baculo, ac vestibus pontificalibus more Episcoporum benedicunt. Alii ut Reges ac Duces induti, quod festum fatuorum vel Innocentium, seu puerorum in quibusdam regionius nuncupastur: alii larvales ac theatrales jocos, alii choreas et tripudia marium et mulierum facientes, homines as spectacula et cachinnationes movent, alii comessationes et convivia iibidem præparant, hæc Sancta Synodus detestans, stuit et jubet.[27]

The council fathers had perhaps missed the point, or else the disturbances were so great that the point was no longer clear. The Christmas liturgy stressed that in the Incarnation were both *magnum mysterium* and *admirabile sacramentum*; the eternal King is born and the Virgin has the joy of being a mother. More obviously than either St Stephen or St John, the Innocents belong to this mystery. As Augustine says in the sermon provided by Pius V for the second Nocturn, the hatred of Herod was more than balanced by the grace and blessing of God who brought them forth to eternal life. This understanding fits well with the way in which the Cross is never ultimately absent from the liturgy. It is the responsories that provide a particular interpretation of the feast. The Innocents are equated with the 144,000 redeemed from the earth, those who are virgins, who have not defiled themselves with women, and who reign with God and with the Lamb. The Matins antiphons will indeed recount the story of Herod's rage and the slaughter of the children, but the responsories, as a sort of counterpoint, return us constantly to the heavenly liturgy *sub altare Dei*, and present a vision of purity and innocence strangely at odds with the reality of Christian life. Grandisson interprets the boy bishop in terms of the Christmas

[26] Martene, *De antiqua ecclesiae disciplina* (Lyons, 1706), p. 101.
[27] Ibid.

mystery when he speaks of him as 'Christum puerum verum et eternum pontificem signans'. That the infant of Bethlehem is both in truth a child and the eternal bridge-builder, the divine mediator, is thus affirmed and enacted, and Grandisson clearly believed that this understanding was the most appropriate one and the one which increased devotion.

The relation of the liturgy to the liturgical plays which depict the slaughter is uncertain. There are four plays which dramatize it, three from France and a fourth from Freising.[28] Philip Pickett holds that the ecclesiastical authorities attempted to divert the spirit of play in the festivities of the octave into the *ludi* of Christmas dramas, utilizing the full potential offered by the story.[29] Young suggests that a trope (or tropes) of the responsory *Sub altare* arose as part of the creative impetus which inspired the great body of liturgical poetry. We find this in a brief and simple form at the monastery of St Martial, at Limoges. The responsory is followed by Rachel's lament and an angelic reply urging Rachel to cease her weeping and rejoice. We know nothing of its performance and can only assume that it was inserted into the office as a dramatic poem rather than as a miniature play.[30]

RESPONSORIUM: Sub altare Dei audivi voces occisorum dicentium. Quare non defendis sanguinem nostrum? Et acceperunt divinum responsum: Adhuc sustinete modicum tempus, donec impleatur numerus fratrum vestrorum.

VERSUS: Vidi sub altare Dei animas sanctorum propter verbum Dei quod habebant, et clara voce dicebant. Quare non.

LAMENTATIO RACHELIS:

O dulces filii,   quos nunc progenui,

[28] Text and studies in K. Young, *Ordo Rachelis = University of Wisconsin Studies in Language and Literature*, no. 4 (Madison, 1919), and *The Drama of the Medieval Church*, 2 (Oxford, 1933), pp. 102–24. English translation of the Fleury play in D. Bevington, *Medieval Drama* (Boston, 1975), pp. 67–72. Specific discussion of the French plays in G. Frank, *The Medieval French Drama* (Oxford, 1960), pp. 31–43.

[29] Pickett, *Feast of Fools*, notes to the recording.

[30] Young, *Drama*, 2, p. 110.

Natalis Innocentum

Olim dicta mater, quod nomen tenui?
Olim per pignora vocor puerpera,
Modo sum misera, naturum vidua
Heu! michi misere! cum possum vivere,
Cum natos coram ne video perdere,
Atque lacerare parum detruncare,
Herodes impius, furore repletus,
Nimium superbus perdit meos partus.

ANGELUS:

Noli, Rachel, deflere pignora.
Cur tristaris, et tundis pectora?
Noli flere, sed gaude potius,
cui nati vivunt felicius.
Ergo gaude!
Summi patris eterni filius
hic est ille quem querit perdere,
qui nos facit eterne vivere.
Ergo gaude![31]

We can surmise that such a trope inspired dramatists to expand the play of the Magi, the *Officium stellae*, as at Laon, or to create a separate play, as in the *Ordo Rachelis* in the Fleury playbook and as performed at the cathedral of Freising. Perhaps the ecclesiastical authorities encouraged the plays in some places, though it seems unlikely. Bishop Grandisson was not alone in disliking the dramas, and if they had been encouraged there would surely be more versions of them rather than the very few we have. The Freising play has remarkably little about the Innocents. Fleury, by contrast, give them a role derived from the liturgical texts. The play began with a procession of boys singing the antiphon *O quam gloriosum*, from the first Vespers of All Saints. A lamb carrying a cross takes its place at the head of the procession, and the boys, singing the antiphon *Emitte agnum*, follow it in an enactment of the Apocalypse (14.4), which was read at Sext. Even as Herod rages, the infants sing to the Lamb, who is removed before the slaughter. The last cry of the Innocents, 'Quare non defendis sanguinem nostrum, Deus noster?' brings us again to Rachel and those who would console her, but before

[31] Text in Paris, BN, MS latin 1139, trop. Martialense saec. xi–xii, fol. 32v–33r; ed. Young, *Drama*, 2, p. 109.

the end the children take their place in choir and sing the praise of Christ. In much the same way that part of the feast that directly concerns the Innocents comes to a close with the Magnificat antiphon, *Ecce vidi Agnum*: 'I saw the Lamb standing upon Mount Sion and with him an army of saints, and his name and the name of his Father are written upon their foreheads.'

The spontaneous nature of the observance of the feasts within the octave had already disappeared before the Tridentine reform imposed the sombre Roman use on the Latin Church. In 1586 Pius V made the Feast of the Holy Innocents a double of the second class. If it fell on a Sunday it was upgraded to the first class, with *Gloria* and *Alleluia*. He also gave it a proper office using Prudentius' hymn, *Salvete, flores martyrum*, part of the twelfth poem in the *Cathemerinon*. The jumble of conflicting observances was sorted out. The Second Vatican Council again reformed the rites and reduced the propers of the feast to the Office of Readings, Morning Prayer, and Prayer during the Day. Evening Prayer throughout the octave is of the Nativity. If it falls on a Sunday, it is not celebrated at all. From the richness of the medieval liturgy just one strand has been chosen: 'Let us adore the new-born Christ; today he gave the Holy Innocents the martyrs' crown.'[32]

Simon of Cyrene Theological Institute,
London

[32] Invitatory antiphon from the Divine Office.

THE BOY BISHOP'S FEAST: A CASE-STUDY IN CHURCH ATTITUDES TOWARDS CHILDREN IN THE HIGH AND LATE MIDDLE AGES

by SHULAMITH SHAHAR

THE main sources for the boy bishop's feast are available in print. These include sections in ceremonial- and service-books, cathedral statutes, councils' decrees, *compotus*, that is, accounts of the gifts and offerings of money the boy bishop received, as well as his expenses, household books that include registrations of the expenses for the annual entertainment of the boy bishop and his retinue, as well as two sermons the boy bishop delivered. Chambers, in his *Medieval Stage*, first published in 1903, dedicated a detailed description to the feast. A short reference to the feast appears in most research works on medieval schools and a number of articles have also been published on the subject.[1] I'll thus refer to the origins of the feast, but describe it only briefly, disregarding variations between places, and then turn to the subject of my paper: the boy bishop's feast, as reflecting the image of childhood, attitudes towards childhood, and medieval educational conceptions. These are expressed in the feast itself and more clearly in the sermons written by adults to be delivered by the boy bishop.

As there was in the Middle Ages a different assessment of the nature of males and females, as well as different goals set to the

[1] *Two Sermons Preached by the Boy Bishop* ed. J. Nichols, Introduction: E. F. Rimbault, Camden Society, ns 14 (London, 1875, repr. 1965), i–xxxvi, 1–29; Ch. Wordsworth, ed., *Ceremonies and Processions of the Cathedral Church of Salisbury* (Cambridge, 1901), pp. 52–7; E. K. Chambers, *The Medieval Stage* (London, 1903, repr. 1967), 2, Appendix M.I, and see also, pp. 72, 282–9, 1, pp. 276–371; A. F. Leach, 'The Schoolboys' Feast', *Fortnightly Review*, 59 (1896), pp. 128–41; E. Howlett, 'Boy-Bishops' in W. Andrews, ed., *Curious Church Gleanings* (London, 1896), pp. 241–50; J. P. Wickersham Crawford, 'A Note on the Boy Bishop in Spain', *The Romanic Review*, 12 (1921), pp. 146–54; J. Lawson, *A Town Grammar School Through Six Centuries* (Oxford, 1963), pp. 15–16; N. Orme, *English Schools in the Middle Ages* (London, 1973), p. 132; R. L. De Molen, '*Pueri Christi Imitatio*: the Festival of the Boy Bishop in Tudor England', *Moreana*, 12 (1975), pp. 17–29; S. E. Rigold, 'The St Nicholas Tokens or the Boy Bishop's Tokens', *Proceedings of the Suffolk Institute of Archaeology*, 34 (1978), pp. 87–101; N. Mackenzie, 'Boy into Bishop: A Festive Role Reversal', *History Today*, 37 (1987), pp. 10–16; E. Duffy, *The Stripping of the Altars. Traditional Religion in England c. 1400–c. 1580* (New Haven, 1992), pp. 13–44.

education of the two sexes conditioned by the ideas about gender roles, different educational modes were also prescribed for them. As the boy bishop and his fellow choristers, as well as the pupils in grammar school, were all boys, the feast was a boys' feast, and the writers of the sermons refer only to the education of boys. In this paper I'll follow them and not deal with the education of girls.

The boy bishop's feast originated from the feast of the Innocents that was celebrated on 28 December. The justification for the officiation of the schoolchildren in church on that day was advanced by the twelfth-century liturgist John of Beleth: 'The children (*pueri*) will perform the office on the feast of the Innocents because the Innocents were killed for Christ.'[2] As Innocents Day commemorated a martyrdom, the chants *Te Deum, Gloria*, and *Alleluia* were omitted from the service, as in Lent and on Good Friday. Honorius of Autun in the early twelfth century writes that these joyful chants should be omitted on Innocents' Day, 'because we imitate their mothers who doubtless felt sadness'.[3] Thomas Aquinas explains that though the Innocents were infants with no free will, and thus could not endure martyrdom voluntarily, they won the glory of martyrdom by God's grace, and the shedding of blood for Christ's sake was a substitute for baptism.[4] Jacob of Voragine found no need to advance an apology. Explaining why of all the feasts of the Old Testament's saints only those of the Maccabees and the Holy Innocents are celebrated by the Western Church, he states that exception is made for the Innocents, 'in each of whom Christ himself was slain'.[5] And Erasmus in his *Homily for the Child Jesus* writes: 'Then straight-away he wished to consecrate his birth with the blood of innocent children, engaging them, as it were, for preliminary skirmish, so that he might enter the war an unconquered leader.'[6]

[2] John Beleth, *Rationale Divinorum Officiorum, PL* 202, ch.LXX, col. 77; the argument is based on a comparison with the feasts of St Stephen (26 December) and of John the Evangelist (27 December); on St Stephen's Day, says John Beleth, the deacons will officiate, because he was a deacon, while on Blessed John's feast the priests will officiate because he was a priest.

[3] Honorius Augustodunensis, *Gemma Animae, PL* 172, pars 3 *Liturgica*, ch. 14, col. 646; and he adds: '*dalmatia vel subile non portatur*'.

[4] Thomas Aquinas, *Summa Theologiae*, 2a 2ae, q. 124, art. 1 (Blackfriars, London, 1972), 42, p. 43.

[5] Jacobi de Voragine, *Legenda Aurea*, ed. T. Grasse (Leipzig, 1850), ch. 10, pp. 62–6; *The Golden Legend of Jacobus de Voragine*, tr. G. Ryan and H. Ripperger (New York, 1948), p. 400.

[6] Erasmus, *Homily on the Child Jesus*, in *Collected Works of Erasmus*, ed. E. Fantham and E. Rummel

It is clear that all the authors attribute to the Innocents' martyrdom a role in the annals of salvation. Notwithstanding this belief, it appears that a playful element was already introduced into the feast by the late tenth century. Ekkehart, the monk of St Gall, who was also master of the school there, recounts the visit of Emperor Conrad I to St Gall on the Vespers of the Innocents. He relates that the Emperor was impressed by the children's procession and ordered his followers to roll apples along the aisles. He could then marvel at their discipline as none even of the smallest children (*parvissimorum*) left the line to get an apple. A serious atmosphere reigned. However, he also recounts that on the next morning the Bishop of Constance, Solomon, who also came to visit, amused himself with the children, who, writes Ekkehart, had the right on that day to capture all guests and detain them until they paid a ransom.[7] In Johan Huizinga's terms it was 'play' as a function of 'culture'.

Gradually the feast became more boisterous and colourful. The joyful chants were no longer omitted,[8] and a clear carnivalesque role-reversal took place. One of the boys from the song school was elected by his fellow choristers to be a bishop. The little bishop carried the various insignia of the office: robe, mitre, ring, and staff, and all the other boys had to do him reverence. He gave benediction, and with the assistance of the other boys performed all the priest's ceremonies, except in the Mass. The proper hierarchical order was reversed both in the church seats and in the procession. The boys took the higher stalls, while the canons took the seats of the choirboys. In the procession they also took the place of the boys and acolytes, carrying the books, censers, and candlesticks. The boy bishop received donations from the canons of the cathedral, and during his visitation to his diocese also from abbots, abbesses, and layfolk. In Toul on the second day of the feast all the boys went masked into the city. A

(Toronto, 1989), 29, p. 61; this homily, written in 1512, is different both in content and tone from the two English sermons. Though it was very popular in the sixteenth century, and was translated into English, it appears that it was not delivered by a boy bishop.

[7] Ekhardus IV, *B. Casuum S. Galli, MGH.SS* 2 (Hanover, 1829, repr. 1963), pp. 84, 91: 'Erat utique ius illorum, sicut adhuc hodie quidem est, quoniam exleges quidam sunt, ut hospites intrantes capiant, captos usque dum se redimant, teneant.'

[8] John of Avranche wrote already in the late eleventh century that in past times the chants had been omitted in some of the churches, however, 'tam quia placuit modernis, placet et nobis ut cantentur': Ioannes Abricensis, *Liber de Officiis Ecclesiasticis, PL* 147, col. 42.

compotus from the year 1441 contains a payment to the boy bishop and his retinue by the abbess of the nearby nunnery. The boys, dressed as girls, danced, sang, and sported before the abbess and the nuns. In other localities mummers performed before the boys. Gradually the feast also became longer. In some places the boy bishop was already elected on St Nicholas's Day, that is, on 6 December, and began his officiation as well as the collection in the streets on that day. In other localities the boy bishop's feast merged with the Feast of Fools (*Festa Fautorum*) which took place on Circumcision Day, 1 January.[9]

All the ceremonies of the feast were an ecclesiastical practice. The details of the ceremonies appear in the service-books.[10] Capitulary acts were sometimes aimed at eliminating abuses and excess and ensuring some control, but not at abolishing the feast. Thus, for example, according to the *ordinarius* of Coutances, the boys had to appoint their superiors to the minor tasks without mockery and impertinence.[11] Or in a capitulary act of the cathedral of York, from the year 1376, it is stated: 'The Bishop of the Boys for the future be he who had served longest in the church and proved most useful . . . provided, nevertheless, that he was sufficiently efficient and handsome.'[12] The capitulary act aimed at curbing the free election of the boys. The councils castigated the behaviour of the adult members of the minor clergy more often and more severely than that of the children. According to one decree, the revelry was permitted only to the young boys under sixteen years of age. Only by the early fifteenth century were there councils that demanded its complete abolition, arguing, *inter alia*, that it had support neither in the Scriptures nor in the writings of the Church Fathers.[13]

While the boy bishop's feast was a common practice, the abbess girl's, which was apparently celebrated in some nunneries, raised opposition. Already Archbishop John Peckham, in the

[9] Chambers, *Medieval Stage*, 1, pp. 291, 337–71; Rimbault, Introduction, *Two Sermons*, pp. vii, xi–xvi.

[10] See *The Sarum Office*, in Chambers, *Medieval Stage*, 2, Appendix M.I.

[11] Ibid., 1, p. 346 and n. 3.

[12] Ibid., p. 356; in 1390 a further qualification was added: he must have a good voice.

[13] *Statuta ecclesiae collegiatae S. Castris, ordinationes et mandata Archidiocesis Trevirensis 1458–1855* (Trier, 1844–59), 1, pp. 361, 365; see also: J. D. Mansi, *Sacrorum conciliorum nova et amplissima collectio* (Florence, 1759–98, repr. Graz, 1961), 24, xvii, col. 142; Jean Gerson, *Contre la fête de fous*, in *Oeuvres complètes*, ed. Mgr Glorieux (Paris, 1966), 7, pp. 409–11; Chambers, *Medieval Stage*, 1, pp. 340–3.

thirteenth century, had issued a mandate forbidding the office and prayers to be said *per parvulas* in the nunneries on Innocents' Day.[14] There are two possible explanations to this opposition which do not exclude each other. First, the Innocents were males. Secondly, as women were to a great extent excluded from the social mechanisms that defined male identity and social status, the consciousness of the multiplicity of statuses and roles that developed from the twelfth century onwards was predominately an awareness of a variety of male roles.[15] Thus a reversal of female roles, despite the fact that a hierarchical order existed in the nunneries, was regarded as pointless. And as modesty and reticence were expected of a girl much more than of a boy, unruliness of girls was probably regarded also as unseemly. It is interesting to note in this context that from a collection of Jewish customs from Germany, it appears that a similar feast to that of the boy bishop's was celebrated in the Talmudical boys' schools, the Yeshivot, on the first Sabbath after the feast of Purim. We have here the materials for a cross-cultural study, the study of shared elements operating in two contiguous societies.[16]

Anthropologists tend to see symbolic reversals as a moment of escape from role and status into an opposite role that ultimately reinforces normal structures. The inversion of the norms always implies the norm which is mocked at, and it emerges reinforced. On the other hand, some historians, such as Natalie Davis, have regarded some of these rituals as harbouring a revolutionary potential, or at least a powerful social and political critique. Emmanuel Le Roy Ladurie, in his *Carnival in Romans. A People's Uprising at Romans 1579–1580*, studied such a case of conjunction of feast and rebellion, or 'masks and massacre', to use the author's phrase. The *mardi gras* carnival in 1580, in the little town of Romans, in the province of Dauphiné, ended in a bloody

[14] Chambers, *Medieval Stage*, p. 361; see also *Regestrum Visitationum Archiepiscopi Rothomagensis 1248–1269*, ed. Th. Bonnin (Rouen, 1852), p. 44.

[15] This lack of acknowledgement of a multiplicity of female roles is very clear in the *sermones ad status*, see: J. Longère, *La Predication médievale* (Paris, 1983), pp. 88–9, 101, 197; G. Hasenohr, 'La Vie quotidienne de la femme vue par l'Eglise: l'enseignement des "Journées chrétiennes" de la fin du Moyen-Age' in *Frau und Spätmittelalterlicher Alltag* (Vienna, 1986), pp. 19–101.

[16] E. Epstein, *Die Wormser Minhagbücher, Literarisches und Culturhistorisches aus denselben*, pp. 314–15; see also: C. Roth, 'The Lord of Misrule. How Jews once Commemorated Purim', *Jewish Chronicle*, 15 March 1935, p. 28.

rebellion against government and against taxes.[17] The manifested view of the medievals was, however, that of the anthropologists. Stephen of Bourbon, the thirteenth-century Dominican and Inquisitor, describing the carnival in Rome, writes that in its wake all seven sins were killed and immediately after it and throughout the year good reigned, and peace and tranquillity prevailed between the pope and his Roman flock.[18] In 1445 the Dean of the Faculty of Theology of the University of Paris addressed a letter to the bishops and chapters of France demanding the abolition of the Feast of Fools. In his letter he strongly refutes the prevailing view of its supporters, which he presents as follows:

> This is not serious; it is just a jest we play following an ancient custom, so that our innate foolishness will abound once a year and then evaporate. Would not the wine bags and casks explode if their air-holes are not relaxed from time to time? We are, indeed, old bags and semi-broken barrels, whereby the wine of wisdom boils excessively [in us]. For the whole year we press and hold it by force in the service of God. It will flow vainly if we don't free it occasionally in games and foolishness. It is freed once in jest so that afterwards we will return stronger to keep our wisdom.[19]

Needless to say that if there was a revolutionary potential in the unruliness and role-reversal in the Feast of Fools which was sponsored by the Church, its defenders, even if they were conscious of this fact, would not admit it. Leaving aside the issue of the Feast of Fools, the point here is that in the boy bishop's feast there was neither a revolutionary potential nor a serious social critique. Biology had the upper hand. It was a children's feast. Children attending song school were generally between the ages of seven and ten. Pupils in grammar school might be anywhere

[17] M. Bakhtin, *Rabelais and his World*, tr. H. Iswolsky (Cambridge, Mass., 1968), pp. 5–12; 'Carnival' in *Encyclopedia of Religion*, ed. M. Eliade (New York, 1987), pp. 948–1103; N. Zemon Davis, 'The Reasons of Misrule: Youth Groups and Charivaris in 16th Century France', *PaP*, 50 (1971), pp. 41–71, *and*, 'The Reasons of Misrule', in *Society and Culture in Early Modern France* (Stanford, 1975), pp. 97–123; E. Le Roy Ladurie, *Carnival in Romans. A People's Uprising at Romans 1579–1580*, tr. M. Feeney (Harmondsworth, 1981).

[18] A. Lecoy de la Marche, ed., *Anecdotes historiques, légendes et apologues tirés du recueil inédit d'Etienne de Bourbon* (Paris, 1877), pp. 423–4.

[19] H. Denifle, ed., *Cartularium Universitatis Parisiensis* (Paris, 1897, repr. Bruxelles, 1964), 4, p. 653.

from eight to eighteen years of age, yet the most common grammar-school age was from ten or twelve to fifteen or sixteen years of age. Sixteen, it should be recalled, was also the maximal age to which one of the councils tried to limit the permission of unruliness on the days of the feast.[20] The feast reflects the conception of churchmen of childhood as a distinct period in human life, distinguished by several stages, as well as an awareness of the special characteristics and needs of children in the respective stages. Children in song school were in their second stage: *pueritia*, which was generally considered to last from the age of seven to fourteen. Boys in grammar school were between the second and the third stage, *adolescentia*, which, according to the most common view, started at the age of fourteen.[21] The feast reflects the recognition that school attendance must have borne down with behavioural and psychological weight that demanded periodic relief. The boy bishop's feast accorded such relief, both through the temporary permitted unruliness and the inversion of the proper order of ages, which was at the same time also a temporary role-reversal. During the feast the binary opposition of child versus adult, or pupil versus master, was reversed. And the temporary reversal was supposed finally to reinforce the normal classification into the various age-categories, each of which had its proper place in society.

Preaching was one of the roles of churchmen. Thus the boy bishop also delivered a sermon. The content of the sermons was serious. If it still had a somewhat comic effect for the audience it was because (a) it was delivered by a child; (b) sometimes mockery and common carnivalesque verbal abuse were incorporated into the sermon. However, things were not without ambivalence. As I shall try to show below, since the child was also presented as an example to adults, his preaching to them was not a classical case of role-reversal. As in all rituals, in those of the boy bishop's feast as well there were different levels of symbolic meaning. While the interpretations of most rituals were socially patterned,[22] those of the boy bishop's feast must have been

[20] J. Heppner Moran, *The Growth of English Schooling 1340–1548* (Princeton, 1985), pp. 64–5; S. Shahar, *Childhood in the Middle Ages* (London, 1990), pp. 105–6, 187–91.
[21] Shahar, *Childhood*, pp. 24–31.
[22] See on this S. Lukes, 'Political Ritual and Social Integration' in *Essays in Social Theory* (London, 1977), p. 67.

patterned by age. They did not have the same meaning for the children, who had the opportunity to retaliate in some way against their masters, as for the adults, who participated or just observed.

Sermons for the boy bishop were already written in the thirteenth century, if not earlier.[23] But the ones that survived are from a much later period. One sermon was written and preached soon afterwards, before the year 1496, at St Paul's Cathedral. The second one was written in 1558 by Richard Ramsey, the Prebendary of Gloucester Cathedral, and preached there in the same year.[24] The year 1558 was the last of the reign of Queen Mary. During her reign the ceremonies connected with the holidays of the saints were restored, including those of St Nicholas and the Innocents, which had been abolished by order of Henry VIII.[25] The sermons were written in English, with some citations in Latin, mainly from the Scriptures. What is remarkable about the two sermons is the total lack of any trace of the new humanistic educational currents. Both sermons clearly express medieval educational theories and conceptions. The same theories and conceptions can be found in various medieval texts such as encyclopaedias, religious manuals, and educational treatises. The few references in the sermons to the curriculum in the schools also reveal a medieval curriculum. J. Heppner Moran has already demonstrated that humanistic curriculum and educational goals hardly penetrated the schools of southern England of the period.[26]

There are two allusions to the Reformation in the second sermon. The writer elaborates on the inherent contrast between the Innocents, who were true martyrs because of their innocence, and those who, despite having also suffered and shed their blood, cannot be considered true martyrs because of their 'lacking the commendacion of innocency'. More bluntly and vindictively he also says: 'For a malefactor that suffreth not

[23] G. R. Owst, *Preaching in Medieval England* (Cambridge, 1926), p. 220 and n. 4; Rimbault, *Two Sermons*, Introduction p. xxxii.

[24] Rimbault, *Two Sermons*, Introduction, pp. xxxv–xxxvi.

[25] E. Duffy, *Stripping of the Altars*, pp. 430–1, 482.

[26] Heppner Moran, *English Schooling*, pp. 214–19; the effect of the Reformation on the standard and scope of English schooling is a matter of controversy; see ibid., pp. 3–20, and H. M. Jewell, 'The Bringing up of Children in Good Learning and Manners: A Survey of Secular Educational Provisions in the North of England, c. 1350–1550', *NH*, 18 (1982), pp. 1–25.

innocently, but for his own gilt and deservyng, is worthy that he suffreth . . .'.[27] The second allusion is in a comparison between children lacking in wit and discretion that are 'caried wyth an apple, or wyth a puffe of wynd as thei that have strength to resist nothing', and the many childish people in the realm of late years 'which waveryd in ther faith and were caried hyder and thyder, from [one] opinion to another . . .'.[28]

A short carnivalesque verbal abuse appears in the first sermon. After recommending to the prayers of the audience all the prelates of the Church, including 'my broder Bysshopp of London' and also 'my worshypfull broder Dean of this cathedral churche', the little preacher beseeches them to pray also for him that he may continue in his office of bishop and thus be spared Jeremiah's rod, meaning his master's stick. He expresses the wish that his master 'whom I love soo well' will make away with himself the way Nero forced his master Seneca to do. As for his other teachers, he expresses the wish that they would be brought before the King's Bench and from there be led to Tyburn (or *via Tributina*), which was the execution-place in London.[29]

Let us turn now to the conception of childhood in the sermons. They present the common division of childhood into stages, the characteristics of each stage, and the way children in each stage should be treated.

The first stage: *infantia*. The prevailing image of the baptized child was one of purity and innocence, on the one hand, and of weakness, helplessness, and lack of reason, on the other. The image of early childhood as a period of inability to control the body, absence of reason, perception, and consistency, was inspired by Aristotle. The image of the innocent child was inspired by the words of Jesus in the Gospel of St Matthew 18.3–6 and 19.14. The propagation of the cult of the infant Jesus from the twelfth century onwards consolidated this image of innocence and purity. Though born in sin, once baptized, the child was seen as sweet, pure, and innocent, a sign of God's wonder. He was believed to be ignorant of both sexual lust and the meaning of death. Thanatos and Eros had no place in his

[27] *Two Sermons*, pp. 17–18.
[28] Ibid., p. 21.
[29] Ibid., pp. 3–4.

cosmogony.[30] The writers of the sermons cite the verses from Matthew as well as the verse from St Paul's First Epistle to the Corinthians, 14.20, which refers both to the child's innocence and lack of understanding: 'Brethren be not children in understanding; howbeit in malice be ye children but in understanding be men.' They also write:

> The litill ones have by nature what the elder have by wrestling and stryvyng with their own affections. Thei have humilitie of mynd and sprite. . . .[31] You shall perceive in them no manner of malice, no envy, no disdayne, no hurtfulness, no synfull affection, no pride, no ambition, no singularitie, no desyre of honor, of riches, of carnalitie, of revenginge, or quitting evyll for evyll . . .

and above all they are innocent, and 'that one vertue includeth all as the general includeth the speciall'.[32] This description is reminiscent of what Petrarch wrote about his little grandson Francesco, who died when he was not yet three years old: 'Often such as these who by innocence and purity even more than by natural instinct gain our favor, are loved more than those who are already grown up, who mix love and hate, and put us of by disdain and disobedience.'[33] As to the child's lack of understanding, the writers of the sermons say that children lack knowledge, discretion, and consistency, and cite also the verse from St Paul's Epistle to the Ephesians 4.21: '. . . be no more children, tossed to and fro, and carried about with every wind of doctrine.'

The writer of the first sermon compares the first stage of life to the first era in the history of mankind, and through it expresses the dominant medieval educational theory relating to this stage. He writes: 'The thre ages . . . is lykened to the thre lawes . . . to the Lawe of Kynde, the Lawe Wryten and the Lawe of Grace.

[30] Gilbert of Nogent writes of children who have not yet reached puberty and are not ashamed of their nudity: 'How great is the joy in the ignorance of little children. Being protected by absence of lust it enjoys the security of angels': *Tractatus de Incarnatione contra Judaeus, PL* 156, col. 497; the English fourteenth-century preacher, John Bromyard, describes the innocent children who do not understand the significance of death and who play merrily with the silk cloth covering the corpse of their father and mother: *Summa Praedicantium* (Antwerp, 1614), p. 338.

[31] *Two Sermons*, pp. 5, 15.

[32] Ibid., pp. 21–2.

[33] Cited in J. D. Folts, 'Senescence and Renascence: Petrarch's Thought on Growing Old', *Journal of Medieval and Renaissance Studies*, 10 (1980), p. 228.

The first age is likenyd unto the Lawe of Kynde.' By the 'Lawe of Kynde', the author means the natural law of the child, or, in other words: he is untamed. Nurture does not yet play a role. The child in this stage is in the state of Adam after the Fall, when he was still under no law whatsoever. 'A childe fyrste whan he is in his infant age is not constreyned unto no lawes; he is not corrected nother beten; and there is no defaute layed unto hym, but utterly he is lefte into the lawe of Kynde. Do he what somever he wyll, no man doth blame hym.'[34] The dominant attitude in the Middle Ages was indeed in favour of lenient treatment and of granting the small child freedom to act in accordance with his natural inclinations. Most of the authors of medieval didactic texts emphasize the importance of play for both the physical and mental development of the child. It was recommended not to enter into conflict with the small child but rather to use diversionary tactics. Since the prevalent conception of the person from the twelfth century onwards was that of a psychosomatic unity, the authors of scientific and medical texts also caution nurses and parents to refrain from angering and saddening the child, as it might harm his health. In none of the texts have I encountered a reference to toilet training. It appears that the child was expected to learn what he had to learn at his own pace, through imitating the adults, without specific toilet training. There is not a word about the need to inculcate in the child control of his drives, and no demand for discipline and self-restraint or for breaking an obstinate child's will.[35] The consensus was that education should begin at an early age, as the foundation of future development was laid in childhood, and that what was spoiled at that stage of life could never be rectified. To substantiate this view maxims were cited: a thin and flexible branch can be bent easily, but once thickened, it cannot be bent without breaking; fresh clay and wax can easily be moulded, etc.[36] However at an 'early age' meant only at the beginning of the second stage of childhood. This goes for both schooling and

[34] *Two Sermons*, p. 5.

[35] See Shahar, *Childhood*, pp. 16–18, 77–120; see also J. Swanson, 'Childhood and Childrearing in *ad status* Sermons by later Thirteenth Century Friars', *JMedH*, 16 (1990), p. 327.

[36] For example: Philippe de Navarre, *Les Quatre âges de l'homme*, ed. M. de Fréville (Paris, 1888), pp. 7–9; John Bromyard, *Summa Praedicantium*, p. 6; *Select English Works of John Wycliffe*, ed. T. Arnold (Oxford, 1871), 3, p. 195.

education in the wider sense. As Aegidius Romanus writes in the late thirteenth century, up to the age of seven a child is almost totally incapable of using his reason. He can be taught neither science nor morals. He can be taught only the vernacular language, and apart from the sacraments of baptism and confirmation, attention should be focused primarily on maintaining a good physical condition.[37]

I have concentrated on the educational theory. The extant sources reveal more about theories, norms, and stances than about their application and the degree of their internalization. From the sources that do give, at least, a partial picture of the reality (and to which I have not referred in this paper), it appears that by and large reality matched the theory. I don't want to idealize medieval childhood. Nor do I mean to belittle the complexity of the issue. I am referring only to the fact that with the exception of those who were placed in monasteries at a very young age, children up to the age of seven generally enjoyed freedom, and few restrictions were imposed on them. Philippe Ariès rightly shows that from the seventeenth century onwards disciplinary demands were increasingly brought to bear on small children. However he attributed the change to dawning awareness of childhood as a distinct stage in life, and to the first glimmers of an educational theory. The gentler treatment of small children in the Middle Ages he attributed to the lack of an educational theory and to benevolent neglect, while in fact it was anchored in an educational theory.

Though according to most schemes of the division of the life-course the second stage was called *pueritia* and the third stage *adolescentia*, the writer of the first sermon passes from *infantia* directly to *adolescentia*. However, from what he says to and about the *adolescenti* it is clear that he is dealing with the second stage of childhood.

The second stage: *pueritia*. It was an accepted view that from the age of seven the child could express himself properly, gradually distinguish good from evil, and choose between them. He reached the 'years of discretion' (*annis discretionis*). Though the 'age of discretion' was not strictly a legal term, it was none the less given some acknowledgement in law. By canon law a

[37] Aegidius Romanus, *De Regimine Principum* (Venice, 1505), L. II, pt 2, ch. 17.

child of seven could be betrothed, as well as have his head tonsured to enter minor orders. According to secular law criminal responsibility began legally only around fourteen years of age. However, unlike infants, children between the ages of seven and fourteen could be placed on trial. Yet they did not receive the same sentence meted to adults for the same crime. The customary punishment imposed on a child was whipping. Only in extraordinary circumstances was the full penalty imposed on a child not yet fourteen years of age. The justification advanced for this relative leniency was that the child at this age was still devoid of malicious intent.[38] The assumption was that the human being grows and develops both physically and intellectually according to the laws of natural development. Concomitantly, however, his tendency to sin grows as well, or, in other words, he is perceived to be controlled by his drives more than by his developing reason. Children in the second stage of childhood were still considered pure. Bartholomaeus Anglicus asserts, in the wake of Isidore of Seville, that *puer* is derived from *puritas*, and *puella* from *pupilla*—the pupil of the eye, because boys and girls at that age are as pure as the pupil.[39] The predilection for sin was believed to reach its peak in youth, but its first sprouting was already in the second stage of childhood. Thus, despite the fact that children in the second stage were considered still pure, a change in the mode of education was expected to take place after the age of seven. Parents were exhorted to teach their children love of God, discipline, and Christian morality; under no circumstances should they postpone the commencement of education and strict insistence on proper conduct, nor should they regard the evil action of children as childish mischief which might be ignored. The time of pampering was expected to be over. As the beginning of the second stage was commonly considered the suitable

[38] See for example: *Die Konstitutionen Friedrichs II von Hohenstaufen für sein Königreich Sizilien*, eds. H. Conrad, T. von der Lieck-Buyken and W. Wagner (Vienna, 1973), Bk I. tit. XIV, p. 22; *Las Siete Partidas del Rey Don Alfonso el Sabio*, Glossadas par G. Lopez (Salamanca, 1555; repr. Madrid, 1974), P. 1, tit. 1, ley 21, p. 10; P. 7, tit. 13, ley 17, p. 51; see also E. Cohen, 'Youth and Deviancy in the Middle Ages' in *History of Juvenile Delinquency. A Collection of Essays on Crime committed by Young Offenders in History and in selected Countries* (Aalen, 1990), 1, pp. 207–10; R. Metz, *La Femme et l'enfant dans le droit canonique médiéval* (Variorum reprints, London, 1985), pp. 18–19, 25–7, 40–2.

[39] Bartholomaeus Anglicus, *Liber de Proprietatibus Rerum* (Strasbourg, 1505), Bk 6, ch. 5; *On the Properties of Things. John Trevisa's translation of Bartholomaeus Anglicus*, ed. M. C. Seymur (Oxford, 1975), pp. 300–1.

age for the commencing of schooling, a demand was addressed to teachers as well to educate and discipline the *pueri*.[40]

The writers of the sermons express the same attitudes and conceptions. They elaborate on the need to educate and instruct the children, as at that age 'is the brekynge of every chylde to goodness or to lewdenes'. They also refer to the commencement of schooling and what it entails for the child: 'Whan that infant age is ended, the fader provydeth for hys childe for a mayster the whyche gyveth instruccyon in small doctrynes, as in hys Donate, Partes of reason and suche other . . . ', as well as in basic Christian morals and devotion ' . . . the whiche mayster comunely is called *Pedagogus* in Latyne.' This master corrects him and punishes him for every fault; sometimes he gives him a hard slap on his hand, and in others he beats him with a rod. This period in life is parallel to the second era in the history of humanity, that of the 'Law Wryten', the law of Moses. It is a rudimentary law, but a severe one, as is attested in the punishments in the Old Testament for the infringement of the law.[41]

In both sermons there is a castigation of ecclesiastical as well as secular dignitaries who fail to fulfil their duties and thus cause a general decline in morals and piety.[42] Special remonstrance is addressed to parents and teachers. The parents are blamed for not teaching their children to do good, and for not chastising them, though it is they who are responsible for their children and will have to give account before God. They fail to fulfil their duty because of a 'foolysh affection and a fond opinion in their child'. In order to gain his love they neglect their duties. To win the words: 'I love father (or mother) best' they dare not displease the child, but pamper him and stroke his head whatever he does. This marrs the child; it makes him think he does well when he does wrong. It is both parents' fault, but especially that of the mothers. Instead of beating the child when he does wrong, they beat the cushion. Why? There is an old saying: 'The rod breaks no bones.' They are too tender to beat their children, and when the child weeps they weep with him. And the fathers say: 'Yf I should beate my child and kepe hym undre and in awe now, I should kill his corage in his youth, and take away his hart that

[40] See on this, Shahar, *Childhood*, pp. 170–6.

[41] *Two Sermons*, pp. 7–8, 10.

[42] Ibid., pp. 6–7.

shall never be bold when he is a man.' But this is exactly the purpose of good education, says the preacher, to discourage youth utterly touching vice and vicious manners, and make them bold in virtue.[43] One finds exactly the same exhortations and admonitions in many medieval sermons, didactic texts, and popular tales about the bad end of those who were not properly educated by their parents.[44]

The remonstrance addressed to the fathers of the school children is in line with the medieval conception of the roles of the father and mother. The accepted view was that up to the age of seven it was the mother's task to rear the child, and that she was the only one responsible for his welfare and physical safety. From the age of seven onwards, once the boy attained the age of understanding, it was the father's duty to educate him. In the presentation of the role of the mother in the various discourses, often the focus is on her biological function, nurturing the foetus during pregnancy, delivery, and nursing, not on an educational function. Thomas Aquinas states that woman was created primarily as a helpmate to man in procreation. The father in whom the rational element is more developed than in woman, and who possesses the authority and power, is assigned the task of educating his sons. He will also know how to punish them.[45]

The second sermon ends with an exhortation to the schoolmasters, whose duty it is to educate the children and teach them both morals and secular learning. They, too, will have to give account before God. Not in vain did Quintilian, 'the flower of scolemasters', call them *tertios parentes*. They mould the child's soul, and 'Good fascionyng of the soule by nurture and vertue is better then the best fascionyng of the body by nature.' The schoolmaster is the worthiest of the three parents. The schoolmasters don't spare the rod. The child in song school is beaten when he sings out of tune; the child in grammar school when he speaks 'false Lattyn or Englysh forbyddyn'. But he is not beaten

[43] Ibid., p. 27.

[44] See Shahar, *Childhood*, pp. 170–4, 178–9.

[45] Thomas Aquinas, *Summa Theologiae*, Prima Pars, q. 92, art. 1 (Blackfriars, London, 1974), 13, pp. 34–6; *Summa Contra Gentiles* in *Opera Omnia* (Milan, 1980), Bk 3, ch. 122, n. 6–8, pp. 100–1; *Bartholomew of Exeter: Bishop and Canonist with the Text of Bartholomew's Penitential*, ed. D. A. Morey (Cambridge, 1937), 9, p. 224; Ivo of Chartre, *Decretum, PL* 161, col. 893; *Diplomatarium Danicum*, ed. M. Skyum-Nielsen (Copenhagen, 1958), 1, p. 144; Bartholomaeus Anglicus, *Liber de Proprietatibus Return*, Bk 6, ch. 7, 14.

when he deserves chastisement most: when he breaks God's commandments and the Church's, when he lies, curses, and blasphemes.[46]

There is only one element that appears in many medieval texts which is lacking in the two sermons: empathy towards the little schoolboy. Though the second stage of childhood was considered a turning-point, at which pampering was expected to come to an end, and controlled whipping was also advocated when all other educational means failed, some medieval authors also recommended that both the boy's exposure to physical hardship and the scholarly and disciplinary demands made on him be introduced gradually. Some authors devoted attention not only to the stages of the curriculum,[47] but also to the need to increase only gradually the demands made of the child over the number of hours devoted to study, and the degree of diligence and concentration which could be expected. Humbert de Romans, for example, writes that it is hard for children who still wish to play to be closed in the schoolroom, but little by little they begin to take interest in their studies.[48] The writer of the first sermon states that 'childerne newely sette to schole, lackynge the use of reason and the habyt of cognycyon' learn first only the simplest things, and small and rude doctrines,[49] thus noting that the curriculum must be graded. However, in both sermons there is no expression of empathy towards the little boys. On the contrary, they, too, are admonished: children in the street, children in song school, and children in grammar school. The main remonstrance is addressed to the adults who fail to fulfil their educational duties, but the children, too, are blamed. They lie, curse, blaspheme, quarrel with each other, mock their elders, and behave irreverently even in church. They are quick to lose their innocence.[50] Recognition that school attendance must have borne down with behavioural and psycho-

[46] *Two Sermons*, p. 28.

[47] The fourteenth-century Dominican friar Robert Holcot, for example, commented that boys when they are first instructed are not able to learn anything subtle but only simple things. Cited in B. Smalley, *English Friars and Antiquity in the Early Fourteenth Century* (Oxford, 1960), p. 332.

[48] Humbert de Romans, *Sermons* (Venice, 1603), 87, p. 87; see also *Le Régime du corps de maître Aldebrandin de Sienne*, eds L. Landouzy and R. Pépin (Paris, 1911), p. 80; Bernard de Gordon, *De Conservatione vitae humanae* (Leipzig, 1570), p. 27.

[49] *Two Sermons*, p. 2.

[50] Ibid., pp. 23–5; see also p. 8.

logical weight seems to have been expressed by the very permission for temporary release, as well as by the short carnivalesque verbal abuse inserted in the first sermon, where the little preacher wishes his teachers dead. There was no need to mitigate the demands made by the schoolboy in the sermons.

As already mentioned, remonstrances are addressed in the sermons not only to the children, their parents and teachers, but also to the prelates and secular potentates and the whole adult audience.[51] A powerless child, whose reason is not yet fully developed, dependent on adults, and who is still under the 'Lawe Wryten', preaching to adults and exhorting them to convert their hearts[52] is a case of role-reversal, but not, however, a clear cut one.

The child represented an image of purity and innocence that is destined to pass away, as Dante wrote in the *Divine Comedy*:

> For faith and innocence are in the heart
> Of children only; both aside are cast
> Before a beard upon the cheeks may start.[53]

There was a belief in the special power of a child's prayer and in his intuitive power that enables him to grasp a significant truth which still remains hidden from adults:[54] 'Thou hid these things from the wise and prudent and hast revealed them unto babes' (Matthew 11.25). In many eucharistic miracle tales, as well as in artistic representations from the High and Late Middle Ages, Christ the child is seen in the Host at the moment of consecration. Sometimes the sacrificed child, who symbolizes both the suffering of the human body and redemption through sacrifice, is revealed to a doubting person who questions the Real Presence in the Host; and sometimes, conversely, the revelation is a special grace bestowed on the pure-hearted believer.[55] In the light of all this, was there a more suitable *persona* than the boy bishop to exhort adults to convert their hearts in the symbolic ritual of Innocents' Day and say: 'Love litill ones, therfor, and

[51] Ibid., pp. 6–7.
[52] Ibid., pp. 8–9, 12, 20.
[53] Dante, *The Divine Comedy*, tr. L. Binyon (New York, 1947), Paradise, Canto 27, p. 511.
[54] A. Vauchez, *La Sainteté en occident aux derniers siècles du moyen âge d'après les procès de canonisation et les documents hagiographiques* (Rome, 1981), pp. 269–70; Shahar, *Childhood*, pp. 17–20.
[55] Shahar, *Childhood*, p. 138 and n. 74; M. Rubin, *Corpus Christi. The Eucharist in Late Medieval Culture* (Cambridge, 1991), pp. 135–9, see also pp. 117, 143, 344.

learn of them how you may have an entre into the kyngdom of heavyn'?[56]

The verse from Psalm 8.2: 'Out of the mouth of babes and sucklings hast thou ordained strength . . .' is not cited in the two sermons, but is implied. The boy bishop who advocated in the sermon the accepted values and norms attested to and reinforced the existing order, including the classification into age categories, each of which had its proper place in society, not only through a temporary reversal, but also explicitly and in an uncoded way. The sermon had the same function as the third and last stage in the carnival according to the anthropological division, the stage that paved the way to the reimposition of order and return to everyday life.[57]

Department of History,
Tel-Aviv University

[56] *Two Sermons*, p. 15, see also pp. 19–20.
[57] E. Le Roy Ladurie, *Carnival in Romans*, pp. 283–4.

CHILDREN, THE LITURGY, AND THE REFORMATION: THE EVIDENCE OF THE LICHFIELD CATHEDRAL CHORISTERS

by T. N. COOPER

THE great interest generated by the theme of this year's conference reflects the central importance of children in the history of the Christian Church, yet at the same time their omission from much of historical writing. For all but the recent past this is largely the result of the difficulties with the source material itself, and this is certainly true for historians of the Church during the medieval and Reformation periods. The main concern of the administrative records of the Catholic Church was with adults and, in particular, ordained men. It is to the schools that we must look for the most useful references to children and, more specifically, to the choir schools for evidence of the role of boys in the liturgy.

Such evidence is, however, sporadic and difficult to interpret. The only extensive surveys of the choristers of individual cathedrals that have been attempted are Robertson's study of Salisbury, which made use of the rare survival there of choristers' accounts, and Orme's invaluable study of the clergy and choir school at Exeter.[1] It was the latter who reminded us that 'The association between the Church and children is as old as Christianity itself.' Indeed, evidence collected from around the country by Edwards for her survey of cathedral administration and, more recently, Lehmberg's study of the effects of the Reformation on the staffing of cathedrals, as well as the work of historians of music, has suggested that increasing use was made of boys in both the spoken and sung liturgy in the later Middle Ages. This development appears to have reached its high point in the later fifteenth and early sixteenth centuries, with an almost universal decline in the number of cathedral choristers in the

[1] Dora H. Robertson, *Sarum Close: a History of the Life and Education of the Cathedral Choristers for Seven Hundred Years* (London, 1938); Nicholas Orme, 'The medieval clergy of Exeter Cathedral, II: the secondaries and choristers', *Transactions of the Devonshire Association for the Advancement of Science, Literature and Art*, 115 (1982), pp. 79–100.

latter half of the sixteenth century.[2] It is the aim of this paper to examine, from the small amount of surviving evidence, the fortunes of the choristers of Lichfield cathedral in the light of the consequences of liturgical development and change for the integration of children into the worship of the Church between the later Middle Ages and the Edwardian Reformation.

The adoption of boys' voices in the liturgy of the great churches in England was initially a consequence of the spread through Europe of Gregorian plainchant. By the mid-eleventh century the popularity of part-singing in a number of monasteries, cathedrals, and collegiate institutions led to the engagement of choristers on a regular basis.[3] Documentary evidence for the presence of choristers at Exeter survives from the 1170s, at which date a master and school were established. An entry in the cathedral's chapter acts for 1236 indicates that there were fourteen boys in the choir, a number which appears to have been set by statute, and which was equalled only at Salisbury. Later medieval chapters were notorious for their rigid adherence to statutes, and some were initially reluctant to increase the size of their choirs in the light of musical developments. A comment made by Bishop Grandisson of Exeter during his visitation of 1337 highlights this, when he demanded to know, 'Are there more than fourteen choristers in the cathedral, and if so, why?'[4]

However, in response to the growing complexity of the musical settings of the liturgy in the later Middle Ages, a number of cathedral chapters were able to amend their statutes in order to accommodate a greater number of choristers. Throughout Europe it was the development of polyphony which was instrumental in promoting greater use of boys' voices in the liturgy.[5] In England the new form was initially used only for the embellishment of the ritual of festivals and was sung by small groups of expert singers.[6] Clear references to the introduction of polyphony appear from the first half of the fifteenth century. An

[2] Kathleen Edwards, *The English Secular Cathedrals in the Middle Ages*, 2nd edn (Manchester, 1967), pp. 307–8, 314; Stanford E. Lehmberg, *The Reformation of Cathedrals: Cathedrals in English Society, 1485–1603* (Princeton, NJ, 1988), p. 198.

[3] Edwards, *English Secular Cathedrals*, p. 308.

[4] Orme, 'The medieval clergy of Exeter Cathedral', p. 86; Edwards, *English Secular Cathedrals*, p. 307; Lehmberg, *The Reformation of Cathedrals*, p. 198.

[5] Edwards, *English Secular Cathedrals*, p. 308.

[6] Frank Ll. Harrison, *Music in Medieval Britain*, 2nd edn (London, 1963), p. 12.

act of the Lincoln chapter of 1434, for example, refers to four of the vicars choral as the 'singers of the daily Mass' and states explicitly that the rendition is to be polyphonic.[7] From about this time, too, appointments of Masters of Choristers become quite common, and by the mid-fifteenth century it was usually specified that they were to teach boys the fundamentals of polyphony.[8]

In the earlier fifteenth century English composers of polyphonic music earned renown throughout Europe for their technical innovations, a position they were, however, to lose later to the master craftsmen employed by the courts of France and Burgundy.[9] Largely in response to the growing adoption within the British Isles of the Sarum Rite, English polyphony developed on a rather different track from its continental counterpart, with composers concentrating on the form and texture of the liturgy.[10] What became a distinctively English style emerged from the increasing trend towards elaboration and decorative adornment of liturgical devotion, which was the express aim of a number of the founders of the great collegiate institutions of the fifteenth century, and which laid the foundations of the developing English choral tradition; a lead which was to be followed by the monasteries and secular cathedrals. Numerous patrons expressed the aim of combating heresy and 'dissonant elements' within the Church through the use of elaborate musical forms which, it was believed, would foster orthodox devotion in the laity. Particular attention was paid to ritual devotion to the Blessed Virgin and to the growing cult of the Name and Passion of Jesus.[11]

The consequence of these developments, then, was the increase in the range of available voice-parts in the choirs of the greater churches, which included a widespread augmentation in the number of choristers. The number at York Minster, for example, was increased from seven to twelve by 1472; at Chichester the earlier provision of ten choristers was increased to

[7] Ibid., p. 177.

[8] *New Oxford History of Music*, III *Ars Nova and the Renaissance 1300–1540*, ed. Dom Anselm Hughes and Gerald Abraham (London, 1960), p. 306.

[9] Denis Stevens, *Tudor Church Music* (London, 1961), p. 11.

[10] Ibid., pp. 12–13.

[11] *New Oxford History of Music*, pp. 303–5; Harrison, *Music in Medieval Britain*, pp. 218–19.

twelve in 1481.[12] The largest complements of cathedral choristers by the end of the fifteenth century were those of Salisbury and Exeter, each with fourteen boys, and all but Hereford could afford to employ more than half a dozen.[13] It was not long before the technical abilities of the English chorister were the envy of the rest of Europe; a Venetian ambassador at the court of Henry VIII in 1515 was moved to describe the singing of the choristers during High Mass as 'more divine than human.'[14]

★ ★ ★

It is from the end of the fifteenth century that the majority of references to the Lichfield choristers occur. Up to this point we know little more than that they appear to have numbered at least eight and had money collected on their behalf from various endowments by the sacrist.[15] Their more frequent appearance in the cathedral records dates from the turn of the sixteenth century, at which time the aged residentiary canon Thomas Milly made a donation of £40 towards the building of a house in the close in which they were to live in common.[16] Houses had been built for the choristers at some of the other secular cathedrals earlier in the period, notably at Exeter in 1276, Lincoln in 1283, and Salisbury and Wells, which date from the early fourteenth century.[17] The comparatively late foundation at Lichfield is evidence of the increased importance of the choristers at this time and of the fact that they had now become well established in the life of the cathedral. From Milly's initial endowment, however, the building of the house proved to be a lengthy affair, occupying much of the following three decades. The major impetus was provided in 1527 when, following its dissolution, the property of the nearby nunnery at Farewell was assigned by the Crown for the use of the choristers.[18] In the same year Bishop Geoffrey Blythe established his obit, part of the endowment of

[12] Harrison, *Music in Medieval Britain*, p. 11.

[13] Lehmberg, *The Reformation of Cathedrals*, p. 198.

[14] Stevens, *Tudor Church Music*, p. 17.

[15] *VCH Stafford*, 3, ed. M. W. Greenslade (London, 1970), p. 156.

[16] Lichfield Joint Record Office [hereafter LJRO], D. 30/3, fol. 37r.

[17] Orme, 'The medieval clergy of Exeter Cathedral', p. 87; Lehmberg, *The Reformation of Cathedrals*, pp. 200–1.

[18] LJRO, D. 30/4, fol. 43r; B/A/1/14 (Register of Bishop Geoffrey Blythe), fol. 97r.

which was to provide for the upkeep of the choristers' house, and Bishop Vesey of Exeter, himself a former canon of Lichfield, made a donation of £20. It is possible that the dean, James Denton, canvassed Vesey's support whilst the two served on the Council of the Marches. Vesey's own cathedral also enjoyed a flourishing boys' choir and song school at this time, and the bishop's interest in the situation at Lichfield provides evidence of an interesting link between the two establishments.[19]

The heyday of the Lichfield choristers was the 1520s. In 1519, presumably at the instigation of the new precentor, Thomas Fitzherbert, a Master of Choristers had been appointed who would have relieved him of direct control of the affairs of the choristers, in particular their training, education, and discipline. Specifically, the Master was employed to instruct the boys in pricksong and descant and teach those interested to play the organ, obligations which were incumbent on the masters of other cathedrals for which documentation survives.[20] The promotion of James Denton to the deanery in 1522, three years after the appointment of Fitzherbert as precentor, provided further stimulus for the integration of the choristers into the life of the cathedral, since he was to become a prominent benefactor of the musical life of Lichfield.[21] Both dignitaries, Denton and Fitzherbert, had attended Eton College and King's Hall, Cambridge, and it is perhaps to these establishments that we should look for the roots of their interest in choral music.[22] Henry VI's foundation of these two institutions, in 1440–1, had included the provision for elaborate sacred music in the emerging florid style through the appointment of ten clerks and no fewer than sixteen choristers, a complement which would have been able to produce part-singing of the highest quality. Both Denton and Fitzherbert were members of the colleges during the period in which choral singing flourished spectacularly. The Eton Choirbook, compiled between about 1490 and 1502, contains the compositions of no fewer than twenty-five musicians, whose work

[19] LJRO, B/A/1/14, fols 46v–47r; A. B. Emden, *A Biographical Register of the University of Cambridge to 1500* (Cambridge, 1963), pp. 182–3, and *A Biographical Register of the University of Oxford*, 3 (Oxford, 1959), pp. 1947–8; Orme, 'The medieval clergy of Exeter Cathedral', pp. 92–6.

[20] LJRO, D. 30/3, fol. 124v; Harrison, *Music in Medieval Britain*, pp. 11–12.

[21] LJRO, D. 30/3, fols 137v, 138v; Emden, *Cambridge*, p. 183.

[22] Emden, *Cambridge*, pp. 182–3, 241.

covered the period from around 1460 to 1523. The collection originally contained sixty-seven votive antiphons for the Virgin; the obligation for the choristers to take part in this daily observance had been enjoined by the college's foundation statutes.[23]

The following ten years, as was the case in a number of other secular cathedrals, saw an increasing involvement of the Lichfield choristers in the liturgy. Evidence of this development was the decision taken by the chapter in 1522 to put the Master of Choristers in charge of the liturgical books and quires of music in the chapter's possession; he was to keep them locked in a chest and was to suffer the full penalties of the statutes should they be removed from the cathedral.[24] The following year it was directed that the choristers should take part in Matins, and groups of four at a time were to take turns after the canons and vicars choral to read the lesson on major feasts, thus giving the boys a formal place in both the sung and spoken liturgy.[25] In a number of secular cathedrals attendance at the daily sung Mass of the Blessed Virgin had been made compulsory for the choristers by the early fourteenth century, but this was not added to the Lichfield statutes until 1524.[26] In the same year they were further required to be present at the obits established by former bishops of Lichfield 'to the greater honour of the church and of God and as required by the vicars choral'.[27] Final confirmation of these new arrangements was made in 1531, when 'to the honour of God and the increase of divine service' the choristers were required to take part in the services in the middle of the night, echoing the late thirteenth-century injunction of Bishop Branscombe of Exeter that the choristers there should 'serve the church by day and night'.[28]

By the 1520s, then, the Lichfield choristers had become fully integrated into the round of worship offered up by the community of the cathedral. By this time, too, their competence was such that they were not restricted to liturgical duties alone. In 1522 the chapter had felt it necessary to make formal arrange-

23 *New Oxford History of Music*, pp. 306–8.
24 LJRO, D. 30/3, fol. 138v.
25 LJRO, D. 30/4, fol. 9r.
26 Edwards, *English Secular Cathedrals*, p. 35; LJRO, D. 30/4, fol. 9v.
27 LJRO, D. 30/4, fol. 12v.
28 LJRO, D. 30/4, fol. 75r; Orme, 'The medieval clergy of Exeter Cathedral', p. 88.

ments for the disbursement of donations made to the choristers by visitors to the cathedral, many of whom would probably have been pilgrims to the shrine of St Chad's head, who were entertained by the boys' performances of vernacular songs.[29] It is from this time, too, that we have evidence to confirm that a boy bishop was being appointed at Lichfield. The ceremony was an integral part of the celebration of Holy Innocents' Day, or Childermas, held on 28 December. This feast has traditionally been viewed as having mainly secular and entertainment purposes, but it has been argued more recently that it was fundamentally a religious ceremony designed to promote the image of innocent childhood as a moral lesson to the adult Christian world.[30] The ceremony was fully incorporated in the Salisbury Use and the coincidence of the possible first appearance of the boy bishop at Lichfield with Bishop Blythe's insistence that henceforth Sarum rather than the traditional Lichfield Use should be adopted in the cathedral is perhaps further evidence of the primarily religious nature of the festival, and would suggest that, as in Salisbury and many other cathedrals and churches throughout the country, the part of the bishop and his entourage was to be played by the choristers as part of a poignant moral and spiritual lesson.[31] It was in the early sixteenth century, when boys were playing an increasing part in cathedral liturgy, that the festival of the boy bishop was at its most popular in this country, though it had become well established at some cathedrals, notably Exeter, earlier in the period.[32] At Exeter, in addition to the part played by the choristers at Childermas, the boys were assigned important roles on All Saints' Day and Christmas Day itself. At the former, the boys were required to represent innocent virgins, a particularly interesting assignation in the absence of a liturgical role for girls and women. The close connection between the duties of choristers and the liturgy of the Blessed Virgin is further attested to by the appearance of one of the boys from behind the high altar at Exeter on Christmas Day to sing in

[29] LJRO, D. 30/3, fol. 137v.

[30] R. L. de Molen, '*Pueri Christi imitatio*: the festival of the boy bishop in Tudor England', *Moreana*, 12 (1975), pp. 17–29; see also now Shulamith Shahar, 'The Boy Bishop's Feast: a case-study in Church attitudes towards children in the High and Late Middle Ages', pp. 243–60 above.

[31] De Molen, 'The festival of the boy bishop', p. 19; *VCH Stafford*, 3, p. 161.

[32] Orme, 'The medieval clergy of Exeter Cathedral', p. 89; de Molen, 'The festival of the boy bishop', p. 21.

her honour.[33] Liturgically, it is clear that a specific use was being made of the poignant symbolism of the boy as innocent and pure, which became increasingly important as the Virgin became the prime focus, apart from the setting of the Mass itself, for the attentions of composers of sacred music in the late fifteenth and early sixteenth centuries.[34]

It is unfortunate that the survival of the sermons preached by boy bishops is so rare; that which was delivered at Gloucester on Childermas Day in 1558 provides a glimpse, albeit in a deliberately moralistic tone, written by adult clergy, of the behaviour of the mid-sixteenth-century choirboy. Here the boy bishop tells his audience

> I kan not let this passe ontouched how boyyshly thei behave themselves in the church, how rashley thei cum into the quere without any reverence; never knele nor cowntenaunce to say any prayer or Pater Noster, but rudeley squat down on ther tayles and justle with ther felows for a place; a non thei startes me owt of the quere agayne, and in agayne and out agayne . . . but only to gad and gas abrode, and so cum in agayne and crosse the quere fro one side to another and never rest.[35]

If there is any accuracy in this vignette of behaviour in the choir it can be said, from the evidence of allegations against the Lichfield vicars choral and those elsewhere, that they were certainly no more badly behaved than their adult colleagues.[36]

In fact, we have very little evidence of the lives of the choristers outside the choir for any part of the medieval and Reformation periods. Only a few names were ever recorded. A charter of endowment by a local gentleman in favour of the choristers in 1530 mentions two, Henry Bylshawe and Richard Shawe, by name.[37] A dispute between the subchanter and the chapter in 1538 over the former's claims to the right of admitting new choristers reveals that one John Audley had been found to be

[33] Orme, 'The medieval clergy of Exeter Cathedral', p. 89.

[34] *New Oxford History of Music*, pp. 306–7.

[35] *Sermon of the Child Bishop, Pronownsyd by John Stubs, Querester, on Childermas Day, at Glocester, 1558*, ed. John Gough Nichols = Camden Society, ns 14, 7 (1875), pp. 24–5.

[36] See, for example, T. N. Cooper, 'Oligarchy and conflict: Lichfield Cathedral clergy in the early sixteenth century', *Midland History*, 19 (1994), forthcoming.

[37] LJRO, Miscellaneous Muniments of the Lichfield Dean & Chapter, L.3.

worthy of admission, whilst a Richard Marshall had not, as well as providing incidental evidence that the roles of the precentor, subchanter, and Master of Choristers were still not clearly defined.[38] It was certainly the case that in some cathedrals a small number of choristers went on to be admitted as vicars choral, but this cannot be proved in any instance at Lichfield. The four boys who were named in the records cannot be positively identified in any later career, and perhaps the most suggestive evidence in this regard comes from the disciplinary action taken by the chapter against one of the vicars choral, Robert Bendbow, in 1523, for gambling with cards and dice. It was recorded that he had been admitted to his stall two years previously as a minor, and it was decided that the sacrist should be appointed as his tutor and guardian to keep him from further trouble.[39] Whilst this does not prove that Bendbow had risen from the ranks of the choristers, it does seem quite likely. The only other reference to education outside the song school during the period comes from injunctions of 1547 and 1559, which enacted that each chorister should be provided with an annual pension of £3 6*s*. 8*d*. for a period of five years after his voice had broken, to enable him to attend the local grammar school.[40] Exactly the same arrangements were made at Durham, Lincoln, Winchester, and Canterbury, whilst at Peterborough and Exeter a provision was added that they should have served the cathedral for at least five years.

* * *

The fifteenth and early sixteenth centuries have been described as witnessing 'a remarkable growth and flowering of musical culture in all parts of the British Isles'.[41] The liturgical stability of the period allowed English composers to establish a strong tradition in form and texture, concentrating on ever greater elaboration of the musical liturgy, a development which culminated in the celebrated work of John Taverner (*c*. 1490–1545).[42] In terms of the musical provision in the major churches of the country, a

38 LJRO, D. 30/4, fol. 118v.
39 LJRO, D. 30/3, fol. 139v.
40 *VCH Stafford*, 3, p. 168.
41 Harrison, *Music in Medieval Britain*, p. 218.
42 Stevens, *Tudor Church Music*, p. 14; *New Oxford History of Music*, p. 339.

direct consequence of these developments had been the augmentation of choirs and, largely due to the increasing devotion to the Blessed Virgin, a particular increase in the number of choristers.

The assumption by Henry VIII of the Supreme Headship of the English Church in 1535 was to provide the first threat to this long period of liturgical stability and, ultimately, the future direction of choral music. From this time composers began to experiment with settings of Marshall's English version of the Sarum liturgy, and by 1540 there had been a number of attempts at producing an acceptable English primer. The upheaval caused by the Dissolution of the Monasteries and its consequent dispersal of the country's leading composers, combined with confusion over the direction that the musical liturgy was going to take, served to stem the flow of sacred compositions. It was not so much doctrinal uncertainty that initially caused problems for composers in these early stages of the Reformation, but musical difficulties. Thomas Cranmer, in particular, appears to have misunderstood the important distinctions between the application of homophonic and polyphonic settings, and attempted to set the simple, rhythmical style of processional music to the liturgy, to which it was technically unsuited. The effect was to force composers into a general simplification of part-writing, albeit with understandable reluctance.[43]

Elaborate church music, of course, had always had its critics. One of the most influential during the early Reformation period was Erasmus, who passed judgement in his commentary on the New Testament that

> Modern church music is so constructed that the congregation cannot hear one distinct word. The choristers themselves do not understand what they are singing, yet according to the priests and monks it constitutes the whole of religion. Why will they not listen to St. Paul? In college or monastery it is still the same: music, nothing but music . . .[44]

Such comments were to gain a sympathetic ear following the accession of Edward VI in 1547. By the time of the Act for the

[43] Stevens, *Tudor Church Music*, pp. 16, 18.

[44] Quoted in Peter le Huray, *Music and the Reformation in England 1549–1660* (Oxford, 1967), p. 11.

Suppression of Chantries in 1547, several of the more important choirs had already been disbanded, and the process continued swiftly thereafter. Most notable among the early casualties were the choirs of the Hospital of St Leonard, York, and the collegiate churches of Newark, Higham Ferrers, St Mary's, Warwick, and Ottery St Mary, in Devon. The second wave of suppression included even more famous institutions, such as the collegiate churches of Beverley and Ripon, the Royal Free Chapels at Fortheringhay and St Stephen's, Westminster, and, perhaps the most significant pointer to things to come, the college choir at Tattershall, in Lincolnshire, where Taverner had been Master of Choristers and had developed his craft.[45]

In 1548 royal commissioners were despatched to enquire into the state of worship at the cathedrals, and it is apparent from their injunctions that a simpler, more 'comprehensible' liturgical style was being envisaged. At Canterbury, for instance, they prohibited the singing of Mass outside the choir and ordered the replacement of sung Lady Mass on feast days, with a sermon or a reading from the homilies. At York they required that the singing of more than one Mass each day be discontinued, along with the lesser hours, dirges, and 'commendations'. The choir was no longer to be allowed to sing responds, and all Latin antiphons were to be replaced by English substitutes. It was demanded of the choir at Lincoln that 'They shall from henceforth sing or say no anthem of Our Lady or other saints, but only of Our Lord, and them not in Latin.' Injunction 28 at Lincoln went into further detail:

> . . . the service of this church called the Lady Matins and Evensong may be used henceforth according to the King's Majesty's proceedings, and to the abolishing of superstition in that behalf, there shall be no more Matins called the Lady Matins, Hours, nor Evensong, nor ferial dirges said in the choir among or after Divine Service, but every man to use the same privately at their convenient leisure, according as it is purported and set forth in the King's Primer.

The consequences of such royal injunctions for the future employment of boy choristers is made explicit by the demands

[45] Ibid., pp. 12–13.

issued to the dean and chapter of St George's Chapel, Windsor, in 1550:

> . . . because the great number of ceremonies in the church are now put away by the King's Majesty's authority and Act of Parliament, so that fewer choristers be requisite, and the College is now otherwise more charged than it hath been; we enjoin from henceforth that there shall be found in this College only ten choristers . . .[46]

★ ★ ★

The decline in importance of the choristers at Lichfield appears to have coincided with the death in 1533 of their patron, Dean Denton. In 1530 he had augmented the endowment of their house through a bequest of land to provide payment for a cook, which would serve to make them independent as a body from the direct hospitality of the canons.[47] Denton's commitment to the boys' part in the cathedral services was expressed in most concrete terms by his testamentary provision for an extra four choristers to bring the total to twelve; only Salisbury and Exeter ever maintained a larger complement.[48]

The decline in the position of the Lichfield choristers was as swift as their initial rise to prominence. The *Valor Ecclesiasticus* of 1535 evaluated the choristers' income as £25 net, which was noted to be insufficient to clothe and feed twelve boys, and they were reliant on additional *ad hoc* payments from the chapter of about £20 per annum to make up the shortfall.[49] By some time in the mid-century their number had been reduced to the eight which had been designated by earlier statutes, and by the 1580s the previous ideal of communal living had been abandoned; the house was leased to local laity, and those boys who remained were lodged in various houses around the city. The tenant was enjoined to return some parts of the house to the boys' use, 'if it fortune the Dean and Chapter to take order that the choristers shall keep commons together in such manner as heretofore they

[46] Ibid., pp. 8–9, 24; Stevens, *Tudor Church Music*, p. 19.

[47] LJRO, Miscellaneous Muniments of the Lichfield Dean and Chapter, L.2.

[48] Emden, *Cambridge*, p. 183; Lehmberg, *The Reformation of Cathedrals*, p. 198.

[49] *Valor Ecclesiasticus Temp. Henry VIII Auctoritate Regia Institutus*, ed. J. Caley and J. Hunter (London, 1810–14), 3, p. 135.

were accustomed.'[50] As a viable institution, the choristers' house had remained in existence for only sixty years, and despite the hopes of the chapter, they were unable ever to restore it to its intended use. There is evidence that by the end of the sixteenth century the chapter was no longer even in a position to pay retiring choristers the pensions that had been stipulated by injunctions drawn up by the Edwardian visitors.[51] This was a far cry from the 1520s, when the cathedral coffers had rung to the sound of rewards earned by the choristers from visitors and pilgrims.

But the decline in the size of the boys' choir and its part in the liturgy from about 1530 was not a phenomenon peculiar to Lichfield. At Salisbury, the cathedral traditionally most dedicated to the use of boys' voices, the number of choristers had fallen from fourteen to eight by 1550. At Lincoln more drastic cuts were made in 1549, with a reduction from twelve choristers to four, although the attachment of some of them to a former chantry foundation went some way to limit the impact of this change.[52] Further evidence of decline from around the country is provided by remarks made during visitation concerning boys' education and training. One of the vicars choral at Hereford, for instance, reported in 1558 that 'He did not know how [the choristers] were trained up in grammar, but in singing, nothing at all to any purpose.' In 1602 the Dean and Chapter of the once-famous Salisbury complained that their choristers 'are not at this present able to sing surely and perfectly but do often miss and fail and are out in their singing to the great shame of the teacher and disgrace of so eminent a church.' In his defence the Master of Choristers replied that it was not his duty to *teach* the children, but only to clothe and feed them. All over the country the training of choristers appears to have gone into decline by the mid-sixteenth century. In 1541 the Winchester chapter paid to bring in a boy from Guildford as a response to the want of trained boys in its vicinity, and in the 1550s both Bristol and Canterbury were paying considerable sums for servants to travel in search of boys with sufficient aptitude to make up the deficiencies in their choirs.[53]

50 *VCH Stafford*, 3, pp. 172–3.
51 Ibid.
52 Lehmberg, *The Reformation of Cathedrals*, p. 198.
53 Ibid., pp. 202–3.

* * *

The growing elaboration of sacred polyphony in England during the fifteenth and early sixteenth centuries led to the development of a choral tradition in this country which was, in fact, to survive the doctrinal upheavals of the Reformation largely intact. The general picture which emerges from this study of the choristers at Lichfield Cathedral and elsewhere, however, suggests that the integration of boys into the liturgy reached its greatest extent on the eve of the Edwardian Reformation, and it is perhaps ironic that the principal agent of change was only a boy himself. From this time onwards, the general trend, apart from a brief respite during the reign of Mary Tudor, was towards a simplification of the choral liturgy and the complete extinction of the Litany of the Virgin and other saints, including the elaborate processional rituals which formed such a prominent feature of the worship of the Catholic Church in the later Middle Ages. It was these features, in particular, which served to promote the integration of the boy chorister into the liturgy, and with the increasingly important position held by choristers in the life of cathedrals, festivals such as Holy Innocents' Day allowed even greater participation on the part of children. They were perhaps never to enjoy such a full part in the Christian liturgy again.

University of Sheffield

COUNTER-REFORMATORY THEORIES OF UPBRINGING IN ITALY

by OLIVER LOGAN

ITALIAN churchmen from the mid-sixteenth to the early eighteenth centuries saw parents as playing a crucial role in forming new generations in the Catholic faith and thus as an indispensable support to the clergy.[1] They stressed the importance of conditioning from the earliest years. They therefore emphasized parental, and more particularly paternal, authority. On the other hand, another major preoccupation was to prevent violation of the wills of young people with regard to religious vocations and marriage. A balance therefore had to be struck between paternal authority and the legitimate desires of young people who had attained the age of discretion. The matter of the all-importance of conditioning raises the question of our writers' views of infant human nature. They emphasized to varying degrees the tractability of unformed infant nature and the need to curb unruly instincts, but by and large the emphasis was on nurture rather than on vitiated human nature, on formation rather than on repression.[2]

Between the fifteenth and the seventeenth centuries, treatises on the family and treatises on pedagogy were overlapping genres. Treatises by churchmen on the Christian upbringing of children are commonly related to these genres and have many points in common with treatises of a more secular character, notably Alberti's *Della famiglia* and Erasmus' *De pueris statim ac liberaliter instituendis*. Discussion of upbringing, however, tended to be closely bound up with that of Christian marriage, particularly evident affinities here being with the Tridentine Catechism and certain model discourses embodied in synodal legislation of the

[1] Silvio Antoniano, *Dell' educazione cristiana dei figliuoli libri tre scritti da M. Silvio Antoniano ad istanza di Monsig. Illustr. Cardinale di San Prassede Arcviescovo* (Verona, B. delle Donne, 1584 and subsequent eds with addition 'e politica'), Lib. 1, pp. viii, ix, asserted that the spread of heresy and sedition in his own age was in large measure due to bad upbringing. Delle Donne was the episcopal printer. For editions see Luigi Volpicelli, *Il pensiero pedagogico della controriforma* (Florence, 1960) [hereafter Volpicelli]. Extracts in ibid. (cf. index at p. 608).

[2] A valuable collection of extracts is Volpicelli.

period.[3] Here it is primarily treatises that will be examined, material in sermons having been discussed by Dr Novi Chavarria in a study of the treatment of the family by Italian preachers between the sixteenth and eighteenth centuries; in point of fact, her earliest examples of discussion of Christian upbringing (as distinct from Christian marriage) come from the early seventeenth century, while, as we shall see, the tradition of treatises on the theme was already well established and the sermon tradition on the theme does seem to be rather impoverished in its thematic.[4]

The major Counter-Reformation treatise on Christian upbringing is Silvio Antoniano's treatise *On the Christian Upbringing of Children* (1584).[5] Antoniano (1540–1603) had risen from being Latin secretary to Pius IV to high curial rank and to the cardinalate. He composed his treatise at the request of Carlo Borromeo, Archbishop of Milan, to whose cultural circle he had belonged in Rome in the 1560s, but it was first published in Verona,[6] evidently under the aegis of another member of that circle, the city's Bishop, Cardinal Agostino Valier, a major lettered pastoral figure. The treatise thus emerged from the milieu of the pastorally conscious prelatical intelligentsia of the immediate post-Tridentine era. It is a vernacular work, written by a major Latinist, cultivated but approachable. It covers family life, upbringing from the earliest years, and Humanist curriculum. Broadly similar in their treatment of family life and upbringing were the Augustinian Andrea Ghetti's *Responsibilities of Fathers and Mothers towards Children* (1572)[7] and Giovanni Leonardi's *Institution of a Christian Family* (1591). (Leonardi (1541–1609) was the founder of a minor congregation of Clerks Regular, that of

[3] *Catechismus ex Decreto Concilii Tridentini ad parochos* (Rome, 1566), pp. 208–19; 'Rubricae seu instructiones de matrimonio' in *Acta Ecclesiae Mediolanensis* (Milan, 1582 and subsequent edns); G. Paleotti, *Archiepiscopale Bononiense* etc. (Rome, 1594), pp. 162–71. Comparable discourses are not uncommon in the *acta* of post-Tridentine provincial synods. This genre appears a more obvious model for our treatises than St Augustine, *De bono conjugali*.

[4] Elisa Novi Chavarria, 'Ideologia e comportamenti familiari nei predicatori italiani tra Cinque e Settecento. Tematiche e modelli', *Rivista Storica Italiana*, 100 (1988), pp. 697–723.

[5] Silvio Antoniano, *Dell' educazione cristiana*; see n. 1 above.

[6] P. Prodi, 'Antoniano Silvio' in *Dizionario biografico degli Italiani* [hereafter *DBI*].

[7] Andrea Ghetti, *Discorso sopra la cura e diligenza che debbono avere i padri e le madri verso i loro figliuoli, sí nella civiltà come nella pietà cristiana* (Bologna, 1572). I have not located a copy; extracts in Volpicelli (cf. index p. 108). On Ghetti, cf. ibid., pp. 594–5.

the Mother of God.)[8] A treatise for pastoral use is Giovanni Pietro Giussano's *Instructions to Fathers on the Ordering of their Households*, another work composed at the behest of Carlo Borromeo, but evidently first published with the pastoral letters of Gregorio Barbarigo, the great Bishop of Padua, in 1690. This was written for the benefit of parish priests convoking assemblies of *padri di famiglia*.[9] An example of an episcopal allocution on the theme is the *Cura famigliare* of Cardinal Federico Borromeo, Archbishop of Milan 1595–1631.[10] A minor work by a senior diocesan administrator is the *Apology for the Catechism* (1607) by Giorgio Polacco, Archdeacon of Venice, quite an authoritative writer of theological compilations, and one of the few members of the shadowy layer of bishops' aides to emerge as a figure with some identity. Polacco composed the treatise as diocesan organizer of the Venetian Oratorio della Dottrina Cristiana, that is, confraternity of lay catechists, for the benefit of its members.[11] Treatises significant for their concept of the parental role in ecclesiological terms are certain *Moral Discourses* of Paolo Segneri, the most renowned Jesuit preacher of the late seventeenth century.[12]

The key Antique model was the *Peri paidon agoges* (*On the Education of Boys*) attributed to Plutarch. Its dominant themes are environment and training. The triad *physis-logos-ethos*, that is, nature, instruction, and habituation (compared to soil, seed, and husbandman), is a central motif of Renaissance and Counter-

[8] Giovanni Leonardi, *Institutione di una famiglia cristiana* (Rome, 1591 and 1673). I have not located a copy; extracts in Volpicelli (cf. index at pp. 609–10). On Leonardi and his work, cf. ibid., pp. 597–8.

[9] Giovanni Pietro Giussano, *Istruttioni e documenti a padri per saper governare la loro famiglia scritti di ordine di San Carlo Borromeo*, in Gregorio Barbarigo, *Lettere pastorali, editti e decreti di G.B. Vescovo di Padova* (Padua, 1690), pp. 214–318. Extracts in Volpicelli (cf. index at p. 609). On Giussano, cf. ibid., pp. 596–7.

[10] Federico Borromeo, *I sacri ragionamenti di F.B. Cardinale e Arcivescovo di Milano fatti in vari luoghi, a diversi stati di persone ed in diverse occasioni*, III *Della cura famigliare* (Milan, 1640). On Borromeo, cf. P. Prodi in *DBI*.

[11] Giorgio Polacco, *Discorso apologetico della dottrina cristiana* (Venice, 1607).

[12] Paolo Segneri, S.J., *Il cristiano istruito nella sua legge. Ragionamenti morali* (Florence, 1686 and subsequent eds), Rag. XIII 'Sopra la debita educazione de' figliuoli'; Rag. XIV 'Sopra due falli grandi che si commettono nella predetta educazione de' figliuoli'; Rag. XV 'Sopra due altri mancamenti, che avvengono nella medesima educazione'; Rag. XVI 'Sopra l'obbligazione c'hanno i figliuoli d'onorare i lor padri'; Rag. XXV 'Sopra il sagramento del matrimonio'. Note also *Quaresimale* (Florence, 1679 and subsequent eds), Serm. XXV. On Segneri, see Celestino Testore in *Enciclopaedia cattolica*, 11, cols 239–41. Reference here will also be made to Fulvio Fontana, S.J., *Istruzioni per vivere cristianamente. Dirette a tutte quelle persone che compongono una famiglia* etc. (Florence, 1714). On Fontana (1648–1723), cf. Emilio Santini in *Enciclopaedia cattolica*, 5, col. 1495.

Reformatory theories of upbringing and education. Training is yet more powerful than nature, as evidenced by the story of Lycurgus, who conducted a controlled experiment with two hounds. Youth, it is emphasized, is impressionable and plastic; just as seals leave their impression on soft wax, so are lessons impressed on the minds of children while they are still young. The responsibility of parents is stressed: the mother must breast-feed herself; later, the father must exercise the greatest care in the choice of teacher. Also significant sources were Plutarch's *Lives*, which often remarked upon the effects of upbringing, lauding the example of Cato, who took personal responsibility for his children's education. Leonardi exploited Xenophon's *Education of Cyrus*, with its ideal of an education in justice and temperance. Our Counter-Reformatory writers were liable to develop the Plutarchan themes with a positively oppressive stress on moulding and conditioning, something not seen for example with Alberti's treatise on the family or Erasmus' on the education of boys, which had made use of Plutarch in their arguments for what could be achieved by good upbringing. These two writers had a concept of an innate human dynamism which is absent from our Counter-Reformatory writers. Overtly Plutarchan are the treatises by Ghetti and Leonardi and, remarkably, the two specifically pastoral ones by Giussano and Polacco; Antoniano is seldom overtly Plutarchan, but is broadly Plutarchan in the thrust of his treatise. Among Christian writers references was often made to Saints John Chrysostom, Basil, and Gregory Nazianzenus, the most important source probably being Chrysostom's *On Vainglory and the Education of Children*. This is in line with the *Peri paidon agoges* in its stress on parental responsibility and on training from the earliest years, while employing a different repertoire of analogies. A significant feature of the treatise is the discussion of parental instruction in the principles of religion and morality adapted to the growing child's understanding. Among our writers, this precedent was most notably followed by Silvio Antoniano, although where Chrysostom would have the developing infant intelligence opened up to the divine by biblical stories, Antoniano suggests examples from the natural world.[13]

[13] Antoniano, *Dell' educazione*, Lib. 2, p. vi.

In our Counter-Reformatory treatises the all-embracing theme is parental responsibility, above all for training in morals and piety, consideration for which must not take second place to that for family status and dynastic advantage. The reiterated and sometimes luxuriantly developed commonplace of a mother's duty to suckle her own children sets the tone.[14] While in part related to an assumption of a close connection between physical factors and character (it was feared that the child might imbibe the evil qualities of a base wet-nurse), this leitmotif may be taken as symbolic of nurture; the theme of the mother's initial duty is echoed in that of constant paternal care for a son's development. The nuclear family is the assumed reality. The key figure, as in Italian treatises on the family generally, is the *padre di famiglia*, to whom is accorded responsibility for a child's upbringing after the age of seven. However, there is some variation among writers as to the emphasis given to the maternal role in the family and in a son's upbringing, Silvio Antoniano's evaluation of it being particularly positive: he saw women as 'the devout sex' and clearly felt that their role in Christian upbringing was crucial, as well as valuing their greater gentleness and patience.[15] In general, our writers' almost obsessive espousal of patriarchy as the foundation of discipline and order and a conviction of female propensity for indulgence is balanced by a concern for respect for wives and some consciousness of the value of maternal influence. Our writers generally deal at length with the father's duty to see to his son's religious and moral instruction, which is not necessarily just a matter of sending him to catechism; Silvio Antoniano expands upon a father's very specific and really irreplaceable contribution in this area.[16] Here it should be remembered that catechization in Italian cities in this period was mainly conducted by lay people.

Our writers, while generally fearful of the ill effects of any relaxation of discipline and parental vigilance, were generally optimistic about what careful upbringing could achieve. The strongest fears seem to have been less about the child's evil

[14] Ghetti, *Discorso*, in Volpicelli at p. 109; Antoniano, *Dell' educazione*, Lib. 2, xxxvi; Leonardi, *Institutione*, in Volpicelli at pp. 120–1; Giussano, *Istruttioni*, cap. xix; Polacco, *Discorso*, p.3; Fontana, *Istruzioni*, pp. 65–9.

[15] Antoniano, *Dell' educazione*, Lib. 1, pp. xlv–xlvii; Giussano, *Istruttione*, cap. xix; Leonardi, *Institutione* in Volpicelli at p. 149; F. Borromeo, *Della cura famigliare*, Ragg. III, VII.

[16] Antoniano, *Dell' educazione*, Lib. 1, p. i, Lib. 2, p. vi; cf. Leonardi, *Institutione*, in Volpicelli at p. 150; Segneri, *Il cristiano istruito*, Rag. XIII.

propensities than about the corrupting influence of servants and ill-selected teachers and threats from the outside world, notably bad companions and Lotharios. Here we are inclined to dissent from Dr Novi Chavarria's statement based on sermon literature that 'The constant recommendations from the pulpit to exercise vigilance over and punish children had their origin in the deeply rooted conviction that the child was by nature evil and corrupt and needed to be trained and tamed like a young animal.'[17] Certainly there were constant assertions of the belief that to spare the rod was to spoil the child and even that the young child should be taught to accept the thwarting of his will; certainly again it was believed that parents should distance themselves from their children; however, the general concern was to strike a balance between excessive indulgence and excessive severity. In point of fact, the Plutarchan motif of the training and taming of animals was not really used as a simple analogy in treatises; a key point was in fact that more could be achieved with young human beings than with animals. There is little evidence in treatises of the theological anthropology that Dr Novi Chavarria assumes. For sure, the insistence on the need for constant vigilance over children and young people is positively paranoid, but the overall impression is of the family under threat from contamination, rather than undermined from the inside by unruly human nature itself, and ultimately there seems to be deep faith in Christian matrimony itself as a moral force. Our writers seem to have regarded authority as a good *per se*, capable of engendering right attitudes, rather than as a means to curb human wickedness.

The Jesuit Segneri, more than any other of our writers, has a theology of the parental role. He sees parents as instruments of and co-operators with divine grace. 'You must, by your diligence', he writes, 'make a way for the Grace of God, directing into the hearts of your children in abundance by your application.' Parents can indeed bring up holy offspring, 'God supporting their intentions and endeavours with efficacious aid, giving water from on high proportionate to the furrow that they have dug.' Segneri adds: 'It was the great good of fathers to have been chosen by divine providence as instruments to help others, both

[17] Novi Chavarria, 'Ideologia', p. 709; cf. also pp. 710–12.

in the order of nature and in the order of Grace, cooperating towards their eternal salvation through their upbringing.'[18] Speaking of the sacrament of matrimony, he writes: 'When he has united husband and wife by so noble a sacrament, one can clearly see that He makes use of both in order to communicate to the creatures born of them the gift of both Grace and glory.'[19] Instruction of children in 'what they have to know as Christians and what they have to do as Christians' is the primary responsibility of parents. When the Church originally permitted the practice of infant baptism it was in view of 'the expectation given by father and mother of not failing to give the necessary instruction, insofar as they were capable', godparents being guarantors of their intentions. Catechization is necessary because parents and godparents have failed in their duty. However, the teaching of morals should not be left to the clergy: they can never do as much good as fathers. Mothers, if they cannot cannot suckle their children, put them out to wet-nurse; priests here are simply in the position of wet-nurses.[20]

Our writers were concerned not only to support parental authority, but also to curb its abuses in the cases of young people on the threshold of adulthood where religious profession or the sacrament of matrimony were involved. The objective was to prevent invalid or disastrous marriages, forced religious professions, or thwarted religious vocations. Parents had no right to decide that a daughter would become a nun; they must not use the male religious orders as outlets for sons with physical disabilities; young persons must not be forced into odious marriages. Again, religious vocations must not be sacrificed to dynastic strategies.[21] It was assumed that fathers would arrange the marriages of offspring—indeed, since fathers were urged to keep daughters in seclusion, there was no other practicable alternative in their case. The emphasis was on the father's duty to find a good future spouse, not allowing considerations of moral qualities to take second place to ones of dynastic advantage. The concern of our writers was that a match should be acceptable

[18] Segneri, *Il cristiano istruito*, Ragg. XIII, v, XIV, ii; cf. also Rag. XXV, i.

[19] Ibid., Rag. XIV, ii; cf. Rag. XXV, i.

[20] Ibid., Rag. XIV, iv, vi.

[21] Ghetti, *Discorso*, in Volpicelli at p. 121; Antoniano, *Dell' educazione*, Lib. 3, pp. lxxxi–lxxxii; Giussano, *Istruttioni*, cap. xxvi; Segneri, *Il cristiano istruito*, Rag. XV; Fontana, *Istruzioni*, pp. 110–20.

both to the young people involved and to their parents. Considerations of the canonical requirement of free consent, emphasized by the Council of Trent, made churchmen the champions of young peoples' rights in the Counter-Reformation era; here, in fact, Church policy was in some conflict with the ethos of lay elites. However, within our sample of texts, the strongest assertions of young people's rights to freedom of choice regarding marriage and religious profession, particularly emphasizing freedom of will, come from two Jesuits, Segneri and his close colleague Fulvio Fontana, writing at the end of our period. Segneri asserts that ultimately a young person's choice of marriage partner must be respected, under pain of grave sin, although children should indeed consult parents, and those who follow their own caprice will surely have cause to regret it.[22] Fontana delivers an exceptionally impassioned diatribe against fathers who force or pychologically manipulate daughters into religious professions or undesired marriages, his definition of violation of the will being broad. His emphasis on freedom of the will *per se* is curiously illustrated by his condemnation of fathers who try to steer sons off marriages of which they disapprove by threats or coldness; the proper way to prevent loss of family reputation through unsuitable marriages is to cut off communication between the son and an undesirable prospective daughter-in-law at an early stage. At the same time he insists that while a young man is free to choose his state in life, he should consult his parents, each meeting the other half-way, the son respecting the parents' wishes in so far, and only in so far, as they are prudent.[23]

In directing a son towards a career, some writers specify, a father should pay regard to inclination and aptitude.[24] The concept of aptitude (*genio, ingegno*) was an important topic in Renaissance pedagogic thought, 'spotting the child's bent' being a common theme.[25] While our churchmen are largely untouched

[22] Segneri, *Il cristiano istruito*, Ragg. XV, v, XXV, xiii.

[23] Fontana, *Istruzioni*, pp. 110–20, 160–1.

[24] Ghetti, *Discorso*, in Volpicelli at p. 192; Antoniano, *Dell' educazione*, Lib. 3, pp. i, lxxxi; Leonardi, *Instituzione*, in Volpicelli at pp. 165–6.

[25] François de Dainville, *La Naissance de l'éducation moderne* (Paris, 1940 and Geneva, 1969), pp. 177–9; Richard M. Douglas, 'Talent and Vocation in Humanist and Protestant Thought', in Theodore K. Rabb and Jerrold E. Seigel, eds, *Action and Conviction in Early Modern Europe* (Princeton, 1967), pp. 261–98.

by Galenic theory of humours and complexions, which often reinforced the concept of *ingegno* in the late sixteenth cenury, the influence of the concept of special aptitude can indeed be found in their work.

At issue in all this are concepts of original sin (or rather its residues), free will, and individuality. In particular, the ideas of our Jesuits can be seen in the context of theological conceptions of free will as a reality and as a value current in their order. Notions of infant psychology are limited. Here there are two main categories of trope. One is a group of commonplaces emphasizing infant malleability: the Aristotelian *tabula rasa*, the Plutarchan wax motif (also employed by St Basil) or that of moist clay.[26] The other is the trope of the field or garden containing useful plants and weeds in first shoot which must be either nurtured or uprooted.[27] Adolescence is seen as a perilous age and in order for him to survive it morally, the small defects in the young child which may later develop into major sins must be eliminated at an early stage, a view expressed in the Tridentine decree on seminary education.[28] Silvio Antoniano, who elaborates the garden trope, does have a relatively developed theory of infant psychology. It should be noted that he treats post-baptismal concupiscence (that is, the proneness to sin which is a residue of cancelled original sin) more as a collective than as an individual problem. Concupiscence in itself offers the individual a challenge through which he can attain merit. However, because men have not curbed their concupiscence, good upbringing has been neglected and hence, in turn, an abundance of iniquity. Human society is corrupt. None the less, in the individual the ill effects of concupiscence can be overcome by discipline from the earliest years. In Antoniano's thought the doctrine of post-baptismal concupiscence is balanced by the assertion that there are in the infant many germs of an inclination to the good; these must be nurtured and cultivated. Antoniano follows St Augustine in seeing in the child the roots of a sinfulness that will in due course become a thing of gravity in the growing person, and he does not, in fact, fall into the trap of a

[26] Ghetti, *Discorso*, in Volpicelli at p. 116 (citing St Basil, *Ecclesiastica hierarchia*, III, ii); Polacco, *Discorso*, p. 9.

[27] Antoniano, *Dell' educazione*, Lib. 1, p. xl; Segneri, *Il cristiano istruito*, Rag. XIII, iv.

[28] Trent, Sess. XXIII, *De Reformatione*, canon xviii, cited in Antoniano, *Dell' educazione*, Lib. 1, p. xlii.

crudely misanthropic reading of St Augustine's vision of childhood; he has grasped the concept of development in Augustine.[29] Both Antoniano and Segneri insist to an extraordinary degree on the capacity of parents to determine whether a child turns out good or ill, the latter, as we have seen, asserting that the gift of divine grace will be proportionate to *their* endeavours. Indeed, our writers do not seem to have an idea of the child as an autonomous, ultimately uncontrollable identity. Although manifestations of maturing individuality are evident from an early stage, the identity of the child in relation to its parent is ambiguous. On the threshold of adulthood, however, the young person has acquired a distinct individuality which must determine the choice of his or her state in life and a will that must be respected, a point especially emphasized by our two Jesuits. Here we should recall the valorization of the exercise of free will which was a key issue in Laxist moral theology, where the value of an individual moral decision *per se* had to be set in the balance against the relative probabilities of the rightness or wrongness of an action.

Our writers were not really concerned to elaborate a theological anthropology of childhood, while for a theory of the evolving stages of childhood and youth one needs to look at the writings of pedagogues concerned with curriculum rather than at treatises on the family. The concerns of our churchmen-writers were not speculative but hortatory: to get parents to discharge their responsibilities for their children's moral and religious formation, but without abusing their powers as those children matured. They were concerned about a prevailing corruption of *mores* and did not, we suggest, see the nature of the baptized child as deeply problematic. *Physis* could be coped with; the main problem was posed by *ethos* in the sense of custom, and the remedy lay in *ethos* as habit.

University of East Anglia

[29] Ibid., Lib. 1, pp. xxxix–xl, Lib. 3 pp. i–iv.

'OUT OF THE MOUTHS OF BABES AND SUCKLINGS': PROPHECY, PURITANISM, AND CHILDHOOD IN ELIZABETHAN SUFFOLK

by ALEXANDRA WALSHAM

IN January 1581 a short black-letter tract in the tiny octavo format favoured by many Elizabethan publishers of sensational news appeared from the press of a London printing house based just outside the City in the Strand. Like other 'three-halfpenny' pamphlets of its ilk, this particular piece of ephemera was a pious tale of the prodigious and strange, but true. It described the 'wonderfull worke of God shewed upon a chylde' by the name of William Withers in the small Suffolk town of Walsham-le-Willows. On the previous Christmas Eve, the eleven-year-old boy had fallen into a deep trance for the space of ten days, 'to the great admiration of the beholders, and the greefe of his parentes'. At the end of this time he regained consciousness and proceeded to deliver a series of vehement prophetic denunciations of contemporary sin and immorality, calling the people to 'spedie repentance'—without which, he announced, the day of destruction was surely at hand. If amendment of life was not quickly forthcoming, the Lord would presently shake their houses on their heads and cause the earth to open up and swallow them alive.[1]

Even as the pamphlet went to press three weeks later, young Withers's extraordinary exhortations continued. Presumably the London publisher had received a manuscript narrative of this rural marvel from some local correspondent, and procured the services of a semi-professional writer, John Phillip, hastily to edit the text, compose a suitably moralistic preface, and append an edifying prayer.[2] The story of the 'Prodigall child' evidently met

[1] John Phillip, *The Wonderfull Worke of God shewed upon a Chylde, whose Name is William Withers, being in the Towne of Walsam, within the Countie of Suffolke* (London, 1581), title page, sigs A8r–v, B1v.

[2] For Phillip's eclectic literary output, which ranges from doggerel verse and broadside epitaphs to small devotional works and a play, see A. W. Pollard and G. R. Redgrave, *A Short Title Catalogue of Books printed in England, Scotland and Ireland and of English Books printed abroad 1475–1640*, 2nd edn,

with the instant approval of a metropolitan populace with an insatiable appetite for providential journalism of this kind. Not only were the rights to the original pamphlet soon after reassigned to a second printer, but the intriguing affair subsequently became the subject of a popular broadside ballad.[3] These published reports of the juvenile wonder reached readers in districts as far away as the Welsh borders, where an anonymous Shropshire annalist considered the incident notable enough to record in his idiosyncratic personal chronicle of Elizabeth I's reign.[4]

This paper considers the significance of this curious interlude in the life of an otherwise unassuming East Anglian community—an episode which became wrenched out of its immediate milieu and transformed into nothing less than a national news item. I want here to relocate the appearance of this schoolboy seer in his parochial environment, and to examine the response of the inhabitants of the surrounding area in relation to developments in provincial Puritan politics. By placing William Withers's trance in a wider cultural context, I hope also to shed some light on the special religious status which late sixteenth-century adults accorded to young children.

Born in 1568, William Withers was the second, and perhaps eldest surviving son of eight children in a family of villein tenants of the ancient manor of Walsham. Since at least the fourteenth century, generations of his ancestors had farmed the high Suffolk wood pasture countryside, eking out a solid, if fairly humble existence, through industrious animal husbandry.[5] His

rev. and enlarged by W. A. Jackson, F. S. Ferguson, and Katherine F. Pantzer, 2 vols (London, 1976–86), entries 19,863–77; *DNB*, 'John Phillips' and 'John Philip'. W. W. Greg establishes that these two separate authors are the same individual, in 'John Phillip—Notes for a Bibliography', *The Library*, ser. 3, 1 (1910), pp. 302–28, 396–423.

[3] See Edward Arber, ed., *A Transcript of the Registers of the Company of Stationers of London 1554–1640 AD*, 5 vols (London, 1875–94), 2, pp. 386 (13 Jan., Robert Waldegrave assigns his rights to 'the thinge of the childe' to Edward White) and 387 (16 Jan., 'master Watkins' tolerates to Edward White a ballad on the same subject). The original pamphlet was entered to Waldegrave on 9 Jan.

[4] Shrewsbury, Shrewsbury School, MS X. 31 [hereafter 'Dr Taylor's Book'], fol. 138r. The 'Strange speeches' of this child were also noted in several printed chronicles, including Raphael Holinshed, *The First and Second Volumes of Chronicles . . .*, continued by John Hooker, alias Vowell (London, 1587), p. 1315; John Stow, *The Summarye of the Chronicles of Englande . . . abridged and continued, unto 1587* (London, [1587]), p. 397.

[5] William Withers's baptism on 4 April 1568 is recorded in the parish register of Walsham-le-Willows: Bury St Edmunds, Suffolk Record Office [hereafter SRO(B)], FL 646/4/1. Wills of a number of members of the family survive, dating from 1477, 1528, and 1552: SRO(B), Hervye 46v;

parents, John Phillip's pamphlet emphasized, were of 'good name and fame' within the rather scattered, but quite prosperous parish of Walsham-le-Willows.[6] Just ten miles from Bury St Edmunds, the town was within earshot of the most critical and formative of the county's current affairs.

William's week-and-a-half-long swoon apparently caused something of a stir both in his own close-knit rural community and beyond. News of the prophesying child clearly carried with the wind, for there was soon 'mutche resort of people' from villages further afield. Many braved the winter weather and crowded into the house where he lay to hear his alarming predictions about the apocalyptic fate of iniquitous England—to witness speeches whose violence was such that the bed itself shook.[7] But it was not only the credulous common sort who flocked to behold the sight of this prodigious small boy. 'Thither came' James Gayton, godly preacher at St Mary's Church, Bury, and 'divers worshipful Gentlemen' of great credit and high rank. '[W]hich of you all', young Withers had declared impertinently in their presence, 'that remembreth the late Earthquake, when the Lord passed by you, as it were, but with one touche of his finger', had heeded the terrible signs of the times? Rehearsing the threatenings of God in the Bible 'in such sorte as though he were a learned Divine', this husbandman's son admonished his 'deaf-eared' social superiors that they could assure themselves that worse plagues and judgements were to come. Unless pride and infidelity were swiftly forsaken, all would imminently taste of 'a farre greater Earthquake' than the minor tremor of the previous 6 April.[8]

Norwich, Norfolk Record Office [hereafter NRO], Attmere 20; SRO(B), IC 500/2/31 (John Wyther, William's grandfather). Fourteenth-century manor court rolls reveal that one 'William Wyther' died in the Black Death of 1349: Ray Lock, 'The Black Death in Walsham-le-Willows', *Proceedings of the Suffolk Institute of Archaeology and History* [hereafter *PSIAH*], 37 (1992), p. 336. Manorial surveys compiled in 1577 and 1581 record William's father's tenements: see Kenneth Melton Dodd, ed., *The Field Book of Walsham-le-Willows 1577* = *Suffolk Records Society* 17, pt 2 (1974), pp. 40, 52, 104, 108, 115, 156–7. I am extremely grateful to Mrs Jean Lock for generously sharing with me her unparalleled knowledge of the records relating to Walsham-le-Willows in this period.

6 Phillip, *The Wonderfull Worke of God*, sig. A8r.

7 Ibid., sig. A8v; 'Dr Taylor's Book', fol. 138r.

8 Phillip, *The Wonderful Worke of God*, sigs B1r–2v. The earthquake of 6 April 1580 seems to have made considerable impact in this area. In Bardwell, the adjoining parish to Walsham, the townwar-

Ironically, the assembled company (as it was 'credibly reported') included some of the most progressive and zealous Puritan magistrates in the county, Sir Robert Jermyn, Robert Ashfield, and Sir William Spring—magistrates whose patronage and aggressive initiatives in favour of leading clerical figures in the campaign for further reformation would, only a year later, bring them into headlong conflict with the conservative Bishop of Norwich, Edmund Freke, and, moreover, into public disgrace.[9] In January 1581 the atmosphere in Bury and its hinterland was probably already tense. Rival factions of reactionary conformists and radical Calvinists were in the process of sharply polarizing. Twelve months earlier, in February 1579, Jermyn and Ashfield had instituted a severe regime of ritual punishments, designed both to eradicate urban immorality and disorder, and as a direct challenge to their 'popishly' inclined opponents.[10] They had, furthermore, begun to apply strong-arm tactics in an effort to oust inadequate local ministers and replace them with preaching pastors, who, like James Gayton and his senior colleague John Handson, shared their own dissatisfaction with the ecclesiastical status quo. Handson and Gayton, who seemingly enjoyed a considerable following in the country thereabouts, were open about their adherence to Presbyterian principles, and audaciously outspoken in the pulpit in their contempt for clergymen who slavishly conformed with the rubrics of the Book of Common Prayer. They were alleged by the adversaries who eventually forced them to resign their lectureships to have reduced services in Bury to little more than 'Geneva Psalmes &

dens purchased the official order of prayer issued after the event to avert God's wrath; possibly the glass window in the church replaced that year had been broken during the tremor: SRO(B), FL 522/11/22. The earthquake also generated a large number of topical tracts and providential pamphlets, including one entitled *Quaedam de terre motu* written by John Phillip himself, and now lost: see Charles Henry Cooper and Thompson Cooper, *Athenae Cantabrigienses*, 2 vols (Cambridge, 1858–1913), 2, p. 99.

[9] For discussions of the 'Bury Stirs', see Patrick Collinson, 'The Puritan classical movement in the reign of Elizabeth I' (London Ph.D. thesis, 1957), pp. 860–930; Diarmaid MacCulloch, 'Catholic and Puritan in Elizabethan Suffolk: a county community polarizes', *Archiv für Reformationsgeschichte*, 72 (1981), pp. 269–78, and *Suffolk and the Tudors* (Oxford, 1986), pp. 199–211; J. S. Craig, 'Reformation, politics and polemics in sixteenth-century East Anglian market towns' (Cambridge Ph.D. thesis, 1992), ch. 3, and, 'The Bury Stirs revisited: an analysis of the townsmen', *PSIAH*, 37 (1991), pp. 208–24.

[10] BL, MS Lansdowne 27, no. 70.

Sermons'.[11] The people of the region, wrote Bishop Freke to Lord Burghley in April and August of 1581, were schismatically divided between those dutiful to the Queen's proceedings and those given to 'fantasticall innovations'—including the 'corrupt and contentious doctryne' disseminated by the separatist Robert Browne. The 'strange dealinges' of several of the Suffolk gentry had much to do with this dangerous state of affairs, which, he feared, would 'in tyme . . . hazarde the overthrowe of all religion'.[12]

Such clashes and controversies inevitably spilt over into the district surrounding Bury—indeed, into the birthplace of William Withers, Walsham-le-Willows itself. In 1583 an obstinately Nonconformist minister, Ezechias Morley, was to write an account of his 'troubles' in this vicinity in the preceding three years. First 'molested', and then arrested by episcopal warrant in view of an underhand attempt to appoint him curate of a key Bury parish, Morley had appealed for protection to another influential Puritan JP, Sir John Higham, who found him a post as preacher in Walsham, where he controlled the advowson. Morley's stay in the town was, however, short-lived. He 'contynued not quiet' there, 'by reason' of powerful 'enemyes', who succeeded in driving him from the parish at Michaelmas 1582, and doggedly pursued him with a writ of excommunication to his next living at Denston, fifteen miles to the south-west. Indicted at their instigation on a trifling matter of liturgical irregularity, Morley was obviously regarded by some individuals as a singularly unwelcome intruder upon the Walsham-le-Willows scene.[13]

[11] See Edmund Freke's articles against Jermyn, Ashfield, Sir John Higham and Thomas Badby, BL, MS Egerton 1693, fols 89r–90r, at 89r. In February 1582, Jermyn answered the charges in full in letters sent to Robert Beale and William Burghley: ibid., fols 87r–v, 91r–100r; BL, MS Lansdowne 37, fols 59r–62v. For allegations about Gayton and Handson's activities, see BL, MS Egerton 1693, fol. 89r; BL, MS Lansdowne 33, no. 13, fols 26r–v; no. 21, fols 41r–v. Three petitions on their behalf signed by inhabitants of Bury were sent to the Privy Council and Burghley between 1578 and 1582. The petition of 6 August 1582 declared that their departure from the town had caused 'greate daunger and unspeakable griefe' to those 'well affected' in the town and 'in the whole countrey aboute': London, Public Record Office, State Papers [hereafter PRO, SP], 12/155/5.

[12] BL, MS Lansdowne 33, no. 13, fols 26r–v (19 April); no. 20, fol. 40r (2 Aug.).

[13] Morley's account of his 'troubles' can be found in London, Dr Williams's Library, MS Morrice A ('Old Loose Papers'), fols 166r–v; calendared in Albert Peel, ed., *The Seconde Parte of a Register*, 2 vols (Cambridge, 1915), 1, p. 164. Morley had similar difficulties at the hands of the Bishop of London in the Essex parish of Ridgwell, being charged in 1584 with refusal to subscribe and comply

What was the real cause of the hostility and antagonism his brief ministry in the town triggered? Could it conceivably be because he was implicated in the 'enthusiastic' excesses that had bred up a young Puritan prophet? While all this remains frustratingly unclear, what does emerge from Morley's tribulations is indirect evidence of a deeply disunited community—a paradigm of the animosity and confrontation fervent Protestant evangelism could provoke. William Withers's coma undoubtedly occurred in the context of one of many sixteenth-century village collisions between passionate advocates of moral and spiritual revolution and diehard defenders of an older religious and cultural order. His outbursts themselves were representative of a more widespread assault on ungodly contemporary manners—a crusade against drunkenness and adultery, sabbath-breaking and swearing, sumptuary excess, and profane sports and pastimes. Perceiving one Smith, a fashionably attired serving-man by his bedside, this eleven-year-old Jeremiah inveighed fiercely against his 'great and monstrous ruffes', advising him 'it were better for him to put on sackcloth & mourn for his sinnes, then in such abhominable pride to pranke up himselfe like the divels darling', the 'very father' of lies. At this the shamefaced manservant 'sorrowed & wept for his offence, rente the bande from his neck, tooke a knife and cut it in peeces, and vowed never to weare the like againe.' Or so, at least, it was said.[14] Perhaps his pronouncements also unsettled townspeople still attached to the traditional customs of the current festive season, the Christmas masking and mumming left over from 'merry', pre-Reformation England. They may even have convinced some inhabitants of the outrageous impiety of maintaining in the centre of their town a public 'game place', an open-air theatre in the round made expressly 'of purpose for the use of stage playes'—to Puritans like

with the liturgical regulations, and with unlicensed preaching. He claimed to have been arrested and committed to the Clink in 1582, where he lay for seven weeks for an unknown cause. See London, Dr Williams's Library, MS Morrice B(2), fol. 91v, calendared in Peel, ed., *The Seconde Parte of a Register*, 2, p. 165. See also Collinson, 'The Puritan classical movement', pp. 685, 895–6. It is not possible to establish conclusively whether Morley was already ensconced as preacher at Walsham by Christmas 1580. The parish was a perpetual curacy, and seems to have been something of a stop-gap for ministers seeking a rectorship or a better living; most stayed only a few years.

[14] Phillip, *The Wonderful Worke of God*, sig. B2r.

a red rag to a bull.[15] '[H]ole household[s]' had supposedly taken young Withers's warnings completely to heart.[16]

In the eyes of John Phillip, pious pamphleteer, God had thus 'raised up a second Daniel' in the form of a meek Suffolk child. William Withers was 'an instrument given to us by the providence of God, if it may be to waken us out of the perilous slumber of our sinne'—to 'terrifie our guiltie consciences' out of hypocrisy, security, and counterfeit Christianity. In the face of the manifest failure both of the ordained ministers of the institutional Church and of recent visible tokens of his wrath to rouse the English people to repentance, the Lord had showed his 'great handie worke' in endowing with divine inspiration this innocent little lad. Since neither 'thy inestimable Levite' nor 'thy . . . heavye comminations' could prevail, and 'pearce our stonye stubberne & flinite hearts', Phillip acknowledged, 'to our shame thou hast opened the mouth of a childe to foreshewe unto us the fulnesse of thy furie.'[17] In entrusting such an extraordinary commission to a boy scarcely out of breeches, God had given living witness to Psalm 8.2: 'Out of the mouth of babes and sucklings hast thou ordained strength because of thine enemies, that thou mightest still the enemy and avenger.'[18]

The historian, however, is inclined to be rather more sceptical and 'scientific' when it comes to assessing the source of William's verbal revelations. It may well be that he was in the grips of an actual physical illness, a genuine victim of delirium brought on by overly austere observance of the devotional practice of prolonged private fasting.[19] Possibly his ecstatic experience was the product of a peculiarly intense Puritan upbringing, testimony to the efficacy of godly methods of educating and indoctrinating the young—to an internalization of regular Bible reading and

[15] The 'Game Place', described in detail in the manorial survey of 1577, was obviously still in much use at that date: Dodd, ed., *The Field Book of Walsham-le-Willows 1577*, p. 92. See also Kenneth M. Dodd, 'Another Elizabethan theatre in the round', *Shakespeare Quarterly*, 21 (1970), pp. 125–56; David Dymond, 'A lost social institution: the camping close', *Rural History*, 1 (1990), pp. 165–92.

[16] 'Dr Taylor's Book', fol. 138r.

[17] Phillip, *The Wonderful Worke of God*, sigs A8r, B1v, B6v, and *passim*.

[18] Ps. 8. 2, echoed by Christ in Matt. 21.16.

[19] According to Phillip, *The Wonderfull Worke of God*, title page and sig. A8r, William Withers took no sustenance for the ten days in which he lay in his trance. On the Puritan practice of public and private fasting, which took on special significance in the early 1580s, see Collinson, 'The Puritan classical movement', pp. 323–45.

frequent catechetical instruction.[20] It is tempting to detect in his exhortations traces of sermon repetition exercises, echoes of the prophetic preaching in the Old Testament mould on which he had presumably been weaned. Had he merely memorized dozens of similar discourses heard on days on which he and his family had 'gadded' in search of true Gospel teaching, or carefully reconstructed shorthand notes taken on such occasions?[21] Was this just the all-consuming Calvinism of a highly precocious child?

On the other hand, the episode also smells suspiciously like a case of adult manipulation—clerical, if not parental, exploitation of a devout and clever boy for honourable proselytizing ends. Could it be that the whole business was master-minded by a fanatically religious father or ingeniously contrived by an enterprising preacher? Driven to desperation by the spiritual apathy and insensibility of country congregations, did James Gayton or even Ezechias Morley himself co-opt a willing pupil as his accomplice in an imaginative evangelizing scheme to galvanize the common people into adopting godly habits? Perhaps William Withers had been coached in the part of child prophet from a script written several weeks before—a script conceivably plagiarized from another printed text. Both striking and suggestive is the marked resemblance his speeches bear to those delivered by an adolescent German girl, reputedly resurrected from the dead the preceding January, whose own foreboding declarations were immortalized in a pamphlet translated from High Dutch and published in London in August of that year.[22] And it may be

[20] On Puritan pedagogy, see Ian Green, ' "For children in yeeres and children in understanding": the emergence of the English catechism under Elizabeth and the early Stuarts', *JEH*, 37 (1986), pp. 397–425; John Morgan, *Godly Learning: Puritan Attitudes towards Reason, Learning, and Education, 1560–1640* (Cambridge, 1986), ch. 8 *passim*, esp. pp. 144–50; S. J. Wright, 'Confirmation, catechism and communion: the role of the young in the post-Reformation Church', in S. J. Wright, ed., *Parish, Church and People: Local Studies in Lay Religion 1350–1750* (London, 1988), pp. 203–27. Cf. Gerald Strauss, *Luther's House of Learning: Indoctrination of the Young in the German Reformation* (Baltimore, 1978).

[21] It is interesting that petitioners to the Privy Council on behalf of Gayton and Handson on 6 Aug. 1582 alleged that the conservative faction in Bury had brought the preachers into question by 'wicked devices', including 'pervertinge the sence and true meaninge of . . . [their teaching] . . . usinge the notes taken by children at their sermons . . .': PRO, SP, 12/155/5.

[22] Eyriak Schlichtenberger, *A Prophesie uttered by the Daughter of an Honest Countrey Man, called Adam Krause* (London, 1580). Jürgen Beyer of Clare College, Cambridge, has discovered numerous other cases in the course of his research on the subject of Lutheran popular prophets in post-Reformation Germany and Scandinavia.

that the 'spontaneous' conversion of Robert Ashfield's pretentiously dressed attendant was actually a brilliantly stage-managed dramatic moral tableau. The self-conscious theatricality of this polished performance is certainly hard to ignore. It does not seem too far-fetched to suggest that William was an adept dissembler, an eager volunteer for an experiment in religious ventriloquism. But in the absence of any firm facts, this, too, is a tentative hypothesis. Who, we might wonder, wrote down—and very probably embroidered—this strange story of events in a relatively sleepy Suffolk town? Who sent it off to be printed for the edification of a broader audience—to be printed on the press of a risk-taking Puritan publisher, Robert Waldegrave, who later that decade would dare to undertake the infamous Marprelate tracts?[23]

There is yet a third scenario and solution to this allegedly providential affair. It could easily be no more than a simple schoolboy prank, a trick played by a young mischief-maker on his unsuspecting elders. Perhaps William was roguishly mimicking his clerical betters, but it is equally likely that he was impudently mocking them. Puritanism, which took an acutely pessimistic view of the human being's inherently depraved nature, encouraged a particularly repressive and authoritarian approach to child-rearing. It reinforced the already rigid assumptions of a severely patriarchal society in which children were expected to display their deference and obedience to their parents through submissive physical gestures and in other ritually symbolic ways.[24] Prophecy, perhaps, was a species of psychological reac-

[23] See R. B. McKerrow, ed., *A Dictionary of Printers and Booksellers in England, Scotland and Ireland, and of Foreign Printers of English Books 1557–1640* (London, 1910), pp. 277–9; *DNB*.

[24] Early modern child-rearing, discipline and attitudes towards the young are controversial topics: the debate can be charted in Phillipe Ariès, *Centuries of Childhood* (Harmondworth, 1962), esp. pp. 24–34; Laurence Stone, *The Family, Sex and Marriage 1500–1800* (London, 1977), pp. 161–79, 194–5; M. J. Tucker, 'The child as beginning and end: fifteenth and sixteenth century English childhood', in Lloyd de Mause, ed., *The History of Childhood* (New York, 1974), pp. 229–57; Linda A. Pollock, *Forgotten Children: Parent-Child Relations from 1500–1900* (Cambridge, 1983). Balanced overviews are to be found in Keith Wrightson, *English Society 1580–1680* (London, 1982), pp. 106–18, and Ralph Houlbrooke, *The English Family 1450–1700* (Harlow, 1984), ch. 6. See also Robert V. Schnucker, 'Puritan attitudes toward childhood discipline, 1560–1634', in Valerie Fildes, ed., *Women as Mothers in Pre-Industrial England: Essays in Memory of Dorothy McLaren* (London and New York, 1990), pp. 108–21; Kathryn Sather, 'Sixteenth and seventeenth century child rearing: a matter of discipline', *Journal of Social History*, 22 (1989), pp. 735–43; Morgan, *Godly Learning*, esp. pp. 144–50.

tion. It was a medium which enabled one momentarily to liberate oneself from an inferior position within this inflexibly hierarchical structure without fear of discipline or recrimination. William Withers's holy misbehaviour and supernaturally-inspired disrespect may additionally reflect subconscious resistance to a religious culture deeply distrustful of the notion of recreation and play as ends in themselves.[25] Children, who, like women, were ordinarily denied access to more conventional vehicles for expression—the pulpit and the printed text—were forced to by-pass them and to represent their utterances as the result of divine dictation. This was a sanctioned mode for speaking out of turn—a strategy for presumptuously articulating opinions in a privileged male, adult, and priestly arena. Yet paradoxically it was an inversion of the established social order which simultaneously endorsed it.[26] Rather like the abolished boy bishop ceremonies of the medieval Church, in which choirboys annually appropriated the ecclesiastical functions of cathedral and collegiate clergy on Holy Innocents' Day (28 December), this world turned upside down was tolerated only because it did not last long.[27] It is a curious coincidence that our Puritan child prophet began his outbursts at exactly the same time of year—post-Reformation Protestantism contains surprising undercurrents of continuity with the proscribed Catholic past.

All such interpretations of the episode are, in the end, entirely conjectural. It is very likely that we shall never know the real reasons for William Withers's mysterious trance, whether it was ingenuous or pretended, whether it embodied some kind of rebellion against or rather a radical absorption of Elizabethan Puritan piety—or a creative combination of both. This does not, however, compromise its cultural significance. The incident in

[25] See Keith Thomas, 'Children in early modern England', in Gillian Avery and Julia Briggs, eds, *Children and their Books: A Celebration of the Work of Iona and Peter Opie* (Oxford, 1989), pp. 45–77, esp.p. 63.

[26] Cf. Keith Thomas, *Religion and the Decline of Magic: Studies in Popular Beliefs in Sixteenth- and Seventeenth-Century England* (Harmondsworth, 1971), pp. 163–4, 177; Phyllis Mack, 'Women as prophets during the English Civil War', *Feminist Studies*, 8 (1982), *passim*, esp. pp. 27–8, 32, 35, 38.

[27] The classic account is E. K. Chambers, *The Medieval Stage*, 2 vols (Oxford, 1903), 1, ch. 15, and 2, appendix M, but see also A. R. Wright, *British Calendar Customs* (London and Glasgow, 1940), pp. 194–8; Richard L. De Molen, '*Pueri Christi Imitatio*: the festival of the Boy-Bishop in Tudor England', *Moreana*, 12 (1975), pp. 17–28; W. W. Wooden, 'The topos of childhood in Marian England', *Journal of Medieval and Renaissance Studies*, 12 (1982), pp. 187–94.

Walsham-le-Willows still has something to disclose about the spiritual authority which late sixteenth-century children could hold.

People in the early modern period were seemingly predisposed to perceive childhood as a stage of life in which one might be afforded at least flashes of startling divine insight. Miscellaneous evidence attests to a more widespread impression that individuals who had not yet reached adolescence were capable of closer mystical communion than adults with God. This derived partly from ideas embedded in the Bible, above all, in the Gospel of St Matthew 18.3: 'Verily I say unto you', declares Christ, 'Except ye be converted and become as little children, ye shall not enter into the kingdom of heaven.' Innocent and untainted by experience of the corrupt and wicked world, the young were supposed to be especially beloved by the Lord—this was why the faithful were themselves called the 'children of God'. Like Samuel, acolyte of Eli in the Jewish temple, they had an intrinsic ability to hear his own voice, a disconcerting tendency to speak the absolute truth. In Tudor and Stuart England this had an enduring folk legacy: it was a piece of proverbial wisdom that 'children and fools cannot lie.'[28]

Scripture complemented and reinforced a web of semi-pagan magical beliefs with the same implications. In the elaborate quasi-ecclesiastical rituals carried out by cunning men in the course of their divinations, pre-pubescent boys and girls could be of crucial importance. '[W]hen a spiritt is raised', observed a Southampton wizard in 1631, 'none hath power to see yt but children of Eleaven and Twelve yeares of age, or such as are true maides.' Their sexual immaturity also made them indispensable as scryers. Virginity was the key to clairvoyance; it gave the child a unique gift for gazing into crystal balls and discerning the location of lost and stolen objects, as well as the identity of the thief.[29] Indeed, it seems to have been quite generally accepted that the Almighty often chose to manifest his omnipotence by using those of tender years to reveal the notorious perpetrators of

[28] Matt. 18.3, I Sam. 3, and Morris Palmer Tilley, *A Dictionary of the Proverbs in England in the Sixteenth and Seventeenth Centuries* (Ann Arbor, 1950), entry C328.

[29] R. C. Anderson, ed., *The Book of Examinations and Depositions, 1622–1644. Vol. II. 1627–1634*, Publications of the Southampton Record Society (1931), pp. 104–5; Thomas, *Religion and the Decline of Magic*, pp. 255–6, 319–20.

concealed crimes. A typical murder pamphlet published in 1606 reported how it had 'pleased God' to bring to light two killers by miraculously endowing with the power of speech a young girl whose tongue they had brutally cut out at the roots.[30] Unborn infants were likewise thought sometimes to cry inauspiciously from the womb, and once delivered to utter hideous forewarnings of impending providential woe before a premature departure from the earthly realm.[31] And while popular fascination with the birth of gruesomely malformed babies may just betray crude curiosity about grotesque anatomical distortion, arguably it also reflects a conviction that children were recurrently selected to be the signposts and mouthpieces of God's wrath. On to their diminutive bodies he projected his ominous messages; their unsightly misshapen limbs were encoded with sinister configurations of his fury. This, asserted ballad-mongers and clerical commentators alike, was one means by which the Lord heralded the dreadful judgements that were hanging over the land.[32] The impact which William Withers's prodigious announcements made was simply one more manifestation of the view that childhood was by way of being an innately prophetic state.

If the rash of cases of demonic possession publicized in this period is any indication, it was also considered to be a phase in which one was particularly vulnerable to the savage onslaughts of Satan. In communities throughout the country, children and teenagers of around William's age were understood to be falling prey to the violent assaults of the devil, to be afflicted by convulsive fits of diabolical frenzy, and to be blasphemously

[30] *The Horrible Murther of a Young Boy of Three Yeres of Age, whose Sister had her Tongue cut out: and how it pleased God to reveale the Offendors, by giving Speech to the Tongueles Childe* (London, 1606), pp. 5–7; and *The most Cruell and Bloody Murther committed by an Inkeepers Wife, called Annis Dell, and her Sonne George Dell* (London, 1606), esp. sigs B3v–C2r. See also *A most Horrible and Detestable Murther committed by a Bloudie Minded Man upon his owne Wife: and most Strangely revealed by his Childe that was under Five Yeares of Age* (London, 1595).

[31] *A Strange and Miraculous Accident happened in the Cittie of Purmerent, on New-yeeres Even last past 1599. Of a Yong Child which was heard to cry in the Mothers Wombe before it was borne, and about Fourteene Dayes of Age, spake certaine Sencible Words, to the Wonder of Every body* (London, 1599).

[32] For just a few examples, see H. B., *The True Discripcion of a Childe with Ruffes, borne in the Parish of Micheham, in the Countie of Surrey* (London, 1566); John D., *A Discription of a Monstrous Chylde, borne at Chychester in Sussex, the xxiiii Daye of May* (London, 1562); G. B., *Of a Monstrous Childe borne at Chichester . . . With a Short and Sharpe Discourse, for the Punishment of Whoredome* (London, [1581]).

ranting and raving at the Tempter's behest. Possession was in a sense prophecy's *alter ego*, an alternative means by which the child of a pious household could express forbidden impulses and legitimately engage in normally unacceptable and punishable conduct. There was always, in fact, a fine line between the satanic and the sacred, a profound ambivalence about what proceeded from divine grace and what from infernal malice. Possession itself could be a form of evangelism: it too could generate juvenile sermons of repentance and exhibitions of steadfast faith.[33] Just such a spectacle had occurred not thirty miles from Walsham only six years before, when the thirteen-year-old son of a Norwich alderman vanquished the fiend that had tormented him for weeks by hurling forth passages from the Bible, in which he proved to be amazingly well versed.[34] Nor were these exclusively Protestant phenomena—pre- and post-Reformation Catholic children were no less prone to be vexed by unclean spirits and to be privileged with supernatural visions.[35] Cultural conceptions of the child as an habitual site of struggle between the forces of good and evil evidently transcended confessional divisions.

Nearly one hundred years later this was still the interpretative framework into which contemporaries fitted the remarkable mental endowments of the three-year-old 'Manchild of

[33] On possession, see Thomas, *Religion and the Decline of Magic*, pp. 569–88; D. P. Walker, *Unclean Spirits: Possession and Exorcism in France and England in the Late Sixteenth and Early Seventeenth Centuries* (London, 1981); Michael MacDonald, ed., *Witchcraft and Hysteria in Elizabethan London: Edward Jorden and the Mary Glover Case* (London and New York, 1991), Introduction; H. C. Erik Midelfort, 'The devil and the German people: reflections on the popularity of demon possession in sixteenth-century Germany', in Stephen Ozment, ed., *Religion and Culture in the Renaissance and Reformation = Sixteenth-Century Essays and Studies* 11 (Kirksville, Miss., 1989), pp. 98–119. A particularly illuminating parallel to the William Withers affair is the celebrated and controversial case of the apprentice musician, William Sommers of Nottingham, exorcised by the Puritan John Darrell in the late 1590s. For a detailed discussion, with references to the rash of contemporary publications on the subject, see Walker, *Unclean Spirits*, ch. 4.

[34] R. A. Houlbrooke, ed., *The Letter Book of John Parkhurst Bishop of Norwich Compiled during the Years 1571–5*, Norfolk Record Society (1974–5), pp. 86–7.

[35] For striking examples of prophetic and demoniac Catholic children, see Thomas More's account of the 'Ipswich miracle' in 1516 in his *Dialogue concerning Heresies* (1529), repr. Thomas L. C. Lawler et al., eds, *The Complete Works of St Thomas More*, 6, pt 1 (New Haven and London, 1981), pp. 92–4; Barnaby Rich, *The True Report of a Late Practise enterprised by a Papist, with a Young Maiden in Wales, accompted amongst our Catholiques in those Partes for a Greater Prophetise, then ever was the Holie Maide of Kent* . . . (London, 1582); and Richard Baddeley, *The Boy of Bilson: Or, A True Discovery of the late Notorious Impostures of certaine Romish Priests in their Pretended Exorcisme, or Expulsion of the Divell out of a Young Boy, named William Perry* (London, 1622).

Manchester', Charles Bennett. When this 'Lancashire wonder' arrived in London in 1679, his alleged linguistic fluency in Latin, Hebrew, and Greek and astonishing familiarity with Scripture were similarly acclaimed as a work of providence, his moralistic exhortations a matter for the reverent admiration and awe of mere mortals.[36] But had William Withers been a child of the late Enlightenment age, his trance might well have shed its religious connotations and portentous overtones, for by then the phrase 'child prodigy' had almost acquired its modern secularized sense. Possibly our young Suffolk oracle would have been regarded as nothing more than an exceptionally able dissenting schoolboy.

Even in 1581 perhaps many of those who travelled to Walsham-le-Willows from locations across the county came solely for entertainment's sake—on a tourist expedition to take in an enthralling East Anglian freak show. And did the avid readers of John Phillip's news pamphlet seek pious instruction or pure titillation from the tale? The ambiguities are, for all that, illuminating: godly Protestantism could obviously, on occasion, be a genuinely popular affair. It may even be that William Withers, senior, was not too high-minded to profit from the Elizabethan pilgrimage to see his 'prodigall' son. At his death in 1617, 'for the love and zeale which he did beare' for his town he left no less than ten pounds for the education of poor children in the parish—an unusually large sum for the average husbandman to set aside for charitable purposes.[37]

By way of an epilogue, the boy himself subsequently fulfilled his prophetic vocation in a rather more mundane fashion. Educated at Corpus Christi College, Cambridge, and in 1594 ordained deacon and priest, he served as the rector of two Suffolk livings for the next fifty-odd years—apparently retaining his strong Puritan sympathies, since he survived the ecclesiastical

[36] William E. A. Axon, *The Wonderfull Child. Tracts issued in 1679 relating to Charles Bennett of Manchester, alleged to speak Latin, Greek, and Hebrew, when three years old without having been taught = Chetham Miscellanies* ns 1, Chetham Society ns 47 (1902). See also Nigel Smith, 'A child prophet: Martha Hatfield as *The Wise Virgin*', in Avery and Briggs, eds, *Children and their Books*, pp. 79–93.

[37] The will itself is not extant; however, a covenant relating to this bequest, dated 23 July 1632, does survive: SRO(B), FL 646/11/92. His sons William and Edmond were appointed to pay this sum to certain parish overseers.

upheavals of the Civil War.[38] How did he recollect the Christmas of 1580 in his sober middle and old age? Did he wince at the memory of an embarrassing aberration, or yearn wistfully for spiritual charisma never fully regained? For a short time William Withers was a public, even cult, figure who wielded extraordinary sway. Refracted through the prism of cheap print, glimpsed through an idealizing adult lens, his trance offers us an oblique angle on the religious subculture of the very young. But, for the most part, the children of early modern England remain neither seen nor, indeed, heard.

Emmanuel College,
Cambridge

[38] John and J. A. Venn, *Alumni Cantabrigiensis*, pt 1 (Cambridge, 1927), 'William Withers'. He was rector of Ickworth from 1595 until at least 1613, rector of Wetheringsett from 1616 until his death in 1647. He may also have been rector of Fersfield, Norfolk, 1613–47. His will survives: NRO, 127. Barker (MF 93).

'FROM FIRE AND WATER': THE RESPONSIBILITIES OF GODPARENTS IN EARLY MODERN ENGLAND

by WILLIAM COSTER

RICHARD HOOKER, in justifying the formula of the baptismal rite of the Elizabethan Prayer Book, objected to the Puritan preference for referring to godparents as *witnesses* '. . . as if they came but to see and to testify what is done', adding,

> It savoureth more of piety to give them their old accustomed name of Fathers and Mothers in God, whereby they are well put in mind what affection they ought to bear towards those innocents, for whose religious education the Church accepteth them as pledges.[1]

By describing sponsors at baptism as 'Fathers and Mothers in God', he stressed the way in which the spiritual facet of parenthood had been assigned outside the natural family. In our modern Western, and in many ways post-Christian, society, it might be assumed that all of the functions of care for a child belong exclusively to the natural parents. But in many other present-day societies the set of responsibilities which we refer to as *parenthood*, including physical care, education, and moral upbringing, may be distributed among a number of individuals or groups, including kin, neighbours, and social superiors, creating what anthropologists refer to as forms of *pro-parenthood*.[2] Hooker implied that this was also true of early modern England, as he indicated that godparents were responsible for the spiritual education of a child.

Prior to the Reformation, at least in theory, godparents took on not only spiritual and educational responsibilities, but also

[1] R. Hooker, *Of the Laws of Ecclesiastical Polity, the Fifth Book*, ed. R. Bayne (London, 1902) p. 338. All spelling in extracts has been modernized, except in the case of personal names.

[2] E. N. Goody, 'Forms of pro-parenthood: the sharing and substitution of parental roles', in J. Goody, ed., *Kinship, Selected Readings* (London, 1971), pp. 331–45.

physical ones.[3] In the Sarum Use these duties were to be stated by the priest after the completion of the baptismal rite when,

> the father and mother be enjoined to preserve their child from fire and water and all other dangers until the age of seven years; and if they do it not, the godfathers and godmothers are held responsible; likewise the godfathers should be enjoined to teach the infant the Our Father, and Hail Mary and I believe in God, or to cause them to be taught them. . . .[4]

Clearly it was not the duty of the godparents to rear the newly baptized infant, rather the natural parents had the primary duty to protect the child 'from fire and water and all other dangers'. Only if they were unwilling or unable to carry them out did these responsibilities devolve upon the godparents. However, it is interesting to note that the rite specifically stated that godparents had a separate and distinct duty towards their spiritual children; they were charged with the rudimentary religious education of the infant, through the teaching of the Lord's Prayer and Hail Mary.

Godparents held this important role in the scheme of late medieval Christianity by virtue of the promises they made in the name of the child, to renounce Satan, his works and pomps, and to state that they believed in God, the Holy Ghost, the Church, the saints, remission of sins, resurrection, and eternal life.[5] Thus, as the Sarum Use explained, 'Men and women who receive children at baptism are appointed their sureties before God.'[6] As the representative of the spiritual side of the infant's character, godparents took on the full responsibility for that facet of the child's life. This role not only placed obligations upon them, but it also gave godparents their right to intervene in the lives of their spiritual children, as the Sarum Use added,

> . . . therefore [the godparents] must frequently admonish them when they are grown or capable of discipline that they guard their chastity, love justice, hold the charity and above

[3] B. Hanawalt, *The Ties That Bound. Peasant Families in Medieval England* (Oxford, 1986), p. 246.

[4] Printed in translation in J. D. C. Fisher, *Christian Initiation: Baptism in the Medieval West. A Study in the Disintegration of the Primitive Rite of Initiation* (London, 1965), p. 175.

[5] Ibid., pp. 172–3.

[6] Ibid.

> all things are bound to teach them the Lord's Prayer and angelic salvation, the symbol of the faith and how to sign themselves with the sign of the cross.[7]

The reference to chastity in particular suggests that even after the coming of age of an infant, godparents were expected to play a part in the spiritual and religious instruction of their godchildren.

The Lutheran Church retained godparents in baptism, attempting to instruct them more carefully on their duties toward the child, and this position was also adopted by the English Church.[8] While Henry VIII's articles of 1536 entrusted spiritual instruction to 'fathers, mothers, masters and governors of youth', interestingly, two years later, Archbishop Lee's injunctions for the diocese of York instructed clergy to 'charge all fathers and mothers, heads of households and godfathers and godmothers and schoolmasters . . . to see their children, servants and scholars well instructed in the Pater Noster, Ave Maria, Creed and Ten Commandments in English and all other things comprised in these injuctions.'[9]

These responsibilities were built into the 1549 Prayer Book.[10] The necessity to spell out the theological significance of baptism as 'a solome vow, promise and profession' was emphasized, and godparents were to teach their spiritual children of its meaning.[11] Additionally, they were to 'call on them to hear sermons', while the specifics of spiritual education were now 'to provide that they may learn the Creed, the Lord's Prayer and the Ten Commandments in the English tongue, and all other things which a christian man ought to know and believe to his soul's health'.[12] Finally, the godparents were charged that 'these children . . . be virtuously brought up to lead a godly and christian life . . .'.[13] The wording of this portion of the liturgy remained almost unchanged in subsequent Prayer Books and became the basis of the English Church's position on the institution.[14]

[7] Ibid., p. 177.

[8] G. W. Bromiley, *Baptism and the Anglican Reformers* (London, 1953), p. 127.

[9] W. H. Frere and W. M. Kennedy, eds, *Visitation Articles and Injunctions of the Period of the Reformation, vol. 2, 1536–1558* = Alcuin Club Collections, 15 (London, 1910), pp. 6, 7 and 48.

[10] *The First and Second Prayer Books of Edward VI* (London, 1910), p. 241.

[11] Ibid.

[12] Ibid.

[13] Ibid., p. 241.

[14] Ibid., p. 399.

Clearly a new emphasis had been placed on the educational and spiritual role of godparents, who were wholly responsible for this part of the child's upbringing. However, while this facet of their duty had been enlarged and emphasized, their potential role as surrogate parents had disappeared from the liturgy; there was no longer any reference to protection from fire and water. This emphasis on religious education by godparents is what might be expected of a moderately reformed Church. It was, in part, a justification for keeping the institution, implying that it had a vital role in the spiritual life of individuals. Calvin and Knox found this position unsatisfactory.[15] For them, and for English Puritans, godparents were superfluous, without a scriptural basis; the swearing of vows for an infant was offensive, and spiritual education should have been the responsibility of the natural parents within a God-fearing household. This position can most clearly be seen in the *Admonition to Parliament* of 1572 which argued that, 'seeing the children of the faithful only are to be baptised, that the father should and might, if conveniently, offer and present his child . . .'.[16]

In replying to this attack Hooker's patron, Archbishop Whitgift, justified the institution by stating that, 'This is the cause why the Church appointed godfathers and godmothers, that the parents of the child being dead, they should take upon them their office, and bring up those in Christian religion for whom they have given their promise to the Church.'[17] This statement could be taken to imply continuity with the pre-Reformation rite (if the 'office' to be taken up by godparents was that of the deceased parents), but it seems more likely Whitgift was suggesting that on the death of the parents the godfathers and godmothers were obliged only to ensure the spiritual well-being of the child.

This debate on the role of spiritual and natural parents in religious education was probably behind a number of prosecu-

[15] However, in Geneva a single godparent was retained and Calvin's baptismal rite did not specify who should present the child. See J. Bossy, 'Godparenthood: the fortunes of a social institution in early modern Christianity', in K. von Greyerz, ed. *Religion and Society in Early Modern Europe 1500–1800* (London, 1981), p. 199. Early English opposition to godparents can be seen in W. Nicholson, ed., *The Remains of Edmund Grindal, D.D., Successfully Bishop of London and Archbishop of York and Canterbury, PS*, 9 (1844) p. 205.

[16] W. H. Frere and C. E. Douglas, eds, *Puritan Manifestoes. A Study of the Puritan Revolt, with a Reprint of the Admonition to the Parliament and Kindred Documents*, 1572 (repr. London, 1954), p. 28.

[17] J. Ayre, ed., *The Works of John Whitgift, PS*, 40, Pt 2 (1853), p. 120.

tions begun in the church courts, like that against Aaron Elsemere of Burstead Magna, Essex, in 1621, who, 'would be godfather to his own child in baptism; openly naming his child and answering for it, contrary to the 29 Canon.'[18] The canon referred to ratified the compromise contained in the 1564 Advertisements, previous to which no parent had been allowed to attend their child's baptism; the Jacobean Church, however, stopped short of permitting natural parents to act as godparents.[19]

Part of the reason for maintaining the distinction between natural and spiritual parents lay in the symbolism of the rite itself, by which baptism was a second birth, the priest a spiritual midwife, and the profane, natural parents replaced with spiritual ones.[20] It was the sacred character of these roles that ensured the child's entrance to the holy world of the Church; to allow the profane parents to take over this role would have destroyed the process. In contrast, Puritans, seeing salvation as a product of faith, understanding, and election, interpreted baptism as merely a confirmation and public profession. To this end children were to be instructed by their parents that they might be brought to a state of belief and all facets of the relationship we know as *parenthood* were invested in the heads of the spiritualized household.[21] It could then be argued that for England, Puritanism played a important role in the development of the modern view of parenthood. However, this is only true to the degree to which this view of responsibilities was successfully disseminated, in opposition to the official view of the Church of godparents as spiritual educators, and also that evidenced in the late medieval

[18] W. Hale, *A Series of Precedents and Proceedings from Criminal Causes, Extending from the Year 1475–1640, Extracted from the Act Books of the Ecclesiastical Courts in the Diocese of London* (Edinburgh, 1973), p. 256; this case was however dismissed on the grounds that 'by error he did stand and that Mr. Pease [presumably the incumbent] did not tell him to the contrary', see also Bromiley, *Baptism*, p. 128, and H. R. Robinson, ed., *The Zurich Letters (Second Series) Comprising the Correspondence of Several English Bishops and Others, with some of the Helvetian Reformers, During the Reign of Queen Elizabeth*, *PS*, 8 (1845), pp. 149 and 133.

[19] *The Constitutions and Canons Ecclesiastical (Made in the Year 1603, and Amended in the Year 1865:), to Which are Added the Thirty-Nine Articles of The Church of England* (London, 1908), p. 16. The 29th Canon referred to stated that 'no parent shall be urged to be present, nor be admitted to answer as Godfather for his own child . . .'. See also D. S. Bailey, *Sponsors at Baptism and Confirmation, an Historical Introduction to Anglican Practice* (London, 1952), p. 92.

[20] A. van Gennep (trans. M. B. Vizedom and G. L. Caffee), *The Rites of Passage* (London, 1960), p. 63.

[21] L. L. Schückling, *The Puritan Family: A Social Study from the Literary Sources* (London, 1969), pp. 56–95.

liturgy and canon law, which made godparents *spiritual kin* and potential surrogate parents. Understanding which of these conflicting views predominated in the society of post-Reformation England may then make a contribution to thc histories of both childhood and religion.

Assessing the degree to which godparents might have influenced and intervened in the lives of their spiritual children is extremely difficult. One place where instances of godparents acting as surrogate parents might be expected to appear is in wills: 7,500 wills were examined from the records of the Exchequer and Prerogative courts at York from the sixteenth and seventeenth centuries.[22] One of the most unusual, and most difficult to interpret, in this sample was that of Hugh Synne, a yeoman from Hull. In 1586 Synne bequeathed his eldest son, John, 'to his godfather Mr. John Lewis', his daughter, Agnes, 'to Mr. George Burrowe, my gossip and neighbour and to Joan his wife, if it please him to take her', and finally his son, James, 'to Bartholomew Burnet, master and mariner and to Elizabeth, his wife, if it please them to take him, [she is] godmother to him.'[23] Synne presents one example of a natural parent attempting to utilize three spiritual relationships in order to obtain adoption for his children. However, it is by no means clear that the 'gifts' Synne was so generous in distributing were not his children, but their portions and property, which would, in effect, have made these patrons guardians, not foster-parents. Synne also indicated that his eldest son might be rejected and if so requested his 'brother' Henry Hubbard 'to put him where he thinketh good and meet for him', implying that what was being sought was not adoption, but apprenticeship.[24]

Peter Clark has observed the ways in which sixteenth-century migrants into Kentish towns used their relationships through family and godparenthood as a basis for relocation and, in at least one case, for employment, when Humphrey Horton of Hornhill, his mother having remarried, 'was put forth to his godfather

[22] York, Borthwick Institute of Historical Research, Exchequer and Prerogative Wills, vols 9 to 52 and boxed wills for 1636 to 1652/3.

[23] Ibid., vol. 23a, fol. 394, will of Hugh Synne, 1586. In this period the term *gossip/godsib* usually referred to the relationship between two godparents of the same child or between a godparent and natural parent of a child; therefore Burrowe is probably the godparent of Agnes.

[24] Ibid.

Butcher' probably at Hythe.[25] How commonly such links were employed is difficult to judge. In one Yorkshire parish, Bilton-in-Ainsty, in 105 sixteenth- and seventeenth-century wills, twenty-seven servants, maids, and apprentices were mentioned, but although a number were clearly natural kin, there is no evidence that any were godchildren, even when use was made of the baptismal register of this parish which recorded the identities of godparents from 1571 to 1604.[26]

From the wills from the diocese of York there was one instance of an employer who was also a godparent. Henry Brigge, a husbandman from Southwood, in 1599 left 'all my goods and chattels movable and unmovable . . . all my lands, tenements and hereditaments whatsoever . . .' to '. . . my well beloved servant and godson Thomas Freke and Alice his wife'.[27] Freke was not Brigge's heir, as the bequest was only 'until such time as Thomas Leeke, my bastard son, do accomplish and come to the full age of twenty and one years'.[28] Although this suggests adoption, this time by a father's godchild, it is probable that what was being established here was simply guardianship.

Wills could be used to nominate guardians, and some godparents were requested to act as tutors, as in the case of James Turner, a yeoman from Sheffield, who in 1583 assigned 'the tuition and government of the said George Turner my son and his goods and lands unto the godly and virtuous government and education of the aforenamed, the right worshipful Jervis Kieve, his godfather . . .'; however, he also made a tutor of a natural relative 'Thomas Turner of London'.[29] Similarly, Robert Caplewood, a husbandman from Ravensfield, allocated the tuition of one of his children to 'Thomas Boland, our vicar of Conisbrough, her godfather', jointly with his brother-in-law.[30] Although the fact that these guardians were godparents was even mentioned may have been significant, it is noticeable that they both shared responsibility with natural kin and, as a civic

[25] P. Clark, 'The migrant in Kentish towns, 1580–1640', in P. Clark and P. Slack, eds, *Crisis and Order in English Towns, 1500–1700, Essays in Urban History* (London, 1972), p. 136.

[26] York, Borthwick Institute, Exchequer and Prerogative Wills, vols 9 to 52, boxed wills for 1636 to 1652/3 and Parish Registers of Bilton-in-Ainsty, Bil. 1 and Bil. 2.

[27] Ibid., Exchequer and Prerogative Wills, vol. 28b, fol. 556, will of Henry Brigge, 1599.

[28] Ibid.

[29] Ibid., vol. 22b fol. 391, will of James Turner, 1583.

[30] Ibid., vol. 28b, fol. 691, will of Robert Caplewood, 1602.

dignatory and local cleric, already presented obvious reasons for being chosen as tutors. In the 105 wills examined from Bilton-in-Ainsty, thirteen allocated tuition to persons outside the nuclear family, but in no instance was there any indication that this was to a godparent. Similarly, in the records of Tuition and Curation for the diocese of York from 1592 to 1611, of 127 bonds which gave the relationship of the guardian, none mentioned any spiritual tie to the child.[31]

Given the number of wills examined for this survey, perhaps the most significant conclusion that can be drawn is that it was unusual for godparents to take on such responsibilities. Children were orphaned much more rarely than might be expected in early modern England, and a child was unlikely to have no natural kin from whom help could be obtained.[32] This was more probable when a child was illegitimate and the father unknown, and it was perhaps to guard against this eventuality that in 1639 the incumbent of the parish of Newchurch, in Lancashire, noted pointedly in his baptismal register that the godparents of a bastard child had promised 'the educating and keeping of the child if the parents do neglect it'.[33]

As this example indicates, godparents were more likely to be called on to contribute to a child's upkeep, education, or moral development than to be asked to adopt it. To this latter end the Church, both before and after the Reformation, attempted to ensure that godparents were fit persons to act as spiritual guardians, by preventing children and non-communicants from taking the role.[34] One example of a godparent intervening in the moral life of her spiritual child is from a church court case from Essex, where a women, finding that her godchild had stolen a chicken, declared, 'Thou art my goddaughter and surely if thy parents will not convert thee I will'; and so 'There and then she beat her.'[35] Less forcefully, Dorothy Leigh suggested to her sons that they extract an assurance from any parents wishing them to act as

[31] Ibid., Register of Tuitions and Curations, 1592–1638.

[32] H. Labras and K. W. Wachter, 'Living forebears in stable populations' in K. W. Wachter, E. A. Hammel and P. Laslett, eds, *Statistical Studies of Historical Social Structure* (New York, 1978), p. 187.

[33] W. J. Kaye and E. W. W. Kaye, eds, *The Registers of Newchurch in the Township of Culcheth* = *Lancashire Parish Register Society*, 22 (1905), p. 9.

[34] Fisher, *Christian Initiation*, p. 178, and *Constitutions and Canons Ecclesiastical*, p. 16, No. 29.

[35] Cited in A. Macfarlane, *The Family Life of Ralph Josselin, a Seventeenth-Century Clergyman: an Essay in Historical Anthropology* (Cambridge, 1970), p. 144.

sponsors that the child would be taught to read the Bible as soon as possible.[36] These examples indicate that some took their duties seriously, but they do not allow the suggestion that even a significant minority of godparents did undertake the responsibilities of spiritual and moral education which the Church placed upon them.

As Dorothy Leigh's advice demonstrates, in the Reformation age religious instruction was closely tied to literacy and education. Here examples of intervention by godparents are more common, such as that of Adam Martindale's godmother, who, when he was aged five, supplied him with his first ABC.[37] Similarly, Adam Eyre in 1648 promised to find for his godson 'clothes for this year to go to school to Leeds and then to provide a calling for him'.[38] According to John Aubrey, George Abbot, born the son of poor clothworker, later Archbishop of Canterbury, had 'several persons of quality' offer themselves to be sponsors at his baptism, adding that his parents being poor 'accepted joyfully, and three were chosen, who maintained him at school, and university afterwards, his father not being able.'[39]

From the sample of Yorkshire wills examined, there is one instance of interest from a godparent in the education of a child. In 1543 Richard Palmes, a gentleman from Naburn, bequeathed to his brother William 'all such sums of money as that he oweth me and he [to give] them . . . to his son Richard my godson to be brought up with learning'.[40] However, the dual relationship (both natural and spiritual) and the nature of the gift make it difficult to stress the significance of this isolated case. Noticeably it was far more common to leave books to members of the clergy than to godchildren. While some godparents could play an important part in their spiritual children's education, it is impossible to escape the conclusion, given the sparseness of the evidence, that for the vast majority in early modern England the

[36] Cited in R. A. Houlbrooke, *The English Family, 1450–1700* (London, 1984), p. 131.
[37] R. Parkinson, ed., *The Life of Adam Martindale, Written by Himself* = Chetham Society, os 4 (1845), p. 5.
[38] C. Jackson and H. J. Morehouse, eds, *Yorkshire Diaries and Autobiographies in the Seventeenth and Eighteenth Centuries*, Surtees Society, 65 (1877), p. 5.
[39] O. L. Dick, ed., *Aubrey's Brief Lives*, 3rd edn (London, 1962), p. 114.
[40] York, Borthwick Institute, Exchequer and Prerogative Wills, vol. 11b, fol. 678, will of Richard Palmes, 1543.

responsibilities and duties of godparents ended when the christening gift was given and the baptismal feast eaten.

In these circumstances the alterations that occurred in the theoretical role of godparents seem likely to have been irrelevant in practice, and the attempt of the English Church to revitalize the institution appears largely to have failed. Still less is there any evidence that the responsibilities of godparents toward the physical care of their spiritual children were significant, and it is tempting to agree with Barbara Hanawalt's conclusion for the late medieval period that godparents rarely played an active role in the lives of their godchildren, or Alan MacFarlane's for the seventeenth century that spiritual kinship 'made little impact on everyday life' and 'obligations to instruct or assist were clearly absent.'[41]

The gap between theory and reality need not lead us to conclude that godparenthood was, or is, necessarily a failed institution, or that the majority of godparents were hypocritical. The symbolic division in the baptismal ceremony into profane and sacred worlds, the distinction between natural and spiritual kinship, meant that godparents were not so much part of the natural kinship system, as in opposition to it. Although in the late Middle Ages godparenthood created a kinship tie in a similar way to birth or marriage, with the same penalties for infringement of incest barriers, the nature of such barriers was not identical; one was due to a natural, biological connection, the other to a sacred, ceremonial bond.[42] Thus the relationship between godchild and godparent was a holy and symbolic one, although perhaps none the less important for all that, vital as it was in the ritual entry of the child into the spiritual family and household of God.[43]

This symbolism remained largely unchanged by the Reformation, and although the reformers, like the medieval Church

[41] Hanawalt, *The Ties That Bound*, p. 248, and Macfarlane, *The Family Life of Ralph Josselin*, p. 145. Interesting comparisons can be drawn with Stephen Guedman's investigations into the parallel complex of *compadrazgo* (co-parenthood) in Veraguas Province, Panama, in 'The Compadrazgo as a reflection of the spiritual and natural person', *Proceedings of the Royal Anthropological Institute* (1971), pp. 41, 56 & 60.

[42] S. Wolfram, *In-Laws and Outlaws, Kinship and Marriage in England* (London, 1988), pp. 22–3.

[43] This concept of baptism as entry to the household of God can be seen in J. Ayre, ed., *The Catechism of Thomas Becon S.T.P., Chaplain to Archbishop Cranmer, Prebendary & C., With Other Pieces Written by Him in the Reign of King Edward the Sixth*, *PS*, 11 (1844), p. 202.

authorities before them, failed in their attempts to graft on to this symbolic role a directly religious one, it was perhaps only from the mid-seventeenth century, with the temporary abolition of godparenthood under the Protectorate and the fragmentation of English religion in the years that followed, that there was a significant erosion of this status.[44] As Hooker observed, 'Ceremonies have more in weight than in sight, they work by commonness of use much.'[45] As an increasing proportion of the population became dependent for their salvation, not on the act of infant baptism and entry to *the* Church, but on membership of the body of *a* church, sect, or denomination, the role of godparents towards their spiritual children would have become increasingly dependent for its significance only on the inclinations of the individual sponsor and their personal piety.

Bedford College of Higher Education

[44] H. Davis, *Worship and Theology in England. From Andrews to Baxter and Fox, 1603–1690* (Princetown, 1975), p. 410.
[45] Hooker, *Laws of Ecclesiastical Polity*, p. 342.

'SUCH PERFECTING OF PRAISE OUT OF THE MOUTH OF A BABE': SARAH WIGHT AS CHILD PROPHET

by SUSAN HARDMAN MOORE

RECOVERING the voice of the child in the Church is hard. Christians must reckon with Jesus' instruction to be like a child, yet the Church usually measures faith by mastery of an adult vocabulary of religious experience. The historian has to dig past adult prejudices and silences. Recent research has done much to rescue the children of early modern England from anonymity. We know, for example, about the ideal of an 'ordered society', in which children and youths took their place as 'inferiors', and yet were valued and loved. We also know that the vision of order was rarely achieved, in a country swarming with juveniles.[1] Attempts to make the vision outward and visible can be seen in arrangements for seating in church, where the young sat apart from their elders, and in the all-pervasive discipline of catechizing, where the assumption that age instructs youth is inherent in the pattern of proceeding by question and answer.[2] Most of the sources that tell us about childhood, however, are heavily prescriptive, or rush past youth after listing a few predictable sins. Even spiritual testimonies provide sparse, brief recollections: vivid memories of a terrifying preacher, 'thundering and beating the pulpit', are the exception, not the rule. Is it possible that 'contemporaries did not regard the

[1] Keith Thomas, 'Children in early modern England', in Gillian Avery and Julia Briggs, eds, *Children and their Books* (Oxford, 1989), pp. 45–78, discusses recent literature; see also Susan Dwyer Amussen, *An Ordered Society: Gender and Class in Early Modern England* (Oxford, 1988); Paul Griffiths, 'Some aspects of the social history of youth in early modern England with particular reference to the period c. 1560–c. 1640' (Cambridge Ph.D. thesis, 1992); Ralph Houlbrooke, *The English Family, 1450–1700* (Harlow, 1984), pp. 127–95; Linda Pollock, *Forgotten Children: Parent-Child Relations from 1500–1900* (Cambridge, 1983); Keith Thomas, 'Age and authority in early modern England', *PBA*, 62 (1976), pp. 205–48.

[2] Margaret Aston, 'Segregation in church', in W. J. Sheils and Diana Wood, eds, *Women in the Church*, *SCH*, 27 (1990), pp. 237–94; Ian Green, '"For children in yeeres and children in understanding": the emergence of the English catechism under Elizabeth and the early Stuarts', *JEH*, 37 (1986), pp. 397–425; John Morgan, *Godly Learning: Puritan Attitudes towards Reason, Learning and Education, 1560–1640* (Cambridge, 1986), pp. 152–6.

experiences of children as intrinsically interesting'?[3] Perhaps, ironically, children's voices shout to us loudest from catechisms: not real children's voices at all, but words devised by adults to be placed in the mouths of the 'young in years and understanding'.

Sometimes, though, real children jumped out of place in a way that riveted adult attention. Such a one is Sarah Wight. She took to her bed for three months in 1647, and the great and good of Puritan London flocked to see. Her speech, her behaviour, fascinated adults. Every word and gesture was noted down. Thus when we listen for voices of children in the Church, we hear from one side the 'ideal' voice represented in catechisms; and from the other, the 'extraordinary' outpourings of a Sarah Wight. The relation between the 'ideal' and the 'extraordinary' is something I want to keep in mind as we look at her case. What assumptions about children's spirituality are revealed by grown-ups' interest in these two different voices? Can we glimpse something of the child's religious world in the interplay between the two? And how could a child leap so dramatically from periphery to centre, from inferiority to authority? What beliefs about the *being* of a child made the leap possible?

The extraordinary drama surrounding Sarah Wight began in the eyes of adults when she collapsed and lay for days, blind, deaf, and motionless. Suddenly she startled those watching her:

> A dying Christ for a denying Peter; a dying Christ for a denying Peter; a dying Christ for a denying Peter . . . Go tell Peter! . . . For a Peter, for a Mary Magdalen, for a Thief on the Cross! That none should despair . . . this is . . . Faith, believing in a full Christ to a nothing creature . . . a nothing creature . . . a nothing creature . . . To me, the chiefest of sinners . . . Christ came in to me . . .[4]

First insensible, and then with more awareness as hearing and sight returned, Sarah captured her auditors with godly words. In fact, not only her words but her whole state of being became a matter of amazement. God sustained her without food. Pressed to take more than sips of 'small beer', she replied 'I would, if I

[3] John Rogers, *Ohel or Bethshemesh* (London, 1653), p. 419; Thomas, 'Children in early modern England', p. 48. See also Steven R. Smith, 'Religion and the concept of youth in early modern England', *History of Childhood Quarterly*, 2 (1974–5), pp. 493–516.

[4] Henry Jessey, *The Exceeding Riches of Grace Advanced*, 6th edn (London, 1652), p. 16 [hereafter *ER*].

could, but I cannot, it makes me sick to think of it, Jesus Christ feeds me.'[5] Sarah was fifteen, and lived with her widowed mother in the London parish of Lawrence Pountney. Her transfiguration came after years of deep religious melancholy, a Puritan condition for which she—young, female, and from a godly gentry family—stood at high risk.[6] Convinced she was 'shut out of Heaven, and must be damn'd, damn'd, damn'd', she 'oftattempted wickedly to destroy herself . . . wretchedly bruising and wounding herself'. She tried to throw herself off a roof; she crossed the Thames to stab herself in a Lambeth ditch; she set off for the dog-house at Moorfields to be eaten alive. Her failure to do the deed simply made matters worse: 'When I had an opportunity against my life, and did not take it, then I beat my self for it most of all.' She believed, 'There's many saints have lived threescore years, that have not suffered so much as I have done in one month.' Her transformation—God 'hath brought Legion to her right minde'—gave her power to counsel her elders.[7] Henry Jessey, a constant note-taker at the bedside, grasped the value of her testimony for a wider audience. Originally from Yorkshire, Jessey ministered to a Baptist congregation in London, but had extensive connections in Puritan circles; he preached on weekdays at the church Sarah and her mother attended. He expected Sarah to die, and started to write his narrative with her end in mind. Yet after seventy-five days without food, 'when in humane reason she was unlike to live two days more', God raised her 'to EAT and ARISE', and soon after, 'to WALK'. Jessey rushed her story into print, and became known for his interest in children's religious experience.[8] As for Sarah, God continued to sustain her on scraps of

[5] Ibid., p. 56.

[6] Robert Burton, *The Anatomy of Melancholy* (New York, 1927), pp. 355–6, 1st edn (London, 1621); Lawrence Babb, *The Elizabethan Malady: A Study of Melancholia in English Literature from 1580 to 1642* (Michigan, 1951), pp. 47–54. 'Youth' was regarded as a particularly vulnerable age: see note 26.

[7] Jessey, *ER*, pp. 6–7, 127–30, 115, 50, N; Mark 5.1–13.

[8] Ibid., pp. 138, L (the tract went through eight editions in Jessey's lifetime, and four thereafter); Henry Jessey, *A Looking Glass for Children* (London, 1672); E[dward] W[histon], *The Life and Death of Mr. Henry Jessey* (London, 1671), pp. 41–2; B. R. White, 'Henry Jessey in the Great Rebellion' in R. Buick Knox, ed., *Reformation, Conformity and Dissent* (London, 1977), p. 142; Barbara Ritter Dailey, 'Youth and the New Jerusalem: the English catechistical tradition and Henry Jessey's *Catechisme for Babes* (1652)', *Harvard Library Bulletin*, 30 (1982), pp. 25–54. Jessey (1601–63) appears in *DNB* and A. G. Matthews, *Calamy Revised* (Oxford, 1934).

food. The publication of a letter of hers nine years later, to comfort those 'bewildernessed' in spirit, shows her lasting authority.[9]

It is tempting to pigeonhole Sarah among female prophets of the 1640s and 1650s—indeed, this is where she is usually placed.[10] But it is misleading to focus on Sarah's gender while disregarding her age, and the fact that Jessey presents her as a *child*. It is also tempting, perhaps, to deny Sarah a voice and see her only through Jessey's eyes: a man wrapped up with signs and wonders of the last days, when 'your sons and daughters shall prophesy'; or a collector of 'improving examples of (inevitably sickly) godly children'.[11] Her experience certainly comes out of the spiritual and political ferment of Civil War London (where the authority of age was at issue); and it has wider connections to conversion narratives, and conventions about the art of dying.[12] However, though Jessey has his own priorities in the narrative, Sarah's voice speaks too. What is more, Jessey's concern with the intrusion of the divine must not be placed in too narrow a context. Children afflicted by witches, or possessed by spirits (often with uncertainty among witnesses about whether the spirits are good or evil) are part of the matrix of children's religious experience in early modern England. Tracts about such children paid detailed attention to their speech and acts.[13] Sarah belongs with these young people, whose disorderly, extraordinary spirituality

[9] [Sarah Wight], *A Wonderful Pleasant and Profitable Letter* (London, 1656), prefatory letter by R. B. (probably Robert Bragge, minister at Sarah's church, All Hallows the Great: Matthews, *Calamy Revised*, p. 70).

[10] Patricia Crawford, *Women and Religion in England, 1500–1720* (London, 1993), pp. 97, 108, 111; Barbara Ritter Dailey, 'The visitation of Sarah Wight: holy carnival and the revolution of the saints in civil war London', *Church History*, 55 (1986), p. 451; Dorothy Ludlow, ' "Arise and be doing": English preaching women, 1640–1660' (Indiana University Ph.D. thesis, 1978), pp. 155–60; Nigel Smith, *Perfection Proclaimed: Language and Literature in English Radical Religion, 1640–1660* (Oxford, 1989), pp. 45–9.

[11] Acts 2.17; White, 'Jessey', p. 142; B. S. Capp, *The Fifth Monarchy Men* (London, 1972), pp. 22, 59.

[12] Smith, *Perfection Proclaimed*, and Dailey, 'Sarah Wight', explore her case in the spiritual and political context of the 1640s.

[13] J. A. Sharpe, *Witchcraft Accusations in Seventeenth-Century Yorkshire: Accusations and Counter-Accusations* = Borthwick Paper 81 (York, 1992), pp. 18–19 (Dr Sharpe developed these themes in a paper given at the Institute of Historical Research, 17 March 1993); D. P. Walker, *Unclean Spirits: Possession and Exorcism in France and England in the Late Sixteenth and Early Seventeenth Centuries* (London, 1981), pp. 49–73; Michael MacDonald, ed., *Witchcraft and Hysteria in Elizabethan London: Edward Jorden and the Mary Glover Case* (London and New York, 1991); Keith Thomas, *Religion and the Decline of Magic* (Harmondsworth, 1978), pp. 569–88; see also John Demos, *Entertaining Satan: Witchcraft and the Culture of Early New England* (New York and Oxford, 1982), pp. 157–65.

betrays a close encounter with supernatural power—whether divine or demonic, the symptoms were remarkably similar. After some spectacular cases in late Elizabethan and Jacobean England, spirit possession became a cause of conflict between Puritans and church authorities. (Jane Hawkins, for example, uttered pious verses from her bed to 200 amazed hearers, with the vicar, curate, and schoolmaster taking notes: discredited by the bishop, she next appeared in Massachusetts, known for 'much familiarity with the devil'.) 'Good possession' revived in the 1640s, and Sarah proved a famous example.[14] Martha Hatfield and Anna Trapnel owe much to her. Ministers who knew Henry Jessey surrounded eleven-year-old Martha, a Yorkshire lass (the dedication of Jessey's tract included his friends there); Anna, somewhat older and later famous for political prophecy, stood at Sarah's bedside in 1647 and fell into her first trance just as Sarah recovered.[15] Such marvels unite soul and body, inspiration and illness, in a tradition that stretches forward to 'religious madness' among early Methodists.[16] The irruption of supernatural power in children therefore provides a broad context for the narrative. Adults of Sarah's day found stereotypes of witches and atheists a powerful aid to defining what it was to be godly.[17] Could the exceptional spiritual experiences of children have served some similar purpose? Did the extraordinary help to shape the ideal? We shall come back to this at the end. First we need to look more closely at Sarah as a child 'out of place'—in her family, in her exercise of authority, and in the extraordinary state of her body; and then turn to her relation with her audience.

Sarah's confession that 'Nothing more burdens me, than my murmurings and disobedience against my Mother' takes us to a critical point of disorder, and shows how Sarah wrestled with the prescriptive voice of Puritan instruction. 'Honour thy father and

[14] Walker, *Unclean Spirits*, p. 78; for Hawkins (1629), Public Record Office, SP 16/141/63, SP16/142/19, and David D. Hall, ed., *Witch-Hunting in Seventeenth-Century New England* (Boston, 1991), p. 20.

[15] Nigel Smith, 'A Child Prophet: Martha Hatfield as *The Wise Virgin*', in Avery and Briggs, *Children and their Books*, p. 80; Jessey, *ER*, pp. R [1647 edn], 139; Smith, *Perfection Proclaimed*, pp. 49–53; C. Burrage, 'Anna Trapnel's Prophecies', *EHR*, 26 (1911), pp. 526–35.

[16] Michael MacDonald, 'Religion, social change and psychological healing in England, 1600–1800', in W. J. Sheils, ed., *The Church and Healing*, *SCH*, 19 (1982), pp. 101–25.

[17] Stuart Clark, 'Inversion, misrule, and the meaning of witchcraft', *PaP*, 87 (1980), pp. 98–127; Michael Hunter, 'The problem of atheism in early modern England', *TRHS*, 5th series, 35 (1985), pp. 135–57.

thy mother' was a vital text for children. Sarah illustrates the effect of this commandment on a young imagination. Jessey presents Sarah as *daughter*.[18] Mary Wight is a powerful but shadowy figure at Sarah's bedside. She had suffered notoriously from melancholy herself, so much so that Sarah lived with her grandmother in her early years. Jessey first met the family when he counselled Mary Wight. An important moment comes when Sarah, reconciled with God, is reconciled to her mother. Still blind and deaf, she cried out: 'Have I not a Mother somewhere?'

> Her mother . . . took her Daughters hand, and put it to her own neck, where her Daughter felt a skare, that was there through the enemy: whereby her Daughter, knowing her, cast her head into her Mothers bosom, and wept greatly and kissed her, and stroaked her face, and said, 'I know you Mother, and I love you with another love, than I loved you before.'[19]

Did the 'skare' mark an attempt at suicide? Sarah's disordered relations with her mother could be approached from a psychological or sociological angle, but here I would like to draw out the implications in the context of Puritan teaching. Puritans rarely forgot what we usually do— the second half of the fifth commandment. A New Testament gloss highlights its importance: ' "Honour your father and your mother" is the first commandment to carry a promise with it: "that it may be well with you and that you may live long on the earth." ' Honour to God and honour to parents were synonymous in early modern Europe.[20] Popular Puritan writers like William Gouge believed obedience to parents was 'one of the surest evidences of our conformity to the whole law'. Obedience included (significantly for Sarah) bearing with a parent's infirmities of fear and grief, even covering up parents' frailties (as Shem 'covered' drunken Noah). Gouge drew a stern corollary from the promise of long life to those who honoured parents: disobedience shortens chil-

[18] Jessey, *ER*, p. 24. Jessey's insistence reflects the notion that mental disturbance could be measured best against the proper patterns of family order: Michael MacDonald, *Mystical Bedlam: Madness, Anxiety, and Healing in Seventeenth-Century England* (Cambridge, 1981), pp. 126–8.

[19] Jessey, *ER*, pp. 5, K, 24–5.

[20] Eph. 6.1–3; John Bossy, 'Moral arithmetic: Seven Sins into Ten Commandments', in Edmund Leites, ed., *Conscience and Casuistry in Early Modern Europe* (Cambridge, 1988), p. 233.

dren's days. John Dod and Robert Cleaver agreed: 'As honouring of parents brings a long and happy life: so dishonouring of parents should make [children] have a short life and miserable; or if a long life, yet full of God's curses, for their unrepented sinne.'[21] So Sarah could moan, 'If all kinds of death were put together in one, it was too good for me. I walked continually in fire and brimstone for rebelling and murmuring against God, and against a Parent.'[22] Her contemporary, Robert Burton, blamed such torments on rigid preachers of predestination. Sarah's plight expressed itself in religious terms, but its root is closer to the recent suggestion that youthful suicide was a mute rebellion against abuse.[23] The ideal voice of Puritan prescription chafed against experience. Her melancholy and self-injury strongly connect with inability to live up to godly expectations of family order.

If Sarah was out of place in her family, she was also out of place in her exercise of authority. Again we can see the interaction of the ideal and the extraordinary. As a well-catechized child, she conjured with a moral universe where small sins had cosmic consequences, and the young stood in particular danger of the devil's assaults. Hilaire Belloc's *Cautionary Tales for Children* (1907) parody such a universe. Jim, who ran away from nurse, gets eaten by a lion: the moral, '. . . always keep a-hold of Nurse/ For fear of finding something worse.'[24] Disobedient Sarah, slipping past her sleeping mother on to the roof to throw herself off, met 'Satan as a roaring lion', 'seeking whom he may devour'.[25] Calvinist preachers believed even an elect child had to be brought to conviction of sin, and invoked the roaring devil, warning of a contest for the soul. 'Youth' was the most 'slippery age', when the development of a godly conscience

[21] William Gouge, *Of Domesticall Duties* (London, 1622), pp. 143–8, 470–1; John Dod and Robert Cleaver, *A Plaine and Familiar Exposition of the Ten Commandments* (London, 1606), p. 193.

[22] Jessey, *ER*, p. 42.

[23] Burton, *Anatomy*, pp. 961–4; MacDonald, *Mystical Bedlam*, p. 224; Terence R. Murphy, ' "Wofull Childe of Parents Rage": suicide of children and adolescents in early modern England', *Sixteenth Century Journal*, 17 (1986), pp. 269–70.

[24] Hilaire Belloc, *Complete Verse* (London, 1991), p. 261. For the influence of Puritan moralism on children's literature of the Victorian era, see Gillian Avery, 'The puritans and their heirs', in Avery and Briggs, *Children and their Books*, pp. 95–118.

[25] Jessey, *ER*, p. 128; I Peter 5.8; Burton, *Anatomy*, p. 878, reflects common use of the image in melancholy talk.

could go awry.[26] Sarah mirrored this teaching back at her teachers: ' "The Devil fights with me, as he did with Michael and his Angels. Do you not see him? Do you not see him?" and she struck with the back of her hand.' Godly children, of course, were not supposed to give imagination free rein: 'Read no Ballads and foolish Books, but a Bible, and the Plaine mans pathway to Heaven . . . read the Histories of the Martyrs. . . . Read also often treatises of Death, and Hell, and Judgement . . . . Sarah's vocabulary reflects this diet, especially when she declares herself worse than 'all the sinners I ever read of or heard of.'[27] She had listened to grown-ups' conversations and read their books. Holding forth from her bed in 1647, she proved her mastery of adult language. Jessey annotated her words to show how close they were to Scripture. The catechized child had turned catechizer.

The extraordinary state of Sarah's body signified to those around her the play of supernatural forces in her soul. First, extreme violence: in her terror, she beat her head against the wall 'till it swell'd abundantly, and the more she dasht it . . . the less she felt it.' Then, a tense stillness that became tranquillity: 'Her hands were clinch'd up together, and so were her feet, as if it were by the Cramp; and her mouth was drawn up, as a purse; & her eyes were with the ey-lids folded up and closed; and her hearing was taken from her.' When her mother ventured to touch her in her trance, she stirred, troubled, saying ' "Why do you hinder my Communion with God?" '[28] Words were part of the physical display. The force of words in early modern England is not something well understood. Here, words threatened to destroy Sarah: she felt impelled to 'blaspheme God and die', but could not get the blasphemy out because God smote her tongue. Then God gave a 'new tongue', lower, quieter, faster: she moved from blasphemy to perfect praise.[29] Jessey emphasized Sarah's fast after she received God's comfort, but she refused food beforehand, too. What changes is not so much her eating pattern, but

[26] Smith, 'Religion and the concept of youth', pp. 497–502; Griffiths, 'Social history of youth', pp. 20–60; Thomas, 'Children in early modern England', p. 46, notes continuity here with medieval perceptions.

[27] Jessey, *ER*, p. 19; [Thomas White], *A Little Book for Little Children* (London, 1660), cited by Avery, 'Puritans and their heirs', p. 97; *ER*, p. 43.

[28] Jessey, *ER*, pp.128, 60–1, 19.

[29] Ibid., pp. 14, 88, 36, 115; Sharpe, *Witchcraft Accusations*, pp. 9–10.

her interpretation of it. Young women who survive on the Eucharist alone are familiar in Catholic piety. Sarah gave this theme a Protestant treatment.[30] In her despair, she felt 'strongly perswaded that what I did eat or drink, it was as the unworthy eating the Sacrament, I did . . . eat and drink my own Damnation.' Later, she explained, 'My stomach was then filld with terror, that I could not eat, and now with joy'; 'God hath given me Christ to feed upon; and his flesh is meat indeed; and his blood drink indeed.' When asked 'What promise have you, that any should live without food?' she answered, 'Man lives not by bread alone but by every word that proceedeth out of the mouth of God.'[31] This must be understood in the context of practices in Sarah's church: frequent fasting, frequent feeding on the Word in preaching, and a well-fenced Lord's Table.[32] Jessey proclaimed her return to health by the simplest of childish acts: she sits up, she combs her hair, she eats broiled fish, she walks. She was Jairus's daughter restored to life.[33] Whatever the cause of her sickness,[34] Sarah's body language took its cues from a rich repertoire of precedents in exciting tales of sin and sinners—'devil in the nursery' tracts on bewitched and possessed children, the suicidal despair of Francis Spira, the melancholy of Joan Drake and Mrs Honywood—not to mention what she learned at her mother's knee (popular belief had it that melancholy could be inherited), and what she picked up in church.[35] The adult witnesses gathered round the bed knew all the precedents for her state better than she. If Sarah did not know what signs they were looking for, no doubt she soon found out.

[30] Caroline Walker Bynum, *Holy Feast and Holy Fast: the Religious Significance of Food to Medieval Women* (Berkeley, 1987); Rudolph M. Bell, *Holy Anorexia* (Chicago, 1985); Fulvio Tomizza, *Heavenly Supper: the Story of Maria Janis* (English edn Chicago, 1991). Walter Vandereycken and Ron Van Deth, 'Miraculous Maids? Self-Starvation and Fasting Girls', *History Today*, 43 (August, 1993), pp. 37–42, discuss cases of extraordinary abstinence from food, from the 1660s to the nineteenth century, as the connecting link between medieval fasting and modern anorexia.

[31] Jessy, *ER*, pp. N, 116, 57.

[32] Murray Tolmie, *The Triumph of the Saints* (Cambridge, 1977), p. 109.

[33] Jessey, *ER*, pp. 137–43; Mark 5.42–3.

[34] Dailey, 'Sarah Wight', pp. 445–6, discusses medical interest in the case; Smith, 'Martha Hatfield', the relation between illness and prophecy; MacDonald, *Witchcraft and Hysteria*, 'Introduction', discusses the character of hysteria.

[35] On children, see note 13 above; for Spira and Drake, Dailey, 'Sarah Wight', pp. 441–4; for Honywood, Thomas, *Religion and the Decline of Magic*, p. 145; for inherited melancholy, Burton, *Anatomy*, pp. 184–8.

The question of audience is crucial, of course, if we are trying to determine how a child could leap from inferiority to authority. Scepticism frequently greeted children's claims, but when the balance tipped from suspicion to credulity, the child held enormous power—as the Salem witch trials show. Jessey knew the need for favourable 'eye and ear-witness'. He reported Sarah's watchers 'so affected, even to admiration, in hearing a Child so speak . . . it cannot affect so much in hearing it at second hand.' He listed about seventy visitors who wondered at her, with a penchant for rank that makes it a Who's Who of Puritan London.[36] Sarah was clearly an object of curiosity, medical and otherwise. People talked about whether she was mad or deluded, possessed by the devil, or a plain counterfeiter. One Dr Cox inferred that people made up tales of despair just to see what she would say, and asked, 'Whether find you a tickling of pride, or hypocrisie, when so many people, and some great ones, come to see you? do you not ask who were the great people, when they are gone?'[37] Henry Jessey allowed scepticism to surface only to despatch it. (Martha Hatfield's credentials were likewise defended by her relator: 'I cannot think that Satan would have bin a mid-wife to help to birth so many masculine sentences . . . as this child hath uttered.')[38] The social dynamics of witch-hunts show the complex circumstantial character of the shift from scepticism to belief, and indeed of interpreting signs as good or evil. Sarah's 'believers' secured her a reputation for sanctity, instead of madness or mischief. For those who accepted her authenticity, her authority came from the particular intensity with which she felt and resolved common patterns of religious anxiety. She marked the boundaries, to show how low you could go, and how high. Since God had brought her 'from the jaws of Hell, to the joys of Heaven', her voice had compelling power.[39]

Sarah's role in testing the extremities of religious experience brings us, in conclusion, to assess what assumptions her watchers made about a child's *being*. That is, what beliefs about a child's

[36] Jessy, *ER*, pp. 39, 36, R, 8–9. Smith, *Perfection Proclaimed*, pp. 46–7, 49, and Dailey, 'Sarah Wight', comment on Sarah's role in cementing communities of piety and politics.

[37] Ibid., p. 119. On discernment and fraud, Sharpe, *Witchcraft Accusations*, p. 13; Walker, *Unclean Spirits*.

[38] James Fisher, *The Wise Virgin* (London, 1653), pp. 17–18.

[39] Jessey, *ER*, pp. 150–1; MacDonald, *Witchcraft and Hysteria*, pp. xxxix–xlvii.

spiritual character made her claims credible? This takes us beyond the function of Sarah's experience (for Sarah herself, or her community), into theological, ontological territory; to the heart of the reasons why children could move from inferiority to authority. Young voices in catechisms and young voices possessed stand as two poles in adult perceptions of children's experience. The important ground between them is the vulnerability of the young to supernatural powers: 'vulnerable' rather than 'innocent', given the taint of original sin. Popular wisdom held that the soul grew with the body, a view perhaps to remember when preachers say that godly conscience developed, with youth as a critical time.[40] So, on the one hand, catechizing kept the devil at bay; yet, on the other, spectacular intrusions of supernatural power, divine or diabolical, could be expected. The exceptional thus strengthened the case for routine catechizing (while catechizing equipped children to give their elders a startling experience, and could both create and discharge tension, as in Sarah's case). It has been argued that accounts of Sarah and her like emerged as a consequence, an extension, of the catechism.[41] This misses the dynamism between 'ideal' and 'extraordinary' voice, in an age when truth was investigated by probing its opposite: as William Gouge put it, 'Contraries laid together doe much set forth each other in their lively colours.'[42] Just as stereotypes of witches and atheists played their part in defining what it was to be godly, so the spiritual traumas of children promoted 'normal' ways of growing up in the Church. Is it too far-fetched to see a parallel between adult fascination with children's spiritual adventures and the popularity of tracts on misshapen births? Sarah's narrative was, after all, a narrative of 'new birth'. Viewing her as a child on the way to adulthood, rather than simply as a woman prophet, sheds a new perspective on her experience—though it is not surprising to find women and children (particularly girls) occupying the same 'abnormal' ground, or even opposing each other on that ground, as when children accuse witches; both are 'muted groups' in the ordered society. Sarah's story, far from being part of a quirky genre of

[40] Thomas, 'Age and authority', p. 210.
[41] Smith, 'Martha Hatfield', p. 79.
[42] Gouge, *Of Domesticall Duties*, 'Epistle Dedicatory'.

'improving stories' of godly children, fits into a dynamic of thought about the spiritual character of the young. Extraordinary stories sowed the seeds for the improving story, of course (Sarah's was reprinted as such in the nineteenth century), but the dynamic changes when witches are confined to fairy stories and childish innocence comes into vogue.[43] A contemporary compared the exceptionally godly child to the prophet Jonah, 'who had bin so close a student in the Whales belly Colledge': the very strangeness of the messenger made the message 'take the more'. When the child steps from periphery to centre, the exceptional shapes the truth: 'such perfecting of praise out of the mouth of a babe'.[44]

King's College London

[43] Avery, 'Puritans and their heirs', and John Sharp, 'Juvenile holiness: Catholic revivalism among children in Victorian Britain', *JEH*, 35 (1984), pp. 220–38, comment on the changing context for children's spirituality.

[44] Fisher, *Wise Virgin*, pp. 135–6; Jessey, *ER*, p. 151.

PRESCRIPTION AND PRACTICE: PROTESTANTISM AND THE UPBRINGING OF CHILDREN, 1560–1700

by ANTHONY FLETCHER

HOW children should be brought up is an everlasting question that vexed our forefathers just as much as ourselves. The most obvious difference between most of the thinking and writing that goes on about it today and that of the early modern period is that a largely secular approach has replaced a fundamentally and deeply religious one. So it is natural that the historian of this period should ask how and in what ways Protestantism changed things in this respect. What emerges in facing this issue, in a peculiarly acute form, is the common historical problem of relating prescription to practice. Patrick Collinson has remarked upon the 'stark contradiction' between 'the austere severity of the conduct books and what little can be glimpsed of the real world outside these texts'.[1] It is this contradiction that my paper addresses. I shall approach it as follows. First I will explore the conduct-book advice about parental duty and practice and about children's obligations to their parents. This provides what we may call the Puritan way of upbringing. I shall relate this to some material from personal sources, like diaries and autobiographies, about what may actually have happened in the home. I will then turn to schooling, which, in its new scale and intensity, can be seen as a crucial social development in Elizabethan and Stuart England, fired in large part by the Protestant evangelizing impulse and its concomitant propaganda of social order. The burgeoning grammar schools, it will be argued, were the principal public instrument of a new and purposeful construction of masculinity. Girls, meanwhile, were being educated, by and large at home, in a conception of femininity which was developed from scriptural teaching. There was less contradiction here between prescription

[1] Patrick Collinson, *The Birthpangs of Protestant England: Religion and Cultural Change in the Sixteenth and Seventeenth Centuries* (London, 1988), p. 78. I am grateful to my wife Tresna and to Elizabeth Foyster for their comments on this paper.

and practice. The overall purpose of my paper is to relate the origins of the construction of gender in early modern England to the process of Protestantization. My argument revolves around contrasts in the values informing the upbringing of boys and girls and between the two worlds of home and school.

The core of early modern thinking about the child was that he was a being lacking in self-control, which came slowly in adolescence and early adulthood as reason and emotional maturity were established. Proverbs equated children with animals, fools, and lunatics. Contemporaries drew upon animal similes from the Old Testament: the young were 'like wild asses and wild heifers' or 'like a young colt, wanton and foolish, till he be broken by education and correction'. 'What wast thou, being an infant', asked Lewis Bayly, 'but a brute having the shape of a man?'[2] Lacking the defences of the adult, the child was prone to evil, 'even', said William Gouge, 'as rank ground is subject to bring forth many weeds'. The crux of the argument about original sin, put most didactically by Puritans, that parents should beat their children was the need to free them from evil. John Robinson, pastor on the *Mayflower*, said that the 'natural pride' of children had to be 'broken and beaten down'.[3] Citing Proverbs 20, 22, and 23, William Gouge described beating children as 'physick to purge out much corruption which lurketh in children and as a salve to heal many wounds and sores made by their folly.' Matthew Griffith based the case for chastisement of the young on the dictum in Proverbs that 'Folly is bound up in the heart of a child.' The question of the role of physical punishment in the upbringing of children is necessarily a principal theme of this paper.

The upbringing of children, in Gouge's view, was a highly demanding task, requiring constant application of admonition and correction, for 'The apprehension of children is fickle and their memory is weak.' 'If they be but once or seldom or slightly instructed', he warned, 'that which is taught will soon slip away and do little or no good.' This was why the inculcation of piety

[2] Citations from K. Thomas, 'Age and authority in early modern England', *PBA*, 52 (1976), p. 218; Michael MacDonald, *Mystical Bedlam: Madness, Anxiety, and Healing in Seventeenth-Century England* (Cambridge, 1981), p. 43. See also C. John Sommerville, *The Discovery of Childhood in Puritan England* (Athens, Georgia, 1992), p. 189.

[3] Cited in Collinson, *Birthpangs of Protestant England*, p. 78.

was the only sure basis for a proper Christian life, for piety held the whole structure of moral adulthood in place. Piety, declared Gouge, was

> the best thing that a parent can teach his child for as reason maketh a man differ from a beast and as learning and civility maketh a wise and sober man differ from savages and swaggerers, so piety maketh a sound Christian much more to differ from the most civil and well ordered natural man that can be.[4]

It is almost thirty years since Christopher Hill introduced us to the notion of the spiritualization of the household as a key feature of the Protestant Reformation. The subject has been much explored in the interim, but others have only added detail to the basic prescriptive case that Hill showed was being promulgated in the decades between Elizabeth's accession and the Civil War.[5] 'Parents and masters of families are in God's stead to their children and servants', insisted John Mayne in 1623. 'Every chief householder hath . . . the charge of the souls in his family', declared Daniel Cawdrey in *Family Reformation Promoted*. 'Let every master of a family see to what he is called', announced Thomas Taylor, 'namely to make his house a little church, to instruct every one of his family in the fear of God, to contain every one of them under holy discipline, to pray with them and for them.'[6] The central texts for the upbringing of children in the godly household which will be drawn upon here are the advice books by John Dod and Robert Cleaver, Gouge, and Griffith. They share a common programme of parental duty which can also be found in outline in works such as William Ames's *Conscience with the Power and Cases Thereof*. It can be summarized as nourishing children until they are independent, nurturing them in the fear of God with good discipline; instructing them in God's ways; providing training for an honest calling, and

[4] William Gouge, *Of Domesticall Duties* (London, 1622), pp. 545, 551, 558, 560; M. Griffith, *Bethel* (1633), p. 366.

[5] E.g. L. L. Schucking, *The Puritan Family: a Social Study from the Literary Sources* (London, 1969); Margo Todd, *Christian Humanism and the Puritan Social Order* (Cambridge, 1987), pp. 96–117; Kathleen M. Davies, 'The sacred condition of equality—How original were Puritan doctrines of marriage?' *Social History*, 5 (1977), pp. 563–80.

[6] Citations from Christopher Hill, *Society and Puritanism in Pre-Revolutionary England* (London, 1964), pp. 452, 455.

arranging a fit marriage. Parents should take all the provident care they could for their children's temporal and spiritual good.[7]

Three aspects of this programme deserve our attention: the demand for outward marks of deference and obedience, the religious education of the young, and the control of their behaviour by admonition and beating. So far as the first is concerned, Dod and Cleaver, Gouge, and Griffith all required silence in the presence of elders and 'no stout answers', uncovering the head, bending the knee, standing in the presence of elders, rising before them and bowing as appropriate. Dod and Cleaver emphasized the general importance of teaching children 'how to behave themselves decently in their going, in their speaking and gesture of their bodies'.[8] They defined a spiritual upbringing as one in 'fear and nurture of the Lord, shamefastness, hatred of vice and love of all virtue'.[9] All the conduct-book writers emphasized the importance of inculcating the habits of reading the Bible and of attendance at church as soon as children could 'sit reverently or fruitfully'. Dod and Cleaver were particularly concerned about an early start in the first principles of religion:

> so soon as by age they are able to perceive and understand the same that they may (as it were) suck in godliness with their mother's milk and straightways after their cradle may be nourished with the tender food of virtue towards that blessed life . . . so soon as the child can begin to speak his tongue should be employed to glorify God . . . by learning some short catechism containing the principles and grounds of Christian Religion.

Gouge stressed the importance of an early start in sabbath observance and in teaching the significance of special observances, such as the 5 November commemoration and fasts marking occasions of plague. There was a good deal of criticism of parents who were seen as slack in these duties. Gouge thought many parents taught their children 'prophaneness, pride, riot, lying, and deceit'; some, he believed, not only neglected catechizing but did not even teach the Lord's Prayer, the Creed, and the Ten

[7] John Morgan, *Godly Learning: Puritan Attitudes towards Reason, Learning and Education 1560–1640* (Cambridge, 1986), p. 150. For a general account see Schucking, *Puritan Family*, pp. 56–95.

[8] Gouge, *Domesticall Duties*, pp. 436–43.

[9] J. Dod and R. Cleaver, *A Godly Form of Household Government* (1614), sigs Q1, R3.

Commandments; many set a bad example by swearing, drinking, and playing unlawful games. Griffith was scathing about parents who pleaded they could not rule their child: 'This may be so indeed but where lies the fault? Is it not because thou did'st pamper him being young? Or not bend him while he was pliable?' 'Wild beasts may be tamed and wild colts by custom be brought to the saddle and are content to be led by the bridle', Dod and Cleaver advised parents who made excuses for themselves.[10]

Robert Schnucker's systematic analysis of twenty-two sources for attitudes to discipline, ranging from conduct books to commentaries on relevant biblical passages, sermons, and catechisms, all published between 1560 and 1634, reveals much general consistency in the rules laid down about the beating of children. We should note that none of this material shows any signs at all of gender distinctions, and it is taken for granted that a mother's disciplinary powers are equal to those of the father, though he was normally expected to take the initiative. She must support him in questions of punishment, as in other matters, whatever her private doubts. In the first place, physical correction should only be applied when verbal reproof failed to have effect. How hard a child was beaten should depend on his or her age, temperament, and state of physical and moral development. The use of wisdom in discipline was strongly enjoined, with warnings in many cases about excessive violence. A parent should never act in anger for, as Robert Cleaver put it, 'He that commeth to reform in anger shall hardly keep a measure in rebuking or chastising.' Every writer insisted that a clear explanation of the offence should precede punishment, and when God's express commandment had been broken, as in cases of swearing, lying, or stealing, this should be made evident.[11]

Reading these texts, for all the limitations that were imposed, one cannot but conclude that Puritan clerics believed that all children would need to be beaten at some time and some more than others. 'Is it not right that they should be?' asks the father in Thomas Becon's *Catechism*, and the model son replies: 'Yes

[10] Gouge, *Domesticall Duties*, pp. 546–51; Dod and Cleaver, *A Godly Form*, sig. Q3.

[11] Robert V. Schnucker, 'Puritan attitudes towards childhood discipline, 1560–1634', in Valerie Fildes, ed., *Women as Mothers in Pre-Industrial England: Essays in Memory of Dorothy McLaren* (London, 1990), pp. 108–16.

most lawfully. For moderate correction is as necessary for children as meat and drink.'[12] The buttocks, according to Batty, were specially created by God to receive just correction in childhood without serious bodily injury.[13] William Gouge insisted that a child was 'much more sensible of smart than words': children were kept by this correction 'in filial awe'; 'as trees well pruned and ground well tilled they will bring forth pleasant and abundant fruit'. 'Stripes and blows', he declared, were 'a means appointed by God to help the good nurture and education of children.' It was, he showed with ample scriptural citation, 'by the Holy Ghost both expressly commanded and also very often pressed'.[14] Levin Schucking described Gouge's system of punishment as 'pietistic' in character. It was more than this for it was also ritualistic: father and child were bound in a collusive bending to God's decree, the one acting in love and lifting up 'the heart for direction and blessing' as he took up the rod, the other bowing the head to receive the stripes inflicted as the physic to purge corruption. Richard Baxter, in the same frame of mind, would have the child read the passages of Scripture on the strength of which the beating was to be given and kneel after it was over to entreat God to 'bless and sanctify' its effects.[15]

So what of practice? The outward marks of deference recommended by the Puritan clerics were almost certainly only shown by children in a minority of strict Puritan households, like that of the widowed Lady Alice Wandesford, where in the 1640s we are told the children knelt daily after the morning Bible reading to receive her blessing.[16] Gouge admitted that he knew this practice was in decay in the homes of members of his Blackfriars congregation and sought to reinforce it by showing its lawfulness in Scripture.[17] John Aubrey reminisced about gentlemen in the Middle Ages who used to stand 'like mutes and fools bareheaded before their parents', which suggests that prescription in this area was probably at a loss in the face of changing custom.[18]

[12] Schucking, *Puritan Family*, pp. 74–5.
[13] Fildes, *Women as Mothers*, p. 117.
[14] Gouge, *Domesticall Duties*, pp. 560–1.
[15] Schucking, *Puritan Family*, p. 74.
[16] Lawrence Stone, *The Family, Sex and Marriage in England 1500–1800* (London, 1977), pp. 155, 171.
[17] Gouge, *Domesticall Duties*, p. 443.

So far as the spiritual upbringing of children in the household is concerned, we have the vivid examples of leadership by those Puritan patriarchs and clerics who, following the model of the advice-book writers, sought to inculcate godliness through household religion. Lay exemplars of this pattern included Sir Nathaniel Barnardiston in Suffolk, John Bruen in Cheshire, Sir James Harrington in Rutland, Thomas Scott in Kent, and Sir Christopher Wandesford, who as Master of the Rolls in Ireland during the 1630s held family prayers three times a day, at 6.00 a.m., 10.00 a.m., and 9.00 p.m. Barnardiston's care for his children's souls, Samuel Clark recorded, showed itself in 'a constant and serious study for their education in the most exact and strict way of pure and paternal religion'. His spiritual counsels were designed towards stirring them up 'to a strict watchfulness over themselves and a close walking with God'. John Bruen, having risen early, would ring a bell to awaken the rest of the family at Stapleford, summoning them to household devotions. These consisted of psalm singing, the reading of a chapter of the Bible, and prayers. Sir James Harrington maintained a regime of weekly catechizing, expounding the Scriptures and repetition of sermons at Ridlington for over twenty years.[19] Thomas Scott prefaced family supper with a Bible reading and sometimes followed it by reading from the sermons of celebrated divines and psalm singing.[20] No doubt many Puritan clerics followed similar lines of household duty. Henry Newcome recorded in his diary how he had adopted Robert Bolton's teaching that he should pray six times daily, twice in secret, twice with his wife, and twice with his family.[21] Samuel Fairclough, Barnardiston's pastor at Kedington, spent Sunday evenings examining his family on the day's sermon, leading them in prayer, and concluding with a psalm.[22]

Children nurtured in households of these kinds could not but receive the imprint of the Protestant faith. Yet such households,

18 Stone, *Family, Sex and Marriage*, p. 171.

19 J. T. Cliffe, *The Puritan Gentry: The Great Puritan Families of Early Stuart England* (London, 1984), pp. 69–70; R. C. Richardson, *Puritanism in North-west England: A Regional Study of the Diocese of Chester to 1642* (Manchester, 1972), pp. 91–2.

20 Stone, *Family, Sex and Marriage*, p. 155.

21 Thomas Heywood, ed., *The Diary of Henry Newcome* = Chetham Society, 23 (London, 1849).

22 Patrick Collinson, *The Religion of Protestants: The Church in English Society 1559–1625* (Oxford, 1982), p. 265.

we must remember, were no more than beacons in the wilderness of a country, from Elizabeth's reign to the Restoration, but half-reformed: they were not typical, they were not even numerous among the gentry, let alone among the population at large.[23] Richard Baxter's instructions to the pastors of his neighbourhood in Worcestershire, in his 1683 tract *The Catechising of Families*, brings us down to earth with a bump:

> If you could but get the rulers of families to do their duty, to take up the work where you left it, and help it on, what abundance of good might be done . . .Go occasionally among them . . . and ask the master of the family whether he prays with them and reads the scripture or what he doth? Labour to convince such as neglect this of their sin.

Baxter wanted the local clergy to persuade every household head to have children and servants repeating the catechism before him on Sunday evenings.[24] What a potent but unrealistic vision of evangelization! The stormtroopers of Protestantism placed huge faith in catechizing and some, like Eusebius Paget, claimed that it worked. He related the catechizing regime of the Ishams in Northamptonshire during the 1570s, asserting that shepherds, carters, milkmaids, and kitchen boys from the estate and household all received some benefit. But, as Patrick Collinson has pointed out, we can be sure that most milkmaids and kitchen boys remained beyond the catechizer's reach. Moreover, all those English children who lacked the peculiar and exacting pattern of religious discipline imposed in the godly household were hardly going to be receptive to learning the catechism. It was not going to be possible, in Collinson's words, 'to implant a religion consisting of patterns of printed words in heads which had little use for words of this kind and which must have found it very difficult to convert the words into authentic and meaningful experience.'[25]

So if the evangelizers failed to bring the vast majority of households to the practice of exacting spiritual exercises, did they at least persuade most parents to beat the sinfulness out of

[23] A. J. Fletcher, 'Oliver Cromwell and the Godly Nation', in J. S. Morrill, ed., *Oliver Cromwell and the English Revolution* (London, 1990), p. 214–16.

[24] Todd, *Christian Humanism and the Puritan Social Order*, p. 105.

[25] Collinson, *Religion of Protestants*, pp. 232–4.

their children? The answer, though our evidence here is thin, must be almost certainly not. 'In the light of all we know about medieval society', writes Shulamith Shahar, 'it is highly implausible to assume that small children were never beaten.'[26] The same goes for early modern society, but, since this is a matter which stirs deep emotions both in the one who inflicts the punishment and the one who submits to it, there seems to be a case for assuming that it is the kind of thing we could expect to find record of in the intimate pages of diaries, personal memoirs, and autobiographies where it occurred. This can be in no way conclusive, but few such records do, in fact, contain such references.[27] Since those that survive are heavily weighted towards Puritans and towards the clergy, it is not surprising that some parents do turn out to have followed the prescriptive line. Henry Newcome beat his twelve-year-old boy: 'I discharged my duty of correction to my poor child, prayed with him after, entreating the Lord that it might be the last correction (if it were his will) that he should need.'[28] One can detect the note of parental anguish, but at the same time a father's settled conviction that his child's inherent sinfulness had to be combated by the use of corrective physical force. Against Newcome we can set Ralph Josselin, who it is fairly clear never took up the rod, a deeply fond father, whose sorrow at the loss of children who died young is palpable, and who, despite all his threats to his unruly younger son John, could not bring himself to disinherit him.[29] Then we have Sir Robert and Lady Brilliana Harley, the model of a Protestant couple, who doted on their heir Edward yet, by his own testimony, had evidently beaten him at times in his childhood: 'My parents were noble, wise and, above all, godly . . . they instructed me in the fear of God and never cockered me in any evil but always corrected it.' Against the Harleys, we can set Sir Nathaniel Barnardiston, who rejected physical punishment of his children altogether in favour of the simple force of his obvious disapproval: 'He would never correct them, nay, not so

[26] Shulamith Shahar, *Childhood in the Middle Ages* (London, 1990), p. 111.

[27] For a general survey see Linda A. Pollock, *Forgotten Children: Parent-Child Relations from 1500–1900* (Cambridge, 1983), pp. 143–56.

[28] Richard Parkinson, ed., *The Autobiography of Henry Newcome* = Chetham Society, 26 (1852), p. 302.

[29] Alan Macfarlane, *The Family Life of Ralph Josselin: A Seventeenth-Century Clergyman* (Cambridge, 1970), pp. 117–25.

much as reprove them in his displeasure, but still waited the most cool and convenient time wherein they seldom discovered he was angry by any other effect but his silence.'[30]

Swopping such examples is not very profitable as a means of establishing how far the prescriptive writers had their way. But strong evidence that they largely failed to do so lies in the stridency of their own tone and their obsession with the issue of cockering. William Gouge was a man who could write highly emotionally to his friend Sir Robert Harley about the loss of his small daughter—'my sweetest child, my only daughter is gone'—yet at the same time advocate fierce discipline on biblical grounds.[31] Most parents at this time simply did not share this cast of mind. There is overwhelming evidence, one must state this clearly since it has been argued that the opposite was the case, that parents loved their children extravagantly and unrestrainedly at this time.[32] From around 1610 to 1640 the clerical advocates of beating children were evidently recognizing that this acted as a considerable restraint upon enforcement of their code. Almost every writer in these decades mentioned that parents spoilt their children.[33] Gouge was particularly scathing about parents who could not endure to hear their children cry, declaring that they thought nothing in their indulgence of God's honour nor their own or the child's spiritual safety.[34] He asked too much in the way of severity of ordinary men and women, with ordinary and spontaneous emotions about the offspring on whom they lavished their care and hopes. But Gouge's authoritarianism, of course, was but one manifestation of a general fear of disorder springing from personal immorality and misbehaviour at this time. In *Measure for Measure*, first performed in 1604, the Duke of Vienna bewailed the same laxity that Gouge made so much of a few years later when he claimed that the rod had become more mocked than feared:

> Now, as fond fathers
> Having bound up the threatening twigs of birch

[30] Cliffe, *Puritan Gentry*, pp. 73–4.

[31] Cited in Collinson, *Birthpangs of Protestant England*, pp. 78–9.

[32] Stone, *Family, Sex and Marriage*, especially pp. 151–218; Keith Wrightson, *English Society 1580–1680* (London, 1982), pp. 108–18.

[33] Schnucker in Fildes, ed., *Women as Mothers*, p. 115.

[34] Gouge, *Domesticall Duties*, pp. 565–6.

> Only to stick it in their children's sight
> For terror, not to use.[35]

Local educational provision was already being improved by the founding of new elementary and grammar schools before Protestantism made its impact in the middle of the sixteenth century, but the Reformation gave it an enormous boost. Both the nature of the religious motivation of founders and the regimes that they identified in founding statutes changed, as we would expect, in the course of the century. William Fettiplace, establishing the free school at Childrey attached to a chantry there in 1526, declared that the master, instructing them in English, was to 'teach the children the alphabet, the Lord's Prayer, the Salutation of the Angel and the Apostles creed . . . the fourteen articles of the faith, the ten commandments, the Seven Deadly Sins, the seven sacraments of the church.' The new grammar schools that burgeoned in market towns across the country between 1560 and 1700 were confined to boys and their curriculum was firmly based on the inculcation of Latin. They were in a real sense religious foundations: the school day included prayers, and attendance of the scholars at the local church on Sundays was normal. These schools were often founded by successful businessmen, whose motives were distinctly evangelical. John Royse, a merchant of Abingdon who had prospered as a London mercer, endowed the grammar school there in 1563 as an emblem of his sixty-three years, establishing a free school for sixty-three boys in a schoolroom sixty-three-feet long. The schoolmaster was to 'teach his scholars as well nurture and good manners as literature and virtuous living and Christian authors for their erudition.' Robert Johnson, founder of Oakham and Uppingham schools, insisted that their masters should be 'painful in the educating of children in good learning and religion'.[36] The Earl of Huntingdon specified attendance at the weekly lecture he had established at Leicester by the boys at his new school there in 1574, as well as at church on Sundays. A visitation order for the parish of Kendal in 1578 designated special seating for the

[35] Anthony Fletcher and John Stevenson, eds., *Order and Disorder in Early Modern England* (Cambridge, 1985), pp. 1–40; *Measure for Measure*, act 1, scene III, lines 23–6.

[36] A. J. Fletcher, 'The Expansion of Education in Berkshire and Oxfordshire 1500–1670', *British Journal of Educational Studies*, 15 (1967), pp. 52–5; Cliffe, *Puritan Gentry*, p. 80.

schoolmaster and his scholars in a chapel to the north of the chancel. David Baker, who later became a Benedictine, has left us an invaluable account of life in the household of the master of Christ's Hospital in the 1580s. Meal times began with a scholar reading a chapter from the Bible; prayers were read each evening; the boys often had to write an account of the sermons they heard in church on Sundays for the master to check.[37]

Whereas previously schoolboys had learnt their books from the clergy, the Reformation involved the establishment of the new profession of schoolmasters.[38] Christopher Rawlins, founding the grammar school at Adderbury, in Oxfordshire, in 1589, made it clear the master should not be a vicar or curate 'for that one cannot supply both offices.'[39] Founders were often emphatic about the kind of man they wanted: he must be 'well reported of for his knowledge, religion and life and known to be an enemy to popish superstition, a lover and forward embracer of God's truth', prescribed the Savilles, West Riding merchants who founded the grammar school at Wakefield in the 1590s. They required 'a man . . . diligent and painful in his own studies, of a sober and amiable carriage towards all men, able to maintain the place of a schoolmaster with dignity and gravity, given to the diligent reading of God's word.' There was a confidence in their mission which shines through the Saville statutes. 'For as much as this school is principally ordained a seminary for bringing up of Christian children', they began, 'therefore we will that especial care be had in the placing of a fit teacher from whom as the root the scholars are to draw the sap and juice of religion, learning and good nurture.'[40] The Protestant movement for the schooling of the English people placed a quite extraordinary degree of faith and responsibility on the first generations of schoolmasters. Moreover, school statutes did nothing to limit their powers beyond cautions against undue severity in punishment.

So again what do we find in practice? No doubt much good Christian education went on through the elements of religious instruction which were attached to the grammar-school regime.

[37] Joan Simon, *Education and Society in Tudor England* (Cambridge, 1966), pp. 323–6.

[38] Rosemary O'Day, *Education and Society 1500–1800: The Social Foundations of Education in Early Modern Britain* (London, 1982), pp. 165–78.

[39] Cited in Fletcher, 'Expansion of Education', pp. 57–8.

[40] Cited in Simon, *Education and Society*, p. 329.

Sir Simonds D'Ewes attested to his 'increase in the knowledge of divine truths and practice of piety' at Bury St Edmunds School, which was 'little inferior' to his progress in scholarship while there.[41] But this was not primarily how educationalists of the period thought about schooling or how contemporaries remembered the experience of their youth. For, in an age in which apprehension of disorder was always rife, the school became more than anything else an instrument of discipline, based on coercion and intended to check youthful high spirits with solid and monotonous learning. 'The prevailing grammar school ethic', writes Keith Thomas, 'was one of instinctual renunciation.'[42] Boys were taught self-control by working long hours at a curriculum which no one pretended would have intrinsic interest for them. The early seventeenth-century ballad *A Table of Good Nurture* details the ways in which scholars should learn 'good manners'. Punctuality, care of basic school possessions like inkhorn, pen, and book, neat attire, clean language, mild and gentle behaviour to schoolfellows, quietness and obedience, steady application: these were the precepts the master sought to inculcate. The coercion, of course, came in the form of the birchrod, figured on school seals, prominent in representations of the classroom at this time, and still occasionally on view, as is one safely put away behind a pane of glass at Royse's schoolroom in Abingdon. 'Therefore be wary you do not offend', runs the ballad,

> Lest stripes do reward you and make you to say
> Your precepts I'll follow, your words I'll obey.

Those who loitered and were lazy 'shall for their labour be brought on their knee'.[43] 'Your points untie' were the schoolmaster's dreaded words.[44]

Whereas the ties of parental love pulled against home beating it was the experience of thousands of boys in this period to submit to kneeling before their fellows with their breeches down to receive the birchrod's stripes. Some suffered under masters who were exceptionally cruel; few, one suspects, were as fortunate as

[41] Cliffe, *Puritan Gentry*, pp. 79–80.

[42] Keith Thomas, *Rule and Misrule in the Schools of Early Modern England* (University of Reading, Stenton Lecture, 1975), p. 8.

[43] W. Chappell, *The Roxburghe Ballads* (Hertford, 1874), 2, pp. 571–2.

[44] O'Day, *Education and Society*, pp. 49–50.

Sir Simonds D'Ewes, whose 'mild and loving' master went no further than denying bad children a share of the raisins he brought to school for his pupils. Many others, besides John Aubrey, who recorded his dreams about them twenty years later, must have remembered these beatings as the chief emotional legacy of their school-days. For masters needed quite exceptional personal authority, given the kind of learning they were inculcating and the crowded conditions of the schoolroom under their sole charge, to maintain order any other way. Francis Cheynell, in a pamphlet of 1646, called the schoolmaster 'a kind of magistrate'. At home he was a symbol of authority: the standard parental threat was 'Your master shall hear of it.' 'At country schools your masters drive you on by fear', noted Richard Baxter.[45]

Protestantism gave birth to the massive expansion of grammar-school education which is such a marked feature of Elizabethan and Stuart society. Scripture sanctioned the harsh rule of the birch, which was, of course, not new, but simply a regime that came to hold very many more children, as many more went to school, at its mercy. In two respects the schooling of this period set the pattern of educational development in England until the present century: it was gender segregated and based on a remote classical tongue that there was no good reason for boys who were to form the nation's social elite to learn. But this, of course, was exactly the point. Many years ago Walter Ong suggested that the Renaissance study of Latin was a puberty rite intended to provide a painful initiation into an exclusive adult society.[46] We can extend his argument, for Latin beaten into boys in the early modern grammar schools was, in fact, the crucial foundation of a whole class and gender system which was beginning to provide a revised basis for English patriarchy. Latin became the male elite's secret language, a language all of its own, a language that could be displayed as a mark of learning, of superiority, of class and gender difference at the dinner table, on the quarter sessions bench, and in those final bastions of male privilege, the Houses of Lords and Commons. The gentry became somewhat obsessive about educating their boys, especially eldest sons, in Latin. Thus

[45] Citations from Thomas, *Rule and Misrule*, pp. 8–9.
[46] Ibid., pp. 9–10.

Henry Slingsby records in his diary for 1640 getting a tutor for his four-year-old Thomas: 'I intend he shall begin to spell and read Latin together with his English . . . he could the last year before he was four years old, tell the Latin words for the parts of his body and of his clothes.' Latin, first at home in cases like this, then at school, became a critical element in the process of gender construction, a process which seems to have entered nobody's mind in quite this form before the late sixteenth and early seventeenth century. The process as a whole can be described as one of hardening, of the inculcation of a sophisticated form of manhood: the objective was to heighten the rational faculty and impose discipline on the emotions. A letter written by Dr Thomas Knipe, master of Westminster School, in 1696 to Lord Herbert provides insight here. It described his difficulties in getting young Henry Herbert to buckle down to the school regime. 'Learning is to children', Knipe reflected, 'as tobacco is to some people, it makes them sick at first.' Hitherto, he explained, Henry

> has been so much a child, that when he had been called from his play to his studies, he has stood in the yard crying and blubbering and roaring, as your own servants have sometimes heard him, because he might not play longer.

'If this infirmity of his leaves him', concluded Knipe confidently, 'I don't doubt but, upon his continuance with me, to finish him.' The classic expression of this set of attitudes, a little beyond our period but impossible to omit, nevertheless, for it tells us so much, is Lord Chesterfield's letter in Latin to his eight-year-old son in 1741:

> This is the last letter I will write to you as to a little boy, for tomorrow, if I am not mistaken you will attain your ninth year; so that, for the future, I shall treat you as a youth. You must now commence a different course of life, a different course of studies. No more levity in childish toys and playthings must be thrown aside and your mind directed to serious objects. What was not becoming to a child, would be disgraceful to a youth.[47]

[47] Citations from Linda Pollock, *A Lasting Relationship: Parents and their Children over Three Centuries* (London, 1987), pp. 148–9, 223.

The Protestant impulse for evangelization through grammar-school education, I would argue, had been hijacked by a social elite seeking a means to reinforce class and gender control. This may seem a curious story, but it is an important one for the understanding of the development of modern British society. So equally, but in a different way, is another story, the final theme of this lecture, the beginnings in this period of the gendered education of girls.

'The breeding of men were after a different manner of ways from those of women', reflected Margaret Cavendish, later Duchess of Newcastle, around 1620, on the upbringing of herself and that of her brothers.[48] Voices had been raised in the sixteenth century for equality of treatment. Was 'the godly instruction of and virtuous bringing up of youth of the female kind' in schools not just as important as for the male kind, asked Thomas Becon? His argument echoed that of Sir Thomas More, justifying the academic education of his daughters, that girls as well as boys were endowed with reason. But girls were denied access to the grammar schools, for the very good cause, in most men's eyes, that their destiny was a different social role from that of boys, and their training must therefore seek to create a quite different gender identity. The founder's statutes for Uffington School, in Berkshire, in 1637 stated that sending daughters to be taught 'amongst all sorts of youth' was 'very uncomely and not decent', so the schoolmaster was not to admit any females.[49] Around 1620 girls' finishing schools started to burgeon in London suburbs such as Chelsea, Stepney, and Hackney. They taught writing, needlework, music and dancing, sometimes with some French.[50] Such schools also began to appear in the provinces. Mr Bevan at Ashford hit exactly the right note in the 1640s to attract the patronage of Kentish gentry who aspired for their daughters to marry well. Henry Oxinden sent his daughters Elizabeth and Margaret to his school at eleven and twelve, after receiving a recommendation from his cousin Unton Dering: Mr Bevan was a 'conscienable discreet man', who besides teaching all the usual

[48] Linda Pollock, ' "Teach her to live under obedience": the making of women in the upper ranks of early modern England', *Continuity and Change*, 4 (1989), p. 238.

[49] Katherine Usher Henderson and Barbara F. McManus, *Half Humankind: Contexts and Texts of the Controversy about Women in England* (Urbana, 1985), pp. 89–90.

[50] O'Day, *Education and Society*, pp. 186–7.

social ornaments 'will be careful that their behaviour be modest and such as becomes their quality and that they grow in knowledge and understanding for God and their duty to him'. A note of class and gender training is clearly struck here.[51] Attending Mr Bevan's establishment would complement the education in religion and domestic roles which the gentry's girls were given at home by their mothers. For it was mothers with whom the main responsibility for their upbringing rested. The foundation of the inculcation of virtue, which was as fundamental for a girl from this social background as Latin was for a boy, was Scripture.

The prescriptive advice which underpinned bringing up girls at home ranges from a series of published funeral sermons lauding godly women to a large pamphlet literature which counselled females to be 'chaste, silent, and obedient'. Popular ballads, such as *The Virgins ABC*, issued the same precepts in a more accessible format.[52] Surveying the Lives of godly women at this society's conference in 1990, Jacqueline Eales concluded that they were didactic pieces which gave a selective biographical account, invariably portraying their subjects as 'pious, charitable, and the centre of religious life within their homes'.[53] The qualities of womanhood that were enjoined and that amounted to a life of virtue included modesty, courtesy, gentleness, grace, zeal, and self-control. The message was always strongly scriptural. Thus Katherine Stubs was alleged never to have brawled or scolded: 'She obeyed the commandment of the Apostle who biddeth women to be silent and learn of their husbands at home.'[54] In the preface to the published version of his 1697 funeral sermon for Elizabeth Dunton, Thomas Rogers drew examples from both the Old and New Testaments to put his subject in context. He commented upon Sarah's 'meekness of spirit' and lauded Rachel as 'pure in her thoughts, honest in her calling and innocent in her life'. The crucial importance of a girl's training in piety was stressed in this genre in several ways.[55] It was a matter of laying

[51] Pollock, *A Lasting Relationship*, p. 223.

[52] Suzanne W. Hull, *Chaste, Silent and Obedient: English Books for Women 1475–1640* (San Marino, 1982), pp. 133–43.

[53] Jacqueline Eales, 'Samuel Clarke and the "Lives" of Godly Women in seventeenth-century England', *SCH*, 23 (1990), pp. 368–9.

[54] P. Stubs, *A Cristal Glass for Christian Women* (1663).

[55] T. Rogers, *The Character of a Good Woman* (1697), epistle dedicatory.

proper foundations. Elizabeth Wilkinson 'was observed from her childhood to be very docile, very willing to learn, industrious in reading of and swift to hear the word of God preached.'[56] The mother's role was to set an example and organize a pattern of instruction. Elizabeth Dunton's regime for her girls is described in detail: how she 'guards them against selfwill and peevishness'; how she has one read while others were sewing bringing useful sayings to the minds of those with their fingers employed; how she catechizes them and how she 'teaches them to think of what is good when they lie down and when they rise.' In all this 'a great calmness and quietness' attended her actions.[57]

Sir Robert Filmer's essay 'In Praise of the Virtuous Wife', written in the 1640s, is a superb summary of the end product that the gentry looked for in the education of their girls. His discourse revolves around two passages from Proverbs: 12.4, 'A virtuous wife is the crown of her husband' and 31.10, 'Who can find a virtuous woman, for her price is above rubies?' Chastity was central to Filmer's conception of virtue but, in his reading, what mattered as much was courage, the self-discipline to live virtuously from day to day: 'That courage is true virtue', he declared, 'it appeareth because true virtue is the moderation of the affections by faith and prudence, that one showing what is lawful, the other what is possible and convenient.'[58] By 'moderation of the affections' Filmer means control of the will. Female gender construction in early modern England was exacting: it required girls to deprive themselves of expectations of initiative and independence and to internalize qualities of modesty and humility.

Whereas I have suggested that there was a very wide gap between prescription and practice with regard to the disciplining of young children, there is good evidence that in the matter of girls' general upbringing the two went closely together. For the kind of prescriptive advice which has just been quoted can be closely paralleled with personal injunctions from parents to daughters. Elizabeth Jocelyn's treatise of advice for her child's upbringing is an authentic account, written in 1622, by a woman fearing she would die in childbirth, which she did. It was

[56] Eales, 'Samuel Clarke', p. 371.

[57] Rogers, *Character of a Good Woman*, pp. 24–6.

[58] Margaret J. M. Ezell, *The Patriarch's Wife: Literary Evidence and the History of the Family* (Chapel Hill, 1987), pp. 132–3.

published and went through several editions. She herself had been educated in languages, history, and piety by her maternal grandfather, Bishop Chaderton of Lincoln, yet she was persuaded that 'sometimes women have greater portions of learning than wisdom.' She declared firmly that, in the case of a daughter, 'I desire her bringing up to be learning the bible, as my sisters do, good housewifery, writing and good works; other learning a woman needs not.'[59] Justinian Isham, a deeply thoughtful Northamptonshire gentleman, composed a code of conduct for his daughters Jane, Elizabeth, Judith, and Susan, the eldest of whom was nine, after the death of their mother in 1642. His advice began with and laid heavy emphasis upon the girls' spiritual development. His charge was

> first of all to instruct in the knowledge of another Father, the Father and Creator of all things. Him you may learn both in his word and works, as of the latter you are daily eye witnesses, so of the first you cannot be too diligent either readers or hearers . . . prayers, meditations and holy treatises I rather commend unto you than knotty disputes; and although your sex is not so capable of those stronger abilities of the intellect, to make you so learned and knowing as men ought to be; yet be sure to keep your hearts upright and your affections to God unfeigned and there is no doubt but that will be more acceptable unto him than all the wisdom of the world besides.

Isham commended the fair examples 'of their own sex and kindred' that his girls could follow, 'there having been of our house both maids, wives and widows, all of a very virtuous and exemplary life.' He warned against reliance in the most serious business of his daughter's lives, finding a husband, on a fair fortune or a fair face:

> I am sure the internal graces of the mind will be your best and surest portion, both unto yourselves, and unto men of such discretions as I believe you would willingly give yourselves unto. A virtuous woman is a good portion which shall be given as a gift to such as fear the Lord.

[59] E. Jocelyn, *The Mothers Legacy* (1625).

He then listed the 'graces and virtues' which Scripture described as 'most proper' for women: 'holiness, chastity, obedience, charity, meekness, modesty, sobriety, silence, discretion, frugality and affability'.[60]

When Sir Ralph Verney, in exile on the continent after the Civil War, heard that his goddaughter Nancy Denton intended to study Hebrew, Greek, and Latin, he reproved the girl's father for his impropriety and had a stern lecture for the girl herself: 'Good sweetheart, believe me a bible (with the common prayer) and a good plain catechism in your mother tongue being well read and practised is well worth all the rest and much more suitable to your sex.'[61] There are plenty of examples of commentaries by adult women on the efforts that their mothers had made to inculcate piety and virtue. Margaret Cavendish, brought up in the 1620s, remembered that her mother 'cared not so much for our dancing and fiddling, singing and speaking of several languages as that we should be bred virtuously, modestly, civilly, honourably and on honest principles'. Henry Slingsby, frantic as we have seen about his son's academic progress, was well satisfied with his five-year-old daughter Barbara in the 1640s when she could 'already say all her prayers, answer to her catechism and write a little'. Margaret Rich, summarizing the care she took of three young nieces entrusted to her on their parents' death in the 1650s, wrote that she had tried to bring them up religiously 'that they might be good and do good afterwards in their generation'.[62]

The upbringing of girls, as Linda Pollock has explored the theme, was about teaching them to 'live under obedience'. The phrase comes from a letter of Sir Ralph Verney's to his friend Dr Denton about young Nancy. The female life-cycle was supposed to move from a schooling in deference along the lines outlined here to acceptance of the governance of a husband. The pressure came from what men were looking for. John Evelyn's eulogy of his daughter Susannah on the eve of her marriage is set in the pattern of male expectation. She was a girl, he wrote, who used her talents 'with great modesty'; she was 'exquisitely shaped and of an agreeable countenance'; 'she is a good child, religious,

[60] Pollock, *A Lasting Relationship*, pp. 249–50.
[61] Ibid., p. 226.
[62] Ibid., p. 206 and 'Making of women', p. 238.

discreet, ingenious and qualified with all the ornaments of her sex.' Edward Montagu was reassured in 1632 that his proposed bride's religion was 'very perfect and her education most modest without exception'. A letter to Peregrine Osborne later in the century sought to persuade him to favour a proposed bride who was 'very modestly bred'.[63] The Bible had proved the starting-point for the English Protestant gentry to elucidate a concept of femininity that, if it could be driven into the mind at home in childhood by mothers trained in the same mould, offered a securely ideological basis for their permanent patriarchal control of women.

Let me conclude with some brief reflections on the legacy of these developments in the perspective of English history between 1700 and the present day. I have argued that the Protestant Church, in its first century and a half, was identified with a set of prescriptions for harsh childhood discipline which parents largely refused to follow. It was also deeply implicated in a system of schooling for boys in which the same kind of prescriptions had much more impact than in the home. Fathers, it seems, by and large supported the schoolmaster's use of the birch, and mothers were in no position to protect their offspring from its stripes. Mary Woodforde, wracked by the news that her son and others 'in rebellion' at Winchester were refusing to be whipped in 1687, wrote in her diary, 'Give them grace to repent and accept of their punishment . . . and let them not run on to ruin, for Christ's sake.'[64] The Church, I have suggested, also leant its authority to a system of gender training of girls for a restricted and restrictive social role in their adult lives. This allegiance, in these several respects, to a particular pattern of English upbringing, I contend, has been immensely powerful, and the results are clearly with us and our society today. There is still a conservative evangelical strain of thought in the church which, based on a pessimistic view of human nature, advocates physical punishment of children. So far as schooling is concerned, it was no coincidence that the first flagellant brothels appeared in London around the 1670s. Thomas Shadwell's comedy *The Virtuoso*, first performed in 1676, contains a scene in which the old libertine

[63] Pollock, 'Making of Women', pp. 244–5, 256.
[64] Pollock, *A Lasting Relationship*, p. 193.

Snarl tells the prostitute Mrs Figgu how he 'loves castigation mightily': 'I was so used to it at Westminster school I could never leave it off since.'[65] The 'English vice' has flourished ever since, though recent reforms in school punishment regimes may spell its decline. But perhaps the most disturbing legacy of all from the biblical teachings which have been considered in this paper concerns the gender construction of girls, in a manner which deprives them of the proper fulfilment of their energies, for this has surely been more pervasive in its effects than an inappropriate ideology of punishment. The narrow and inhibiting view of femininity which some seventeenth-century Protestants took authoritatively from the Bible has lain like a pall, in the intervening centuries, across many women's lives. It obviously contributed to the reactionary position in the recent debates on women's ordination. The Church, I believe, has never repudiated a series of dire legacies of certain biblical teachings; it has never spoken out about what has been done to children in the name of Scripture. Perhaps it is about time it did so.

University of Durhan

[65] Ian Gibson, *The English Vice: Beating, Sex and Shame in Victorian England and After* (Duckworth, 1978), p. 12.

THE BIBLE FOR CHILDREN: THE EMERGENCE AND DEVELOPMENT OF THE GENRE, 1550–1990

by RUTH B. BOTTIGHEIMER

BOOKS for children have existed for centuries. Their contents range from instructional manuals to flights of fancy. In children's literature, a variety of narrative forms have emerged, developed, flowered, and faded, but one genre, Bible stories for children's use, has remained in existence as long as print itself.

Bibles for children were and are special-purpose Bibles. Their number is legion, their form varied, and their titles attest to closely defined readerships: *Bible Stories for Use in Country Schools*,[1] . . . *for Reflective Youths*,[2] . . . *for Children*,[3] *pour M. le Dauphin*,[4] . . . *for children from eight to twelve years old*,[5] . . . *for the use of children who are learning to read and write*.[6] They share, however, a single purpose, namely, to give their young readers a correct idea of the contents of Holy Scripture.

Children's Bibles have generally contained stories from Old Testament histories, the Apocrypha, New Testament Gospels, and Acts. As a group, these books included paradigmatic tales of creation, fall, and deliverance, stories of patriarchal heroes, and New Testament fulfilments of Old Testament 'patterns' (also called 'types' or 'figures') and prophecies. The profile of stories offered to the reader and the proportion of space allotted to the Old and New Testaments changed dramatically from the late sixteenth to the twentieth centuries: in the sixteenth and seventeenth centuries the Old Testament outweighed the New, reflecting the composition of the canonical Bible. But these

[1] [Georg Gessner], *Biblische Geschichten zum Gebrauche der Landschulen* (Zurich, 1774).

[2] Johann Caspar Lavater, *Christliche Religionsunterricht für denkende Jünglinge* (Zurich, 1788).

[3] Johann Jakob Altdorfer, *Sammlung des Gemeinnützlichsten aus den Schriften des Alten Testaments zum Gebrauch der Jugend* (Winterthur, 1788).

[4] Both Nicolas Fontaine's and Claude Oronce Finé de Brianville's Bible stories (both Paris, 1670) were dedicated to the dauphin.

[5] François Martin de Noirlieu, *Histoire abrégée de l'Ancien et du Nouveau Testament, Bible de l'enfance* . . . (Liège, [1847?]).

[6] Anon., *Petit cours d'Histoire Sainte à l'usage des Enfants qui apprennent à Lire et à Ecrire* (Paris, 1828).

proportions changed in the course of the eighteenth century, until the New Testament overtook and finally displaced the Old Testament in many nineteenth-century compilations.

In a long-range study of the Bible for children in Europe and the United States,[7] I have explored the ways in which twenty or so Bible stories have been told over the last 800 years, with reference to their underlying and embedded messages about the nature of God, parent-child relationships, work, drinking, sexuality, male beauty, municipal pride, miraculous events, the Crucifixion, and the fall from grace. What people took for granted about these subjects has fluctuated dramatically, and the lines along which opinion has divided have sometimes been social, sometimes national, sometimes historical, sometimes confessional.

In the history of children's Bibles, five stand out from the rest. The first is the *Historia scholastica* (1170) of Peter Comestor, because it marks the absolute beginning of the genre and because it provided a common narrative fund of Bible stories for Europe as a whole.[8] The second is Hartmann Beyer's *Biblische Historien* (1555), which set the table of contents for children's Bibles for their first century. The third is Nicolas Fontaine's *Histoire du Vieux et du Nouveau Testament* (1670), because it was *the* Catholic children's Bible from its first publication for the following century, and because it dominated the French children's Bible market for nearly two centuries; fourth, Johann Hübner's *Zweymahl zwey und funffzig Biblische Historien* (1714), because it dominated the German market for 150 years; and finally Christian Gottlob Barth's pietistic *Biblische Geschichten* (1832), because it furnished the text that international Bible societies most often translated into scores of exotic languages for proselytizing throughout the non-Christian world.[9]

Each of these children's Bibles consisted of many stories, but the stories themselves change dramatically over time. One such story, that of Jael's murder of Sisera, encapsulates and demonstrates the kind of change made to Bible stories for children.

[7] *The Bible for Children from the Age of Gutenberg to the Present* (Yale University Press, forthcoming).

[8] I am leaving out of consideration at this point the Bible stories of Geoffroy de Latour-Landry's *Der Ritter von Turn* (Basle, 1493), because it does not purport to be a Bible in the sense that subsequent collections of Bible stories for children do.

[9] For additional publishing information see Rudolf Schenda, *Volk ohne Buch* (Munich, 1970), p. 169.

The oldest document in the canonical Bible is generally held to be the Song of Deborah in the fifth chapter of Judges. A Hebrew judge, she was 'a mother in Israel' who '[led] out the host' of Hebrew 'kings' fighting the 'kings of Canaan'. And when the Canaanite general, Sisera, fled the battlefield, it was a woman, 'Jael, blest above all women in the tents', who secured Israel's ultimate victory by slaying him and vanquishing the enemy.

The story is a gripping one and warrants retelling: In those days, the Bible says, God had given Israel into the power of Canaan. The people of Israel cried unto the Lord, because Sisera, the commander of the Canaanite army, 'had 900 chariots of iron and oppressed the people of Israel cruelly for twenty years. Now Deborah, a prophetess, the wife of Lappidoth, was judging Israel at that time. She used to sit under the palm of Deborah . . . and the people of Israel came up to her for judgment.' She summoned one of Israel's strong men, Barak, and told him that God commanded him to gather 10,000 men to fight Sisera. Barak replied, 'If you will go with me, I will go; but if you will not go with me, I will not go.' Deborah responded to his faintheartedness by predicting that 'The Lord will sell Sisera into the hand of a woman'.

When the enemy, Sisera, was told that Barak had gathered troops in the field, he called out all of his 900 chariots of iron and all his men, but Barak's 10,000 routed Sisera's army, and 'Sisera fled away on foot to the tent of Jael, the wife of Heber the Kenite' because Heber was allied with Canaan.

> And Jael came out to meet Sisera, and said to him, 'Turn aside, my lord, turn aside to me; have no fear.' So he turned aside to her into the tent, and she covered him with a rug. And he said to her, 'Pray, give me a little water to drink; for I am thirsty.' So she opened a skin of milk and gave him a drink and covered him. And he said to her, 'Stand at the door of the tent, and if any man comes and asks you, "Is any one here?" say, No.' But Jael the wife of Heber took a tent peg, and took a hammer in her hand, and went softly to him and drove the peg into his temple, till it went down into the ground, as he was lying fast asleep from weariness. So he died. And behold, as Barak pursued Sisera, Jael went out to

> meet him, and said to him, 'Come, and I will show you the man whom you are seeking.' So he went in to her tent; and there lay Sisera dead, with the tent peg in his temple.
>
> (Judges 4.2–22)

Deborah's song about Jael's deed climaxed dramatically at the killing:

> She put her hand to the tent peg
> and her right hand to the workmen's mallet;
> she struck Sisera a blow,
> she crushed his head,
> she shattered and pierced his temple.
> He sank, he fell,
> he lay still at her feet;
> at her feet he sank, he fell;
> where he sank, there he fell dead.
>
> (Judges 5.25–7)

This text's venerable age and historical importance mark it as the documentary beginning of the Bible as we know it. Yet nothing sets it apart for the ordinary Bible-reader, except for its remarkable content, which would deeply trouble first Protestant authors and later all authors during its brief history as a component of children's Bibles. The authors of children's Bibles were nearly all men, and for them, audacious women of wit, wisdom, courage, and brutality posed a perplexing problem.

⋆ ⋆ ⋆

There is much evidence that the issues in the story of Jael and Sisera that discommoded Protestant children's Bible authors and editors were not moral, but social. In the Bible Jael occupies a position of independence strangely alien to most of the Old Testament. She was married, yet appears to have exercised dominion over her own tent, not as a discarded wife, but as an equal partner.[10] In sixteenth- and seventeenth-century Europe, on the other hand, an independent woman in her own tent must have

[10] Mieke Bal, *Death and Dissymmetry* (Chicago, 1988), pp. 26, 212. I take issue with Bal's interpretation of the murder of Sisera as a reverse rape; Bal has, however, raised important issues about our understanding of the facts of the biblical text. For further criticism of theological exegesis of Judges, see Bal, *Murder and Difference* (Bloomington, 1988).

been a familiar concept. There was Queen Christina of Sweden. And in France, Marie de Medici, a powerful Italian princess, was Henri IV's second wife, regent for their son Louis XIII, and a woman who lost power only when Richelieu forced her out of the country in 1631. Her son's wife, Anne of Austria, was similarly regent for Louis XIV during his minority. At the court of Louis XIV and his immediate successors, looked to by courts all over Europe as a model to be emulated, women were often conduits of power and preferment.[11] There was a veritable gallery of powerful women, as the title of a mid-seventeenth-century French volume said.[12] French women were admired by Italians for their practical ability. In 1616 Stefano Guazzo wrote that they were capable of 'conducting lawsuits, and frequenting the houses of judges and lawyers, and keeping with their own hands the registers of credits and debits.'[13] And in England, Queen Mary was ultimately followed by Elizabeth, who ruled for forty-five years, and John Foxe, in his *Acts and Monuments* had made the point, *inter alia*, that she 'was a second Deborah'.[14] And in the Glorious Revolution of 1688, Parliament first offered the English crown solely to Mary, the daughter of James II, though eventually her husband William required that he and she rule jointly.

Against this background, most seventeenth-century children's Bible authors wrote easily about Jael's deed, though none of these woman rulers performed recorded deeds as terrifyingly brutal as Jael's. She appeared in nearly every seventeenth-century German Bible for children,[15] and the same held true in France. In Paris, in 1670, Nicolas Fontaine and Claude Oronce Finé de Brianville each produced a children's Bible dedicated to Louis XIV's young son, the dauphin, in which the story of Jael appeared.[16] Finé abbreviated his version somewhat; Fontaine expanded his, enlarging on Jael's wisdom and courage. The fact

[11] For contemporary commentary on the power of women in seventeenth-century France see Charles Montesquieu's *Lettres Persanes* (1721).

[12] Pierre Le Moyne, *La Galerie des femmes fortes* (Paris, 1647).

[13] *La civil conversazione* (Venice, 1616), p. 118, cited in *The Pentamerone of Giambattista Basile*, ed. and tr. N. M. Penzer (Westport, Conn, 1979) 1, p. 172, n. 6.

[14] Rosemary O'Day, *The Debate on the English Reformation* (New York, 1986), p. 20.

[15] Salomon Glassius (Nuremberg, 1654?, 1686); Sagittarius (Altenburg, 1679); Lenderich (Nuremberg, 1677, 1717).

[16] Fontaine, *L'Histoire du vieux et du nouveau testament* (1670); Finé de Brianville, *Histoire Sacrée*.

that this woman was seen battling for the people of God, he wrote, made it apparent that if God wished to do so he could give women as well as men wisdom and power to direct 'les grandes affaires'.[17] He expanded his praise to include Deborah's organizational and martial accomplishments, which, he noted, showed that men can be weaker than women, and women more 'genereuses' than men.

The second half of the seventeenth century was the period in which prototypes for modern children's Bibles began to appear, the eighteenth century the period of their proliferation. In the seventeenth century the story of Jael existed in both German Protestant and French Catholic children's Bibles; after 1700, however, the story's appearance or suppression depended on confessional distinctions. It lived on in Catholic France for nearly two hundred years, but it underwent immediate change and erasure in Protestant Germany. The narrative's fate in Protestant England was similar to that in Protestant Germany. A couplet in Benjamin Harris's *Holy Bible in Verse* (first edition 1698) must have made Jael's name familiar to many young English readers,[18] but when the anonymous author of *A Compendious History of the Old and New Testament* produced the first English children's Bible a few years later, in 1726,[19] Jael disappeared. Her story was equally absent in eighteenth-century America, where the children's Bible tradition derived almost completely from English models.

If we observe the publishing history of the story of Jael from a long perspective, we perceive a single pattern for editing the story. Initially it was cast in positive terms, as the Bible itself prescribed. Subsequently, however, authors looked askance at Jael's deed, found her form of heroism unacceptable, and eventu-

[17] Fontaine, *L'Histoire*, pp. 133–4: '. . . cette femme combattent encore pour le peuple de Dieu . . . que Dieu peut donner aux femmes mesme quand il luy plaist, le conseil & la force, aussi-bien qu'aux hommes pour gouverner les grandes affaires.'

[18] (1717) np: And Heber's Wife whose Name was Jael/Thro' Sisera's Temple drove a Nail.

[19] I used the London, 1726 edition. There may be an earlier edition, but it is the earliest recorded edition among the comprehensive computerized listings of the Research Libraries Network. Fontaine's version of the tale entered England when his Old Testament history was translated and published for adults in 1690. A second adult Bible story book, Howel's *Compleat History of the Holy Bible* (London, 1716), gratuitously doubted Deborah's judgeship and disapproved of Jael's act; moreover he erroneously stressed a non-existent vicious component of her act by borrowing words from the act of decapitation from the story of Judith and Holofernes to insert in the final scene in Jael's murder of Sisera (1, pp. 301–3).

ally rejected it. This pattern of gradual erasure repeated itself with uncanny exactness in all children's Bible publishing and editing traditions. But the pace and timing of the sequence—philogynous inclusion, misogynistic commentary, and ultimate erasure—is completely confession-dependent until the twentieth century.[20]

I have couched the discussion so far in terms of country and century to sketch the broad outlines of the geographical and historical distribution of Jael's story. The chief dividing-lines in this distribution, however, are confessional. The boundaries that define—and determine—an author's or editor's treatment of Jael and her murder of Israel's enemy Sisera are mainly those that separate Catholic from Protestant. Within Protestantism itself, a secondary divide in the treatment of the story separated Reformed—that is, more or less Calvinist—from Lutheran (in Germany) or Calvinist Dissenter from Anglican (in England).

For Catholic children's Bibles, the most influential Jael story was that of Nicolas Fontaine. His version, first published in Paris in 1670, appeared decade after decade for nearly two centuries. It provided a standard telling of the tale; its heroine was a woman battling for the people of God, a woman whose wisdom and courage Deborah celebrated in her ancient song. Its built-in commentary told its young readers that the story demonstrated that God could give women (as well as men) as much wisdom and strength to govern as he liked. Fontaine expressed further gender heresy when he wrote that the story demonstrated that men could be weaker than women and that women, for their part, could be more noble and courageous than men.[21] Fontaine's example proved a durably powerful one when other French Catholic authors began to produce children's Bibles. French children's Bible authors valorized a woman's initiative when they related how 'Jael took advantage of Sisera's sleep to

[20] Usually the children's Bibles that included Jael's story in periods that otherwise ignored it occurred in Bibles that were collections of emended canonical text. See Foster, *The Story of the Bible* (Philadelphia, 1884); Robinson, *The Children's Bible* (1911); *Passages from Holy Writ* (Philadelphia, 1894); Rogers, *The School and Children's Bible* (London, 1873); *The Child's Bible* (1883); Smith, *The Children's Bible* (London, 1911).

[21] (1670), pp. 133–4.

deprive him of life'[22] or how she was 'inspired by God'.[23] Lest one suspect Jael of 'dishonesty and treason', the Catholic author of an 1853 children's Bible insisted that

> One may assume that in the moment in which she invited Sisera to enter her tent, she wasn't thinking at all of killing him, and that God only inspired her to do so after he had fallen asleep and made her understand in her heart that he wished to use her too as an instrument to deliver his people from this enemy.[24]

And deliver Israel she and Deborah did, as French Catholic children continued to learn well into the nineteenth century.[25] By the mid-twentieth century, however, Catholic acceptance of a heroic woman in children's Bibles had mostly disappeared, and those that *did* include Jael's story offered the narrative in reservedly lapidary style ('Jael killed him'),[26] and often diminished the story's visual significance by presenting it bare of illustration.[27]

Those seventeenth- and eighteenth-century German Catholic children who had a children's Bible would probably have read the German translation of Fontaine's *History*. With various titles it issued from south German presses for nearly a century from 1684 to 1782, spreading Fontaine's view east of the Rhine of a wise and courageous female patriot. This lasted only until indigenous German Catholic authors produced Bible stories for children; then they adopted a drier, more neutral, tone in their descriptions: Jael 'drove a tent-peg into his temple',[28] or 'Israel was thus liberated.'[29]

[22] *Bible en Estampes* (Paris, 1817), p. 66: 'Jael profita du sommeil de Sisera pour lui ôter la vie.'

[23] Gustave Essards, *La Bible des Enfans* (Paris, [*c.* 1850]), p. 180: 'inspirée par Dieu'.

[24] *Abrégé de l'histoire et de la morale de l'ancien testament* (Paris, 1853), p. 93: '. . . de mensonge et de trahison' and 'on peut supposer que, dans le moment qu'elle invita Sisera à entrer dans sa tente, elle n'avait point encore la pensée de le tuer, et que Dieu ne la lui inspira qu'après qu'il fut endormi, lui faisait entendre au fond du coeur qu'il voulait se servir d'elle pour délivrer son peuple de cet ennemi.'

[25] Essards (see n. 23), p. 180: 'Jael delivra ainsi le peuple d'Israël de celui qui l'avait tant opprimé.'

[26] *La Bible Illustrée* (Paris, 1969), p. 198: 'Jahel le tua.'

[27] René Berthier, *Bible* (Paris, 1969).

[28] Johan Ignaz von Felbiger, *Geschichte des alten Testaments*, 1st edn (Cologne, 1777, here 1801), p. 66: Jahel 'schlug . . . ihm einen Zeltfloch in die Schläfe.'

[29] Josef Anton Fuetscher, *Die heilige Geschichte*, 2nd edn (Bregenz, 1791), p. 119: 'Israel wurde hiedurch befreyt.'

In Protestant Europe, Reformed children's Bibles, particularly those emanating from Zurich and its environs, were notable for their philogynous view of Jael. In that religious environment, the story's history made a strong showing in the first book of Swiss children's Bible stories, those of the verbose Abraham Kyburz. His catechetically rendered Bible stories called Deborah 'the faithful mother in Israel', whereas Jael was the person who drove 'the nail of her tents through the temple of the commander Sisara'.[30] The publication of Swiss Bible stories began in earnest in the 1770s, with the appearance of Lavater and Hess's small book of Bible stories. For them Deborah was 'a heroic woman . . . a prophet and a teacher in Israel'. People turned to her in important matters to learn the will of God.[31] Jael was a Kenite, who wanted to use her abilities to be of service to the Israelities.[32] Lavater wrote that Deborah's song commemorating Jael's deed, 'in the Book of Judges [was] extraordinarily worth reading.'[33] Lavater and Hess's version was as foundational for nineteenth-century Swiss Reformed retellings as Fontaine's *History* had been in neighbouring France. The result was that even when the story was attenuated by Swiss authors and editors in the nineteenth century, it maintained a philogynous hue by telling the story in words tinged with admiration: 'It even happened that valiant women, like Deborah, for example, won great glory for themselves',[34] or simply by telling it in its entirety.[35]

Non-Reformed Protestant readings of Judges 4 and 5, however, ranged from perplexed confusion through reluctant acceptance to angry denunciation and outright erasure. All over Europe and North America the story undermined society's expectations for women's behavior. There was also a fundamental tension between God's will in this story and the treatment of women in much of the rest of the Bible. Some Protestants called Jael's killing of Sisera an 'assassination', even though the Biblical

30 Abraham Kyburz, *Catechetische Kinder-Bibel*, 2nd edn (Zurich, 1763), p. 184: '. . . die treue Mutter in Israel'.

31 Johann Caspar Lavater and Johann Jakob Hess, *Biblische Erzählungen* (Zurich, 1772), pp. 293, 298: '. . . ein heldenmütiges Weib . . . eine Prophetin und Lehrerin in Israel'.

32 Ibid., p. 300.

33 Lavater and Hess, *Biblische Erzählungen*, 3rd edn (Zurich, 1807), p. 119.

34 Johann Andreas Hofmann, *Erzählungen aus der Geschichte des Menschgeschlechts* (Zurich, 1842), p. 56.

35 Peter Scheitlin, *Biblische Geschichte* (St Gallen, 1843, 1844), pp. 136–8.

Israelites had praised her for her act. 'Sin is sin . . . Jael could have sent him away from her tent', said Johann Philipp Trefurt.[36] To eighteenth-century Protestant English and American eyes, Jael's action was 'seemingly ungenerous and cruel', despite the fact that it had been 'Pre-ordained by the all-wise Creator, to let the Israelites see that the weakest instrument in his hands, were more effectual than all the might and power upon earth.'[37]

For a while Bible-story authors were entrapped by textual tradition into entitling the story 'The Woman who Saved Israel', yet their revulsion at the story's narrative content made them rewrite it in terms of the 'guile' of Sisera's 'treacherous hostess', whom they called a thoroughly 'treacherous woman'.[38] Authors adopted a variety of strategies in their efforts to deal with Jael's deed. Some vented their angry feelings by creating a new title like 'Jael's Treachery', yet knowledge of the Bible constrained them to reproduce Deborah's contradictory salutation to Jael, 'Blessed above women.'[39]

Social expectations and biblical text warred with one another. In the eighteenth century women had been defined according to their reproductive, maternal, even lactating, potential, and here, too, the story's content inverted the concept of women's nurturing function, because Jael had offered Sisera that form of sustenance. The very word 'milk' awakened the expectation of maternal nurturance in Jael's character. Kyburz had called Deborah a mother in Israel; Jael, however, he continued, killed Sisera. Implicit in Kyburz's 'however' was a denial of real or potential maternal, or matronly, solicitude, and, indeed, a suggestion of an opposing set of emotions. Jael's offer of milk seems to some Bible-story authors to have been of sufficiently treacherous intent that they excised precisely *that* element of the tale in order to make the story conform to reader expectations.[40] Thus prevailing social norms outweighted Bible content.

Above all, Deborah's judgeship and Jael's courage alarmed non-Reformed Protestants. In the eighteenth- and nineteenth-century world they shared with their readers, female heroism

[36] Johan Philipp Trefurt, *Biblische Erzählungen nach Hübner*, 4th edn (Hanover, 1828), p. 87.
[37] *The Children's Bible* (Philadelphia, 1763), p. 73.
[38] James Baikie, *The Bible* (New York, 1923), p. 137.
[39] Edward T. Bartlett and John P. Peters, *Scriptures Hebrew and Christian* (London, 1886), pp. 167, 171.
[40] Sigisbert Frisch, *Historia dil veder e niev Testament* (Cuera, 1823), p. 60.

must have been a preposterous idea that contravened palatable gender roles. They responded by reformulating her role from one of national significance into a family one. It is worth exploring the portrayal of Jael in England's first family Bible,[41] because its text exerted considerable influence on England's children's Bible tradition. Its author, Laurence Howel, believed that the reputed appearance of women like Jael and Deborah, '*said* [my italics] to have judged Israel at that time', could only have resulted from the fact that 'the Severity of the [Israelites'] Servitude' had left them utterly 'degenerated and dispirited'. In his version, Deborah warned Barak 'pleasantly' that it wouldn't be honourable for Sisera to 'fall into the Hands of a Woman'. Howel's embedded message was clear: the identity of each woman was primarily that of a deferential wife (Deborah was Lepidoth's wife; Jael was Heber's); women's efforts must needs be inconsequential—so insignificant, in fact, that recognition of their efforts inevitably diminished their husbands' stature; and victory brought about by a woman's agency must necessarily be dishonourable. Howel concluded his version of Jael and Sisera this way: when she perceived him asleep,

> she took a Hammer and a long Nail or Tent-pin; and pitching it to the Temples of his Head, she struck it with such Force, that it pierced through his Head, and pinned him to the Ground; after which she cut off his Head, and so left him.

Howel demonized Jael by using the more violent of the two biblical accounts of the incident, that from the Song of Deborah (Judges 5.26), rather than the narrative account of Judges 4.21. He intensified her act by increasing the length of the murderous instrument, a 'long' Nail, by adding the words 'with such Force' and by construing the King James translation, 'smote off' as a beheading like Judith's of Holofernes (Judith 13.8), and by concluding the story with the words 'and so left him', which do not occur in either of the two versions.

Howel seems to have derived his much touted 'facts' more from popular tradition than from theological training, and his

[41] Laurence Howel, *A Compleat History of the Holy Bible* (London, 1716). Family Bibles in eighteenth-century England were Bible story collections, much like children's Bibles, but intended for an adult readership.

misogynistic outlook was one that endured into the twentieth century. The many Jaels who followed Howel's creation were no longer inspired by God; instead, they perpetrated 'a cruel *devilish* trick [my italics]'.[42] By the middle of the twentieth century, children's Bible authors of whatever country and confession rejected Jael's heroism and denigrated Deborah's stature. 'For lack of a man and a leader, the people went to [Deborah].'[43]

ERASURE

The more usual (non-Reformed) Protestant response to the story of Deborah and Jael was simple erasure. The process, in its simplest stage, removed Jael's name from the story-title. Justus Gesenius did this in 1684 when he introduced the story with this phrase: 'About Deborah the Judge and Barak / how . . . field marshall Sissera was put to death.' Gesenius's illustration, however, supplied the identity of the executioner that the title's passive voice was able to obscure.[44] It was a simple and short step to erase the entire story. Some authors announced their intention abruptly. With reference to Judges 3–5, Georg Friedrich Seiler wrote, 'These chapters are not to be read.'[45]

Seiler gave no reason for blotting out Deborah and Jael. But we may easily guess at the motivations that drove him and other Bible-story authors to do so. Discomfort with a woman's martial exploits led some to denigrate or even to castigate Jael, despite the importance of the victory she achieved for Israel. Both of the children's Bibles that dominated the eighteenth and early nineteenth centuries in America, *The Holy Bible Abridged* and *The History of the Holy Bible*, presented a non-Jael canon to their child readers. One mid-nineteenth-century French Catholic children's Bible did the same, but its author's name, Elisabeth Müeller, suggests the presence of non-French influences.[46]

[42] Charles R. Brown, *Ten Short Stories from the Bible* (New York, 1925), p. 29.

[43] Meindert DeJong, *The Mighty Ones* (New York, 1959), p. 207.

[44] Justus Gesenius, *Biblische Historien* (Braunschweig, 1684), pp. 199, 201.

[45] Georg Friedrich Seiler, *Das grössre biblische Erbauungsbuch* (Erlangen, 1788–95), no vol., p. 66. Seiler's sixteen-volume book was meant for pulpit use, and we can assume that its contents echoed off many hallowed walls.

[46] *Bible du jeune age* ([1850]). Many Catholic children's Bibles, some of them very influential, have omitted Jael's story in the twentieth century. See J. M. Rovira Belloso, *Die neue Patmos Bibel* (Düsseldorf, 1990) and the many translations of Anne de Vries' children's Bible.

The Book of Judges is full of terrifying stories, one of which describes Jephthah's sacrificing his own daughter to satisfy a rash battlefield vow. It is notable that many of the children's Bibles that have omitted Deborah and Jael have included this grisly tale.[47] That suggests that it was not the avoidance of gore *per se*, but gender constraints that determined excision: a male could cause a female's death, but it was illicit for a female to kill a male. By the twentieth century it was usual for Jael to be erased from story titles,[48] from the illustrations,[49] and from the text itself:[50] the process of erasure had become international, supraconfessional, and apparently inexorable. Deborah herself was reduced from a judge who exercised power in her own day to a prophetess who addressed a parlous future.[51] Women were not to be admitted to power, and so we are hardly astonished when a modern German-language Catholic children's Bible for children of the South Tyrol denied the existence of female judgeship and omitted Deborah entirely by stating that 'The men, whom God awakened in those days as deliverers were called judges.'[52]

For many children's Bible authors it was easier to postpone all battlefield glory and to transfer it to Gideon in the following chapters of Judges. For barbarism and primitively bloody executions (Judges 7.25), his conquests equalled or surpassed Jael's, but Gideon was a man, and hence unthreateningly heroic to a world that required female gentleness.[53]

In far more cases, however, Jael disappeared because her story offered a negative example and thus contravened a new educational imperative in the eighteenth century. The first and most consequential erasure of this sort occurred in Johann Hübner's

[47] Some examples are [Biber], *The Child's Own Bible* (London, 1838); Georg Ludwig Jerrer, *Erzählungen aus der Bibel* (Nuremberg, 1820); Sophie Ségur, *Bible d'une grand'mere* (np, 1976); the first edition was about a century earlier.

[48] As in *The Bible for Boys and Girls* (London, [1952]).

[49] Ernst Hülle, *Hundert-Bilder Bibel* (Berlin, [*c.* 1910]).

[50] *The Child's Bible* (London and New York, 1912); Marina Battigelli, *Il Vecchio Testamento* (Brescia, 1953); *Biblische Geschichte* (Bozen, 1959); Pat Alexander, *The Puffin Children's Bible* (Harmondsworth, 1983); A. Rutgers van der Loeff, *De Bijbel voor Kinderen* (Leyden, nd).

[51] Daniel-Rops, *Histoire sainte* (Paris, 1st edn 1948, 1961), p. 100.

[52] *Biblische Geschichte* (Bozen, 1959), p. 65.

[53] Johann Gottfried Zeidler, *Neu-Ausgefertigte Bilder-Bibel*, 2nd edn (Magdeburg, 1701), or Lewis Browne, *The Graphic Bible* (London, 1950), pp. 36–7.

Bible stories (1714 ff.). His book dominated the eighteenth-century German market by the sheer force of numbers.[54] Most children's Bibles followed Hübner's pattern in one way or another.[55]

Acceptance and valorization characterized Catholic treatment of the story of Deborah and Jael from 1670 into the nineteenth century; appreciative acknowledgement typified Swiss and German Reformed versions; discrediting and erasure marked other Protestant treatments of the story. And yet, the story has stubbornly and regularly reappeared. The precipitating causes for each of Deborah's and Jael's various returns are themselves equally various: the pre-existence of illustration material, the story's inclusion in Latin-language school texts, and the predilection of women authors for including Jael.

The emergence of the 'higher' or 'scientific criticism' of biblical texts also seems to have had a philogynous effect on tellings of Deborah and Jael's story in the later nineteenth century, a time generally marked by pervasive gender prejudice against women. Modern textual analysis of the Bible had begun tentatively in France in the seventeenth century with Richard Simon's work,[56] and it had emerged as a vigorously developing discipline at Tübingen in the 1820s. German scholars, who led the way in dating Bible texts, concluded that the Song of Deborah comprised the most ancient of Old Testament writings. As knowledge of the German school's findings spread throughout the Western Christian world, it appears to have precipitated a renewed interest in the fourth and fifth chapters of Judges. In the 1870s, 1880s, and 1890s a great many Bible-story collections for school use appeared, consisting of texts from the canonical Bible, and as a result Jael returned to many Bible-story collections for

[54] Christine Reents, *Die Bibel als Schul- und Hausbuch* (Göttingen, 1984), pp. 240–74.

[55] Some omitted all or most of the book of Judges as did [Christoph von Schmid], *Biblische Geschichte*, 2nd edn (Munich, 1806); Didier Decoin, *La Bible Illustrée* (Geneva, 1980); Nathaniel Crouch, *Youth's Divine Pastime* (London, 1691); Kaspar Friedrich Lossius, *Moralische Bilderbibel* (Gotha, 1821); some cut out Joshua and Judges as did Johann Peter Miller, *Erbauliche Erzählungen*, 1st edn (Helmstedt, 1753); J. Davidson, *Selectae e veteri testamento* (Philadelphia, 1789); some left out Judges, 1 and 2 Samuel, and 1 and 2 Kings as did Johann Gottlieb Seidentopf, *Moral der biblischen Geschichte* (Berlin, 1803–6); and some leapt from Moses to Samson as did Abbé Pascal, *Bible de la Jeunesse* (Paris, *c*. 1840); Johann Hübner, *Zweymahl zwey und funffzig Auserlesene Biblische Historien*, 1st edn (Leipzig, 1714).

[56] Richard Simon, *Histoire critique du Nouveau Testament* (Rotterdam, 1690).

home use, her tale now told not in disapproving but in neutral language.[57]

The most recent return of Jael to the pages of children's Bibles has taken place within the last five years. Authors' evaluations have been mixed: for one, Jael brought about a great victory; another author wrestled with the contradictory requirements of hospitality and patriotism; yet another concluded that Jael was a traitor to her husband.[58] Still others simply recounted the facts laconically.[59]

CONCLUDING THOUGHTS

Both Catholic and Protestant traditions began with a generally philogynous view of Judges 4 and 5. Catholics and Reformed Protestants maintained that view, while Lutherans and Anglicans gradually reformulated Jael as a woman more to be reviled than revered. In the eighteenth and nineteenth centuries confession determined how individual children's Bible authors would render the story contained in that most ancient of biblical texts. Jewish children's Bibles followed a similar course. In the first vernacular Jewish children's Bible, a German one of 1823, Jael was glorified, but in subsequent editions a footnote first commented reservedly on her act, then absorbed that part of the story, which later disappeared altogether.[60]

Through examination of these permutations of the story of Jael, we see how a sacred text, solemnly handed from generation to generation, sets up a dissonance in societies whose values differ from those that produced those stories. The Bible is supposed to mould and prescribe the morals and manners of succeeding ages—and it may succeed in doing that to some extent. But a study of its adoption for children over two

[57] *New Illustrated Bible for the Young* (Philadelphia, 1874), p. 128; *Bible for Infant Minds* ([1885]), pp. 43–4; John William Mackail, *Biblia Innocentium* (Hammersmith, [1892]), pp. 97–8; William Canton, *The Bible Story* (New York and London, 1915), pp. 136–41.

[58] J. F. Allen, *The New Illustrated Children's Bible* (London, 1970), pp. 142–5; *Die Bibel im Bild* (Stuttgart, [1980s]), 3; Paul Roche, *The Bible's Greatest Stories* (New York, 1990), p. 135.

[59] Bridget Hadaway and Jean Atcheson, *The Bible for Children* (London, 1974), p. 102; Sandol Stoddard, *The Illustrated Children's Bible* (London, 1984), pp. 95–7; Esther Tusquets, *Despues de Moises* (Barcelona, 1989), pp. 16–19.

[60] Moses Mordecai Büdinger, *Der Weg des Glaubens* (Stuttgart, 1823).

continents and several centuries shows us also how it beats powerlessly on autonomous and changing human values, which endlessly alter and even subvert the original message.

State University of New York,
Stony Brook

THE EYE OF HIS MASTER: CHILDREN AND CHARITY SCHOOLS

by W. M. JACOB

THE aim of this paper is to examine the evidence from a number of charity schools, for attitudes towards the childhood of the 'poorer sort' in the early eighteenth century. Conventionally it has been claimed that lack of affection, and even brutality, characterized the relationship between parents, especially fathers, and their children. Lawrence Stone, in particular, has promoted the view that, as a result of the very high mortality rate among children until the late eighteenth century, parents did not invest much affection in them in order to insulate themselves from the sorrow resulting from their likely deaths before reaching adulthood.[1] This view was also taken by Ivy Pinchbeck and Margaret Hewitt. They pointed out the formality of address seen in letters between children and parents of the upper classes, and suggested that cruelty to children and flogging was commonplace at all levels of society.[2] These views have been challenged by Linda Pollock, who has suggested that, when examined carefully, the evidence suggests that, from the sixteenth century at least, nearly all children seem to have been wanted, loved, and cared for. She claims that the majority of children were not subject to brutality, and that physical punishment was used relatively infrequently and as a last resort. Pollock suggests that from the eighteenth century onwards parents were much concerned with 'training' a child in order to ensure that he or she absorbed correct values and beliefs and would grow into a model citizen.[3]

The evidence derived from attitudes displayed towards charity-school children is particularly interesting, for it illustrates the attitudes of the 'better sort' towards the children of the

[1] Lawrence Stone, *The Family, Sex and Marriage in England 1500–1800*, abridged edition (Harmondsworth, 1979), p. 293.

[2] Ivy Pinchbeck and Margaret Hewitt, *Children in English Society I: From Tudor Times to the Eighteenth Century* (London, 1969), pp. 303–4.

[3] Linda Pollock, *Forgotten Children: Parent-Child Relations from 1500 to 1900* (Cambridge, 1983), pp. 268–9.

'poorer sort', as well as illustrating the attitude of those exercising Christian charity towards their needy infant neighbours.

The first thirty years or so of the eighteenth century saw a burst of activity aimed at providing very basic schooling for the children of the poor. Detailed research in Kent, Gloucestershire, Lincolnshire, Devon, Cheshire, London, Norfolk, and the East Riding of Yorkshire[4] shows that benefactors and subscribers were energetically providing for education, either by means of benefactions and donations or by subscriptions, to pay for teachers and/or school premises for poor children to receive instruction. In 1729 the Society for the Promotion of Christian Knowledge (SPCK)'s *Account of Charity Schools* listed 1,419 new schools established in England since the beginning of the century. The number of children thought to be attending them was reckoned at 22,203. The true figure was well in excess of that, for in many schools pupil numbers remained unknown to the SPCK. Even the number of schools may be underestimated: for example, Sheffield had five schools founded between 1710 and 1724, but only two appear in the SPCK's 1724 list, Cheshire had twenty-nine schools founded after 1699, but only thirteen appear in the SPCK's list.[5] In almost all cases of the establishment of a school the motive would seem to be religious. But this was not a clerical movement; in many rural parishes where a school was established, usually by endowment, the incumbent was named as a trustee, but he was usually associated in this trust with two lay officials elected by the ratepayers, the churchwardens, and in towns it was usually laymen who formed the bodies of trustees who managed the schools.

An examination of the aims and motives of the originators of these schools may throw some light on their attitudes towards childhood. The preamble to the List of Subscribers at the estab-

[4] R. Hume, 'Educational provision for the Kentish poor 1660–1811: fluctuations and trends', *Southern History*, 4 (1982), pp. 128–40; A. Platt and G. H. Hainton, *Education in Gloucestershire: A Short History* (Gloucester, 1954), pp. 24–41; C. M. Rose, 'Politics, religion and charity in Augustan London c1680–c1720' (Cambridge Ph.D. thesis, 1988); M. F. Lloyd Prichard, 'The education of the poor in Norfolk 1700–1850', *Norfolk Archaeology*, 33 (1965), pp. 321–31; D. H. Webster, 'A charity school movement? The Lincolnshire evidence', *Lincolnshire History and Archaeology*, 15 (1980), pp. 39–46; Arthur Warne, 'Church and society in eighteenth century Devon' (Leeds Ph.D. thesis, 1963), pp. 225–40; D. Robson, *Some Aspects of Education in Cheshire in the Eighteenth Century* (Manchester, 1966); J. Lawson, *Primary Education in East Yorkshire 1560–1902* (York, 1959).

[5] Geoffrey Holmes, *Augustan England: Professions, State and Society 1680–1730* (London, 1982), p. 53.

lishment of the charity school at Diss, a market town in south Norfolk, provides an apt illustration of the aims and motives of subscribers to this, and many other schools.

> Whereas Prophaneness and Debauchery are greatly increased owing to a gross Ignorance of Religion especially among the lower sort and nothing is more likely to promote the practice of Christianity and Virtue than an early and pious Education of Youth and hath been experienced from many Charity Schools erected in this Kingdom for Teaching children of the poor who were desirous of having them taught but were not able to afford them Christian Education, Wee whose names are underwritten doe agree to pay yearly at two equal payments (during pleasure) the respective sumes of money against our names subscribed for the Maintenance of a Charity School at Disse. . . . For teaching 30 poor boys to read and to sustain them in the knowledge and practice of the Christian Religion as professed in the Church of England and for learning such other things as are suitable to their Condition and Capacity. And doe alsoe agree to Cloath some of them that have most need once in a year and to putt them out to Apprenticeshippes or Services as they are capable (out of the moneys soe collected).[6]

The promotion of Christianity according to the 'Practice of the Primitive Christians', who it was believed had established schools in Alexandria, for which it was thought that Clement's *Catechetical Discourses* had been written, was the chief aim of charity schools, according to Bishop Trimnell of Norwich in his sermon at the opening of the Norwich charity schools in 1708.[7] The movement for the development of basic education for the poor in the first decades of the eighteenth century, in which the SPCK played a very important part, was a response by Anglican laypeople and clergy to what they perceived as a very great threat from Dissenters and Roman Catholics, whom they saw as competing for the souls of the poor on equal terms with the Church

[6] Norfolk and Norwich Record Office [hereafter NNRO], 17608 38 D 5 Diss Charity School, List of Subscribers, 1715.

[7] *A Sermon Preached at St Peter's Mancroft in Norwich on Sunday the 13th of June 1708 Upon the Ocassion of the Charity Schools lately set up in several Parts of the City, by the Right Reverend Father in God, Charles, Lord Bishop of Norwich* (Norwich, 1708), pp. 2, 5 and 6.

of England, following the Toleration Act of 1689.[8] The SPCK's initial aim was to encourage schools in London, but soon they resolved to 'establish a correspondence with one or more of the Clergy in each County, and with one Clergyman in each great Town or City of England, in order to erect Societies of the same nature with this, throughout the Kingdom'. Shortly afterwards the correspondence was extended to include laymen.[9] The object was to encourage local community activity to promote the education of the poor in the principles of the Christian faith as found in the Church of England.

A chord was struck in the consciences of many of the 'middling sort' for, particularly in London, but also in most large towns and cities, in market towns and villages, schools were established to provide a basic grounding in the Catechism of the Prayer Book, to teach children to read, and possibly to write, and even to 'reckon'. It was a popular and communal movement, considerably assisted by financial ideas borrowed from the late seventeenth-century development of the joint stock company, which enabled people of the 'middling sort' to collaborate in charitable activities which were previously possible only for the rich, or through bequests after death.[10]

The motive of Christian charity provided the framework for subsidiary motives. In a sermon preached to raise funds for the Norwich charity schools in 1721, a country clergyman reminded the congregation, led by the mayor, alderman, and common councilmen, that they

> whom God hath blessed with a greater Abundance of the good Things of this Life . . . can, by providing for [the poor] good Nurture and Admonition . . . compensate to 'em the Disadvantage of their obscure Birth and its appendent Evils; free them from the Darkness which uninstructed Nature must have left 'em in, and set them in that respect upon a

[8] For the role of the SPCK as a ginger group promoting the establishment of charity schools (among a number of other activities) see Robert Unwin, 'The Established Church and the schooling of the poor: the role of the SPCK 1699–1720', in Vincent Allen McClelland, ed., *The Churches and Education: Proceedings of the 1983 Annual Conference of the History of Education Society of Great Britain* (Leicester, 1984).

[9] Unwin, 'The Established Church', p. 16.

[10] B. Kirkman Gray, *A History of English Philanthropy: From the Dissolution of the Monasteries to the Taking of the First Census* (1905, new edn. London, 1967), p. 105.

> level with Children born to better Fortunes and the Benefit of a more liberal Education.

He reminded the congregation that they had a vested interest in the education of the poor:

> If your own Temporal Good and Welfare as well as your Eternal [welfare] is consulted and advanc'd by this ingenious Education of the Children of the poorer Sort'.

He went on to point out that

> the Business of this City in the necessary Dispatch of it requires the Hands of many Hundreds, some Thousands of the meaner Sort of its Inhabitants . . . But . . . What are their Hands, how feeble and insufficient, how little to be relied upon, without their Hearts and Consciences to guide them in the Discharge of the Trust that may be repos'd in 'em, in the several Offices in which they may be imploy'd for their Master's Service during the course of their whole lives?

The preacher saw the importance of the education of the whole person.

> Is it not obvious to everyone, that Diligence, Obedience and Fidelity, are qualifications most necessary in a Servant; yet what is it lays upon 'em so strict an Obligation to the sincere Exercise of these Virtues as Principles of Religion and the Knowledge of their Duty imprinted upon their Minds in their tender Years . . . 'tis only a well grounded Sense of Goodness that sets the Head and Hands at work, to promote the Master's Advantage, when he is absent; 'tis Religion that teaches him, That tho' his Master's Eye may sometimes be off yet the Eye of his Master which is in Heaven never is; and consequently that he ought to behave so in his Business as to please not only Men but God.[11]

A complex set of motives combined to encourage people to invest in and subscribe to charity schools. Christian charity called for the salvation of children from the ignorance of sin into which

[11] *The Charitable Education of the Poor Recommended In a Sermon preach'd in the Cathedral Church of Norwich on Ashwednesday February the 7th 1721, by William Sutton, Vicar of Saxthorpe* (London, 1722), pp. 19–21.

they were born, whilst commercial prudence suggested that investment in employees who could read and write and count, and respected the deferential divine order into which they had been born, would pay good dividends. People who had themselves been rewarded with a modest surplus of the good things of the world could devote a proportion of this surplus to promote the honour of God and the well-being of their poorer neighbours' children, thus ensuring their salvation, the defence of the Anglican settlement, and a steady supply of well-motivated and literate apprentices. This combination of motives may explain the detailed care that was taken by trustees, subscribers, and benefactors in the establishment and management of charity schools.

It certainly explains why there was substantial provision for the education of girls as well as boys. In Norwich by 1719 there were eight schools for 240 boys and four schools for 160 girls.[12] Girls as well as boys had souls, and they too needed to be taught about the saving grace of the Christian faith. Girls too would be apprenticed and employed, and so would benefit from the ability to read, write, and count. In particular, girls were important, for it would be their responsibility, in due course, to manage Christian households, the basic unit of the Church, and teach their children their duty towards God and their neighbour, as set out in the Catechism. Not only girls were taught; in London there is at least one reference to a black boy sent to the Cordwainers Ward and Bread Street Schools by his master, Sir John Fellows.[13]

Norwich, a leading provincial centre in early eighteenth-century England, provides considerable evidence of the attitudes of its leading citizens towards childhood in the children of the poor educated in the city's charity schools. The provision of education and the supervision of the schools was a significant and onerous task for some of the leading citizens. In 1712 thirty of them were trustees, including the Chancellor of the Diocese, Thomas Tanner, an archdeacon, the recorder and steward of the borough, the sheriff, and three aldermen.[14] They met weekly to

[12] Society for the Promotion of Christian Knowledge [SPCK] Archives, Society's Reports 1715–1725. Report for 1719.

[13] Guildhall Library MS 1775, Minute Book of Cordwainers Ward and Bread Street Schools 1716–1727.

[14] This and subsequent information relating to the Norwich Charity Schools is derived from NNRO, Late Diocesan Box 1 P125D, Charity School Minute Book 1711–1761.

deal with business relating to the schools. They appointed masters and mistresses, ordered in which parts of the city schools should be, supervised fund raising and income, and expenditure, and generally kept a close eye on the schools. From February 1717/18 some trustees were appointed as Visitors to the schools and were required to report monthly to the full meeting of trustees. From June 1719 usually only six or seven trustees attended meetings, which settled down to a monthly pattern. The regular attenders included Thomas Tanner, the Chancellor, a distinguished Church Whig, and subsequently Bishop of St Asaph, and Alderman Risebrow, a leading Tory, indicating a community of interest across party lines. During the 1720s there are frequent complaints about trustees not undertaking their responsibilities in visiting the schools.

A similar high level of supervision was common in other towns. At King's Lynn the common council itself maintained the 'writing school', which was regularly inspected by three alderman, one of whom was often the mayor.[15] At the charity school supported by the religious society at St Mary-le-Bow, in London, the eleven directors, elected by members every half-year to manage the society, met twice a month and deputed two of their number to visit the school and to report monthly.[16] This random sample suggests a high level of investment of time in the management of schooling for the children of the poorer sort by at least a small number of energetic representatives of the middling sort and urban elites.

It is not easy to calculate the cost of charity-school education. However, significant sums were raised annually to pay for the education of the poor. In 1710 it cost £71 to educate fifty boys at St Mary-le-Bow Charity School. In 1719 the Society of Trustees for Charity Schools estimated that £10,000 a year was raised to support London charity schools.[17]

At Norwich the masters and mistresses were required to find their own premises; elsewhere there could be large expenditure by individuals or trustees on grand buildings for charity schools. The trustees of the Kensington Charity School included

[15] King's Lynn Borough Archives, KL/C7/13, Hall Book 1731–1761.

[16] Sir John Cass Foundation Archives, Records of the Cornhill, Limestreet and Langbourn Ward Schools, 1B/5/9 Minute Book for the Charity School 1709–1712.

[17] Rose, 'Politics, religion and charity', p. 102.

Hawksmoor, who was employed to design a large new building with separate boys' and girls' schoolrooms on the upper floors.[18] The surviving Bluecoat Schools in Westminster and Liverpool suggest considerable investment. Although fittings and furnishings of schools were of the simplest and sparsest, basic comforts were provided, such as fuel for heating the schoolroom.

The provision of uniforms for charity-school children illustrates a positive attitude to the childhood of poor children. The most obvious motive was the need to alleviate the financial burden on parents, who would otherwise be required to forgo the child's earnings and to bear the expense of clothing him or her. The provision of clothes, usually 'Gowns and Petticoats' for girls and 'Capps, coats and bands' for boys, ensured that they looked respectable and, by emulating the example of older foundations, such as Christ's Hospital in London, attracted and pleased benefactors, and this visible token of their generosity provided an example for others. This is vividly illustrated by a monument in All Saints' Northampton, recording that Mrs Dorothy Beckett (who died in 1747 aged ninety) and her sister Mrs Anne Sargent (who died in 1738 aged sixty-eight) 'jointly settled an Estate in Trust, for cloathing and teaching Thirty poor Girls of this Parish.' Above the tablet is a relief of a uniformed charity-school girl, holding a scroll inscribed, 'Go and do thou likewise.'[19]

Provision of uniforms, usually annually, was a significant element in the cost of maintaining a charity school. At Norwich £50 a year was spent on clothes for boys. At Diss, where things were managed on a more homely scale, in 1716 '6 Coatts and 6 westcoatts' cost 12*s*., six 'pr of Leather Breeches' cost 12*s*. and '6 Shirts 6*s*'; five boys also had 'shoose' and four 'stockings'. They were also provided with 'Capps and Bands'. Uniforms also assisted in discipline and the reinforcement of the teaching in the schools. At Diss it was required

> That no Charity Child shall appear publickly without his Cloaths, Cap and Bands upon pain of Expulsion if upon proper Admonition from the Minister of the parish such child shall refuse to reform . . . [and] That if any Charity

[18] Kerry Downes, *Hawksmoor* (London, 1970), p. 66.

[19] All Saints' Church Northampton, monument on west wall of north aisle.

> Child shall be heard Cursing or Swearing in the Streets or be guilty of any other offence contrary to Religion or Good Manners and shall not reform upon Admonition as aforsd such Child shall be expelled from the School.[20]

Children in uniforms reassured subscribers that their money was being appropriately invested in deserving children and that the public behaviour of children could be properly monitored.

After the provision of school buildings and clothing, the appointment and supervision of teachers is an indicator of the attitudes of trustees to children in their schools. There is considerable evidence that trustees of town schools, at least, were scrupulous in seeking godly and respectable teachers for the children under their care. Usually they were required to be practising Anglicans, for an important part of the nurture of children in godliness and good manners was attendance at their parish church. At Raine's School, in London, attendance was required at Morning and Evening Prayer on Sundays, and at St George's in the East on Holy Days as well. At Archbishop Tenison's charity schools in Croydon attendance was additionally required every Wednesday and Friday, and at St Margaret's Westminster charity school, attendance was required daily at Evening Prayer.[21]

The SPCK played perhaps its most useful role in relation to charity schools in providing advice about appointing teachers. Their *Rules for Charity Schools* recommended that a master must be at least twenty-five years old, a communicant, of 'a meek temper', able to stand up to an examination in the Christian religion, 'a keeper of good order in his family', and approved by the minister of his parish.[22] The Norwich trustees adopted these rules. With eight schools to staff, they were regularly seeking staff, and resolved that

> no Person's Testimonials shall be admitted to Stand as a Candidate for either a Master or a Mistress . . . without first having obtained a Certificate under the hand of the Minister of the parish where in they live that he or she are of Sober

[20] NNRO, MS 17607 38 D Diss Charity School, Account Book 1716–1773.
[21] Rose, 'Politics, religion and charity', pp. 117–18.
[22] W. K. Lowther Clarke, *The History of SPCK* (London, 1959), pp. 37–8.

> life and Conversation and constant frequenters of their Parish Church.

Both the Norwich and Diss Trustees expected teachers to be of exemplary behaviour, both in school and in church. The Norwich trustees, through Alderman Risebrow, used the good offices of the SPCK to recruit a London-trained master. The Secretary of the SPCK expressed the hope that

> his Example may Animate other Masters in yor Neighbourhood to discharge this Trust with equal Zeal, if not with equal skill. If the Master of Hethersett could spend a Day or two with Mr Mansel, he would acquire the London methods of Teaching and redeem that time by the Expeditious way of instructing his Children.[23]

As has been noted, trustees played a part in supervising schools. In Norwich inspectors noted when a school was 'very much out of order' and the master was 'desired to amend for the future or to be turned out.' Threats were carried out. In 1725 'Joseph Gunton for his great and repeated neglect of the School committed to his care was then discharged.' At Great Yarmouth in July 1742 William Herring was 'dismissed as School Master for his misappropriating school funds', but a successor was appointed at a salary of £45 a year 'providing he payed £10 a year out of his salary and allowances to William Herring during his lifetime' because 'of his great poverty and Inability of providing for himself'.[24]

Whether the punishment of children was monitored is not clear but occasionally there is criticism. In October 1712 the Norwich trustees noted, 'Upon sufficient testimony before us of the undue severity of Thos Hostler one of the schoolmasters exercised upon one or more of the poor Children under his care. Itt is . . . ordered that [he] be dismissed.' In September 1762 it was noted, 'Whereas Several Complaints have been made of Mrs Good's Behaviour to the Children in her School by Inhumanly beating them without reasonable Causes—Ordered that she be

[23] SPCK Archives, Society Letter Book 1714/5–1716, Henry Newman to John Risebrow, 18 October 1715.

[24] NNRO, Great Yarmouth Papers L3/3, Yarmouth Hospital School Committee, Minute Book 1704–1758.

admonished to forebear such Usage for the future.' Whether such meagre references are the tip of an iceberg, it is not possible to guess.

Despite the evidence for popular Jacobitism in Norwich after the Hanoverian succession,[25] the trustees of the Norwich charity schools were not as perturbed as the London trustees by the distubances surrounding the Hanoverian succession and the Jacobite uprising in 1715. The trustees of the charity school sponsored by the St Mary-le-Bow religious society were especially anxious that they and their school should not be regarded as disaffected towards the government. Consequently they fiercely disciplined a boy who was found to have in his possession 'a paper of Verses very much reflecting upon Seaveral great persons'. The boy was examined in front of all the children and, when the Steward was satisfied that the boy had not obtained the verses from the master, the trustees ordered that the boy should be 'required to kneel before all the scholars and the Society and ask pardon for misusing his education, and then should have his coat and school clothes removed by two great boys and then be expelled from the school.'[26]

In some London schools masters proved their political loyalty by whipping boys who on 29 May 1716 had been 'at a bonfire' and worn 'bows in their caps' or cried 'High Church and Ormonde for ever!'[27] This outburst of violent discipline may reflect a sense of paranoia among some charity-school trustees and religious societies in 1716–18 over fears of government attempts to frame them for Jacobitism.[28]

The prime purpose of charity-school education was the salvation of the children of the poorer sort. The curriculum therefore was primarily religious. *The Christian Schoolmaster* by Edmund Talbot, published by the SPCK in 1707, which probably represented the most widely circulated attempt at a common curriculum, recommended that children should begin by learning the alphabet and the first rudiments of reading in the hornbook

[25] See Nicholas Rogers, 'Popular Jacobitism in provincial context: eighteenth century Bristol and Norwich', in Evelyn Cruickshanks and Jeremy Black, eds, *The Jacobite Challenge* (Edinburgh, 1988).

[26] Guildhall Library MS 1775, Minute Book of Cordwainers Ward and Bread Street Schools 1716–1727.

[27] Leonard Cowie, *Henry Newman: An American in London 1708–1743* (London, 1956), p. 89.

[28] Rose, 'Religion, politics and charity', pp. 136–54.

primer and spelling book. They should then pass on to the Psalter and the New Testament for their reading matter, and then to the Old Testament. Recommended books for older children were Aesop's *Fables* and *The Whole Duty of Man.* Only when they had mastered reading did children pass on to writing. Instruction in arithmetic was limited to those who mastered writing.

Talbot recommended that each Saturday and at the end of term exercises should be set in accordance with the abilities of pupils, for example, to learn a psalm or part of the Catechism or a 'practical' chapter of the Bible or, for those learning to write, to copy a religious passage, and for those learning arithmetic, an arithmetical problem. Each child was to be seated in school according to learning proficiency. When the master took them to church, a careful seating order was also to be observed, with precedence being given to those who had distinguished themselves in piety.[29] The centrality of orthodox Anglican teaching is illustrated by the Charitable Society of St Michael's Cornhill, which in 1716, ordered that

> the following Books be taught in this School and no other, viz *The Bible, The Principles of the Christian Religion explained by the Present Lord Archbishop of Canterbury, The Duty of Public Worship* by Mrs Fox, *An Exposition of the Church Catechism* by Mr Lewis, *The Church Catechism broke into Short Questions and Answers* and *A Dialogue between Master and Scholar.*[30]

The rote learning which characterized most of the teaching in charity schools was relieved by singing psalms. The St Michael's Cornhill Religious Society agreed with a master to 'teach the Boys and Girls to sing Psalms'. The books listed in the SPCK's Report for 1711 for use in charity schools included 'a common prayer book with the singing psalms', 'some book of psalmody', Dr Bray's *Baptismal Covenant*, which had ten psalm tunes as an appendix, and *Hymns for the Charity Schools.*[31] The trustees of the Newcastle charity schools paid £2 a year to a master to teach

[29] See R. W. Unwin, *Charity Schools and the Defence of Anglicanism* (York, 1984), pp. 25–6.

[30] Sir John Cass Foundation Archives, 1B/5/10 Order Book and Minute Book of the Charitable Society of St Michael's Cornhill 1711–1732.

[31] Quoted in Nicholas Temperley, *The Music of the English Parish Church*, 1 (Cambridge, 1979), p. 104.

[32]

psalmody, which was taught professionally, for they also paid 'the Painter for drawing lines on the Psalmody Board in the School'.[32] When the vicar of Box, in Wiltshire, began in 1717 to teach his charity children to sing psalms by notes, other children (up to 100, he claimed) wanted to join them, so he gave them books and practised them every Tuesday, Thursday, and Saturday night in church for about one and a half hours, to sing two or three psalms before and after Sunday afternoon service. He found that this induced 'the greater Number of my Congregation to joyn in the Singing of Psalms', and that subsequently the church was full. Perhaps charity schools and psalm singing not only recruited children to church attendance, but also drew in other backsliders.[33]

In many schools, especially from the 1730s onwards, emphasis was placed on inculcating the discipline of work in children. Henry Newman, as secretary of the SPCK, kept a list of 'working schools' to which he referred inquirers for further advice. These included the schools in Lambeth, where they spun stocking and mop yarn, Spitalfields, where they wound raw silk, St Clement Danes and St Martin-in-the-Fields, where children were employed by a third at a time, so that every boy worked two days in the week, and St George's in the Fields, Southwark, where the master was 'bred a woolcomber'.[34] Work might also help to finance the school by the sale of the products of the children's labours. As the London examples suggest, work was often related to local occupations. In Beverley, where 'the People mostly supported themselves by working at Bone-lace', the children in the charity school there 'work this sort of Lace'.[35] At Diss, in Norfolk, the boys were taught 'Spinning in the Wooling Manufacture'.[36] The introduction of 'work' into schools where it had not previously been part of the curriculum could prove unpopular with parents. At Norwich parents began to withdraw their children from the schools when, in the 1780s, on the initiative of a new bishop, Lewis Bagot, spinning was

Northumberland County Record Office EP9/83, All Saints Newcastle Charity School Accounts 1747–1787.

33 Donald A. Spaeth, 'Parsons and parishioners: lay-clerical conflict and popular piety in Wiltshire villages 1660–1740' (Brown University Ph.D. thesis, 1985), p. 16.

34 Cowie, *Henry Newman*, pp. 96–7.

35 Lawson, *Primary Education in East Yorkshire*, p. 11.

36 NNRO, PD 100/311, Papers relating to Diss Charity School.

introduced into the schools. The parents were reported not to like 'the Children not having the Benefit of their Earnings', which were applied to the maintenance of the schools. When the initiative was dropped, recruitment to the schools immediately recovered.[37] Work silenced the main objections to the charity schools that, while they cared for the minds and morals of the children of the poor, they unfitted them for the life of industry which would be their lot.

The ultimate aim of the charity-school trustees and benefactors was to provide suitable apprenticeships for the children of their schools in order to assist them to the next stage of becoming devout Christians and loyal citizens. The evidence suggests that trustees took very great care in placing their boys and girls in apprenticeships or domestic service. Benefactors like Edward Colston, an immensely rich merchant of Bristol, who left over £25,000 for religious and charitable purposes, were as concerned to fund appropriate apprenticeships as to fund schools.[38] The trustees of the London charity schools took considerable care over apprenticing children from their schools. The trustees of St Botolph's Aldgate Charity School in 1732 rejected a master gardener's application for an apprentice because he was a Dissenter.[39] The rules of the St Michael at Cornhill Religious Society required that 'no Child be placed out before Enquiry be made whether the Person who is Intended for the Master or Mistress be of the Church of England as by law Establisht and of good Life and Conversation.'[40] It is quite clear that the Cordwainers Ward and Bread Street Schools sponsored by the St Mary-le-Bow Religious Society regarded apprenticeship as the sole aim of the education provided in their school.[41] At Diss, too, the advertisement for the charity school describes the objective of the school as to 'putt them out to Apprenticeshippes or Services as they are capable (out of the moneys soe collected)'.[42]

[37] NNRO, P 125 D, Norwich Charity School Minute Book 1759–1811.

[38] Inscription on monument to Edward Colston, died 1721, in south aisle of All Saints,' Bristol.

[39] Sir John Cass Foundation Archives, 1B/2/1A St Botolph's Aldgate Charity School, Rough Copy of a Minute Book 1701–1764.

[40] Sir John Cass Foundation Archives, 1B/5/10 Order Book and Minute Book of the Charitable Society of St Michael's Cornhill 1711–1732.

[41] Guildhall Library MS 1775, Minute Book of Cordwainers Ward and Bread Street Schools 1716–1727.

[42] NNRO, MS 17607 38D Diss Charity School, List of Subscribers 1715.

That the trustees' labours were rewarded with some success is indicated in a letter in 1744 from Mr Blundell, who had for thirty years been treasurer of Liverpool's charity schools. He noted that he had been responsible for putting out nearly 200 children as apprentices, 'Some of which are now masters of ships, some mates in the Ginney [Guinea] trade and that trade to other parts [presumably the slave trade], and many that have attained to be masters in other trades on shore.'[43]

This cumulative, if random, evidence from the charity schools suggests a positive attitude among the 'middling sort' and urban elites during the first half of the eighteenth century towards the children of the 'poorer sort'. They were concerned to train them not only in the discipline of work and labour, but also in an understanding of the Christian faith, as taught by the Church of England 'by Law Establisht'. This would help them to understand their own place in a divinely ordered society and show them that they too might have reasonable expectations of justice and mercy from their masters who, in their turn, were accountable to their 'Master in heaven'. Pollock's view that children were not subject to brutality seems proven, as also her view that childhood was regarded as a period of preparation for citizenship.

Lincoln Theological College

[43] Clarke, *History of SPCK*, p. 48.

REPRESENTATIONS OF CHILDREN IN THE SERMONS OF PHILIP DODDRIDGE

by FRANÇOISE DECONINCK-BROSSARD

WHEN one realizes how small a percentage of eighteenth-century pulpit literature consists of sermons to, or about, children,[1] one may wonder whether the much-vaunted new 'awareness of childhood'[2] ever influenced preachers in the Augustan age. The most prominent minister to address the theme being Philip Doddridge of Northampton, the influential Dissenter,[3] it seems worth investigating how he and his contemporaries chose to represent children.

The most striking feature is the preachers' vivid sense of infant and child mortality. Unlike some of their contemporaries, they could not overlook this dreadful reality.[4] In spite of slow improvements in personal hygiene, the encouragement of breast-feeding, the Lockean demise of swaddling bands, and the training of better midwives, death still took a heavy toll on very young lives. There had been no revolution in this field. The figures in Doddridge's own family[5] differ very little from the statement made by Adam Smith, three-quarters of a century later, about the Highlands of Scotland. Although modern demographers[6] are

[1] The *English Short-Title Catalogue*'s 1992 CD-ROM can provide 21, 186 references with 'sermon$' as a keyword, only eighty-six of which were published in England and can be accessed by specifying 'child$' as a keyword. Unfortunately, this search brings about much 'noise', so the figures quoted above need qualification. They confirm, however, such data as are to be found in Letsome's (1753) and Cooke's (1782) *Preacher's Assistant*, with, respectively, eleven references about children out of 13, 734, and nineteen out of 24, 277 entries.

[2] The pioneering study was Philippe Ariès' famous work, *L'Enfant et la vie familiale sous l'Ancien Régime*, 2nd edn (Paris, 1973). Though the book is not without its critics (among others, Adrian Wilson, 'The infancy of the history of childhood: an appraisal of Philippe Ariès', *History and Theory: Studies in the Philosophy of History*, 19 (1980), pp. 132–53), it was seminal in that it raised the issue of the history of childhood. On the new social attitudes towards children, see J.H. Plumb, 'The new world of children in eighteenth-century England', *PaP*, 67 (1975), pp. 64–95.

[3] The most recent biography is by Malcolm Deacon, *Philip Doddridge of Northampton* (Northampton, 1980).

[4] Richard Wall, 'Mean Household Size in England from Printed Sources', in Peter Laslett and Richard Wall, eds, *Household and Family in Past Time* (Cambridge, 1972), argues (p. 172) that the factor was overlooked in many contemporary printed sources.

[5] Philip Doddridge's mother had borne twenty children, two of whom survived.

[6] The classic work is by E. A. Wrigley and R. S. Schofield, *The Population History of England 1541–1871: A Reconstruction*, 2nd edn (Cambridge, 1989).

wont to show that the curve edges down in the latter half of the century, they also reckon that in the period 1700–49, mean female and male mortality rates in the first nine years of childhood stood at 263 and 277 per 1,000, respectively,[7] which implies that, on average,[8] fifty-four per cent of English children never reached their tenth birthday. The estimates confirm Samuel Eaton's statement in one of his sermons on *The Mortality of Children Considered and Improved*, published in 1764:

> The Mortality of Children, as well as of Parents, needs no Proof. Daily Observation evinces this awful Truth. . . . Yea many die from the womb, and give up the Ghost, when they come out of the Belly. In short, not one half live to the Age of Man. May I not say, not one half survive the Term of Childhood?[9]

The preacher was referring to a traditional distinction between the different stages of human life, according to which childhood 'extended to about *twelve* years', and manhood began at the age of twenty.[10] Ariès' theory about the late discovery of adolescence,[11] or 'youth', as it was then called,[12] cannot therefore apply to England. Teenagers were considered as a separate category, who deserved enough attention for sermons to address them specially, seemingly twice as often as children. Apparently 'young persons' were just as vulnerable, and therefore needed 'admonition', 'advice', 'warnings', 'caution', and reminders of their 'duties'.[13] Though they had survived childhood, they could not easily dismiss the haunting spectre of premature death.

[7] Wrigley and Schofield, *Population History of England*, p. 249.

[8] It should be borne in mind, however, that there was considerable variation from one parish to another; as Wrigley and Schofield have shown, the issue should not be oversimplified.

[9] Samuel Eaton, *A View of Human Life, In a Series of Sermons on the Following Subjects* (London, 1764), p. 27.

[10] Ibid., p. 4.

[11] Ariès, *L'Enfant et la vie familiale*, p. 369.

[12] To quote one example, see Samuel Eaton, *A View of Human Life*, p. 4.

[13] See Cooke's *Preacher's Assistant, passim.* I am grateful to John Gordon Spaulding for lending me his computerized version, known as 'Spaulding's Cooke', while I was on sabbatical leave at the IBM Almaden Research Center in Spring 1992. A printout of his data is on deposit at the Huntington Library.

The samples of sermons for children and young persons are too small for a numerical comparison to be statistically valid.

That, as Doddridge said, 'few Parents [were] exempt from' that 'common Calamity'[14] of mourning the loss of one or several children led not to indifference or resignation, but to genuine grief and persistent parental anxiety about their surviving progeny, has long been documented.[15] It is reasonable to assume, however, that in previous centuries such sorrow had remained private.[16] What may be new in Doddridge's attitude is the public acknowledgement of his distress and indignation at the death of his five-year-old daughter:

> It is not so easy to get rid of every repining Thought, and to forbear taking it, in some Degree at least, unkindly, that the GOD whom we love and serve, in whose Friendship we have long trusted and rejoiced, should act what, to Sense, seems so unfriendly a Part: That he should take away a Child; and if a Child, *that Child*; and if that Child, at that Age . . . and all this, when he could so easily have recalled it; when we know him to have done it for so many others; when we so earnestly desired it; when we fought it with such Importunity, and yet, as we imagine, with so much Submission too:—That, notwithstanding all this, he should tear it away with an inexorable Hand, and leave us, it may be for a while, under the Load, without any extraordinary Comforts and Supports, to balance so grievous a Tryal.[17]

The grieving father voices a very modern view of other people's deaths as the major metaphysical stumbling-block, and implies that the decease of a young child is even more disquieting. Thus he showed great sensitivity to the special nature of childhood. However indignant he may have been at the apparent indifference of Providence, who brings no reward for regular service, the minister of religion was not shaken in his faith. Unlike continental libertines or *philosophes*, he did not seem aware of the conflict, or transition, between traditional Christian teaching and a radically new outlook. Alternatively, it can be argued that he

[14] *Submission to Divine Providence in the Death of Children, Recommended and Inforced, in a Sermon Preached at Northampton, On the Death of a very Amiable and Hopeful Child, about Five Years Old. Published out of Compassion to Mourning Parents*, 2nd edn (London, 1740), p. 32.

[15] Keith Wrightson, *English Society 1580–1680*, 2nd edn (Rutgers University Press, 1984), pp. 109–11.

[16] Linda Pollock's anthology, *A Lasting Relationship: Parents and their Children over Three Centuries* (Hanover and London, 1987), provides useful evidence from primary sources, pp. 123–32.

[17] *Submission to Divine Providence*, Preface, p. iv.

was trying to keep a balance between the world views of the Church and the Enlightenment.

In the bitterness of his heart he still believed that heavy afflictions are acts of God, and referred to them in the same terms as natural disasters. Such 'mournful Providences'[18] as disease, earthquakes, and the deaths of innocent children 'are but second Causes, which owe all their Operations to the continued Energy of the great original Cause'.[19] Not until the latter half of the century and Voltaire's poem on the Lisbon earthquake would theodicy be questioned systematically. All calamities had to teach wise and pious men to recollect their sins and repent accordingly, to remind them of the vanity of the world, warn them of their own approaching deaths, and therefore quicken them in their sense of duty and resignation to the divine will, as the title of the sermon implies. However, Doddridge took an active part in trying to remove one of the major causes of infant and child mortality by fighting a crusade for inoculation against smallpox,[20] at a time when others felt that this practice involved meddling in divine affairs. In his correspondence he conveyed his concern with the issue and exclaimed: 'Oh, when shall we see the Importance of inoculating Children!'[21] Once more Doddridge's ambivalence between traditional and modern attitudes is noteworthy.

The indignation at young children's deaths results from their innocence. 'It is, indeed, impossible for us to say, how soon Children may be capable of contracting personal Guilt' conveys a more Lockean than Calvinistic viewpoint. Indeed, Doddridge had already quoted Locke's educational writings favourably in his earlier sermons on the religious education of children.[22]

[18] Ibid., p. 15. Compare with Doddridge's sermons on natural disasters, *The Guilt and Doom of Capernaum* (1750) and the *Sermon Preached at Wellingborough* on occasion of the Great Fire (1739). The theme was also popular both with Anglicans and Dissenters.

[19] *Submission to Divine Providence*, p. 8.

[20] *The Case of Receiving the Small-Pox by Inoculation, Impartially Considered, and Especially in a Religious View* (1725) by David Some, published from the original manuscript by P. Doddridge (London, 1750). On the conquest of smallpox, see Raymond Phineas Stearns, 'Remarks upon the Introduction of Inoculation for Smallpox in England', *Bulletin of the History of Medicine*, 24, 2 (March–April 1950), pp. 103–22, and Peter Razzell, *The Conquest of Smallpox: The Impact of Inoculation on Smallpox Mortality in Eighteenth-Century Britain* (Firle, 1977).

[21] Geoffrey F. Nuttall, *Calendar of the Correspondence of Philip Doddridge DD 1702–1751* (London, 1979), letter 1679, p. 345.

[22] *Sermons on the Religious Education of Children, Preached at Northampton*, 3rd edn (London, 1743), p. 33.

Although Calvinism soon lurks back with the idea that 'the Corruptions of Nature begin early to work, and shew the Need of sanctifying Grace',[23] there seems to be a short, privileged age of innocence.

Hence, mourning parents need not 'torture themselves' with the thought that their dead children might be damned.[24] On the contrary, they can rest assured that their dear little ones have 'shot up, on a sudden, from the Converse and the Toys of Children, to be Companion[s] with Saints and Angels, in the Employment, and Blessedness of Heaven!'[25] The idea that God's compassion—a recurrent theme[26]—cannot pass a damnatory sentence on any child, who will automatically go to Paradise, confirms the well-documented seventeenth- and eighteenth-century 'decline of Hell', even among Free Church circles.[27] However, Doddridge did not renounce Calvinist predestination, and argued that 'Perhaps, as some pious divines have conjectured, they may constitute a very considerable Part of the Number of the Elect.'[28] It is reasonable to assume that the qualified innocence of the young creatures, who had not yet entered the adult world, and still needed to be diverted with specific activities, such as playing with toys, accounted for assurance of their salvation.

The loss of a young soul spurred parents to pay great attention to the education of surviving children, so that 'the Death of one may be the Means of spiritual Life to many.'[29] Characteristically, the preacher whose family motto read as 'Dum vivimus, vivamus', turned his own grief into concern for others, and his reflections on an appalling experience into a life-giving lesson. Convinced that Heaven was the ultimate goal and the only reality that matters, compared with the 'vain, delusive, transitory joys of this world',[30] he preferred to look to the future rather

---

The reference edition of *The Educational Writings of John Locke* is by James L. Axtell (Cambridge. 1968).

23 *Submission to Divine Providence*, p. 23.

24 Ibid., p. 24.

25 Ibid., p. 26.

26 Ibid., e.g. pp. 22, 25.

27 The classic study is by D. P. Walker, *The Decline of Hell: Seventeenth-Century Discussions of Eternal Torment* (London, 1964).

28 *Submission to Divine Providence*, pp. 22–3.

29 Ibid., p. 20.

30 Ibid., p. 15.

than concentrate on the past. Hence the insistence on the need for religious instruction. Although he considered his sermons as 'practical',[31] he would say little on child-rearing or school curricula. 'Our truest Kindness to them will be to endeavour, by Divine Grace, to form them to an early Inquiry after GOD, and Christ, and Heaven, and a Love for real Goodness . . . that [they] might be farther assisted in the Preparations for Death and Eternity'.[32] No gloom should be read in such statements, but rather the awareness of living 'in a dying World',[33] and the need to hand the congregation's faith down to future generations, so as to avoid breaking a line of continuity in the life of the community:

> *Our Fathers, where are they?* [Zech. 1.5] Sleeping *in the Dust*, as we must shortly be. We are sure, that in a little, a very little while, these *Places must know us no more* [Job 7.10]: And when we are mouldering in the *House of Silence*, who must *fill our Places* in the *House of GOD?* Who must *rise up in our stead* for the *Support of Religion* amongst those that succeed us? From what can it be expected, but from *our Children?*[34]

If a minority church was to survive and keep its identity, particularly in a context of toleration that seemed to encourage more defections than the heroic period of ejection and persecution, it was important that boys and girls should be entrusted, from an early age, with the dissenting tradition, so that they might duly act as the repositories of their fathers' principles.

Affection pervades Doddridge's sermons on children. In a long paragraph, he describes the parents' heavy emotional investment in that source of delight: 'Their Words, their Actions, their very Looks touch us . . . in a tender, but very powerful Manner; their little Arms twine about our Hearts; and there is something more penetrating in their first broken Accents of Indearment, than in all the Pomp and Ornaments of Words.'[35] The keyword that best expressed the warm feelings of family relationships, in Dod-

[31] *Sermons on the Religious Education of Children*, p. 75.
[32] Ibid., p. 20.
[33] Ibid., p. 43.
[34] Ibid., p. 43.
[35] Ibid., pp. 15–16.

dridge's view, was 'tenderness', referring both to parental affection and to the vulnerability of young minds.

Parents also found a source of satisfaction and expectation in their offspring. They greeted each new achievement with pride and joyfully recorded the development of the child's personality: 'Five, or four, or three, or two Years, make Discoveries which afford immediate Pleasure, and which suggest future Hopes. . . . Every Infant-Year increases the Pleasure, and nourishes the Hope.'[36] That he began the enumeration with the five-year-old is probably a personal note, but modern psychologists would not belie the statement. Educationalists now agree that the first five years of life are of paramount importance. Doddridge felt that it was 'the *most impressible Age*',[37] when children could 'imbibe'[38] the maxims which would be 'deeply ingraven [*sic*] upon their Minds'.[39] The metaphors hint at the Lockean outlook of the *tabula rasa* or blank slate, which made it important to provide a proper course of education, for young minds were essentially malleable.

The preacher insisted on the need to give children the right environment, not only because of the high rate of infant mortality and low life expectancy among adults, but also because of 'their Minds being then incapable of judging and acting for themselves in Matters of Importance.'[40] In a race against time, it could be hoped to impress upon them a moral set of values before the human propensity for evil could take hold of them.

The first notions they had to learn, namely the existence and providence of God, and an afterlife of eternal rewards or punishments, looked like the heads of polemical sermons or treatises on theodicy, or the first chapter of a catechism.[41] Yet 'great Care

[36] Ibid., pp. 15–16.
[37] Ibid., p. 39.
[38] Ibid., p. 20.
[39] Ibid., p. 28.
[40] Ibid., p. 25.
[41] On apologetics, see my article, 'L'Apologétique dans la prédication anglaise', in Maria Cristina Pitassi, ed., *Apologétique 1680–1740: sauvetage ou naufrage de la théologie?* (Geneva, 1991), pp. 73–99. On catechisms, see Marcel Brosseau's doctoral thesis, 'Essai sur les livres de spiritualité et de dévotion populaires en Angleterre de 1680 à 1760', 3 vols (doctorat d'Etat, Paris III-Sorbonne nouvelle, 1979), and Ian Green, ' "For children in yeeres and children in understanding": the emergence of the English catechism under Elizabeth and the early Stuarts', *JEH*, 37 (1986), pp. 397–425.

should be taken not to confine our Discourses to these awful Views, lest the *Dread of* GOD should so *fall upon them*, as that *his Excellencies* should *make them afraid* to approach him [Job 13.11].'[42] As a man of his time, Doddridge did not base his preaching on fear.[43] His religion was not of the gloomy or repressive strain. Besides, he was acutely aware of the frailty of young minds, and apprehensive of the 'Danger in over-loading [children's] tender Spirits'. There was no need to force their development or turn them into adults in miniature. In this respect Doddridge echoed the post-Lockean awareness of childhood as a specific stage of development, when there was still scope for introduction 'into the Amusements nay perhaps, where Circumstances will admit it, into the Elegancies of Life, as well as its more serious and important Business.'[44] As often happens, toys, games, and other forms of recreation imitated life in the adult world, including social divisions.

Yet, the child was a person in his own right, who could be taught to pray, not only with ready-made forms, but also in his own private words, 'were they ever so weak and broken.'[45] Even though one may detect a hint of the Dissenters' taste for extemporization, the dignity and individuality here conferred on children is of particular interest, as well as Doddridge's insistence on the slow process of mastering language.[46]

The religious curriculum moved on from theology to social morality. Obedience to parental authority and integrity ranked high on the list of the virtues that had to be taught patiently; so did the typically Augustan virtue of benevolence. The father who rewarded his family for giving their mite to charity out of their pocket money[47] was implicitly acting as God's representative on earth—a very traditional idea indeed.

[42] Ibid., p. 21.

[43] I have shown elsewhere that English eighteenth-century pulpit literature was not founded on fear: *Vie politique, sociale et religieuse en Grande-Bretagne, d'après les sermons prêchés ou publiés dans le Nord de l'Angleterre 1738–1760*, 2 vols (Paris, 1984), 1, pp. 347–50. The basic study on the Continental religion of fear is by Jean Delumeau, *Le Péché et la peur: la culpabilisation en Occident XIIIè–XVIIIè siècles* (Paris, 1983).

[44] *Submission to Divine Providence*, p. 15.

[45] *Sermons on the Religious Education of Children*, p. 22. The idea is repeated later in a direct address to the children, p. 88.

[46] Cf. above p. 384, n. 35.

[47] *Sermons on the Religious Education of Children*, p. 27.

Diligence would equip any child, 'in whatever Station of Life [he] may at length be fixed',[48] with the necessary qualities to secure employment. One could not escape from the work ethic or from the commonplace idea that idleness is evil, of course! However, the ideology here apparently applied to all social classes, whereas charity sermons found it particularly relevant for the poor.[49] Diligence being therefore a classless virtue, prudent parents would ensure that children did not remain idle, and 'quickly assign them *some Employment* for their Time: an *Employment* so moderated, and so diversified, as not to overwhelm and fatigue their tender Spirits.'[50] Far from the horrendous stories of child labour that were to be recorded later at the time of the Industrial Revolution, the notion of specific, unproductive tasks, well adapted to the particular abilities of the young, shows that children were not a source of labour. No immediate economic return was to be expected from them.

Humility would prove a social quality, more so than a moral virtue. It resulted in giving a very strong sense of the social hierarchy, by teaching the proper respect due to one's superiors, and the forms of civility appropriate to address one's equals, bearing in mind that arrogance towards one's servants was not to be tolerated.[51] Likewise, cruelty to animals, inferior creatures though they were, did not provide a permissible form of entertainment.[52] Doddridge's affection could not blind him to children's natural sadism, which Hogarth also was to depict a few years later in *The Four Stages of Cruelty* (1751). That youngsters can be very nasty indeed probably confirmed the Dissenter's views on the depravity of human nature. Hence, no hint of sentimentality is to be traced here. Only later in the century would preachers, including at least one of Doddridge's former

[48] Ibid., p. 27.

[49] Having spoken at length elsewhere of the issues raised in charity sermons, I shall not repeat them here, given the limitations of this short paper: see *Vie politique, sociale et religieuse*, 2, pp. 536–768, as well as 'Sermons sur les oeuvres charitables', in C. d'Haussy, ed., *Le Sermon anglais* (Paris, 1982), pp. 91–121; 'La Représentation de la pauvreté dans la prédication du milieu du siècle', *Actes du congrès d'Amiens* (Paris, 1987), pp. 221–38, and 'Pauvreté et assistance dans la prédication du XVIIIè siècle', *Revue française de civilisation britannique: Religion, politique et société en Grande-Bretagne* [1992], pp. 31–41. See also Donna Andrew, *Philanthropy and Police: London Charity in the Eighteenth Century* (Princeton, 1989).

[50] *Sermons on the Religious Education of Children*, p. 27.

[51] Ibid., p. 31.

[52] Ibid., p. 26.

pupils, verge on mawkishness in their hagiographies of dead children.[53]

The course of education had to be given 'in the *most endearing Language*'.[54] The father who had dared to voice his grief publicly even advised other parents not to suppress any tears while they were speaking to their sons and daughters,[55] for 'a *weeping Parent* is both an *awful*, and a *melting Sight*.'[56] This statement reflects not only an affectionate author's sensitivity, but also a more general shift towards sentimentalism that became fashionable in the 1740s.[57] Tears of emotion conveyed delicacy of sentiment, tenderness, and sympathy, particularly when children were so young as to be speechless, in the etymological meaning of 'infant'. Such language of feeling, mediating between silence and words, was an ideal means of unfettered communication between adults and their offspring.

Should, however, the child disobey his parents, punishment would be used as a last resort. Common sense probably prompted Doddridge to suggest sparing the rod as much as possible. He also showed psychological acumen when he advised mothers against smothering their children with too much affection. More traditional was the idea that 'a Parent's *correcting his Child* should be regarded as an Act of *domestick Justice*.'[58] Here the *pater familias* was acting as a judge, hence, again, as a representative of God on earth. The parallel between the family and the state also underlines the social nature of education.

[53] Benjamin Fawcett, *Children Shouting their Hosannas to Christ. A Sermon Occasioned by the Death of a Child, who was Eight Years Old; With Some Account of her Pious Temper, while she was in Health; and of her Remarkable Expressions in her Last Illness. Preached at Kidderminster, October 22, 1769* (Shrewsbury, 1770), and James Bowden, *The Affection of Christ to his Young Disciples; or, Fervent and Early Piety Recommended and Encouraged. A Sermon, Occasioned by the much Lamented Death of Thomas Bowden, who Departed this Life March 15th, 1795, Aged Ten Years; Preached at Lower-Tooting, in Surry, March 22d, 1795* (London [1795]). Benjamin Fawcett had been one of Doddridge's many pupils.

[54] *Sermons on the Religious Education of Children*, p. 57.

[55] On 'the right to weep,' see Michel Vovelle, *La Mort en Occident de 1300 à nos jours* (Paris, 1983), p. 443.

[56] *Sermons on the Religious Education of Children*, p. 57.

[57] The best attempt at definition of eighteenth-century sentimentalism is that of R. F. Brissenden, *Virtue in Distress: Studies in the Novel of Sentiment from Richardson to Sade* (London, 1974), pp. 11–55. See also John Mullan, *Sentiment and Sociability: The Language of Feeling in the Eighteenth Century* (Oxford, 1988).

[58] *Sermons on the Religious Education of Children*, p. 63. Doddridge's interest in psychology was reflected in his lectures on 'pneumatology', several manuscript copies of which have been preserved, for instance, at Doddridge and Commercial Street Church. Northampton, and at Manchester College, Oxford.

Let us note briefly that parental concern did not end there. 'Settlement in the World', for which education had provided the necessary preparation, was riddled with as many dangers. Here Doddridge seemed to recommend endogamy, for '*Apprenticeships* and *Marriages*, into *irreligious Families*, have been the *known Sources* of innumerable *Evils*.'[59]

Interestingly enough, the post-Lockean, and at times inconsistent, images of children in Doddridge's sermons have revealed an affectionate[60] minister's representations of God. Therefore, one may wonder whether it is by pure coincidence that two-thirds of eighteenth-century sermons to young persons should have been preached by Dissenters.

University of Paris—X

[59] Ibid., p. 68.

[60] On the notion of affectionate religion, see Isabel River's clear study, *Reason, Grace and Sentiment: a Study of the Language of Religion and Ethics in England 1660–1780*, Volume 1 *Whichcote to Wesley* (Cambridge, 1991), pp. 164–204.

'MISSIONARY REGIMENTS FOR IMMANUEL'S SERVICE': JUVENILE MISSIONARY ORGANIZATION IN ENGLISH SUNDAY SCHOOLS, 1841–1865

by BRIAN STANLEY

JUVENILE associations in aid of foreign missions made their appearance both in the Church of England and in the Nonconformist churches in the wake of the successful campaign in 1813 to modify the East India Company charter in order to open British India to evangelical missionary work.[1] The fervour which the campaign engendered led to the formation of numerous local associations in support of the missionary societies. In some cases these associations had juvenile branches attached. However, until the 1840s children's activity in aid of foreign missions was relatively sporadic.[2] Children's missionary literature was almost non-existent. Such children's missionary activity as did take place was confined largely to the children of church and chapel congregations; before the 1840s there was little perception of the vast potential for missionary purposes of the Sunday-school movement.[3]

From the early 1840s the four principal evangelical missionary societies in England—the Church Missionary Society (CMS), London Missionary Society (LMS), Baptist Missionary Society (BMS), and Wesleyan Methodist Missionary Society (WMMS)—began to exploit the juvenile constituency of their respective denominations on an unprecedented scale. The children of both the congregations and the Sunday schools were for the first time seen not only as a fund-raising agency, but also as the key to implanting a missionary spirit in the rising generation.

[1] Brian Stanley, 'Home support for overseas missions in early Victorian England, c. 1838–1873' (Cambridge Ph.D. thesis, 1979), pp. 261–6. I owe thanks to the Methodist Church Overseas Division (Methodist Missionary Society) and the Council for World Mission for permission to cite from their archives.

[2] The significance of the 1840s is not noted by F. K. Prochaska in his study of juvenile missionary organization in *Women and Philanthropy in Nineteenth-Century England* (Oxford, 1980), pp. 73–94.

[3] [Jemima Luke], *Early Years of My Life* (London, 1900), p. 134.

Initially, the financial motive was the dominant one. The decision to cultivate the juvenile constituency was taken at a time when economic depression was compelling the missionary societies to search desperately for new sources of income.[4] However, the more the societies explored the potential of juvenile organization, the more it became apparent that the new movement opened up both possibilities and dangers of a different kind. The Sunday schools were the churches' most substantial beachhead amidst the hostile expanse of working-class irreligion. Whilst there is no doubt that their pupils were primarily working class in provenance, T. W. Laqueur's claim that their teachers and managers came from a similar background has not won universal acceptance. The thesis that the Sunday schools represented a primary instrument whereby the ideals of respectable religion could be implanted in the minds of the poor remains a plausible one.[5] The advocates of missionary organization in the Sunday schools were convinced that the dissemination of missionary enthusiasm in the schools would not merely guarantee the future of overseas missions, but could also be a critical manœuvre in the battle to preserve vital religion within England itself. However, some of the methods which they urged on the missionary societies aroused fears that the exploitation of Sunday-school children for missionary purposes might imperil the very process of integrating the schools into the denominational fabric which was so marked a feature of the evolution of the Sunday-school movement in the mid-nineteenth century.

Two individuals stand out as the primary advocates of the expansion of juvenile missionary organization from the 1840s onwards. One was Thomas Thompson, a wealthy lay Congregationalist and founding member of the Sunday School Union.[6] In January 1841 Thompson issued the first of a series of published letters to Sunday-school teachers, urging them to take every means to interest the children in foreign missions—to set them

[4] Stanley, 'Home support for overseas missions', pp. 29–32.

[5] T. W. Laqueur, *Religion and Respectability. Sunday Schools and Working-Class Culture 1780–1850* (New Haven and London, 1976); Philip B. Cliff, *The Rise and Development of the Sunday School Movement in England 1780–1950* (Nutfield, 1986), pp. 150–2; Malcolm Dick, 'The myth of the working-class Sunday School', *History of Education*, 9 (1980), pp. 27–41.

[6] For Thompson see Jemima Luke, *Sketches of the Life and Character of Thomas Thompson* (London, 1868).

reading missionary literature, collecting for the cause, and praying for the 'heathen'.[7] Thompson combined his public campaign on behalf of juvenile missionary organization with private representations to the missionary societies, in particular the LMS. On 31 May 1841 the LMS Board evinced its appreciation of the financial potential of children's missionary activity by adding Thompson to its committee of funds and agency, the body responsible for organizing the financial support of the Society.[8]

For Thompson, the financial proceeds of children's missionary activity were of secondary importance. His lifelong commitment to the Sunday-school movement derived from his belief that it 'might be made . . . effectual for the moral regeneration of England, and through England of the world.'[9] Thompson viewed the distress among the labouring classes in 1841, and feared for the future of Christian society; the remedy lay in a system of Christian education which would teach the poor 'how to bear privations with subjection and without repining, or running into all the evils of anarchy under designing leaders.'[10] Of central importance in this strategy was instruction in the Christian duty to love our neighbour as ourselves, and what more appropriate vehicle could there be towards this end than the support of foreign missions? Thompson's first published letter to Sunday-school teachers thus pointed out that the diffusion of the missionary spirit among their pupils would not only swell the ranks of missionary recruits, but also inoculate the young against a variety of spiritual diseases, from the 'cold, stagnating breath of Oxford heresy' to 'all the darker suggestions of socialism and infidelity'.[11]

Not everyone in the churches shared Thompson's confidence that collecting for foreign missions would exert an uplifting influence on the working-class children who filled the Sunday schools. His third letter to Sunday-school teachers, issued in July

[7] The letters (which first appeared in denominational or Sunday-school periodicals) were reprinted in T. and J. Thompson, *Sunday-schools and Missions. Or, Outlines of Correspondence with Sunday-school Teachers, During the Years 1841, 1842* (London, 1843).

[8] London, School of Oriental and African Studies, Council for World Mission archives [hereafter CWMA], LMS Board minutes, box 27, p. 336.

[9] Luke, *Sketches*, pp. 99–100.

[10] CWMA, LMS Home Office Incoming Letters, Thompson to J. J. Freeman, 16 Aug. 1841.

[11] Thompson, *Sunday-schools and Missions*, p. 7.

1841, was 'principally intended to answer objections which began to be felt in some quarters'; it urged teachers to be watchful to prevent 'the leaven of self-confidence and self-elation' from entering the hearts of their pupils, robbing them of 'that humility and simple-mindedness which, in the sight of Jesus, are childhood's chief ornament.'[12] Thompson's proposals soon ran into difficulties of another kind. In November 1841 he had letters published in the *Patriot* newspaper, suggesting that the customary Christmas treat observed in many Sunday schools should on the coming Christmas Day be made into a nationwide juvenile missionary festival.[13] Thompson originally suggested that, as part of the festivities, the children should carry 'missionary banners'. It is clear from subsequent correspondence between Thompson and the LMS that this proposal aroused particular concern. The display of decorated banners carrying texts or mottoes was a common feature of Sunday-school processions and gatherings, at least in the provinces, as Thompson hastened to point out to the Society.[14] Nevertheless, the prospect of simultaneous meetings throughout the country filled with banner-waving working-class children seems to have alarmed some of the more conservative metropolitan spirits within English Congregationalism.

Largely frustrated in his plans for a juvenile missionary festival at Christmas 1841,[15] Thompson turned his thoughts towards Easter 1842. His hope was to persuade the LMS Directors to hold a vast missionary meeting for Sunday-school children in Exeter Hall. The LMS committee of funds and agency jibbed at such an audacious project, proposing instead to organize four separate London meetings for the young over the Easter weekend.[16] However, confronted by threats from Thompson's daughter, Jemima, that if the LMS failed to act, 'We have some idea of putting the Wesleyans up to something of the kind', the LMS

[12] Ibid., pp. 10–11.

[13] The letters are reprinted in ibid., pp. 13–16.

[14] CWMA, LMS Home Office Incoming Letters, Thompson to J. J. Freeman, 13 Nov. 1841. It is claimed that Sunday-school banners were the parent of banners in trade union marches; see Cliff, *Rise and Development*, p. 91.

[15] Thompson repeated the project in 1842, and succeeded in gaining the support of the *Sunday School Teachers' Magazine*; see new ser. 13 (1842), p. 847.

[16] CWMA, LMS Committee Minutes, Home Occasional, box 1, book 1, pp. 23–4.

Board overruled the recommendation, and resolved to hold a meeting in Exeter Hall on 29 March.[17]

The LMS set about preparing for the Exeter Hall meeting with a thoroughness that betrayed its anxiety. Admission was to be by ticket only, and no child under eight years of age was to be admitted. The scope of the meeting was widened from the original restriction to Sunday-school children to include the chapel-going children of the juvenile missionary associations. The Sunday-school children were to use the Exeter Street side entrance, and the children of the juvenile associations the main door in the Strand. The two social categories were to be similarly segregated in the Hall itself, as were the sexes. The chairman was to state that the object of the meeting was not 'to collect money of the Sunday school children', but to excite a missionary spirit. Most telling of all was the stipulation that 'Police Officers be engaged to attend at the doors.'[18]

With such prudent precautions, the meeting was a decided success: 'About 6000 children were there, and though a second and a third room were opened to receive the overflowing numbers who sought admission, it was calculated that above 1000 went away. . . . The arrangements were so well made, that notwithstanding the numbers, no confusion or accident occurred.'[19] However, the same fear of 'confusion or accident' which had nearly destroyed the project at the outset prompted the LMS Board to decide that in Easter 1843 juvenile meetings should be held in five separate chapels, rather than in Exeter Hall.[20] The Exeter Hall children's meeting in 1842 was a controversial experiment which was not repeated. Nevertheless, it proved a stimulus to children's missionary organization throughout the country. In London itself, teachers and children were fired with a new determination to organize their own school or congregation.[21] In the provinces, a series of large

[17] CWMA, LMS Home Office Incoming Letters, J. Thompson to J. Arundel, 26 Feb. 1842; LMS Board Minutes, box 27, p. 516. The threatened letter to the Wesleyans was written; see London, School of Oriental and African Studies, Methodist Church Overseas Division archives [hereafter MCODA], WMMS Home Correspondence, T. Thompson to WMMS secretaries, 1 March 1842.

[18] CWMA, LMS Committee Minutes, Home Occasional, box 1, book 1, pp. 24–7.

[19] Thompson, *Sunday-schools and Missions*, p. 29.

[20] CWMA, LMS Board Minutes, box 27, p. 544, and box 28, pp. 103–4; cf. *Evangelical Magazine*, 21 (1843), p. 151.

[21] Thompson, *Sunday-schools and Missions*, pp. 20–1.

children's meetings ensued, organized by the LMS, though often attended by children of all denominations. At many of these the main attraction was Robert Moffat from South Africa, who seems to have been uniquely effective as a speaker to the young.[22] Impressive attendances were recorded: 2,400 in Great George Street Chapel, Liverpool; over 2,000 in Grosvenor Street Chapel, Manchester; 3,000 in Birmingham Town Hall; 3,250 in Edinburgh; and these estimates are for numbers of children alone, excluding teachers. The series culminated in the largest meeting of all, on 27 October 1842, when Moffat addressed the children of the Glasgow Sunday schools in the City Hall, Glasgow. The LMS directors had already decided not to hold an Exeter Hall meeting in 1843, but the reports from Glasgow can only have confirmed their decision:

> The immense hall was crowded to overflowing, there being present, old and young, nearly seven thousand persons, six thousand of whom were children, while thousands more were disappointed in not obtaining admission. The children were carried into the hall by the pressure of the crowd, and Mr Moffat himself was almost squeezed to death on making his way to the platform.[23]

Even allowing for a measure of hyperbole in this account of Thompson's, it is clear that children's meetings on this scale posed problems of crowd control that were sufficiently serious to question the validity of his conservative vision of the antiseptic value of juvenile missionary organization. None the less, Thompson must have been well pleased with the flowering of children's missionary periodicals which soon followed in order to service the newly expanded juvenile market. The CMS got in first, with the *Church Missionary Juvenile Instructor*, first published in 1842, which reached a circulation of between 63,000 and 80,000. In 1844 the WMMS and the LMS followed with, respectively, the *Wesleyan Juvenile Offering* and the *Juvenile Missionary Magazine*; the latter initially had a circulation of 100,000, which later steadied to 85,000. The BMS published the *Juvenile Mission-*

[22] William Walters, *Life and Labours of Robert Moffat, D.D., Missionary in South Africa* (Derby, nd), pp. 151–2.

[23] Thompson, *Sunday-schools and Missions*, p. 31.

ary Herald in 1845, with an initial circulation of 40,000.[24] Children's missionary literature had become big business, and remained so well into the twentieth century.[25]

The second individual who laboured unceasingly for the expansion of juvenile activity on behalf of foreign missions was a Wesleyan Methodist from Harrow, Joseph Blake. It was in the Wesleyan connection that the broader domestic purposes of the movement were most clearly perceived, perhaps because the Wesleyan Mission House was not merely the headquarters of overseas missionary operations, but also the seat of power within the denomination. Nevertheless, the movement also encountered its most serious obstacles within the Wesleyan connection, for it became caught up in the tussle for control of the Sunday schools between lay managers and teachers, on the one hand, and Conference preachers, on the other.

Three years before Thomas Thompson launched his campaign, Blake, a shoemaker and Sunday-school teacher,[26] had begun to urge the WMMS to train a new generation of missionary collectors drawn from the Wesleyan Sunday schools.[27] For three years the Mission House turned a deaf ear to Blake's suggestions. But in December 1840 Blake was appointed circuit steward for the Hammersmith circuit, and thus from May 1841 occupied a seat on the London District Meeting, whose chairman was the ageing Methodist patriarch, Jabez Bunting.[28] Blake had instituted his own system of juvenile missionary collecting among the Harrow Sunday-school children, whereby each child was invited to collect eight weekly subscriptions of a halfpenny each, entering the names of subscribers in a collecting book, and paying in the subscriptions every Sunday to his or her Sunday-school teacher. From July 1841 Blake used his new access to the fountain-head of Wesleyan power to urge Bunting to promote the Harrow system of weekly collecting throughout the

[24] Stanley, 'Home support for overseas missions', pp. 219–20.

[25] Prochaska, *Women and Philanthropy*, pp. 91–2.

[26] E. Armstrong, 'A J.M.A. History', *The Kingdom Overseas* (April, 1952), p. 67.

[27] MCODA, WMMS Home Correspondence, J. Blake to E. Hoole, 16 Jan. 1838, and box 'Joseph Blake', Blake to [Hoole], 5 June 1838. This box, formerly located at the headquarters of the Methodist Church Overseas Division, has unfortunately been lost.

[28] Joseph Blake, *The Day of Small Things or a Plain Guide to the Formation of Juvenile Home and Foreign Missionary Associations in Sunday and Day Schools and Private Families*, revised edn (Sheffield, 1868), p. 10.

connection.[29] Although he received some initial encouragement,[30] the Wesleyan missionary secretaries hung back from lending their official sanction to Blake's plan, for Bunting had already decided on an alternative expedient better calculated to meet the pressing financial needs of the Society. The plan, adopted by the WMMS General Committee on 6 October, was that all pew-holders in Wesleyan chapels were to request their children to 'collect or beg' a sum of one shilling each, to be presented to the Missionary Committee on Christmas Day 1841. The scheme was confined to the children of pew-holders, so that it would not 'press heavily on the very poor, who are not, generally, renters of pews in our chapels.'[31] Furthermore, since pew-holders represented the core of the Wesleyan faithful, Bunting could be assured that his project would remain within the bounds of connectional order, whereas Blake's scheme, whose primary focus was in the Sunday schools, would be less amenable to ministerial control.

The 1841 Christmas Offerings were an astounding success. A sum of almost £5,000 was raised, which enabled the Society to avoid its anticipated deficit for 1841. Suggestions were made that the Offerings should be repeated in 1842.[32] Blake continued to write to the Mission House pressing the merits of his own scheme, which he predicted could be worth £10–50,000 per annum to the Society; he did not scruple to tell Bunting that his 'systematic and regular' method was to be preferred to any repetition of the Christmas Offerings: 'Collecting by these fits and starts will not do.'[33]

At the same time, however, Bunting was being urged by Thomas Thompson to repeat the Christmas Offerings: 'Our Sabbath and other schools must form one grand missionary camp and the descendants of John Wesley must do their duty in forming these missionary regiments for Immanuel's service.' No

[29] Manchester, John Rylands University Library, Methodist Church archives [hereafter MCA], Blake to [J. Bunting], 1 July 1841; MCODA, box 'Joseph Blake', Blake to Bunting, 22, 26 and 30 July 1841.

[30] *Wesleyan Methodist Magazine* [hereafter *WMM*], ser. 3, 20 (1841), pp. 790–1; Blake, *The Day of Small Things*, pp. 10–11.

[31] MCODA, WMMS General Committee Minutes, Box 549, p. 173; *WMM*, ser. 3, 20 (1841), pp. 1054–5.

[32] *WMM*, ser. 3, 21 (1842), p. 260.

[33] MCODA, box 'Joseph Blake', Blake to WMMS Secretaries, 11 March 1842; MCA, Blake to Bunting, 14 Oct. 1842.

doubt Bunting was attracted by Thompson's argument that the diffusion of a missionary spirit among the Sunday-school children would be an antidote to 'Popery Puseyism, Chartism and all the errors of the day'.[34] Perhaps still more cogent to Bunting's mind was the potential of another Christmas Offering to stave off a further accumulation in the Society's debt. On 23 November 1842 the General Committee decided, after 'mature and long consideration', to repeat the Christmas Offerings at the coming Christmas.[35] The decision had been taken too late to ensure a response from the circuits on an equivalent scale to 1841. Less than £2,000 was raised. The Society's annual report for 1842 expressed the hope that the hesitation which had impaired the success of the second Christmas Offering would not again occur, and that in future the project would be promoted in every circuit.[36] In July 1843 the Missionary Committee of Review reiterated this call for 'the *diligent* and *universal* repetition of such efforts in *all* our Circuits'.[37] The crisis-induced expedient of 1841, hesitantly repeated in 1842, had by 1843 become a regular connectional project. Furthermore, the scope of the scheme was now extended. The appeal for the 1843 Offering was addressed 'to children and young persons, especially to such as belong to families who are seat-holders in Wesleyan chapels'.[38] In subsequent years all reference to the original limitation disappeared; the Offerings were widely adopted by Sunday-school children, as well as by the children of the chapel juvenile associations. The title of the Wesleyan juvenile missionary periodical first issued in 1844, the *Wesleyan Juvenile Offering*, indicated that the Offerings now had behind them the full weight of the Mission House establishment, as circuits which failed to remit an Offering found to their discomfiture.[39] By 1859 the Christmas Offerings accounted for 9.5 per cent of WMMS ordinary receipts from Great Britain.[40]

[34] MCODA, WMMS Home Correspondence, Thompson to WMMS Secretaries, 11 Feb. 1842; see also his letter of 1 March 1842.

[35] MCODA, WMMS General Committee Minutes, Box 549, p. 216.

[36] *WMM*, ser. 3, 22 (1843), pp. 501, 524.

[37] *Minutes of Several Conversations between the Methodist Ministers* . . . (1843), p. 93.

[38] MCODA, Circulars 1819–1904, circular dated 7 Dec. 1843.

[39] MCODA, WMMS Home Correspondence, Jan.–May 1845, letters 28–82.

[40] *Report of the Wesleyan-Methodist Missionary Society for the year ending April 1860*, pp. 2–4; cf. Prochaska, *Women and Philanthropy*, p. 82.

While Jabez Bunting remained alive, the Mission House continued to promote the Christmas Offerings and resist Joseph Blake's repeated pleas on behalf of his weekly collecting scheme. However, within a few weeks of Bunting's death, on 16 June 1858, Blake wrote to the missionary secretaries urging them to 'get the Christmas Offerings out of the Way' in favour of his more systematic scheme.[41] At the same time he petitioned the Wesleyan Conference, requesting them to replace the Christmas Offerings with permanent juvenile missionary societies on the Harrow pattern. The Conference referred the matter to the WMMS Committee, which informed Blake in October that it was 'very favourably impressed' with the advantages of forming juvenile societies on the Harrow pattern; it also recommended that such societies should be formed where suitable leadership was available, and that where such juvenile societies were already in existence, the Christmas Offering need not be raised that year.[42] In May 1860 the Society relented a stage further, and sent one of its secretaries, William Arthur, on a deputation tour with Blake to the north of England, and in particular to Bradford, where the Bradford West circuit had set up a Juvenile Home and Foreign Mission Association in close liaison with Blake. Arthur was much impressed, and inserted an article in the *Wesleyan Methodist Magazine*, remarking that the weekly system produced a considerably larger annual return than the Christmas Offerings in those circuits which had abandoned the latter in favour of the former, and expressing the hope that many Sunday-school friends would adopt the weekly system.[43] Five years later the Conference gave its official sanction to such circuits as so desired to set up juvenile missionary associations on the Bradford model and dispense with the Christmas Offerings.[44] Although Blake was denied his wish to see the Offerings entirely abolished, his persistence had borne fruit in the genesis of the Juvenile Missionary Association (JMA), an organization which was to exert a considerable influence in Methodism for generations to come.

Why did the Wesleyan authorities maintain such a protracted resistance to the entreaties of so loyal a servant as Joseph Blake?

[41] MCODA, box 'Joseph Blake', Blake to [WMMS], 24 July 1858.

[42] MCODA, WMMS General Committee Minutes, Box 549, pp. 395–6.

[43] *WMM*, ser. 5, 6 (1860), pp. 1041–3.

[44] *Minutes of Several Conversations between the Methodist Ministers* . . . (1865), p. 171.

No doubt Bunting resented Blake's impudent insistence on the moral and organizational superiority of his weekly system, in which no child was permitted to enrol more than eight subscribers, in order to prevent a spirit of unseemly rivalry. Blake did not help matters by adopting as the patron of his cause Samuel Jackson, who was no friend of Bunting's, and the successful anti-Buntingite candidate for the presidency of the Conference in 1847. Yet the arguments advanced by Blake and Jackson on behalf of the weekly scheme appeared well calculated to appeal to the Mission House authorities. They suggested that making adolescents missionary collectors could halt the drift of this age-group from the Wesleyan Sunday schools to the Anglican National schools, which had followed the success of the Conference in eliminating writing classes from the Sunday schools.[45] Missionary organization within the Sunday schools would tie children to the Wesleyan family with bonds which would prove too strong for the Anglicans to 'sever by entreaties or paltry gifts'.[46]

To Bunting and some other Wesleyan ministers, however, the prospect of missionary organization in the Sunday schools presented alarming possibilities for lay insubordination. Blake's insistence on the complete autonomy of juvenile missionary organization from the regular circuit structures was disturbing to those who complained that the structures of neither the Sunday schools nor the local missionary auxiliaries were sufficiently under the control of the preachers.[47] Such fears were expressed as late as 1863, when Blake, touring the north of England on behalf of his cause, found that the Leeds and Bradford ministers regarded the proposal of the school managers for a single juvenile movement throughout the circuits as an infringement of their prerogatives.[48] To Wesleyan ministers still insecure in their relationship with the Sunday schools the idea of missionary organization controlled by lay enthusiasts and crossing circuit boundaries could be threatening. By the mid-1860s, however,

[45] Blake, *The Day of Small Things*, 1st edn (London, 1849), pp. 68, 71; W.R. Ward, *Religion and Society in England 1790–1850* (London, 1972), pp. 135–40; Laqueur, *Religion and Respectability*, pp. 124–46.

[46] MCA, Blake to [Bunting], 6 May 1844.

[47] MCA, Blake to Bunting, 10 Feb. 1844; cf. W.R. Ward, ed., *Early Victorian Methodism. The Correspondence of Jabez Bunting 1830–1858* (Oxford, 1976), p. 175.

[48] MCODA, WMMS Home Correspondence, Blake to [WMMS Secretaries], 4 July 1863; cf. M. Cranswick to W. Arthur, 18 Jan. 1862.

the connectional battle for control of the Sunday schools was effectively won, and the gulf between Sunday-school and chapel children was narrowing. Once Bunting was removed from the scene, the continuing unease in some quarters at the implications of Blake's scheme was outweighed by the financial attractions of a scheme which promised regular and systematic income.

The denominations took up the idea of children's missionary activity in the early 1840s in rapid succession. Both the keen interdenominational rivalries which ran beneath the placid surface of evangelical ecumenism and the immediate pressures of financial stringency moved the societies to action. The two chief advocates of the movement—Thomas Thompson and Joseph Blake—conceived of its potential benefits in terms whose scope extended well beyond the financial sphere. For them the missionary education of the young, and especially the young of the working classes who filled the Sunday schools, offered a shining example of the general providential principle that Britain's benevolence to the world through the missionary movement would redound to her own temporal and spiritual benefit. Those within the missionary societies who had the responsibility of implementing their vision were not always so sanguine: the potential for loss of control, whether of vast children's meetings or of autonomous organizations in the Sunday schools, was never far from their minds. In the long run, however, the allure of children's money-raising power proved powerful enough to override such hesitations. By the end of the century income from juvenile sources accounted for an extremely large proportion of missionary society domestic receipts—Prochaska estimates about twenty per cent in the case of the Methodist Missionary Society by 1901.[49] Constance Padwick, surveying in 1917 the story of the missionary societies' nineteenth-century discovery of the potential of juvenile support, commented that 'Missionary committees had discovered not children but a copper-mine.'[50] That comment was cited by Roland Allen in *The Spontaneous Expansion of the Church* as an example of the 'overwhelming materialism' of

[49] Prochaska, *Women and Philanthropy*, pp. 82–3.

[50] Constance E. Padwick, 'Children and missionary societies in Great Britain', *International Review of Missions* (Oct. 1917), p. 566.

the missionary movement which he so much deplored.[51] Whether or not these strictures are justified, the significance for popular British attitudes to the non-Western world of the type of literature and imagery which fuelled the flow of juvenile copper into missionary coffers cannot be underestimated.

Trinity College,
Bristol

[51] Roland Allen, *The Spontaneous Expansion of the Church and the Causes which Hinder it*, 4th edn (London, 1960), p. 102.

SUNDAY-SCHOOL BOOK PRIZES FOR CHILDREN: REWARDS AND SOCIALIZATION

by DOROTHY ENTWISTLE

THIS paper considers the reward books given to children as Sunday-school prizes in the north-west of England between 1870 and 1914. From the titles presented and from the authors considered to be suitable, it was possible to select a number of books which were representative of these prizes. An examination of these stories showed that there were themes which were repeatedly stressed, and that those for boys and girls were noticeably different. In the light of what is already known about the organization and purposes of Sunday schools, the choice of a particular genre of books for prizes suggests that their contents were seen as one way of socializing children into appropriate attitudes and behaviour.

Today there is considerable concern in the churches, and across society in general, about the possible harmful effects of television on children's attitudes and morals. It is not just the 'video nasties', but the everyday diet of materialist values which arouses that concern. There has also been active interest in the content of children's books, in particular to see what gender roles are being endorsed by authors. At the turn of the century there was a very similar anxiety being expressed about working-class children. For example, William Groser, author of many Sunday-school teachers' manuals, warned that the 'penny dreadfuls diffuse subtle poison among tens of thousands of youthful readers' and 'brought ruination to hundreds of our brightest and best lads and lasses'.[1]

The reason for this long-lasting concern can be found in the nature of socialization. It is accepted that children learn by

[1] William H. Groser, *The Opening Life* (London, 1911), p. 30. For examples of widespread religious and secular contemporary concern about the circulation of undesirable juvenile literature see Edward Salmon, *Juvenile Literature as It Is* (London, 1888), pp. 184–99; Charlotte M. Yonge, *What Books to Lend and What to Give* (London, 1887), pp. 5–14; 'Penny fiction', *Quarterly Review*, 171 (1890), pp. 150–71; G. R. Humphrey, 'The reading of the working classes', *Nineteenth Century*, 33 (1893), pp. 690–701.

imitation, initially of parents and family, later of teachers, and increasingly of peers. But children are also strongly influenced by the characters of the 'heroes' or 'heroines' depicted in literature, and nowadays in films and television. It was the imitation of the inappropriate role models found in popular fiction which alarmed the nineteenth-century commentators as much as their twentieth-century counterparts. Such literature often presents heroes in successful conflict with authority, showing in the words of Hanna and McAllister, 'Vice, brutality, moral and physical degeneration . . . foul and offensive language . . . unhealthy horrors . . . and a disregard for law and order, and a flouting of authority, [all] shown to be humorous, glamorous, or smart'.[2]

Of course, it is already well known that Sunday schools awarded book prizes to their pupils, and it has been assumed that these books concentrated solely on moral and religious themes. But surprisingly little is known in any detail about which particular books were given as prizes, which individual authors were considered 'safe', and which specific themes were contained in typical prize books. Some evidence on these aspects has now been collected and analysed, and forms the main basis of this paper.

First of all, which titles were given? To answer this question, a survey was carried out of books in second-hand bookshops. Books with labels inside the covers showing that they had been given as Sunday-school prizes were noted and analysed to find which titles and authors were given frequently. Next, which of these authors were considered safe? The approach here was to examine denominational magazines. They contained reviews of children's books, with comments about their suitability and reasons for that judgement. Certain authors were consistently 'approved'. Finally, from the previous analyses, particular books could be chosen as typical and carefully examined to establish categories of themes which the authors introduced.

In the survey of twelve second-hand bookshops in Lancashire and Yorkshire, we found 1,278 books given by a variety of religious institutions between 1870 and 1914. Of course, even

[2] G. R. Hanna and M. K. McAllister, *Books, Young People, and Reading Guidance* (New York, 1960), p. 140.

such a substantial set of books cannot be regarded as necessarily representative of what was actually given. Inevitably, only some books find their way into the bookshops and some of these are not on display. However, we were also able to look at library records from the undenominational Stockport Sunday School, over the same period. These showed similar authors and titles to those found among the prize books and so suggests that the sample of prize books was not atypical.

The information from the books and bookplates enabled us to record not just author and title, but also publication date, the name and place of the institution, together with the date and reason for giving the prize—usually for attendance or good behaviour. Most of the prizes had been given in areas of industrial north-west England, where mainly working-class children would have attended the Sunday schools. The analysis of titles and authors immediately gave a more precise idea of what had previously been a rather amorphous grouping called 'Sunday-school prizes'. Although only 252 titles occurred more than once, there were still clear favourites, and several authors featured frequently in the sample. The most popular authors and titles are shown in the Appendix. The sample made it difficult to separate authors preferred by different denominations, but there were some distinguishable preferences. The temperance novel *Danesbury House* had been given *only* by Nonconformist Sunday schools, which also preferred books by Silas Hocking, 'Pansy', and Mrs Henry Wood. Favourite authors in Anglican Sunday schools were A. L. O. E. and W. H. G. Kingston.

Of course, the main concern of this study was to identify how prize books were thought to influence children's values and behaviour. One way of looking at this was to examine denominational magazines. These reflected the official policy of the Sunday-school movement and also had regular reviews of books for both adults and juveniles. Of the eight denominational magazines chosen, the *Church Times* and the *Methodist Recorder* represented the two main religious streams of the prize sample, while the *Sunday School Chronicle* was a largely interdenominational magazine produced for Sunday-school teachers.

Frequent comments about literature for young people were made across the range of magazines and contained a rich source of information, advice, and criticism. Again they illustrated the contemporary concern about the spread of undesirable juvenile literature, but they were too idiosyncratic to be easily categorized. Book reviews, on the other hand, had more in common. These discussed the relative merits or demerits of books in terms of their general moral tone, and gave relevant information about the themes they contained. From them, the popularity of authors and titles in the prize sample could be assessed, as could the reasons why such books were considered appropriate as prizes. 1,361 reviews were traced. They were of three different kinds. Some of them specifically recommended books as prizes; others were of titles given often as prizes; while the majority were of books by authors who occurred frequently in the prize sample. So, not only was there a group of authors, but there was also a *type* of literature, considered particularly suitable for Sunday-school pupils.

Most of the reviews described broad themes from the books. The reviewers' selection of particular themes seemed to indicate their own concerns, as well as the content of the stories. Sometimes the comments highlighted the character of the hero or heroine in ways which drew attention to approved role models and associated values. A content analysis of the reviews produced a series of categories describing the themes which recurred most frequently. How these categories were related to the comments can be illustrated from specific reviews. For example:

> The hero tries all play and no work and finds that it is no good either for body or soul. He commences by neglecting his work, chumming with boys worse than himself, covering up his faults by falsehoods and apparently going from bad to worse until finally his downward career is arrested and he turns over a new leaf. A capital school story for boys.[3]

This review was categorized as *inculcation of virtues* which was an aspect of 'character training', while the next extract came under the heading of *woman's role*.

> A story of a long-suffering cab-driver whose one indiscretion, his marriage to a frivolous shop-girl wrecks the happiness of his life but whose patience and forbearance at length

[3] Harold Avery, *All Work and No Play* (London, 1901). Reviewed in *Primitive Methodist Magazine* [hereafter *PMM*] 1901.

meet with their reward. The deeper moral is the utter unfitness for marriage which generally results from bringing up without proper fitness of training in housewifely habits.[4]

Table 1 *Reviews of book titles grouped into the main themes identified*

1 *Feminine Role*: 'self-sacrifice leading to rewards', 'female biographies for emulation and example', 'service to Christ and/or conversion of others', 'woman's role and nature', 'woman's beneficial influence', 'development of self-reliance', 'schoolgirl stories'.
2 *Masculine Role*: 'male biographies for emulation and example', 'development of Christian manly virtues', 'true adventure tales for inspiration', 'self-sacrifice leading to rewards', 'service to Christ and/or conversion of others'.
3 *Character Training*: 'homilies on inculcation of virtues', 'virtues of a Christian life', 'lessons in contentment', 'moral lessons', 'models of character'.
4 *Vices*: 'smoking, drinking, gambling, opium', 'emptiness and danger of society life', 'corrupting effect of money', 'dangers within upperclass life', 'superficiality of outward appearance versus inner values'.
5 *Family*: 'duty to parents by both sexes', 'love and marriage', 'child rearing'.
6 *Social Concern and Philanthropy*: 'social concern', 'philanthropy', 'foreign missionary work'.
7 *Self-improvement*: 'self-help and improvement', in both fiction and non-fiction.
8 *Relevant to Lower Classes*: 'for servants', 'for both sexes of humble/rural background', 'effect of changed environment on lower classes'.
9 *Emigration*: 'Colonial information and interest'.
10 *Denominational Bias*: 'anti-popery', 'anti-dissent'.
11 *Occupational Life*: 'industrial life and problems', 'business or clerical life'.
12 *Nature*: 'items related to the natural world'.
13 *Russia*: 'political and religious problems' in fiction.
14 *Reviews with adverse criticism.*

The full content analysis produced fourteen categories which are shown in Table 1. An appropriate gender role, both male and female, was the salient feature in approximately a third of the sample of reviews. Character training, the dangers of certain vices (notably smoking, drinking, and gambling), and family

[4] Florence Wilford, *Tender and True* (London, 1882). Reviewed in *Church Times* [hereafter *CT*], Dec. 1882.

matters were the next most important categories. Social and philanthropic concerns, and self-improvement, were not as frequently mentioned as might have been expected, and there were even fewer comments indicating 'denominational bias'.

The next step was to read fifteen of the reviewed books, chosen from within these fourteen main categories, to see how far their contents related to the reviewers' themes. The books consisted of non-fiction for both sexes, and also girls' and boys' fiction.[5] It was tempting to look for the subtle, the covert, and even the ideological slant within the contents of these books. The main concern, though, was to examine the generally accepted aims of the authors, that is, communication with the unsophisticated reader. For that reason, only the most obvious themes were selected, producing seventeen broad categories, which proved to overlap substantially with those derived from the reviewers' comments.[6]

The most commonly mentioned items among these seventeen categories were 'trust in God', 'self-sacrifice', 'philanthropic work', 'good temper', 'teetotalism', 'industriousness', 'studiousness', and 'the influence of mothers'. Books written specifically for girls emphasized additional qualities of 'unselfishness' and 'kindness to animals'. Literature for boys also had additional features; the ideal type was 'manly', 'considerate', 'courteous to women', 'dutiful', 'devoted to parents', 'helped his neighbours', and 'wished to improve himself'. These characteristics indicated the type of adult the Sunday schools, and specifically those in the industrial north-west, were aiming to produce. Consciously or

[5] Unless otherwise stated in the books listed below, the place of publication is London. *Books for girls*: Stella Austin, *Uncle Philip* (1878); 'H. M. B.', *Ida Royton's Village Life* (Bristol, 1875); Alice J. Briggs, *Margaret Bishop's Life Work* (1908); Evelyn Everett-Green, *My Black Sheep* (1889); Mary Paull, *Mary Hazeldine's Desk* (1879); Annie S. Swan, *Dorothea Kirke* (Edinburgh, 1884); Florence Witts, *The Sisters of Trenton Manse* (1902).

Books for boys: Harriet Boultwood, *Clerk or Carpenter* (1890); Emma Marshall, *Nature's Gentleman* (1893); 'Pansy', *Man of the House* (1887); James Jackson Wray, *Paul Megitt's Delusion* (1879).

Non-fiction books: Sabine Baring-Gould, *Sermons to Children* (1879); Jenny Chappell, *Women Who Have Worked and Won* (1904); William J. Forster, *Sergeant's Adventure* (1904); Henry Page, *Leaders of Men* (1880).

[6] Seventeen categories came from 136 content items: feminine attributes; masculine attributes; marriage; character models; mother; homelife (positive and negative models); religion; inner versus worldly life (positive and negative values); fashionable people and society; self-sacrifice in both sexes; self-improvement in both sexes; deference; attitudes to money; books; vices; positive qualities in both sexes; negative qualities in both sexes.

subconsciously, schools appeared to promote qualities and values in their pupils as an antidote to inappropriate models in juvenile literature and working-class life.

The prize books cast girls and women in the traditional social mould of the time. The role model was very precise, combining the concepts of wifehood, motherhood and 'queen of the home'. To reinforce this idea, there were very few examples in these fifteen books of women who were employed in an economic capacity outside the home; two millworkers, one dressmaker, one village shopkeeper, and one children's nurse. Similarly, there was no suggestion that women's roles might extend beyond traditional boundaries, although in real life a high proportion of working-class women did work outside the home. Both before and after marriage they were employed as servants, dressmakers, shop assistants, and, especially in the north-west, textile workers.[7] Many women also acquired experience in organizing activities and public speaking, often involving local government or trade union work, and philanthropic ventures. The conspicuous absence of role models portraying either employment or outside activities was matched by frequent descriptions of married working-class women coping with domestic problems, poverty, and alcoholic husbands.

> She had told him of . . . her husband's increasing passion for drink, which was fast bringing misery and ruin on them all . . . and debt and difficulty; of bad language and cruel deeds. She thought of the happiness and peace which might reign in their humble dwelling but for the home blasting influence of strong drink.[8]

Reviewers similarly paid minimal attention to stories concerning the occupational lives of working-class girls. Religious organizations apparently had little interest in helping female pupils to prepare for future work experience, with so few books offering alternative models to those of housewife and mother. Only

[7] Specifically, in Preston, Burnley, and other Lancashire weaving centres, nearly a third of married women worked in the 1880s, along with as many as three quarters of unmarried women. See Jill Liddington and Jill Norris, *One Hand Tied Behind Us* (London, 1978), p. 58; Jane Lewis, *Women in England, 1870–1950* (Brighton, 1984), p. 156; also John Walton, *Lancashire: a Social History, 1558–1939* (Manchester, 1987), pp. 286–93; Angela John, *Unequal Opportunities* (Oxford, 1986), p. 12.

[8] Wray, *Paul Megitt's Delusion*, pp. 46–7.

two stories within the reviews were about girls in service, while two others concerned a newspaper vendor and a flower-seller. A further two were about dressmakers, one of whom used her talent for sewing and also her capacity for self-sacrifice to 'deliver her church from a crushing debt in a short time'.[9] Only two reviews acknowledged new employment opportunities. One was about pupil teaching, although it offered little encouragement to working-class aspirants, while the other described a clerical occupation, in which a lame girl became an office clerk, was falsely accused of theft, and finally married her employer.[10] The extension of female employment, drawing as it did on the stereotype of the 'New Woman', created a feeling of independence which seemed to offend Sunday-school reviewers and authors alike. 'To Uncle Philip, it was a new light to him that the vexed question of "Women's Rights" should occupy the minds of schoolgirls, and put into their heads such uncomfortable cracked notions.'[11]

The discrepancy between the models of femininity approved by Sunday schools and changing social realities points to a way of thinking that was inappropriate and dated, and the same approach can be seen in literature specifically for boys. If the presentation dates of each of the books in the prize sample is compared with its publication date, the conclusion is that the schools selected well-established material, with many books being given up to twenty-five and some up to sixty years after first being published. By the end of the century religious magazines thought so too, and confirmed that the Sunday schools were 'grinding on in the old style'. Similar explanations, however, for this time-lag cannot be applied equally to books for both sexes. As seen above, prizes for girls rejected a more realistic approach to women's roles, while examination of boys' prizes shows different considerations.[12]

[9] Review of *Miss Priscilla Hunter* by 'Pansy', *PMM*, March 1880, p. 187.

[10] Charlotte M. Yonge, *Our New Mistress* (London, 1888), reviewed in *CT*, 9 Nov. 1888. 'With the so-called improvement in education, the daughters of ex-servants emerge under school board influence from their grubby existence into butterfly form and not infrequently have a longing to fly into the world of teachers.' L. T. Meade, *A Brave Poor Thing* (London, 1900), reviewed in *Baptist Magazine*, June 1900, p. 303.

[11] Austin, *Uncle Philip*, p. 106.

[12] Dorothy Entwistle, 'Children's reward books in Nonconformist Sunday schools, 1870–1914' (Lancaster Ph.D. thesis, 1990), pp. 294–6, 304–7, 326–35.

The literature written for boys, in both the sample of prize books and the reviews, shows marked contrasts. Many reviews emphasized roles which were appropriate up to the end of the period, but the settings and plots of such books were dull to the adolescent boy. Yet the favourite books in both sets of data were by three popular authors of adventure fiction, R. M. Ballantyne, W. H. G. Kingston, and Gordon Stables. Not only did they have an enthusiastic secular following, but prizes by Ballantyne and Kingston showed the longest time-lag between publication and presentation.[13] There were noticeable differences, however, between their heroes and those of the Sunday-school stories recommended specifically for boys. The popular genre put more emphasis on physical prowess, imperialism, patriotism, and outdoor adventure away from parents and from city and clerical life. It offered to Sunday schools an acceptable compromise between the approved but dull book and the sensational juvenile literature which attracted such hostile criticism. However, these images of the manly hero inevitably clashed with the staid religious values of patience, self-discipline, and self-negation shown by the Sunday-school ideal. Running away to sea, for example, was appropriate in adventure tales, but reprehensible in the Sunday-school story.[14] Even physical manliness, a prerequisite for both types of hero, was qualified in Sunday-school stories. 'Bodily strength and courage do not always mean moral courage wherewith to face difficulties and withstand temptations which after all try the real making of the man.'[15]

The books recommended for Sunday schools offered a model of a mature, responsible man rather than one of prolonged adolescence and boyish behaviour. Emphasis was placed on being dutiful to parents and a reliable economic provider, and on learning a trade, doing a job, or preparing for a career. The portrayal of a steady, dependable hero in Sunday-school literature was probably encouraged for two reasons. Firstly, the underlying philosophy dictated hard work and, secondly, the realities of working-class life demanded a form of preparation to face the often abrupt transition from childhood to adulthood.

[13] Books by R. M. Ballantyne and W. H. G. Kingston were still popular as prizes at the turn of the century and thereafter, although the authors' creative period had ended in the 1870s and 1880s.

[14] Marshall, *Nature's Gentleman*, p. 24.

[15] Ibid., p. 2.

'Alan, at twenty-five years . . . had risen by his industry . . . had a slight stoop, his face lined with deep thought which made him look older than his years and had grey in his hair.'[16]

Why were Sunday-school pupils given such books? As many of the books were both dated and dull, it is strange that they were seen as an incentive to continued good attendance and behaviour. But, in fact, these qualities were part of a broader value system—that of 'respectability', itself synonymous with the Victorian era. The concept of respectability contains additional elements, most of which were found in the fifteen prize books.[17]

There was, for example, the value of thrift and the economic independence which it protected. Related to that independence was the attitude to education and its effects on employment opportunities and subsequent social status. Prize books for boys sometimes portrayed auto-didactic heroes, again in contrast to those of popular adventure stories. For example:

> Alan used his evenings after work to study instruction books: 'he was really an instance of self-help and self-education, which has in other cases besides his, achieved unlooked for results'. Martin similarly prospered; 'he became all the better workman because he is well educated'. But Jack, hero of a popular adventure tale, 'was apt in his lessons to give a false quantity, and sometimes a translation of his Caesar, which put him down to the bottom of the class'.[18]

Respectability also involved a belief that women should conform to the traditional domestic role, and provide a level of household skills which would ensure the physical well-being of the major breadwinner. Descriptions of home baking abound in prize books, along with domestic accomplishments. Daughters were 'pleased to be instructed in the art of putting on a neat patch'.[19] This emphasis on home life also involved avoiding undesirable neighbours and keeping up standards, such as tidiness, within the home. These values are reflected in the following extract from one of the fifteen books. The author, here, is

[16] Ibid., p. 5.

[17] Entwistle, 'Children's reward books', p. 402.

[18] Marshall, *Nature's Gentleman*, p. 150; Boultwood, *Clerk or Carpenter*, p. 93; W. H. G. Kingston, *The Three Midshipmen* (London, 1873), p. 4.

[19] Briggs, *Margaret Bishop's Life Work*, p. 126.

trying to strengthen his moral message by placing it in a biblical setting. The effect, however, is perhaps not as intended:

> What was Christ's first thought (on Easter Sunday)? To escape the tomb; to see his mother? No. He first folded up his grave clothes and put them properly in their proper place. You may be quite sure that, unless tidiness were a Christian grace, Christ would not have provided that his gospel should record this striking instance of it for all ages to read. . . . (And) what were the boys and girls doing in Jerusalem on Good Friday? In good homes, the girls were doing needlework and tidying the houses: the boys were going to school. They had thoughtful, decent parents who kept them off the streets. In bad homes, disorderly children were playing truant from school, running about the streets, indulging in insulting gestures.[20]

It may seem self-evident that literature associated with religious institutions is usually religious and moral. But this was true only up to a point, at least for the period 1870 to 1914. Prizes, and denominational book reviews, certainly emphasized moral themes, but these were not specifically religious, nor distinctively denominational. Many themes were surprisingly secular in outlook, reflecting concern about respectability, character training, and traditional gender roles. It seems that prize books were being used by teachers, acting *in loco parentis*, partly to convey secular moral messages, as a form of protection against undesirable models in working-class children's lives and reading matter. In so doing, they were probably trying to guard the more vulnerable members from the worst aspects of their own culture.

Department of Education,
University of Edinburgh

[20] Baring-Gould, Sermons 3 and 9.

Appendix: Titles and authors found most frequently in the sample of prize books

Preferred titles

Westward Ho! (1855), Charles Kingsley, given 11 times; *Uncle Tom's Cabin* (1852), Harriet Beecher Stowe; *Danesbury House* (1860), Mrs Henry Wood, given 9 times; *From Log Cabin to White House* (1881), William M. Thayer; *Basket of Flowers* (1851), Christoff von Schmid; *Infelice* (1889), A. J. E. Wilson, given 6 times; *Martin Rattler* (1858), R. M. Ballantyne; *Pilgrim's Progress* (1678), John Bunyan; *What Katy Did* (1872), Susan Coolidge; *From Jest to Earnest* (1876), E. P. Roe; *Mark Desborough's Vow* (1884), Annie S. Swan; *Wide, Wide World* (1850), Elizabeth Wetherall, given 5 times. Among titles given on 4 occasions was R. M. Ballantyne's *Coral Island* (1858).

Preferred authors

W. H. G. Kingston 22 titles; Evelyn Everett Green, Silas Hocking 21 titles; R. M. Ballantyne 19 titles; A. L. O. E. 15 titles; Annie S. Swan 13 titles; Jenny Chappell 11 titles; Gordon Stables 10 titles; Emma Marshall, 'Pansy', Hesba Stretton, Mrs Henry Wood 9 titles.

FACT AND FICTION: CHILDREN AND THE CRUSADES

by ELIZABETH SIBERRY

IN addition to those who could bear arms, the crusade armies included numerous camp-followers. They came in a variety of forms—the old and infirm, women (who posed a different set of problems), the clergy, and children.[1] It is the latter who are the subject of this paper. In the first part I will examine the evidence for children on the crusades in contemporary sources—histories of individual expeditions written by participants or drawing upon eyewitness accounts. I will then go on to examine how the image of children on the crusades has been passed on to subsequent generations. I do not intend here to offer a comprehensive survey of children's literature about the crusades. I will merely try to highlight some themes, in particular, from British historical novels and adventure stories written in the nineteenth and early twentieth centuries.

To start with the fact. Children are mentioned in passing in a number of crusade sources, but hitherto, as far as I am aware, have not been studied in their own right. Substantive references to *pueri* or *infans* are rare, and it is really a question of assembling pieces of a jigsaw. The best evidence comes at either end of the crusading scale, so to speak, where one has the relative wealth of sources for the First Crusade (1095–9) or a first-hand account of a participant such as Jean de Joinville, biographer of St Louis (Louis IX of France, 1214–70). Then there is the ill-fated Children's Crusade of 1212, which I will mention briefly.

Children who went on the crusades fall under several different headings. First, there were those who accompanied their parents on the journey from Europe or who were born during the expedition. Thus Baldwin of Boulogne, brother of Godfrey of Bouillon, and subsequently King Baldwin I of Jerusalem, went on the First Crusade with his wife, Godwera of Tosny, and their small children. Albert of Aachen relates that Godwera died at Marash, in Lesser Armenia, and their children did not long

[1] See J. E. Siberry, *Criticism of Crusading, 1095–1274* (Oxford, 1985), pp. 25–46.

survive her.[2] A century and a half later, King Louis IX of France went on his first crusade to Egypt with his wife, Margaret, and their two young children. Two more children were born during the expedition—John Tristan, so called because he was born three days after news reached the Queen of the King's capture, and the Lady Blanche, who was born in happier circumstances at Jaffa. According to Joinville, whilst awaiting the birth of her son at Damietta the Queen dreamt that the room was full of Saracens, and for reassurance, she made an old knight lie down beside her bed and hold her hand. The day after the birth she had to summon the defenders of Damietta to her bedside to prevent them deserting.[3] The ill-fated John Tristan, of course, died with his father on the latter's second crusade outside the walls of Tunis. A more fortunate royal crusading family was that of Prince Edward, later Edward I of England. His daughter Joan was born at Acre in 1272 and subsequently became known as Joan of Acre.

In crusade sources and vernacular poetry there is almost a standard formula of the crusader's sacrifice—leaving behind his wife, family, and lands in order to serve in God's war.[4] In practice, however, it was not just kings and nobles who travelled on crusade accompanied by their families. There are a number of references to children on the journey to the East and in the crusading camp on the First Crusade. For example, Fulcher of Chartres mentions children amongst the non-combatant camp-followers, and Guibert of Nogent describes a motley crew of peasant families who set out for Jerusalem with little idea of what this meant or the distance involved. At every castle or town they reportedly asked if this was the Holy City.[5] The Second Crusade was similarly encumbered with non-combatants and there are references to children taking the cross and, for example, at the capture of Damietta on the Fifth Crusade.[6]

[2] Albert of Aachen, *Historia Hierosolymitana, Recueil des Historiens des croisades, Historiens Occidentaux* [*hereafter RHC occ*], 5 vols (Paris, 1844–95), 4, p. 358.

[3] Jean de Joinville, *Histoire de Saint Louis*, ed. N. de Wailly (Paris, 1868), pp. 141–2, 212.

[4] For example, Fulcher of Chartres, *Historia Hierosolymitana*, ed. H. Hagenmeyer (Heidelberg, 1914), pp. 162–3; Odo of Deuil, *De profectione Ludovici VII in Orientem*, ed. V. G. Berry (New York, 1948), p. 8. See also J. E. Siberry, 'Troubadours, trouvères, minnesingers and the crusades', *Studi medievali*, ser. 3, 19 (1988), pp. 21–3.

[5] Fulcher of Chartres, *Historia*, p. 183; Guibert of Nogent, *Gesta Dei per Francos, RHC occ.* 4, p. 142.

[6] James of Vitry, *Lettres*, ed. R. B. C. Huygens (Leiden, 1960), p. 77; John of Tulbia, 'De Domino Iohanne rege Ierusalem', ed. R. Röhricht, *Quinti belli sacri scriptores* (Geneva, 1879), p. 139.

Travel to the East was perilous. Joinville relates how the King and his family were nearly shipwrecked on rocks off Cyprus on their outward journey, and on their safe return to France, the Queen presented a silver ship, with figures of herself, the King, and their children, to the shrine of St Nicholas at Varangeville, in fulfilment of a vow made at the moment of danger. Another ship was less fortunate, and everyone on board perished, except one woman and her child, who floated to safety on a piece of timber. They were subsequently given shelter by the Count of Joigny.[7]

There were also, of course, the casualties of war. Although the sources have relatively little to say on this subject, many children no doubt died in battle, others from illness or starvation. And Fulcher of Chartres writes of the cries of women and children during the battle of Dorylaeum and their suffering from excessive hunger during the protracted siege of Antioch.[8] For a variety of reasons, children became separated from their families, and Guibert of Nogent mentions a regiment formed by a group of First Crusade orphans, who armed themselves with rudimentary homemade weapons.[9] After the defeat at Mansurah, Joinville seems to have taken charge of a young boy, Barthelemy, son of the lord of Montfauçon, 'lest the Saracens should take him away', presumably into slavery. And after his own release from captivity, King Louis was apparently particularly concerned about the fate of young children who remained in the Muslims' charge and had been forced to renounce their faith.[10]

No discussion of this subject would be complete without reference to the Children's Crusade of 1212. The main elements of the story are well known. Against the background of crusade preaching in Northern France and the Rhineland, there was a movement of children, who, we are told, believed that God would surrender the Holy Land to them rather than the rich and powerful. The leaders were Nicholas, from Cologne, and a French shepherd boy, Stephen, who claimed to have had a vision of Christ. The 'army' dispersed as it travelled through Europe; some arrived at Marseilles, set sail for the East, but were in fact

[7] Joinville, *Histoire*, pp. 14–15, 223, 225–6.
[8] Fulcher of Chartres, *Historia*, pp. 196, 225.
[9] Guibert of Nogent, *Gesta Dei*, p. 241.
[10] Joinville, *Histoire*, pp. 117, 145.

tricked and sold into slavery. The traditional interpretation of this 'crusade' has been a pilgrimage of innocents, reacting against the failure of crusades led by the kings and nobles of Western Europe, which ended tragically in betrayal, slavery, and slaughter. Modern research and scrutiny of the sources, however, has begun to challenge this, showing that rather than children, the participants were probably young adults, and linking the movement with the cult of apostolic poverty.[11]

How has this rather harsh reality of children on the crusades been developed in fiction? Bibliographies of children's literature reveal a sizeable corpus of crusade stories, and as a subject the crusading movement naturally appealed to the romantic and the writer of the adventure story, combining Christian heroism with the exoticism of the East.[12] Crusaders provided an example for children to emulate. Thus in Susan Coolidge's novel *What Katy Did*, published in 1872, the heroine declares, 'I mean to do something grand . . . perhaps . . . I'll head a crusade and ride a white horse, with armour and a helmet on my head and carry a sacred flag.'[13]

The doyen of the Victorian adventure story was George Alfred Henty, by career a war correspondent, who wrote some seventy historical novels on subjects as diverse as Ancient Rome and the Crimean War. Henty tended to follow a standard formula: his teenage hero goes to war, performs brave deeds, and often marries the girl he has rescued somewhere *en route*. Henty's crusade novel, published in 1882, is entitled *Winning His Spurs*. It tells the story of Cuthbert, who goes on the Third Crusade with Walter, Earl of Evesham. Henty wrote, 'Life in the castle and hut was alike monotonous, and the excitement of war and adventure was greatly looked for.'[14] Cuthbert certainly found both. He was made the Earl's esquire and seems to have had the

[11] The traditional interpretation is epitomized by P. Alphandèry, *La Chretienté et l'idée de croisade*, 2 vols (Paris, 1954–9). For an alternative interpretation, see P. Raedts, 'The Children's Crusade of 1212', *JMH*, 3 (1977), pp. 279–333. See also J. M. Powell, *Anatomy of a Crusade, 1213–21* (Philadelphia, 1986), pp. 8–11.

[12] See E. A. Baker, *A Guide to Historical Fiction* (repr. New York, 1968); D. D. McGarry and S. H. White, *World Historical Fiction Guide* (Metuchen, New Jersey, 1973); J. R. Townsend, *Written For Children* (repr. London, 1990); H. Carpenter and M. Prichard, *Oxford Companion to Children's Literature* (Oxford, 1984).

[13] S. Coolidge, *What Katy Did* (London 1872), p. 33.

[14] G.A. Henty, *Winning His Spurs* (London, 1882), p. 57.

knack of being in the right place at the right time. Amongst his heroic deeds, he saves the life of Richard the Lionheart and is rewarded by being knighted. With the minstrel Blondel, he later rescues the imprisoned Richard and, finally, after further trials and tribulations, is created Earl of Evesham and marries the late Earl's daughter, whom he had rescued from a wicked baron in chapter 2.

Henty also wrote a novel about the Knights Hospitallers and the siege of Rhodes—*Knight of the White Cross*, published in 1896. Again the central figure is a gallant English boy, Gervaise Tresham, who performs many valorous deeds on behalf of the Order. In the end he marries a wealthy Genoese heiress, whose cousin he had freed from a corsair galley.

The same structure can be found in a historical novel, *Between Two Crusades*, by Gertrude Hollis, published by the SPCK in 1908. Subtitled *A Tale of AD 1187*, it tells the story of Henfrid de Castellan and Ralph of Kingston, pages in the service of Sir Wakelin de Ferrars, and was no doubt intended as an improving moral tale. The boys witness the Battle of Hattin, and after the defeat and capture of the Christian army, Henfrid is sent by Saladin as an emissary to Tiberias and then Jerusalem. There he manages to save Saladin's life from an assassin, and receives 2,000 bezants, Saladin's own bejewelled scimitar, and his freedom as a reward for his bravery. The story ends with a hint of the Third Crusade. Ralph declares, 'Sir Wakelin saith that if Richard of Aquitaine doth take the cross, he shall return hither. . . . Then, perchance, I shall see the Holy Sepulchre, and it may be, we shall take it out of Saladin's hands again.'[15] Hollis also wrote a novel about the Seventh Crusade, entitled *A Slave of the Saracen*.

The Third Crusade seems to have been a particularly popular theme. Another example is *For Cross and Crescent*, by Gordon Stables, a regular contributor to *Boy's Own Paper*, who trained in medicine at Aberdeen, became a naval surgeon, serving in a whaler in the polar regions, and took up the pen after he was invalided out of service. His hero is the young Lord Lovegrace, Ethelred, whose father had been a Knight Templar:

> The boy was a crusader already at heart. He longed for wild adventures at sea, but he longed also to be a true Knight

[15] G. Hollis, *Between Two Crusades* (London, 1908), p. 247.

> Templar, to fight against the wild Saracens, to break a lance on the blood red field of battle in far off Palestine and to come back covered with honour and glory.[16]

Ethelred, of course, has various adventures, serves his king loyally, and shares his captivity before returning home to marry his childhood sweetheart.

Finally, on the boundary between the children's novel and the adventure story, there is Rider Haggard's *The Brethren*, published in 1904. Haggard attributed his inspiration to a visit to the Horns of Hattin:

> Whilst musing on these strangely contrasted scenes enacted in one place, there arose in his mind a desire to weave, as best he might, a tale wherein any who are drawn to the romance of that pregnant and mysterious epoch, when men by thousands were glad to lay down their lives for visions and spiritual hopes, could find a picture, however faint and broken, of the long war between Cross and Crescent waged among the Syrian plains and deserts.[17]

The Brethren tells the story of Rosamond, a fair English maid, who is the daughter of an English knight and Saladin's sister; the latter's attempts to persuade her to settle with him in the East, and two English brothers and knights, Godwin and Wulf, who rescue and protect her.

The boy-hero formula apart, there are some common threads in these books which it is worth drawing out here. First, whilst the crusades appealed to these authors of children's literature and the adventure story because they combined the exoticism of the East with tales of Christian chivalry and heroism, virtues to be emulated and admired by Victorian and Edwardian youth, they were not uncritical of aspects of the crusading movement. For example, in *Winning His Spurs* Henty refers to the dissension between the French and English contingents even as the forces assembled in France. King Philip of France reminds his nobles, perhaps with a hint of irony, in view of his own behaviour later on the expedition:

[16] G. Stables, *For Cross and Crescent* (London, 1897), p. 112.
[17] R. Haggard, *The Brethren* (London, 1904), Preface.

> Do you forget the mission upon which you are assembled here? Has not every knight and noble in these armies taken a solemn oath to put aside private quarrels and feuds until the holy sepulchre is taken? . . . Shall we show before the face of Christendom that the knights of the cross are unable to avoid flying at each other's throats, even while on their way to wrest the holy sepulchre from the infidel?

The hardships and defeats suffered by earlier crusaders were attributed to 'a punishment from heaven, because they have not gone to work in the right spirit'.[18] Moreover, the boy heroes did not set out believing that their undertaking was free of danger. The grandfather of Ethelred Lovegrace had been a member of the ill-fated Second Crusade, and died of wounds received in battle against the Turks not long after his return to the West. And an old family servant tells the young lord, 'All the dreams of success and glory that your brave grandfather had entertained had ended in failure.'[19]

Secondly, it is not simply a question of noble crusader versus wicked Saracen. Saladin is portrayed as a noble, if exotic, foe. To quote from Hollis:

> A white turban, with a single ruby set in an ouche of filigree of gold, was wrapped around his head, and his costume, quite plain and made of tanned leather, was yellow in colour, with deep cuffs of black cloth to the under vest. A wide belt of goldsmiths' work richly encrusted with jewels, supported a simple leather scabbard from which protruded the gold hilt of his scimitar, and one of the toothed clubs like those worn by his guards. . . . His complexion was of the usual dark hue of the East.

Saladin's nobles were even more richly dressed and armed, a dramatic contrast to the bloodstained, unwashed, and exhausted Christian prisoners.[20] Saladin is described as a noble monarch, a devout Muslim, inspiring devotion and even adoration from his followers, and, in a reversal of what one might expect, Stables writes that Richard 'proved himself so mighty a warrior that

[18] Henty, *Winning His Spurs*, pp. 47, 64–5.
[19] Stables, *Cross and Crescent*, pp. 150–1.
[20] Hollis, *Between Two Crusades*, pp. 35–6. See also Henty, *Winning His Spurs*, p. 131.

even Saladin was feign to own him the bravest of the brave.' Elsewhere, Stables refers to the 'vile Turk or Saracen (who) would cut us off from the holy city itself'.[21] But Haggard offers a Muslim perspective of the crusades. Saladin comments to Wulf:

> I desire peace and to save life, not to destroy it. It is you Christians who for hard upon a hundred years have drenched these sands with blood, because you say that you wish to possess the land where your prophet lived and died more than eleven centuries ago. How many Saracens have you slain? Hundreds of thousands of them. Moreover, peace with you is no peace.[22]

Finally, it is worth noting that in all the books which I have mentioned the crusading heroes have Saxon rather than Norman names, and the two races are seen as set apart, the original occupants of the land and the foreign invader and ruler. Thus Henty makes Father Francis, preacher of the crusade, comment:

> Methinks that it will do good service to the nation that Saxon and Norman should fight together under the holy cross. Hitherto the races have stood far too much apart. They have seen each other's bad qualities rather than good; but methinks that when the Saxon and Norman stand side by side on the soil of the Holy Land, and shout together for England, it must needs bind them together, and lead them to feel that they are no longer Saxons and Normans, but Englishmen.[23]

The Saxon–Norman divide is, of course, also a feature of Sir Walter Scott's *Ivanhoe*, published in 1819, and set against the background of the Third Crusade. Scott also produced three other novels which deal with various aspects of the crusading movement: *The Betrothed* and *The Talisman*, printed together as *Tales of the Crusaders* in 1825, and the last Waverley novel, *Count Robert of Paris*, printed in 1831. The action of *The Talisman* takes place during the Third Crusade itself. A poor Scottish crusader, known as Sir Kenneth or the Knight of the Leopard, encounters a Saracen emir, with whom, after an inconclusive combat, he

[21] Stables, *Cross and Crescent*, pp. 135, 152, 216.
[22] Haggard, *The Brethren*, p. 244.
[23] Henty, *Winning His Spurs*, p. 48.

strikes up a friendship. The emir appears in the crusading camp and cures the ailing Richard. After various twists and turns he proves to be Saladin, and Sir Kenneth, King David of Scotland. Again, therefore, the portrayal of the Muslims is sympathetic, and Scott was by no means an uncritical observer of the crusades, writing elsewhere of the participants' 'reckless and intolerant zeal'.[24] His novels were, of course, highly popular and influential; they are quoted specifically by Gordon Stables, but would probably have been read by Henty and others.

Not surprisingly, the Children's Crusade also attracted the children's novelist, with a variety of titles listed in the bibliographies.[25] There was also a musical, *La croisade des enfants*, composed by Gabriel Pierne in 1907, based on a story by Marcel Schwob, and the Royal Academy catalogue lists a painting entitled 'The Departure—an episode of the Children's Crusade', by a Mrs Henry Tanworth Wells, exhibited in 1860. Worth quoting as a curiosity is a book by Eileen Heming, published as recently as 1947, and entitled *Joan's Crusade*. Inspired by a history book about the Children's Crusade, Joan and her friend Wendy decide to go on their own crusade, not to the Holy Land, but on a 'crusade of helping people'.

And finally there was a collection of stories about Louis IX's last crusade and the subsequent expedition of Prince Edward.[26] An example of this, with the same sort of central boy hero, is Charlotte M. Yonge's *The Prince and the Page: A Story of the Last Crusade*, published in 1866. She took as her central figure Richard, the fourth son of Simon de Montfort, about whom little in practice is known. An old Hospitaller tells the young Richard:

> No cause is worth the taking of a life, save the cause of the holy sepulchre. What be these matters of taxes and laws to ask a man to shed blood for? Alack, the temper of the cross bearer is dying out. I pray I may not see this crusade end like half those I have beheld and the cross on the shoulder become no better than a mockery.

[24] Sir Walter Scott, *Essay on Chivalry* (1818), written for the *Encyclopaedia Britannica*.

[25] For example, Sheppard Stevens, *The Sign of Triumph: A Romance of the Children's Crusade* (London 1904); E. Everett Green, *The Children's Crusade: A Story of Adventure* (London, 1904); W. Scott Durrant, *Cross and Dagger. The Crusade of Children* (London, 1910).

[26] For example, C. H. Butcher, *The Oriflamme in Egypt* (London, 1904); J. G. Edgar, *The Boy Crusaders—a Story of the Days of Louis IX* (London, 1865).

Richard goes on to save the life of the future King Edward, although he is mortally wounded in the process. And reference is made to a legend that the block of stone forming Edward's tomb in Westminster Abbey came from Acre itself.[27]

Whilst, therefore, the reality of children on the crusades was often hard, with perils on land and sea and suffering from hunger and thirst, the fiction presents a more heroic picture, with children playing a key role in the heat of battle and often saving the day: the classic ingredients of an adventure story.

London

[27] C. M. Yonge, *The Prince and the Page* (London, 1866), pp. 139, 320.

THE CHILD AS MAKER OF THE ULTRAMONTANE

by BERNARD ASPINWALL

THE Revd Gerard Manley Hopkins, S.J., after two months' residence in Glasgow wrote that though repulsive to live in yet there are alleviations, the streets and buildings are fine and the people lively. The poor Irish among whom my duties lay are mostly from the North of Ireland. . . . They are found by all who have to deal with them very attractive; for though always very drunken and at present very Fenian, they are warm hearted. . . . I found myself very much at home with them.[1] [Their horrific lives gave] a truly crushing conviction, of the misery of town life to the poor and more than to the poor, of the misery of the poor in general, of the degradation of our race, of the hollowness of this country's civilisation: it made even life a burden to me to have daily thrust upon me the things I saw.[2]

The 1869 Royal Sanitary Commission[3] had shown a catastrophic increase in poverty in Glasgow: one third of the population lived in a single room, and there was a weekly death rate of 4.6 per cent. Prejudice similarly persisted: a boy worker could be dismissed for attending Mass.[4] Exile, abject poverty, death, and bigotry made the bulk of potential faithful nowhere at home. In such conditions how could an ultramontanist children's loyalty be manufactured to prevail over class and nationalist ideology?

[1] G. M. Hopkins to A. W. M. Baillie, 6 May 1882, Claude Colleer Abbott, ed., *Further Letters of Gerard Manley Hopkins* (London, 1935), pp. 248–9.

[2] G. M. Hopkins to R. W. Dixon, 1 Dec. 1881 in C. C. Abbott, ed., *The Correspondence of Gerard Manley Hopkins and Richard Watson Dixon* (London, 1935), p. 97.

[3] Professor W. T. Gairdner, *Evidence to the Commission* (1869), pp. 433–43.

[4] Glasgow, Mitchell Library, Strathclyde Regional Archives, St Andrew's school logbook, 3 Nov. 1865. All school logbooks cited hereafter,—St Mary's, St John's, St Mungo's, Holy Cross, etc.—are in the Stratchlyde Regional Archives.

Catholic strategy required an educational framework within which to mobilize ethnic loyalty, to provide a social network, ameliorating self-help and integration up to an 'acceptable' level. Denied an idealized family, with access to Catholic influences, the child became a ward of the school. It was to exclude the proselytizer, the atheist, the Utopian. A new composite identity, rejoicing in struggle, emerged from the school to give order and continuity to Catholic life. If the child was the father of ultramontanism, local loyalty prefigured the larger ultramontanist collective: the small, the school, the provincial, was beautiful.[5] Locally that meant the ultramontane leadership of the English archbishop Charles Eyre, 1869–1902. A man of considerable personal fortune and a founder of the Scottish Society for the Prevention of Cruelty to Children (1883), he brought Tridentine Catholicism to fruition in Glasgow. Aristocrats like the Marquess of Bute, substantial entrepreneurs like Robert Montieth, and migrant masses from the Highlands and Ireland helped to build a future for Catholic children. Far from conspiratorial social engineering, it was a voluntary enterprise of ethnic, lay, and clerical interests in concern for the child. Each group viewed the 'Protestant' environment with distaste in their differing ways: all were united behind a purer Catholic system. Together, they sustained a more positive self-perception, a moral superiority, and inevitable triumph within the child's mind. Consolidating his predecessors' zeal, Eyre began a seminary, and built and expanded numerous churches and schools throughout his archdiocese. Their mass-produced, Puginesque, neo-Gothic achitecture helped to manufacture a local tradition of deference, common endeavour, and social romanticism: laity and clergy, classes, and ethnic notions united for the common ultramontane good. The restoration of the Scottish hierarchy in 1878 was equally the restoration of a certain sense of community.

The parochial school provided that base community in those poor areas with heavy concentrations of Catholic children. Clergy mobilized the older loyalties of their intensely poor folk. Folk memories of migrant parents, and Catholic evangelicalism blended with the developing child, 'frontierslike', to shape the future character of the Church. Catholicism, like the larger

[5] Cf. J. H. Newman, *On the Present Position of Catholics in England* (London, 1851).

society, was shaping its own new identity. Mutual interests or common grievances bred union. Far from being manipulative, clergy responded positively to parental demands: schools tried to meet consumer demands for higher standards.[6] The parish, essentially a close-knit village community, was gradually eroded by social and economic mobility from 1920: the extensive city tramways, improved education, wider social gradations, metropolitan employment, and leisure opportunities. In 1891 Catholic children were still concentrated in poorer areas,[7] but they were already asserting independence: geographic, intellectual, and spiritual. An interim ultramontane strategy wonderfully worked in a peculiar crisis: new sustained initiatives have been slow to follow.

First, the establishment by Eyre of a local seminary in 1874 would produce local clerical leaders and 'professionalized' managers of schools. Second, the education of the poor and middle classes and the higher literary and scientific education of the layman, too, would eventually be reinforced to combat permeating, corrosive rationalism:

> Instead of implicating ourselves in a sinking wreck, it is the prudence of common sense as well as the obligation of Catholic duty, to keep ourselves free, not only from all entanglements with it, but as far as possible from the vortex it makes in going down. We earnestly hope that Catholics while they manifest to their fellow countrymen the largest social charity and the truest public fidelity, will keep themselves from all contact with the traditions of anti-Catholic policy and education. We repeat again that an education deprived of the light of faith and the guidance of the Church is essentially anti-Catholic. There can be no neutrality: 'He who is not for Me, is against Me.'[8]

Assertive ultramontanism coincided with and confirmed the social ideas of those who by 1870 aspired to better status and modest affluence: the needs of both were satisfied. The discipline of the ultramontane, hygienist, and educator co-operated for the

[6] E.g. St John's, 28 April 1864.

[7] Source: Robert Howie, *The Churches and the Churchless in Scotland* (Glasgow, 1893), p. 97; *Scottish Catholic Directory* (1891); Glasgow, Strathclyde Regional Archives, School Board Minutes, 1891.

[8] [H. E. Manning], 'The work and wants of the Catholic Church in England', *DublR*, ns 1 (July, 1863), pp. 139–66, at p. 165. Manning was a patron of Archbishop Eyre.

[9] See my 'The formation of the Catholic community in the West of Scotland', *InR*, 33 (1982), and

communal good: refining, integrating, yet preserving an Irish identity within a *British* Catholic context.[9]

Schools could save the children of sordid homes: their products would become better parents and better Christians.[10] Woman would be the third stabilizing element. Idealized in Mariolatry, in religious orders, as a teacher, in frequently sung hymns and reproduced paintings, she was to nurture the family unit like the localized priestly formation. Finally, omnipresent death and cultural adjustments made ultramontane Catholic evangelicalism an attractive identity in a world of threat.[11]

As much as any priest, the vocation of the very low-paid, certificated teacher supported by pupil-teachers with few prospects, zealously served the ultramontane cause. Overwork in under-resourced schools, instructing pupil-teachers before and after classes, for scanty financial rewards, made schoolteaching a religious vocation. Like the contemporary Church, the teacher imposed discipline rather than stimulated independent critical thought: since the qualified teacher-pupil ratio remained unchanged, around 1:150[12] between 1850 and 1877, sheer numbers militated against anything else. Their pay lagged far behind that of the Glasgow School Board Schools.

A small schools system had got under way by 1815, supported by voluntary contributions of the poor faithful and by beneficent Protestant merchants. Expansion followed the arrival of Franciscan and Sisters of Mercy nuns in 1847 and 1849. Twelve city Catholic schools with some 2,500 pupils in 1851 grew in 1866 to twenty-three schools with almost 4,500 children.[13] The Scottish Education Act, 1872, introduced compulsory education, forced

---

'Robert Monteith and the origins of modern British Catholic social thought', *Downside Review*, 97 (1978), pp. 46–68.

10 [J. G. Wenham], 'Our elementary schools and their work', *DublR*, 85, 3rd series, 2 (Oct. 1879), pp. 417–48. See Thomas Walter Laqueur, *Religion and Respectability: Sunday Schools and Working Class Culture, 1780–1870* (New Haven, 1976).

11 St Mungo's, 11 Dec. 1874, gives one instance of many epidemics.

12 Martha Skinnider, 'Catholic elementary education in Glasgow, 1818–1918', in T. R. Bone, ed., *Studies in the History of Scottish Education* (London, 1967), pp. 24–34, esp. pp. 24–5.

13 *Education Commission (Scotland) P.P. XXV (*1867), containing James Greig and Thomas Harvey, *The Condition of Schools in Glasgow* (Edinburgh, 1866).

14 On the background see J. M. Roxburgh, *The School Board of Glasgow, 1873–1919* (Edinburgh, 1971); T. A. Fitzpatrick, *Catholic Secondary Education in Southwest Scotland Before 1972* (Aberdeen, 1986), pp. 25–42; *Report of the Committee of the Council on Education in Scotland, 1898–99* (1899), p. 418.

standards to be raised in the new curriculum, and brought further pressures.[14] By 1885, 13,000 children were enrolled, as schools were remodelled and rebuilt: much criticized school board officials compelled attendance. Evening classes supplemented that basic education to a limited degree.[15] In 1891 over 27,000 children were in Catholic schools of the Glasgow archdiocese: by 1921, these had almost trebled to nearly 76,000, almost a fifth of the total Catholic population.[16] The opening of Notre Dame, the first Catholic teacher training college in Scotland, in 1894, partially contained the problem: some 1,400 teachers had graduated by 1918. In this 'feminization' of the schools, many trained women teachers worked on the cheap: many committed women sacrificed their celibate lives to the community. Without them the strained system might have collapsed.

The continuously growing schools were vital components in the ultramontane endeavour: discipline, cohesion, and simple answers to urban industrial complexity were the means of personal, group, and religious survival.[17] Children of more literate, more politically conscious recent migrants posed further strains. But lavish liturgical or non-liturgical services, rosary, medals, and numerous voluntary religious associations focused obedient attention on Rome, the priest, and the teacher.

The school, the flagship of ultramontanism, linked priest and people; it grew as an increasing number of disciplined, professionalized priests emerged from the Scottish seminaries, and Catholics acquired property, careers, and families rooted in the Glasgow area.[18] It provided an entrée to the profession of teaching, uniting vocation, service, status, and self-improvement; it formed part of the network of voluntary parochial organizations characteristic of the prevailing ultramontanism; it fostered a communal devotional outlook through the various pupils' organizations, rosary and prayers, statues and pictures in the school,

[15] Skinnider, 'Catholic elementary education', pp. 24–34; *The Statistics of Glasgow* (Glasgow, 1891) has 16,170 Catholics (19%) with 84,986 in Glasgow and Govan board schools.

[16] See James Darragh, 'The Catholic population of Scotland, 1878–1977', *InR*, 29 (1978), pp. 211–47, at p. 233.

[17] See Skinnider, 'Catholic elementary education'. The Revd Tom Bourke, O. P., a popular visiting Irish preacher in Glasgow, promoted these views in his sermons published by the Protestant Nationalist, John Ferguson, in Glasgow.

[18] See my 'The Catholic Irish and wealth in Glasgow', in T. M. Devine, ed., *Irish Immigrants and Scottish Society in the Nineteenth and Twentieth Centuries* (Edinburgh, 1991), pp. 91–115.

and increasingly regular visits of the parochial clergy. It gave pride, sanctions, and interest in their communal property and achievement. In the process the school may have encouraged a clerical perception that the poor were a self-perpetuating class for whom limited literacy and numeracy were sufficient for spiritual and economic life:[19] or perhaps, realistically, little more could be done. A morally innocent and corruptible laity in an amoral capitalist world must be protected.[20] But respect for hierarchies, temporal and spiritual, remained: as Coventry Patmore said,[21] relations between landowner and labour were 'free, cheerful and exhilirating because . . . it was the only equality worth regarding, that of goodwill' and 'a very great good to all parties'. These attitudes inculcated asceticism and self-denial, stifled ambition and envy in a world of careers often closed to their talents and aspirations: a superior self-image was vital in a not infrequently discriminatory world. The school provided a basic Catholic survival-kit. That emphasis upon religious formation can readily be seen in the school timetable below.[22] About one-fifth of the day was devoted to religious matters: later the proportion was about a quarter of the longer, six-and-a-quarter-hour day.

Teachers in Glasgow schools reflected these values. They self-consciously welded themselves into a cohesive body with a strong sense of vocation: in fact, a number did enter the religious life.[23] Recruited from English, Highland, and Irish migrant backgrounds, they trained in England: men at St Mary's, Hammersmith, or women at Mount Pleasant, Liverpool, or at Wandsworth, until the foundation of Notre Dame Training College, Glasgow, in 1894. The religious orders equally seem to have trained far more members in France than in Scotland or Ireland.

[19] See Barry M. Coldrey, *Faith and Fatherland: The Christian Brothers and the Development of Irish Nationalism, 1838–1921* (Dublin, 1988), pp. 87–8, 181; Tom Garvin, *Nationalist Revolutionaries in Ireland, 1858–1928* (Oxford, 1987), p. 8.

[20] Ibid., pp. 23, 56.

[21] Quoted in Osbert Burdett, *The Idea of Coventry Patmore* (Oxford, 1921), pp. 179–80.

[22] St John's, frontis., 1864. Also see 20 Oct. 1873 for post-Education Act timetable.

[23] At least two pupil-teachers, John Hackett and John Young, became priests in Ireland: St Mungo's, 9 Jan. 1870. Some fifty-six women teachers became nuns.

[24] St Andrew's, 22 Feb. 1866, 19 Aug. 1870; St Mary's, 7,8 Sept. 1870, 13 Sept. 1875, 10 March 1876, 20 March 1885; St John's, 17 March 1894; St Mungo's, 20 Sept., 6, 13, 15 Nov. 1867, 26 May

Table 1 *St John's School Timetable 1864*

Hours	*First Class*		*Hours*	*Second Class*
taught by principal teacher and pupil-teacher			*taught by assistant teacher, one pupil-teacher, and four monitors*	
1st Division:	2nd Division:	3rd Division	1st Division:	2nd Division
10.00 am	Morning Prayers followed by		Catechism	
Writing on paper	Arithmetic	Reading and spelling	10.30 am Spelling:	Tables and object lesson
10.45 am Reading and History or Mental Arithmetic	Dictation or transcribing	Writing on paper	11.00 am Tables and object lesson	Reading and spelling
11.20 am Catechism and Religious Instruction			11.30 am	Writing on slates
12.00 noon	Singing			
12.30 pm	Angelus and Recreation			
1.00 pm	Prayer followed by			
Arithmetic	Writing on paper	Reading and tables	Reading	Arithmetic numeration and notation
2.00 pm Grammar and Geography alternate	Reading and tables	Arithmetic	2.00 pm Arithmetic numeration and notation	Reading and spelling
2.45 pm Dictation or composition	Grammar or geography Drawing on	Dictation or transcribing Wednesdays	2.45 pm	Religious instruction
3.15 pm	Evening	prayers	and	dismissal

Source: St John's 1864 frontis. Also see St John's 1873 timetable.

Teachers vigorously prevented clashes with neighbouring Protestant schools. Irish songs were markedly absent from school-books: 'Men of Harlech' and other British airs abound.[24] Overwhelmingly English-trained until 1894, teachers were loyal to an ultramontane, supranational Church.[25] Basic education, order, hygiene, and industrious, obedient zeal provided a social and religious survival-kit for the English-speaking world: many pupils were likely to migrate to America or the British Empire. These influences echoed those of the Scottish Catholic Superior-General of the Irish Christian Brothers: avoid dissension, involvement in politics, and seize the democratic opportunities within the United Kingdom.[26] And at the least financial cost.

An ultramontane church nurtured the 'right' Catholic values in a sanitary home and a sanitized school, 'more arduous and difficult to do than competing with others in mere secular instruction.'[27] Catholic schooling was part of a strategy for social amelioration. In focusing on the school the community was united. Pupils' soirées were but one form of cohesion: some 340 turned out at St Mary's in 1875.[28] By intimately linking people and priest, the school blocked any Protestant evangelical wedge between them.[29] Irish sympathies mellowed: critical comments diminished, particularly after 1872. Although C. J. H. Cox,[30] principal teacher at St John's, scoffed at 'heretical Glaswegians observing the Queen's birthday on Corpus Christi', many pupils preferred English Catholic to Irish textbooks. At first attendance fell on days of Irish National Society meetings, but radical notions shifted: as the day book noted 'The Prince of Wales visit to Glasgow, therefore, as no other benefit accrued to our poor, we gave them the satisfaction of a holiday.'[31]

1868, 8 Sept. 1869, 24, 25 Aug., 12 Oct. 1870, 10 Oct. 1871, 24 Aug 1877. On songs see St John's, 17 Jan. 1879, 7 Dec. 1883, I found only one on 28 June 1897; St Mary's, 8 Jan. 1874; St John's, 27 May 1869; and St Mungo's, 9 Aug. 1864.

25 See my forthcoming article on the training of Scottish Catholic teachers from 1850 to 1920, in *InR*.

26 Coldrey, *Faith*, p. 224.

27 Ibid., p. 425.

28 St Mary's, 19 Nov. 1875.

29 See David Hempton and Myrtle Hill, *Evangelical Protestantism in Ulster Society, 1740–1890* (London. 1992), p. 82, 92.

30 St John's, 27 May 1869 and St Mungo's, 9 Aug. 1864.

31 St Andrew's, 19 March 1866, 8 Oct. 1868.

That close identity was fostered in other ways. The parish through the priest and the St Vincent de Paul Society provided free education, shoes, and clothes for the poorest children: St Mary's, St John's, and others gave dozens of pairs of boots every winter.[32] Lunches were provided for the poorest from an early stage, for health, attendance, and charity: St Mary's even provided them during Christmas vacations.[33] As the headmaster of St John's said of his 50 hungry 'very destitute looking' poor, 'The wonder is they attend.' A continuous litany of poverty rallied the community.[34] The priests and local school board officials chased up absentees, with threats of spiritual and legal penalties.[35] Priests and the St Vincent de Paul and St Elizabeth Societies helped with school fees or clothes and boots for the poorest. Even the *Daily Record* once gave fifty pairs of boots.[36] At St John's over sixty pairs of boots were given to pupils in December 1903: two years later seven boys received clothes from the City Educational Endowment Fund.[37] In 1885 St Mary's St Vincent de Paul Society provided a special Christmas lunch for over 200 children.[38] The school, already feeding around forty pupils a day, began a penny lunch scheme in 1886: in the first week over 1,000 meals were served. The parish priest provided all books and classes free for 180 in the evening school.[39] Not surprisingly, through the Marist, Brother Walfrid, Celtic F. C. emerged from the parish to raise considerable funds to feed the poor.[40] Often more than ten per cent of the pupils depended on such aid.

Even more pertinent, the schools mobilized Catholic women, gave them a lay vocation, a low-paid career, and a wider sense of family. Contemporary Mariolatry coincided with the 'feminization' of Glasgow schools: the cult of Mary, rosary, hymns, and

[32] E.g. St Mary's, 17 Dec. 1875; St John's, 23 Jan. 1891.

[33] St Mary's, 24 Dec. 1884, Archbishop Eyre and Madame Kuefke, the wife of a flour importer, paid; 9 Jan. 1885.

[34] St John's, 5 Dec. 1890, 24 Oct. 1864; St Mary's 13 March 1884.

[35] E.g. St Mungo's, 23 Nov. 1865.

[36] E.g. St Mungo's, 17 April 1869; 30 May 1870; St Mary's 17 Dec. 1875, 12 Dec. 1879, 9 Dec. 1885; 12 Dec. 1890, 14 Dec. 1894, 10 Jan., 22 Feb. 1895, 11 Feb. 1898, 15 Dec. 1899, 4 Dec. 1901; St John's 11 Jan. 1895, 5 Feb., 15 Oct. 1897, 1 June 1900, 7 Nov. 1904, 25 Jan. 1907.

[37] St John's, 4 Dec. 1903, 12 May 1905.

[38] St Mary's, 9, 24 Dec. 1885, 11, 25 Jan., 29 Oct. 1886; 21 Dec. 1888.

[39] St Mary's, 7 Nov. 1893.

[40] See James Handley, *The Celtic Story* (London, 1960); St John's, 13 Nov. 1865. Even so, St Mary's raised £10.10 *s.* 0 *d.* for the Red Cross: 21 June 1918.

[41] *Report of the Committee . . ., 1898–9.*, p. xxvi and *1903–04*, p. 18.

processions paralleled the increase in numbers of women teachers. Between 1897 and 1899,[41] the Catholic women Queen's Scholars in Scotland grew from fifty-two to sixty-nine; three women, but no men, were attending Glasgow University classes. Within five years there were 114 women scholars, with five at Glasgow University, and still no men.

Hitherto, concentration on 'the least unworthy and most ill-conditioned' had alienated the 'careful, industrious, sober and orderly' faithful.[42] Now communal unity, reinforced by juvenile literature and hymns, ensured 'a body who are ready to choose individual sacrifice for the sake of gaining united success.'[43] Intellect might lag behind faith, discipline, and deference. Like Newman,[44] they doubted fulfilment through the trained mind: 'Who was ever consoled in real trouble by the small beer of literature or science?' Even in early twentieth-century Glasgow, Catholics had little opportunity in sciences or advanced arts courses.[45] While the annual reports of even the poorest schools invariably reported excellent staff commitment, discipline, order, and singing, they often found academic deficiencies.[46] Inculcating basic faith, literacy, and hygiene among poor children in often cramped rooms proved a massive burden.[47] The result was obvious from the comment of one apocryphal layman: 'Your reverence, I'll manage for the faith, it's the moral that bates me.'[48]

Schools shared the philosopy of Dr Arnold, Manning, Newman, and Hopkins. The Boys' Brigade and the Boy Scouts

[42] *DublR*, 85, ser. 3 (1879), p. 445.

[43] 'Literature for the Young', *DublR*, 89, ser. 3, 6 (Oct. 1881), pp. 354–77, at p. 364. See the hymns and illustrated biblical schoolbooks of Henry Formby, the popular novels of Lady Georgiana Fullerton, and others.

[44] Lee H. Yearley, *The Ideas of Newman: Christianity and Human Religiosity* (Penn State, University Park, 1978), p. 122.

[45] *Report of the Committee . . . 1903–04*, p. 495.

[46] See Annual Reports in almost every school logbook.

[47] St Mary's, 14 Oct. 1864. Also 15 March 1869; HMI Annual Report, St Mary's, 1869.

[48] J. G. Wenham (1820–95), a Catholic schools inspector, p. 423 in 'Our elementary schools and their work', *DublR*, 85, ser. 3, 2 (Oct. 1879), pp. 417–48.

[49] See John Springhall, *Sure and Stedfast: A History of the Boys' Brigade, 1883 to 1983* (London, 1983), and *Youth, Empire, and Society: British Youth Movements, 1883–1940* (London, 1977), pp. 43–4, and Michael Rosenthal, *The Character Factory: Baden-Powell and the Origins of the Boy Scouts Movement* (New York, 1986), esp. pp. 92–3.

[50] Norman Vance, *The Sinews of the Spirit: The Ideal of Christian Manliness in Victorian Literature and Religious Thought* (Cambridge, 1985), p. 51.

similarly stressed discipline and team work.[49] But Catholic clergy never became part of the clerisy: they were allegedly imprudent, unmanly, and unpatriotic.[50] The school then was an opportunity to determine the character of the future Church. Religion had a high profile in the curriculum: prayer, instruction, and devotions occupied almost a third of the daily timetable. It gave children a structured world: they could cope with prejudice and failure within a consoling spiritual universe of *patron* saints and a sustaining material community. Medals, rosaries, and hymns linked the two.

Frequent visits from clergy and Archbishop Eyre made clericalism familiar, friendly, and acceptable.[51] Priest-managers visited the schools every week, some virtually every day. Bishop Gray[52] had waxed lyrical about school announcements as on a par with church regulations. Archbishop Eyre as far as possible visited each school every six months. All invariably urged Sunday school and Mass attendance, particularly in school holidays. Mass on Sundays and holy days of obligation was a *school* activity: children were successfully brought out for the services. The almost panic concern of early days subsided; the practice later became a routinized professional practice.[53] School board truancy officers, although heavily criticized, did bring many children into an ultramontane ethos.[54] Regularity in religion, cleanliness, and work were part of the same package.

Teaching staff were dedicated, but few were professionally trained. Nuns were prominent in the infant and girls' schools. As the 1866 Education Commission reported,[55] their influence was impressive: 'Good manners and respectful tone of children contrasted favourably with any other school of the same class in Glasgow', their 'tranquillity and refinement', and 'the considerable taste and neatness displayed in school arrangements . . . seem visibly to have affected the children who are unduly affectionate in their bearing.' They won respectful gratitude among both children and parents. A similar atmosphere prevailed in

[51] E.g. St Mary's, 8 Sept. 1876, 20 Sept. 1878; St Andrew's, 8 Sept. 1865.

[52] St Andrew's, 14 Sept. 1868.

[53] The careful checks on Mass and school attendance on holy days of obligation in the early log-books later became a routine mention of the holy day.

[54] E.g. St Mary's, 28 Jan., 20 May, 3 June, 27 Aug, 2 Dec. 1887, 13 Jan. 1888, 28 Aug. 1903.

[55] *Commission on Education*, p. 81.

[56] Ibid., p. 84.

evening classes: 'The tone and bearing of the teachers cannot but refine and temper the girls.'[56] Their good conduct medals were constant reminders of that discipline. Nuns further cemented the ultramontane wall.

Marists from 1858, short-lived Christian Brothers' junior schools, and Jesuits from 1859 in the limited secondary field gave solidity to the boys. But generally over those between the ages of seven and twelve, the laity dominated. Many were pupil-teachers: almost entirely male until about 1888. Some would progress to training college, but many failed to stay the course, through illness, migration, or violence towards their charges. A headmaster might remain in post for many years, but turnover among assistants and pupil-teachers continued at high levels until the Second World War. A number emigrated: one went to Cape Town as early as 1866, while another left for America without notice in August 1889.[57] Some pupil-teachers gave up or found more lucrative jobs.[58] Some had chequered careers: John McQuade[59] taught, went to Ireland, then America, and tried to join the Royal Navy, before returning to St John's. Many died from fever and other infections.[60] Occasionally parents objected to inadequate pupil-teachers.[61] Some too readily beat their charges, a constant if not always justified charge from parents: it might be a pretext to remove children from a particular school or from any school.[62]

A pupil-teacher's lot was onerous: he was to inspire devotion by pious reception of the sacraments.[63] Any shirking of his burden met severe reprimand.[64] Some 200 boys were cajoled to Saturday Mass at St Mary's in 1873: a similar number were taken

[57] St Andrew's, 6 Aug. 1866; St John's, 9 Aug. 1889.

[58] St John's, 22 April 1870, 22 April 1872. Hugh Brady continued his summer factory job at 8 *s.* a week, 9 Aug. 1872.

[59] St John's, 14 Aug. 1896.

[60] E.g. Daniel Carrigan, St Mungo's, 23 May 1865; Philip Mooney, St John's, 30 April 1875; J. Melia, St Mary's, 26 April 1889; Thomas Dunnigan, St John's, 6 Jan. 1893.

[61] St John's, 28 April 1865.

[62] St John's, 4 Sept., 16 Nov. 1865, 23 Aug. 1866, 2 Oct. 1871; St Mary's, 19 Oct. 1868, 23 May 1881; St Andrew's, 3 Oct. 1876, 5 Sept. 1879.

[63] St Mary's, 17 June 1873.

[64] St Mary's, 11 Jan. 1872. The Revd Peter Forbes attacked smoking.

[65] St Mary's, 1 Nov. 1873, 11 Jan. 1875.

[66] St Mary's, 23, 24 May 1870, 30 Sept. 1872, 15 Oct. 1875; St Mungo's 24 Aug., 14 Sept. 1868.

[67] St Mary's, 23 Sept. 1870.

to the requiem Mass of a former parish priest.[65] Pupils who missed Mass or were found at employers' obligatory Protestant Sunday schools were pursued.[66] The distribution of church collecting cards to children was another chore.[67] Constant supervision, local social pressures, demands for attendance at evening classes, at regular school confessions, Sunday Mass, and Sunday school began to incorporate them into ultramontane discipline.[68] A pattern was set.

But commitment was not enough: professionalism was essential. Mr Cox, principal teacher of St John's, received a crushing assessment in 1873: 'This school is in a very unsatisfactory state and it is difficult to believe that the master has, before giving up charge of it, sufficiently exerted himself to bring it into a proper state of efficiency.'[69] Following the 1872 Act, the renewed ultramontane zeal and somewhat more settled state of the migrant body, newly trained teachers appeared. James Harper, a former pupil-teacher, trained at St Mary's, Hammersmith, 1871–2, returned to transform St John's. His tough discipline and uncompromising stand against weak pupil-teachers, disgruntled parents, and low standards turned the school around. Backed by his priests, the school rapidly improved: 'I shall use strict corporal punishment till such time as it will have to be dispensed with.'[70] By 1877 the school '*is* in vigorous working order.'[71] The rigour of the contemporary church was reflected in the vigorous punishments even for small infringements.[72] Misbehaviour at Sunday Mass could mean corporal punishment.[73] Even attendance at 'immoral' and 'forbidden' shows outside school hours was punished.[74] Teachers were both loved and feared by tidy, cheerful, well-mannered children: ultramontane deference and discipline extended far and wide.[75]

68 E.g. St Mary's, 29 June 1870, 18 June 1871, 1 Dec. 1873; St Mungo's, March, 26 May, 1 Aug. 1864, 29 Sept. 1865.

69 St John's, Inspector's Annual Report 1873.

70 St John's, 4 Sept. 1874, 25, 26 March, 11 Aug. 1873.

71 St Johns, Inspector's Annual Report 1877.

72 St Andrew's, 5 June 1867.

73 E.g. St Mary's, 1 Dec. 1873.

74 St Mary's, 14, 17 Dec. 1868.

75 St Mungo's, 9 April 1866; HMI Annual Report, 1865, 1875, 1876; HMI Annual Report, St Peter's, Partick, 7 May 1897.

76 St Mungo's, 12 Nov. 1868, 18 Jan., 5 April 1868. A French bishop and two French priests were astounded by barefoot children, 19 Sept. 1890. Crowded 'adventure' slum schools, invariably

A further difficulty was attendance. Children, inadequately fed and clothed and frequently barefoot, came from desperately poor families: some went to appalling squalid 'adventure' schools which were slowly eliminated.[76] Careless parents neglected education. In 1866 a Gorbals priest[77] had claimed less than a third of all Catholic children were in any school: exhortations from the pulpit and in person had little effect. He put the blame on illiteracy, imprudence, and drink. More probably, local economic conditions meant disproportionate unemployment among unskilled parents. Cold weather or need of seasonal labour further reduced attendance.[78] Many had to leave at an early age to sustain the family. Others were unable to pay the tiny school fee or buy the required books, paper, and slate: even by 1887 more than a hundred children, a fifth of St Mungo's pupils, could not buy the books:[79] three years later half the pupils had no books.

Schools were overcrowded and under-resourced in a poor community struggling to sustain basic facilities. In 1912, for example, a coal strike severely affected children and parents.[80] But under Archbishop Eyre a massive expansion of buildings took place. Although pressure on space and limited Catholic resources were immense, Inspectors nevertheless could begin to note improvements in 'the highest state of efficiency'.[81] By 1898 St Mary's was described as 'in every respect excellent. Criticism is unnecessary as a very pleasant air of intelligence, cheerfulness and industry prevails in this school.'[82] In the circumstances, with 600 to 950 pupils placing impossible demands upon the handful of qualified teachers, the disciplined ultramontane achievement was considerable.

Not surprisingly, a preoccupation with hygiene was marked in most schools. Visitors to St Mary's noticed far greater cleanliness than in the average Scottish school.[83] In some schools

taught by Irish Catholics, faded: *Education Commission, Glasgow*, pp. 52, 68. One teacher, an alleged Glasgow University graduate, had peculiar vocabulary, pronunciation, and spelling.

77 Ibid., p. 80. On the background see J. McCaffrey, *SCH*, 24 (1987), pp. 359–70.

78 St John's, 11 Dec. 1874.

79 St Mungo's, 6 May 1887, 24 Jan. 1890.

80 St Mary's, 22 March 1912.

81 HMI Annual Report, St Mary's, 1867.

82 HMI Annual Report, St Mary's, 1898–9.

83 St Mary's, 19 Aug. 1870.

84 St Mary's, 10 Aug. 1868, 8 May 1869, 23 Jan., 9 May 1871; HMI St Mary's Annual Report 1869; St Mungo's, 20 Feb. 1865 and timetables with cleanliness inspections.

each day began with a cleanliness inspection. Prizes were given for the cleanest pupils but HM Inspectors noted a deterioration as overcrowding increased.[84] Even by 1895 at St John's, children sent home to wash were being confronted by even filthier parents.[85]

Returning home became a disciplined activity. Pupil-teachers marched children to a street closest to home.[86] Orderly group behaviour avoided clashes with Protestant schools. Pupil-teachers and pupils sought out absentees and urged them to school.[87] High turnover rates during the school year, accentuated by the annual renters' 'flitting day' in May were greatly reduced by the turn of the century.[88] Parents often pressured priests and teachers to advance their children, partly from pride, but partly to speed them into the labour force. Many left before the legal age, with few formal qualifications, and so individual advance was limited.[89] Even pressure from priests and Archbishop Eyre had little effect: he even urged children to remonstrate with their parents if kept away from school.[90] Whatever their failings, children invariably received great credit for their exceptional discipline. In rapidly growing St Peter's, Partick, the school Inspectors captured that ambivalent spirit. They typically reported: 'Excellent discipline prevails throughout the school. The pupils are seldom sufficiently advanced for their years.'[91]

Priests and teachers resorted to the stick and carrot approach to retain pupils. Attendance at evening instruction was encouraged with promises of spiritual benefits and tangible rewards.[92] At Hallowe'en there were sweets and fruit; at Christmas

[85] St John's, 13 Sept. 1895.
[86] See St Andrew's, 7 Feb. 1872, 23 April, 2 Oct. 1872.
[87] See St Andrew's, 14 Jan. 1870, 10, 24 Jan. 1872.
[88] Cf. St John's, 27 May 1866 and late 1890s.
[89] See St John's, 24 March 1876, 5 April 1878. Poverty affected all denominations but Irish children were allegedly the main victims of inadequate education. See James R. Russell, *The Children of the City: What Can We Do for Them?* (Edinburgh 1886), p. 89 and David Watson, 'Child Life in Cities', in *Child Life in Cities and Some Aspects of the Social Problem: Papers Read before the Social Christian Union, June 6th 1901* (Glasgow, 1901), pp. 5–11.
[90] See St Mary's, 15 Oct. 1872; St John's, 7 March 1864.
[91] Annual HM Inspector's Report, St Patrick's, 24 March 1909. Also Annual HMI Report, St Martin's, 1 March 1910 on 'the discrepancy between attainment and age'.
[92] St Mary's, 26 May, 7 June 1865, 29 Oct. 1875; St Mungo's, 2 May 1865.
[93] St John's, 11 April 1864; Holy Cross has numerous entries.
[94] St Mary's, 17 Dec. 1882 and 15 Oct. 1872.

special parties; in summer, outings, occasional soirées, and several lantern light shows.[93] At Christmas, cards were given to those in attendance.[94] At Holy Cross, the first middle-class parish,[95] gramophone evenings were used in the early twentieth century. Passing showmen presented a wider view of Africa, China, Buffalo Bill, Barnum and Bailey's circus acts. At the close of the century, school board officials varied in enthusiasm in rounding up truants: headmasters often felt they were indifferent.[96] But by 1900 attendance levels were well above ninety per cent.

Within the school, Catholic values were emotionally and aesthetically consolidated through hymns. Singing was vital in creating a portable ultramontane religion. It was Sister Mary Xavier Partridge of Mount Pleasant Training College, who wrote the hymn, 'Lord for Tomorrow and Its Needs': it embodied the desired values. St John's had earlier begun hymn classes as a means of promoting communal identity and encouraging Mass attendance.[97] Hymn-books were quickly introduced into St Andrew's. May devotions further developed hymn-singing.[98] The quality of singing was invariably high, thanks to clerical interest or peripatetic professional music masters. Even the poorest school might boast a new harmonium.[99] Alto singers were carefully selected while Fr Dobbleacre presented the score of a French Mass to his little choir.[100] Music lessons before the clergy and at school Masses excited the imaginations of the children:[101] 'to inspire some of them with a taste for school'. Their Vespers and psalms impressed the much travelled Mgr Munro: they invariably impressed the government schools inspectors.[102]

[95] Holy Cross, 11 Dec. 1895, 30 Nov. 1898; St John's, 13 Oct. 1870; 'an African' came on 11 Jan. 1878 and 13 Oct. 1882.

[96] E.g. St John's, 5 June, 9 Oct. 1896, 21 April 1899; St Mary's, 14, 22 Aug., 5 Sept., 7 Nov. 1890; St Mary's, 6 Sept. 1907.

[97] St John's, 25 April 1866.

[98] St Andrew's, 8 Aug. 1870 and St Mary's, 26 May 1864.

[99] St Mary's, 10 Aug. 1870.

[100] St John's, 24, 26 Oct. 1870.

[101] St Mary's, 16 Dec. 30 Nov. 1872; St John's, 6 June 1871.

[102] See St Andrew's, 21 Aug. 1871, Annual HMI Report, 7 Aug. 1874.

[103] St John's, 23 Nov., 12 Dec. 1871, 10 May 1895; St Mary's, 7 June, 30 Aug., 13 Sept. 1865; St Mungo's, 8 Oct. 1866.

Choirs, brass bands, the distribution of medals, competitive selection for processions, for altar-servers and, latterly, for swimming and soccer helped to maintain group identity.[103] Provision of a playground football dramatically increased punctual attendance: so, too, did gifts of holy picture cards.[104] St Mary's even provided full football kit and winners' watches for special games.[105] School libraries took ultramontanism into poor homes.[106] Class photographs were used to stir group consciousness.[107] Communal outings helped: Christmas pantomimes, spring and summer picnics. As early as 1865 some 500 pupils from St Mungo's went to Pollokshaws for a picnic: a year later 500 pupils and 150 adults took a special excursion train to Cambuslang. St Peter's, Partick, had 918 children at the Christmas party in 1903.[108] Such events suggest sophisticated organizational skills.

Poverty remained both a challenge and response to unify the group: even in 1908, 200 pupils from St John's qualified for the poor children's civic outing to Rouken Glen.[109] The school's priest-manager treated the rest to an outing to Bishopbriggs. Not surprisingly, even the poorest pupils, the HMI reported, in St Mary's are 'in every respect excellent. Criticism is unnecessary.'[110]

The children's lot slowly improved. Holy Cross, the first Catholic middle-class parish in Glasgow, emerged in 1882. Significantly, the first parish priest, the Revd J. Linkh, was a cultured German social Catholic refugee, with social Catholic notions. The headmistress, Margaret McGinlay, 1889–1914, gave the school high standards, reflecting the upwardly mobile flock. Operetta, drill, educational gramophone concerts, and limelight shows followed: in 1905 and 1906 the school received an excellent rating in all three departments from the inspector-

[104] St Mary's, 6 Aug. 1866, 1, 17 Sept., 3 Nov. 1868, 7 March, 29 May 1871, 24 Sept., 7 Oct., 6 Nov. 1872, 28 April 1876.

[105] St Mary's, 28 May, 4 June, 23 Dec. 1897.

[106] St Mary's, 26 Jan. 1874, 25 Jan. 1886.

[107] St John's, 31 Oct. 1902.

[108] St Mungo's, 21 Sept. 1865, 13 Sept. 1866, 12 Feb. 1870; St Peter's, 16 Jan. 1903.

[109] St John's, 22 May, 5 June 1908.

[110] St Mary's, HMI Annual Report; St Mary's, 15 Oct. 1872.

[111] Holy Cross, 7 Dec. 1882, 27 Jan. 1888, 6 Aug., 11 Dec. 1895, 15 March 1899, 13 Jan. 1905.

ate.[111] It was a symptom of slow-running changes in the Catholic body.

Catholic evangelicalism was reinforced by visits during church missions. For example, Redemptorists gave instruction before and after lessons in St John's School during 1875 and 1892: others visited St Mary's.[112] In 1865 Passionists took over St Mungo's parish and school. Soon classes were using Abbé Gaume's *Catechism of Perseverance*: school missions and confessions followed.[113] Pupils as a corporate body attended Holy Week services.[114] Communal observance naturally followed the shared experience of folk memory in later life.

Latin liturgy, a shared mystical experience, increased the need for more English hymns and devotions. An early end of formal schooling increased the need for more organizations to sustain immediate Catholic sentiment and solidarity. Faith was anything but remote. The profusion of parish guilds, particularly St Aloysius' for boys, and Angels' and St Margaret's for girls, furthered group consciousness. Adult bodies, the Confraternity of Christian Doctrine, the Apostleship of Prayer, the Sacred Heart Society, the St Vincent de Paul Society, the Catholic Young Men's Society, and the League of the Cross, with recreational rooms and Penny Savings Bank schemes, prospered. All reinforced domestic devotional discipline within the locality, neighbourhood, and city.[115]

That universal Catholic spirit was consolidated by a sense of being part of wider world of achievement and effort. Numerous visitors spoke to schools: English, French, and Germans; Archbishop John Keane of St Louis, the Glasgow-born Conservative Bishop Gilmour of Cleveland, priests from Colorado or Egypt.[116] Former teachers and pupils bolstered that perception: one Marist

[112] St John's, 16 April 1875, 27 May 1892; St Mary's, 30 June 1865.

[113] St Mungo's, 7, 30 Aug. 1866, 1 April 1867, 9, 15 Nov. 1869. See my 'Formation', and Ann Taves, *The Household of Faith: Roman Catholic Devotions in Nineteenth Century America* (Notre Dame, 1986).

[114] St Mungo's, 28 March 1864, 19 April 1867.

[115] See my 'Formation', John Ferguson, the Glasgow Protestant Irish Nationalist, maintained that organization was an end in itself: 'educational, improving and it indicates life'; quoted in Hugh Heinrick, *A Survey of the Irish in England, (*1872), ed. Alan O'Day (London, 1980 edn.), p. xvii.

[116] See St John's, 27 Aug. 1875, 20 May 1896; St Andrew's, 1 Nov. 1877; St Mary's, 17 Aug. 1882; St Mungo's, 27 Aug. 1897.

[117] St Mary's, 30 April 1897.

returned as Provincial in New Zealand, and another after thirty-three years in Australia.[117] Pupils might be at the bottom of the *Glasgow* social heap, but their self-perception was bolstered by a sense of ultramontane world community, European strength, and achievement against the odds. Shared experience, hardship, and folk memory were reconciled in the ultramontane world of the late nineteenth and early twentieth century. The boy was father of the ultramontane.

Glasgow University

CHOIRBOYS AND CHOIRGIRLS IN THE VICTORIAN CHURCH OF ENGLAND

by WALTER HILLSMAN

I INTRODUCTION

ALTHOUGH the roles played by children in recent centuries in English church music have varied enormously, it is probably fair to say that choirs with at least some boys' or girls' voices have proven more important in musical, ecclesiastical, and social developments than those with none. The most obvious example of this is the choir of men and boys, which has constituted a conspicuous feature of cathedral and some collegiate music since the Middle Ages, except, of course, during the Commonwealth. As women and girls have until very recently been regarded as inappropriate in such music, it is difficult to imagine that the breadth of achievement in musical composition and performance standards associated with these choirs would have been possible if they had contained only men and no boys.

In the parochial sphere, the first significant choral developments took place after the Restoration. In the late seventeenth and early eighteenth centuries in urban areas, many charity schools were founded, and boys and girls from those schools gradually came to form 'the choir' in local churches. Although their repertoire was simple—psalm tunes in one or two parts, hymns sometimes arranged to sound like arias, and occasional anthems in a limited number of parts—they came to constitute a distinctive feature in the life of many town churches. Sitting usually around the organ in the west gallery, they increasingly assumed responsibility for singing service music, while congregations grew more silent.[1]

In country churches, a different but equally distinctive type of musical ensemble began to emerge in the late seventeenth century, namely, a group of instrumentalists and singers of both

[1] N. Temperley, *The Music of the English Parish Church*, 2 vols (Cambridge, 1979), I, pp. 102, 116, 132, 134.

genders, also based in the west gallery. Such groups—which sometimes included boys and girls[2]—were often called Old Church Bands or West Gallery Minstrels. They, too, assumed primary responsibility for music in services, to the detriment of congregational singing.

The apparent musical impressiveness of the charity children—at least in their gigantic annual festivals in St Paul's Cathedral—and the social contribution of the West Gallery Minstrels to village life[3] afforded both types of choir a seemingly assured place in Anglican parochial music. Both, however, effectively remained aloof from clerical control, and either directly or indirectly contributed to the increasingly cold, slovenly, and indevout character of many parochial services. Men and women minstrels, for example, often flirted in the west gallery during services.[4]

II VICTORIAN CHOIRBOYS

The above-mentioned parochial groups, not surprisingly, became prime targets for early Victorian, High-Church clerical reformers, who were seeking, as a first objective, to raise the devotional tone of services. As one means of achieving this, many Tractarian and moderately High-Church clergy began to cause the installation of choirs of surpliced men and boys in facing chancel stalls in parish churches—choirs which had been virtually unknown parochially since the Reformation. The proximity of surpliced choirs to similarly attired clergy and acolytes visibly strengthened the impression that singers were participating integrally in the work of the sanctuary. The supposedly unemotional[5] and angelic sound and demeanour of choirboys represented an ideal of liturgical austerity.[6] To Tractarian clergy at least, men and boys were also seen as most fit to

[2] F. Helmore, *Church Choirs, containing Directions for the Formation, Management and Instruction of Cathedral, Collegiate and Parochial Choirs Being the result of 22 years' experience in Choir Training* (London and Stratford-on-Avon, 1865), p. 9.

[3] Temperley, *Music of the English Parish Church*, I, pp. 157–8.

[4] Ibid., p. 162.

[5] Helmore, *Church Choirs*, p. 58.

[6] 'Ladies' surpliced choirs', *The Musical Times* [hereafter *MT*], 30 (1 Sept. 1889), p. 526.

encourage congregations to sing plainsong hymns, responses, psalms, and canticles.

The second reason High-Church clergy were promoting surpliced choirs lay in the social function they served in church life. These choirs acted as draw-cards to boys,[7] who might be interested in filling a gap in their schooling, as music frequently bypassed them, while almost forcing itself on girls—more so as the century progressed.[8]

In the 1840s and 1850s surpliced choirs spread rapidly in Tractarian and moderately High-Church parishes. Subsequently they appeared in middle-ground and Evangelical churches. By about 1870, twenty-one per cent of Greater London churches[9] and fifty per cent of Birmingham churches had them.[10] In 1884 the London figure had risen to fifty-seven per cent.[11] By 1900 most town churches of any importance maintained them. With only one exception, cathedral voluntary choirs founded in the Victorian era were made up of men and boys. Even that exceptional group—the St Paul's Voluntary Choir—saw the replacement of its women with boys shortly after the 1872 appointment of the High-Church organist John Stainer.[12]

The fact that surpliced choirs became status symbols is evidenced in part by the increasing amount of direct and indirect financial support which parochial and cathedral authorities lavished on them. Such subsidies also helped to foster and reflect the growing sense in these choirs of an increasing obsession of Victorian men (and of some older boys), namely, professionalism.

Parochial choirboys in town churches were normally paid—the term 'voluntary choir' to Victorians generally meant unpaid *men*.[13] Boys often earned between sixteen shillings and two

[7] 'The social aspect of the church choir', *The Choir and Musical Record* [hereafter *CMR*], 16 (4 Oct. 1873), p. 207.

[8] B. Rainbow, 'Music in education', in N. Temperley, ed., *Music in Britain, The Romantic Age* (London, 1981), p. 43.

[9] C. Mackeson, *Guide to the Churches of London and its Suburbs for 1884* (London, 1884), p. 171.

[10] Temperley, *Music of the English Parish Church*, 1, p. 279.

[11] Mackeson, *Guide to the Churches of London*, p. 171.

[12] G. L. Prestige, *St Paul's in its Glory: a Candid History of the Cathedral 1831–1911* (London, 1955), p. 154; London, St Paul's Cathedral Library, 'Chapter Minute Book 1874–1889', p. 320 (25 June 1887).

[13] 'Church music', *The Musical Standard* [hereafter *MS*], ns 17 (6 Sept. 1879), p. 154.

pounds a year, and could earn between five and ten pounds.[14] Solo boys were sometimes paid twenty or twenty-five pounds, an impressive amount when one considers that many contemporary farm labourers earned about fifty-two pounds a year, and some schoolmasters and curates around a hundred.

The greatest benefit enjoyed by some parochial and many cathedral choristers, however, lay in subsidized schooling, which varied enormously in educational, boarding, and semi-boarding arrangements. The cost of a good education and full board for each boy normally totalled fifty pounds a year, the same as in non-choir boarding schools.[15] St Paul's Cathedral, which provided thirty boys with free board and education, thus spent £1,500 each year on its choir school. St Saviour's, Eastbourne, spent twenty pounds on each of twenty boys, that is, £400 a year, and each set of parents paid a further thirty pounds.[16] The most attractive musical establishments to parents were, of course, those where all choristers were boarded and educated free. Until the mid-1880s, these included St Paul's Cathedral, as already mentioned; All Saints, Margaret Street;[17] the Chapel Royal; St Peter's, Bournemouth; St John's, Torquay;[18] Magdalen College, Oxford; and King's College, Cambridge.[19] However, because of financial difficulties, all parish choir schools except Margaret Street abolished residential arrangements, and cathedrals from the mid-1880s failed to increase them.

Arrangements for *day* schooling throughout the country remained numerous and often attractive. St Peter's, Eaton Square,

[14] For sixteen shillings, see E. West, 'How to raise a choir, and keep it', *The Organist and Choirmaster*, 3 (15 July 1893), p. 51; for two pounds, J. S. Curwen, *The Boy's Voice. A Book of Practical Information on the Training of Boys' Voices for Church Choirs, &c.* (London, 1891), p. 21; for £5–£10, G. Fleming, *A Treatise on the Training of Boys' Voices, with Examples and Exercises and Chapters on Choir-Organization, Compiled for the Use of Choirmasters* (London, 1904), pp. 75, 80, and Advertisements: Wood-street, *MT*, 14 (12 Apr. 1870), p. 609.

[15] 'Educational [Trent]', *The Rock*, no. 1,102 (27 Aug. 1886), p. 1.

[16] For St Paul's Cathedral, see 'St Paul's Choir Boys. Sir George Martin vindicates their absence', *MS*, illus. ser. 16 (24 Aug. 1901), p. 120; for Eastbourne, 'The Warden', 'Choir schools', *The Musical World*, 59 (15 Oct. 1881), p. 669.

[17] For St Paul's, see Misc.: St Paul's, *The Church Times* [hereafter *CT*], 18 (26 Nov. 1880), p. 801; for Margaret Street, Misc.: Margaret Street, *CT*, 24 (15 Jan. 1886), p. 47.

[18] For Chapel Royal, see 'Clerical and organists', *CT*, 26 (23 Nov. 1888), p. 1,029; for Bournemouth, Advertisements: Bournemouth, *MS*, 3rd ser. 19 (11 Dec. 1880), p. 365; for Torquay, Advertisements: Torquay, *MT*, 21 (21 Aug. 1880), p. 377.

[19] For Magdalen, see Misc.: Magdalen, *CT*, 23 (2 April 1885), p. 279; for King's, Advertisements: King's, *MS*, 4th ser. 20 (7 May 1881), p. 289.

for instance, provided its own free education at non-National schools.[20] Other churches with choir schools or school arrangements for choristers included St Michael's, Paddington; St Matthias, West Brompton; All Saints, Clifton;[21] Christ Church, Blackfriar's Road; St Alban's, Holborn (until 1879); St Paul's, Brighton; St John the Divine, Vassall Road;[22] Malvern Priory Church; Dunster Parish Church; St Andrew's, Wells Street; St Nicholas, Liverpool;[23] Annunciation, Bryanston Street; Holy Trinity, Bournemouth; and Newland, near Malvern.[24]

As the century wore on, the size of surpliced choirs increased. In 1854, when an average cathedral choir numbered twelve boys and six men, the Cathedral Commissioners noted that such small numbers did not provide much insurance against illness.[25] By 1874, the editors of the *Musical Standard* were agreeing with one writer who thought that cathedral choirs on Sundays should number about a hundred![26] Although no cathedrals enlarged their principal choirs to that extent for ordinary Sunday services, some did, in fact, expand, increasing the number of choristers. Ely, for instance, by 1890 had twenty trebles, St Paul's in 1901, thirty.[27]

Parish choirs were larger. The average size of a surpliced choir in the early 1880s in central London was apparently about

[20] 'Our leading organists. XIV.—Dr Huntley at St Peter's, Eaton Square', *Church Bells* [hereafter *CB*], 26 (29 May 1896), p. 800.

[21] For Paddington, see Advertisements: Paddington, *CT*, 10 (26 April 1872), p. 195; for West Brompton, Advertisements: West Brompton, *CT*, 10 (22 Nov. 1872), p. 535; for Clifton, Advertisements: Clifton, *CMR*, 16 (19 July 1873), p. 33.

[22] For Blackfriar's Road, see Advertisements: Blackfriar's, *CT*, 17 (21 Nov. 1879), p. 738; for Holborn, 'St Alban's, Holborn', *CT*, 17 (20 June 1879), p. 391; for Brighton, Advertisements: Brighton, *CT*, 13 (8 Oct. 1875), p. 507; for Vassall Road, Advertisements: Vassall-road, *MT*, 15 (1 Oct. 1871), p. 248.

[23] For Malvern, see Advertisements: Malvern, *CT*, 16 (19 July 1878), p. 415; for Dunster, Advertisements: Dunster, *MT*, 22 (1 July 1881), p. 337; for Wells Street, 'Church news. St Andrew's, Wells-street', *CT*, 27 (13 Dec. 1889), p. 1,175; for Liverpool, Advertisements: Liverpool, *MT*, 21 (1 May 1880), p. 211.

[24] For Bryanston Street, see 'Lay workers, organists, &c. [Bryanston-street]', *CT*, 38 (6 Aug. 1897), p. 146; for Bournemouth, 'Church and organ music [Bournemouth]', *MT*, 42 (1 May 1901), p. 317; for Newland, O. Chadwick, *The Victorian Church, Part II*, 2nd edn (London, 1972), p. 180.

[25] T. Hopkinson, 'Sunday choral festivals', *MS*, ns 7 (8 Aug. 1874), p. 88, and Parliamentary Papers 1854, xxv, p. 27.

[26] Hopkinson, 'Sunday choral festivals', pp. 77–8, 88.

[27] For number of choristers, see Salisbury, Salisbury Cathedral Library, Chapter Acts Books, xxvi, p. 46 (22 Nov. 1864), and York, York Minster Library, MS Add. 157/2 (Scrapbook 1859–1908), p. 341h (1874); for Ely, Curwen, *The Boy's Voice*, p. 80; for St Paul's, 'St Paul's Choir Boys. Sir George Martin vindicates their absence', p. 120.

twenty; in Greater London about the same time, nearly thirty.[28] In 1904 George Fleming assumed that the 'ordinary' parish church choir numbered between thirty-six and forty-six, that is, twenty to thirty boys and sixteen men.[29] Some churches had larger ones before that. For example, All Souls, Leeds, had forty-seven; Sheffield Parish Church, almost fifty; Halifax Parish Church, sixty; St Anne's, Soho, sixty-four; and Marylebone Parish Church, eighty to ninety.[30] St Mary Abbotts, Kensington, subdivided: there were 'two full choirs for the Sunday services and one for the children's services. The number of choir-boys exceeds one hundred.'[31]

Until the 1870s Victorian parochial choirboys were in most respects in an enviable position compared with their counterparts in cathedrals. John Jebb in 1843 condemned the choirs of St Paul's Cathedral, Lincoln Cathedral, and Westminster Abbey as 'degenerate'. The same year, the Precentor of Ely, W. E. Dickson, described the music at King's College, Cambridge, as 'radically bad'. Four years later a writer in the *Parish Choir* maintained that the choir of Christ Church, Oxford, was 'possibly the worst in England'.[32] The only apparent exceptions were Norwich and Durham.[33]

Abysmal performance standards were matched by slovenliness in other respects. Choristers often noisily distributed anthem word-books before services, and behaved with levity during them. Some cathedrals had no orderly entry of singers in proces-

[28] C. Box, *Church Music in the Metropolis: Its Past and Present Condition* (London, 1884), *passim*; Temperley, *Music of the English Parish Church*, 1, p. 282.

[29] Fleming, *A Treatise on the Training of Boys' Voices*, pp. 25–6.

[30] For Leeds, Sheffield and Halifax, see W. Spark, *Musical Reminiscences: Past and Present* (London, 1892), pp. 69, 179, 193; for Soho, J. S. Curwen, *Studies in Worship Music (First Series) Chiefly as Regards Congregational Singing*, 2nd edn (London, 1888), p. 376; for Marylebone, 'Chats with the clergy. The Rev. Canon Baker, Rector of St Marylebone', *CB*, 30 (8 June 1900), p. 581.

[31] 'Canon Pennefather and his work. St Mary Abbotts, Kensington: the church, the vicar, and the parish', *CB*, 29 (13 Oct. 1899), p. 956.

[32] J. Jebb, *The Choral Service of the United Church of England and Ireland: being an Enquiry into the Liturgical System of the Cathedral and Collegiate Foundations of the Anglican Communion* (London, 1843), p. 246; W. E. Dickson, *Fifty Years of Church Music* (Ely, 1894), p. 23; 'Laicus Oxoniensis', 'Church music at Oxford', *The Parish Choir* [hereafter *PC*], no. 22 (Oct. 1847), p. 54.

[33] For Norwich, see B. Rainbow, *The Choral Revival in the Anglican Church 1839–1872* (London, 1970), p. 245; for Durham, 'Alto', 'Report on church music in the Diocese of Durham', *PC*, no. 17 (May 1847), p. 135, and W. Hillsman, 'Trends and aims in Anglican church music 1870–1906 in relation to developments in churchmanship' (Oxford D.Phil. thesis, 1985), p. 309.

sion. Cassocks were not generally worn, and surplices were often soiled or torn.[34]

Cathedral chorister education at mid-century was by all accounts terrible. Ely and Chester boys suffered because their chapters spent too little money on them; those at Westminster Abbey would reputedly have been better off in a National School.[35] In 1854 Cathedral Commissioners attributed this to choristers' long hours of practice, which took priority over general studies. An extreme example of this was at Norwich, where the boys were engaged in rehearsals or services from about 8.30 a.m. until 5.30 p.m. (except for a lunch-break) and were instructed academically for only two hours from 5.00 until 7.00 p.m., during which time their schoolmaster sometimes fell asleep.[36]

Matters gradually improved because better state education presented a challenge, chorister schools (where they existed) merged with larger, more viable ones, and chapters increased boarding arrangements for choristers, at least until the mid-1880s, when cathedral income shrank considerably.[37] Salisbury and Lincoln were possibly the only cathedrals at mid-century to board even some of their choristers. However, the insistence of musicians like Samuel Sebastian Wesley and William Done (organist of Worcester Cathedral) and of one Dean of Canterbury[38]

[34] For distribution, see 'J.A.', 'Defects in the cathedral service', *PC*, no. 6 (July 1846), p. 47; for entry, Jebb, *Choral Service*, p. 229; for cassocks and surplices, Rainbow, *Choral Revival*, p. 253.

[35] For Ely, see 'Cathedral musical enquiry. no. 1—Ely Cathedral', *MS*, ns 9 (2 Oct. 1875), p. 223; for Chester, P. C. Moore, 'Cathedral worship in England from the Reformation to the nineteenth century' (Oxford D.Phil. thesis, 1954), p. 371; for Westminster Abbey, 'Musical opinion', *MS*, ns 1 (27 May 1871), pp. 44–5.

[36] For Commissioners, see Parliamentary Papers 1854, xxv, p. 42; for Norwich, F. G. Kitton, *Zechariah Buck, Mus. D., Cantuar. Organist and Master of the Choristers at Norwich Cathedral 1817–1877. A Centenary Memoir* (London, 1899), p. 62.

[37] For merged schools, see York, York Minster Library, 'Chapter Minutes 1883–1909', p. 101 (5 Oct. 1887), and F. A. G. Ouseley, 'On the education of choristers in cathedrals', in J. S. Howson, ed., *Essays on Cathedrals. By Various Writers* (London, 1872), pp. 216–17; for boarding arrangements, see J. S. Bumpus, *The Organists and Composers of S. Paul's Cathedral* (London, 1891), pp. 185–6; for reduced cathedral income, see York, York Minster Library, MS Add. 157/2, Scrapbook 1869–1908, p. 371b (14 Jan. 1887).

[38] For Salisbury and Lincoln, see *The Wiltshire Archaeological and Natural History Magazine* (Dec. 1937–Dec. 1939), p. 214, and Parliamentary Papers 1854–5, xv, pp. 74–9; for Wesley, S. S. Wesley, *Reply to the Inquiries of the Cathedral Commissioners, relative to the Improvement in the Music of Divine Worship in Cathedrals* (London, 1854), p. 16; for Done, P. Barrett, 'English cathedral choirs in the nineteenth century', *JEH*, 25 (Jan. 1974), p. 34; for Canterbury, Parliamentary Papers 1871, lx, p. 199.

that boarding would ensure a higher class of applicant for choristerships led to the establishment of boarding arrangements in many places.

Lack of boarding facilities had left choristers vulnerable to bad influences, as noted by the founder of St Michael's College, Tenbury, the Revd Professor Sir Frederick A. Gore Ouseley, Bart.:

> And is not this a wretched training for a young and susceptible lad? Again, he has to go through the streets and lanes of the city to and from home. There he sees and hears vicious and immoral sights and sounds most defiling to a boy's mind. Surely such a daily practical commentary on the good precepts he hears in church and school cannot but exercise a most deleterious influence on his whole religious and moral character.[39]

Ouseley had established his foundation at Tenbury deliberately to serve as a model in all respects for existing choral foundations. Although well-intentioned, he apparently failed to recognize that boarding sometimes entailed other problems, as at Magdalen College, Oxford, in the 1880s, when choristers sought refuge in chapel or in the streets from disciplinary anarchy in the boarding-house.[40]

Chorister education at many choral foundations eventually drew praise, particularly at Winchester, Worcester, Bristol, Salisbury, the Temple Church, Lincoln Cathedral, Christ Church (Oxford), Tenbury, and the Chapel Royal.[41] The only negative report I have seen on such education late in the period concerned Westminster Abbey, where arrangements were called 'erratic'.[42]

[39] Ouseley, 'On the education of choristers in cathedrals', p. 225.

[40] E. M. Venables, *Sweet Tones Remembered: Magdalen Choir in the Days of Varley Roberts* (Oxford, 1947), preface, pp. vii–ix.

[41] For Winchester, see W. R. W. Stephens, 'Cathedral choristers', *The Guardian* [hereafter *GD*], 53 (20 July 1898), p. 1,142; for Worcester, H. H. Woodward, 'Cathedral choristers', *GD*, 53 (20 July 1898), p. 1,142; for Bristol, Moore, 'Cathedral worship', p. 372; for Salisbury, D. H. Robertson, *Sarum Close: A History of the Life and Education of the Cathedral Choristers for 700 Years* (London, 1938), p. 319; for the Temple, D. Lewer, *A Spiritual Song: The Story of the Temple Choir and a History of Divine Service in the Temple Church, London* (London, 1961), p. 224; for Lincoln, 'Dotted Crotchet', 'Lincoln Cathedral', *MT*, 45 (1 May 1904), p. 299; for Oxford, Tenbury and Chapel Royal, H. Fisher, *The Musical Profession* (London, 1888), p. 16.

[42] E. Pine, *The Westminster Abbey Singers* (London, 1953), p. 228.

Performance standards among cathedral choirs rose dramatically from the 1870s, and were nourished by better schooling for choristers; increased full practice time; establishment of men's-voice services, which gave boys a much-needed weekly break; an annual holiday for the whole choir;[43] and more stringent demands by choirmasters.

III GIRLS IN VICTORIAN CHOIRS

At least three features of surpliced choirs proved obstacles to Victorian girls' membership. First, wearing surplices was, to many Anglican minds, an activity reserved for men and boys, as these were clerical vestments indicating that wearers were extending the work of the altar. Secondly, earning money, as choirboys usually did, would, to early and mid-Victorian upper- and upper-middle-class girls at least, have represented a 'loss of caste'.[44] Thirdly, pursuing musical performance standards to the level some surpliced choirs achieved would also have been thought unladylike by the many parents who discouraged their daughters from overachieving.[45] With the overwhelming success of surpliced choirs, Victorian girls were reduced to sparsely documented and ignominious or purely supportive roles in English church music. In some town churches, and even more frequently in villages, girls (or women, or both) were sometimes used to prop up the treble line when choirboys were weak.[46] They never wore surplices and almost never occupied choir stalls. Front pews in the nave, or pews hidden behind chancel choir stalls, constituted their most frequent seating. In at least one Victorian Anglican monastery, Claydon, girls in the organ gallery added musical assistance to boys singing from stalls in the middle of the chapel.[47]

[43] For standards, see 'Cathedral progress', *MS*, 4th ser., 39 (11 Oct. 1890), pp. 301–2; for men's-voice services, Cambridge, Cambridge University Library, EDC 2/1/8 ([Ely] 'Dean & Chapter Order Book 1863 to 1888'), pp. 349–50 (14 June 1888); for holidays, Lichfield, Lichfield Joint Record Office, 'Lichfield Chapter Acts Book vol. 16 1896–1908', p. 136 (7 March 1902).

[44] D. Gorham, *The Victorian Girl and the Feminine Ideal* (London and Canberra, 1982), pp. 8, 51.

[45] J. N. Burstyn, *Victorian Education and the Ideal of Womanhood* (London and Totowa, NJ, 1980), p. 42.

[46] L. Coleman, 'The music of the English Church', *The Church Magazine* (Sept. 1886), p. 234.

[47] *Church Music in Town and Country. By 'The Stranger Within Thy Gates'* (London, 1881), p. 34; L. Coleman, 'The music of the English Church', p. 234; and C. Walker, *Three Months in an English Monastery: A Personal Narrative* (London, 1864), p. 58.

Girls singing extra-liturgical music by themselves in special services, that is, without boys or adults, constituted a rarity, but did feature occasionally in some churches, notably in Lancashire. As the Revd Brian Findlay, currently Vicar of St Augustine's, Tonge Moor, Bolton, relates:

> Most parishes [in Lancashire] had (and some still do) an annual 'School Sermons Sunday', on which the children of the church schools paraded in their Sunday best, and special preachers were engaged to persuade the congregation to dig deep into their pockets for school expenses. Of course, the services were sung by the usual men and boys choir, but as a special treat, selected girls were brought forth to sing a few sentimental items, dressed (usually) in white dresses and shawls. They were (and are) called the Little Singers—always female, and always in addition to the 'resident' choir. Their appearance is so exceptional in a culture where male choirs still flourish much more than elsewhere that it is almost a 'feast of misrule', with the normal scheme of things being turned upside down![48]

Institutions founded from the late nineteenth century where liturgical choirs of girls did not contradict the 'normal scheme of things' were, of course, girls' boarding schools. Of these, publications concerning a limited number of High-Church establishments speak most of the centrality of chapel services to the life of the school, and of the importance of chapel music. At St Mary's School, Wantage (managed at that time by the Community of St Mary the Virgin, Wantage) and Heathfield School, Ascot, music was dominated by plainsong, and the choirs were small—eight at Wantage and ten (including two girl cantors) at Ascot. At Wantage they wore 'beautiful blue veils' and sat 'in stalls that continued along the walls from the Sisters' stalls'.[49]

[48] Personal letter to the author from the Revd Brian Findlay of Bolton, 17 June 1993.

[49] For High-Church foundations, see G. Avery, *The Best Type of Girl: A History of Girls' Independent Schools* (London, 1991), p. 155; for Wantage, 'Reminiscences of Wantage', *S Mary's School [Wantage] Magazine* (Christmas 1908), p. 17, and Sr Phyllis, C.S.M.V., *St Mary's School: a Personal History* (Wantage, 1973), p. 12; for Ascot, 'School notes', *Heathfield School Magazine* [hereafter *HSM*] (1899–1901), p. 5, and G. O. F. Griffith, 'The Chapel of the Ascension', *HSM* (1903), p. 44.

The most lavish chapel music at any High-Church girls' boarding school was apparently at St Anne's School, Abbots Bromley, in Stafforshire—a Woodard School. There,

> since the beginning of the School [in 1874], plainsong has been . . . used for the psalms, for canticles on Friday, and for the Communion service throughout Lent and Advent. At other times Anglican services were sung, such as Stanford in B [Flat] and Baden Powell in F. . . . Later in the Nineties, came . . . Tours in F, Woodward in A, Woodward's Communion Service in E flat and Gounod in C . . . . The hoods and cloaks now worn [1924—see plate 1] had been established since early times, and of this occasion the famous story is told.
>
> 'Who are the Nuns in the organ loft?' asked a stranger. 'There are none,' was the reply.[50]

Evidence points to vocal help from women (staff or wives of men on the staff), to accompaniment of the choir in chapel festival services by violins, piano, and organ, and to manuscript arrangements for treble voices of the above-mentioned four-part music by the chaplain, at least from 1895 to 1902.[51]

IV THE TWENTIETH CENTURY

Proportionally speaking, boys in the twentieth century have played a gradually less important, and girls a more important, role in Anglican church music. Parochial surpliced choirs of men and boys have declined in number, and cathedral voluntary choirs have mostly replaced boys with women—Worcester being a notable exception.

The reasons for this change are complex, but two may be singled out here. First, problems of recruiting and keeping boys in parochial and cathedral voluntary choirs—already evident in

[50] V. M. Macpherson, *The Story of S Anne's, Abbots Bromley, 1874–1924* (Shrewsbury, 1924), pp. 123, 128.

[51] Ibid., p. 124.

Plate 1 The Choir of St Anne's School, Abbots Bromley, in 1903, from V. M. Macpherson, *The Story of S. Anne's, Abbots Bromley, 1874–1924* (Shrewsbury, 1924), p. 128 [Bodleian shelfmark G. A. Staffs. 4° 37]. Reproduced by permission of The Bodleian Library, University of Oxford.

the late nineteenth century[52]—have been growing more severe, partly because ecclesiastical funds to pay them or subsidize their education have been eroding. Secondly, the assumption that only men and boys should wear surplices and play quasi-clerical roles in Anglican services has been held by a declining number of churchmen. The surplicing of women, which began creeping in to Anglican services very late in the nineteenth century,[53] has continued apace, and that of girls has followed as a matter of course.

Partly because of their relatively greater financial resources and ability to appeal for funds, most cathedrals have remained able to attract boy trebles by offering subsidized private schooling. Opportunities for girls in regular cathedral services have only recently begun to emerge, with precedents being set outside England. Since the mid-1970s, St Mary's Cathedral in Edinburgh has been offering chorister scholarships in its school to girls as well as boys, and both sing together in the cathedral choir—in the proportion of about 25 per cent girls to 75 per cent boys.[54] Also in the mid-1970s, girls were mixed with boys at Bury St Edmunds (a practice which ceased in the 1980s). Since 1991, at Salisbury, money to endow scholarships for girls in the cathedral girls' choir has been coming in. At the moment, this choir is singing about one service a week by itself, and a further one with the altos, tenors, and basses of the cathedral choir, that is, when the boys of the cathedral choir do not sing.

The Salisbury experience may yet prove to be a turning-point for girls in English church music. For the first time ever, carefully selected and rigorously trained girls can be compared as a group with equivalent boys in the liturgical choral sphere, in respect of vocal timbre, artistic polish, and demeanour. As a recent article in *The Times* notes, girls' choirs are due to be founded in late 1993 at Bristol Cathedral, in 1994 at Wells, and 1995 at Exeter.[55] Perhaps these noteworthy precedents will further enhance girls' usefulness in parish choirs, where there is less likelihood of an

[52] Hillsman, 'Trends and aims', p. 165.

[53] Ibid., p. 164.

[54] Much of the information in this paragraph is drawn from conversations with Denis Townhill of Edinburgh (20 July 1993), Paul Trepte of Ely (19 July 1993), and Richard Seal of Salisbury (13 July 1993).

[55] R. Gledhill, 'Girls strike a sour note in the cloisters', *The Times* (17 July 1993), p. 8.

artificial, enforced end to a girl's singing career at age thirteen than there would be in many cathedral choir schools. They obviously do not experience as dramatic a vocal change at puberty as boys.

From the dawn of the Victorian age until recently, girls in Anglican church music have constituted what might be termed the *de facto* 'trebles of last resort', that is, material regarded as better than nothing, but certainly not to be compared with boys or women, and, above all, not to function seriously in cathedrals. Arguments concerning the composition of treble lines have been revolving around the relative merits of only two types of singers—boys and women. In the twenty-first century, the battle may well be more three-cornered.

Faculty of Music,
University of Oxford

THE PURLEY WAY FOR CHILDREN

by CLYDE BINFIELD

THE Sunday school was an art form. Its classical age has been explored by T. W. Laqueur and its totality by P. B. Cliff.[1] Like those of great art, its creative moments were the simultaneous issue of evolution, system, and individual genius. Those moments were intensest in their Nonconformist aspect, for Nonconformists, though often thwarted, were born educationists. Their buildings reflected this: theological colleges, for instance, which grew from overgrown houses to imitations of Oxford, and eventually to Oxford itself; or proprietory schools, strait-jacketed between the financial constraints and social aspirations of an enlarged middle class trying to reconcile Manchester's values with those of Thomas Arnold. And there were the Sunday schools themselves, complexes of hall, parlour, and classroom, enfolding the chapel, reflecting the activity, mentality, and spirituality of a particular society, encompassing therefore a concept of the Church, and designed with considerable ingenuity to meet the needs of a rounded yet carefully graduated community. By the turn of the twentieth century they housed daily activities for all ages. Their influence reached far. Fuelled by the Word proclaimed from the pulpit, and empowered by the decisions of representative meetings taken in hall or vestry, the Sunday school broke chapel bounds to teach more people than could be met with in chapel pews.

Such places were sophisticated institutions, as prone as any others to the operations of Parkinson's Law or the Peter Principle. They were also *constitutions*, hives of internal politics, seen sometimes as outposts of Empire, sometimes as fomenters of Home Rule. Their purpose was to create and to improve; and they offered a vocation to a variety of people—young men, perhaps, for whom this was a first lesson in the handling of

[1] See T. W. Laqueur, *Religion and Respectability: Sunday Schools and Working Class Culture 1780–1850* (Yale, 1976); P. B. Cliff, *The Rise and Development of the Sunday School Movement in England, 1780–1980* (Redhill, 1986).

others; and women of all ages, for whom here was an unassailable sphere of influence, responsibility, and development.

If the Sunday school were an art form, then George Hamilton Archibald was its Diaghilev. More accurately, he was a Sunday composite of Oberlin, Pestalozzi, Froebel, and Maria Montessori. Archibald was the Canadian who took the American Sunday-school world of teachers trained in psychology and of schools graded into departments and syllabused according to age, and translated it into the language of Edwardian Nonconformity. Archibald's English moment came in 1905 with the prospect of a demonstration school at Cadbury's Bournville. That offer led to West Hill, built in 1907 as Britain's first training college for Sunday-school teachers.[2] Here was explicated the power of play in child culture;[3] an emphasis that education began with the child rather than the lesson, that children were best taught through their senses and their actions and were best appealed to through their imaginations, that recitation and rote should give way to story, play, and nature-study.

Yet could such art be liberated for all children? The plant and programmes of Edwardian Sunday schools and institutes demonstrate popular and comprehensive intentions. Given a situation in which social divisions were nicely reinforced by the division between the children of the church, whom it was a duty to nurture, and all other children, whom it was a duty to reach, could those intentions be convincingly squared with the practicalities of a class-conscious society or the polities of gathered churches? The answer was no easier for churches in the new, few, but growing suburbs, whose children were sent away to school, than it was for churches at the social frontier, where the surrounding children were so different from those of the church, and Social Darwinism became all too plausible in the face of lice and smells.[4] Such issues were not ignored. They were attacked

[2] For Archibald, see Cliff, *Sunday School Movement*, pp. 205–8; Ethel A. Johnston, *George Hamilton Archibald: Crusader for Youth, 1858–1938* (London, 1945). His ideas were promoted within Anglican circles from 1908, especially by Hetty Lee (Mrs Richard Holland), and led to St Christopher's College, Blackheath: see Margaret M. B. Bolton, 'Anglican Sunday Schools, 1880–1914' (University of Kent at Canterbury, M. A. thesis, 1988), esp. pp. 44–6, 54–7.

[3] G. H. Archibald, *The Power of Play in Child Culture* (London, 1905).

[4] The pungent smell of the children of Woodberry Down Baptist Church's Sunday school, off Seven Sisters Road, and the frequency with which they were suddenly and unavoidably sick, is a memory of the 1940s recalled by one whose sister taught there. Yet even if Woodberry Down had slipped

with verve in a host of places. Indeed, thanks to West Hill and the National Sunday School Union, not to mention Nonconformists' consciences, fine-honed by educational agitation, there was a network of responses.[5] One response, select yet representative, and admirably documented, was that of Purley's Congregationalists. Here West Hill took root in Surrey's White Highlands.[6]

Purley, whose railway station is the essence of the London, Brighton, and South Coast Railway, as its churches are the essence of London, Brighton, and South Coast Religion, is the quintessence of what outsiders believe to be Surrey. Its perfection, however, was slow in developing. Although the railway reached the area in 1841, there were by 1870 only twenty-four private houses, three public houses, an asylum for fatherless children, and a boarding school for the dependents of clerks and warehousemen. Anglicanism arrived with a chapel of ease in 1878, Congregationalism began in 1892, Methodism in 1906, the Baptists in 1908. Of them all, it was the Congregationalists whose church was the pearl of Purley. It was also its soul:

> A society has a soul of its own which far exceeds the sum-total of the individual souls who compose it. Thought, emotion, enthusiasm, and strength come to an individual from an inspired community which he could not realise without it. The soul-life of each is enhanced by the general

---

since its Edwardian peak, it had retained a socially respectable congregation, instituting a children's church for its morning children in the 1930s; but chronic poverty, poor diet, and the habit of sewing children into their winter clothes were still normal urban facts in the 1940s.

[5] For aspects of this, with particular reference to Vivian and Dorothy Pomeroy at Greenfield Congregational Church, Bradford, from 1911 to 1923, and to Wilton E. Rix at Ealing Green Congregational Church from 1922 to 1939, see C. Binfield, 'True to Stereotype? Vivian and Dorothy Pomeroy and the Rebels in Lumb Lane', in S. Mews, ed., *Modern Religious Rebels* (London, 1993), pp. 185–205, esp. pp. 198–201, and 'Freedom Through Discipline: the concept of Little Church', in W. J. Sheils, ed., *Monks, Hermits and the Ascetic Tradition, SCH*, 22 (1985), pp. 405–50.

[6] I am particularly grateful for permission to use the records of Purley United Reformed Church, and for help and recollections extending from the 1920s from Mr and Mrs J. Artingstall, Ms Rosemary Green, Mr and Mrs Charles Kersley, Mr D.B. Pascall, Mr. R. Pye-Smith and Miss Lois Watson. The church's records are generously contexted. This section is particularly based on Mary Rose Jenkins, 'An Inquiry into the Growth of the Congregational Church at Purley', unpublished thesis, Caloma College, West Wickham, Kent, 1975 [hereafter Jenkins]; Vera Kersley, 'Purley United Reformed Church Diary', typescript 1984; G.M. Pinnell, *Pringle of Purley: 10 May 1866–22 January 1933* (Purley, 1966) [hereafter Pinnell]; *Purley Congregational Church 1895–1954* (Purley, 1954).

> soul . . . .Not only through visible example and spoken word, but through telepathy, through the subtle working of psychological and spiritual influences, unseen and mystic, whose ways we are only now beginning to trace, the power of the corporate life acts upon the individual . . . .A church whose atmosphere is charged with spirituality of a healthy and practical, as well as richly spiritual kind, will draw men irresistibly into the sweep of its power, and will not need to justify its existence by theoretical argument.[7]

There, caught consciously creedless in 1914, is the world of Independents turned Congregationalist, earthworms spiritualized into so many Sir Oliver Lodges. Who were they? How were they nurtured?

They had names to set the antennae twitching.[8] By 1933 there were nearly 800 in membership, with over 100 waiting for sittings. They paid their minister £1,000 a year. They were drawn from all denominations and all sections of the middle classes. They were the sort to own motor cars, to have university degrees, and to be Justices of the Peace. Since 1904, the year when the tin tabernacle turned into Hampden Pratt's folksy free Gothic, their church had been steadily and ingeniously enlarged at seven-yearly intervals until it became a thousand-seater. The reason for that was Arthur Pringle: 'Proud Prelates of a sister church are summoned to the House of Lords, amidst the pomp and ceremomy of the world. Our church has no dignities to confer but nevertheless there is an honour attaching to the plain description of Pringle of Purley."[9] Pringle came to Purley in 1904.[10] He was advanced. That is to say, he was a New Theologian, the sort of man for whom the Twelve Apostles were the first

[7] Purley Congregational Church, *Manual* (1914), p. 1.

[8] As Purley Congregational Church, 'Membership, Marriage and Baptismal Register, c. 1905–46' and a bound volume of Manuals, Reports and Statements of Accounts, 1908–33, demonstrate, they include names which betray superior ministerial descent (Jukes, Newth, Creak, Pye-Smith, Campbell-Finlayson); the Silcocks made cement and the Pascalls made sweets; the Beaumont Shepheards were solicitors in the City; there were Surrey county councillors and Croydon borough councillors; there were also a Harrod of Harrods, a meat-importing Vestey (Sir Edmund, his first wife, a son and a daughter) and the widow, daughters and a lay-preaching son of J.M. Dent the publisher; and there was a gratifying mix of men from Whitehall, home and colonial knights and titled wives and widows. Their doyen was Henry Sell (1851–1910) of Sell's World Press.

[9] Epigraph to Pinnell from a speech given by F. H. Elliott, 23 September 1929, MS in church archives.

[10] For Pringle see Pinnell and *Congregational Year Book* (1934), pp. 273–4.

modernists, and when he became Chairman of the Congregational Union in 1924 his addresses were suggestively titled 'The True Fundamentalism' and 'New Testament Modernism and the Church of Today'.[11] He was hot and strong for social idealism, conferences on pressing issues, and daringly churchy practices. He made Purley's communion table look altar-like by pushing it back against the wall and putting a cloth with an embroidered cross on it. Had he dared he would have placed a wood or metal cross there.[12] He used liturgical forms of prayer, introduced printed orders of worship,[13] and encouraged the chanting of the Lord's Prayer. He liked processions. As his church concertinaed out, so he embarked on a steady campaign of interior gentrification. The chancel was panelled in oak, and hassocks were placed in the pews. There were a side pulpit, a Willis organ, and a war memorial window by Christopher Whall. From 1920 the choir was discreetly robed in black gowns, with mortar-boards for the women since berets or caps might be worn at too rakish an angle.[14] Although one member had feared lest this 'addition of further ritual might weaken the directly spiritual element', and Purley's Baptists had begun as a secession fuelled by fear of New Theology, most of the changes were trouble free.[15] That, too, was Pringle's doing.

Pringle was credible. He combined the arts of authority as opposed to autocracy, and diplomacy as opposed to pragmatism, and cloaked them in character. 'There is a child in the transept coughing—try and curb it', he might announce.[16] After Sunday worship there was no question of him shaking hands in the porch: anxious enquirers might see him in his vestry, by appointment. He visited punctiliously once a year, sending a warning card ahead of him, to intimate whether or not he might be offered tea. He was president of Rotary, then very new. His devotion to tennis, cricket, and football meant that he never missed Wimbledon, The Oval, or Crystal Palace. He was the 'compleat minister'.

11 *Congregational Year Book* (1925), pp. 84–109.

12 A bronze cross was given for the table in 1946.

13 Bound Volume of Orders of Service, 1933.

14 The black robes were replaced by blue, and the mortar-boards by caps, in 1961.

15 Jenkins, pp. 55, 31.

16 Pinnell, p. 5.

Such was the context for Purley's most characteristic contribution to Congregational attitudes: the Children's Church that was Purley's singularly easy and successful solution of the challenge presented not so much by children as by those church children for whom the traditional Sunday school was not quite the thing. Purley's way for Christian children was neither unique nor the first, but it was infectious throughout English Congregationalism.

Arthur Pringle was the childless pastor of a family church which had its Guides (4th Purley, 1918) and its Scouts (1st and 13th Purley, 1919 and 1932) as well as its Pucoga Amazuti and Pucoga Owani Groups, with their Guardians of the Fire. And from February 1918 there was Children's Church. This was the creation of May Silcock, a deacon's daughter. She was a trained teacher. She had the National Froebel Union's Higher Certificate and had spent two years at West Hill. It is indicative of her class, her generation, and her training that she found her vocation in Sunday-school teaching.[17]

It began when Arthur Pringle met May Silcock on Woodcote Valley Road. He had been greatly impressed by what he had seen on a recent Sunday in Enfield, where just before his sermon the children left 'Big Church' for their own 'Nursery Church'. Miss Silcock was the right person to adapt this Enfield practice to the needs of Purley. The idea was no sooner planted than it took root and flowered. Yet, although the Children's Church began at once, its further development was a suggestive evolution. At first Children's Church was for the Sunday morning children (nineteen of them to start with, although only five had been expected); Sunday school continued as a separate Sunday afternoon institution, although it changed its name to Junior Church in 1925 and closed down completely in 1939.

At Purley it was Children's Church that held the stage until its post-war fulfilment as Family Church.[18] The metaphor is apt, for Children's Church countenanced drama and ritual of a kind that few adult Congregational churches would contemplate: the gift

[17] This section is particularly based on 'Purley Congregational Children's Church 1918–1939', an album presented to Miss W.M. Silcock in 1939 [hereafter *Album*], and W.M. Silcock, 'Some Experiments in The Religious Training of Children as applied (1) In a Children's Church, (2) In a Nursery School', MS October 1932 (hereafter 'Experiments').

[18] *Album*; Pinnell, pp. 7–8; Jenkins, pp. 57–8.

service in 1921, when each child brought a teddy bear for the Purley day nursery; the Clyppen Service in 1926, 'when the children returned to the Big Church, for the singing of the last hymn, and made a ring round the centre of the Church as an expression of their love for the Mother Church'; in 1927, 'We held our first "Passing on the Light" Ceremony, and on Rogation Sunday we had an out-of-door procession and prayed for a blessing on the crops'; in 1928 there were bunches of violets to take home to mother on Mothering Sunday, and in 1929, 'We celebrate the special Sundays by a procession with our banner. Our special Saint is St. Christopher, of which we have a picture on our banner.' A specially commissioned triptych of St Christopher followed in 1936.

Service was a responsibility to be enjoyed. Palm Sunday 1938 saw 'our usual . . . procession in the Big Church, when the children were handed green palm-branches as they came down the aisle to the Children's Church, which they found already decorated with palms.' Then

> Once more the deacons came early on Easter morning to decorate the Children's Church with spring flowers. The best white cloth and the Easter picture were put out and the Cross to remind us of all that had gone before. Then, with bunches of primroses in our hymn books, we sang and shared in the Easter Joy of the Church.
>
> The children brought an offering of new laid eggs for distribution to the hospitals in the district.

That such prosperous usefulness was far horizoned was underlined at Christmas when, 'By means of a "television set" [in fact, a model constructed to look like one] we were able to see how the children of other countries kept Christmas.'

In the 1930s the surest way of enlarging Congregational imaginations to include the children of other countries was still the London Missionary Society's ship, *John Williams V*, one of a long succession to ply the South Seas. In 1938 Children's Church held a Missionary Cruise Party when the church hall became the *John Williams*:

> A hundred and seventeen young sailors, complete with caps and collars, went for a 'cruise' on the *John Williams V* in

> October. They were marshalled by smart, peak-capped officers along the narrow 'gangway', over the frothy 'sea' on to the deck. They brought with them ship halfpennies, missionary boxes, parcels of silver paper and stamps which were received by the 'ship's purser'. Then they sailed from Island to Island of the South Seas; they played games or sang on deck; dropped anchor and had tea on an Island and 'visited' the other Islands by a film.

That Sunday the morning service was held on board ship 'and the children sang on their way as they visited many of the Islands carrying the message of Jesus'.[19]

Such jollity was in the great Edwardian tradition of themed missionary bazaars, but there was more to it than mere extravaganza. Successive *Church Manuals* mediated the purpose of Children's Church to the congregation at large:

> By story, parable, singing, and all kinds of happy ingenuities, the interest is maintained at high pressure . . . the methods adopted are surely calculated to produce reality, reverence, simplicity and sweetness in the formation period of child life. Upon such a foundation the noblest Christian character is sure of being reared [1921].

> The devotion and worship in the Children's Church is very active. We often sing our hymns in procession; we show our thankfulness in action, our joy in helping one another. We are very free and yet we enjoy ceremony and a certain amount of ritual. We are interested in all churches and their traditions, and we are ready to be friends with children of all denominations, of all countries and all classes. We try to be Catholic in its true sense. Is this the cradle of the Re-union of the Churches? [1922]

> People never collect in two companies and march in definite order into their Church. Why should we? So we gather at each entrance door, talk quietly together about anything and everything, until we hear the soft strains of a voluntary, when we walk into our Church, receive a hymn book if

[19] *Album*, passim. The obverse side of the halfpenny coin had a sailing ship on it, hence its appeal to missionary-minded Congregationalists. The London Missionary Society's collecting box was no less suggestive: it was in the form of a native hut.

> necessary, advance up any of the three aisles, choose our seats . . . and settle ourselves comfortably . . . But we can't quite be grown-ups. *They* are so prosaic and like the same pew every Sunday; *we* like a change and sometimes we like to leave our families and go and sit with a friend; and what we *do* like very much, sometimes almost to the extent of fighting for it, is to have a baby child of three or four to sit with and look after. Then the choir files in, and we all kneel in silence for a few moments and prepare ourselves for worship. [1924][20]

That worship's incidentals were steadily accumulated: a Children's Choir, gowned and surpliced, from 1922, with its own front row in the oak choir-stalls of Big Church, dedicated to Pringle's memory in 1935; the same hymn-book as Big Church from 1924; an alms dish; a reed organ, a reading-desk and a hymn-board, all in the 1930s. There was also an essay in Congregational polity: in 1928 seven children, four boys and three girls, each with a badge of St Christopher suspended on a blue ribbon edged with gold, were formed into a diaconate, with one of them as Children's Church secretary. For Children's Church was seen more consciously than most Sunday schools were then seen as a nursery for church membership. It was in 1925 that two of the earliest Children's Church members 'were received into the Mother Church and took their first communion'; and by 1933 over 700 children had been connected with Children's Church, and over fifty of them had gone on to become members of Big Church; by 1937 over 100 had done so.[21]

In 1930 May Silcock described her intentions to a wider audience:

> In forming the Children's Church at Purley, we have made use of the instinct of imitation shown in early childhood. The child of a 'Church-going' family is ready to imitate his parents at worship, and since there is great inspiration to be gained from simultaneous action, we hold our children's service at the same time as that of the parents . . . their Church is part of the Mother Church, which itself is part of

[20] Bound Church Manuals; 'Experiments', pp. 73–4.
[21] *Album*, passim.

> the 'Church throughout all the world'. . . . Little ones attend as early as two to three years of age, bringing their parents, nurses or governesses if they wish.[22]

That last touch was pleasantly, sensibly, Purley. It was underlined two years later when Miss Silcock turned her experiences into a thesis:

> A mother, applying at an employment agency for a nurse for her children, was asked whether she had any preference with regard to the religious views of the nurse. She replied 'No, provided her God is a God of love and joy, and not an unpleasant old gentleman who spies on little boys and girls.'[23]

Here she explained what church manuals could only hint at. 'The value of a creed', she quoted, 'lies in the experience that has preceded and caused it, and that experience must be personal.' To achieve that her aim was 'not the "saving of souls", but to put before the children such a beautiful picture of Jesus, that they cannot do otherwise than like Him, and liking Him, love Him, and in consequence will dedicate their lives to His service.' Since love 'is the only magnet which will attract children', the teacher is duty-bound to present God 'in the most lovable and beautiful form we can offer'; that duty takes one directly to Jesus and therefore to the New Testament for, though the child 'cannot understand doctrines and theology . . . he can understand the Father and Friend, and later, the appeal of the Hero and Master.'[24] At this point the Froebel-trained teacher came into her own. She began with daily life's foundational impressions—a mother's tenderness, a father's protectiveness, a home's harmony: 'Will anyone deny that these are impressions of God?' Then, turning to a child's natural curiosity, that sense of something beyond control ('He begins to wonder, and it is not long before worship follows'), she annexed the world of nature:

> At this stage of his life comes his own joy in creating. . . . he will try to copy God in Nature. In his care of plants and pets he learns more of what God is like. His forethought and

[22] May Silcock, 'The Children's Church', *Teachers and Taught* (May, 1930), cutting in 'Experiments', p. 78.

[23] 'Experiments', p. 4.

[24] Ibid., pp. 4–6.

> tenderness are called into action, and the attributes of God are being developed in him. . . . Gradually will come to him the sense of kinship with all living creatures, and from this will grow the realisation of sonship, brotherhood of man, and Fatherhood of God.[25]

Such a child was now ready for church:

> interest will be shown in the high arches and pillars, the stained glass windows, the pulpit, the organ, music and flowers. . . . Colour, form and sound play a large part in the lives of little children . . . unconsciously the child feels the unity of life in 'the coming of people together in assembly'.[26]

That, too, was Froebel, but it was also Purley, since Hampden Pratt's ever-enlarging building allowed for all those things. Order and ceremony held no terrors for one who had studied the rituals of childhood games, but here her inherited Nonconformity came into play, for there must be *reason* behind every action, as well as art:

> As long as the service appeals only to his sight and hearing, pageantry and ceremony may hold him, but in adolescence he will, and must use his thinking powers to a far deeper extent, and his demand for free expression of thought and feeling must find an outlet.
>
> Rigid forms of worship, too, will cripple our progress in the search for truth. Let us use them therefore in their rightful place, as a means to an end, guides and helps for the child, until he can 'walk alone'.[27]

That approach explained the development of Purley's Children's Church from the straightforward, if up-to-date, graded Sunday-school class of February 1918 to a miniature church with choir, sidesmen, and elected officers:

> One Sunday, the children were asked to bring in their missionary boxes, which they had had for a year, and the money collected in them would be counted. In order to impress the children with the realisation that their missionary

[25] Ibid., pp. 8–13.
[26] Ibid., p. 15.
[27] Ibid., p. 19.

> offering was to God, it was arranged that they should make a procession up the centre aisle of the Church, and their boxes, being received by the minister, would then be placed upon the Communion Table, the children passing out by the chancel door to their own service. This little ceremony proved so impressive and effective that a decision was made that day whereby a similar processional exit of the children should be made on each subsequent Sunday, a special voluntary being played meanwhile. . . . Several years later, at the suggestion that the children appeared unshepherded, I took the end seat of the choir stalls, and now, when the voluntary is played, I stand at the chancel steps to receive them, and when all have passed, I follow them to their own service in the hall. . . .[28]

May Silcock, standing there in her black mortar-board and her black gown with its red band worn over a long grey dress, and with a gold chain round her neck, remains in many Purley memories. Her power was that of intuitive good sense. Thus, though the deacons of Children's Church met regularly, it was usually quarterly, at a Saturday tea-time, after school games or scout and guide meetings were over: homework made weeknight meetings impracticable. At one such meeting the question arose of the felt strips which rubbed on bare knees when the children knelt to pray. Should not hassocks be provided? 'But miners come before hassocks', urged a deacon, drawing attention to the rival claims of the Miners Distress Fund. In 1932 there was debate about more active leadership in worship:

> no one was particularly keen, and one remarked, 'The chaps who would do it are the very chaps who shouldn't do it, and if you asked any of us, we should be too nervous to do it properly, then the others would laugh, and not listen to what we were reading, but only to how we were reading.'[29]

Miss Silcock knew that participation must emerge; it should never be imposed. She accepted other limitations. Boarding school was one of them. As John Elliott wrote from The Larches, Woldingham:

[28] Ibid., pp. 22–4.
[29] Ibid., pp. 25–9, 35.

> As I am going to Oundle School next term, I wish to resign my position as a deacon and treasurer of the Children's Church.
>
> Thank you again and again for all that you have done for me. It has all been a very great help to me.
>
> Hoping that you will have very happy holidays.
>
> With best wishes from your tennis partner.[30]

Whether or not Children's Church was the best preparation for Oundle Chapel, May Silcock developed an unbeatable combination of the predictable and the daring in her recommendations for worship's setting. Since ' "seeing is believing", particularly in the young', the worship-room 'must express thoughts of Him'. That meant symbol: 'Surely this is God's own method of teaching—the whole world is symbolical?'

> A table or small Altar, if adorned, adorned simply and beautifully, will be found helpful, and on it may be placed a picture of Jesus, the Children's Friend. Some will like to place a Cross there, but since the children are full of life, will it not be better for them to dwell on the Life of Jesus rather than on the death, and to use the Cross only occasionally . . .

That raised the question of quality: 'There are not enough pictures in the world yet, which may be considered suitable for children in their religious training.' But Miss Silcock listed several by Margaret Tarrant, as well as Harold Copping's 'The Hope of the World' and 'Jesus and the Children' and other older classics—Raphael's Sistine Madonna, Bouguereau's 'Madonna of the Angels', Holman Hunt's 'Light of the World', Hoffmann's 'Gethsemane' (to be used only occasionally), and there was Eleanor Fortescue Brickdale's 'St Christopher'. Indeed, she had the temerity to recommend a visit to Mowbray's in Margaret Street, and felt that sometimes a statuette—Allouard's 'Madonna and Child' perhaps—could take a picture's place.[31]

As for stories, hymns, and prayers, she could be as satisfied with those contemporary Free Church classics, John Oxenham's

[30] Ibid., letter of 3 August 1928.

[31] Ibid., pp. 40–2. She used as illustration a plate of 'Apparatus suggested by Messrs. Mowbray and Co. Margaret St. W.1.'

The Hidden Years and Basil Matthews's *The Splendid Quest*, as she was saddened by the swing of the hymnodic pendulum 'from mystery to . . . cheap doggerel'; she determined to 'see to it that our hymns are big and grand in style'.[32] The style of prayers was quite another matter: there 'simple litanies were found to be helpful', the Prayer Book General Thanksgiving was entirely adaptable, though the Lord's Prayer should be sparingly used, since it was hard to understand. With silent prayer she was bolder yet: 'At least the young worshippers are given an opportunity for their own communion with their Heavenly Father, when they will not be influenced by adults, however well-meaning.'[33]

It was with 'picture forms of worship'—the sort 'found in the records of the saints and in early Church activities'—that May Silcock was most at ease ('It is an interesting and significant fact, that news has come to us from missionaries in Central Africa, that these dramatic religious celebrations are most helpful to the child races of the world').[34] So she prepared specimen services: one for Epiphany, another for Rogation Sunday, a third for Palm Sunday:

> Tall palms stood on either side of the Lord's Table wearing its green cloth. There were Lent Lilies in the vases beside the picture of the Christ-Child standing with his arms outstretched in the form of a cross. . . . The children were reminded of the baby game they used to play with their mothers, 'How much do you love me?' and the answer they gave by stretching their arms open wide showing the amount. Jesus, the Christ-Child, was asked 'How much do you love the people?' He answered 'Sic te amo. Thus much do I love you', and He opened his arms to the extent of the Cross for love of His people.

On Trinity Sunday, 'Each child carried home with him a purple iris he had made to remind him of the meaning of Trinity Sunday', while on Whit Sunday there were 'White flowers on the red cloth on The Lord's Table', and 'no handwork after the

[32] Ibid., pp. 52, 58.
[33] Ibid., pp. 60–1.
[34] Ibid., pp. 64–5.

closing prayer, but the children went quietly out to show in their homes, what God's Spirit in their hearts might mean to others.'[35]

For children reared on A. A. Milne, Kenneth Grahame, Arthur Ransome, E. Nesbit, and Arthur Mee, Purley's chapel Sundays held few terrors, and should they move on to school or college chapel, or even to parish church, they would be able to do so with some discrimination. Should they remain in Nonconformity their influence would be incalculable:

> There was a look of surprise on the children's faces as they came into their church and found nothing but chairs and hymn-books placed ready for them. . . . In the talk, the children began to understand why there was no accustomed Lord's Table. Two big boys were asked to fetch it and put it in its place at the head of the Church. Its name was discussed and its meaning. Since the children come from homes of different denominations, the name 'Lord's Table' was found to be most suitable to its use. [A girl covered it] with a beautiful red velvet cloth, others arranged vases of flowers, laid out the deacons' badges and offertory bags, placed a picture of Christ, the Children's King, in the centre, and lit the candles, while the choir robed themselves in their clean white surplices. As each symbol or ornament was put in its place, its meaning and use were discussed. Then came the readiness to sing: 'We love the place, O God, wherein Thine honour dwells'. [Next, however, came Timothy's story] who, having arranged his own little chapel for worship, showed himself dependent on the symbols and ornaments. An angel seeing this showed him a vision of John Bunyan with his friends holding a very real and true service in Bedford gaol, and Timothy realised how a bare prison may become a Church; and a worshipper, bound fast in his worship by the symbols and ornaments of his Church, may be almost in prison. . . . Now beginning to realise that true worship lies not in the beauty of the Church, but in the holiness of the worship, the children were able to sing one or two verses of the hymn 'O worship the Lord, in the beauty of holiness'.[36]

[35] Ibid., pp. 66–9.

[36] Ibid., 'Symbols and Ornaments', p. 70.

They were, after all, ready for Big Church. Arthur Pringle's not-so-chance winter encounter with May Silcock on the Woodcote Valley Road had more than served its purpose. In 1932 Miss Silcock could list twenty-four 'Other Children's Churches started from this one' and a further eighteen with a separate origin. Most of them were Congregationalist, but at least two were Methodist, and one was Anglican; and not all were in Surrey's White Highlands or their Sussex and suburban outliers.[37] Thus are attitudes changed while values are reinforced, but it is seldom that the route can be so easily followed. As Frank Elliott of The Larches, John's father, put it in 1925:

> Family responsibility in the old days was one of the strong character building assets of the state. The state has weakened this responsibility by many of its social and political activities, and its conduct is reflected in the loss of self reliance and independence that we see all around.
>
> I venture to think that the teaching and associations of our Church have developed a sense of parental and family responsibility, of self sacrifice and courage, which has bred a spirit of sturdy self-help, while not unmindful of the claims of the weak. I am very glad that my own sons are having the opportunity of growing up in the reverent atmosphere and spirit of sturdy manly Christianity of our Church.[38]

University of Sheffield

[37] They are listed in ibid., p. 79.
[38] Speech delivered 28 September 1925: MS.

THE FOUNDRESS AND THE FOUNDLINGS: THE 'MORAL PANIC' OF 1893 IN THE ORPHANAGE OF MERCY

by STUART MEWS

CHILD abuse sometimes seems to be a discovery of the closing decades of the twentieth century. Academic attention was focused on the problem by a conference sponsored by the Royal Society of Medicine, chaired by the Health Minister Dr David Owen, in 1976. Among the twenty-six contributors was a member of our society, Professor Gordon Dunstan, and Dom Benedict Webb. The publicity for the published proceedings claimed that 'Child abuse and neglect provide some of the most important and difficult problems in Western Society.'[1]

Ten years later academic debate had trickled down to clinical practice. The resulting diagnoses were catapulted into media headlines in the Cleveland child abuse panic, which the local MP attempted to chronicle and explain under the title *When Salem Came to the Boro*, published in 1988.[2] Amongst the consequent theological reflections on the same incident was an article in *New Blackfriars* on child abuse and the reality of sin, in which the Dominican author made some sensible comments about the way in which what was once seen simply as cruelty is liable to be demonized under the new category of 'abuse'.[3] Moving from semantics to sociology, he observed that 'The present growth *in attention* [my italics] to child abuse seems to emanate from countries which are predominantly Protestant in ethos (the United States leads the field, of course).' He continued: 'The same countries are also the most industrialised, or post-industrial and the wealthiest. These facts are not unconnected. It is in these countries that we see the most breakdown in traditional family

[1] *The Challenge of Child Abuse. Proceedings of a Conference sponsored by the Royal Society of Medicine, 2–4 June 1976*, Alfred White Franklin, ed. (London and New York, 1977).

[2] Stuart Bell, *When Salem Came to the Boro: The True Story of the Cleveland Child Abuse Crisis* (London, 1988). For the official view: *The Report of the Inquiry into Child Abuse in Cleveland* (London, 1988).

[3] Michael Doyle, 'Child Abuse and the Reality of Sin', *New Blackfriars*, 69 (1988), p. 431.

organisation.'[4] At this point he played down the denominational aspect, but did briefly touch on the function of secrecy in the overall Catholic approach to sexuality.

Five years later that secrecy, at least in non-Catholic environments, seems to have been substantially eroded. In his 1993 Christmas message the Pope said that he had been reduced to tears of anguish by reports of sexual abuse by Catholic priests. His remarks follow the setting up of a commission by the Vatican to investigate clerical paedophilia.[5]

Allegations about the abuse of children and women by the personnel of religious institutions, both Catholic and Protestant, have surfaced in England at regular intervals. They belong to some extent to the historical pathology of the English people, and the task of the historian is to sift fact from fiction and explain both the circumstances which enabled things to happen, and to account for the persistence of salacious but sometimes untrue or exaggerated beliefs in popular mythology.

In *The Erosion of Childhood* Lionel Rose maintains that the 1880s were 'a period of growing sensitivity to the problems of child cruelty and neglect'.[6] Child neglect had been covered by statute for the first time in 1857 by the introduction of industrial schools, into which stray children caught begging in the streets or associating with thieves might be placed. Yet the Vagrancy Act of 1824 still applied to vagrants of all ages, and in 1887 J. W. Horsley, chaplain of Clerkenwell Gaol, protested at the imprisonment in solitary confinement of two homeless orphans, aged six and seven.[7] Nevertheless, the public mind was moving. The number of children born into middle-class families began to fall in the 1880s, and this may have conferred greater value on the significance of each individual child's life.[8] Attitudes towards children were changing, even though they had to react to a variety of conflicting demands. There was primarily the requirement of public policy for the suppression of a subordinate class which might otherwise threaten public order. There was the wider framework of Victorian Christian moral values. Finally

[4] Ibid., p. 435.

[5] *The Times*, 22 Dec. 1993.

[6] Lionel Rose, *The Erosion of Childhood. Child Oppression in Britain 1860–1918* (London, 1991), p. 236.

[7] Ibid., p. 96.

[8] F. M. L. Thompson, *The Rise of Respectable Society: A Social History of Victorian Britain, 1830–1900* (London, 1988), pp. 53–4.

and usually last in importance were the needs of the child, physical, mental, and spiritual. Meeting them might, however, conflict with the rights and responsibilities of the parent, which opened considerable areas for conflict.

It was in 1880 that elementary education to the age of ten became compulsory, and to the age of eleven in 1893. The National Society for the Prevention of Cruelty to Children had been set up as a voluntary body in 1883 and was soon looking into 10,000 referrals a year. Its efforts were, however, hampered by a reluctance to interfere in the domestic sphere, though its activities, reports, and warnings aroused sufficient concern to lead to the passage of the Children's Act of 1889.

The late Victorians were suspicious of total institutions. In 1882 negotiations between Edward Benson, Bishop of Truro, and William Booth for the incorporation of the Salvation Army into the Church of England foundered in part on the newspaper revelations of the Army's methods with children and young people. It was alleged that children were encouraged by the Army to denounce their parents as unrepentant sinners and to transfer their prime allegiance to the General and his officers. Matters came to a head with the Charlesworth case, when an Anglican vicar, Samuel Charlesworth, alleged that his seventeen-year-old daughter, Maud, had been improperly influenced by the Booths to renounce her family and move to France, where she was sent out into the streets of Paris selling copies of the *War Cry*. The consequent correspondence in the church papers revealed the deep-seated Anglican fear that the authority of the Victorian father was being undermined.[9]

It was partly to win back alienated public support that the Army broadened its focus from being an exclusively evangelistic movement, seeking to save souls, and became also concerned with saving bodies. The campaign waged with W. T. Stead, the crusading editor of the *Pall Mall Gazette*, and Josephine Butler to outlaw teenage prostitution not only led to the raising of the age of consent to sixteen in 1885, but also focused attention on the plight of abandoned young women and girls in London.[10] These

[9] Stuart Mews, 'The General and the Bishops: alternative responses to dechristianisation', *Later Victorian Britain 1867–1900*, Alan O'Day and T. R. Gourvich, eds (Houndmills, 1988), pp. 225–6.

[10] Edward J. Bristow, *Vice and Vigilence* (London, 1977), ch. 5; Deborah Gorham, 'The "Maiden

were sections of the population which various religious groups felt compelled to try to help.

One aspect of the problem was presented by the plight of orphans. It was to meet their needs that the Irish evangelical Dr Thomas Barnado founded his homes, and the Wesleyan Thomas Bowman Stephenson had founded the National Children's Homes in 1869. In addition to these great national institutions were smaller local initiatives in parishes. When Luke Paget became vicar of St Pancras in 1887, he found a section of the gallery occupied by the St Pancras Female Orphans, attired in their eighteenth-century dress—mob caps, tippets, prim dresses, aprons, and long mittens. His widow recalled being told that before the church acquired hymn-books it was the duty of the Female Orphans to copy out the hymns for the forthcoming Sunday, adding their names and ages, so that the pew-holders could assess the improvement in their writing and so ensure that they picked the neatest if they needed a new housemaid or tweeny. On Orphanage Sunday guest preachers were advised not to mention the charity by name too often because at the first mention of it the girls would rise and from then on give a grateful curtsy to every subsequent mention. After the service the orphans would be grouped around the collection plates in the porch, where they would again curtsy and chorus, 'Thank-you, sir', 'Thankyou, madam', whenever they saw a gift of half a crown or over.[11]

The St Pancras Female Orphans were organized on conventional Church of England lines, but there were other Anglican ventures which sometimes seemed to late Victorians like the social investigator Charles Booth to 'go beyond the bounds of prudence and perhaps of principle also'.[12] That was his opinion, as quoted by Peter Anson, of what were popularly called the Kilburn Sisters. They were responsible for the Orphanage of Mercy or Homes for Orphaned and Deserted Children set up by the Church Extension Association in Kilburn, Broadstairs, Mar-

Tribute of Modern Babylon" re-examined; child prostitution and the idea of childhood in late Victorian England', *Victorian Studies*, 21 (1978), pp. 353–79; Paul McHugh, *Prostitution and Victorian Social Reform* (London, 1980).

[11] Elma K. Paget, *Henry Luke Paget; Portrait and Frame* (London, 1939), p. 123.

[12] Charles Booth, *Life and Labour of the People of London: Religious Influences*, I (1902), p. 209, quoted in Peter F. Anson, *The Call of the Cloister*, 2nd rev. edn (London, 1964), p. 442.

gate, and Brondesbury. The Kilburn Sisters were officially known as the Sisters of the Church, a High-Church religious order founded in 1870 by Emily Ayckbowm (or Ayckbown). In 1895–6 they were to be at the centre of a storm of criticism which for a time placed them under a cloud, but from which they have long since emerged to continue their much valued ministry of prayer and service in England, Canada, and Australia, even to this day.

Women's religious orders were by the 1890s accepted warily as permanent features of Anglicanism. Their emergence and significance has been the subject of much recent scholarly attention.[13] I doubt whether Martha Vicinus is wholly correct in describing the Sisters of the Church as 'one of the most characteristic sisterhoods',[14] because in its period of fastest growth, from 1880 to 1895, it seems to have been most distinctive in the boldness of its plans and the independence of its operations.

Emily Ayckbowm's father was of German extraction, and she had been born in Heidelberg in 1836. Her mother died when she was five, and Emily was brought up by a stepmother in Chester where her father was vicar of Holy Trinity, a ramshackle church which was declared unsafe in 1862. The poverty and squalor close to her home made a permanent impression. When she was eighteen Emily was sent to Germany and Italy for two years to improve her German and develop her appreciation of art. What made most impression on her was the dignified worship of cathedrals and the sight of rich and poor worshipping side by side. On her return to Chester she attempted to share her vision of a Church renewed and open to all by raising money for the restoration of the church and instructing groups of uneducated children, women and men. Installing some of her pupils in cushioned rented pews, she was dismayed when they were ejected by indignant pew-holders. In 1864 with a dozen friends she formed the Church Extension Association (CEA) in her stepmother's drawing-room in Chester. Emily, now twenty-eight,

[13] Martha Vicinus, *Independent Women, Work and Community For Single Women 1850–1920* (London, 1985); John Shelton Reed, 'A female movement: the feminization of nineteenth-century Anglo-Catholicism', *Anglican and Episcopal History*, 57 (1988), pp. 199–238; Michael Hill, *The Religious Order. A study of virtuoso religion and its legitimation in the nineteenth century Church of England* (London, 1973); Sean Gill, 'The power of Christian ladyhood: Priscilla Lydia Sellon and the creation of Anglican Sisterhoods', in Stuart Mews (ed.), *Modern Religious Rebels* (London, 1993), pp. 144–65.

[14] Vicinus, *Independent Women*, p. 82.

became the first secretary. The Association's aim was to provide funds so that new churches could be built in poor areas, and to provide free pews. It also took a special interest in children, their education and welfare.

Four years later Emily moved to London. When she heard that one of her clerical subscribers, R. C. Kirkpatrick, was likely to become first vicar of a new church, planned to provide for Kilburn the type of worship and teaching already offered at All Saints', Margaret Street, and St Alban's, Holborn, she wrote to him offering to organize a sisterhood. In 1870 she was clothed by Kirkpatrick as first novice of a new community—the Sisters of the Church.[15]

The growth of the Church Extension Association was spectacular. Its headquarters moved to Kilburn Park Road in 1873, close to St Augustine's Church, then in course of erection. Two years later a 'Free Orphanage for the most destitute children in the Kingdom' was opened. These were children in need, it was claimed, 'for whom hitherto nothing has been done by the Church.'[16] Twenty years later, when the Association was under attack, a pamphlet on *Homes for Orphaned and Deserted Children* was issued. There were many institutions for orphans of the respectable, it argued, 'but for the forlorn waif, the outcast child without a penny, there existed at that time, no home of charity under the wing of the Church.' Emily and her Sisters were only too well aware of thousands of orphans and foundlings. Whether illegitimate or born in wedlock, no distinction was made by the Sisters when they began this work. In their defensive pamphlet an appeal was made to church history. In the sixth century, it was claimed, foundling homes existed in Rome. There were distinct institutions for them at the time of Charlemagne. Dalbius in 787 founded a home in Milan to prevent infanticide. A charitable order was founded at Montpellier in 1070, primarily to bring up foundlings and orphans. St Vincent de Paul, with royal support, set up a sisterhood for looking after foundlings. Further east, the Russian people were generally regarded as barbaric by the British, yet thousands of foundlings were looked after annually in

[15] [Sisters of the Church], *A Valiant Victorian. The Life and Times of Mother Emily Ayckbowm* (London, 1964), pp. 1–20.

[16] *A Short History of the Church Extension Association* (nd), copy in Lambeth Palace Library: Benson MS 158, fos 115–28.

Moscow and St Petersburg—'Those of exceptional talent are sent to the University, and many of Russia's best engineers, artists, and teachers are foundlings.' In New York the State Legislature provided a site and 100,000 dollars for the Sisters of Charity to open a home for 2,000 foundlings. 'May the time be near at hand when the English Government—roused at last to action by the appalling increase of child *massacre*—will supplement the efforts of the CEA in as liberal a spirit!'[17]

To mobilize support and appeal for money, a lively quarterly magazine, *Our Work*, began to appear in 1878. Through its pages appeals were made for voluntary help to sort and sell cast-off clothes and left-over food. A nourishing soup was once made from the water in which several large hams had been boiled for a Member of Parliament's party to celebrate the Queen's Diamond Jubilee. Emily realized that there were considerable numbers of keen church-going ladies with time to devote to raising money for good causes. The CEA began to open what they called their 'depots' in 1882. They provided cheap goods for the poor and raised useful funds for the Association. They were only gradually closed down after the Second World War, when the welfare state seemed to have removed the need for them. The last depot closed in Kilburn High Street in 1956, when it was thought that in the coming Age of Affluence there would no longer be any need for charity clothes shops.[18]

In less than twenty-five years the Church Extension Association had become a significant independent force within the Church of England. Emily understood the importance of networks and publicity. She sought the support of influential people in both Church and society, and secured the Archbishop of Canterbury as patron, and Earl Nelson as President. Wealthy and titled people were ever ready to lend support and provide financial backing. Orphanages near Stroud and Brondesbury were donated, and a home opened at St Annes-on-Sea.

New initiatives were for ever springing from the enterprising mind of the foundress. They were a strategic mixture of headline-catching pressure-group politics, often involving social or political leaders, but always reinforcing her religious message and

[17] Copy in Benson MS 158.
[18] *Valiant Victorian*, p. 68.

social ideals. In 1882 she started the Church Teachers Union, with Kirkpatrick as warden. In 1884 seventy teachers came to a retreat conducted by the well-known Anglo-Catholic priest E. F. Russell. *Our Work* commented, 'The life of a school or college teacher in these days is one of constant unrest, and wearing responsibility.'[19] In 1885 Emily was the driving-force behind the Religious Education Union set up to protect, defend, and support church schools. It made grants to Anglican schools in danger of closing, and in 1887 made the enormous effort of collecting 250,000 signatures on a petition in defence of religious education which was presented to the Royal Commission on Education. In 1894 the fourth petition got up by the Association was presented to the Commons by the future Prime Minister, A. J. Balfour.

Petitioning was tiring work, but it did establish the Sisters of the Church as front-line defenders of the faith. It also brought them the mantle of Establishment respectability. Earls and countesses were regularly to be found supporting the work of the CEA. The Old Palace, Croydon, had been bought by the Duke of Newcastle while an Oxford undergraduate and offered to the Sisters in 1887. In the same year HRH. Princess Frederica of Hanover had opened their home in Broadstairs. Their bazaar in the late eighties was graced by the presence of three princesses, two duchesses, marchionesses, countesses, and other titled ladies.[20]

The Sisterhood was growing rapidly. In 1895 there were ninety-eight professed sisters, forty-four novices, and seventeen postulants.[21] Work was being carried out in Canada, India, Burma, and Australia. There were 600 orphans in their homes and over 5,000 children in their schools. Income had risen from £500 to £38,000, which made it one of Victorian England's largest charitable organizations.[22] At a time of fierce competition for charitable funds it inevitably attracted suspicion and resentment. Criticism came from several directions. Other providers of welfare questioned their methods, paranoid Protestants resented this High-Church success; some High-Church sisters were estranged by the energetic expansion, by the relentless activism of the Order; church authorities were apprehensive at the growth

19 *Our Work* (September, 1884), p. 268.

20 *Valiant Victorian*, pp. 85–6, 91–2.

21 Ibid., p. 166; Vincinus *Independent Women*, p. 82.

22 Ibid., p. 147.

of this church within a church, apparently a law unto itself. In several respects Peter Anson was right to draw comparisons between Emily Ayckbown and General Booth.[23] They both founded authoritarian orders dedicated to holy worldliness, and both began within a year of each other in inner London. Within Anglicanism, Bernard Kent Markwell has rightly remarked that 'The real counterpart to the women's orders was not men's orders but ritualist slum priests.'[24]

Irritation was caused by what were often considered over-emotional publicity methods, which tugged at the heart-strings and opened the purse strings. A leaflet in Archbishop Benson's papers at Lambeth Palace tells its own tale. Under the heading SAVE THE CHILDREN, we read, next to a photograph of an emaciated child:

> Reader, do you see this miserable little specimen of humanity? Notice how shrunken are its limbs; how fixed and hollow are its eyes; how unnaturally sharpened are its features!
>
> No smile plays over the little wasted face; no joy shines in the baby eyes. A look of helpless misery is alone apparent.
>
> There is no need to ask its story. It is written plainly enough in every lineament. Starved! Neglected!
>
> Your eyes turn, perhaps, to your own plump, rosy darlings, and then fill with tears as you murmur, 'How could anyone so ill treat a poor helpless creature?' How indeed!

The leaflet moves on to quote from an NSPCC report:

> Fancy hanging a child up by the neck on a slip-strap to a hook in the ceiling till black in the face and unconscious! Thrusting a red-hot poker in the mouth through the closed lips into the mouth—burning lips, gums and tongue! Putting bare little thighs on the top of a hot ironing stove! Immersing a tender form for half-an-hour in a freezing tank out of doors. Starving and imprisoning in attics and cellars for days without so much as a drop of water.
>
> Yet such things have been done and are being done daily!

[23] Anson, *Call of the Cloister*, p. 442.

[24] Bernard Kent Markwell, *The Anglican Left, Radical Social Reform in the Church of England and the Protestant Episcopal Church, 1846–1954* (New York, 1991), p. 39.

> On behalf of babies so tormented so ill-used, we have lately opened a Foundling Home, and close upon a hundred little ones have already been received. It was quite pitiful to notice the way in which some of these even shrank from the caresses, lifting up pleading eyes fearfully as if expecting a blow, afraid almost to join in play with other children, sitting apart mournfully, *ignorant of the way to smile.*[25]

For the Sisters of the Church 1893 was their highpoint of both success and vulnerability. Their rapid growth and high visibility marked them as an easy target for those who resented their achievements. In 1893 Mother Emily was beginning to feel the strain of overseeing such a large and multifarious operation. Work was being carried out in Australia, Canada, India, and Burma, as well as in Britain. She was now fifty-six years of age, and was much affected by the death of Sister Elizabeth, who was two years her junior, and had been with her from the beginning.[26] Four months later nearly twenty members of the community withdrew.

They complained that they were being over-worked and inadequately consulted, and that the religious life of the community was suffering from the heavy demands of their caring responsibilities. They also disapproved of the advertisements for illegitimate children and the internal arrangements in the orphanage.[27] It was often claimed that the dissidents were largely responsible for the damaging allegations which now began to be voiced publicly.

The official biography of the foundress links the spate of rumours with 'certain ladies and others who were circulating sensational reports about the Orphanages'.[28] Harmful reports did certainly circulate, but the earliest public concerns seem to have been expressed by representatives of the Ladies Associations in London for Rescue and Preventative Work. Whilst the Kilburn Sisters expressed their prime concern for abandoned children, these particular ladies were more interested in the social implications of appearing too accommodating to the mothers. They protested to the Archbishop of Canterbury that 'The principles

[25] Benson MS 158, fol. 10.
[26] *Valiant Victorian*, p. 148.
[27] Ibid., pp. 148–9.
[28] Benson MS 158, fol. 2.

on which the Homes for Illegitimate Children are conducted . . . are calculated to increase immorality amongst society at large and are entirely opposed to all sound principles of rescue work.'[29] This view was expanded in a further submission to the Archbishop, which began with the assertion that the Kilburn homes encouraged immorality among men

> by making them believe that a sum of money can relieve any girl they may lead astray from all the consequences of her sin and also that the child or children can thus be happily provided for under the fostering care of a religious community. That the offer comes from a Religious Body does but intensify its ill effects as it is these very circumstances that provide the man with a plausible excuse for adopting such a line of conduct.[30]

But that was not all. By taking and caring for illegitimate babies, the Sisters were offering help 'to the mother while still in a life of sin'. There was thus no incentive for her to abandon her wicked ways. By taking full charge of the child, the mother was offered freedom 'from maternal responsibilities and a screen from her sin'. The price to be paid was 'a fixed sum of money *and her own child*'. After handing over money and baby, the mother might walk away, 'apparantly a free woman'. All the responsibilities and 'the joy of motherhood which is the strongest incentive on the girl's side to prevent her from falling a second time' are left behind. Her sense of right and wrong are confused, because after handing her child over unconditionally to the Sisterhood, she is left with the belief that 'She no longer owes any duty to her child.'[31]

The Sisters reacted with indignation to the sanctimony of their detractors. The implication of the criticisms seemed to be that 'If an erring sister fell she was to be sternly prevented from rising again.' 'Babies of this kind have no right to be born at all', many churchgoers seemed to think, and the inescapable logic would seem to be 'so the sooner they are put to death the better.' By contrast, at Kilburn foundlings were admitted, provided the mother was not living in sin, and only when she was unable to

[29] Ibid., fols 3–4.
[30] Ibid., fol. 5.
[31] Ibid., fol. 4.

bring the child up herself. 'We only take children that are about to be handed over to the baby-farmer. We say (in effect) give us what you would give the baby-farmer and we will bring your child up.'[32] The lady critics of Kilburn insisted that 'It is cruel to deprive children of a mother's love.' They were not convinced by the Sisters' claim to take the mother's place. There had been cases where the Sisters had acted in ways which were inconceivable for parents.

> No mother would throw her child upon the Rates. . . . This the Sisters have done. If a girl proves unfit for their Home they can and do turn her out to face the world and its temptations without a single friend to care for them. They are in this less like parents than are the Guardians of the Poor who in all cases hold the responsibility for the welfare of any girl under their care until she is 16 years old.[33]

The London Ladies were emphatic that this type of rescue work could only be effective if parents could be made to take responsibility for the children they had brought into the world. That meant providing financial support and taking an interest in the child: 'At stated times the mother should be encouraged to visit her child.'[34] When a child was placed with the Kilburn Sisters it was claimed that £40 was handed over, and the parent was freed from any further obligation. The critics argued for a different policy. Why could not the mother have been advised to place her child with a nurse 'while she herself goes into training and redeems her character after which, she can take a situation and continue to support her child by her own exertions.'

The lady critics were appalled by what they had heard about the ruthlessness of the Kilburn Sisters when things went wrong. Girls of fourteen and sixteen should not be thrown out of orphanages or be despatched to the workhouse. The ladies objected to the ease with which unmarried mothers could get rid of their babies. They could not ignore the tales they had heard of cruel treatment of the girls at Kilburn. There was anger at the emotional stories carried in *Our Work*.

[32] *Our Work* (October 1894).
[33] Benson MS 158, fols 3–4.
[34] Ibid.

These allegations found a test case in Dora Hill. Dora had been 'found' by a Miss Long on the doorstep of her house in Berkeley Square (Oscar Wilde, whose *The Importance of being Earnest* was first performed in 1895, might have considered Berkeley Square a superior birth-place to a handbag with a first-class ticket to Worthing!). Miss Long placed the baby, presumably her own illegitimate daughter, in the care of the Kilburn Sisters, and agreed to pay £16 a year in advance for her upkeep. Miss Long was not a little shocked and distressed to be asked in July 1893, after paying for Dora for fourteen years, to transfer her payments to another orphan, on the grounds that Dora was too troublesome to remain there. Miss Long demanded a fuller explanation: what had Dora done wrong, and where was she? After some correspondence, it emerged that Dora had already been removed from the Home and sent to the workhouse, 'And this', wrote Miss Long's friend, Edith Wethered, 'without any communication with the lady who had paid for her for all these years.' Together Miss Long and Edith Wethered went to Kilburn, but the Sisters 'couldn't say where Dora was now'; they had 'washed their hands entirely of the girl.' The concerned ladies went to the workhouse and found the clerk more helpful. Dora, they discovered, was one of a group of six from the Orphanage who had been left at the workhouse without warning. 'The clerk was so horrified', reported Edith Wethered, 'at these women and girls being sent there that he spent a whole day going from institution to institution and finally provided for them all.' Dora Hill, it was discovered, had been placed in service, but was found to have been so badly trained that she was sent to another home, 'where she is doing well.'[35] When *Truth* took up its investigation of the Kilburn Sisters, it quoted the minutes of the Paddington Guardians, which specifically referred to the admission of girls from the Orphanage of Mercy.[36]

Archbishop Benson was alarmed by these complaints and allegations and wrote to Mother Emily in May 1894 asking for a copy of any circular about the terms on which illegitimate children could be taken into the orphanage. There then followed months of polite skirmishings between Mother Superior and

[35] Ibid.
[36] *Truth* [Supplement] (18 June 1896) p. 10.

Archbishop, which resulted in a statement by Mother Emily that the terms for the reception of illegitimate children had been changed, and all copies of the outdated circular had been destroyed. In his next letter, on 17 November, the Archbishop moved to the matter of registration. It was the practice of the Kilburn Sisters to give their orphans new names. This produced the complaint that due to confusion in the orphanage a parent in search of a child did not discover until months later that the child had died. This incident provided another emotive issue with which to arouse the late Victorian public. Although the Sisters produced and published photographs of their register, showing entries for each child, with details of her or his former identity, the incident added to the unease about the rescue work of the Sisters.

Archbishop Benson next proposed to nominate a responsible person to visit the orphanage on his behalf, but Mother Emily raised objections to each of his three successive nominations, imploring him to make a personal visit. Her opposition to Benson's nominees seems unreasonable until their appropriateness is examined. One is then left wondering whether the Archbishop was genuinely looking for unbiased information or seeking a pretext for severing relations with the Sisters. One of his nominees, for example, was W. E. Knollys, an Assistant Secretary at the Local Government Board. He theoretically met Mother Emily's criteria; she had suggested that 'someone accustomed to inspect Homes might be appointed such as a Poor Law Inspector.'[37] But Knollys had already supervised the investigation of the wire cages or cubicles in which the Sisters kept the smaller children. These were intended to keep the children apart and reduce the possibility of mischievous behaviour or carnal exploration. Knollys found himself accepting the judgement of Dr Downes from his department that they were a fire risk. With forty-eight beds packed into the largest dormitory, there seemed a real danger of some child being trapped and burned.[38] To Emily, this opinion was sufficient evidence of bias. She claimed the wire cubicles to be an innovation which 'will probably be

[37] Benson MS 158, fol. 217, E. Ayckbowm–E. W. Benson, 28 November 1894.
[38] Benson MS 158, fol. 70, Copy of Local Government Board Report.

largely adopted by those who watch over the purity of the young people under their charge.'[39] They were patented in 1894.

In January 1895 the Archbishop announced that he did intend to accept her invitation to make a personal visit, but required her to agree to abide by his findings. This was not an undertaking which the Mother Superior was willing to give. She passed his letter on to sixteen of the senior Sisters, who offered to 'prayerfully consider' any suggestions, but not give pledges in advance. Perhaps realizing that the notoriously short-tempered Archbishop[40] was unlikely to be mollified by this response, the senior Sisters took pre-emptive action by informing the Archbishop that they had decided to dispense with all their distinguished male patrons:

> We trust that this will save our former patrons much annoyance. . . . We know that our work is likely to become more unpopular as time goes on. Our warm espousal of the cause of religious education, foundlings, starving men and tortured animals, all goes against the spirit of the age, and brings us much ill-will and opposition.

Benson was thus firmly rebuffed. It is unlikely that he would have been much impressed by the decision to axe the male patrons, which meant removing all the bishops and retaining only women patrons. It was put to the Archbishop that 'As the work of the Church Extension Association has always been carried on by women, and has largely to do with young children, does it not seem appropriate that the aid of Patronnesses only should be sought?'[41] Rumours about the Kilburn Sisters were now gradually seeping out. The Protestant Alliance, ever ready to make mischief, sent the Revd Alexander Reger to investigate. He visited one of the seceding Sisters, who told him that not only had they caned children of Protestant parents for refusing 'to bow down to the image', but that the Archbishop of Canterbury, the Bishop of London, and the Bishop of Marlborough were holding an enquiry into irregularities. She also handed him documents, 'which would cause the whole of England to rise at

[39] Benson MS 158, fol. 234, E. Ayckbowm–E. W. Benson, 30 January 1895.

[40] G. W. E. Russell, *The Household of Faith* (London, 1902), p. 161.

[41] Benson MS 158, fol. 202, E. W. Benson–E. Ayckbowm, 12 January 1895; Benson MS 158, fol. 218 Sisters–E. W. Benson: 25 January 1895; *Church Times*, 8 Nov. 1895.

once.' Young women aged between eighteen and twenty, it was alleged, 'were sometimes confined in rooms which were practically iron cages, for 3 weeks at a time, simply because they would not submit to discipline, which they considered too severe.'[42] Reger presented his findings in the *Protestant Echo* in May 1895, which gleefully reported the scandal of the willingness of the Sisters to accept foundlings 'with no questions asked', and the use of wire cages to separate the children.[43] Protestant extremism had long known what to expect from sisterhoods, whether Roman or Anglo-Catholic, and unsavoury stories about the Kilburn Sisters could be fitted easily into a salacious conspiracy theory to undermine national wholesomeness.

The Kilburn Sisters rightly ridiculed the more fanciful allegations of the Protestant Alliance, but it was not so easy to shrug off the displeasure of the Archbishop when it was made public in *The Times*. On 20 June 1895 it was announced that he had ceased to be a patron of CEA, and his entire correspondence with Mother Emily was published in September.[44] This told its own story, which was reinforced by the publication in December of a report, highly critical of the Association's charitable work, by the Charity Organization Society.

The Charity Organization Society (COS) had come into existence to co-ordinate the many charitable societies providing help for the poor in London, and also to set examples of good practice in contrast to the impulsive charity handouts which were believed to demoralize character and undermine self-help. The COS in 1895, and its secretary, C. S. Loch, could count on the unswerving support of its chairman, Frederick Temple, Bishop of London.[45] The COS produced its report on the Kilburn Sisters and their charity work at a moment when its own methods were being called increasingly into question. In July 1895 Canon Samuel Barnett, one of the founders of the COS, had confronted its council with his criticisms of its approach. Their well-known distinction between the deserving and the non-deserving poor had in Barnett's view sometimes led to

[42] *English Churchman*, 23 May 1895.

[43] *Protestant Echo*, 15 Sept. 1895.

[44] *The Times*, 20 June, 28 Sept. 1895.

[45] *Charity Organisation Review*, ii (1886), p. 52; see also *Social Policy 1830–1914*, ed. Eric J. Evans (London, 1978), pp. 204, 208–9; *Guardian*, 2 January 1895.

enquiries which had 'not always been undertaken in Christ's spirit of tenderness'.[46]

If there was one body which represented a standpoint opposite to that of the Church Extension Association, it was the COS, whose secretary, the dour C. S. Loch, was temperamentally as opposite from Mother Emily as any two people could ever be. Not surprisingly, the COS was scathing in its denunciations of the Kilburn Sisters and of what it described as the 'unsatisfactory' management of the orphanage and its other charitable work, especially for the unemployed, which ran the risk of creating a culture of dependence.

Although the approach of the COS was itself coming under criticism (Beatrice Webb described it as 'my friend the enemy'),[47] its *Report upon the Orphanages and other Charitable Institutions conducted by the Church Extension Association*, published in 1895, appeared authoritative. It seemed to confirm the wisdom of Archbishop Benson in calling for the inspection of the community and its work. In the absence of any response from Kilburn, the friends and supporters of the CEA welcomed the efforts of a church paper, *Church Bells*, to provide a refutation. Unfortunately *Church Bells* seemed to rely overmuch on the assertions of the Sisters rather than on in-depth investigations.

It was in an attempt to get to the heart of what seemed a complex and confusing storm of assertion and innuendo that the radical Liberal MP Henry Labouchere decided to launch a comprehensive enquiry in his paper *Truth*. Founded in 1876, this journal had a reputation for exposing deception and championing the down-trodden. A lifelong agnostic, Labouchere had no religious preferences. In 1894 he won the gratitude of the Roman Catholic *Tablet* for catching out Dr Barnado in whipping up anti-Catholic prejudice in his fund-raising.[48] In its unravelling of the treatment of children at the Kilburn orphanages, *Truth* appeared to be offering a plausible interpretation.

For our purposes, we limit our consideration to what the COS report called 'the panic of suspicion', which seems to have broken out in May or June 1893, when some of the children

[46] *Canon Barnett. His Life, Work and Friends by his Wife* (London, 1921), p. 658.

[47] Carole Seymour-Jones, *Beatrice Webb: Woman of Conflict* (London, 1992), p. 77.

[48] *Tablet*, 28 April, 19, 26 May, 9, 23 June 1894; *Truth*, 24 May, 7 June 1894.

were caught acting improperly. One response was the wire cubicles to separate the children, and the other was a determination to root out those who had introduced and persisted in what seemed unnatural acts. Young women, aged from fourteen to eighteen were, without warning, taken to another home and accused of immorality. They were told that they would only be allowed to rejoin their friends if they admitted their guilt.

> If the girl declined to confess, she was placed in a room by herself, sometimes under lock and key; otherwise she was deprived of her frock, so that she was virtually a prisoner and was given to understand that she would not be released until she had confessed. . . . The duration of the confinement ranged from a few hours to a week or two. The girls were generally kept on a low diet, and in some instances subjected to severe punishments. . . . They were threatened with the workhouse, the nature of the offence with which they were charged was stated to them, and they were told that their most intimate companions had denounced them. Helpless, isolated, without power of appeal, anxious to end their misery, the girls with few exceptions finally made the required admissions, which many of them have since repudiated. They were made to wear a distinctive dress and subjected to other degradations. Before their release they were as a rule required to give a promise that they would say nothing about their treatment.[49]

This promise obtained under duress was disregarded when they got back to their friends and they then discovered 'how they had been induced by false representations to denounce one another, and how they had been falsely represented as having denounced one another'. The COS elicited statements from young women in England and Canada and placed them before a group of three who came unanimously to the conclusion

> that the mass of the girls in question were innocent of the offences charged against them; that admissions were obtained from them under great physical and mental suffering, and sometimes by means of false representations; and that im-

[49] *Truth* [Supplement], 18 June 1896, p. 7.

> modest notions, of which they had no previous conception, were suggested to their minds by the accusation.[50]

These were the allegations dismissed by *Church Bells*, but generally corroborated by *Truth. Church Bells* was able to produce many testimonies of gratitude from orphans and to dismiss the evidence of the seceding Sisters and the expelled orphans. The seceders it considered vindictive, and the expelled were viewed as brazen hussies who refused to admit their guilt.[51] Perhaps that was true of some of the accusers, but unlikely to be true of all. Before 1893 probably most of the orphans led happy lives, by the standards of the times, but in 1893 some of the Sisters found themselves confronted by a situation of which they had no previous experience, and for which they had no training. Not surprisingly, it produced panic reactions. As Labouchere conceded: 'They discovered evidence of the existence in their homes and schools of an evil of a very insidious character, pernicious alike to the moral and physical well-being of the children.'[52]

When Labouchere met the Sisters he found that 'the substance of the COS allegations was not even denied. The answers of the Sisters rather took the form of extenuation and explanation.'[53] Labouchere interviewed several of the expelled young women himself. 'They spoke in all instances with modesty, and were far from displaying any animus or hostility to the Sisterhood as a body.' All of them were still indignant about their interrogation and expulsion.

> Practically the girls were prisoners under solitary confinement, broken only by periodical visits from a Sister or matron, who endeavoured to extort a confession. . . .
>
> Three of the girls state that they were struck during such visitations either by the Sister or the matron (house-keeper). One girl said that, on one occasion, when she persisted in her denial of the charge against her, the Sister became very angry, threw her on the bed, thumped her, and pulled her hair till she screamed.

[50] Ibid., pp. 7–8.
[51] *Church Bells*, 27 March, 2, 10, 24 April 1896.
[52] *Truth* [Supplement], 18 June 1896, p. 8.
[53] Ibid., p. 8.

Labouchere offered the following case as specially significant because there was independent corroborrative testimony on one important point. It concerned a sixteen-year-old pupil-teacher, who had been at Kilburn for seven years.

> I was sent for on Sunday morning, and taken to the Orphanage of Mercy, where Sister K. locked me in the airing room on the top floor. I was questioned, and told I should go to the workhouse . . . unless I confessed. I was not told of what I was accused, but Sister K. and Miss M. told me that I was aware of what had taken place, and that certain girls (mentioning names) had accused me. She also asked me for the names of my friends. I denied that I had been guilty of anything. I remained in the same room till Thursday, my dress and boots being taken away. Miss M. came several times, and told me she would make me confess. She struck me on the arms and in the face. . . . On Wednesday Sister K. removed me to Mother's sitting room, where I remained over Wednesday and Thursday without my dress and boots. Every time they brought me my meals they pressed me to confess. On Wednesday Sister K. told me that if I did not confess she would walk me about the house without my dress and boots. She became very angry, and took me by the shoulders with both hands and thumped me against the wall. She then struck me on the right eye with her hand. My eye became black.

As corroborative evidence of the black eye Labouchere offered the support of Lord Salisbury's chaplain, who had personally gone to Kilburn to make his own enquiries.[54]

A woman of twenty-one, who had been at Kilburn since she was nine, described her experience:

> I first heard of the difficulties in this way: Sister K. had half a dozen little ones in the second class room. She was 'rowing' them, and the children were crying. They made a great noise and I tried to go in. The door was fastened. I heard Sister K. Say, 'If you don't tell, I will thrash you till you do.' The children were there from six o'clock till nine. This was the

[54] Ibid., p. 11.

> beginning. Afterwards the whole of the children in the Orphanage were gradually questioned.

This testimony continued with an account of the events of one Friday, when Sister K. sought her out and demanded to be told what was going on.

> She took me upstairs. . . . She emptied my pockets, and kept asking me to confess. I said I had nothing to confess, and she said she would keep me there till I did. I said I would not stay [Remember this is a girl of 21—Ed. *Truth*]. She then took a pair of scissors and split my dress and tore it off me, and left, but I heard where she went and fetched my dress. . . .
>
> At 10–30 Sister K. came again, and told me I was to sleep there, and took away my dress and slippers.

The account continues with the happenings of the next five days, during which the suspect refused all food, whilst continuing to demand that she might confront her accusers. On the fifth day of the ordeal she had another visit from Sister K., who had brought some medicine mixed with mustard, which was refused. It was on this day that at long last she was brought face to face with her accuser—a little girl of eight, who was accompanied by a Miss F. When asked why she had made the allegation the little girl said, 'Please—, I did not mean to say it. Sister K. made me say it.' When asked what harm the older woman had done, the girl said, 'You didn't do anything, Sister K. made me say it.' That evening Sister K. made a final attempt to get a confession, this time holding out the prospect of an excellent reference and a good situation—but again to no avail. After another five days this resilient young lady was sent to the Victoria Orphanage and told that she was excommunicated, to which she replied, 'Only the Bishop can do that'![55] The result of what Labouchere called 'the Inquisition' was, according to him, that around 150 of the older girls were expelled. The Sisters disputed this figure and replied that it was only thirteen, but this refers only to those sent to the workhouse. Other girls were either returned to friends, found a job, or sent to Canada, but no numbers were provided. According to the Community's

[55] Ibid., p. 12.

Archivist in 1994, the number of girls who went to live apart from the Sisters was—150.[56]

The frequent references to Sister K. in the various accounts led to a request from Labouchere to meet her. This was refused on the entirely convincing grounds that her health had broken down. When Mother Emily was asked about meeting Sister K., she replied that 'The state of her health was such that the doctor would not sanction an interview.' 'I draw special attention to this', commented Labouchere, somewhat allusively, 'because it may in the future become a point of considerable importance.'[57] But it didn't, and the Sisters were right in claiming that 'This scurrilous attack fell wide of the mark.'[58] For this they could largely thank Dr Jameson, who became a national hero in 1895 through his famous raid on the Transvaal. By denouncing 'the fighting doctor and his bold buccaneers' in *Truth* and being in a minority on one of the Parliamentary committee of enquiry, Labouchere became widely unpopular, and *Truth*'s findings on other issues were consequently discredited.[59] As the Sisters thankfully reported, 'Recent revelations—connected with the South African enquiry—have since rendered it quite harmless.'[60]

Total institutions like convents and orphanages were on the fringe of late Victorian respectable society. There was anxiety about some of the charity work which might be undertaken by respectable ladies. In its courageous attitude to illegitimate babies, the CEA was risking its reputation. The rapid growth of the sisterhood and expansion of the work raised problems about authority and control. A situation was easily created in which a caring but confused woman like Sister K. could fan the flames of a moral panic and make the link between foundlings and what Stanley Cohen has called 'folk devils'.[61] The need to maintain the Home of Mercy in Kilburn as a zone of purity and drive out pollution with all its dangers could easily have become obsessive in those Sisters disturbed by the secession, frustrated by the

[56] *The Sisters of the Church. Reply to certain Statements addressed by two ladies to the Bishops of the Lambeth Conference* (privately printed), copy at St Michael's Convent, Ham Common, p. 3; Sr M. Mae Eamon–Diana Wood, 13 June 1994.

[57] *Truth* [Supplement], 18 June 1896, p. 9.

[58] *The Sisters of the Church*, p. 6.

[59] *Truth*, 9 January 1896; Hesketh Pearson, *Labby. The Life of Henry Labouchere* (London, 1936), pp. 274–80.

[60] *The Sisters of the Church*, p. 6.

[61] Stanley Cohen, *Folk Devils and Moral Panics—the Creation of the Mods and Rockers* (Oxford, 1980); see also Mary Douglas, *Purity and Danger; an analysis of concepts of pollution and taboo* (London, 1966).

inaccessibility of Mother Emily, and convinced of the reality of evil.

The evidence makes it likely that some children and young women were abused, physically and emotionally, but Lord Nelson was surely right in maintaining that no one 'could for a moment believe in the charge of *systematic* cruelty [my italics].'[62] The children, however, even if not all were abused, were used. They were pawns in a series of moves between Archbishop and Mother Superior, extremist Protestants and Anglo-Catholics, and those who held different concepts of the religious life, different views of charity work, and different Christian moral traditions.

In 1897 the Bishop of Marlborough, Alfred Earle, wrote to Frederick Temple, now Archbishop of Canterbury, 'It appears that the Sisters are urgently trying to extend their Foundling work and are advertizing for Diamond Jubilee children. This will do further harm if not checked. But who can check them? They are in my opinion no more within ecclesiastical control than Harrod's Stores.' It was in an attempt to deal with this type of situation that the 1897 Lambeth Conference had a long debate on sisterhoods.[63]

Mother Emily died in 1900 at the early age of sixty-three. Under her successor, an Episcopal Visitor was appointed in 1903. But whether the Visitor, the easy-going new Bishop of London, A. F. Winnington-Ingram, would have been much of a match for 'the heroic foundress',[64] as Michael Ramsey described Emily Ayckbowm, may be doubted. In the New Year's Honours List of 1934 Sister K. was awarded an M.B.E. for her work with children.[65]

Cheltenham and Gloucester College of Higher Education

[62] *Church Bells*, 1 May 1896.

[63] Lambeth Palace Library, F. Temple MS 4, fol. 358: A. Earle–F. Temple, 14 April 1897; Stuart Mews, 'Lambethkonferenzen', *Theologische Realenzyklopadie*, Band XX, Lieferung 3/4 (Berlin and New York, 1989), p. 420.

[64] Michael Ramsey, 'Foreword', *Valiant Victorian*, p. viii.

[65] I owe this information to Sister Marguerite Mae Eamon, CSC, Archivist to the Community of the Sisters of the Church, who read the proofs with great care and helped to improve the article, although she disagrees with my interpretation, insisting that 'none of the accusations were ever proven'; letter to Diana Wood, 13 June 1994.

APPENDIX

For The Ecclesiastical History Society

INTROIT: OUT OF THE MOUTHS . . .

Ps. 8 Vincent H. Packford

is thy name in all the world:
is thy name in all the world:
is thy name in all the world:
is thy name in all the world:
mp
thou that hast set thy glo - ry a -
mp
thou that hast set thy glo - ry a -
mp
thou that hast set thy glo - ry a -
mp
thou that hast set thy glo - ry a -
- bove the heavens!
- bove the heavens!
più mosso
mp
cresc.
- bove the heavens! Out of the mouths of
- bove the heavens! Out of the

ve - ry babes and suck-lings hast thou or- dain'd
cresc.
mouths of ve - ry babes and suck-lings hast thou
mf
cresc.
Out of the mouths of
mf
Out of the
dim.
strength, Out of the mouths of babes and
dim.
or - dain'd strength, out of the
ve - ry babes and suck - lings
cresc.
mouths of ve - ry babes and
suck - lings hast thou or - dain'd
mouths of babes and suck - lings

f
hast thou or - dain'd strength, be - cause of thine
suck - lings hast thou or - dain'd strength, be - cause of thine
strength, or - - dain'd strength, be - cause of thine
hast thou or - dain'd strength, be - cause of thine
dim. e rall.
p
en - e - mies: that thou might - est still the
pp
e - ne - my, and th'av - en - ger.

INDEX

NOTE: Page references in *italics* indicate illustrations.